OBJECT-ORIENTED
C++
PRIMER

This book is a comprehensive and easy to understand introductory and intermediate course of C++. It gives in depth detailed knowledge of all the features of C++ in a clear and easy to read manner. Most theoretical points are illustrated by the programs or the explicit examples. The book contains hundreds of programs. Each of them has been tested on at least two C++ compilers.

The book can be used by any category of people who want to get a hands-on experience in object-oriented C++. It covers object-oriented C++ used on almost any operational system or environment (for instance, DOS, Windows, Windows 95, Windows NT, OS/2, UNIX, Macintosh and others). The book is highly recommended as a course book for the universities and colleges. It is a perfect book for the students, engineers, scientists, programmers. It can also be easily used by the people with no or very limited exposure to programming, science and engineering.

The fact, that the book gives a truly in depth knowledge of C++ and can be used by different groups of readers can be attributed to a unique experience of the author. This course has been written by a scientist and engineer, who has spent many years in science. He also participated and managed different cutting edge engineering development and scientific projects. The author combines a university level teaching experience with engineering and scientific experiences.

OBJECT-ORIENTED C++ PRIMER

LEON POSKAR

MBSL Communications Co
Boston, MA

MBSL Communications Co.,
P.O. Box 15492
Boston, MA 02215
U.S.A.

For information about translations, how to order, or book distributors
inside or outside of the U.S.A., please write to MBSL Communications
Co. at the above address.

Object-oriented C++ primer

Library of Congress Catalog Card Number: 96-79017

ISBN 1-890005-00-2

MBSL Communications Co., Boston

To my mom, whose patience and love have made this book possible.

L.P.

Contents

PREFACE

We want to welcome you to C++. C++ has been developed from the computer language C. We hope computer object-oriented language C++ does not need any push from our side to make you understand its importance in the modern society. It is becoming one of the leading languages in professional programming. It offers a great power, enormous flexibility, incredible efficiency, when used correctly.

This book will teach you programming in C++. It can be used by those who have no experience in programming at all and C++ in particularly. This book will be equally educational for professional programmers, who want to study C++. So, this book will teach you C++, does not matter whether you know or do not know programming and language C. Our goal was to create an object-oriented C++ textbook for the introductory university-level courses. Our goal was also to create a book suitable for people who would want to study C++ on their own.

There can be different situations when people have to learn such widely used language as C++. They can be students taking a course or studying it on their own, or working people trying to improve their professional level, engineers, programmers, scientists. Each of those categories of people has a different background. But they still have to learn the object-oriented language C++, which they do not know. We tried to make this book very clear and transparent for those who will read it without sacrificing the depth or the completeness of treatment of the theory and practice. The book will start with the simple material and end up with very sophisticated object-oriented programming features. By the time you finish reading this book, you will become a knowledgeable C++ programmer.

Many educators believe, C++ must be taught only for the people knowing computer language C. This book offers another approach. It teaches the object-oriented language C++ to everybody from scratch. However, C++ is not a completely object-oriented computer language. It allows the procedural and object-oriented programming. The procedural programming is enabled by the tools of C++ and the tools existed in C language.

This is why we choose to begin the book with introducing the concepts, that C++ inherited from C and slightly modified in some cases. They are the data types, control structures, functions, arrays, pointers, structures, strings, unions. We also introduce to you the C style input and output, library functions. The book gives you in depth knowledge of object-oriented programming tools, such as classes, operator overloading, inheritance, polymorphism, virtual functions, template classes and functions, exception throwing. We also give a thorough treatment of the C++ input and output tools, such as **iostream** library.

Each theoretical concept is supported by a complete working C++ program example. The text provides and discusses an output of each program. Each program example is reviewed, sometimes, on a line by line basis. The book contains hundreds of exercises.

The programs have been tested on a number of compilers, for instance, Symantech C++, Borland Turbo C++, Microsoft Visual C++, Think C++, etc. The book will be equally helpful to those who work in DOS, Windows 3.XX, Windows 95, Windows NT, OS/2, UNIX, on PC, VAX/VMS, Macintosh. For the most part, the programs discussed in this book would work in those environments and operating systems with no or little modifications.

The text concentrates on good software engineering principles. It emphasizes the ways of correct program structuring, error checking. The text offers you not only the theory of C++, but also discusses the best use for certain language features.

The text is based on American National Standards Institute (ANSI) and International Standard Organization (ISO) C standards. It is also based on ANSI C++ Standard draft. It interprets different theoretical concepts from the standardization and unification point of view. However, a number of modern compilers use similar features, that are not specified in the standards. Where it makes sense, the text offers those features to the readers.

You must understand, the best way to study any computer language is to combine theoretical material with the practical work. We offer you a good textbook. The rest is up to you. You must not only read it, but try to run on your computer the programs given in this text. Try to solve the excercises given in each chapter.

If you have any comments or suggestions, please do not hesitate to write us. Our address is: MBSL Communications Co., P.O.Box 15492, Boston, MA 02215.

CHAPTER 1

INTRODUCTION TO C++ LANGUAGE.

1.1. Language and computer.

Before starting to learn about C++ programming language, we have to understand the communication process between the computer and C++ code. Programmers can just skip this part of our introduction. Those who just begin their journey in the world of programming should know how C++ interacts with a computer.

Computer is just an electronic device. It operates mainly with two types of signals: "low" or "0" and "high" or "1". Both "0" and "1" are just two levels of voltage. These signals "go back and forth" inside computer's electronic circuits. They either carry some information (data) or represent commands to be performed. They also carry the status of command execution and states of different devices. An example of the data is the numbers or characters you enter stored as the combinations of "0" and "1" or in their *binary* representation. A command can, for instance, send the data to a location in memory or perform an arithmetic operation. Whenever you play games on the computer or type in a text, you create the sequences of "0" and "1". There are special programs between you and a computer. They interpret or translate human actions into those sequences of "0" and "1", that your computer can understand.

Those sequences are generated, when you program in C++ or any other language. A computer "does not know" language C++ or any other language. A program goes through different stages of translation and execution before it becomes a binary sequence, that is clear to a computer. In fact, at the dawn of programming people had to enter the combinations of those "0" and "1" directly to program a computer. These days, people discovered other ways of doing it better. One of them is language C++.

In nutshell, a simple computer consists of: Central Processing Unit (microprocessor) with Arithmetic and Logic Unit (ALU), memory and input/output devices. Microprocessor or Central Processing Unit (CPU) is the main element of the computer. The CPU is the "mind" of the computer. It gives orders to all other devices, checks their execution, performs all the calculations. Sometimes, there is more than one processor in one computer. Each additional processor can perform its specific functions. For instance, a complementary processor can be used for some complicated math calculations. But there always is a processor in the system, that among other things is used to control all others.

Computer memory is a storage device for storing those combinations of "high" and "low" level signals that represent the data and commands. The sources of the memory are: the very CPU, additional memory chips, hard drive or drives, floppy or CD drives. Input/output interfaces are used for communications with the external world. The examples of input and output devices are: monitor, keyboard, printer. A microprocessor operates by means of a set of internal instructions. Those instructions are translated into a "machine code" or a sequence of "0" and "1", corresponding to a certain action. This set is an internal processor language called assembler. Devices inside the computer (such as hard drive, floppy disk drive and so on) also perform actions handled by those combinations of "0" and "1". The computer "understands" the machine code. The machine code is processor dependent. The set of instructions, called assembler, consists of a number of commands, that perform certain actions. Each assembler command is translated into a machine code. An internal assembler language also varies for different processors.

An assembler command, usually, performs a very particular action. For instance, it moves the data from one register to another. A register is an electronic cell, where the data is stored. Usually, one register stores one value of data. Computer memory is, loosely speaking, a set of the registers. A microprocessor also has a set registers as its memory. A microprocessor also has a number of the registrars that are used for performing arithmetical actions on the data.

Assembler requires a number of commands to write some procedures. For example, to add two numbers can require 3 or four commands. This is why people created *higher level languages*. They permit the user to write one command. This command can consist of many assembler sub-commands. The higher level language will be eventually translated into an assembler language and then into a machine code. A user has a convenience of writing one instruction instead of many.

There are common operations that the computer should perform. They deal with handling files, internal memory organization and other aspects. One can write routines handling the files, memory organization, communication between different parts of the computer, etc., using assembler instructions. One, for instance, can write a routine to copy the content of the floppy disk to a location on hard drive. That can be time consuming even though that is only one task. Thus, it was a good idea to write and organize those routine operations as one program called "Operating system". There are a few popular operating systems like DOS, OS/2, UNIX. There also are environments written on top of the operating systems. For instance, Windows is an environment that gives you a pictorial view of the tasks. Each operating system has its commands. Some of them you should know.

Before programming a computer, one shell choose an operating system or environment to work in and read a bit about it. You should know how, for instance, to create the files, move them around, I/O the data. The program that permits you to write a code in some programming language (such as C++ for example) and then translates it into a machine code is called a compiler. A compiler that translates C++ code into a machine code is called C++ compiler. You would need to select a compiler, if you plan to program in C++ on your computer. You choose C++ compiler that can run in an operating system that you like. A compiler is operating system or environment dependent. Compiler is also system dependent.

We said, that a compiler is just a program that analyzes and translates C++ code into a machine code. The machine code is different for different computer systems. Different computer systems use different processors. Those processors have different machine codes. This is why compiler is system dependent. Choose compiler for PC if you intend to write programs for PCs. If you intend to do the software for Apple computers, choose a compiler for those computers. Make sure, that the compiler is written for a microprocessor that is used in your computer. The compiler and your program are operating system or environment dependent, because they use the system tools. Thus, choose, whether you want to program in Windows, or in DOS, or in OS/2, or in UNIX.

You should install a compiler on the computer, before it can be used. You have to read a compiler manual for the installation instructions. Usually, they are very easy. You insert a floppy in a floppy drive or a CD in a CD drive and type install word. If you are a student, your computer facility has C++ compilers already installed. So, you just have to learn how to use them before starting to program.

Now we come to a question, how to write a program. A compiler provides you with the space where you have to write a program. It, then, converts the code that you write in that space into a machine language and executes it. How to get to this space? Wait for couple moments. We will come to it. Before writing a code, one should first start *running* or activate that compiler program. How to start a compiler program depends on a particular compiler. Each compiler comes with a manual that you should read to know how to start a compiler. Compiler program allows to start or create a *project*. A project consists of the files that you embody into it. Compiler permits you to create and open the *source* and *data* files. A project can consist of a few source files. You have to make those files a part of a project. How to create, open and add a file to a project is described in a particular compiler manual. The source files contain the C++ code. This is the place in which you write C++ code that is later translated into a machine code and executed. The data files contain the data. We will teach you how to handle data files by means of C++. This book teaches you the rules of how to create C++ code, that should be entered in the source files. A program code in C++ written in a source file is called a *source* code. You type in a program into a *source* file from a keyboard. One can also always make the changes in the source code.

After the code is written, it can be compiled by using a special compiler command. That is, when you translate a C++ code into a set of instructions, that a computer can finally comprehend and execute. To find out about this command, you will have to go to the compiler manual. During the first step of compilation, compiler examines each of your program statements for conformance with the syntax and semantics of the C++ language. Then, a compilation goes through the preprocessing stage, at which the compiler processes special program instructions called *preprocessor directives*. You will study them. They are a part of C++ language.

The further compilation translates C++ code into an assembler and then into the machine code. During the compilation a form called *object code* is generated. It is an intermediate stage between the source and machine code. This stage is needed, because the program often consists from more than one file. Each of those files can be compiled separately. They should be *linked* to produce a fully executable program. The program execution begins after the complete translation.

The compilation creates a file with the extension .**EXE**. It contains the compiled code. This file is the final product of the compiler. You can move this file to another computer, that does not have C++ compiler on it. You type the name of this file in DOS or click on its icon in Windows, and the program that you created starts its execution. You might often need some other library and data files along with this file to be transferred to another computer to be able to run a program without a compiler.

A program and its compiled code can be saved at any time. A program can be changed as needed. The program execution creates an output containing the results of the run. A program rarely runs correctly first time. There usually are more than enough program "bugs" to take care of. They will be driving you crazy, sometimes. Unfortunately, this is a part of the job. Some of the bugs you would catch after program compilation. A compiler usually displays all the errors. Those are mostly syntax errors. They happen, because you did not write the C++ statements and operators correctly. You would have to fix each of them. Even if no errors are found after program compilation, you can find many problems when you run a program for the first time. For instance, you can create an infinite loop, and the program will be going in cycles until you interrupt it using system tools. Another example can be when the results might be way off, because a program does not do what you thought it should.

When your program runs without bugs and is translated into a machine code, it can be made independent from the compiler. You can load those translated files on a separate disk and use them on the computers, that do not have C++ compilers installed on them. Those are the applications, games, etc., that you buy in stores. You cannot access their programs. But you can use their results. They will run only in an operating system they are created for. Also the application can run only on certain computer systems.

There are many C++ compiler vendors and too many compilers. They all have a lot in common. One can figure out how to work on any of them knowing how to work with one compiler. Volumes of manuals come with each compiler that describe how to use its different features. Those features are more important for debugging, graphics and some other tools. But the main thing remains unchanged - you should know C++ language. And it is a subject of our book.

1.2. C++ history.

C++ language has not been created from a scratch. Its ancestor was the language C, that has evolved from two other languages, BCPL and B. The BCPL language was created in 1967 by Martin Richards primarily for developing operating systems and compilers. Ken Thompson was one of the creators of the language B, used to create some early versions of the UNIX operating system. The C language was created by Dennis Ritchie at AT&T Bell Laboratories in the early 1970s. It was developed for UNIX based systems for DEC PDP-11 computer architecture. The language became very popular and is used for any known operating system and computer architecture.

Unfortunately, as the language progressed in late 1970s, a number of modifications have been made. In some cases those changes were incompatible with each other. This had become a serious problem and required a development of a standard. This is why the American National Standards Institute (ANSI) has standardized language C. All the compiler vendors in USA had to conform with the ANSI Standard X3.159-1989. C also was standardized worldwide by the International Standard Organization (ISO). ISO has adopted a standard ANSI/ISO 9899:1990 for C language. Both standards are essentially identical to each other.

C++ was developed in the early 1980s at Bell laboratories by Bjarne Stroustrup. It is an extension of C language, that has certain advantages over C. Those advantages are: improvement of type checking, support of abstract data types, *object-oriented programming*, capability of function and operator overloading, improvement in modular programming,

C++ language is hardware independent. A code in C++ can work on different computer systems. This means, that a carefully created source code can be transferred among different computer systems virtually unchanged. You would still have to select a compiler to translate it at least once into a specific machine code for each computer system. A compiler that translates the code into a machine code is computer dependent. But you, as C++ programmer, do not program the details of the translation. It means, that you can write a program that can be applied with some minor changes to any computer system.

C++ differs a bit from compiler to compiler. However, knowing the material given in this book, will make you highly proficient in C++. You will study some additional details by reading a specific compiler manual and books and practicing on a computer. There are efforts under way to standardize C++ language. Today there exists a draft of a standard C++ library, which will eventually become a standard. This book is based on this draft. It gives a user a view of tomorrow's C++. Our book also offers a number of specific features presently implemented on a majority of compilers.

1.3. Writing a program in C++.

We will begin from a fragment of C++ program given below in **Program 1.1**. It has more less common components of a C++ program. In this chapter we just introduce some of them. Do not try to understand how they work or how to use them. At this point just try to remember their names and definitions where we give them.

```
#define MAX  10            //preprocessor directives
#include <stdlib.h>        // header files inclusion
#include  <iostream.h>

void main  (void)          // you begin any C or C++ program
 {
int x1, x2;                // introducing type of data
float y1, z3;
...                        // other statements
cin >> x1;
 }
```

Program 1.1.

1.3.1. Tokens of C++.

Computer language C++ consists of some basic elements, called *tokens*. Token is a part of a program, that compiler does not break into the components. It understands a token as a separate element. Word can serve as an example of token in English language. A word in English, even though it consists of letters, has a certain unique meaning. Take away a few letters, and it can get a different meaning. It can become a new word. The words in English are used to communicate by creating sentences. So are the tokens in C++. C++ is a computer language. Its tokens are different from those in English. You divide words in English on nouns, verbs and so on. C++ has its classification of the tokens. They are: keywords, identifiers, constants, operators, punctuators.

The *keywords* are the words reserved for use, because they have a special meaning for the compiler. One should know how to use each of given below words, and use them only for that purpose. You cannot use them for anything else, for example, to name a variable, because this will be misinterpreted by a computer. The 32 keywords are used in both C and C++ languages:

auto	break	case	char	const
continue	default	do	double	else
enum	extern	float	for	goto
if	int	long	register	return
short	signed	sizeof	static	struct
switch	typedef	union	unsigned	void
volatile	while			

Beside those keywords inherited from C, there are additional words used only in C++.

asm	friend	private	this
catch	inline	protected	throw
class	new	public	try
delete	operator	template	virtual

Two above listings constitute the standard set of keywords for C++ language. Any C++ compiler should have them. Along with this set, many compilers also inroduce some other compiler-specific keywords. We will study each of the standard keywords. We just want you to see them now, because they are the tokens of C++ language. Look at the programs in this book and find some of the keywords.

The *identifiers* are the names you give to variables, objects, classes, functions and so on. They are also used as the labels in your program and for some other applications. They consist of any combinations of uppercase and lowercase English letters, underscores (_) and numbers. No other special characters should be used. First character can be only a letter or underscore (_). A number of characters in the identifier are limited. Modern compilers allow to use up to 32 characters and even more for the identifiers. Microsoft Visual C++, for example, permits to write the identifiers up to 247 characters long. Upper and lower case letters are different in C++. For example, names of the variables "**AbC33**" and "**aBc33**" are different names in C++.

Some examples of identifiers are given below:

```
    a04nfm389jr    or_mwll    x    z1    qASjen20    _1pw3
```

Some of the identifier examples from the **Program 1.1** are

```
    x1    x2    y1    z3
```

They are the names of the variables in this program. You will learn to handle them. We caution you against using two leading underscores in identifiers, as (__). Some compilers can use words beginning with two underscores for some other purposes. Since you do not know everything about C++, you are likely to make up an identifier with two underscores that can lead to some unexpected event. So, it is better to avoid them.

The *constants* are the entered values or characters, that will not change during the program. They are the ways of presenting the data to the computer. There are four basic types of constants: integer, floating-point, enumeration and character. We will discuss them thoroughly in the next chapter. One can also define the string constants, often called *strings* or *string-literals*. The *string-literals* are just the sequences of characters. They can contain letters, numbers, some special characters as **; ' " ? \n** and so on. Strings are surrounded by double quotes from both sides. For example,

```
"How are you";
```

will be a string. We will have a special discussion about them in the later chapters.

The *operators* are symbols and words that specify an operation to be performed. That operation can be a calculation, or a comparison, or some other action. We will study operators. Examples of operators are:

```
+    –    *    ++    ==    >>
```

The *punctuators*

```
[ ]    { }    ( )    *    ,    ;    :    #    =    ...
```

are symbols separating one language element from another one. The presence of those symbols can be required by C++ language. However, the punctuators do not perform an operation yielding a value. Examples of punctuators are: each C++ statement terminated by **;** punctuator, list of variables separated by a comma. For example,

```
int x1, n, m;
```

Here, a comma separates different identifiers.

Let's draw an analogy between C++ and English. The C++ punctuators serve the same purposes as those commas, semicolons, dots separating different phrases in English. The punctuation marks are required in English. The punctuators are also required in C++. Now, how do we recognize a word in English? Review an example

```
Doyouseeanywordatall?
```

What happens if we rewrite it

```
Do you see any word at all?
```

The words are separated by the blanks. A new word can even start from a new line. The same principle is used in C++. The tokens in C++ are separated by so called *white space characters*. They make a program readable for a compiler and for you.

The white space characters are: space, tab, carriage-return, linefeed, formfeed, vertical-tab, newline character and comments. They do not specify any operation and are used to separate tokens. In the **Program 1.1** we used blanks to separate the keyword **int** from variable **x1**. We could have written

```
int
x1,
x2;
```

And that would have had the same meaning. Here, we use newline white space to separate **int** and **x1**. One can use as many white spaces as needed to make a program look readable. Pay attention that we also use a white space between the comma after **x1** and **x2**. The white space used after punctuator has no effect on a program. Why? Because it is a white space between a punctuator and another token. The comma already separates two variables **x1** and **x2**. We use it only to improve the program readability for us. There is also no difference in how many white spaces are used between tokens. The white spaces are ignored by a compiler unless you use them as character constants or string-literals. Use at least one white space to separate tokens. One cannot write

```
intx1;
```
The same statement rewritten correctly is
```
int x1;
```

1.3.2. Comments in C++.

We want to introduce to you a *comment*. It is an important feature of C++. A comment is a sequence of characters that is ignored by the compiler. The compiler does not "see" comments, as if they do not exist. The C++ compiler does not evaluate the comments. Therefore, they cause no actions. Programmers use comments to write messages to themselves. You can explain to yourself, what each particular program fragment is supposed to do. It will save time if you try to look at the program later, when you might not remember each of your steps. There are two ways of writing comments in C++.

The first way is inherited from C. Comments in C++ begin with a forward slash and asterisk combination **/*** and end with asterisk and forward slash ***/**. For instance,
```
/* this is a comment */
```
Compiler treats a comment as a single white character. Whenever a compiler encounters the **/*** sequence, it disregards any characters after it until it encounters ***/**. Whatever you write between **/*** and ***/** has no effect on a program. It is ignored by a compiler. A comment can occupy more than one line and appear anywhere a white character is allowed. It can include any character excluding ***/**, because this will eliminate a comment. Nested comments or comments inside comments are not allowed. The
```
/*.../*...*/...*/
```
will not work.

The second way of writing a comment in C++ begins with two slashes (**//**). All the characters typed after these two slashes up to the next line are considered to be a comment. In this case, the comment is concluded by a newline character (or return) not immediately preceded by the backslash (****). It is called a "single line comment". For instance,
```
int x    // this is your comment
```
We also have to talk about the backslash character (\), that concatenates two lines together. If a line ends on a backslash followed by pushing the return, as for instance,
```
// Hi, \
programmer.
```
it will be considered as one line
```
// Hi, programmer
```
Both **Program 1.1** and **Program 1.2** illustrate the comments.

1.3.3. Structure of C++ program.

Now let's consider a structure of C++ program. It can begin with the preprocessor directives (statements). ANSI C Standard even recognizes the *preprocessing-tokens* (or

components of those directives) as the separate tokens. Preprocessor statements are ana-
lyzed before the compiler analyzes the whole C++ program. We will study preprocessor
statements and tokens later in this book. Now, you should only be aware of their existence. **Program 1.1** introduces some of those directives. We also duplicate them below

```
#define MAX   10
#include <stdio.h>
#include   <stdlib.h>
```

You can have no preprocessor directives at all in a program. Most often you will use at
least the **#include <...>** statements.

The **#include <...>** statements will be often present in your program for the following reason. We have identified the tokens of C++ language. However, they cannot perform a number of actions. For instance, C language cannot perform the data input or
output. A computer language is useless without being able to enter the data and to get the
results.

Those problems were solved by creating C library. Small programs were written for some
additional operations. Those small programs or routines are called functions. If you need
them, just call them to do the work. You will study, how to do it as well. Those functions
are called *library functions*. Functions were combined in groups and put into files called
header files or *library files*. Each header file contains a separate group of functions. A
library of functions comes along with each C++ compiler. Libraries of functions were
inherited from C. Later you will also study the classes, that are the powerful tools of
C++. Compiler vendors supply a number of classes with each C++ compiler. They are
called a *library of classes*. Those classes are stored in a number of files. The classes can be
used to write a program. Do not try to imagine how to use them at this point. You will
understand how to write new classes and use the prepared ones after reading this book.

A compiler cannot use library functions or classes, unless you include in the program the
files in which they are described. So, to use a certain function or class, you have to
"include" a header file containing it by writing

```
#include <...>
```

This statement is, usually, written before the program. The name of the header file is
contained inside those brackets **<...>**. If more than one header file should be included,
use a separate **#include** statement for each one.

Some of the header files are specified by the ANSI C Standard. We will call header files
specified in the ANSI C Standard the *standard library files*. They were inherited from C.
Many C++ compilers also have some similar library files, that have not been specified in
the ANSI C Standard. They vary a little for different compilers. Their content is very close
to proposed C++ ANSI Standard Draft. We will study those files as well. They describe
the classes and the objects. Many of those objects are used to perform certain actions. We
will study them.

At the beginning you will be told which header files to include for particular functions,
classes or objects. You should know them after reading this book. Many compilers supply
additional compiler-specific header files. It means, that only one or a very limited number
of the compilers has them. Those header files and their content are not a subject of this
book. To know them, you shell read a compiler's manual. You can also create the header
files on your own. Just write some routines or classes, put them in the files, and include

those files as the header files.

There are four groups of header files. The first one is a group of header files specified by ANSI C Standard. The second one is C++ specific group common for a majority of compilers that is likely to become a standard with some minor changes after approval of the new C++ Standard. There also are additional header files created by the compiler vendors. They can vary from vendor to vendor. You can also create the header files.

After writing the preprocessor directives, you begin to write a code. Every C++ program begins with **main()** function as in **Program 1.1**. It is written in the form:

```
main ( )
  {
 . . . .
 . . . .
  }
```

All the operators and statements are written between those brackets. **main** is a special word indicating the point, from which the program execution begins. We mentioned, that **main()** is a function. As a function it can have arguments, but we postpone this discussion until later. Some routines and statements can be written outside **main()** function. We will consider them. One should understand that every C++ program should have **main()** function. The text of the program should be contained between opening **{** and closing **}** brackets.

One usually begins a program in C++ with introducing all the players, i.e., all the variables, arrays and any other kind of data to be handled by the program. This is followed by the data input functions or statements. You have to introduce the data and to assign it the initial values.

One proceeds the code by writing statements and functions for performing operations on this data. The program is, usually, concluded by writing the data output.

Then you compile or run the program. Do not be embarrassed, if it does not run correctly for the first time. One has to put an effort to make a program run without the errors. Just try to find, what has gone wrong. You should also remember that *every statement in C++ is terminated by a semicolon*. A semicolon constitutes the end of a statement in C++. Consider **Program 1.2** as a simple example.

```
#include <iostream.h> /* it is a preprocessor directive*/

main ( ) // presence of this function is obligatory
{
cout << "This is my first C++ program.\n";
}
```

Program 1.2.

The program will display a message on a screen.

```
This is my first C++ program.
```

The above program has a typical C++ style not known to classic C programmers. The whole line of code terminated by the semicolon

```
cout << "This is my first C++ program\n";
```

is a statement of language C++. The **cout** is the output operator called *standard output stream object*. The < < operator is *called a stream insertion operator*. It inserts the string to the right of it into the output object **cout**. We will study the input/output in the next chapter and in chapters 17 and 18 in details. For now, we just want to show them to you. As you see, the string has **\n** character, that is not displayed on the screen. This character is called an *escape sequence*. It moves the cursor to the next line. Thus, if there were any words after it they would have been printed from the next line.

   C++ is a very rich language. It can use the tools of C language. It also has its specific features. We will study them. We introduce **Program 1.3** to show another way to output a message. It is a classic C program. It will also run under C++.

```
#include <stdio.h>

main ( )
{
printf ("This is my C++ program.\n");
}
```
Program 1.3.

The output of the program is
```
This is my C++ program.
```
Here we used function **printf()** to display a message. We will study this function throughout this book. Whenever you use input/output functions, the **<stdio.h>** header should be included. We have demonstrated the way to do it.

CHAPTER 2

DATA PRESENTATION.

As you already know, the data is stored in a computer in a binary form as a sequence of "1" and "0". For example, consider binary number "00100110". There are 8 positions in this number, and each of those positions can be either "0" or "1". Each of those positions is called a *bit*. Eight bites are called a *byte*. Any value can be converted to a binary form (Appendix 1). We use decimal representation of values in everyday life, for instance, numbers 21, 8492. Decimal numbers can be converted to binary, octal, hexadecimal base in C++. We discuss it in Appendix 1. A computer operates on the numbers in their binary representation. Even though the values and the keyboard characters are also manipulated by a compiler as binary, you, in most cases, do not even have to deal with this form. C++ permits to enter and read the data in most comfortable form: decimal, octal, hexadecimal.

2.1. Introduction to variables.

Here, we introduce two notions: a variable and a constant. You are familiar with the variables from the math. Some knowledge about a variable from math is pretty much applicable here. You can assign a value to a variable and use them in the expressions. So, there is nothing unusual that a variable in C++ is capable of changing its value during program execution as many times as needed.

To introduce a variable you first declare it, usually at the beginning of a program, by a statement like

```
int x;
```

A variable is declared by stating its data type and name. The first word **int** in that statement defines the data type. The second word **x** is the name of this variable. This short statement tells the compiler to allocate some memory space, that can hold one value of type **int**. This space will store a value, and the computer will know this cell by its name **x**. If you assign value to **x**, it will be placed in that particular memory cell. The memory cell is allocated during program compilation. The size of that memory cell varies for different data types. Integer and floating-point numbers occupy different sizes of memory. C++ is designed to efficiently allocate memory for the data. Each data type requires different standard number of memory bytes to be reserved. Some types of data are: **char**, **short**, **int**, **long**, **float**, **double**.

How do you create a name of a variable? A familiar to you from the previous chapter identifier is used to name a variable. In our example it is the variable **x**. You know the rules of how to create an identifier. We have given them in the previous chapter. Some examples of variables declarations are

```
int  x1, x2, x3;
```

```
char my_name_let, z2, z3;
float NhmI34;
```

Here we have three variables of type **int**, three of **char** type, one **float** type variable.

Suppose, program has a few variables of the same data type. For example, you need to declare three **int** type variables **x1**, **x2** and **x3**. You can write the declaration of some or all of them in one statement as we did below

```
int   x1, x2, x3;
```

Thus, different variables of the same data type can be declared in one statement. Each of the variables should be separated by the comma from the previous one. It is shown in the above declaration of **x1**, **x2** and **x3** variables. But one could also write them as

```
int   x1;
int   x2;
int   x3;
```

One can assign a value to a variable anywhere in the program. There are a number of ways to assign a value to a variable. It involves an assignment operator (**=**). We will study it in more details later in this chapter. However, we have to introduce you to this operator now. What does **x=5** mean? It means, that the variable **x** is equal to 5. The assignment operator makes a variable on the left of it equal to a value or an expression on the right. In other words, the assignment operator copies the value on the right into the memory cell corresponding to the variable on the left. Thus, the expression **x=5** places the value 5 into the cell reserved for the variable **x**.

One can assign a value to a variable (or initialize it) when it is declared. For example,

```
int m=2;
```

Here we have assigned 2 to a variable, while declaring it in the program. An example is given in **Program 2.1**.

```
#include <stdio.h>

main ( )
{
int   m=3;
printf ("m=%d \n", m);
}
```

Program 2.1.

The output of the program is

```
m=3;
```

We assigned a value to the variable **m** and displayed it on the screen using **printf** (**"m=%d \n"**, **m**) function. The **printf()** function is used for the data output. It will be discussed later in this chapter. We also included **<stdio.h>** file to be able to use the **printf()** function. We wrote a C style program using the **printf()** function that has been inherited from C. We did it, because we firmly believe, that a good C++ programmer should also know language C. This will broaden your horizon in solving practical programming problems.

A value can be assigned to a variable, after it is declared by an assignment "**=**" operator.

For example,

```
int m;
m=2;
```

Program 2.2 illustrates this way of assigning a value to a variable.

```
#include <iostream.h>

main ( )
{
int m;
m=2;
cout << "x=" << m << endl;
}
```
Program 2.2.

The output of the program is

```
x=2;
```

This program is similar to the previous except it uses another way of assigning a value to a variable. It also uses a C++ output style.

One can assign a computed value of an expression to a variable, as shown below.

```
#include <iostream.h>

main ( )
{
int x, m, k=2;
m=3;
x=(m+5)*k;
cout << "x=" << x << endl;
x=3*(m+5)*k;
cout <<"x="<< x << "\n";
}
```
Program 2.3.

The output of the program is

```
x=16
x=48
```

We assign two different values to the variable **x** in the above program. We assign a numerical result of the calculations of **(m+5)*k** expression to the variable **x** by

```
x=(m+5)*k;
```

Calculate the result of **(m+5)*k=(3+5)*2=16**. It is equal to 16. We display its value using the first **cout** object. Later, we assign a value to **x** again by

```
x=3*(m+5)*k;
```

This changes the value of **x** to 48. We display this value on the screen using **cout**. We changed the value of **x** to show, that the same variable can change its value in the program.

The value of **x** has changed from 16 to 48, when we needed it. We include the **<iostream.h>** header file in the program to be able to use the **cout** object.

We realize, that the word "object" applied to **cout** might bother you at this stage. As you read this book, we will clarify it. Later in this chapter we will show, how to use this **cout** object. Do not worry, if we call it an object. You do not have to understand now, how to write using the **cout** object. We want you just to see the programs. You will learn how to use this and many other objects later in this book.

A value can be assigned to a variable by the user from a keyboard, while a program is running. It is done using the C input function that we will study later in this chapter.

```
scanf ("%d", m);
```
It is called a console input and is illustrated by the following program.

```
#include <stdio.h>

main ( )
{
int m;
printf ("enter a value. \n");
scanf ("%d", &m);
printf ("m=%d \n", m);
}
```
Program 2.4.

The program displays a message on the screen
```
enter a value.
```
You enter a value, for instance 45, and press **ENTER**. The output is
```
m=45
```
This program displays a message prompting to enter a value. The **scanf()** reads the value entered from the keyboard. The entered integer number is displayed by the last **printf()** function.

A C++ style console input can be performed by means of the **cin** object. This is demonstrated in the following program.

```
#include <iostream.h>

main ( )
{
int m;
cout << "enter a value\n";
cin >> m;
cout << "m=" << m;
}
```
Program 2.5.

The program displays the message

```
enter a value
```
Let's assume, we enter number 20 and press **ENTER**. The program output is
```
m=20
```
We display a message prompting the user to enter a value by the first **cout** object. We read the value entered from the keyboard with **cin** object, and display that value using the second **cout** object. Both objects **cin** and **cout** require an inclusion of the **<iostream.h>** header file.

A variable can get its value from another file or device. We will learn it later.

2.2. Fundamental data types.

A programmer has to be able to see a value and evaluate its data type. It is necessary, because C++ programmer should declare in advance the types of the data to be used in the program. A variable, an array, a string, a structure or an object should have their data types specified before one can use them.

You choose the data type of a variable, when you declare it at the beginning of the program. You should approximately evaluate what kind of values will that variable accept. Will it be used for integers, floating-point numbers, or characters? What will be the range and the precision of those values? You determine the data type of the variable considering that. If you cannot estimate any of those factors, choose the safest type that will definitely cover your variable.

You should understand, better precision and larger estimated value can require more memory. You might occupy more memory than needed, which is a bad programming. It can also slow down your program a bit. Thus, choosing a data type is a trade.

The data in C++ can be subdivided on the data of *fundamental* and *derived* types. The fundamental types are considered in this chapter. Examples of fundamental data types are: **int**, **float**, **double**, **char**, **void** and so on. The derived data types in C++ are: enumeration types, structures, unions, classes, etc. None of the derived types is described in this chapter. We will explain the derived data types later in the book. Each derived data type can occupy a chapter in this book.

2.2.1. Integer data types.

They are used for integers, i.e., the values having no decimal points. For instance,
```
100, 20, 48, 681, 1, 7
```
We will consider following data types: **short**, **unsigned short**, **int**, **unsigned int**, **long**, **unsigned long**. Even though we will consider all of them, but you will most often deal with **int**, **unsigned int**, **long**, **unsigned long**.

The first data type we consider is **int**. It is used to represent the integral numbers. The length of the cell reserved by a computer for each integral value of **int** data type is typically two bytes, although some computers reserve four bytes. This type can be used to represent integral numbers in the range from -32767 to 32767 for two byte cells and -2,147,483,647 to +2,147,483,647 for four byte cell computers. If you do not know, which one is applied to your computer, write the program, then assign a number greater than 33000 to your variable, and see if you get an error displaying it.

The **unsigned int** data type is used only for positive integers. Numbers range from 0 to 65535 for two byte memory cells or from 0 to 4,294,967,295 for four byte cells.

The **long** (sometimes written as **long int**) type is used for numbers in the range from -2,147,483,647 to +2,147,483,647. A value of this type occupies four bytes of memory. Type **unsigned long** is used for positive values in the range from 0 to 4,294,967,295. It also occupies four bytes of memory.

Type **short** is pretty much like **int**. **short** is used for storing integral numbers with the values ranging from -32767 to +32767. It occupies 2 bytes of memory per value. Also used **unsigned short** differs only by its range from 0 to 65535. For many compilers those data types are identical to **int** and **unsigned int**.

2.2.2. Data types for floating-point values.

The examples of floating-point numbers are
  29.37, 9.728351, 729.192836
The floating-point numbers are written, sometimes, in a scientific notation as
  4.8e-3, 8.234e+4, 3.343e+2, 2.8e-1
The number after **e** (as in **e-3**, **e4**) represents a power of 10. It is called an *exponent*. The part before the exponent is called *mantissa*. For the value **4.8e-3** the mantissa is **4.8** and the exponent is **-3**. Value **4.8e-3** can be rewritten in a regular notation as $4.8*10^{-3} = 0.0048$. Thus, **4.8e-3** is, in fact, **0.0048**. The value corresponding to **8.234e+4** is **8.234*10** ^{4} **=82340.0**.

You can express the integers as floating-point numbers in C++, just add a point and at least one zero. For instance, the floating-point representation of integers **8, 20, 482** is
    8.0, 20.0 or **2.0e+1, 482.0** or **4.82e+2**.
Type **float** is used for the floating-point values. Each **float** value typically occupies 4 bytes of memory or 32 bits. One bit is usually used for the sign, 8 bits for the exponent and 23 for the mantissa. A floating-point number of this type typically ranges from **3.4e-38** to **3.4e+38**. It displays 8 digits with up to 7 digits of precision. Precision has a double meaning for different compilers. For some compilers it refers to the number of digits after the decimal point. Some compilers consider the precision as a total number of digits in a value.

Type **double** is also used for the floating-point values, but it has better precision and wider range. One value of this type occupies 64 bits of memory. One bit is used for the sign, 11 for the exponent and 52 for the mantissa. It ranges from **1.7e-308** to **1.7e308**. It gives up to 15 digits of precision.

The **long double** type is used for the floating-point values. It has a range from **3.4e-4932** to **1.1e4932** and contains 80 bits (1 for the sign, 15 for the exponent and 64 for the mantissa). It can have 19 digits of precision.

The ranges and the precision can vary for different compilers. Some of them can have smaller or greater range and precision. We urge you to look in the compiler manual. You will learn how to get the maximum and minimum data values for different data types later.

2.2.3. Character data types.

Every keyboard character, whether it is printable or not, corresponds to a certain number. The binary or numerical representations of those characters are standardized. One of those conventions is called the ASCII code. ASCII requires only 7 bits per character. Some computers use other codes than ASCII, although they also work fine with C++. A number is sent to the computer when you enter space, return, tab or a character, like "**e**", "**r**" and so on from the keyboard. There exists a special data type that handles those characters. It stores a character as an integral number, and displays it as a character when needed.

Type **char** is used for declaring a variable, that stores characters. It is used when you anticipate your variable to be a symbol or some character. The value corresponding to that character ranges from -127 to + 127. For **unsigned char** value range is from 0 to 255. Types used for character representation usually occupy 1 byte of memory.

2.3. Constants.

Constants are tokens that represent some fixed numeric or character values. When you assign a value to a variable, this value is a constant. For instance,

```
float k=3.92;
```

Here, the value 3.92 is a constant. C++ language recognizes following classes of constants: integer, floating-point, enumeration, character constants and string-literals. We will consider enumeration constants and string-literals later in this book.

2.3.1. Integer constants.

The *integer* constant is a decimal (base 10), octal (base 8), or hexadecimal (base 16) number representing integral value. Open Appendix 1, if you want to read more about octal and hexadecimal numbers. A decimal constant consists of digits from 0 to 9. It normally begins with a non-zero digit or sign (-), as for instance,

```
-7, 9183, -638152, 29, 5
```

An octal integer constant consists of digits ranging from 0 to 7. It should begin with the leading zero. The (-) sign usually precedes leading zero, if it is a negative value. This way you and computer would know that it is an octal number, as for instance

```
0374, 01, 02, 05,-022, 063
```

A hexadecimal integer constant consists of the digits ranging from 0 to 9 and the lowercase (uppercase) letters **a, b, c, d, e, f** (**A, B, C, D, E, F**). It should begin from either **0x** for the lowercase or **0X** for the uppercase letters. The (-) sign usually precedes leading **0x** or **0X**, if it is a negative value. For example,

```
0xb45, -0x3c8a, 0X77BBE
```

Whenever an integral constant is entered, the compiler places it in the smallest memory cell. You do not have to specify a data type when you enter a constant, because it is a numeric value. Computer evaluates the size of the memory needed for that value and automatically gives it a correct standard data type. The constant is placed in the memory cell of the size corresponding to its data type. If you want a constant to be explicitly a long integer (**long**), then a letter **l** (or for some compilers **L**) should be added to the end of the numeric value, as for example,

```
291, -1001, -0771, 024L, -0x9a2l, 0xb9aL
```

Letters **u** or **U**, added to the end of the constant, specify it as an **unsigned int** type. For instance,

```
225u, 15U, 066u, 073U, 0xd5u
```

A constant can be entered as **unsigned long**. In this case, both **l** (**L**) and **u** (**U**) letters should be added to the end.

2.3.2. Floating constants.

We know the data types used for the floating-point values. A floating-point constant can be also entered directly in a decimal notation with the leading (-) sign if needed

```
34.81, -891.66
```

It can be entered in a scientific (exponential) notation with the leading (−) sign, as

```
3.2e-3, 7.4e-2, 8.3953e2, -6.3332e1
```

You already know, there are three types that are used to store the floating-point values: **float**, **double**, **long double**. Any floating-point constant is treated by a computer as type **double** by default. It means, the computer automatically determines the data type of an entered constant as **double** and allocates corresponding to this data type size of memory. Then, the constant is placed into that memory cell. If you want a constant to be treated as a **float** explicitly, a letter **f** (or on some compilers **F**) should follow the entered number. For instance,

```
28.43f, -28.43F, 28.43f
```

To explicitly specify a **long double** type add **l** (or for some compilers **L**) to the end of the number. For example,

```
28.43l, -28.43L
```

2.3.3. Character constants.

A *character constant* is a sequence of one or more characters enclosed in the quotation marks as, `'q'`, `'t'`, `'2'`, etc. A character constant can contain any characters, digits and special combinations of characters called *escape sequences*. An escape sequence consists of a backslash (\) followed by a letter or certain combination of digits. This backslash character combination is regarded as a single character. Those escape sequences are typically understood by a computer as some action orders. They can, for instance, specify carriage return, or cursor tab movement on the screen. Table 2.1 gives some escape sequences and the kind of action they specify.

If a backslash is followed by any other character, C++ just disregards the backslash and understands it as a character by itself. For example, **\y** is understood as **y**. **Program 2.6** illustrates the use of some escape sequences.

```
#include <iostream.h>

main ( )
{
cout << "It is me.\tHow are you?\nHave a nice day.";
}
```
Program 2.6.

The output of the program is

```
It is me.                How are you?
Have a nice day.
```

The **\t** character starts the second sentence from the horizontal tab. The **\n** character starts the third sentence from the next line. We can now partially discuss I/O functions. This will allow us to perform the input and output of different type data.

Table 2.1. Most common escape characters.

Sequence	Meaning
\v	moves the cursor to a vertical tab
\t	moves the cursor to a horizontal tab
\r	performs printer's carriage return
\n	newline character; (next character after that sequence will start from the new line
\f	formfeeding, i.e., cursor goes to line 1, column 1 on the next page
\b	backspace
\a	alerts by sound
\'	displays a single quotation mark
\"	displays a double quotation mark
\\	displays a backslash
\?	displays literal question mark
\ooo	displays an ASCII character, but writes it as an octal number
\xhhh	displays ASCII character in hexadecimal notation

2.4. C style console data input and output.

There are a few ways of entering data. You can enter the data from some data file, interface device, or the keyboard. The result or data output can also be displayed on the screen or written to any device or file. File input/output is considered later in this book. Here, we will consider C style functions for direct data entering from a keyboard and displaying the data on the monitor, called *console* input/output (I/O) functions.

2.4.1. Console data output.

Message or the result of calculations can be displayed on the screen by using the **printf()** function. The **printf()** function is described in **<stdio.h>** header file. Therefore, it should be included, when you use the **printf()** function as

```
#include <stdio.h>
```

One can use **printf()** to display the messages, as for example, in **Program 2.7**.

```
#include <stdio.h>

main()
  {
printf ("How are you?\n I am writing in C.");
  }
```
Program 2.7.

The output of the program consists of two lines displayed on the monitor

```
How are you?
I am writing in C.
```

The **printf()** function is written in the form

```
printf ( ".........");
```

Here, the characters inside the double quotation marks "**...**" are called a *format string*. The **printf()** function displays the characters inside the double quotation marks "**...**" on the screen. In other words, the **printf()** function displays its format string on the monitor screen. If there are any escape characters in the format string, **printf()** function performs an action specified according to Table 2.1.

For example, we use **\n** escape sequence in **Program 2.7**. Computer treats **\n** as an order to move to the next line. Anything displayed after this character starts from a new line. This is why it is called a newline character. As you can see, the next phrase (**I am writing in C.**) in **Program 2.7** is, indeed, displayed from the new line. You can use any number of escape characters anywhere within the double quotation marks.

Sometimes, you might have to use the double quotation mark " as a character inside the format string. It can be tricky, because it is, in general, treated as the end of the format string. The only way to use it in the format string as a part of the text, is to use it with a backslash as **\"**. Consider **Program 2.8** illustrating how to use the **\"**.

```
#include <stdio.h>

main ( )
{
printf (" I am \"writing\" in C.");
}
```
Program 2.8.

The output of the program is

```
I am "writing" in C.
```

We add a few words about the backslash character (\). If used at the end of the line in a format string, the backslash character indicates that this line continues to the next line. If you just need to have that character (\) in a text and not concatenate the lines, write double backslash (\\) in a format string. Do not confuse a backslash in a format string with the backslash written outside of any statement, that stands for a comment.

We now return to the **printf()** function. It has more features, that you should learn. There is another form of writing **printf()** as

```
printf ("......%d....", var);
```

Here, the format string in the double quotes is followed by a comma and an identifier **var**. We also show **%d** character inside the format string. The identifier **var** after the comma stands for the name of the variable to be displayed. It is called *argument*. The **%d** character 'tells' the computer the data type of that variable and how it should be displayed. This is why the **%d** character is called the *format specification field* or *format*. Thus, we call **%d** a *format*, because it specifies how or in what format to display a variable.

Function **printf()** displays an exact copy of its format string including all the white spaces. It does not display the escape characters. They perform their actions according to the Table 2.1. The **%d** character is substituted by the value of the variable **val**, i.e., it is replaced by the corresponding argument. Consider **Program 2.9**.

```
#include <stdio.h>

main ( )
{
int out_test;
out_test=10;
printf ("Variable out_test is equal to %d.", out_test);
}
```

Program 2.9.

The output of the program on your screen is

```
Variable out_test is equal to 10.
```

Here you see, instead of typing **%d** on your screen, the computer substitutes it with the value of the variable **out_test** equal to 10. The displayed message is called an *output* of the **printf()** function.

Let's consider the **%d** character. We know, the format specification field **%d** 'tells' the computer how to display a variable. The format specification field begins with the percentage sign **%**. In our case it is followed by **d**, so we have **%d**. There can be other letters and even numbers following **%**. The letters are different for different data types. We will consider, how to display different data types.

The characters **%d**, **%o**, **%x** (**%X**) are used to display respectively decimal, octal and hexadecimal integral numbers of type **int** or **short**. The **%u** format specification field is used for **unsigned short** or **unsigned int**. **Program 2.9** is an example of an output with **%d** format specification field. Following **Program 2.10** uses **%o**, **%x** and **%u** format specification fields.

```
#include <stdio.h>

main ( )
{
int m=31;
unsigned int k=100;
printf ("octal m=%o, hexadec m=%x, k=%u\n", m, m, k);
}
```

Program 2.10.

The output of the program is

```
octal m=37, hexadec m=1f, k=100
```

Here, the value of 31 is displayed as octal number 37 and as a hexadecimal number 1f. The format specification field is used three times by the **printf()** function. There are also three variables to be displayed **m, m, k**. In our case, **printf()** function displays the same variable **m** twice. In general, one **printf()** function can display a number of variables of different data types. Each argument should be separated by the comma, as we showed. Computer will associate the first format specification field **%..** with the first variable, second **%..** with the second variable, and so on.

If you need to display a **long** or **unsigned long** integral number, just add letter **l** (for some compilers **L**) to those format specification fields, as **%ld, %lo, %lx, %lu**.

One can also use numbers in the format specification fields, as for example, **%6d, %101d, %5o**. We explain them on an example of **Program 2.11**.

```
#include <stdio.h>

main ( )
{
int m=31;
printf ("m=%10d \n", m);
}
```

Program 2.11.

The output of the program is

```
m=          31
```

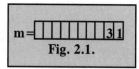
Fig. 2.1.

We requested to display **m** as **%10d**. The number 31 is displayed on 10 positions as shown in Fig. 2.1. The number 10 in **%10d** is called a *field width*. It specifies the number of positions used to display a value of one **int** type variable.

We would like to discuss another feature of **printf()** function. One can use a format specification field containing a dot followed by the numbers. For instance, **%.6d, %.101d, %.5o**. Review **Program 2.12**.

```
#include <stdio.h>
```

```
main ( )
{
int m=31;
printf ("m=%.10d \n", m);
}
```
Program 2.12.

The output of this program is
    m=0000000031

We intentionally used almost similar to previous example format specification field **%.10d**. Here, number 10 follows a point. The form **.10** specifies how many digits of an integer to display. If there are not enough digits, it displays leading zeros. You can count, there are precisely 10 digits in the number 31 displayed this way. The number after the point is called *precision*. In our example the precision was 10.

An integral number can be displayed with specified field width and precision. For instance, if we display number 31 in the format **%10.4d**, it will occupy 10 positions and consist of 4 digits. Therefore, two leading zeros would be added to the number 31.

A number can be displayed using "**+**" sign in the format specification field, as **%+d**, **%+20.101d** and so on. Normally, **printf()** displays a number only with the "**-**" sign if needed. Specifying a sign in the format specification field (like **%+d**), will always display a number with leading "**+**" or "**-**" sign.

Program 2.12 uses the precision **.10** in a format **%.10d**. As you know, the **%d** format is used to display the integers. We will see in a moment, the precision can have a different meaning when used with the floating-point value formats.

The floating-point values are displayed using **%f**, **%e** and **%g** format specification fields. We will consider **%f** and **%e** floating-point number formats in **Program 2.13**.

```
#include <stdio.h>

main ( )
{
float   x=10.673;
double  y=23.98765433489366;
printf ("x=%f, x= %e \ny=%f, y=%e \n", x, x, y, y);
}
```
Program 2.13.

The output of the program is
    x=10.673000, x=1.067300e+01
    y=23.987654, y=2.398765e+01

We declare **float** variable **x** and **double** type variable **y** at lines 4, 5. (We count the lines from the beginning of the program.) The **printf()** function at line 6 displays them. Let's concentrate on how those values are displayed. The **%f** format displays floating-point value in a regular notation with a decimal point. We have displayed the values **x=10.673000** and **y=23.987654** in this format. The **%e** format displays the floating-point numbers in an exponential notation. The values **x=1.067300e+01** and **y=2.398765e+01** are displayed in this format. Both **%f** and **%e** display up to six, in some cases, seven digits after the decimal point. However, some compilers display the floating-point values as the numbers with up to seven or eight digits total. In this case, the eight digits are split between the integral and fractional parts of a value.

We declared variable **x** to be of type **float** and **y** of type **double** in **Program 2.13**. Both values have been displayed similarly with 6 digits of precision after the point. What if we need more precision in displaying **double** and **long double** floating-point values? The answer is to use a precision in the format specification field, that we discussed for integers. The precision for the floating-point values specifies the number of digits after the decimal point to be displayed. However, the precision defines a total number of digits in a floating-point value on some compilers. Review **Program 2.14** illustrating the precision.

```
#include <stdio.h>

main ( )
{
double y=23.98765433489366;
printf ("y=%.14f, y=%.14e \n", y, y);
}
```

Program 2.14.

The output of the program is
```
y=23.98765433489366, y=2.39876543348937e+01
```
Here, 14 digits after the decimal point are displayed.

The format **%g** is used for the floating-point numbers as well. It displays those values either in **%f** or **%e**, whichever format takes less space for the same precision.

One can use the field width and the sign "**+**" in the format specification fields for the floating-point numbers. They have the same meaning as for the integers.

2.4.2. Console data input.

We now consider a function, that allows a compiled and running program to read the information from the keyboard. It is the **scanf()** function. You will find similarities in writing **scanf()** and **printf()** functions. The **scanf()** is written in the form
```
scanf ("%d", &x);
```
It consists of a *format string* **"%d"** enclosed in the double quotation marks and the address of the variable to be entered **&x**. The address of the variable to enter is called an *argument*. The format string and the address of the variable are separated by a comma (**"...", &x**).

Look carefully at the name of the variable **&x**. It does not look as a conventional name of a variable, because there is a **&** character in front of the identifier **x**. The **&x** is, in fact, not a name of a variable. Character **&** in this case is an address of the variable **x**.

When you define a variable, for instance **x**, a memory cell is allocated for it during the compilation stage. The **scanf("%d", &x)** places an entered from the keyboard value in the memory cell allocated for **x**. This is why the argument of the **scanf()** function is not the variable **x**, but rather its address **&x**. You do not have to worry, what is the address of the variable **x**. You just type **&x** and computer finds this address. We will study how to refer to a variable by its address in more details in the Chapter 8.

You see a familiar character **%d** in **scanf()** format string. It is a *format specification field* or a *format* as in **printf()** function. The **%d**, **%o** and **%x** formats are used for entering respectively decimal, octal and hexadecimal integers of type **int**. Formats **%D** or **%ld**, **%O** or **%lo**, **%X** or **%lx** are used for reading **long** decimal, octal and hexadecimal numbers respectively. Capital letter or additional letter **l** indicates that this is a **long** type. Any of the formats **%f** or **%e** can be used for reading the data of type **float**. Those values can also be entered in an exponential notation. Any of the formats **%F**, **%lf**, **%E** and **%le** can be used for reading the **double** and **long double** data types.

It is very important to use each of the formats very strictly for the proper data type. Otherwise, you can get unpredictable errors in data reading. We urge you to experiment with your computer to see it. Consider **Program 2.15** demonstrating the input function.

```
#include <stdio.h>

main ( )
{
int m;
long k;
float x;
double y;
printf ("\nenter an int number\n");
scanf ("%d", &m);
printf ("m=%d \n", m);
printf ("enter a long number\n");
scanf ("%ld", &k);
printf ("m=%ld \n", k);
printf ("enter two floating numbers\n");
scanf ("%f, %le", &x, &y);
printf ("float x=%f, double y=%.10e \n", x, y);
}
```

Program 2.15.

The variables **m**, **k**, **x** and **y** are declared at lines 4-7. The **printf()** function displays a message
```
enter an int number
```
After that, you can enter an integer of **int** data type. Its value is assigned to **m** by
```
scanf ("%d", &m);
```
After entering a value, you must press **ENTER**. That constitutes the end of data entry for the **scanf()** function. Following **printf()** displays the value stored in **m**. Then, the program prompts the user to enter a **long** type number. Second **scanf()** performs an

input of variable **k**. It is followed by the **printf()** function, that displays this variable **k**. The program is quite readable up to the line containing

```
scanf ("%f, %le", &x, &y);
```

You can enter two floating-point numbers as either regular or exponential numbers, that will be read by the **scanf("%f, %le", &x, &y)**. You should separate those two values with the comma, because there is a comma in the format string **"%f, %le"**.

The **scanf("%f, %le", &x, &y)** illustrates a number of interesting features of the **scanf()** function. First, the **scanf()** is a multiargument function. This means, it can read a number of variables every time you call it. It should have equal numbers of format specification fields **%..** and the arguments. First format specification field specifies the format of an input for the first argument, the second format specification field specifies how to read the data into the second argument and so on. In our example first **%f** provides an input for the **&x** argument and **%le** - for **&y**.

A format string can contain any other characters beside format specification fields **%...**. In that case, you should enter the data and all other characters in exact order, as they follow in the format string. *Function* **scanf()** *reads the input, until it reads the values for all the arguments or finds the first discrepancy between the format string and the input.* Naturally, you enter values instead of **%..** characters. The white spaces separating the characters are ignored by the **scanf()**. So, you can write any number of white spaces in an input.

For example, you write a program containing a line

```
scanf("first value: %d, second value: %d", a, b);
```

When the program is running, you can enter from the keyboard

```
first      value: 200, second value 100
```

Here, you lost the second colon (**:**), when entered the data. Therefore, **scanf()** will read 200 and will not read 100. Also, it does not matter how many white spaces were between the words '**first**' and '**value**'.

We also want to illustrate another aspect in reading the data by **Program 2.16**.

```
#include <stdio.h>

main ( )
{
int m;
printf ("\nenter a number\n");
scanf ("don't forget %d and all other characters", &m);
printf ("m=%d \n", m);
}
```

Program 2.16.

When the program prompts you

```
enter a number
```

You enter

```
don't forget 200 and all other characters
```

The program extracts 200 from the line and displays it by the **printf()** function

```
m=200
```
The **scanf()** function reads a value of each argument until it encounters:
-a first white character;
-a character of a different data type than specified by the format field of that argument.
You entered "**forget 200 and ...**" in the above program. Number 200 was followed by a blank. The computer treated the blank as an end of the number. This is why it understood, that you have entered 200. If you enter "**forget 200and ...**", the computer would recognize letter '**a**' as **char** type and stop before it. Why is it so? The **scanf()** expects to read an **int** data type in **Program 2.16**, because the format specification field is **%d**. The data reading should stop, when the **scanf()** function has encountered white space or character '**a**' of **char** data type. Thus, the read value should be 200 in both cases.

The **scanf()** used with all the discussed above formats skips any white or escape character preceding the value to be read. In other words, if we use

```
scanf ("%d", &x);
```
you can enter any number of white or escape characters, or **ENTER** before entering a number. All the white spaces, preceding an **int** value will be ignored.

The **scanf()** function can use a field width in its format specification field. In this case, the field width indicates the number of positions to be read as one value. Consider **Program 2.17**.

```
#include <stdio.h>

main ( )
 {
int n;
scanf ("%3d",&n);
printf ("%d\n", n);
 }
```

Program 2.17.

If you type a number 12345678 and hit **ENTER**, the **scanf()** function will only read 3 positions, that is number 123. Thus, the output of the above program is: **123**. You can use field width, when reading a few values at once, as shown in **Program 2.18**.

```
#include <stdio.h>

main ( )
{
int n, m  ;
scanf ("%3d %3d", &n, &m );
printf ("n=%d, m=%d \n", n, m);
 }
```

Program 2.18.

You can enter 123456789. The output of this program is
```
n=123, m=456
```
The first three positions of the number 123456789 are considered as the first value **n**. The next three positions are treated as the value of **m**. Even though we entered more then six positions, but only six of them specified by the field widths have been read.

2.4.3. Console character input/output.

You are already familiar with **printf()** and **scanf()** functions. Everything you know about them by now is applicable to the I/O of characters. What is different? You shell use a **%c** format specification field for a character I/O. Format **%c** is used to read or display only one character. This one character can be anything: letter, one digit, special character, escape character, or white space. Thus,
```
scanf ("%c", &x);
```
will read the *first character you enter*, whatever it is. The
```
printf ("the output is: %c \n", x);
```
will substitute **%c** by one character and display that character, whatever it is.

We know, that variables of type **char** are used to represent a character. The characters are stored as integers internally in the computer. Therefore, one can use both **char** and **int** data types to store the characters. Furthermore, you can enter a character under **%c** format by **scanf()**, and its integral value can be displayed using the **%d** format in **printf()**. Consider a few examples.

```
#include <stdio.h>

main ( )
{
char k;
printf ("\n enter a character \n");
scanf ("%c", &k);
printf ("it is: %c \n", k);
}
```
Program 2.19.

The program prompts you to enter a character. For example, we enter **a**. It will display **a** on the screen. Consider next example.

```
#include <stdio.h>

main ( )
{
char k;
printf ("\n enter a character \n");
scanf ("%c", &k);
```

```
printf ("it is: %d \n", k);
}
```

Program 2.20.

Let's enter a character, for instance **a**. The program displays the argument **k** of the **printf()** function in the **%d** format, which produces a numeric value of **a**.

    it is: 97

One can enter a character in **%c** format and display its value in **%d**. Review an example.

```
#include <stdio.h>

main ( )
{
char k;
printf ("\n enter a number \n");
scanf ("%d", &k);
printf ("it is: %c \n", k);
}
```

Program 2.21.

The program asks to enter a number. You enter a number, that is read by the **scanf()** function. The **printf()** function displays a character corresponding to it. We enter an integer in **%d** and display a character in **%c** formats. If you enter, for instance, number 114, the message will be

    it is: r

Pay attention, we use a variable **k** of **char** data type in all three programs above. They will also work, if you change the type of the variable **k** to **int**. But the value of the entered integral numbers can not exceed the maximum allowed for type **char**.

We want to elucidate this important point about characters. A character is represented internally as an integer. Therefore, in C style programs you can assign to **int** or **char** variables a numeric value or a character. Those variables will store an integral number in any case. You can display this number or corresponding to it character by choosing respectively **%d** or **%c** format in the **printf()** function. It is illustrated in **Program 2.22** below.

```
#include <stdio.h>

main ( )
{
int m=97, p='a';
char k=98, r='b';
printf ("m=%d, p=%d  ", m, p);
printf ("m=%c, p=%c \n", m, p);
printf ("k=%d, r=%d  ", k, r);
printf ("k=%c, r=%c \n", k, r);
```

```
}
```
Program 2.22.

The output of the program is
```
m=97,  p=97   m=a,   p=a
k=98,  r=98   k=b,   r=b
```
 This program illustrates, among other things, how to assign a character to a variable directly. It is done as for a regular variable. In our program it is
```
p='a';
```
Variable **p** should be declared as **int** or **char** type. We can assign a character to it in the same way as to any other type variable. The character that you assign should be enclosed in the quotation marks (' '). If we display variable **p** in the character format, we will get the letter **a** on the screen.

 We initialize all the variables at lines 4, 5 in **Program 2.22**. We have chosen two **int** and two **char** variables. We assign the value 97 and corresponding to it character 'a' to **int** type variables **m** and **p** respectively. We assign the value 98 and corresponding to it character 'b' to the variables **k** and **r** of type **char**.

 The first **printf()** displays the integral values corresponding to character 'a' stored in both **m** and **p**. The second **printf()** displays the character 'a' stored in **m** and **p**. A point to remember is, that we assigned an integer to the variable **m** and a character to **p**, and displayed the integral values of both **m** and **p**. We were also able to display the values stored in **m** and **p** as the characters. We performed the same operation with the **char** type variables **k** and **r**.

2.4.4. More about console character input/output.

 Let's discuss **getchar()** and **putchar()** functions. The **getchar()** function reads a single character from a keyboard. It reads the first incoming character, even if it is a white space or an escape character. The function does not have an argument. We offer you an example of how to use this function in the assignment below.
```
x=getchar( );  where
```
x can be declared as either **int** or **char**. When a character is entered from the keyboard, its numeric value is stored in the variable **x**. One can display that character using **printf("%c", x)**. The value corresponding to the character stored in **x** can be displayed by choosing **%d** format in **printf()**. **Program 2.23** illustrates the use of the **getchar()** function.

```
#include <stdio.h>

main ( )
{
char k;
printf ("\n enter a character \n");
k=getchar( );
```

```
printf ("it is: %c \n", k);
printf ("its value is: %d \n", k);
}
```

Program 2.23.

Program prompts you to enter a character. If you enter **b** and press **ENTER**, it displays
```
it is: b
its value is: 98
```
The program displays a character or its integral decimal value depending on which format **%c** or **%d** we use in **printf()** function. The program will work, even if you change the data type of variable **k** to **int**.

The **putchar()** function displays a single character on the screen. We will study it on the example of **Program 2.24**.

```
#include  <stdio.h>

main ( )
{
int m, p=98;
char k;
k='a';
putchar (k);
putchar (p);
putchar ('\n');
m=putchar ('r');
printf ("%c \n", m);
}
```

Program 2.24.

The output of the program is
```
ab
rr
```
The **putchar(x)** function displays on the monitor screen a character stored in its argument **x**. The function always displays a character. Its argument can have **int** or **char** type. You can even assign an integral number to an argument of **putchar()** function, but it always displays a character corresponding to that integral value, if the character exists. In our example, **k** was assigned to be 'a', and variable **p** has received the value 98, corresponding to character 'b'. The **putchar()** function with **k** and **p** arguments displays the characters 'a' and 'b' respectively. We also used a newline character '**\n**' as an argument of **putchar()**. You can see, letters '**ab**' are displayed on the same line. The **putchar('\n')** moves the cursor to a new line. Two other characters are displayed on the next line. Therefore, the escape characters perform their actions, when used as the arguments of the **putchar()** function.

The **m=putchar('r')** demonstrates, that you can use a character directly as an argument of the **putchar()** function. In this case, a character should be surrounded by the quotation marks. We used character '**r**' as **putchar()** function argument. It was displayed on the screen. Another important lesson is, the **putchar()** function not only writes an argument to the output (or screen). The character in the argument can be assigned to a variable. We have assigned it to **m** and displayed **m** by means of the **printf()** function.

We want to demonstrate rather an interesting property of the character input functions. It occurs when you use **scanf()** or **getchar()** functions a few times for reading the characters. It will be clear, after you go over **Program 2.25**.

```
#include <stdio.h>

main ( )
{
char x;
printf ("\nEnter lowercase characters. \n");
scanf ("%c", &x);
x=x-32;
printf ("%c", x);
scanf ("%c", &x);
x=x-32;
printf ("%c", x);
scanf ("%c", &x);
x=x-32;
printf ("%c", x);
}
```

Program 2.25.

The program first asks you to enter some characters
```
Enter lowercase characters.
```
Let's enter a few characters at once and press **ENTER**.
```
alskdf ENTER
```
The output of the program is
```
ALS
```
The program reads and converts lowercase letters into the uppercase letters. Its fourth line declares the variable **x** of **char** type. The fifth line displays a message on the screen prompting a user to enter a character. After that line the program consists of three identical blocks
```
scanf ("%c", &x);
x=x-32;
printf ("%c", x);
```
Here, the **scanf()** function reads a character from a keyboard and stores its value in **x**. The formula (**x=x-32**) subtracts 32 from the integral value corresponding to the entered character. The integral value of a lowercase character is greater its uppercase version by 32. Thus, if '**a**' corresponds to 97, then '**A**' corresponds to 65. Also, '**b**' corresponds to 98, and '**B**' corresponds to 66. This is why a value corresponding to an uppercase character

can be obtained from its lowercase value by subtracting 32 from the last one. Why 32? This is the way in which the ASCII character set has been set. Used in our program **printf("%c", x)** displays this converted uppercase character.

We repeated this code fragment three times in **Program 2.25**. Since there are only three **scanf("%c", &x)** functions in the program, only three characters can be read from the input. The first **scanf()** reads the first character 'a' in the line, the second **scanf()** reads the character '1', and the last function reads the third character. We entered more characters to show you, that no more than three of them will be read. Thus, each character input function should read the next character in the line.

The numbers are read by the **scanf()** function one by one. We just remind you, that one uses **%d**, **%f**, **%e** and other formats for reading the numbers. The numbers can be entered in two ways. You can enter numbers separately. You enter a number, push **ENTER**. It is read by the first **scanf()**. Then, you can enter another number and press **ENTER**. In will be read by the second **scanf()** and so on. You can enter as many numbers as needed this way. Try to push ENTER after each letter in Program 2.25 and see the difference. The second way is when you can enter all the values at once, as for example, **23 432 81 2 5** and only then push **ENTER**. The effect must be the same. The first **scanf()** reads the first value, the second **scanf()** reads the second one.

2.5. Object-oriented input /output.

This section is meant to be an introductory to the C++ style I/O, because you have not learn all the prerequisite information for that subject. We will come to the C++ style I/O later in this book in a separate chapter, that will give a thorough treatment of this subject. Here, we just want to give you fundamentals in specific for C++ *stream I/O*. We will consider **cin** and **cout** used for the C++ I/O. Both are not functions but rather the objects. We avoid calling them the objects, because right now we do not want to switch you to the definition of objects. We will do that later. Just know, that they are the objects used for I/O. We will show you how to use them for the input and output. You should include the **<iostream.h>** header file when using any of those objects.

```
#include <iostream.h>
```

We used the word "stream" for the C++ I/O. The notion of stream is applicable to both C and C++. We will return to it later in the book. For now, think about a stream as a sequence of bytes. At this stage you just have to understand that a stream I/O provides the bytes flow between different devices and the memory. So, entering the data from a keyboard, can be called a stream input, while displaying the data on the monitor screen can be called a stream output.

2.5.1. Object-oriented output.

We will consider the **cout** object first. Programmers say, that **cout** writes the data to the standard output. This means, it displays the data on the screen. It is used along with the *stream insertion operator* (<<). Object **cout** can display the numbers, values stored in the variables and produced by the expressions, and messages. To produce an output using

cout object, insert any value or message into that object by the stream insertion operator. For example,

```
cout << "This is the message.";
```

produces an output

```
This is the message.
```

A message should be surrounded by the double quotation marks (" ").

You insert a number of messages using a separate insertion operator for each of them.

```
cout << "How are you? " << "I am fine.\n" << "Good.";
```

The output of that statement is

```
How are you? I am fine.
Good.
```

The second phrase is terminated by the newline character. This moves the screen cursor to the next line, so the third string "**Good.**" is displayed on the next line. You can see, that the escape sequences work with the **cout** object.

One can display the constants of any data type using **cout**. It is also very important, that one can also insert different kinds of entries (values, messages, expressions) into the same object. For example,

```
cout << "x=" << 200 << ", y=" << " " << 4.39 << ".";
```

The output of the last statement is

```
x=200, y= 4.39.
```

Here, one **cout** object displays two constants 200 and 4.39, and a number of strings, like "**x=**", "**, y=**" and others. Each of the entries is displayed in the order it follows. For example, "**x=**" precedes the number 200, so it goes the first followed by 200, then "**, y=**", blank space, value 4.39, and the dot. Each entry is inserted with a separate insertion operator.

You can insert an expression into the **cout** object. For example,

```
cout << x*y/z;
```

Each of the variables **x**, **y** and **z** should be assigned a value before inserting that expression into an output object. The object displays a numeric value of the expression. One can also calculate a numeric value of an expression of constants. For example,

```
cout << (1+2);
```

produces 3 as its output.

The output object can end with the **endl**. This moves the cursor to the next line on the screen, so the subsequent output will begin from the next line. The **endl** should be the last entry in the cout object. It terminates the object in which it is inserted. The **endl**, however, produces no output. For instance

```
cout << "Have a nice day." << endl;
cout << "This will start from the next line.";
```

The output of the last sequence is

```
Have a nice day.
This will start from the next line.
```

The semicolon should always conclude the last entry inserted into the **cout** object.

We shell now consider a few programs illustrating the output object. We will start with **Program 2.26.**

```
#include <iostream.h>

main ( )
{
cout << "It is easy.\n";
cout << "One can display " <<"a few messages"
     <<" by one object.\n";
}
```
Program 2.26.

The output of the program is

```
It is easy.
One can display a few messages by one object.
```
We use two **cout** objects here. The first one displays only one message. The message is surrounded by the double quotation marks. We also show, that one **cout** object can display a few messages. They all are inserted into **cout** by a separate stream insertion operator (**<<**). The semicolon concludes the last message inserted in the **cout** object.

Program 2.27 also demonstrates some of the features of the output object **cout**.

```
#include <iostream.h>

main ( )
{
int m=2, k=5;
cout << 100;
cout <<"\n";
cout << k;
cout <<"\nThe value of m="<< m
     <<". Sum of two values is "<<(10+25) << endl;
}
```
Program 2.27.

The output of the program is

```
100
5
The value of m=2. Sum of two values is 35
```
This program demonstrates, that one can insert a number and display it by the **cout**. We also insert the variable **m** and display its value by the **cout** object. The last **cout** object in **Program 2.27** displays multiple messages, the value of the variable **m**, and even an expression **(10+25)**. It is called to concatenate the messages. The messages are displayed in the order they follow.

Program 2.28 shows the floating-point number output, performed by the **cout** object.

```
#include <iostream.h>
```

```
main ( )
{
double x=3.9286987456321;
cout << x;
}
```
Program 2.28.

The output of this program is
```
3.9287
```
One can ask how to display a character using C++ programming style. It can be done by different means. It can be displayed using **cout** object and insertion operator. We illustrate it in **Program 2.29**.

```
#include <iostream.h>

main ( )
{
char x='a';
cout << x <<'b';
}
```
Program 2.29.

The output of the program is
```
ab
```
The program demonstrates, that a character can be displayed in the same manner as a number. The value of a **char** variable is always displayed as a character by the **cout** object. In our case **x='a'**. If we have written **x=97**, the **cout** object would have displayed it as **a** anyway.

A character can be displayed by **cout.put()** combination. The **cout.put('c')** will display a character **c** on the screen. The **put()** is a function. The **cout.put(x)** will display a character assigned to its **char** type argument **x** on the screen. One can concatenate calls to **put()**. For example,
```
cout.put ('H').put('o').put('w');
```
will display the word **how**. It is illustrated by **Program 2.30**.

```
#include <iostream.h>

main ( )
{
cout.put ('H').put('o').put('w');
}
```
Program 2.30.

The output of the program is
```
How
```

2.5.2. Object-oriented input.

As you know, the **cin** object reads the data from a standard input. The standard input is the keyboard. It is used along with the *stream extraction operator* (**>>**) that takes the read data and "furnishes" it to the memory. Thus, the expression **cin >> x** reads the data and places its value in the cell **x**. It will make **x** equal to the read value. The input object **cin** permits to enter integers, floating-point numbers, individual characters and character sequences (strings). Let's consider, how to enter the data on an example of the following program.

```
#include <iostream.h>

main ( )
{
int x;
char y;
float z;
cout <<"Enter integer, character, "
     << "floating-point number.\n";
cin >> x;
cin >> y;
cin >> z;
cout <<"x="<< x <<" y=" << y <<" z=" << z;
}
```
Program 2.31.

The program prompts the user
```
    Enter integer, character, floating-point number.
```
Let's say, we enter
```
    20   a   1.123456789
```
The program displays
```
    x=20 y=a z=1.12346
```
The user has an option, whether to enter all the values at once and press the **ENTER**, or to press the **ENTER** after each value. The first **cin** input object reads an integer. The second **cin** looks for a character. The third **cin** looks for the floating-point number. *The type of data to be read is determined by the data type of the variable to which the stream extraction operator passes the data.* In the first case we use **int** variable **x**, so the input should read an integer. Second time we pass the input data to the **char** type variable **y**. Therefore, the second entry shell be a character.

How does **cin** determine the end of an entry? When we read a value or a character with **cin**, the end of the value is determined by the white space, or by the data of another type. For example, if the **cin** object expects an integer and we type 23 or 23c, the value 23 will be assigned to the input variable. Here, the end of the value 23 is determined either by the blank character after it, of by the **c** character after the value 23. The **c** character is not an integral number. Thus, the **cin** object determines the end of an entry similarly to the **scanf()** function of C. One can also ask how does the **cin** object treat the leading white spaces before each entry. *The input object cin ignores the leading white space characters.* It applies to any data type. It means, that if you need to entry, for instance, an integer 23, you can use any number of blanks, newline and other white characters before it. Only after you type 23, it will be entered.

One can use the **get()** function with the input object **cin**. The function **get()** used as **cin.get()** reads a single character (even a white space) from the standard input. The read character can be passed to any variable using an expression like

```
x=cin.get( );
```
Consider following example.

```
#include <iostream.h>

main ( )
{
char a;
a=cin.get( );
cout << "You entered: " << a;
}
```

Program 2.32.

This program does following. You enter any character: letter, number, punctuator, a white space, escape character. It will be read and displayed, if it can be printed on a screen. A **ENTER**, for instance, would just move the cursor to the next line.

We do not consider any other features of the input object, because they will require to get deeper into material for which you are not ready yet. We will have a chapter about the C++ style I/O later in this book. By that time you shell be ready to appreciate all the features. Now you have enough knowledge of I/O to go over a part of this book.

2.5.3. Object-oriented formatting capabilities.

C++ permits to format the data. The first formatting capability is that C++ allows the user to display an integral number as a decimal, octal or hexadecimal one. The integers are normally displayed as the decimal numbers. To display the integers as octal numbers, you should insert the word **oct** into **cout** before inserting the value to be converted into octal number. To display a hexadecimal number, one should insert the word **hex**. If you want to go back to decimal numbers after working with octal or hexadecimal numbers, insert **dec** into **cout**. This would reset the stream back to the decimal values. The **oct**, **cout** and **dec** are called the *stream manipulators*. **Program 2.33** demonstrates the use of the manipulators.

```
#include <iostream.h>
```

```
main ( )
{
int m=189;
cout<<"Octal of "<<m<< " is "<<oct<<m
    <<",  decimal is "<<dec<<m;
cout<<"\nHexadecimal of "<<m<< " is "<<hex<<m;
}
```

Program. 2.33.

The output of the program is

```
Octal of 189 is 275, decimal is 189
Hexadecimal of 189 is bd
```

C++ allows a user to specify the precision of the floating-point number to be displayed. The *parametrized stream manipulator* **setprecision(m)** and the function **precision(m)** are used for that. The manipulator **setprecision(m)** can be inserted into the **cout** object by means of known to us stream insertion operator (< <). Its argument **m** specifies the number of digits that will be displayed after the decimal point. You have to include the **<iomanip.h>** header file

```
#include <iomanip.h>
```

in order to be able to use the **setprecision(m)** manipulator. The **precision(m)** function does not require the inclusion of the **<iomanip.h>** header file. The function should be used in a construction like

```
cout.precision (m);
```

This statement stipulates the output displaying a value with **m** digits after the decimal point. Some compilers understand the precision as the total number of digits in a value. Consider following program illustrating setting the precision.

```
#include <iostream.h>
#include <iomanip.h>

main ( )
{
double x=1.123456789123456787;
int k;
cout <<"\nEnter the precision you want.\n";
cin >> k;
cout<< setprecision(k) << x << setprecision(10)
      <<" For precision 10 x=" <<x;
cout <<"\nEnter the precision you want.\n";
cin >> k;
cout.precision (k);
cout <<x;
}
```

Program 2.34.

The program prompts the user to enter a precision to display the value of **x**.

    Enter the precision you want.

Let's assume, we enter 11. The output is

    1.12345678912 for precision 10 x=1.1234567891
    Enter the precision you want.

We enter any number, for instance 8. The output is

    1.12345678

One can set the field width using **width()** function and **setw()** manipulator. The **cout.width(m)** function and **setw(m)** manipulator specify the number **m** of digits or characters to be displayed. The **setw()** requires an inclusion of **<iomanip.h>** header file. **Program 2.35** demonstrates their use.

```
#include <iostream.h>
#include <iomanip.h>

main()
{
int x=22,y=3;
cout << "123456789" << "\n" << setw(5) << x;
cout.width(4);
cout <<y;
}
```

Program 2.35.

The output of the program is

    123456789
       22   3

We specify the output width of the **x** variable to be 5 characters. Its value is displayed on the field 5 positions wide. We specify the output field width for the **y** variable to be 4 positions. Since the second variable immediately follows the first, the four positions of **y** come next immediately after **x**. We also display numbers 123456789 in one line as a grid, so you would see, that **x** is displayed on 5 positions and **y** on 4.

2.6. Assignment and arithmetic operators.

2.6.1. Assignment operator.

The *assignment* operator is one of the first we shell study. It is written in the form:

    operand 1=operand 2;

An operand can be a constant, variable, structure, expression, function and so on. It means, that the **operand1** on the left side gets the value of the **operand2** on the right. Let's explain this statement on some examples.

So far, we have been intuitively accepting the assignment operator. Remember, when we discussed how to assign a value to a variable? We used the form

```
x=5;
```
This is nothing else but an assignment operator. The value 5 on the right side of this
equality has been assigned to the variable **x**. It means, that 5 has been put into the memory
cell, reserved by the computer for the variable **x**. This is a simplest assignment operator.
Now, we can go one more step ahead. We write

```
x=y;
```
It means, that the current value of variable **y** is assigned to **x**. Let's say, before that
statement variable **y** was equal to 3. From this statement on, the value of **x** is equal to 3,
if you do not change it again later. The value of **y** has not changed. It was just copied to **x**.
Consider **Program 2.36**. It will help you to understand the assignment operator.

```
#include <iostream.h>

main ( )
{
int x=1, y=2;
cout << "x=" << x;
x=y;
cout << " x=" << x;
y=3;
cout << " x=" << x;
}
```
Program 2.36.

The output of the program is

```
x=1  x=2  x=2
```
It illustrates a few very important points about the assignment operator. We have already
discussed in **Program 2.3**, that variable can change its value during the program. We
change the values of the variables in **Program 2.36**. We declare variables **x=1** and **y=2** at
the beginning of **Program 2.36**. The first **cout** object prints the value of **x** equal to 1 on
the screen. After that, we assign the current value of **y** to **x** by **x=y** statement, and display
x again. The computer prints number 2, as you would expected.

We change the value of **y** to 3 and print **x** again. The computer displays 2 again. The
value of **x** has not changed, even though we made **y**, assigned previously to **x**, equal to 3.
This indicates, that the assignment **x=y** copied the current value of **y** to **x**. The current
value at that moment was 2. We changed the value of **y** after that, and it had no effect on
x. Thus, the assignment **x=y** does not establish any connection between the two variables
x and **y**. It just copies the current value of the variable on the right to the variable on the
left. In our case, it copies the current value of **y** into **x**. If you change the value of **y**
afterwards, it has no effect on **x** whatsoever.

One can assign an expression to a variable, for instance,

```
x=(8s-3z+82)/5y;
```
where **s**, **z** and **y** are some other variables. *One of the most important properties of an
assignment is, that it can assign a variable to itself.* For instance, something like

```
x=2x+4;
```

is a quite legitimate assignment. The **x** will get a new value after that assignment. Its new value is on the left. The right side is the expression **2x+4** with the *old* **x**. This assignment makes the new value of **x** equal to the result of some operation **2x+4** on the current **x**. Let's make **x** equal to 3 before the assignment statement and write our operator **x=2x+4**. New **x** will be **2*3+4=10**. **Program 2.37** demonstrates this feature of the assignment operator.

```
#include <stdio.h>

main ( )
{
int x;
x=5;
printf ("%d ", x);
x=x+10;
printf ("%d ", x);
x=x+10;
printf ("%d ", x);
}
```

Program 2.37.

The output of the program is
```
5 15 25
```
We will not explain this program, because it should be clear to you. As you see, each **x=x+10** increases the value of **x** by 10, as you would expect. We intentionally used **printf()** not **cout** for the output to remind you, that you have this way of output in your disposal.

2.6.2. Arithmetic operators.

You must understand the arithmetic operators and their actions, such as addition (**+**), subtraction (**-**), multiplication (*****) and division (**/**). They are used for arithmetic expressions in the program. The priority or precedence of the arithmetic operations is the same as in math. Just to remind you: the operations in the parentheses are evaluated and executed first, the multiplication and division are evaluated second and the last priority goes for the addition and subtraction. The unary minus operator (**-**) though has a preference over any other arithmetic operators. **Program 2.38** illustrates those arithmetic operators.

```
#include <iostream.h>

main ( )
{
int x, y=7, z=4, m;
m=5;
```

```
x=z*(m-3*y)/2;
cout << "x=" <<x;
}
```

Program 2.38.

The output of the program is

```
x=-32
```

Another fairly straightforward operator is the modulus (**%**). Do not confuse it with the format specification field character **%** in the **printf()** and **scanf()** functions. You can distinguish the modulus operator, because it is used independently of any function. Consider an example.

```
30%4
```

This operator gives a remainder of the first value 30 divided by the second value 4. It is equal to 2 in our case. The result of the operation can be assigned to a variable as, for example,

```
x=21%8
```

Here, **x** will be equal to 5.

We also want to introduce a *unary minus* operator. For example, the unary minus operator applied to the variable **x** is written as **-x**. We can use it with the assignment operator as well. For instance,

```
a=-y;
```

Another example is

```
x=-z+3*y;
```

The unary minus operator acts on a single variable or a constant. The value of variable **x** is *negated* by the unary minus operator **-x**. This means, that if the value of **x** were positive, the **-x** will make it negative. If **x** were a negative number, the **-x** will make it positive. Do not mix it with the subtraction operator, that is used to subtract one value from another one. If we rewrite

```
x=3*y-z;
```

This will be a regular subtraction, not a unary minus. Thus, unary minus should not be written between two values or variables.

One can ask, what is the difference between an assignment and a formula for math calculation. For example,

```
x=7*(6z-28b/k) + 5y;
```

What is it: an assignment or an arithmetic expression for calculations? The value of this expression on the right **7*(6z-28b/k)+5y** will be calculated and the result will be assigned to **x**. So, deep down, a math expression is an assignment operator as well.

2.6.3. Data type conversion.

We now know almost all data types and can do arithmetical operations on numbers. We also know an assignment operation. But what happens when you assign a **float** type value to a variable of type **int**? Can we add **int** and **double** type variables? You can have mixed data types in an expression, or assign a variable of one data type to another data type variable. One can also cast one data type to another. In all these cases, you will have to deal with the data conversion conventions, that are very simple.

We first write a chain of data types:

long double -> double -> float -> unsigned long -> long ->
-> unsigned int -> int -> unsigned short -> short-> char

Each data type in this chain either occupies more memory or can accept greater value than its successor (right neighbor). For example, data having **long double** type occupies more memory and can have wider range than data of type **double**. Another example, data of **unsigned long** type can accept greater positive number than that of **long** type. Let's call **long double** type a "higher precision" type than **double**, **double** a "higher precision" type than **float**, **float** a "higher precision" type than **unsigned long** and so on along the chain.

When there are different data types in the arithmetic expression, all the values are converted to the data type of the variable or constant having the highest precision data type. The result will have that highest precision data type. For example, we have to add **x** having **float** type and **y** of **int** type. The highest precision type in this expression is **float**. The **y** will be converted to the **float** type. The result of **x+y** will have the **float** type as well. You can ask how an **int** value can be converted to **double** or any other higher type? It will be padded with zeros after the point. So, if a lower precision data type value is converted to a higher precision data type, it is padded with zeros to bring it to the precision of that higher data type. The conversion of data type is called *promotion* in C++. What happens when a number with the sign is converted to a higher precision unsigned type? The sign will retain. The promotion of unsigned types to signed can, sometimes, lead to peculiar results shown in **Program 2.39**.

```
#include <iostream.h>

main ( )
{
unsigned long x;
int y=-10;
unsigned long z=20;
x=y+z;
cout << "x=" << x;
}
```

Program 2.39.

The output of the program is **x=10**. We can see, that **y** has retained its negative sign.

One interesting point. What if you have to compute a value of an expression containing all the integers and the result of this expression is a floating-point value? For example, the result of computing the value of the expression (2+3)/2 will be an integer 2. To get the correct floating-point value, we should express one of its values as the floating-point number. If we rewrite this expression as (2+3)/2.0, the answer will be 2.500000. We made 2.0 a floating point value, and got the correct result. The result should be assigned to a **float** type variable. Write a program that will do this calculation. It is a very important point to remember. If you want a result to be a higher precision data type, use at least one of the values of that precision in an expression.

In an assignment the passed from the right side of the = operator data is converted to the data type of the left side operand. The sign of the right side operand normally does not change. Thus, if the value of **y** is assigned to **x** (**x=y**), then data type of the value passed from **y** to **x** is converted to that of **x**. Data type in an assignment is converted to the type of the variable to which the assignment is made. The value stored in **y** does not change.

If a higher precision data passed from the right is converted to a lower precision operand on the left, the information can be lost. The conversion to the lower type is performed by the value truncation. If **y** has type **double** and **x** has the **int** type in the assignment **x=y**, the value of **y** will be truncated to **int**. If the value of **y** is beyond the range of **x**, the assignment can give an error. **Program 2.40** shows an assignment truncating a value.

```
#include <iostream.h>

main ( )
{
int x;
float y=1.23456;
x=y;
cout << "x=" << x;
}
```

Program 2.40.

The output of the program is number 1. It is a fairly straightforward program so we do not go into details. The value stored in **y** of type **float** is passed to **x** and truncated to the data type **int** of the variable **x**. **y** is still equal to 1.23456 after the assignment.

C++ permits the *data type casting*. For example, you have an expression

```
7*(6z-28b/k) + 5y
```

Its variables can have any data type, but you want the **int** type result. You can write

```
res= (int)( 7*(6z-28b/k) + 5y);
```

The form **(int)**, in which the data type name is surrounded by the brackets, casts the expression to the **int** type. You can also achieve it by declaring the variable **res** as an **int** data type. Type casting is more important in other areas of C, that we will study.

2.6.4. Compound assignment operator.

Let's consider so-called compound assignment operators. Those operators represent a shorter way of writing the arithmetic operations and an assignment. We will review multiplication assignment (***=**), division assignment (**/=**), remainder assignment (**%=**), addition assignment (**+=**) and subtraction assignment (**-=**). You will also learn some other compound assignment operators later in this book. The compound assignment operators are given in Table 2.2.

We hope, the table below is easy to read. However, let's consider a few examples of the

compound assignment operators. For instance, an addition assignment
```
x +=10;
```
is a shorter form of
```
x=x+10;
```
By analogy
```
var_val *= 2;  is  var_val = var_val*2;
```
Consider something more difficult.
```
x /= y+10;  is nothing else but  x=x/(y+10);
```

Table 2.2. Compound assignment operators.

Assignment operator	Example	Explanation
+=	x+=5	x=x+5, if x was 3, then x=3+5=8. It assigns 8 to x.
-=	x-=5	x=x-5, if x was 3, then x=3-5=-2. It assigns -2 to x.
*=	x*=5	x=x*5, if x was 3, then x=3*5=15. It assigns 15 to x.
/=	x/=5	x=x/5, if x was 20, then x=20/5=4. It assigns 8 to x.
%=	x%=5	x=x%5, if x was 18, then x=18%5=3. It assigns 8 to x.

This concludes present chapter. Following exercises will deepen your understanding of the chapter.

EXERCISES.

1. If you have an access to a computer that supports C++ programming language, type and run all the programs presented in this chapter.
2. Find valid names of the variables among following.

x423	4x23	Lx423	float
$x	%d	variable	integer
_yz	abcdefg	abc_abc	abc#ab1

3. Following are the constants. Determine which of them are integer, floating-point or character constants.

a	1234	23.23	1029300
2.34e+10	\vsd	$	0

3. Try to find appropriate data types for the data given below.

0	@	2938475	3999999999
29384.36	39.123362514	70000	r

4. Enter and display following data using C and C++ style I/O.

?	w	180	43.89
-100000	-	1.2987e+88	-387.256
0667	982	af7	aaa
a	8	!	"

5. Write a program for finding an area **S** of a triangle in Fig. 2.2 using a formula **S=(1/2)*c*h**, and find it for

a) c=10.5cm, h=2cm;

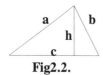
Fig2.2.

b) c=3cm, h=5cm;
c) c=30.12345678987cm, h=2cm.
The data type of the variables can be chosen only once and it should be able to accommodate each of those values. In the real life you have to take an assumption of how precise should the entered numbers and the result be. Use your judgment in each case if you need the sides as precise as they are.

6. Write the programs capable of calculating the value of
   100+(298.87654378923456*6.9283/(10 +100000/1.59) -66) -921
   a) the result should be an integer;
   b) the result should have not more than six digits after a point;
   c) the result should have up to 14 digits after a point;

7. Assign each of the values in exercise 4 to a variable and display them as: **int** (decimal, octal, hexadecimal), **unsigned int** (decimal, octal, hexadecimal), **long** (decimal, octal, hexadecimal), **unsigned long** (decimal, octal, hexadecimal), **float**, **double**. Write two programs. One of them should display the data using C style I/O, the second one should use the C++ I/O.

8. As an exercise write a program displaying in **%f** and **%e** formats following values of type **double**: 1.23456789123, 12.3456789123, 123.456789123, 1234.56789123, 12345.6789123, 123456.789123, 1234567.89123. See for yourself, how many digits after a decimal point will be displayed, when the value increases.

9. Write a program for converting 100° in Fahrenheit (**F**) to the Celsius scale (**C**), using the formula
   C=(F-32)*(5/9)

10. Write two programs that produce a bank statement. Both of the programs should ask a user to enter the opening balance, total amount of deposits and withdrawals. Both programs should print a statement on the screen in the form

Opening Balance	Deposits	Withdrawals	Closing Balance
1000	500	-200	1300

The first program should use the C style input/output. The second program should use C++ I/O tools.

11. Write two programs that read a character from a standard input and convert it to a hexadecimal and octal number. Both numbers should be displayed on the screen with the proper message, like:
   The hexadecimal representation of the character ...is... .
The first program should use C style I/O. The second program should use C++ style.

12. Write two programs that display a graph y=2*x. Use asterisk character (*) for every point of the line. The first program should draw the graph using C style I/O. The second

program should use C++ style I/O.

13. Discuss the meaning of **cin**, **cout**.

14. Predict an outcome (if it exists) in the following cases:

    a) **cout << 2*x+3;** **x** is an integer with value 5;

    b) **cout << " The output is x+x";** where **x=10**;

    c) **cout << " The output is " << x+x+x;** where **x=7**;

    d) **cout << " The output is   << x+x+x;** where **x=7**;

    e) **cout << "y" << "=" << x+x+x;**

    f) **cin >> "input";**

    g) **cin >> y >> x >> z;**

        cout << x << ", " << y << ", " << z;

If you have an access to a computer, run a program with each of those statements and see how they work.

15. Write two programs that print following

    1 2 3 4

      4 5 6 7

        7 8 9 0

The first program should use C style I/O. The second one should use C++ I/O style.

16. Write a program that prompts the user to enter a radius of a circle and displays its circumference and area. Use the value 3.141592653 for π.

17. Write a program that reads four digit integral number like 2345 and displays each of its digits separated from the others by a comma and a space. For example, for the input like 2345 the output should read 2, 3, 4, 5.

CHAPTER 3

CONTROL STATEMENTS.

3.1. Loop, relational, increment, decrement statements.

There are three loop statements in C++: **for, while, do-while**. The loops are the attributes of every computer language and C++ is no exception. They have been inherited from C language. Those statements are almost identical in C and C++.

3.1.1. The *for* statement.

We will begin with a simple problem to give you a feeling of when and how the **for** looping statement can be helpful. Let's calculate a sum of first 10 numbers from 1 to 10. Forget for now a simple math formula allowing you to do it. Do not forget math when you program a computer though. A good programmer should be a good mathematician.

So, we want to calculate this sum. We intend to use the C++ tools known to us from the material covered in this book up to this page. It produces the following program.

```
#include <iostream.h>

main ( )
{
int m;
m=1+2+3+4+5+6+7+8+9+10;
cout << "m=" << m;
}
```

Program 3.1.

The output of this program is **m=55**. It can be written even easier as shown below.

```
#include <iostream.h>

main ( )
{
cout << "m=" << (1+2+3+4+5+6+7+8+9+10);
}
```

Program 3.2.

In this case, we got away relatively easy. What if you have to calculate a sum of 1000 numbers, or a sum of the numbers changing somehow? Instead of writing the repetitive statements, one can write one statement that will substitute all of them. Do not try to imagine how do the loops work. You cannot understand how to create a loop yet. Just go with us step by step.

The **for** statement is written in the form

```
for (initial expression; loop condition; loop expression)
    C statement;
```

It should be written correctly with all the punctuators as shown above. We will learn the loops on an example of **Program 3.3**. It finds a sum of 10 numbers from 1 to 10.

```
#include <iostream.h>

main ( )
{
int n, x;
x=0;
for (n=1; n<11; n=n+1)
x=x+n;
cout << "The sum is " << x << "." << endl;
}
```

Program 3.3.

The output of the program is

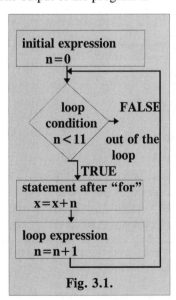

Fig. 3.1.

The sum is 55.

The program is pretty straightforward by itself. It first declares two variables **x** and **n** of type **int**, and assigns zero to **x**. The **for** statement computes the sum of numbers.

```
for (n=1; n<11; n=n+1)
x=x+n;
```

The result is displayed on the screen by the **cout** object. Let's discuss **for** loop. Our *initial expression* is n=1, the *loop condition* is n<11, the *loop expression* is n=n+1. The variable n in **for** statement is called an *index* variable. Statement x=x+n immediately following the **for** statement is a part of the *body of the loop*.

The execution of the **for** loop can be broken into following steps shown in Fig. 3.1. The computer first executes the initial expression **n=1**. The index variable **n** is set to a value called *initial* value. In our case **n=1**. Then, the loop condition **n<11** is evaluated. In our example the condition is **n<11**. The current value of **n** is 1. If the condition is true, computer executes the statement right after the **for** statement. This statement, as we

mentioned, belongs to the loop body. Our statement is **x=x+n**. After executing this statement, computer executes the loop expression. The loop expression in our program is
n=n+1. **n** becomes equal to 2. The first loop cycle is over. Follow the arrows in Fig. 3.1.
The computer begins another loop. It evaluates the loop condition **n<11** and, if it is true,
executes the statement **x=x+n** of the loop body. Your computer again executes the loop
expression **n=n+1**. This completes the second loop. Then, as shown by arrows in Fig.
3.1, it checks the loop condition. Now **n=3**. Hence, the condition is still holding. Computer executes **x=x+n** statement. This completes the loop execution again.

The computer loops time and again for as long as **n** is less than 11. The loop condition
(**n<11**) becomes false, when **n** is equal to 11. Then, the program follows the exit "**FALSE**"
in Fig. 3.1. The computer leaves the loop and executes the second after **for** statement. It
is the **cout** object in **Program 3.3**.

We shell now figure out how does the algorithm of computing the sum work. It is done by
the **x=x+n** statement inside the **for** loop. You set **x=0** before the loop. At the beginning,
x=0 and **n=1**. Follow the Fig. 3.1. The first loop sets **x=x+n=0+1=1** and **n=n+1=1+1=2**.
Thus, the value of **x** changes to 1, and **n** becomes 2. The second loop sets **x=x+n=1+2=3**
and **n=n+1=2+1=3**. Next loop cycle yields **x=x+n=3+3=6**. Each cycle increases the
previous value of **x** by the current value of **n**. This is, in fact, the sum **1+2+3+4+5+....**

3.1.2. Relational, increment and decrement operators.

Recall the form of loop condition, that was **n<11** in **Program 3.3**. The **n<11** condition
specified, that **n** was "less than 11". The "**<**" character is called *relational operator*. Table
3.1 gives the relational operators and specifies their meaning.

Table 3.1. Relational operators.

Operator	Usage
==	compares if left side is equal to right side
<	compares if left side is less than right side
>	compares if left side is greater than right side
!=	compares if left side is not equal to right side
<=	compares if left side is less than or equal to right side
>=	compares if left side is greater than or equal to right side

The relational operators have lower precedence than arithmetic operators. It means, if an
expression consists of arithmetic and relational operators, the arithmetic operators will be
executed first. If we make a loop condition **n<11*2**, the compiler would first execute
11*2=22, and only then compare **n** to 22. So, **n<11*2** is the same as **n<22**. We wanted
the loop to run only when **n** was less than 11 in **Program 3.3**. Consider almost similar
program. It uses another relational operator.

```
#include <iostream.h>

main ( )
```

```
{
int n, x;
x=0;
for (n=1; n<=11; n=n+1)
x=x+n;
cout << "The sum is " << x << ".";
}
```

Program 3.4.

The output of the program is

```
The sum is 66.
```

The condition **n<=11** requires **n** to be "less or equal" than 11. The loop has stopped after **n=10** in **Program 3.3**. The loop stops after **n=11** in **Program 3.4**. The relational operators can be used in different loop and condition statements that we will study in this book. They can also be used independently.

One can write **n=n+1** and **n=n-1** in a shorter form. The **n=n+1** expression can be written as **++n** or "add one". The **++** is called the *increment operator*. The **n=n-1** can be written as **--n** or "subtract one". The **--** is called the *decrement operator*. Again, **n=n+1** and **++n** are two ways of writing the same expression. They mean the same action, that increases the value of **n** by one. Both ways are equivalent in C++. One has to be very careful with the increment and decrement operators. There are two increment operators, and each of them is called differently:

++n - is called a *pre-increment* operator, because **++** is placed before the operand **n**;
n++ - is called a *post-increment* operator, because **++** is placed after the operand **n**;
The effect of both of those operators will be an increase of the variable **n** by **1**, or

```
n=n+1;
```

There also are two decrement operators: *pre-decrement* **--n** and *post-decrement* **n--**.

You can try to run **Program 3.3** using

```
for (n=1; n<=11; ++n) or
for (n=1; n<=11; n++)
```

There will be no difference in the results. Therefore, it does not matter, which of the increment operators you use in the **for** loop. The increment and decrement operators can be used anywhere, not only inside the **for** loop. You can see the difference in the results produced by the post- and pre-increment (decrement) operators, when they are used in some compound assignment statements. To illustrate this, let's introduce a second variable **m**. Let's assign an increment or decrement of variable **n** to **m**. It can be done by writing an assignment and increment operators together as shown.

```
m=++n;
```

Let's assume, the value of **n** was equal to 1, before we wrote the above line of code. The above expression first increases the value of **n** by 1, making **n** equal to 2. Then 2 is assigned to **m**. The result of **m=++n** operation is **m=2** and **n=2**. It is equivalent to

```
n=n+1;
m=n;
```

We rewrite the increment expression, changing the position of the **++**.

```
m=n++;
```

The above statement first assigns the initial value of **n=1** to the variable **m**. Only then, it increments **n** by 1. This produces **m=1** and **n=2**. It is equivalent to

```
m=n;
n=n+1;
```

The post- and pre-increment operators are demonstrated in **Program 3.5**.

```
#include <iostream.h>

main ( )
{
int n=1, m;
m=n++;
cout << "n=" << n << " m=" << m;
}
```

Program 3.5.

The output of this program is

```
n=2, m=1
```

Change the fifth line in **Program 3.5** from **m=n++** to **m=++n** and run it again. You get

```
n=2, m=2
```

Everything you learned about increment operator is true for the decrement operator as well. Run **Program 3.5** to prove that **n=- - m** and **n=m - -** produce different results.

3.1.3. More about *for* statement.

Often one needs more than one statement to be executed every time inside the loop. We have indicated so far, that only a statement following **for**, is executed inside the loop. If more than one statement should be executed inside the loop, write it as

```
for (initial expression; loop condition; loop expression)
{
statement 1;
statement 2;
...
}
next statement after loop;
```

Part of the program contained inside **{}** brackets belongs to the loop body and will be executed every loop cycle. When the loop is completed, the computer will execute next statement outside and after the brackets.

Be careful with the brackets. The fragment within the brackets is executed many times. Do not forget to close the bracket, because the program will search for the closing bracket. This will cause an error. If you forget to write a loop condition, or the loop condition will always be true, the loop will run forever. You have to use compiler or even system tools to terminate that loop.

The group of statements inside the **{}** brackets is called a *compound* or, sometimes, a *block* statement. It is used with the loop and decision statements. The block statements can be also used by themselves. C++ permits to use a block statement by itself not only inside the body of decision or loop statements.

We will demonstrate a loop containing a number of statements in **Program 3.6**. This program finds a sum of factorials from 1 to any entered number. A factorial of an integral number **n** is **n!=1*2*3*...n**. The **n!** is a standard factorial writing form in mathematics. For example, a factorial of **4!** is **4!=1*2*3*4=24**. We have to write a program, that adds those factorials, as **1!+2!+3!+....** We did a simple summation so far. Here, each loop cycle would have to calculate a factorial and to do an addition. It is implemented in **Program 3.6**. We even made it interactive. It asks a user to enter how many values to add. After the number is entered, it finds the result. For instance, if you enter 4, it will find **1!+2!+31+4!**.

```
#include <iostream.h>

main ( )
{
int n, k, p=1, x=0;
cout << "Enter how many numbers to add? \n";
cin >> k;
for (n=1; n<=k; ++n)
{
p=p*n;
x=x+p;
}
cout << "The total is " << x << ".";
}
```

Program 3.6.

The program prompts you first

```
Enter how many numbers to add?
```

If we enter 5, the answer is

```
The total is 153.
```

We first declare the variables **n**, **k**, **p=1**, **x** in **Program 3.6**. The **cout**, then, prompts a user to enter how many numbers to add. The object **cin** reads the value of the variable **k** that is the number of factorials to be added. Let's assume, **k=5**. We have to explain the fragment

```
for (n=1; n<=k; ++n)
{
p=p*n;
x=x+p;
}
```

Here, the **for** statement sets **n=1** and checks if **n<=5**. Since the condition is true, two lines of code inside **for** statement are executed next. We had initially **p=1** and **x=0**. First cycle produces **p=p*n=1*1=1**, and **x=x+p=0+1=1**. The second loop cycle sets **n** to 2 by **n=n+1=1+1=2** and checks the condition **n<=5**. The condition is true. The second cycle produces **p=p*n=1*2=2** and **x=x+p=1+2=3**. You can trace this up to the last cycle and confirm, that the program does what it claims to do. Each time the value of **p** is equal to previous value of **p** multiplied by **n**. It will be equal to **1*2*3** after 3 cycles, to **1*2*3*4** after 4 cycles and to **1*2*3*4*5** in 5 cycles. The variable **x** is increased by the current value of **p** each loop cycle. We had **x** equal to **1+1*2=3** after two cycles. It becomes **1+1*2+1*2*3** after three cycles. Four cycles produce **1+1*2+1*2*3+1*2*3*4**.

3.1.4. Nested *for* statements.

One can use loops within the loops. This is called *nested* loops. A nested loop consists of the outer and the inner loops. The

```
for (m=2; m<=20; m++)
for (k=40; k>2; k—)
x=x*m+y*k;
cout << x;
```

is an example of a nested loop containing the outer **for(m=2; m<=20; m++)** and the inner

```
for(k=40; k>2; k—)
x=x*m+y*k;
```

loops. There are two nested levels in the above sample. The **x=x*m+y*k** statement belongs to the inner loop. The inner loop belongs to the body of the outer loop. The **cout<<x** statement does not belong to any of the loops. It will be executed after both loops are completed.

Both the inner and the outer loops can have a number of statements in each of them. In this case, one can write.

```
for (m=2; m<=20; m++)
{
...
for (k=40; k>2; k—)
{
...
}
...
}
```

All the statements of the inner loop are contained inside the inner braces **{}**.

```
for (k=40; k>2; k—)
{
...
}
```

The inner **for** loop is a part of the outer loop. Besides, there can be other statements inside the outer loop body. So, the outer braces **{}** should surround all the statements of the outer loop as well. We showed it in the above fragment.

One can have three and more nested levels of a **for** statement. For example,

```
for (...)
{
...
for (...)
{
...
for (...)
{
...
}
...
}
...
}
```

This fragment demonstrates three nested levels of a **for** statement. As you see, it has three sets of opening and closing brackets **{ }**.

Consider **Program 3.7**, that demonstrates the nested loops.

```
#include <iostream.h>

main ( )
{
int n, k, p, x=0;
cout << "enter how many numbers to add? \n";
cin >> k;
for (n=1; n<=k; ++n)
{
x=x+n;
for (p=1; p<=x; ++p)
cout << '*';
cout << '\n';
}
cout << "the total is " << x;
}
```

Program 3.7.

This program computes the sum of integral numbers from 1 to any number. It also prints an elementary graph using "*****" character. Each line of the graph corresponds to the sum of consecutive numbers. The number of stars at each line corresponds to the value of this sum. This graph is called a *histogram*. The program first prompts user to enter the largest value in the sum. Let's assume, it is 3. The output of the program is

```
*
***
******
the total is 6
```

The first line is 1. The second line is the sum of $1+2$. The third line is $1+2+3$ and so on. We requested a sum of the first three numbers. Therefore, there are only three displayed lines. We display a message containing the sum at the end.

Program 3.7 is pretty straightforward. It declares all the variables. It, then, prompts a user to enter the greatest integer in the sum, and provides an input for this number. The plotting and the calculations are performed by two nested **for** loops. One of them is inside the other one, as shown below.

```
for (n=1; n<=k; ++n)
{
x=x+n;
for (p=1; p<=x; ++p)
cout << '*';
cout << '\n';
}
```

You will know how does a nested loop work, after we consider one from **Program 3.7**.

The program first encounters the outer loop

```
for (n=1; n<=k; ++n)
```

It treats this loop as a regular one. The loop sets **n** to initial value 1 and checks the loop condition **n<=k**. It, then, executes the statements inside its body, beginning from

```
x=x+n;
```

Then, the outer loop finally comes to the inner loop

```
for (p=1; p<=x; ++p)
cout << '*';
```

This inner loop is treated as a regular statement. Hence, it should be executed in full. The program cannot leave this statement before it runs **p** through all the values it can accept,

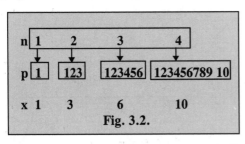

Fig. 3.2.

i.e., from 1 to **x**. You already know, to execute a loop in full means to run it, until its condition becomes false. In this sense, the inner loop in our program is executed as a regular loop, until the condition **p<=x** becomes false. When the inner loop is completed, the outer loop can execute the next command

```
cout << '\n';
```

At last, the outer loop increments **n** to 2. This is the end of the first cycle of the outer loop. After that, the outer loop begins its second cycle. The program checks the outer loop condition **n<=k** again. It, then, continues executing every statement of the outer loop body, until it reaches the inner loop. The inner loop is executed completely again. The computer, then, executes **cout<<'\n'**, increments **n** to 3, begins the next outer loop cycle. The execution of the outer loop stops, when the loop condition **n<=k** becomes false. Hence, the inner loop variable **p** runs through all the allowed values per each **n** increment of the outer loop in our program. It is shown in Fig. 3.2.

The outer loop, in our example, finds the sum of the numbers **x=x+n**. The inner loop just prints a line of stars. The loop condition of the inner loop is made sum dependent **p<=x**. The number of stars displayed every time is determined by the maximum value of

p. The number of stars **p** displayed during each loop cycle is equal to the sum **x**. We used **cout<<'\n'** after the inner loop, because we wanted to print the stars from a new line for each outer loop cycle.

The loop condition **p<=x** makes the maximum value of the inner loop variable **p** equal to **x**, where the variable **x** is calculated during each outer loop. It is not the rule. The index variables of the inner and outer cycles can be independent. We have discussed a double nested loop. Triple nested loop works in the same way. One can even have a hierarchy of a number of nested loops inside each other. It is limited though. The limit varies for different compilers.

3.1.5. Variation of *for* statement.

Sometimes, an index variable already has an initial value at the time, when the loop execution begins. Let's assume, it was calculated or entered before the loop. Then, you do not need to write the initial expression. The **for** statement in this case can be written in the following form

```
for (  ; n<100; ++n);
```

C++ allows to substitute with a semicolon (;) an initial condition, loop expression, or loop condition of a **for** loop. The semicolon constitutes the end of an absent part in a **for** statement. We have given you an example of the **for** loop without an initial condition. The above statement does not have only an initial condition. However, a **for** loop can have any other parts of it missing. For example, the loop

```
for ( ; ; )
```

is perfectly legal. However, it is a potentially infinite loop.

C++ allows to use a semicolon as a statement

```
;
```

This statement performs no action. It seems, probably, silly to have a statement doing nothing. And, yet, it is useful, specially, with loops. You know, the statement in the loop body will be executed during every loop cycle. What if you just want to run a loop without executing any statement in it? In this case use a semicolon statement.

To illustrate our point, we introduce **Program 3.8**, that is a copy of **Program 3.3**. In the latest program a semicolon follows the **for** statement. Now, **x=x+n** is no longer inside the body of the loop. In fact, there is no statement inside the loop body, because of the semicolon statement following **for** loop (**for (n=1; n<11; n=n+1)   ;**).

```
#include <iostream.h>

main ( )
{
int n, x;
x=0;
for (n=1; n<11; n=n+1)   ;
x=x+n;
cout << "The sum is " << x << "." << endl;
```

```
    }
```

Program 3.8.

The output of the program is

    The sum is 11.

So far, we have dealt with the increment and decrement operators as **for** loop expressions. In C++, you can write almost any mathematical assignment operation as the loop expression. You can, for instance, decrease or increase the index variable by any number. For example,

    for (n=0; n<6; n=n+2)

Here, the loop expression is **n=n+2**. It increases the variable **n** by 2 every loop cycle. Write **n=n-1** to decrease the index variable by 1 every loop cycle. **Program 3.9** shows a multiplicative loop expression.

```
#include <iostream.h>

main ( )
{
int n,   x=0;
for (n=1; n<=20; n*=2)
x=x+n;
cout << "The total is " << x << ".";
}
```

Program 3.9.

The output of the program is

    The total is 31.

You can understand this program by now. The compound assignment operator **n*=2** is, in fact, **n=n*2**. It should also be known to you.

You can also use more than one index variable in the loop. More than one expression can be used as well. A **for** loop with two variables would look like

    for (x=2, y=0; y<=20; -x, y=y+2);

Here, **x** is set to 2, and **y** to 0 initially. It works similarly to loop with one variable, except that each cycle will subtract 1 from **x** and add 2 to **y**. Computer just executes all loop expressions for both variables during every cycle of the loop.

One can use more complex loop conditions. For example,

    for (x=100; x>(6*y-3); x-)

Here, the loop condition **x>(6*y-3)** consists of two operands **x** and **(6*y-3)**, and the relational operator **>**. The operand **(6*y-3)** is an arithmetic expression. *Thus, a loop condition can consist of two operands connected by a relational operator from Table 3.1. Each operand can be a variable, constant, math expression, etc.*

Index variable can be declared and initialized inside a loop in C++. For instance,

    for (int m=0; m<10; m++)
    . . .

The variable **m** is declared in the above form inside the loop initial condition instead of doing it separately in a program. This variable can be used by the program beginning from the point of its declaration. This means, that the variable declared inside the loop can be used by the loop statements and any other statements after the loop.

3.1.6. The *while* statement.

The **while** statement is written in the form
```
while (condition)
C statement;
Second statement after while;
```
The **condition** in the **while** statement is typically an expression of type
```
while (x>2*y)
```
Usually, a condition consists of two operands connected with a relational operator. Two

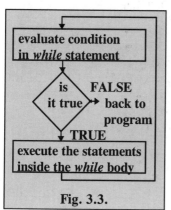

operands **x** and **2*y** in the expression **x>2*y** are connected by the relational operator **>**. Each operand can be an expression consisting of different operators. One of our operands **2*y** is an arithmetic expression. The conditions in **while** and **for** statements are very similar. They can be created by the same rules. You already know how to create the loop conditions in **for** statements. Creating the conditions in **while** statements is similar to **for** loops. We will also study the use of logical and bitwise operators in conditions later.

The **C statement** is called the loop body statement. It is a statement inside the body of the loop, because it

Fig. 3.3. is executed during every loop cycle.

The execution of the **while** statement begins with evaluation of the *condition* in parentheses as shown in Fig. 3.3. If the condition is true, **C statement** following **while** is executed. This is the end of the first loop cycle. After that, computer returns to the **condition** in **while** and evaluates it again. If it is still true, the C statement is again executed. This constitutes the end of the next loop cycle. It continues, until the condition in **while** statement becomes false after some cycle. This stops the loop. The computer exits the loop. It proceeds executing the program beginning with the **Second statement after while**.

The **while** statement also allows an execution of a number of statements during each loop cycle. In this case, the statements that ought to be executed inside the loop should be enclosed in the parentheses **{}** as
```
while (condition)
{
C statement;
...
C statement;
}
...
```

The statements surrounded by the **{ }** brackets belong to the body of the **while** loop.

One can use nested **while** statements. They work in the same way as the nested **for** statements. We will consider a few examples showing how to use the **while** statement. Consider **Program 3.10**, that computes cumulative yearly interest rate per $1000 of a mortgage. You pay off a mortgage yearly. Thus, the amount you owe decreases each year, so does the amount of interest. This program finds yearly interest rate without that correction. It can be used just for a crude estimate.

```
#include <stdio.h>

main ( )
{
int year_max, year=1;
float rate, sum =1000.0, bank=0.0;
printf ("Enter the mortgage interest rate \n");
scanf ("%f", &rate);
printf ("enter the number of years for mortgage \n");
scanf ("%d", &year_max);
printf("Table1. Cumulative interest and amount on $1000 \
          borrowed \n");
printf (" year  |interest |total amount | \n");
while ( year<=year_max)
{
bank=bank+10*rate;
sum=sum+10*rate;
printf ("%5d    %10.2f         %6.2f  \n", year, bank, sum);
year++;
}
printf ("the yearly interest is $%.2f \n", 10*rate);
}
```

Program 3.10.

The program first prompts you to enter the interest rate.

```
enter the mortgage interest rate
```

For instance, we enter 8.5. It, then, asks in how many years you will pay off the mortgage.

```
enter the number of years for mortgage
```

Let's enter number 3. The output of the program is

```
Table1. Cumulative interest and amount on $1000 borrowed
   year  |interest |total amount |
    1        85.00    1085.00
    2       170.00    1170.00
    3       255.00    1255.00
   the yearly interest is $85.00
```

We first declare **int** and **float** type variables. Next four lines provide the input of the yearly interest rate **rate** and the duration of the loan **year_max**. The **printf()** function displays a message, that prompts the user to enter the interest rate. It is read by the **scanf()** function. Then, we ask to enter the duration of the loan and read the value of **year_max**. Two **printf()** functions right before the **while** loop display the table name and the table head.

The **while** loop condition **year<=year_max** compares the current value of **year** to the value of **year_max** entered earlier. The **while** loop executes four statements during each of its cycles. The first one finds the cumulative amount of interest by computing **bank=bank+10*rate** during each loop cycle. Here, the yearly interest is **10*rate**. The second statement **sum=sum+10*rate** finds the total owed amount. The third statement prints both values in a form of a table. The last statement **year++** increments the variable **year** by one. The loop works as follows.

The first loop begins with checking the condition. It is true, because we set **year** to 1 at the beginning. The **10*rate** is added to **bank**. Next statement adds **10*rate** to **sum**. Both variables **bank** and **sum** are then displayed by **printf()**. The first loop cycle concludes with increasing the value of **year** by one. The next loop cycle begins with checking the condition. It, then, adds another **10*rate** to the value of **bank**. We get sum of two yearly interests after two loop cycles. The previous value of **sum** is also increased by **10*rate**. Both values are displayed by the **printf()** function. The value of **year** is increased again by one. The loop repeats, until the condition becomes false. In our case, it happens after the third cycle. The total amount of interest for the loan period is computed as **bank=bank+10*rate**. If you compute the value of this expression three times, the final value of **bank** will be the total interest for three years. We also calculate the total amount one owes on **$1000** borrowed.

To calculate the amount you owe to the bank for three years, we add three times the amount of yearly interest to **$1000**. It is done by **sum=sum+10*rate**. Each cycle increases the previous value of **sum** by the yearly interest **10*rate**. Run it for three cycles, and you add three yearly interests to it. This will be a total amount you owe for three years. A **printf()** function is used in the **while** loop to display **sum** and **bank** after every mortgage year.

```
printf ("%5d    %10.2f     %6.2f \n", year, bank, sum);
```
The **printf()** function uses the field width and precision. We wanted to organize the output as a table to illustrate that one can use the printing formats to organize the data output in a convenient way.

Our **while** loop is analogous to following **for** statement.

```
for (year=1; year<=year_max; year++)
{
...
}
```
Thus, **while** and **for** loops are interchangeable. The **for** statement

```
for (initial expression; loop condition; loop expression)
{
...
}
next statement after loop;
```
can be substituted by

```
initial expression;
while (loop condition)
{
...
loop expression
}
next statement after loop;
```

The **while** statement is more convenient to use than **for** in some cases. **Program 3.11** demonstrates one of those cases.

```
#include <iostream.h>

main ( )
{
char  x;
cout << "Enter lowercase characters.\n";
cin >> x;
while ( x >= 97)
{
x=x-32;
cout << x;
cin >> x;
}
cout << "  end\n";
}
```

Program 3.11.

This program first prompts you

```
    Enter lowercase characters.
```

Let's enter

```
    program=
```

The output of the program is

```
    PROGRAM   end
```

The program converts lowercase letters to their uppercase equivalent. The code begins with variable declaration. It, then, displays a message prompting to enter a sequence of characters. First **cin** reads the first entered character. It is followed by **while** loop.

Remember, that **cin** has already read the first character, and stored it in **x** before the loop. The **while** loop compares, if the integral value of **x** is greater or equal to 97 (**x >= 97**). Number 97 corresponds to '**a**'. Any other lowercase letter ('**b**', '**c**' and so on) corresponds to greater integral values. So, the loop condition checks if a lowercase letter has been entered. If the condition is true, the internal loop statements will be executed. We get the uppercase equivalent of the first letter by calculating **x=x-32**. The character corresponding to the value stored in **x** is printed by the **cout**. We, then, acquire another character using **cin** object inside the **while** loop. This character is stored in **x**.

Loop is repeated again producing the same sequence of statements. The loop stops, when we enter a character, which integral value is less than 97. In our case the last character is =. It terminates the loop, because its value is less than 97. When the loop is completed, the **cout << "\nend\n"** is executed.

  The program also permits to enter the characters one by one. This means, you type in the first character, press **ENTER** and the computer displays it. Then you can type in the next character, press **ENTER** and it is displayed and so on. The program stops and prints "**end**", when you enter a digit or some special character. If we have used the **scanf("%c", &x)** function inside the loop for performing the input, we would have to enter all the characters at once and then press **ENTER**. We would not be able to enter each character and press **ENTER** after it. Why? Because, if we enter a character and press **ENTER**, that **ENTER** is interpreted as another character as well. Do not forget, that we use **%c** input format. This format reads any character from the input. And **ENTER** is one of those characters. To be able to enter characters one by one, we would have to use **scanf("\n%c", &x)**. This is not necessary with **cin** object, that reads the characters at once or one by one.

  One can use a condition like **while(y)**. It is the same as **while(y!=0)**. It tests, if **y** is not equal to zero. It is true, when **y** is not equal to zero.

3.1.7. The *do-while* statement.

  The **do** statement is written in a form
    do
    C statement;
    while (*loop condition***);**
So far, all the loops first evaluated conditions, then executed the loop statements. The **do-while** construction first executes the *C statement* between **do** and **while**. That *C statement* belongs to the body of the loop. Then, the computer evaluates the *loop condition* in **while** statement. This is the end of one loop cycle. If that condition after the first loop cycle is true, it again executes C statement between **do** and **while**. This is the end of the second loop cycle. After that, your computer again evaluates the condition. If it is true, it executes the statement inside the **do-while** body again. It is the third loop. This process continues again and again, until the loop condition becomes false. Only then, the computer leaves the loop, executing next statement after **while** and proceeding with the program. There can be more than one statement in the body of the loop. You enclose them in **{ }** braces and they all will be executed every loop cycle. Example is given in **Program 3.12**.

```
#include <stdio.h>

main ( )
{
int year=1;
float rate, sum =1000.0, bank=0.0;
printf ("enter the mortgage interest rate \n");
scanf ("%f", &rate);
```

```
printf("Table1. Cumulative interest and amount on $1000 \
borrowed \n");
printf ("  year  |interest total| amount | \n");
do
{
bank=bank+10*rate;
sum=sum+10*rate;
printf ("%5d    %10.2f        %6.2f  \n", year, bank, sum);
year++;
}
while ( year<=3);
printf ("the yearly interest is %.2f \n", 10*rate);
}
```

Program 3.12.

This program is a shorter version of **Program 3.10**. The only difference is that we use **do-while** loop here instead of **while** loop used in the **Program 3.10**.

3.2. Decision statements.

Why do we need a decision statement? You often make the decisions in your life. Decision capability is known to be a very important feature of any computer language. Those decision statements are similar to real life decision process. For example, you want to go somewhere and you look at the weather. You decide to wear a coat, if the weather is cold. You do not wear the coat, when the weather is warm. Same happens with decision statements. If the tested condition is true, the program is forced to execute some statement or group of statements and to continue. If it is false, another statement or group of statements can be executed.

3.2.1. The *if* statement.

Let's consider the **if** statement, first. It is written in the form
```
    if (test condition)
    program statement;
```
Execution of this statement begins with testing the **test condition** inside the brackets. If it is true, the program statement immediately following **if** is executed. The computer, then, executes the program starting from the second after **if** statement. If the condition is false, the first program statement after **if** is skipped. The program execution still follows the same path starting from the second statement after **if**. The conditions inside the **if** brackets are similar *to the loop conditions in the loop statements*. The **if** conditions are created in the same way as in the loops. Review **Program 3.13**. Pay attention, how we compare if **x** is equal to `'y'` by **x=='y'**.

```
#include <iostream.h>
```

```
main ( )
{
char x;
cout << "If you want condition to be true enter 'y'"
     << ", otherwise enter anything.\n";
cin >> x;
if (x=='y')
cout << "This is the next after if line.\n";
cout << "This is executed first if condition is false.\n"
     << "We go further.\n";
}
```

Program 3.13.

The program first displays a message

```
If you want condition to be true enter 'y',
otherwise enter anything.
```

If you enter **y**, the displayed messages are

```
This is the next after if line.
This is executed first, if condition is false.
We go further.
```

If you enter any other character, the condition **x=='y'** becomes false. Then, the first statement after **if** is skipped and following messages are displayed

```
This operator is executed first if condition is false.
We go further.
```

One can, sometimes, see a conditional expression written as

```
if (x)
...
```

This is a shorter way of writing **if(x != 0)**. **Program 3.14** illustrates it.

```
#include <iostream.h>

main ( )
{
int m;
cout << "Enter a number from 0 to 9.\n";
cin >> m;
if (m)
cout << "m is not equal to 0 \n";
cout << "you will see it first if m=0 \n";
}
```

Program 3.14.

If you enter a number not equal to zero, a message is displayed on the screen

```
m is not equal to 0
you will see it first if m=0
```

So far, we stated that if the condition is true, the first statement after **if** is executed.
What happens, if instead of one statement, we want to execute a group of statement? As
you have, probably, guessed, it is possible in C++. Only one condition - that group of
statements should be surrounded by the **{ }** parentheses, as shown below

```
if (condition)
{
statement ;
...
statement;
}
```

The group of statements surrounded by the parentheses is executed, if the **condition** is
true. The **if** statement can contain any statements and even loops, and vice versa. Consider **Program 3.15**.

```
#include <stdio.h>                          /*line1*/

main ( )                                    /*line2*/
{                                           /*line3*/
int n, m, limit, remain, no_prime=1;        /*line4*/
printf ("non-prime|prime numbers \n");      /*line5*/

for (n=3; n<=20; n++)                       /*line6*/
{                                           /*line7*/
limit=n;                                    /*line8*/
for (m=2; m<limit; m++)                     /*line9*/
{                                           /*line10*/
remain = n%m;                               /*line11*/
if (remain==0)                              /*line12*/
{                                           /*line13*/
no_prime=0;                                 /*line14*/
limit=m;                                    /*line15*/
printf ("%5d\n", n) ;                       /*line16*/
} }                                         /*line17*/
if(no_prime)                                /*line18*/
printf ("          %8d \n", n);             /*line19*/
no_prime=1;                                 /*line20*/
}                                           /*line21*/

printf ("end\n");                           /*line22*/
}                                           /*line23*/
```

Program 3.15.

Program 3.15 displays a table of prime and non-prime numbers in the range from 3 to
20. A prime number is a number, that can be divided only by 1 and itself without a
remainder. An example is 7. It can be divided without a remainder only by 1 and 7.

Before you write a program, think how to solve it. Try to develop an algorithm for doing this problem. First, let's take 3. Try to divide it by 2 with zero remainder. You cannot do it. Therefore, 3 is a prime number. Try to divide number 4 by 2 and 3 without a remainder. You can divide it evenly by 2. Thus, it is a non-prime number. Then, try to divide 5 by 2, or 3, or 4 evenly. You cannot do it. This is why it is a prime number. Do you see the algorithm? The solution is, to try dividing every number **n** in the range from 3 to 20 consecutively by **m** in the range **2, 3...n-1**. Number **n** is a prime number, if it cannot be divided evenly by any of those divisors. The test of number **n** should also stop after the first division with zero remainder. For instance, if 15 divides evenly by 3, there is no use in trying to divide it by 4, then 5 and so on. Number 15 is not a prime number, if it can be divided evenly by 3. If we stop the test of **n=15** there and go to the test of **n=16**, it will definitely save some time. This is implemented in **Program 3.15**. We numbered the code lines in that program, so it is more convenient to discuss it.

Lines 4 and 5 declare the variables and print the table head. The outer **for** loop begins with **n=3**. This is the first value to be tested. The outer loop generates the numbers from 3 to 20. Each of those numbers is checked if it is a prime number. The inner loop

```
    for (m=2; m<limit; m++)      /*line9*/
```

has **m<limit**. The **limit** is the maximum value of the divisor **m**. Each of the values **n** will be tested by dividing it by all the numbers in the range from 2 to **limit-1**. The **limit** variable is assigned a value of **n** at line 8, because we want the maximum divisor number to be limited by **n-1**, where **n** is the tested number. We find the remainder of **n** divided by **m** at line 11. The **if** statement at line 12 compares the remainder **remain** to zero. If the remainder is zero, we have a non-prime number. In this case, we print it in the non-prime number column (line 16) and set the variable **limit** to **m**. When **m** changes by one in the next cycle, it will not pass the loop condition **m<limit**. We do it to stop the test of number **n**, if it is known to be a non-prime number. The third statement inside **if** sets the variable **no_prime** to 0 for zero remainder.

After the inner loop has been completed, we have to know whether any of the remainders were equal to zero during the loop. This is what **no_prime** variable is for. If **no_prime** is not equal to zero after the end of the inner loop, that indicates that we are dealing with a non-prime number. This decision is made by the **if** statement at line 18. It contains two statements. If **no_prime** is zero, the current value under the test **n** is printed as a prime number. We also set **no_prime** back to 1 as it was set at the beginning at line 20. We do that, because we have to use it again during next loop. The program ends with printing the message "**end**" on the screen by the function **printf()** at line 22.

3.2.2. Logical operators.

Sometimes, it is necessary to make a decision, based on evaluating a few conditions. For example, we write a program performing some arithmetical calculations. We want to know, when the result of those calculations will be within the range from 1 to 10. One can write a few test conditions inside **if** condition brackets. Those conditions are called *compound relational tests*. The conditions should be connected by **||**, **&&**, or **!** characters, which are called logical operators.

The || is a logical **OR** operator. Computer evaluates all the conditions connected by **OR** operator. For example,

```
if (x<y || x>z)
```

The result of evaluation of the whole bracket is true, when at least one of those separate test conditions inside the brackets is true. Thus, the whole bracket is true, when either **x<y** or **x>z**. It is illustrated by **Program 3.16** given below.

```
#include <iostream.h>

main ( )
{
int x;
cout << "Enter x within the range from 0 to 20.\n";
cin >> x;
if (x<1 || x>10)
cout << "The value is beyond the range of 1 to 10.\n";
cout << "Have a nice day.\n";
}
```

Program 3.16.

The above program checks whether the value of variable **x** is within the range from 1 to 10. The program prompts first to enter a value within the range from 0 to 20. We read the value of **x** by **cin**. The first condition **x<1** checks, if **x** is smaller than 1. The second condition is **x>10**. If **x** were equal to 5, for example, then the first and the second conditions are false and the second statement after **if** is executed. It prints

```
Have a nice day.
```

Let's assume, **x** was equal to 12. Then the first condition is false, but the second is true, because **x** is, indeed, greater than 10. The whole bracket is now true. The first operator after **if** displays a message on the screen

```
The value is beyond the range of 1 to 10.
Have a nice day.
```

Character **&&** is called logical **AND** operator. All the test conditions connected by **AND** operator are evaluated. For example,

```
if (x<y && x>z)
```

The whole bracket is true only when *all* the test conditions inside the brackets are true. Therefore, both **x<y** and **x>z** should be true. Consider **Program 3.17** as an example.

```
#include <iostream.h>

main ( )
{
int x;
cout << "Enter x beyond the range from 0 to 20.\n";
cin >> x;
if (x>=1 && x<=10)
```

```
cout << "The value is within the range of 1 to 10.\n";
cout << "Have a nice day.\n";
}
```

Program 3.17.

It looks almost alike the previous fragment, but it is a bit different. Let's say, you enter **x=3**. Then, the first (**x>=1**) and the second (**x<=10**) test conditions are true. You will get a message on your screen

```
The value is within the range of 1 to 10.
Have a nice day.
```

If you enter **x=12**, then the first condition is true, 12 is greater than 1. But the second condition is false. One of conditions is false. Hence, the whole bracket is false. Program skips the first and goes on to the second statement.

```
Have a nice day.
```

Character **!** is a logical **NOT** operator. Condition used with this operator is reversed. For instance,

```
if (!x)
```

is a shorter way of writing

```
if (x==0)
```

The logical operators can be used not only in the decision operators. They can be, for instance, used in the loop statements as well. For instance,

```
while (x>'A' && x<'z')
```

Any logical operator has lower precedence than any arithmetic or relational operators. Thus, it will be executed only after arithmetic or relational operators execution. Among logical operators **&&** has higher precedence than **||**. The **||** has higher precedence than **!** operator.

One can use combinations of those operators in the programs. For example, you have to test, if a number **x** can be divided by 2 and 5 evenly, or only by 3. The condition will be

```
if ( (x%2==0 && x%5==0) || x%3==0)
```

3.2.3. The *if-else* statement.

The **if-else** statement can be written in the form

```
if (test condition)
statement A;
else
statement B;
```

The execution of **if-else** statement begins with evaluating the **test condition** inside the brackets. If it is true, **statement A** is executed and **statement B** is skipped. Then, the computer executes the next statement after **statement B**. If the test condition is false, **statement A** is skipped and **statement B** is executed. Then, again, the computer executes the next statement after **statement B**. Again, in nutshell, if the test condition is true **statement A** is executed, **B** is not. If the condition is false, **statement B** is executed and **statement A** is not. In both cases the computer proceeds starting from the next statement after **B**. Review **Program 3.18**.

```
#include <iostream.h>

main( )
{
int x;
cout << "enter an integral number \n";
cin >> x;
if (x>=0)
cout << "the absolute value is: " << x;
else
cout <<"the absolute value of " << x << " is: " << -x;
cout << "\nend of execution \n";
}
```

Program 3.18.

The program prompts a user to enter an integral number. If you enter a positive value, for instance 3, the output is
```
the absolute value is: 3
end of execution
```
If the entered value is -3, the output is
```
the absolute value of -3 is: 3
end of execution
```
Program 3.18 finds an absolute value of a number. It first declares the variable **x**. Next two lines prompt the user to enter a value of variable **x** and provide its input by means of **cin** object. The entered value of **x** is compared to zero inside the **if-else** statement. As you saw, the message displayed on the screen depends from the decision made by the **if-else** statement.

To execute more than one statements inside **if-else**, use the **{ }** parentheses
```
if (test condition)
{
...
}
else
{
...
}
```
The **else-if** statement, or sometimes it is called a construction, is written in the form
```
if (test condition 1)
statement A;
else if  (test condition 2)
statement B;
else
statement C;
```

```
    next statement;
```
Here, the C++ statements A, B and C belong to the **else-if** construction. The **next statement** is the next program statement following that construction. Program begins the execution of the **else-if** statement with evaluating the **test condition 1**. If it is true, the **statement A** is executed. Then, the program executes the **next statement** and goes on executing the rest of the program. If **test condition 1** is false, then the **test condition 2** is evaluated. If it is true, the **statement B** is executed followed by the **next statement** with the rest of the program. If both **test condition 1** and **test condition 2** are false, then, **statement C** is executed. It is succeeded by the **next statement** and the rest of the program.

Basically, this statement consists of two **if-else** constructions. You can see them, if we rewrite the statement

```
if (test condition 1)
statement A;
else
if (test condition 2)
statement B;
else
statement C;
C next statement;
```

The **test condition 1** belongs to the first **if-else** statement. If it is true, **statement A** is executed. Otherwise, as you know, the next after **else** statement is executed. This statement happens to be the next **if-else** statement. C++ "does not care" how many white spaces separate **else** and **if**. Hence, those two forms are identical.

The **if-else** statement is used when you need three way decisions in a program. It is illustrated by **Program 3.19**, that classifies entered by you character.

```
#include <iostream.h>

main ( )
{
char x;
cout << "enter a character\n";
cin >> x;
if (x>='A' && x<='z')
cout << "it is a letter\n";
else if (x>='0' && x<='9')
cout << "it is a digit\n";
else
cout << "it is a character\n";
cout << "\nend of execution";
}
```

Program 3.19.

You can enter any character and the program will determine whether it is a letter, or a digit, or a special character. The program first declares the variable **x**, prints "**enter a character**" message on the screen, and provides the data input using **cin** object. The **else-if** checks, if the value of **x** lies within a certain range. If **x>='A' && x<='z'**, it is a letter. The program displays a message, that it is a letter. If **x>='0' && x<='9'**, the entered character is a digit. The corresponding message is displayed. Otherwise, it is a special character and the program states, that this is a character. All these three messages are the part of the **else-if** statement. After executing the **else-if** statement, the program goes to the next program statement, that does not belong to the **else-if** construction. The next program statement is

```
cout << "\nend of execution";
```

3.2.4. Nested *if* statements.

The **if** statement allows nested constructions, as

```
if (condition1)
if (condition2)
if (condition3)
inside_statement;
next statement;
```

The program evaluates the **condition1** of the outer **if** statement first. If it is true, then, the **condition2** of the second **if** statement is evaluated. Why? Let's assume, any other statement or operator was used after the first **if** statement and the condition of that first **if** were true. Then, the following it statement would have been executed.

That following statement happens to be another **if** statement. Hence, this is the one to be executed. If **condition2** of the second **if** statement is true, the program evaluates the **condition3** of the third **if** statement. Why? Treat the third **if** as any other statement of C++. If the **condition2** is true, the following after the second **if** statement should be executed. It is, again, an **if** statement. If the third condition is true, the program executes the **inside_statement**. After that, the program carries out the **next statement**. If a condition in any of the **if** statements in this chain is false, the program simply skips the **inside_statement** and executes the **next statement**. We have shown a triple nested **if** statement. One can create the nested **if** statements ranging from double to multi-level. We demonstrate it in **Program 3.20**.

```
#include <iostream.h>

main ( )
{
float x=10.0, y=2.5, z;
if (x>5)
if (x>y)
if (y!=0)
{
z=x/y;
```

```
cout << z;
}
cout << "\nif you see no number, something is wrong";
}
```

Program 3.20.

The output of this program is

    4

    if you see no number, something is wrong

This program finds a result of a division. It performs the division only when all three **if** conditions are true. Try to make **x** less than 5, or **y** greater than **x**, or **y=0**. The division will not be performed in any of those cases.

It is interesting to consider nested **if-else** constructions. Following program demonstrates them.

```
#include <iostream.h>

main ( )
{
float z, x=1, y=0;
if (x>y)
if (y!=0)
{
z=x/y;
cout << z;
}
else
cout << "error";
cout << "\nend of nested ifs.";
}
```

Program 3.21.

The output of the program is

    error

    end of nested ifs.

Outer **if** is a separate statement. The **else** belongs to the inner **if**, making it an **if-else** construction. *In C++ the first **else** in a code always belongs to the last **if** statement*. If the first **if** condition **x>y** is true, then the inner **if-else** statement will be executed. If **x>y** is false, the whole **if-else** construction, following it, will be skipped. The program will simply display the "**end of nested ifs**" message.

Consider **Program 3.22** illustrating how to use the nested **if-else** constructions.

```
#include <iostream.h>                           /*line1*/

main ( )                                        /*line2*/
```

```
{                                          /*line3*/
int guess=1, number =232, giveup=1000;     /*line4*/
cout << "Try to guess the number I hide.\n"; /*line5*/
cout << "To give up enter 1000.\n";        /*line6*/
while (guess != number || guess != giveup)  /*line7*/
{                                          /*line8*/
cin >> guess;                              /*line9*/
if (guess !=giveup)                        /*line10*/
if (guess == number)                       /*line11*/
cout << "You won.\n";                       /*line12*/
else                                       /*line13*/
if (guess > 100 && guess < 300)            /*line14*/
if (guess > number)                        /*line15*/
cout << "You hit higher.\n";                /*line16*/
else                                       /*line17*/
cout << "You hit lower.\n";                 /*line18*/
else                                       /*line19*/
cout << "You are not even close.\n";        /*line20*/
else                                       /*line21*/
cout << "Can't beat me? Ha.";               /*line22*/
}}                                         /*line23*/
```

Program 3.22.

You have to guess a number concealed by the program. We made this number equal to 232.
If you guess it correctly at the first entry, a message will be displayed
        You won.
Entering a number beyond the range from 100 to 300 will display a message
        You are not even close.
If you enter a number within the range from 100 to 300, then the message
        You hit higher.
is displayed if **guess>higher**. Otherwise, the message will be
        You hit lower.
If one chooses to give up and enters 1000, the program replies with a message
        Can't beat me? Ha.
   Our program uses a number of nested **if-else** constructions inside the **while** loop.
The loop stops after you find the right number or give up. The most outer **if-else**
statement is written at lines 10, 21, 22. It checks if you entered number 1000. If you enter
this number, it displays the message "**Can't beat me? Ha.**". If the entered number is
not 1000, then the first inner **if-else** statement written at lines 11, 12, 13 checks if
guess == number. If you predicted the number right, the program displays the message that you won. Otherwise, it executes the **else** part of this statement, which is, in
fact, another nested **if-else** construction. It consists of the outer **if-else**, written at
lines 14, 19, 20. This statement checks, if the entered number lies within the range from
100 to 300. If that number is beyond the range, it displays the message that you are not
even close to the hidden value. This statement, as we have mentioned, consists of another

if-else construction, given at lines 15-18. It guides our actions by displaying whether the entered number is greater or less than the hidden one.

3.2.5. The *switch* statement.

The **switch** statement can be replaced by nested **if** constructions. It is written as

```
switch (expression)
{
case value 1:
statement;
statement;
...
break;
case value 2:
statement;
statement;
...
break;
...
case value n:
statement;
statement;
...
break;
default:
statement;
statement;
...
break;
}
```

The **switch** statement consists of different fragments contained inside **case value...** and **brake**. For example,

```
case value n:
statement;
statement;
...
break;
```

The keyword **case** indicates the beginning of the code fragment corresponding to the **value n**. The keyword **brake** indicates the end of that fragment. The fragment consists of a number of statements. To execute a fragment means to carry out all its statements, operators, etc., that lie between the colon of the **case value ...:** and the **break** statement. Hence, the keyword **break** (called also a statement) indicates the end of execution of a particular fragment.

Computer begins an execution of **switch** by first calculating a numeric value of the

expression in the brackets. Sometimes, the ***expression*** can consist of a single variable. In this case, its value should be somehow specified before the **switch** statement. The result of the ***expression*** is compared with the values of ***value 1, value 2...value n***, which are just simple constants or constant expressions. If this result matches the value of one of those ***value 1, value 2...value n***, the computer executes that matching ***case value...*** fragment. Only one **case value ...** fragment inside the **switch** statement can be executed. This concludes the execution of the statement **switch**. The program, then, completes the statements after the closing bracket "**}**" of the **switch** statement.

There is a keyword **default** used in **switch** statement. You can have situations, when the result of the ***expression*** inside the **switch** parentheses does not match any of those values ***value 1, value 2...value n***. If it happens, then the program executes the **default** fragment. The presence of the **default** fragment is optional and depends on your task. Hence, you do not necessarily have to have the **default** fragment in the **switch** statement. The example is given in **Program 3.23**.

```
#include <iostream.h>

main ( )
{
char x='1';
int y=0, z;
cout << "enter any number of digits\n";
while (x>='0' && x<='9')
{
x=cin.get ( );
switch (x)
{
case '0': cout << "zero ";  z=0 ;        break;
case '1': cout << "one ";   z=1 ;        break;
case '2': cout << "two ";   z=2 ;        break;
case '3': cout << "three ";              z=3 ;   break;
case '4': cout << "four ";  z=4 ;        break;
case '5': cout << "five ";  z=5 ;        break;
case '6': cout << "six ";   z=6 ;        break;
case '7': cout << "seven ";              z=7 ;   break;
case '8': cout << "eight ";              z=8 ;   break;
case '9': cout << "nine ";  z=9 ;        break;
default : cout << " ";      z=0 ;        break;
}
y=y+z;
}
cout << "The sum is " << y;
}
```

Program 3.23.

The program prompts a user to enter a number of digits. Enter any combination of digits, for instance 12345, and press **ENTER**. The output is

```
one two three four five
the sum is 15
```

This program reads a sequence of numbers from the input and converts it into a sequence of words. Each number is substituted by its name: 1 by "**one**", 2 by "**two**" and so on. The program begins with declaration of **x**, **y** and **z** variables. The **while** loop is set to read the characters using **cin.get()**. You pretty much understand how the **while** loop reads the character data. The new solution, is to use the **switch(x)** statement. It uses **x** as its condition. If you entered 3, the **switch** fragment

```
case '3': cout << "three ";        z=3 ;        break;
```

is executed. This prints "**three**" on the screen and sets the value of **z** to 3. We also find a sum of all entered digits. We read each digit as a character. Thus, the character 3 is stored as a binary value corresponding to its ASCII (or other convention) representation. This is why we set the **int** type variable **z** to be equal to 3. So, if a computer reads the character "3" from its terminal, the value 3 is assigned to another variable **z**. That variable **z** will be used to calculate a sum of all entered digits. The sum of all entered digits is found by computing **y=y+z**.

The **while** loop reads the entered digits. For instance, you enter: 42 and press **ENTER**. When **while** starts its first cycle, the condition is satisfied, because we initialized **x** as **char x='1'**. The **cin.get()** is inside the loop. It first reads '4'. Loop is executed, the message "**four**" is printed. Next loop begins with **x='4'**, and reads 2 from the input. It displays the message "**two**". A subsequent loop checks again the condition in **while**, where **x='2'**. The **ENTER** is read as the last character. Unfortunately, the decision to stop the loop is made only during the next cycle after this one. Therefore, the program makes one extra loop cycle with **x='ENTER'**. This is why we set **z=0** in the **default** fragment of the **switch** statement. That fragment adds 0 to the sum, when the entered character is not a digit. If we have not done it, the program would have executed **y=y+z** for the **ENTER** character using the value of **z** from the previous loop. It could have resulted in adding an extra value. We used this not very elegant solution of the problem to indicate some important pitfalls of the **while** loop.

We wrote each **case** fragment in the **switch** statement of **Program 3.23** in one line. It is done to save some space and to make the program more readable. We do not want to make the program look long and complicated. Remember, you can use white spaces between the tokens in any convenient for you way. You can write the tokens on the same line or on separate lines. It is all right as long as you have at least one white space between the tokens.

3.2.6. The *conditional expression* operator.

We shell study now so-called conditional expression operator. It has a form

```
operand 1 ? operand 2 : operand 3;
```

Both question mark "**?**" and the colon "**:**" are used in this operator. The **operand 1** is a condition. **operand 2** and **3** are just the expressions. Execution of this operator begins with evaluation of **operand 1** (condition). If the condition is true, then **operand 2** is executed. If the result of condition evaluation is false, then the program executes the **operand 3**. Let's illustrate this operator on an example.

```
#include <iostream.h>

main ( )
{
int x, y;
cout << "Enter the value of y. \n";
cin >> y;
x=(y<=3) ? 2*y : 1;
cout << "See, the value of x is equal to " << x << ".";
}
```

Program 3.24.

This program displays a message on the screen

```
Enter the value of y.
```

Our program uses the conditional expression and assignment operators together. We wrote **x=...**, that, in fact, is an assignment operator. The result of the conditional expression operator **(y<=3) ? 2*y : 1** is assigned to **x** by

```
x=(y<=3) ? 2*y : 1;
```

Let's assume, you entered 2, then **y=2**. The condition **y<=3** is true, because you entered **y=2**. Thus, the **operand 2** should be executed. It is the expression **2*y**. A numeric value of that expression should be assigned to **x** on the left. We have **x=2*y=2*2=4**. The result is **x=4**, and the output is

```
See, the value of x is equal to 4.
```

In case if we enter **y** equal to 5, the condition becomes false. The value of the **operand 3** will be assigned to **x** and displayed

```
See, the value of x is equal to 1.
```

Again, operands 2 and 3 are just the expressions. Expressions can be algebraic, logical, etc. They can also be constants not necessarily integers. We wanted to show some diversity of operands in our example. We chose **operand 2** to be a mathematical expression, and a number as an **operand 3**. One can write the condition as

```
x=(y) ? 200 : 100;
```

Here, we compare **y** to zero.

We can use this operator to make the decisions in the programs instead of **if-else** construction. Consider another example.

```
#include <iostream.h>

main ( )
{
char state;
cout << "Enter the state: 'L' for low, 'H' for high. \n";
```

```
cin >> state;
state=='H'? cout <<"high state\n" : cout <<"low state\n";
cout << "End of test\n";
}
```

Program 3.25.

The program first prompts a user to enter a state of a system. This program displays a message, indicating whether some hypothetical system is in high or low state, depending on what letter '**H**' or '**L**' you enter. It displays the end of test message in both cases.

3.2.7. Flags.

A notion of the flag is a very important one. We have already dealt with the flag in **Program 3.15**. It was **no_prime** variable. An idea of a flag is very simple. One wants to have a variable, that will be set to certain value in case of certain events. We set the variable **no_prime** to zero, when we knew, we were dealing with a non-prime value in **Program 3.15**. Usually the flag is set to 1 or to 0, although you can choose another convention for yourself. Consider following **Program 3.26**, that finds the least common divisor of two integral values not equal to one.

```
#include <iostream.h>

main ( )
{
int y, z, r, x, n, m, k=1, flag=1;
cout << "Enter the integral values of x and y.\n";
cin >> x;
cin >> y;
if (y!=0 && x!=0)
{
z=x/y;
if (z>=1)
r=y;
else
r=x;
while (flag ==1 && k <= r)
{
k++;
n=x%k;
m=y%k;
if (n==0 && m==0)
flag=0;
}
if (!flag)
```

```
cout << "The common divisor is " << k <<"." ;
else
cout << "There is no common divisor.\n";
}
else
cout << "There are zeros among entered numbers.\n";
}
```

Program 3.26.

The program prompts
```
Enter the integral values of x and y.
```
Let's enter two integral numbers: **10   15**
The program displays the message
```
The common divisor is 5.
```
Think about the algorithm for solving this problem. In order to find the least common divisor of two entered numbers, one shell try to divide them consecutively by 2, 3, 4 …10. The first of those values that divides both 10 and 15 evenly is the least common divisor. The maximum divisor value to try should be equal to the least of those two values. You also have to stop your trials, whenever the first common divisor is found. There also can be a case, when no such divisor is found. The algorithm is implemented in **Program 3.26.** The program begins with declaring the variables. It provides the input for **x** and **y** by means of **cin** object, and looks for the least common divisor for those **x** and **y**. **Program 3.26** is written inside the **if-else** statement
```
if (y!=0 && x!=0)
... (the whole program)
else cout << "There are zeros among entered numbers.\n";
```
There is no point in looking for the divisor, if one of the entered values is equal to zero. This is what is tested by that **if-else** construction. If at least one of the variables is equal zero, a proper message is printed and the program is terminated. If none of the values is zero, one can look for the possible common divisor.

We first find **z=x/y**. If **z>=1**, then variable **y** is less than **x**. Otherwise, **x** is less than **y**. We assign to **r** the least value of **x** and **y** by
```
if (z>=1)     r=y;
else          r=x;
```
This will be the maximum value of the number that will be tried as a divisor for both values. The actual divisor is found by the **while** loop. It has two conditions as
```
while (flag==1 && k<= r)
```
We start from **k=1**. Every loop cycle increases it by one, until it reaches **r** - the least value of both variables **x** and **y**. If in any loop cycle both **x** and **y** can be divided by any divisor evenly, the flag variable **flag** is set to zero. This stops the next loop. We also use **flag** in **if(!flag)** statement. This tells us, whether the common divisor was found. If the condition is true, the current value of **k** is the least common divisor. Otherwise, the common divisor cannot be found.

3.3. Addition to loop and decision statements.

We will introduce here some statements associated with looping and decision making in C++. Some of them are not used too often. Some are considered as a bad taste. But those statements exist. So, we must review them.

The **break** statement that is used inside the **switch** statement has a wider application in C++. It is, sometimes, used in **switch**, **for**, **while** and **do** statements. Execution of **switch** statement terminates, when a program encountered the first **break** statement. Sometimes, you need to terminate the loop, when certain condition is reached. You can do it using the **break** statement. It causes all the subsequent statements after it to be skipped, and the loop to be terminated. This is shown in a following example.

```
for ( n=0; n<10; ++n)
{
x=x+n;
if (x>100)
break;
cout << "x=" << x << endl;
}
```

That loop adds **n** to **x** every cycle. We set a condition **if(x>100)** inside the loop. If the value of **x** during a cycle is greater then 100, the **break** statement is executed. Computer skips all the statements after **break** and terminates the loop. In our case, the computer skips the

```
cout << "x=" << x << endl;
```

statement and terminates the loop.

If you use **break** statement in the nested loops, better use it in the innermost loop. In this case, it terminates only the innermost loop. Use of **break** statement, in general, is not desirable, because it interrupts the sequential flow of the program, makes it more difficult to follow. We recommend to use a flag in those cases, and to use a value of the flag in the conditional loop expression, as we have shown in this chapter.

The **continue** statement has a format of writing

```
continue;
```

Any statements in the loop appearing after **continue** are skipped. But the computer does not terminate the loop. It proceeds normally, only without execution of those statements, as shown in an example.

```
#include <iostream.h>

main ( )
{
int x=10, y=0, n;
for (n=1; n<15; n++)
{
y=2*x+n;
if (y==(3*x))
```

```
continue;
cout << n << ", " ;
} }
```

Program 3.27.

This program computes the value of the expression **y=2*x+n**. When **y=2*x+n** becomes equal to **3*x**, the **if(y==(3*x))** statement permits the execution of the **continue** statement. The **cout** object in that particular loop cycle is skipped. Thus, the output of the program is

```
1, 2, 3, 4, 5, 6, 7, 8, 9, 11, 12, 13, 14,
```

The number 10 is missing in the output. For this value of **n** we have **2*x+n=3*x**. The **continue** statement is usually used to avoid a group of statements. The same goal can be better achieved by the **if** statements.

The **goto** statement can be used in the loops and by itself in the program to direct the computer to execute a certain statement. The format of writing this statement is

```
goto label;
...
label :   statement;
```

The **label** in **goto** is, basically, an identifier. This **label** becomes *attached* to this particular **goto** statement. You see another line beginning with the **label**. That **label** is separated from the **statement** by a colon (**:**).

When a computer encounters the **goto** statement, it reads the **label** attached to it. The computer looks for a statement following **label:**. The **statement** following **label:** is executed. The computer proceeds the execution from the next statement after the labeled statement. The labeled statement can be anywhere in the program where it is needed. You can place it before or after the **goto** statement. The example of **goto** use is given in **Program 3.28**.

```
#include <iostream.h>

main ( )
  {
int y=0, n=1;
a1: y=y+n;
n++;
if(n<=10)
goto a1;
cout << y;
}
```

Program 3.28.

The program displays the number 55. It is a sum of the first 10 integral values. The familiar to us loop is implemented with **goto** statement. Use of **goto** statement is highly discouraged in C++ programs. One can use loops, decision statements, flags instead of this statement.

EXERCISES.

1. Run all the programs given in this chapter, if you have an access to a computer.

2. Write a program that reads a binary number from the standard input and converts it to a decimal number.

3. Write a program converting a decimal number into:
   a) binary;   b)octal;   c)hexadecimal.

4. Write a program that reverses an order of the digits in any entered integral value. Make it working for the positive and negative numbers. For instance, if you enter 12345, the program output should be 54321. Try to develop at least a few algorithms for doing this task.

5. Write a program that adds the squares of the integral numbers $1^2 + 2^2 + 3^2 + \ldots$ from 1 to **n**. Display the square of each number you add by every loop cycle.

6. Write a program, that rounds off the floating-point numbers.

7. Write a program that computes real amount of interest and total amount paid for each $1000 borrowed. The duration of the mortgage and interest rate should be read from the standard input. You pay off all the interest during the first half of the mortgage period. Only after that, you can pay off the actual $1000 borrowed. The yearly payments should be equal during the time of the mortgage.

8. Write a program that allows you to enter two numbers and divide the first one by the second one. The program should check for the division by zero. If the numbers can be divided evenly, it should display a message.

9. Write a program that allows you to enter three numbers and prints them in increasing order.

10. Write a program that adds or subtracts fractions (like 3/5 +5/9 and so on) entered from the standard input.

11. Write a program that reads integral numbers entered from a keyboard and displays them in words. For instance, you enter 1995. The output is: **one thousand nine hundred and ninety five**.

12. Write a program that acts as a calculator. It should check for division by zero.

13. Write a program that prints your monthly telephone bill. The monthly service fee is $15.95. For this fee you can call up to 20 minutes free. Each additional minute is $0.13. Make the number of minutes a variable that is entered from the keyboard.

14. Print a histogram of the function $y = 5x^3 - x^2$. **x** changes in the range from 0 to 5.

15. Find a value of the function
$$y = 3 \times x^2 - z + 9, \text{ when } 0 \le x \le 5.8 \text{ and } z \prec 0;$$

$$y = \frac{9 * x^3}{6z - 5}, \text{ when } x \prec 0 \text{ and } z \succ 0.$$

16. Write a program for identifying even and odd numbers.

17. Write a program that finds a special math constant **e=2.71828...** from its definition. It is defined as
$$e = \lim_{x \to \infty} \left(1 + \frac{1}{x}\right)^x$$

18. Write programs for finding the sums of the following mathematical rows

a) $1+\dfrac{1}{1!}+\dfrac{1}{2!}+\dfrac{1}{3!}+\dfrac{1}{4!}+...+\dfrac{1}{n!}+...;$

b) $\dfrac{1}{1\times 2}+\dfrac{1}{2\times 3}+\dfrac{1}{3\times 4}+...+\dfrac{1}{n\times (n+1)}+...;$

c) $1+\dfrac{1}{2^2}+\dfrac{1}{3^2}+\dfrac{1}{4^2}+...+\dfrac{1}{n^2}+...$.

19. Write a program that finds the result of $(x+y)^n$ operation. Here **n** is an integral number. **x** and **y** can be the floating-point numbers. The binomial formula for finding it had been discovered by Sir Isaac Newton and is given below

$$(x+y)^n = x^n + n\times x^{n-1}\times y + \frac{n\times (n-1)}{2!}\times x^{n-2}\times y^2 + \frac{n\times (n-1)\times (n-2)}{3!}\times x^{n-3}\times y^3 + ... +$$

$$+ \frac{n\times (n-1)\times ..\times (n-m+1)}{m!}\times x^{n-m}\times y^m + ... + n\times x\times y^{n-1} + y^n$$

20. Write a program that converts a hexadecimal number to a decimal, octal to a decimal and vice versa. It should prompt the user what base does he or she want to enter a number in and to what base to convert that number. The number should be converted and displayed with the proper message. For instance,

```
You have entered hexadecimal number ... .
Its decimal   equivalent is ... .
```

21. Write a program that prompts a user to enter two sides of a triangle (for example **a**, **b**) and the hypotenuse **c**. It then checks, if the entered sides belong to a triangle that has a direct angle in it. Those triangles have a property: $a^2 + b^2 = c^2$.

22. Write a program that plots a histogram of a **sin(x)** function, where **x** changes in the interval from 0 to π. (Hint: look up the last chapter on standard library functions to find out how to use the standard library **sin(x)** function in a program).

23. Write a program, that finds integral numbers **a**, **b** and **c** satisfying the famous condition $a^2 + b^2 = c^2$. Examine the numbers from 1 to 20. The program should display its results as a table with three columns. The first column is the variable **a**, the second - is **b** and the third is **c**.

24. Write two programs that print a histogram in a form of a circle. The first program should use the C language I/O, and the second one must use C++ tools.

25. Write a program that finds and prints all the perfect numbers in the interval from 1 to 800. The main property of a perfect number is that its factors add up to the number. For instance, 6 is a perfect number, because its factors are 1, 2, 3 and 1+2+3=6. The 28 is a perfect number, because its factors are 1, 2, 4, 7, 14 and 1+2+4+7+14=28.

CHAPTER 4

ARRAYS.

4.1. One-dimensional arrays.

Sometimes, a particular problem requires a user to work with many parameters, that are changing. For instance, consider a problem of keeping salary and names of all the employees at a big firm. Another example is keeping student grades and displaying them as you need. One might have to operate with a significant number of variables in those cases. That can make a program long and too compli-cated. C++ as well as C allows to organize all the variables in the ordered sets called *arrays*. An array consists of a number of variables organized in a certain way. Each of its variables is called an *element*. An array is a powerful tool. If used wisely, it makes the programs more efficient.

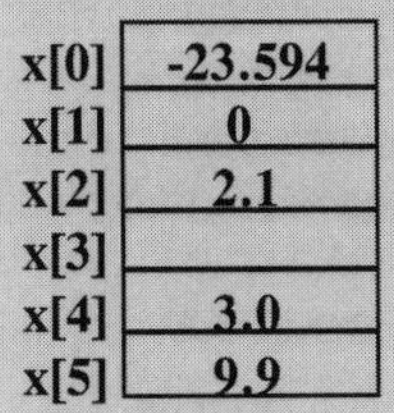

x[0]	-23.594
x[1]	0
x[2]	2.1
x[3]	
x[4]	3.0
x[5]	9.9

Fig. 4.1.

The arrays must be declared prior to their use. It is usually done in the beginning of a program, when all the data is declared. They are declared as follows

```
char zq[20];
int temp_nor[30];
```

An array declaration consists of three components: the data type of each array element (**int**, **float**, **double**, etc.), the array name and number of elements inside the array. The array names are the identifiers. The square brackets **[]** immediately follow a name of an array. There are no white spaces between the array name and the brackets. An optional number appearing within those brackets in declaration statement indicates the number of the elements in the array. It indicates how many cells of memory must be reserved by the computer to store the values of all the array elements. Each of these cells should be capable of storing a value of an array element of a declared type.

Let's declare an array

```
float x[6];
```

We have declared an array named **x**. It contains 6 elements or six variables, if you will. Each of those elements has type **float**. This declaration tells the computer to allocate 6 cells of memory, each capable to store one value of type **float**. Let's stipulate an important point. Even though the array as a whole can be of any data type, but all the elements of the same array must have the same data type. In other words, if you declare an array as having an **int** type, you cannot have some elements of that array of **int** type and some of other data types.

Each array element can be used absolutely independently in the program as a regular variable. The name of an array element is formed by the special rules. For instance,

```
x[4]=3.0;
```

This assigns the value 3.0 to the array element **x[4]** in Fig 4.1. If you need to use the third array element, you can call it as any variable by its name **x[2]**. So, treat the array elements as separate variables. You have learned by now input/output, loops, decisions and other material. We have applied them to the variables. All those tools can be used for the arrays as well. It would be a pity, if you are afraid to use them for the array elements. An array is just an organized collection of the same variables you know. And there is nothing magic about them.

There are some specific things you need to know, when you handle the arrays. They allow more flexibility in handling along with the traditional ways of dealing with the variables, that you have learned. We will study those additional features, that arrays allow you to do.

The first specific feature of an array is an ambiguity of the numbers inside the brackets. They have one meaning, when you declare an array. They have another meaning, when you use the array elements in the program.

When you declare an array, the number inside the brackets **[4]** corresponds to the total number of elements in an array. Thus, when we have declared at the beginning

```
float x[6];
```

we have specified, that this array contains six elements. Look at Fig 4.1. It, indeed, consists of six elements.

After the array has been declared, the number within the brackets acquires a new meaning. An array notation anywhere in the program now indicates a particular element of the array. The first array element always has number **[0]** inside the brackets. Look, at the Fig 4.1. The **x[3]** refers to the fourth array element, for instance. So, if you see **x[4]** in any statement after declaration, it now refers to the fifth element of the array. And **x[2]** refers to the third element. So C++ statements now operate with fifth, or third elements, without doing anything to other elements. For example,

```
if (x[1] >= 0)
```

uses second array element **x[1]** in the condition of the **if** statement.

The number inside the brackets **[]** is called an *index* number, or simply an *index*, or a *subscript*. You can also see an array element written without the index number, as

```
x=10;
```

Using an array element without the index number refers to the first element of the array, i.e., it is the same as

```
x[0]=10;
```

The second very important feature is, that you can address an array element in the program as

```
x[n]
```

Here, the index number **n** is a variable, that can accept only integral values. This gives an enormous flexibility for array handling. If you want to assign a value to fourth array element **x[3]**, just write it as

```
n=3;
...
x[n]=20.567;
```

Here, **n** is assigned the value 3. When we call **x[n]**, we, in fact, call the element **x[3]**. So, by changing **n** in **x[n]** one can call any array element.

The memory cells for the array elements are allocated according to a special order. Fig 4.1 shows us how those cells are allocated. The array elements are always located in the neighboring memory cells. Computer allocates a cell for the first array element **x[0]**. The second array element **x[1]** is placed in the cell next to **x[0]**. The third array element **x[2]** should be in the cell next to **x[1]** and so on as shown in Fig 4.1.

Let's say, you want to enter twenty values from the keyboard and store them in the array of twenty elements **int data[20]**. You do not have to use **scanf()** or **cin** twenty times for entering each value. You can write a loop, where you let **n** change from 0 to 19 as shown

```
for (n=0; n<=19; n++)
cin >> data[n];
```

The above loop will assign a value to each array element from a keyboard. There will be twenty cycles. You can code it in two lines. It is not only advantageous for input or output. You can reach any array element by changing **n**. This will simplify almost any operation you want to do using arrays. For instance, you can code to sort the array array elements in a few lines.

Program 4.1 illustrates known to us way of dealing with the arrays as with the collections of variables. It assigns the values to the array elements directly one by one and displays them in the same manner. We are dealing only with four elements. See for yourself, how sloppy and ineffective this way can be.

```
#include <stdio.h>

main ( )
{
int t[4];
t[0]=10;
t[1]=20;
t[2]=30;
t[3]=40;
printf ("t[0]=%d, t[1]=%d, t[2]=%d, t[3]=%d. \n",
        t[0],t[1],t[2],t[3]);
}
```

Program 4.1.

The output of that program is

```
t[0]=10, t[1]=20, t[2]=30, t[3]=40.
```

Here, we assign the value to each array element directly, by calling it by name. We use the same way of output, to get the value of each array element directly.

Program 4.2 illustrates loop input/output. This way can be used to input/output the array elements by changing the index number.

```
#include <iostream.h>
```

```
main ( )
{
int index;
float test_array[5];
cout << "Enter all 5 elements.\n";
for (index=0;  index<5;  ++index)
cin >> test_array[index];
index=0;
while (index<5)
{
cout << "enter element number to see or number greater"
      << " than 4 to exit.\n";
cin >> index;
cout << "The element test_array[" << index
      << "]=" << test_array[index] << endl;
  }  }
```

Program 4.2.

All the array elements are entered using the loop statement **for**. The value of a particular array element can be displayed on the screen by the **while** loop. We display the array
number by reading the index number **index** inside the brackets **test_ array[index]**
with **cin** object. Then, **cout** object displays the array element, which corresponds to that
index. One can terminate the **while** statement by entering the **index** value greater
than 4. It makes the condition false.

You know, one can assign initial values to the variables, when they are declared. Same
can be done with the arrays as well, because they are just the collections of variables. It is
called an array *initialization*. If an array is initialized when it is declared, one should add
the word **static** before the declaration on some compilers. Many compilers and C++
do not require to add the word **static**. Two initialization forms are shown below.

```
static int abc[5]={1, 8, 4, 6, 2};
int abc[5]={1, 8, 4, 6, 2};
```

Here, we initialize the array of 5 elements. The values are assigned to all its elements in
the parentheses **{ }** in the corresponding order. The element **abc[0]** is assigned 1, element **abc[1]** is equal to 8, element **abc[2]** to 4 and so on. One can assign an initial
value not to all but to some of the array elements. For example,

```
int abc[10]={167, 8, 45, 63, 2};
```

declares an array of 10 elements **abc[10]**. The initial values are assigned only to the first
five elements of that array. The first value in the parentheses **{ }** is assigned to the first
element **abc[0]**, second to **abc[1]**, and so on, until the last value is assigned. The
remaining array elements have not been assigned the initial values. Their initial values are
usually 0 by default. Any array element can get its value any time later.

If an array has less elements than there are values inside the **{ }** brackets, it causes an
error. When the number of array elements is not specified in the initialization procedure

```
int abc[ ]={ 1, 8, 4, 6, 2};
```

compiler presumes, that the number of the array elements is equal to the number of values inside the **{ }** parentheses.

Another aspect, worth to be discussed here, is the use of increment or decrement operators. Assume, we write an assignment

    x=a[n++];

If **n** was equal to 3 before this assignment, the statement will first assign

    x=a[3];

Only then it will increment **n** by one. The statement

    x=a[++n];

where **n** was equal to 3, will first increment **n** to 4. It will, then, assign

    x=a[4];

Those cases are true for the assignments with decrement operators **x=a[--n]** and **x=a[n- -]**. Instead of adding, it will subtract one from the current value of **n**.

One should exercise caution working with the arrays. We will explain it on an example. Suppose, you have declared an array consisting of 20 elements **x[20]**. You can attempt to access any and even not existing array element. For instance,

    x[60]=5;

This assignment, basically, attempts to assign 5 to the 60-th array element. But we have declared an array with only 20 elements. What will happen? It will be an error, that can lead to very unpleasant surprises. Unfortunately, too many compilers do not inform a user about attempting to access the elements that do not exist.

We offer a program to illustrate the arrays and some formatting capabilities of C++.

```
#include <iostream.h>
#include <iomanip.h>

main ( )
{
int k[4], m;
cout << " Enter four integer numbers\n";
for (m=0; m<4; m++)
cin >> k[m];
cout << setw (10) << "Entry" << setw (10)
     << "Value" <<"\n";
for (m=0; m<4; m++)
cout << setw (10) << m << setw (10) << k[m] << "\n";
}
```

Program 4.3.

The program prompts a user to enter 4 integers. If we enter 82 3 201 58, the output is

Entry	Value
0	82
1	3
2	201
3	58

The program demonstrates an array application and creation of tables in C++.

4.2. Multi-dimensional and character arrays.

Suppose, we have a table containing numbers or a matrix. We want to store all the numbers as an array. We may have two options of handling this situation. We can enter each of those values consecutively in one-dimensional array. Sometimes, one wants to be able to access a table value by pointing at the column number and row number. In this case, one has to specify a multi-dimensional array. It is a two-dimensional array for a simple table. An example of two dimensional array having 4 elements in one dimension and 6 in other is

```
int abc[4][6];
```

Three dimensional array will have three sets of brackets, four dimensional - four, and so on. The total number of elements in **abc[4][6]** is **4*6=24**. The total number of elements in a multi-dimensional array can be obtained by multiplication the indexes of all the dimensions. **[..]** × **[..]** × **[..]** × **[..]** . Even though, all the elements of multi-dimensional array can be put in one dimension, sometimes, it is more convenient to deal with the multi-dimensional arrays. Compilers have different maximum number of dimensions. You can always explore what is the maximum number of dimensions for your compiler. Everything applicable to a one-dimensional array applies to a multi-dimensional array as well. However, we will illustrate the multi-dimensional arrays.

Let's consider a table or a matrix to learn how to create a two-dimensional array.

	Column number				
	0	1	2	3	4
Row number					
0	12	65	23	99	31
1	85	82	37	18	12
2	-7	59	-36	84	11

Let's assume, the variable **n** represents the row number and **m** the column number. Then, any element of the table can be referred to by those numbers. You can declare an array based on this table. If we want the first index to denote the row number, then we have 3 rows (**0, 1, 2**). The second number will stand for the number of columns. There are 5 columns in the table (**0, 1, 2, 3, 4**). So we have total of **3*5=15** elements in the array, and the array will be declared as

```
int table[3][5];
```

This statement should reserve 15 cells each capable of storing one value of type **int**. From that point on, the numbers inside the brackets refer to a particular element, as in one-dimensional array. The table element can be accessed by **table[n][m]**.

For example, **table[1][3]** would refer to the row 1 and column 3, and the value of the array element there is 18. Therefore, the **table[2][1]** has value 59. One has to remember, the count begins from the **table[0][0]**.

Initialization of multi-dimensional arrays, as everything else, is analogous to one-dimensional case. But we want to emphasize a few points. If an array is declared with the initial values, one can write

```
int x[2][3]={ {24, -5, 93},{100, 29, 4}};
```

The word **static** is required to declare and initialize an array in the same statement by a number of compilers. However, you can get away without using that word on many compilers. C++ proper does not require to use the word **static** to initialize an array. The above example can be interpreted as having two rows and three columns. As you see, each row is entered in the internal **{}** parentheses. The sets of **{}** parentheses inside are separated by the commas. There are only two rows in the given example. Commas are required after each **{}** brace. But inner pairs of braces are not required. You can write

```
int x[2][3]={ 24, -5, 93, 100, 29, 4};
```

and this statement is identical to the one given above.

Two above code lines demonstrate how does the computer initialize an array. You had an array with 2 rows and 3 columns. The computer first assigns the values to the array elements **x[0][0]**, **x[0][1]** and **x[0][2]**. When the second index has gone over all the values, the first index is increased by one. The computer assigns the values to **x[1][0]**, **x[1][1]**, **x[1][2]**. Thus, the first index stands for the number of internal braces. The second index indicates how many elements are in the braces. If you partially initialize a two-dimensional array, the inner pairs of braces are required to prevent an ambiguity in reading.

How to initialize a multi-dimensional array? Use the same method. We offer you a program that initializes a three-dimensional array. This will give you an idea how to deal with the higher dimensions.

```
#include <iostream.h>

main ( )
{
int x[2][3][4]={{{10, 20, 30, 40}, {50, 60, 70,
       80}, {90, 100, 110, 120}}, {{130, 140, 150, 160},
       {170, 180, 190, 200}, {210, 220, 230, 240}}};
cout << "x[0][0][2]=" << x[0][0][2] << ",  "
     << "x[0][1][2]=" << x[0][1][2] << ",  "
     << "x[1][1][2]=" << x[1][1][2] << endl;
}
```

Program 4.4.

The output of the program is

```
x[0][0][2]=30,   x[0][1][2]=70,   x[1][1][2]=190
```

Here, the initialization of a three-dimensional array has six sets of brackets, each containing four elements. We combined all the braces into two groups. Each group contains three sets of braces. Each group is surrounded by the extra set of braces. You access each of those two groups by the first index. For example, the **x[0][..][..]** accesses the group

```
{{10, 20, 30, 40}, {50, 60, 70, 80}, {90, 100, 110, 120}}
```

The second index accesses each of the three sets of brackets inside any of those two groups. Each of those four elements in the most inner braces is accessed by the third index. For instance, the **x[..][..][2]** accesses the third element in those braces.

We demonstrate, that **x[0][0][2]** accesses the third element of the first bracket of the first group. Its value is 30. The **x[0][1][2]** accesses the third element of the second bracket of the first group. Its value is 70. The **x[1][1][2]** accesses the third element of the second bracket of the second group. Its value is 190.

Again, we did not have to surround the initial values by the multiple sets of braces. We could have put all of them in just one set of external braces, as

```
int x[2][3][4]= {10, 20,  30,  40,  50,  60,  70,  80,  90, 100,
                110, 120, 130, 140, 150, 160, 170, 180, 190,
                200, 210, 220, 230, 240};
```

The computer would have assigned them in the same order to the same array elements anyway. Hence, when a computer initializes an array, it assigns the values to the array elements in a certain order. This order is a rule of C++ and C++. The form of writing the initialization procedure is also a rule of the language. Do not mix it with assigning the values to the array elements by you. We have already learned in this chapter how you can access and assign the values to the array elements. You can do it in any order.

Couple words about the character arrays. Character arrays obey to the same rules as one- and multi-dimensional arrays. They are declared to have the **char** data type. Each element of such an array is entered surrounded by the single quotation marks ' '. Consider, for example, an initialization of such an array illustrated in **Program 4.5**.

```
#include <iostream.h>

main ( )
{
int k;
 static char sam[ ]= {'l', 'a', 'n', 'g', 'u', 'a', 'g',
                     'e'};
for (k=0; k< 8; ++k)
cout << sam[k];
}
```
                          Program 4.5.

The output of the program is
```
    language
```
We display each element of the array on the screen with the **for** loop.

4.3. Array application examples.

We have to learn how to use the arrays and how to create the programs with them. The next couple sections will illustrate a few applications of programs with the arrays. You will learn how to use the arrays in a program and what are the advantages of using the arrays.

We will solve a few problems and try to show you how to do it.

4.3.1. An election program.

The first problem is to create a program for the primary elections. Suppose, there are six candidates for some office. Each voter has one vote. Each voter presses a number from 1 to 6 once. Each number corresponds to certain presidential candidate. The program has to read a number corresponding to each candidate. The votes given for each candidate should be stored. The program should also print the names of the candidates and the number of votes given for them.

```
#include <stdio.h>                      /*line1*/

main ( )                                /*line2*/
{                                       /*line3*/
int vote[6], m, k, stop;                /*line4*/

static char name[6][8]= {{'A','b','e','l','0'},
   { 'A','b','r','a','h','a','m','0'}, {'A','n','n','0'},
  {'A','d','a','m','0'},  {'A','d','r','i','a','n','0'},
   {'A','g','a','t','h','a','0'}};        /*line5*/
for (m=0; m<=5; m++)                     /*line6*/
vote[m]=0;                               /*line7*/
do                                       /*line8*/
{                                        /*line9*/
printf ("enter the candidate number from 1 to 6 or 7 to
         exit. \n");                     /*line10*/
scanf ("%d", &m);                        /*line11*/
vote[m-1]=vote[m-1]+1;                   /*line12*/
}                                        /*line13*/
while (m<=6);                            /*line14*/
printf(" votes | names\n");             /*line15*/
for (m=0; m<=5; m++)                     /*line16*/
{                                        /*line17*/
printf ("%5d  |", vote[m]);             /*line18*/
stop=7;                                  /*line19*/
for (k=0; k<=stop;k++)                   /*line20*/
{                                        /*line21*/
if (name[m][k]!='0')                     /*line22*/
printf("%c", name[m][k]);                /*line23*/
else                                     /*line24*/
stop=k-2;                                /*line25*/
}                                        /*line26*/
printf("\n");                            /*line27*/
```

```
} }                                    /*line28*/
```
Program 4.6.

Program 4.6 gives you a version of performing this task. The logical way to solve this problem is to declare the data, to enter the votes, and to display them.

The arrays and the variables are declared at lines 4, 5. The two-dimensional array **name[6][8]** is initialized at line 5 of the program. We used the first dimension **[6]** for the candidate's number. The second dimension **[8]** stores the candidate's name. For example, the element **name[1][..]** displays the name of the first candidate. An array **vote[m]** will record the number of votes for each candidate.

The next step should be to set all the **vote[m]** elements to zero. This way we know, each element was zero at the beginning. The array elements are set to zero by default on many systems. But in critical applications you might want to set them to zero. It is very important to know in this case, that each element was zero at the beginning. We use **for** loop at lines 6, 7 to set all the array elements to zero.

The next step is to enter the votes. Each **vote[m]** array element corresponds to one candidate. We do the following. Every time you enter a number from a keyboard, the corresponding array element is called and its value is increased by one. For example, you enter number 3, you call the third array element. The value stored in **vote[2]** is increased by one. As you know, we call **vote[2]** not **vote[3]**, because the array starts from the element **[0]** and **vote[2]** is the third array element. We increase **vote[m-1]** instead of **vote[m]**, because you enter the numbers from 1 to 6 for the candidates, but the array starts from **vote[0]**. We can certainly ask you to enter numbers from 0 to 5, but they would be a bit awkward for humans. If you call element **vote[2]** ten times during the elections, its value will be 10. You can print this value.

The vote input is implemented at lines 8-14 by **do-while** loop. It prompts us to enter the candidate's number and reads it by means of **scanf()** function. When you enter the number, the value of the corresponding array element is increased by one. It is coded at line 12 of **Program 4.6**.

```
vote[m-1]=vote[m-1]+1;
```
The loop is terminated by entering a value greater than 6.

The rest of the program is a code that provides a proper output. You want to print the number of votes **vote[m]** for each candidate. This is coded as the outer **for** loop. But you also want to display the name **name[m][k]** of the candidate. Here comes the inner **for** loop, because for the candidate number **m** you want to display all **k** letters of his or her name. It is very easy to follow those loops. We also want to point to one very important feature. Consider a fragment of **Program 4.6**.

```
for (k=0; k<=stop; k++)              /*line21*/
{                                    /*line22*/
if (name[m][k+1]!='0')               /*line23*/
printf("%c", name[m][k]);            /*line24*/
else                                 /*line25*/
stop=k-2;                            /*line26*/
```
Now take a look how did we initialize the array **name[m][k]** at the beginning of the program. We entered character '**0**' at the end of each name. Why? Each name has different

length, or different number of letters in it. We did not want to display all eight positions for a name consisting of four characters. So, we added the last character '**0**' to every name, and introduced a check for it by **if(name[m][k]!='0')** statement. The name is printed normally, until the compiler encounters '**0**'. This sets the **stop** to **k-2**, and makes the condition **k<=stop** in the **for** loop false. The name printing is stopped and the computer goes to the next candidate in the outer loop. We use

```
printf("\n");   /*line28*/
```

to start printing each new record from a new line.

We used C I/O functions for the output in the above program. We will be coming to the C style programs in this book from time to time. We do it to remind about the existence of C tools in C++ language. You can rewrite the previous program using C++ I/O tools.

4.3.2. Sorting program.

We introduce following sorting program for an array of ten elements. However, one can modify it for an array of any number of elements. You enter ten integral numbers in any order and our program will display them in the increasing order. Using this idea one can modify the program to display the array elements in decreasing order. One can do it with the floating-point numbers. More complicated sorting can be used for arranging words in alphabetic order. The sorting has a great number of applications in life. One can sort and display the students according to their scores. You can sort experimental results and display them accordingly in a convenient way.

There are many sorting algorithms. One of them is illustrated in **Program 4.7**.

```
#include <iostream.h>

main ( )
  {
int a[10],n, m,  x;
for (n=0; n<10; n++)
cin >> a[n];
for (n=0; n<9; n++)
for (m=n+1; m<10; m++)
if (a[n]>a[m])
{
x=a[m];
a[m]=a[n];
a[n]=x;
}
for (n=0; n<10; n++)
cout << a[n] << " ";
}
```

Program 4.7.

You enter ten integers of **int** type separated by the space. The program displays them in ascending order. This program is relatively simpler and easier to follow than the previous one. This is why we have not numbered each program line. The program declares the array and the variables and uses the **cin** object for reading all the elements of **a[]** array. The next step is to sort them. The third step is to print the sorted array. Since the array printing is fairly easy, we shell concentrate on the sorting procedure.

We want to sort the array elements in increasing order. You first take **a[0]** and compare it to the rest of the elements from **a[1]** to **a[9]**. If the value of **a[0]** is less than the value of any other element, the **a[0]** should be at the first position. How to be if we, for example, have an array **{300, 25, 100, -73...}**?

If **a[0]=300** is greater than **a[1]=25**, we want them to trade their places. So, **a[0]** becomes 25 and **a[1]=300**. If we now compare new **a[0]=25** to **a[2]=100**, they should remain as they are. We want to swap **a[0]=25** with **a[3]=-73**, because the smallest value should be stored in **a[0]**. After that, **a[0]=-73** is compared with the next element **a[4]** and so on. Thus, we compare **a[0]** to other elements in order from **a[1]** to **a[9]** and swap them with current **a[0]** if **a[0]>a[k]**. Here, **[k]** stands for an index of any current array element. It will yield the minimum value for **a[0]**.

We can now compare **a[1]** to the elements beginning from the **a[2]** to **a[9]**. We will swap any of the elements from **a[2]** to **a[9]** with current **a[2]**, if they store smaller values. This will place the second smallest value at the second position inside the array. Then, you compare the third array element against the **a[3]** to **a[9]**, and switch any of those elements less than **a[2]** with **a[2]**. Then, you start placing the minimum of the existing values in the **a[3]** by comparing **a[3]** with all other elements with the indexes greater than **[3]**. You keep doing it, until comparing **a[8]** with **a[9]**. In general, you compare **a[n]** to every other element **a[m]**, where **m** should be greater than **n**. If **a[n]>a[m]** you swap the values by

```
x=a[m];
a[m]=a[n];
a[n]=x;
```

You cannot just swap the values. The value of **a[m]** should be stored in the third variable **x**. The old a[m] value could be lost, if you do not store it somewhere. We, then, assign the value stored in **a[n]** to **a[m]**. After that, the old **a[m]** value stored in **x** can be assigned to **a[n]** by **a[n]=x**.

The sorting procedure consists of two loops. The element **a[n]** is compared to **a[m]**. The inner loop chooses different **a[m]** every cycle to be compared and swapped with the current **a[n]**, if necessary. The variable **m** in the inner loop should vary from **n+1** to 10. Why the lower limit is **n+1**? Remember, **a[0]** was first compared to **a[1]** and so on. We have to "walk" over all the elements with **a[n]**. The index variable **n** changes from 0 to 8. We do not need to do the operation with the last element. It will be arranged in the cycle, that compares **a[8]** to **a[9]**.

4.3.3. Program for solving systems of linear equations.

Suppose, there is a system of two equations with two unknowns

$$a_{11}x_1 + a_{12}x_2 = b_1$$

$$a_{21}x_1 + a_{22}x_2 = b_2$$

We will solve this system using Cramer's rule. The program below would be an example of a program utilizing mathematical calculations. The solution of this system is

$$x_1 = \frac{b_1 a_{22} - b_2 a_{12}}{a_{11}a_{22} - a_{12}a_{21}} \quad \text{and} \quad x_1 = \frac{a_{11}b_2 - a_{21}b_1}{a_{11}a_{22} - a_{12}a_{21}}$$

Each variable is a result of a division. The denominator should not be equal to zero in our case. There are special solutions, when it is zero. We do not consider them. We will not go deeply into math, because our readers can have different background in math. We do not want to scare them away from language C++, that is the subject of our book. The above algorithm is implemented in **Program 4.8**.

```
#include <iostream.h>

main ( )
{
float a[2][2], num[2], x[2], det;
int   n, m, k;
for (n=0; n<2; n++)
for (m=0; m<2; m++)
{
cout << "enter a[" << (n+1) << "][" << (m+1) << "]\n";
cin >> a[n][m];
}
for (k=0; k<2; k++)
{
cout << "enter num[" << (k+1) << "]\n";
cin >> num[k];
}
det= a[0][0]*a[1][1]-a[0][1]*a[1][0];
if (det!=0)
{
x[0]=(num[0]*a[1][1]-num[1]*a[0][1])/det;
x[1]=(a[0][0]*num[1]-a[1][0]*num[0])/det;
for (k=0;k<2; k++)
cout << "x" << (k+1) << "=" << x[k] << "\n";
}
else
cout << "determinant is zero\n";
}
```

Program 4.8.

The program prompts the user to enter the coefficients of each variable in the system.

After you enter them, a solution of the system of equations will be displayed. Suppose, we want to solve the system of linear equations

```
28*x1+3*x2=31                    and              20*x1-7*x2=51
```

When we enter 2 for **a[1][1]**, 3 for **a[1][2]**, 20 for **a[2][1]**, -7 for **a[2][2]**, 31 as **num[1]**, 51 for **num[2]**. The result should be displayed as

```
x1=5
x2=7
```

Program 4.8 is pretty straightforward. Pay attention to the way we code the value input for a two-dimensional array **a[n][m]**. We use double nested loop to do that. The program also checks for a zero denominator. If it is zero the message is displayed

```
determinant is zero
```

EXERCISES.

1. Run all the programs given in this paragraph, if you have an access to a computer.
2. Write a program for the elections that has the features we have described. It should also be able to display the candidates according to the number of votes they received.
3. Write a program that displays your name on the terminal as

```
D D         A         N   N
D  D       A A        NN  N
D  D      A A A       N NN
D D      A    A       N   N
```

Use two dimensional array to display your name.

4. Write a program that keeps student names along with their scores and displays students according to those scores. The program should display the student name, score and grade together. It should be able to find an average class score. It should be able to give the names of the students below certain score. The program should also assign a letter grade to each score: A for the score greater than 90, B for the score from 70 to 90, C for the score within the range from 50 to 70, D for the score from 40 to 50, and F for the scores below that.

5. Write a program that performs matrix
a) multiplication;
b) additions and subtractions;

6. Write a program that finds and inverse matrix.

7. Write a program that first declares an array with twenty elements and assigns the values to eight of them. The program should allow to add an element or to insert it anywhere between those eight values. To insert an element **x[4]** means to put it in the fifth cell. The previous values of the cells beginning from the fifth element up should move one position up in the array, as shown in Fig 4.2.

before insertion

10	32	1	88	55	21	7	-6			
[0]	[1]	[2]	[3]	[4]	[5]	[6]	[7]	[8]	[9]	[10]

we insert x[5]=99

after insertion

10	32	1	88	55	99	21	7	-6		
[0]	[1]	[2]	[3]	[4]	[5]	[6]	[7]	[8]	[9]	[10]

Fig 4.2.

8. Every even integer greater than 2 can be expressed as a sum of two prime numbers.

Write a program that allows the user to enter a number, checks if it is positive and even, and finds those two prime numbers.

9. Declare a two dimensional array 7×80. It will hold 7 phrases. Each phrase consists of a number of words. The total number of the characters in one phrase should not exceed 80. Write a program that enters words from the keyboard into that array. The program should be able to search for a certain word in this array and display a phrase in which it is found. (Hint: You can use dots before and after the phrase to find the beginning and the end of the proposition.)

10. Write a program that reverses the order of characters in the entered string.

11. Write a program that finds a solution of the system of three equations with three unknowns.

12. Write a program that reads the floating-point numbers from the standard input and sorts them in the decreasing order.

13. Write a program arranging 10 words up to 8 characters each in an alphabetic order in a two dimensional array. You should be able to enter those words from the keyboard.

14. Write a program that prompts a user to enter his or her name, hourly wage and number of hours worked per two week. Assuming the tax is roughly 30%, it prints a pay stub in a form of a table. It should display the gross earning for two weeks, number of worked hours, amount of taxes withheld and the amount to go in a pay check.

15. Improve the program that you would have to write for the previous problem by assuming a graduate income tax. A tax begins from 14% for biweekly earning of $300 and increases by 2% on each additional $50 until reaches 30%. For instance, a person making $350 for two weeks would pay 16% income tax, for $400 biweekly one would pay 18% and so on.

16. Write a program that reads a phrase from an input and counts the number of digits in it. The program, then, prompts a user to enter a number of a character. The program displays the rest of the phrase beginning from a character whose number was specified by the user.

17. Write a program, that reads a phrase. It, then, should display that phrase printing the uppercase letters in the beginning of each word of the phrase. It should also add a dot, if you forget to terminate a phrase with a dot.

18. Write a program that declares an array of 30 elements, reads integral numbers from a keyboard and places them into that array. An integer is places into the array only, if it has not been read previously. For simplicity use the integers in the range from -200 to 200.

19. We will make a previous problem more complex by adding one more condition to it. When a read element is placed into our array, it should be placed in ascending order among the array elements.

20. Write a program for a stock room. The room contains different electronic parts. The program should store a name of a part, its price, starting and ending quantity. The program has to be able to keep a record of about 10 of such parts. After all the parts are entered, a program displays a menu:

```
Select following:
Edit an element - 1;
Display all the parts - 2;
End -3;
```

If you select 1, it prints additional menu:

```
Write the name of a part to edit.
```

You write the name of the part to be edited. The program displays how many pieces of that part are now in stock and prompts you to type a positive number to add or negative to withdraw the required number of pieces. After you enter that number, it confirms it and prints the current balance for the part. The program then returns to the previous menu.

If you select 2, it displays all the elements in one table. The table has following columns: part name, price, ending balance. The program then returns to the previous menu. Selection 3 ends the program.

CHAPTER 5

FUNCTIONS.

You already used functions in C++, but you have never actually thought about them. Examples of the functions are: **printf()**, **scanf()**, etc. We have dealt with the **main()** function. Any C++ program must have this function. A program can have only one **main()** function. A program begins and ends inside **main()** function. The word **main** is not a keyword. It should not be used anywhere else in the program. C++ allows you to write other functions in the program.

One can run into having to write a very long code for solving a problem. Functions permit us to break a program into a number of fragments. Each fragment is a new function, that performs its particular operation. This permits programmer to concentrate on each fragment separately. Sometimes, a project requires a combined effort from a group of people, each working on their fragments. This approach brings us to a point of "structured programming", when a program is organized in those easy to work with and debug, logically complete routines or functions.

The functions give us certain advantages. First, each function is independent. Therefore, it can be developed, tested, and debugged separately. This makes easier team software development. Second, it simplifies the debugging. One can test separate program fragments. If the program does not work, you can check it function by function. It makes it also easier to debug, if you can rely on some function, that have been tested. Third, it can eliminate the needless repetitions of parts of the code and prevent some errors with naming and using the variables and other data.

5.1. Function syntax.

5.1.1. Introduction.

We will consider some primary definitions for working with functions. We will refer to **Program 5.1** introduced on pages 105-106 to show them on an example. We will consider how that program works a bit later.

A function can be *called* or *invoked* by another function. That another function is called an *invoker* or *caller*. When the function is called, it begins its execution. The **main()** function (invoker) in **Program 5.1** calls the **number_function()** by

```
number_function (m);
```

The **number_function()** is the invoked function in this program. To *call* a function means to call it by its name with the right arguments. Here, the argument is **m**. The value of **m**, as a value of any argument, should be obtained prior to the function call. The arguments pass the data from the invoker to the called function. The called function needs them to perform its task. The called function can have any number of arguments or no arguments at all. It can do calculations and return the result to the caller. We will study how to do it later in this chapter. The same function can be called any number of times with the arguments having the same and different values.

void number_function (int p)	**Header**

{
int k;
float x, y=0;
for (k=1; k<=p; ++k)
{
cout << "Enter any value.\n";
cin >> x;
y=y+x;
}
y=y/p;
cout << " Average is "
    << y << "\n";
}
	Body

Fig. 5.1.

5.1.2. Function declaration and definition.

To use a function, one must *define* and *declare* it. Let's talk about defining a function first. Loosely speaking, to define a function means to, actually, write it. Every function definition consists of a *header* and a *body*. Therefore, to define a function means to write its header and its body. The body immediately follows the header. Fig. 5.1 shows the header and the body of **number_function()** used in **Program 5.1**.

The header of the function consists of one line here

```
void number_function (int p)
```

The first word **void** specifies the data type of value returned back to the caller. A function can do some calculations and give their result back to the caller function. The caller can use that value. It is called "to return a value". One can use any data types, such as **int**, **char**, **float** and so on. We used **void** type. This type is used for the function, that does not return a value to the caller. We will consider it later in this chapter in more details. If you do not write the data type at all, most compilers will presume, that the returned value is of type **int**. Thus, the returned value is assumed to be an integer by default.

The second word **number_function** is the name of the function, which is just an identifier. The **int p** inside the braces is called a parameter. We named it **p**. It has type **int** in our case. Sometimes, it is also called a *formal parameters* list. One should specify all the parameters along with their data types. The formal parameters indicate the types and the number of values that will be passed to the called function, when it is called. If there are more than one parameter in the called function, they should be separated by the commas from each other. For instance, consider a function header

```
one_func (int x, float y, int z)
```

This function has three parameters, each separated by the comma from another one.

The values passed during a call are called the arguments. When a function is called, the caller should pass the arguments of the same data type and in the same order as they appear in the header. For instance, we have specified **p** to have an **int** type in **Program 5.1**. If we call it from the **main()** function as

```
number_function (a);
```

where **a** has type **float**, it might lead to an error. We have to pass to this function an integer. If you call the **one_func()** from some program as

```
one_func (2, 3.5, 8);
```

it should have the same number and type of arguments. The first argument will be passed as a value of the first parameter **x**. The second argument will pass a value to the second parameter **y**, and the third argument will respectively give a value to the third parameter **z**.

As you see, the arguments in the call to a function should be separated by the comma from each other as well. *Thus, you can consider the formal parameters of a function as the placeholders for the expected values.*

Some sources call the formal parameters the arguments or even call them, sometimes, as the parameters and, sometimes, as the arguments without any distinction. There is no big problem if you call the parameters the arguments and vice versa. But you should know, how do they work.

The *body of the function* is located inside the **{ }** braces in Fig. 5.1. It can consist of any statement, operator or function, except another function **main()**. Furthermore, one cannot call the primary **main()** function from any other function. This might lead to some very strange effects.

A function is defined outside the **main()** or any other function. Functions can not be defined inside other functions. Each function should be a separate entity. You have already dealt with the functions like **printf()**, **scanf()** and so on. Those functions are already defined in the header files that you include. This is why you can just use them without definitions.

We have discussed how to define a function. Now we have to find out how to declare a function. It will be clear to you after going over **Program 5.1** with us. That program computes an average of all the values entered from the standard input.

```
#include <iostream.h>

main ( )
{
void number_function (int p);
int m;
cout << "How many numbers to expect?\n";
cin >> m;
number_function (m);
cout << "The control is back.\n";
}
void number_function (int p)
{
int k;
float x, y=0;
```

```
for (k=1; k<=p; ++k)
{
cout << "Enter any value.\n";
cin >> x;
y=y+x;
}
y=y/p;
cout << " Average is " << y << ".\n";
}
```

Program 5.1.

It prompts you

```
How many numbers to expect?
```

We can for simplicity enter 2. The program displays

```
Enter any value.
```

Let's enter 4 and push **ENTER**. Next message will appear immediately.

```
Enter any value.
```

If we enter 5 the answer is

```
Average is 4.5.
The control is back.
```

The program consists of two routines: **main()** and **number_function()**. The **main()** function contains the code that prompts the user how many numbers will be entered, reads them with **cin** object, and calls the **number_function()**. The number of the values to be read is passed to **number_function()** by the argument **m**. We also use **cout** object after call to **number_function()** to show you, that the control will be given back to the caller after the called function completes its execution.

The **number_function()** uses **for** loop to read the values of the variable **x** from the input and add them up by **y=y+x**. The number of cycles is limited by the loop condition **k<=p**. Therefore, one can enter only **p** values. The value stored in **p** is passed as an argument of the **number_function()**, when it is called. After the loop has been completed, the average value of all the entered values is computed by **y=y/p**. This value is then displayed by

```
cout << " Average is " << y << "\n";
```

Let's learn how to operate with the functions. We pointed earlier, when a function is called, it begins the execution. **Program 5.1** calls the **number_function(m)** from the **main()** routine. When the execution of **number_function()** function ends, the control is given back to the caller. In our program the caller is the **main()** routine. Program execution inside the caller function resumes normally from the next code statement or operator after the execution of the **number_function()**. The **main()** routine in **Program 5.1** continues with carrying out the following statement.

```
cout << "The control is back.\n";
```

This is why the message

```
The control is back.
```

is displayed at the output.

As you saw, we defined **void number_function(p)** having the formal parameter named **p** and called this function from **main()** with the argument **m**. It does not matter, that the variable names in the calling function do not match. Only the number and corresponding types of arguments and formal parameters should match. *The formal parameters can be used by the function in which they are declared. You declare the formal parameters in the function header. They do not need additional declarations. You can use them inside that function's body. But no other function including the caller can access those formal parameters.*

For example, **Program 5.1** defines the **number_function()** with the parameter **p**. It is declared in the function header. As you see, we use it without any declarations in that function. However, the **main()** function "does not know" if that variable exists. It can pass a value to that variable only by calling the function.

We also want to point to rather shadowy to you so far first line in **main()** routine

```
void number_function (int p);
```

It is called function *declaration*. We have declared the variables and arrays. We should have some idea about declaration in general. To declare a function is to inform a compiler about the name of the function, the type of the value returned by it, number and data type of the arguments. The declaration looks exactly like the header in Fig. 5.1. The declaration is almost an exact copy of the function header from its definition. The only difference is the presence of a semicolon at the end of function declaration. The function declaration form is called *function prototype*.

Declaration of a function can be done inside the caller or outside of any function at the beginning of the program. We would recommend to declare a function in the beginning of the program, outside of any function and before writing any function. This can, hopefully, prevent a number of errors. Remember a very important rule. *You should declare a function in a program prior to calling it. The very definition of the function can be coded even after a call to it. If the definition of a function is coded later in a program than a call to this function, you cannot use the function without prior to its call declaration. If the definition of a function is coded earlier than a call to this function, the definition acts also as a declaration. So, you do not need an additional declaration. However, if you write a declaration in the last case, it is not considered as an error.*

We coded the definition of the **number_function()** after the **main()** routine in **Program 5.1**. This is why we needed the function declaration. The **main()** function is the caller in our case, this is why we declare **number_function()** in it. The program will not need a declaration, if we define the **number_function()** before the **main()**. It is shown in **Program 5.2**, that has the same output as **Program 5.1**.

```
#include <iostream.h>

void number_function (int p)
{
int k;
float x, y=0;
for (k=1; k<=p; ++k)
{
cout << "Enter any value.\n";
```

```
cin >> x;
y=y+x;
}
y=y/p;
cout << " Average is " << y << ".\n";
}

main ( )
{
int m;
cout << "How many numbers to expect?\n";
cin >> m;
number_function (m);
cout << "The control is back.\n";
}
```

Program 5.2.

We want to add couple additional words to the function declaration and definition. C++ allows to write the declaration in which you can just state the data type of each formal parameter. You do not have to indicate the names of those parameters. It can be done only in function declaration. However, the definition header needs both the types and the names of the formal parameters. Thus, the declaration in **Program 5.1** can be

```
void number_function (int );
```

Here we did not specify the name of the formal parameter in the function declaration.

You might ask how to prototype a function with no parameters. It is a function, that does not expect any arguments. Let's assume, you want to prototype function **tree()** that returns a **float** value and does not take any arguments. Its prototype is

```
float tree (void);
```

The type **void** inside the ( ) braces indicates the absence of any arguments. Those forms of prototyping are endorsed by the ANSI standard for C. C++ supports that form. However, it permits another form of writing a prototype of a function without any formal parameters. For example,

```
float tree ( );
```

The absence of formal parameters in function prototype and the definition header specifies, that there are no formal parameters in the function.

5.1.3. Functions and *return* statement.

Let's consider another example. It calculates an integral of any math function of one variable $y=f(x)$, as shown in Fig. 5.2. Do not mix mathematical function with C++ language function.

The integral of any function on the interval $[x_1, x_n]$ is equal to the area of a figure, contained between a graph of the function on that interval and the **x** axis. There are many algorithms calculating a numeric value of an integral on a given interval. We break the big

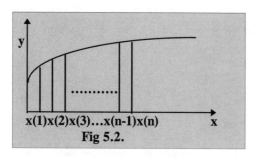

x(1)x(2)x(3)...x(n-1)x(n)   x

Fig 5.2.

interval onto small intervals approximated as rectangles. Let's consider some **i** to **i+1** sub-interval inside $[x_1,x_n]$. One side of that rectangle is equal to the length of the small sub-interval Δx. We assume the length of the other side to be equal to the average value of the function **y=f(x)** on that interval. It is equal to **[y(i)+y(i+1)]/2**. Taking the average minimizes an error. The whole area of the graph in Fig. 5.2 on that interval will be a sum of those rectangle areas. To minimize an error, one should increase the number of sub-intervals, which is equivalent to making them smaller. Unfortunately, this increases the computing time. A case of computing a value of an integral is given in **Program 5.3**.

```
#include <iostream.h>

float square_area( float inner, float outer, int num );

main ( )
{
int n;
float a, b, result;
cout << "Enter the interval, smallest value first.\n";
cin >> a;
cin >> b;
cout << "Enter how many intervals do you want.\n";
cin >> n;
result= square_area(a, b, n);
cout << "The result is " << result << ".";
}



float square_area( float inner, float outer, int num )
{
float sum=0, y, x, del_x;
int   k;
del_x= (outer-inner)/num;
x=inner;
for (k=1; k<=(num-1); k++)
{
y=del_x*(5*(x+k*del_x)+3+5*(x+(k-1)*del_x)+3)/2;
sum=sum+y;
}
return (sum);
```

```
}
```

Program 5.3.

The program first asks you
```
    Enter the interval, smallest value first.
```
You enter the interval, for example,
```
    1   10
```
and hit ENTER. The program displays a message
```
    Enter how many intervals do you want.
```
We can enter any number, for example 100. This displays the calculated integral of the function **y=5*x+3** on the given interval.
```
    The result is 269.750305.
```
Why did we pick this function? We picked it up just as an arbitrary one.

The above program consists of two routines: **main()** and **square_area()**. The **main()** provides an input of the integration interval variables **a** and **b**. It also provides for reading the number of integration sub-intervals **n**. The integral is calculated by **square_area()** function. We call it by
```
    result= square_area(a, b, n);
```
This call invokes the **square_area()** function, that calculates a value of the integral and returns it back to the point of call. The returned value is assigned to the variable **result**, which is then printed by
```
    cout << "The result is " << result;
```
We isolated the calculation of an integral in a separate **square_area()** function. This function is organized pretty analogous to what we have seen so far. It declares the variables **x**, **y**, **sum**, **del_x**, **k**. The header formal parameters **inner**, **outer** and **num** can be used inside the **square_area()** function without any other declaration.

The algorithm is clear. We first find the sub-interval

$$\Delta x = \frac{a-b}{n}$$

It is found as
```
    del_x= (outer-inner)/num;
```
The following loop finds the sum of the small square areas using the **for** loop.
```
    x=inner;
    for (k=1; k<=(num-1); k++)
    {
    y=del_x*(5*(x+k*del_x)+3+5*(x+(k-1)*del_x)+3)/2;
    sum=sum+y;
    }
```
The **return(var)** statement stops function execution, and returns the value of the variable **var** in its **()** braces back to the caller. The value is returned to the point from which the function was called. We used **return(sum)** in **Program 5.3**. The **square_area()** function returns a value of the variable **sum** inside the braces to the caller. Since **square_area()** was called by the assignment statement inside the **main()** function, this is the point to which it will be returned.

One can return the result of the expressions by the **return** statement. The form

```
return (x*x);
```
will return to the caller the numeric value of the square of the variable **x**. Naturally, that the variable should be declared and assigned a value, before one can use it in this statement. One can use **return** statement without the brackets on some compilers. The

```
return x;
```
will return a value stored in **x**. One can return constants. For instance, **return 2** returns 2. Sometimes, one can find the **return** statement used without an argument as

```
return;
```
This will simply stop the function execution and return the control to the caller.

5.2. Functions and variables.

The first step for writing a function is to declare its variables. When we were dealing with the program consisting of one routine, it was pretty straightforward. You had to specify its fundamental data type and name. It was enough to declare a variable. The variables in a multi-function program might need more information for the declaration. You might need the information about its *storage class*, *scope*, *linkage*. A variable declaration can also include additional *qualifiers*.

There are four storage classes: **auto**, **register**, **extern**, **static**. Those words can also be included in the variable declaration. They determine how long does the variable exist in the memory. It can exist during all the program execution, or only when a particular function is called. The storage class also determines, where the computer will allocate the memory for that variable. Normally, the computer allocates the space for the variables in the RAM memory. You will learn, that the **register** class variable can be placed in CPU register. We review storage classes in this chapter.

A variable can have following visibility scopes: *function scope*, *file scope*, *block scope*, *function-prototype scope* and *class scope*. In programming, a scope of visibility means the ability of certain parts of the program to access the variables, i.e., to assign and read the values contained in this variable. The function scope variables are visible only inside the function, where they are declared. No other function "knows", that this variable exists. The file scope variables are visible only inside the same source file. A program can consist of many source files. We can make a variable visible inside a source file to all the functions. It becomes a global variable. A variable can be visible only inside a block of statements and we will discuss it later. The variables used in the function prototype have function-prototype visibility scope. The class scope we will learn later in this book, when we come to classes in C++. This is a specific feature of C++. The visibility scope is also a subject of this chapter. You will learn how to declare the variables with different visibility scopes. A variable can have a qualifier used with it. We will consider **volatile** and **const** qualifiers in this chapter.

5.2.1. Local *auto* variables.

Program 5.4 calculates the volume **v** of a parallelepiped with the sides **a**, **b** and **c**.

```
#include <iostream.h>

float paral (float , float , float );

main ( )
{
float a, b, c, v;
cout << "Enter three sides as a b c\n";
cin >> a;
cin >> b;
cin >> c;
v=paral (a, b, c);
cout << "v=" << v;
}

float paral (float x, float y, float z)
{
float volume;
volume=x*y*z;
return (volume);
}
```

Program 5.4.

Here, the **main()** routine is used to enter and to display the variables. It also calls the **paral()** function, that computes the volume. If we enter **2 3 4**, the function calculates the volume and displays **v=24**.

The variables declared inside the body of each function are called *auto local variables*. Local variables can be accessed only inside the function, in which they were declared. They cannot be accessed by any other part of the program. In other words, no other function in the program "knows", that those variables have been declared.

For instance, variables **a**, **b**, **c** and **v** act only inside **main()** function of **Program 5.4**. If you use those names in **paral()** function, the program will ask you to declare them. They do not exist for **paral()** function. You can even use the same variable names in **paral()** function. They have no effect on the same names of the variables in **main()**. They will be different variables. Therefore, if you use the same names within another function or routine, it will be treated as a different variable.

In programming it is called the *scope of visibility*, as we have mentioned above. Again, visibility means the ability of certain parts of a program to access the variables. The local variables are visible only inside the function, where they are declared. You can ask, what is the scope of visibility of the variables declared in the header of a function. We have talked a little bit about it in the 5.1.2 section. The variables declared inside a function header are visible only inside that function. You can use them without any redeclaration inside the function. They have a function scope visibility. Some sources also call it a *function-prototype scope* visibility. Hence, the variables **volume**, **x**, **y**, **z** are visible only inside the **paral()** function.

It is also worth to note, why do we call the variables inside the body of a function the auto variables? *The auto variables are declared by specifying their types and identifiers (names), as we have studied before. They are declared inside a function. They are called auto variables, because they are automatically created and activated every time we call the function, in which they are declared. The computer allocates the memory cells for them, only when the function, where they are declared, is called for an execution. The computer destroys the local auto variables and frees the allocated for them memory, after the function, where they are declared, terminates its execution.* It is done for the purpose of saving the memory. The memory space, that holds those local variables during function execution, can be used for something else, when the function is not used. If such a variable is given an initial value, this value will be reassigned to this variable every time the control is given to its function. Every time a function is called, its local variables "do not remember" their last value from the previous call.

Why? Again, because the local variables are created as the brand new ones every time when the control is given to the function in which they are declared. The memory cells allocated for the local auto variables in a function are freed every time that function completes its execution. In other words, when the function execution is finished, the computer discards those variables from the memory.

The auto local variable can be declared as

```
auto float a;
```

C++ compiler allows to skip the word **auto**, when we declare auto local variables. The word **auto** is assumed by C++. Thus, you have to specify only the data type and the name (identifier) of the auto variable to declare it inside a function. For instance,

```
float a;
```

We used different names for arguments and parameters for the **paral()** function in **Program 5.4**. It was called from **main()** with the arguments

```
v=paral(a, b, c);
```

The parameters in the definition were

```
float paral (float x, float y, float z)
```

The names of the formal parameters and the arguments do not have to coincide. Only the number and the types of the arguments and the formal parameters should correspond to each other. We wrote the function declaration without the names of the parameters to remind C++ specific declaration form.

```
float paral (float , float , float );
```

We offer **Program 5.5**, that illustrates a local variable visibility.

```
#include <stdio.h>

void test (void);

main( )
{
int x;
printf("Enter an integral value.\n");
scanf ("%d", &x);
```

```
test ( );
}
void test (void)
{
printf ("x=%d\n", x);
}
```

Program 5.5.

An error message will be displayed if you attempt to run this program. The message would state, that the variable **x** is not defined. Indeed, the **test()** function does not know about variable **x**, because it has been declared in the **main()** routine.

5.2.2. Global variables.

So far, we have dealt with the functions that used only local variables. C++ lets you declare a variable in such a manner, that it is visible for all the functions of your source file. It is a *file visibility scope*. Those variables are called *global*. Global variables are declared by the same rules as we have studied before. A declaration of a global variable should contain the data type and the name of that variable. For example,

```
int x;
```

The difference is that the global variables should be declared outside of any function. It is better to declare them in the very beginning of the program.

A global variable does not belong to a particular function. It belongs to a source file, in which it is declared. It is visible to all the functions inside the same source file. Any function of that file can use it. Any function of that file can access that variable and change its value. That changed value will be in effect for the whole program, until any other function changes it. This happens, because the global variables are not discarded after every function execution. The computer allocates the memory for the global variables and initializes them, when the execution of the whole program starts. They exist for as long as the whole program is executed. The global variables are discarded only after the whole program has been completed. **Program 5.6** demonstrates them.

```
#include <iostream.h>

void test ( );
int x;
main( )
{
cout << "Enter an integral value.\n";
cin >> x;
test ( );
cout << "new x=" << x;
}
```

```
void test ( )
{
cout << "x=" << x << endl;
x=x+1;
}
```

Program 5.6.

The program prompts to enter a value. If we enter 5, it displays following messages
```
x=5
new x=6
```
The variable **x** is now declared as global variable. Therefore, it is visible to any function of the same source file. Since the whole program is written in one source file, variable **x** should be visible within the whole program. We code the **main()** function, so it allows to enter the value of **x**. The **test()** routine prints it. We also change its value by one in **test()**. When the control comes back to **main()** function, it displays the new value of **x=6**. Here, we observed that each function can access and change the value of **x**. This value is stored, until the next change by other function.

Global variables are meant to be used in the programs, where their values are accessible to many functions. It is, sometimes, a better way of writing programs, rather than having to pass the function arguments. Consider **Program 5.7**, that finds the **Sin x** value for any entered value of **x**. It illustrates the concept of the global variables, and demonstrates a program consisting of a number of functions.

```
#include <iostream.h>

double x, y=0, z=1;
char angle;
void read_x (void);
void conv_rad (void);
void Sin_fun (void);

main ( )
{
read_x( );
conv_rad ( );
Sin_fun( );
cout << "final " << y << "\n";
}

void read_x (void)
{
cout << "Will you enter the angle in radians or degrees?"
     << "\n";
cout << "If radians press 'r', if degrees press 'd'.\n";
cin  >> angle;
```

```
cout << "Enter the angle.\n";
cin  >> x;
}

void conv_rad (void)
{
if (angle=='d')
x = 3.142*x/180.0;
}

void Sin_fun(void)
{
long n, m, p=-1;
double k=1;
for (n=0; n<=16; n++)
{
for (m=1; m<=(2*n+1); m++)
{
z=z*x;
k=k*m;
}
p=p*(-1);
y=y+z*p/k;
}  }
```

Program 5.7.

The program consists of 4 functions: **main()**, **read_x()**, **conv_rad()** and **Sin_fun()**. The **read_x()** function reads an angle from the standard input. It asks, if an angle is measured in degrees or radians. The **conv_rad()** function converts the angle entered in degrees into radians. The **Sin_fun()** function calculates the **Sin x**.

The calculation is based on the idea, that sine of an angle **x** expressed in radians can be approximately expanded in series as

$$Sinx = x - \frac{x^3}{3!} + \frac{x^5}{5!} - ... + (-1)^n \frac{x^{2n+1}}{(2n+1)!} \pm ...$$

The **Sin_fun()** function finds the sum of this expansion. It is implemented by two nested **for** loops. The inner loop for **m** finds x^{2n+1} as **z=z*x**, and $(2n+1)!$ as **k=k*m**. The outer **for** loop adds all the fractions and adjusts the sign by calculating **p=p*(-1)** every loop cycle.

We use the **main()** routine for organizing the program. Each required action is separated in one of the other three functions. The **main()** calls them in the required order. We need to enter the angle first, and it calls the **read_x()** function. After the function completes its execution, the control is given back to **main()**. Then, **main()** calls the **conv_rad()** function to perform possible angle conversion to radians. When the control returns back to **main()**, it calls the **Sin_fun()** function to perform the calculations.

The result is displayed by following it **cout** object.

None of those functions has an argument. As you know, it is not necessary. We declared global variables. Each of the functions can access them and change. The next function will be working with already changed value of the same variable. We used local variables in **Sin_fun()** function. We wanted to show, that one can use different storage classes of variables (local auto, external and so on) together.

An argument against the extensive use of the global variables is that they can reduce the flexibility for writing functions and, sometimes, the readability of a program.

5.2.3. Variables visible to all source files.

We pointed, the global variables are visible to any function inside the same source file, where they are declared. Sometimes, the programs consist of more than one source file. The variables that are visible in a number of source files are called the *external variables*. The question is how to make a variable visible to the functions in all the source files. The answer can be demonstrated on an example of **Program 5.8**.

We create a project called **book**. We add two source files to this project. We call the first file **msone.cpp**, the second - **mstwo.cpp**. File **msone.cpp** contains the code.

```
#include <iostream.h>

int m;
void display (void);

main ( )
{
cout << "enter an integer value.\n";
cin >> m;
display ( );
cout << "new m=" << m << "\n";
}
```

File **mstwo.cpp** contains the following code.

```
#include <iostream.h>

void display ( )
{
extern int m;
cout << "m=" << m << "\n";
m=m+1;
}
```

Program 5.8.

The output of the program is similar to that of **Program 5.6**. The variable **m** can be read and accessed in both source files. We declared it in the source file **msone.cpp** as global. In order to make it visible in the **mstwo.cpp** file, it should be declared as

```
extern int m;
```

In order to make a variable external to multiple-source files, it should be declared as global in one of them, typically in the one containing **main()**. This variable should be redeclared in each source file, in which it should be readable. One should use the word **extern** in the source files in which the variable is redeclared as local. We have shown the redeclaration of **m** inside the **display()** function in the file **mstwo.cpp**. We had to redeclare **m** with the word **extern**. To declare a global variable in a number of source files to be visible in all those files, the word **extern** must be used in all but one of the files. We would recommend to redeclare an external variable outside of any function in any source file. Thus, if you declare variable **m** outside of any function in both source files in **Program 5.8**, the

```
extern int m;
```

form can be put in any of them. Naturally, another file in this case should contain the declaration of **m** as a regular global variable.

If you want your function to be visible in different source files, write its prototype in each of the files, in which it will be used. In this case, you can also define a function with the word **extern** in its header. However, it is not required to use the **extern** in the function definition to make it visible in the programs with multiple source file. It will work with or without that word. Just write its prototype in each source file.

One can ask how to deal with the included files in case of programs with multiple source files. Suppose, some source files use object **cout** from the **<iostream.h>** header file. You have to include **<iostream.h>** header in every source file that uses **cout**. It is also illustrated in **Program 5.8**.

Another way to write a program using multiple source files is to create the files with the extension **.h**, as, for example, **myprob.h**, and to include them as the header files in the beginning of the program as **#include "myprob.h"**.

5.2.4. Static variables.

It is important to clear out the concept of static variables. So far, we have used the word **static** only for the arrays. One can declare not only a **static** array, but also a variable. The word **static** should be included in the declaration. For example,

```
static float x;
```

Here, we declared **x** as a static variable. Static variables can be declared inside the body of a function. In this case, they are called *local static* variables. They can be declared outside of any function body as well. Those variables are called *global static* variables.

We know, auto local variables are created and initialized, when the control is given to the function, where they are declared. If you do not specify their value, they most likely to have zero value. Their values and the very variables are discarded, after control is transferred from the function, in which they were declared. It works differently for the local static variables. They are visible only inside the function, in which they have been declared. A static variable is initialized once, when the program execution starts. This means, that if we write a local static variable

```
static int a=3;
```
It will be assigned the value 3 once, when the storage is allocated for it. If you change its value, it will have this new value when the function is called again. Local static variable will exist during the program run. It will be discarded when the program terminates its execution. This is why you can change the value of a local static variable every time you call the function that declares it. We illustrate them in **Program 5.9**.

```
#include <iostream.h>

void variable (void)
{
static int stat_variable=2;
int aut_variable=2;
cout << "Static variable is " << stat_variable
     << ", automatic variable is "
     << aut_variable << "\n";
stat_variable *=10;
aut_variable *=10;
}

main ( )
{
int n;
for (n=0; n<=3;++n)
variable ( );
}
```

Program 5.9.

The output of that program is
```
Static variable is 2, automatic variable is 2.
Static variable is 20, automatic variable is 2.
Static variable is 200, automatic variable is 2.
Static variable is 2000, automatic variable is 2.
```
This program consists of **main()** and **variable()** functions. The **variable()** function declares and initializes two variables: local auto variable **aut_variable=2** and static local variable **stat_variable=2**. The **main()** function calls the function **variable()** four times. The **variable()** performs the same action on both auto and static variables.
```
stat_variable *=10;
aut_variable *=10;
```
The auto variable **aut_variable** is initialized with the same value 2 every time, when the control is given to the **variable()** routine. Even though its value increases ten times during **variable()** routine, it is discarded every time the control leaves this

routine. This is why the value of **aut_variable** remains equal to 2 every time you call the **variable()** function. The computer initializes the static variable **stat_variable** with the value 2 only once. Every time the **variable()** function is executed, its value is increased ten times. The value of **stat_variable** is saved, even after the control is given back to **main()**, because the computer does not destroy it after leaving the **variable()** function. This is why the value of **stat_variable** is increased from 2 to 2000. Since we print its value before the multiplication, its value will be even greater than the one displayed after the last cycle. It will be 20000.

Global static variables act pretty much as a regular global variables. They are visible, and accessible only inside the source file, where they were declared. They cannot be accessed by other source files. They exist for the duration of the program run.

5.2.5. Register variables.

You declare a register variable by declaring it along with the word **register**, as

```
register int x;
```

This declaration requests, that the variable should be stored in a CPU (processor) register. You can run into cases when one or a few variables are very heavily used during a program. The CPU register can be accessed faster, than a memory location. Thus, declaring a variable with a **register** storage class can speed up a program.

The computer can disregard your request for register variable. At the other hand, many modern compilers perform optimization during compilation. If they encounter a frequently used variable, they might automatically place it in the CPU register. You might rarely need this type.

Register variables shell be declared inside the functions as auto local variables, although they can be used as the function parameters, sometimes. Their behavior in the program is similar to auto local variables. Unfortunately, the address operator **&** cannot be used with the register variables, because they are stored in CPU, not in the internal memory. Therefore, one cannot use the **scanf()** function for the register variables.

The register variables should have the narrowest possible visibility scope to more effectively use the available registers. Those variables should have short integer types, such as **char**, **int**, **short**, **int** for the best fit into the registers.

5.2.6. Variables visible inside a block.

As you remember, a block is a number of statements enclosed in the curly brackets **{ }**. We have dealt with them in the loop and condition statements. One can declare the variables, that are visible only inside the block. Let's demonstrate it.

```
#include <iostream.h>

main ( )
{
int x=5;
```

```
x=x+10;
cout << "x before the block is " << x;
{
int m=3, k=4;
k=k+m;
x=x+20;
cout << ", k inside the block is " << k << "\n"
         << "x inside the block is " << x;
}
cout << ", end of code\n";
}
```

Program 5.10.

The output of the program is

```
x before the block is 15, k inside the block is 7
x inside the block is 35, end of code
```

The above program consists of only **main()** function. We declare the variable **x=5** at the beginning of the function. We change its value **x=x+10** and display it by the first **cout** object. It is followed by the opening **{** brace. Since the variable **x** declared at the beginning of the **main()** function is visible within that function, the value of **x** can be accessed inside any block within this function. We demonstrate it by changing its value **x=x+20** again inside the block. We also display the new value of **x** by means of the second **cout** object inside that block. Two variables **k** and **m** are declared inside the block. They are visible only inside that block. We change and display the value of the variable **k**, that is visible only inside the block. The block ends with the closing **}** brace. It is followed by

```
cout << " end of code\n";
```

If you try to add any statement, that involves any of the variables **k** or **m** outside the block, an error message will occur. This happens because the variables **k** or **m** are visible and accessible only inside the block. They do not exist outside of it. Try to add

```
cout << k;
```

after the block closing brace and observe, that it is true. Modify the above program to display the variable **x** by **cout << x** written outside the block. You should see, that **x** would still be equal to 35. *So, the value of a variable whose declaration in a function precedes a block is accessible and can be changed inside the block. The value remains changed, even when the block completes its execution. However, a variable declared inside the block cannot be accessible outside of that block neither before nor after it. This is true when a block is written inside a function.*

In case of nested blocks, one can declare the same variable name in both the outer and the inner blocks. The variable with the same name in the inner and outer blocks acts as two independent variables even though it has the same name. Same is true for a function and a block inside it. If a block redeclares a variable declared in a function, that variable acts as two different variables inside and outside the block. Consider an example illustrating the redeclaration of a variable with the same name inside a block.

```
#include <iostream.h>
```

```
main ( )
{
int x=10;
x=x+2;
cout << "x before the block is " << x;
{
int x=3;
cout << ", x inside the block is " << x;
}
cout << "\n x after the block is " << x << "\n";
}
```

Program 5.11.

The output of the program is

```
x before the block is 12, x inside the block is 3
x after the block is 12
```

This program declares **x** and assigns 12 to it before the inner block. It, then, declares **x** again and makes it equal to 3 inside the inner block. The **x=3** is the variable, that acts inside the inner block. When the execution of inner block is completed, variable **x** equal to **12** from the outer block becomes accessible again. This indicates, **x** inside and outside the block acts as two independent variables. The **x** has a block visibility scope.

5.2.7. The scope resolution operator.

If a local and global variables have the same name, C++ choose to operate with local variable, rather than with global. However, C++ permits to use either the global or local variable at your choice. This requires adding a special *scope resolution* operator (::) before a variable. Consider following program.

```
#include <iostream.h>

int x=250;
main ( )
{
int x=10;
cout << "local x=" << (x+1);
cout << ", Global x=" << (::x+5);
}
```

Program 5.12.

The output of the program is

```
local x=11, Global x=255
```

We were able to access the global variable referring to it as **::x**. This operator allows to select a global variable over the local. It does not provide an access to the outer local variable in the nested blocks. The scope resolution operator is vital for classes. We will study how to use it in connection with classes.

5.2.8. Variable qualifiers.

C++ like C permits to use the **const** qualifier. When it is used with the variables, it turns them into the constants. The values are assigned to those variables only through the initialization and cannot be changed in the program. Thus, after initializing **const** variables, you will only be able to read their values. Consider following example.

```
#include <iostream.h>

main ( )
{
const int x=3;
int m;
float arr[x];
for (m=0; m<x; m++)
cin >> arr[m];
for (m=0; m<x; m++)
cout << arr[m] << " ";
}
```

Program 5.13.

You enter three array elements and get them displayed on the screen. The program uses variable **x** with the **const** qualifier. It precedes the data type. The value of **x** cannot be changed. Suppose, we modify **Program 5.13** to somehow change **x**. The compiler would display an error message, when we attempt to run that program. This is why we did not do it in **Program 5.13**. C++ allows to use a **const** variable in an array definition, as **arr[x]**. C does not permit that. C++ also permits you to put **const** declarations in the header file. It is impossible in C.

One can use a variable with the **volatile** qualifier. An example of such declaration is given below.
```
volatile int x;
```
This qualifier (modifier) indicates, that the object can be changed any moment by some hardware or software event, such as interrupt or I/O port. A variable of that type will not be made a register variable by the compiler. It might change the way how the value is assigned and read from those variables. If this value is called a few times, the compiler always checks it instead of using its last read value.

One can ask, does C++ permit to declare a variable as
```
const volatile int x=3;
```
This declaration is permitted. It informs the compiler, that we have a **volatile** type variable, that cannot be changed. The system would only be able to read its value. C++ permits the use of some other qualifiers. You might not ever need them.

5.3. Calling and called functions.

When one function calls another, the information may be passed and returned. There are four possible combinations with respect to passing and receiving the information
1) caller does not pass the data to called function, the invoked does not return a value;
2) caller passes the data to called function, but the invoked does not return a value;
3) caller does not pass the data to called function, but the invoked returns a value;
4) caller passes the data to called function, and the invoked returns the value;
We will discuss those possible communication schemes now. This will also teach you how to operate with functions. Here we will consider only local variables. You should also remember, the information can be also passed and received indirectly by means of the global and external variables.

5.3.1. Call without arguments and returned value.

A function can be called without passing any arguments to it and without getting any returned values from it. We illustrate this way by **Program 5.14**.

```
#include <iostream.h>

void display ( )
{
cout << "This is the display( ) function.\n";
}

main ( )
{
cout << "Calling the function.\n";
display ( );
cout << "End of execution.\n";
}
```
Program 5.14.

The output of this program is
```
Calling the function.
This is the display( ) function.
End of execution.
```
The execution of the program begins with **main()** function. It prints the first message and calls the **display()** function, that prints the second message. After the execution of **display()** function is over, the control is given back to **main()**. The control is returned to the next program statement, expression, operator, object or a function after the one, that called the **display()** function. It happens to be the **cout** object in our program.

As you can see, the **display()** function is called without any arguments. It was defined without any parameters as well. The header in the definition statement looks as

```
void display ( )
```

A function that does not receive the data from a caller has no parameters. Thus, no data can be passed as the arguments from the caller to the called function. The **main()** routine cannot pass any values to the **display()** function in **Program 5.14**, because the later does not have any parameters.

Presence of **void** data type before the name of the function specifies that the function does not return any values. The **display()** function does not give back any values to the point of call. This is why we say, "function returns no value". The **display()** function could use **return** statement without any arguments as terminating statement. *Thus, a function that has **void** return type and no parameters receives no data from a caller and returns no data to the caller.*

5.3.2. Call with arguments and no returned value.

A function can be called with the arguments. But it can complete its execution without returning any values to the point of call. In this case, a function to be called will have arguments. Consider the **Program 5.15**, that illustrates it. The program finds a sum of first **n** members of geometrical series.

The first member is equal to 2, so $a_1 = 2$ The second one is obtained by multiplying a_1 by the number **q=3**. The third member is obtained by multiplying the first member by the square of **q**. The n-th member is equal to $a_n = q^{n-1} a_1$. The sum of first **n** members of the geometrical series s_n is computed by $s_n = a_1 (q^n - 1) \div (q - 1)$.

```
#include <iostream.h>

void sumgeom (int a1, int q, int n)
{
int q1, n1;
q1=q;
for ( n1=2; n1<=n; ++n1)
q1=q1*q;
cout << "The result of calculation is "
     << (a1*(q1-1)/(q-1));
}

main ( )
{
int b=2, p=3, m=5;
sumgeom(b, p, m);
cout << "\nend\n";
}
```

Program 5.15.

The output of this program is

```
The result of calculation is 242.
end
```

The program consists of two functions: **main()**, **sumgeom()**. The **main()** routine declares the variables **b**, **p**, **m**, and initializes them. It calls the **sumgeom()** function to compute the sum of 5 member geometrical series, where the first member is **b**. The **sumgeom()** function calculates this sum. The only fancy thing there, is the calculation of q^{n-1} using **for** loop.

We declared variable **q1** and made it equal to

```
q1=q1*q;
```

It will be equal to the **n**-th power of **q** after the loop execution. We have used similar statements previously. The sum is calculated by the expression **(a1*(q1-1)/(q-1))** inserted into **cout** object.

The **sumgeom(b, p, m)** in the **main()** routine calls the **sumgeom()** function. The **sumgeom()** function is executed completely. To complete a function execution means to execute all the statements inside its body. After that the control is passed back to the next statement after the one that called **sumgeom()** function. The **main()** completes its execution. The **sumgeom()** function is defined as a function of returning type **void**. This indicates, that the function does not return a value. That is why no value is given back to **main()**. This is why we say, that it does not return any value to the caller. The **sumgeom()** not only computes the sum, but also displays it. The **sumgeom()** function does have a list of formal parameters. Therefore, it can receive the arguments from the caller. *A function that has **void** return value type and the list of parameters can receive the data from a caller. However, it does not return any data to the caller.*

We call the **sumgeom()** function in **Program 5.15** from **main()** as

```
sumgeom(b, p, m);
```

The header in the definition of the **sumgeom()** function looks like

```
void sumgeom (int a1, int q, int n)
```

A function is called with the same number and types of arguments as specified in its header in the definition. The names of the arguments and parameters are different. The compiler "understands", that the value of variable **b** is assigned to **a1**, the value of **p** to **q**, the value of **m** to **n**. Since we set in **main()** function **b=2**, **p=3** and **m=5**, the **sumgeom()** is called with the following arguments

```
sumgeom(2, 3, 5);
```

The programmers say that compiler matches the first argument **b** to the parameter **a1** and so on. It is the same thing, but expressed in professional language. The values are matched in the order they go - first argument to the first parameter, second argument to the second parameter and so on. The arguments should have numeric values, before they can be passed. The arguments can, sometimes, contain the constant expressions. One can call a function directly with the numbers plugged-in as arguments, as we showed.

There is another important point about passing the arguments. Consider a program.

```
#include <iostream.h>

main ()
```

```
{
void look (int k, int p);
int n=1, m=2;
look (n, m);
cout << "n=" << n << " m=" << m;
}

void look (int k, int p)
{
k=k+1;
p=p+1;
cout << "k=" << k << " p=" << p << "\n";
}
```

Program 5.16.

The output of the program is

```
k=2, p=3
n=1, m=2
```

This program consists of two functions: **main()** and **look()**. We declare variables **n** and **m** in **main()**. They are passed as the arguments to the **look()** function. We, then, change the values of the formal parameters **k** and **p** inside the **look()** function. The **look()** function displays their current altered values. The control returns back to **main()**. The next statement of **main()**

```
cout << "n=" << n << " m=" << m;
```

displays the values of **n** and **m**.

We wanted you to see, that any operation on the parameters **k** and **p** cannot change the values of **n** and **m**. The values of **n** and **m** can be passed as the arguments of the **look()** function. However, the **look()** function cannot change them in any way. This happens because the called function operates on the copies of the arguments it is called with. Thus, it cannot change the values of the arguments passed to it. Call of a function, with passing the arguments to it, is called a *call by value. When a function is called by value, it receives the copies of the arguments. It can change the values of those argument copies. When the control comes back to the caller, the variables passed to the function will have the same values as before the call. A called function cannot change them.*

5.3.3. Call without arguments returning a value.

A function can be called without any arguments, but it can return a value. *A function can return only one value.* We will consider the functions returning arrays later in this book. Here, we will concentrate on the variables. Consider **Program 5.17**, that shows us how to write another kind of function calls.

```
#include <iostream.h>
```

```
float smallnumber ( )
{
float x, y;
cout << " Enter two numbers to compare as x y \n";
cin >> x;
cin >> y;
if (x>y)
return (y);
else
return (x);
}

main ( )
{
float z;
z=smallnumber ( );
z=z*z;
cout << "the value of square is equal to " << z << "\n";
}
```

Program 5.17.

The output of this program is first a message

 Enter two numbers to compare as x y

If we enter 2 and 3. Then, the result is 4.

 The above program consists of two functions: **main()** and **smallnumber()**. When two numbers are entered, it compares them and calculates a square of the smallest one. The **smallnumber()** function reads two numbers and compares them. If **x>y**, it returns the value of **y** to the **main()** routine. Otherwise, it returns the value of **x**.

 There are two **return** statements in the above example. Functions usually have one **return** statement. There, we demonstrate how to use more than one **return**. In our case, if **x>y**, the first **return(y)** statement is executed. The computer exits called function and goes to **main()** routine. The value stored in **y** is returned. If the condition is false, the **return(y)** is skipped and the **return(x)** is executed instead. The computer gives the control and returns the value stored in **x** to **main()**.

 The **smallnumber()** function has no arguments and is defined as

 float smallnumber ( )

having no formal parameters. However, its header includes the data type of the returned value. This means that the function can return a value of type **float**. To return a value means, loosely speaking, that the point from which the **smallnumber()** function is called will become a value. The very function will become a value, when the control is passed back to the caller. The returned value can be used in the expressions, in the assignment operators and so on. The value returned to **main()** routine in our program is assigned to the variable **z** by

 z=smallnumber ( );

It, as you know, makes **z** equal to that value. The smallest of two entered by us values is

2 in the above program. It will be returned by the **smallnumber()** function and assigned to **z**. Hence, **z** will be equal to 2 after function execution. Both the returned value
of **smallnumber()** and **z** have **float** data type. You do not necessarily have to use
the returned value in any expressions. The call

```
smallnumber ( );
```

is perfectly legal. However, you do not use the returned value in this case.

The **main()** routine in our program computes the square of that returned value by

```
z=z*z;
```

Here, the new value of **z** will be a square of its old value. Our program, therefore, finds
a square of the smallest of two entered numbers.

*A function that has no formal parameters and non-**void** returned value type receives no
data from a caller, but returns a value to it.*

5.3.4. Call with arguments returning a value.

A function can be called with the arguments and the computed value can be returned
back to the caller. It should be defined with the parameters and returned value different
from **void** type. An example is given in the **Program 5.18**, that rounds off the entered
value and prints the result.

```
#include <iostream.h>

int round_off (float x);


main ( )
{
float y;
int res;
cout << "Enter a value to round off.\n";
cin >> y;
res=round_off (y);
cout << res << "\n";
}

int round_off (float x)
{
int m;
m=x;
x=x-m;
if (x>=0.5)
return (m+1);
else
return (m);
```

}

Program 5.18.

The output of this program is
```
Enter a value to round off.
```
If we enter, for example, 4.39 the output is 4.

The program consists of two functions: **main()** and **round_off()**. The **main()** reads the value to be rounded off. This value is passed as an argument **y** of the **round_off()** function. The **round_off()** function computes the rounded off value of its parameter **x** and returns it as variable **m**.

We get the rounded value as follows. The **float** value of **x** gets assigned to **int** type variable **m**. The fractional part of this assignment is truncated. We get the lost fractional part by calculating **x=x-m**. It is compared to 0.5 by **if-else** statement. If **x>=0.5**, the function returns the value of **m+1**, i.e. it rounds off to the next number up. Otherwise, it rounds off to **m**.

*A function with a list of parameters and non-***void*** returned value receives the data from the caller and returns a value to it.*

5.4. Handling functions with global variables.

We have considered four cases of handling the data between the caller and the called function. Each of these four cases has been examined by means of the local variables. One can do the same thing with the global variables as well.

What does it mean to pass a value to the called and to return a value to the caller? The called function can still be defined with no parameters and as returning no values. When called, it can change the value of the global variable. That changed value can be printed by the caller afterwards. The global variables do not need to be passed as the arguments or returned back. You can enter their values in one function, do the calculations with them in another function and so on. We showed you an example of their use in **Program 5.7**. The **read_x()**, **conv_rad()** and **Sin_fun()** functions did not have arguments and could not return any values. However, we were able to access the global variables from each of them and print the result.

This does not mean, that you should not have arguments in your functions and use only global variables, or you should use only local variables. One should use all the features of the language. The same function can have arguments and use the global variables as well. Since a function can return only a value of one variable, you can also use the global variables. This way you can change any number of variables by one function. All of them can be used by the caller. You have learned, that there are four ways of passing the data. You do not have to remember these four ways. Just know, the functions can give and take the data from each other.

We also offer you another program, in which the called function **dat()** does not have the arguments. It does not return the value to the caller **main()** as well. The data is transferred from **main()** to **dat()** by means of the global variables.

```cpp
#include <iostream.h>

int date, week_d;
void dat (void);

main ( )
{
int a=1;
cout << "Enter the day of month and the day of the week,
        as\n"
    << "date  weekday\n"
    << "Day of the week enter as number. Sunday is
        1.\n";
cin >> date;
cin >> week_d;
while ( a==1)
{
dat( );
cout << " Press 1 to proceed or any number to stop.\n";
cin >> a;
}
cout << "The end.\n";
}

void dat (void)
{
static char name[7][10]={{'s', 'u', 'n', 'd', 'a', 'y',
 '0'},{ 'm', 'o', 'n', 'd', 'a', 'y', '0'},{'t', 'u',
 'e', 's', 'd', 'a', 'y', '0'},{'w', 'e', 'd', 'n', 'e',
 's', 'd', 'a', 'y', '0'},{'t', 'h', 'u', 'r', 's', 'd',
 'a', 'y', '0'},{'f', 'r', 'i', 'd', 'a', 'y', '0'},{'s',
 'a', 't', 'u', 'r', 'd', 'a', 'y','0'}};
int rem, m, k, n, stop=9;
cout << "Enter the date of the same month and get what
        day of the week is it.\n";
cin >> n;
rem=(n-date)%7;
m=week_d +rem;
if (m<=0)
m=7+m;
if (m>7)
m=m-7;
for (k=0;k<=stop; k++)
{
cout << name[m-1][k];
```

```
if (name[m-1][k+1]=='0')
stop=k-2;
}
cout << "\n";
}
```

Program 5.19.

You enter the day of the month and corresponding to it the day of the week. The program will give you the weekday for any other entered date of the same month. For instance, the 23rd of the month falls on Saturday. Saturday is the 7th weekday. The program prompts the user

```
Enter the day of month and the day of the week, as
date  weekday
Day of the week enter as number. Sunday is 1.
```

We enter 23   7

Now we can enter any day of the month at the prompt

```
Enter the date you need and get what day of the week is
it.
```

and get what day of the week is it. For example, we enter 10. It will display

```
Sunday
Press 1 to proceed or any number to stop.
```

You enter any number to stop or 1 to inquire about another day of the month.

The program consists of two functions: **main()** and **dat()**. The **main()** function is used to enter the initial setting of the date and the weekday. It also reads this initial setting by means of **cin** objects. Two entered values are stored in **date** and **week_d** global variables. The **main()** routine includes **while** loop, that calls the **dat()** function as many times as needed. The program asks, if you want to proceed, and reads the response. If the response is not '1', the loop is terminated.

Function **dat()** does not have any arguments. It receives the data through those external variables **date** and **week_d**. It declares and initializes two-dimensional array **name[7][10]**, containing the names of the weekdays. The proper weekday is displayed by the **for** loop.

The weekday is determined by the first subscript **m** in **name[m][k]**. The **k** subscript is used to display all the letters in that name. For example, for printing **Monday**, one would have to display all **name[1][k]**. It can be done by displaying all the elements **name[1][k]** with **k** running from 0 to 10. You will print **Tuesday** choosing **m=2** and displaying the **name[2][k]** elements with **k** running from 0 to 10. Therefore, the problem of displaying the correct weekday can be narrowed down to finding **m**.

Think how to solve this problem. You enter the current date **date** and the weekday **week_d** at the beginning. The same weekday will appear every 7 days. If the entered date **n** differs by 7, 14, 21, etc., it will come on the same weekday. If **(n - date)** cannot be divided by 7 evenly, the entered date will be a different day of a week. The remainder **rem** of **(n - date)%7** is the number of days you have to add or subtract from **week_d** to get the weekday corresponding to that **n**. Thus, the weekday **m** is determined by

```
m=week_d +rem;
```

This formula for **m** can, sometimes, give the values greater than 7 and less or equal to 0. Calculate manually **m**, when the input is **n=27**. You will find, the weekday for the 27th day of the month. The **rem=(27-23)%7=4**. The **m=7+4=11** is greater than the number of days in a week. Here, the 7th day is the same weekday as **week_d**. To find the day of the week, we subtract 7. The result will be **11-7=4**. This is **Wednesday**. Thus, you would have to introduce **if** loops in the program to take care of **m** being outside the range from 1 to 7.

We hope, you now pretty much understand the implementation of **dat()** function given in **Program 5.19**. It declares the **name** array and all the variables. The function then reads the value of **n**. Next two lines find **rem** and **m**. The **if** statement

```
if (m<=0)   m=7+m;
if (m>7)  m=m-7;
```

corrects for **m** being beyond the range from 1 to 7 by either adding or subtracting 7.

We then print the corresponding **name[m-1][..]** by means of the **for** loop. We have discussed an analogous loop in Chapter 4. It uses '**0**' characters on the end of each day for loop termination. Changing **k** permits to display all the **name[m-1][k]** elements for given **m**. The loop stops when '**0**' character is encountered. We display **m-1** element, because the array elements are in the range from 0 to 6, and the entered days change from 1 to 7. The first day of the week we enter as 1. But the first array element is **name[0][..]**.

5.5. Nested function calls.

So far, we have discussed the cases, when a function is called from the **main()** routine. In general, one can call a function from any other function. One can also have a situation, when a program code calls a function, that calls another function. That other function can at some point call some other function, and so on. This is called *nested function calls*. Nested function calls are often used in programming. Consider **Program 5.20** illustrating nested function calls.

```
#include <iostream.h>

main ()
{
int m;
int sum (int k);
cout << "Enter an integer.\n";
cin >> m;
cout << "The result is: " << sum(m);
}

int sum (int k)
{
int fact (int z);
int n, y=0;
```

```
for(n=1; n<=k; n++)
y=y+fact(n);
return(y);
}

int fact (int z)
{
int p, w=1;
for (p=1; p<=z; p++)
w=w*p;
return (w);
}
```

Program 5.20.

The program prompts a user to enter an integer. Do not enter big numbers, because the result will be a huge number and can cause an error. We enter number 5. The program displays the value 153. If you need to enter greater integers, rewrite the program using **double** type variables.

This program calculates the sum of the series

```
1+2!+3!+4!+...+m!
```

You enter the number **m** of the maximum factorial in the sum. The program consists of three functions: **main()**, **sum()** and **fact()**. The **main()** function is used to enter the value of **m** and to display the result by

```
cout << "The result is: " << sum(m);
```

The **fact()** function computes the value of **m!**, using the **for** loop. Each loop yields

```
w=w*p;
```

The value of that factorial is returned to the **sum()** function. The summation of all the factorials is implemented in **sum()** function. It adds up all the factorials

```
y=y+fact(n);
```

inside the **for** loop.

The **main()** function calls the **sum()** function. The **sum()** calls the **fact()** function. It is an example of a nested function call. The first call to **fact()** function is made inside the **for** loop, when **n=1**. The argument of the **fact()** function is equal to 1. The **fact()** function computes the factorial of 1 and returns it to the expression **y=y+fact(n)** of **sum()** function. This computes **y=y+fact(n)=0+1=1**. Next loop cycle with **n=2** calls **fact()** with the argument 2. After the **2!** is computed, its value is returned back to the same point in the expression. The result is **y=1+2=3**. The loop proceeds, until the whole sum is calculated and its value is returned to **main()**.

The nested function calls work in the same way as calls from a function to a function. We coded the **fact()** after the **sum()** function to show you the need in prototyping the **fact()** function before its use in **sum()**. Since **sum()** is coded after **main()**, it should be prototyped before its use. Again, if you write all the function prototypes at the beginning of the program, it will minimize a chance that you can forget to write it.

5.6. Functions and arrays.

So far, we have considered how to pass a value of a variable to a function. It is also possible to pass an array element to a function. It is also possible to pass the whole array to a function. Consider **Program 5.21**.

```
#include <iostream.h>

float triplevalue (float x[5], int m )
{
float z;
z=3*x[m];
return (z);
}

main ( )
{
static float a[ ]= {2.5, 3.0, 1.5, 4.2, 5.0};
int n;
for (n=0; n<5; n++)
{
cout << a[n] << "   ";
a[n]= triplevalue(a, n);
cout << "triple: " << a[n] << ", ";
} }
```
Program 5.21.

The program triples and displays each array element **a[n]** before and after the tripling.
```
2.5 triple 7.5,  3.0 triple 9,  1.5 triple 4.5,  4.2
triple 12.6, 5.0 triple 15
```
It consists of functions: **main()**, **triplevalue()**. The **triplevalue()** has two formal parameters. One of its parameters is the array **x[5]** of **float** type. The **a[]** array is declared in **main()**. The **for** loop calls each array element **a[n]** and triples its value. Each of the array elements is tripled by the **for** loop using a call
```
a[n]= triplevalue(a, n);
```
The **triplevalue()** function triples passed to it array element. A call to function **triplevalue(a, n)** has two arguments. The first one is the name of the array **a**. It passes the array **a[]** to the function. The second argument **n** is the array subscript. The **triplevalue()** function triples the array element **a[n]**
```
z=3*x[m];
```
and returns it back as a value of variable **z**. We assign the returned value to **a[n]** in **main()** to change it. We display the initial and tripled element by the same **for** loop.

Above example shows, that *to call a function with an array as an argument, one has to define a function with array formal parameter. This formal parameter should specify the*

data type, array name and the number of elements in the array to be passed. The second
formal parameter in our first example is a particular array element number. When that
function is called, an array argument should contain only the name of the array. In our
example we have done that. The function is called as

```
triplevalue(a, n);
```

You can use other arguments as well. We pass a particular index of an array element in our
second argument. Therefore, our function takes a particular array element number **n** as its
second argument.

Program 5.21 handles the array, but it still approaches the array just as a collection of
variables. The array elements are tripled in the same manner, as you would triple five
different variables. However, the program illustrates the definition of a function taking an
array argument. It shows how to pass an array as an argument. The arrays can be handled
in a different manner. We demonstrate it in the following program.

```
#include <iostream.h>

void triplevalue (float x[ ], int m)
{
for (m=0; m<5; m++)
x[m]=3*x[m];
}

main ( )
{
static float a[ ]= {2.5, 3.0, 1.5, 4.2, 5.0};
int n=5;
triplevalue(a, n);
cout << "The tripled values are\n";
for (n=0; n<5; n++)
cout << a[n] << ", ";
}
```

Program 5.22.

The output of the program is

```
The tripled values are
7.5,  9, 4.5,  12.6,   15,
```

This program looks very similar to the previous one, but has some drastic differences. It
consists of the same functions: **main()** and **triplevalue()**. The **main()** function
declares and initializes the **a[]** array and the variable **n=5**. It, then, calls the function
triplevalue(a, n). After the function has been executed, the control is given back
to **main()**. The **main()** routine displays all the elements of **a[]** array using the **cout**
object inside the **for** loop.

Each of the array elements is tripled by the **triplevalue()** function. The function is
of type **void**. It does not return any values. But it is still able to change the elements of the
initial array. It takes the whole array as an argument. Pay attention, that the header in the

definition is

```
void triplevalue (float x[ ], int m)
```

The array parameter is used as **x[]** without specifying the number of elements in the array. We could specify the number of the array elements as **x[5]**. Therefore, the array formal parameter does not necessarily have to have the total number of the array elements specified in the brackets. The second argument in this header is the number of array elements **m**. The function uses **for** loop to access and triple the value stored in each array element. It is done by the **x[m]=3*x[m]** assignment inside the **for** loop body. This statement triples current value of an array element. The loop performs this assignment for each array element. We triple **x[0]** during first cycle, **x[1]** during the second cycle and so on.

The changed values of the array elements are displayed in **main()** by the **cout** object. It is very important. The **triplevalue()** function receives an array as its argument. It changes the values of the array elements. The change remains in effect even after the function terminates its execution. We display the new values of the array elements in **main()**. Thus, a function can change the values of the elements in the array, that is passed to it as an argument.

The program illustrates a very important relation between the arrays and the functions. *If an array is passed as an argument to a function, the values of its elements can be accessed and changed by that function.* This is an important difference in passing a variable and an array as an argument. Why is it possible? When an array is passed as an argument, it is written by name, as **triplevalue(a, n)**, for example. We will study later, that **a** represents an address of that array in the memory. Thus, we pass an address of the array to the called function. Hence, the called function is able to access the memory in which the original array is stored and change the values of its elements.

Next program finds a sum of all the array elements. It uses only one argument to pass an array. We define the parameter as an array of **float** type with 5 elements.

```
#include <iostream.h>

float sum (float x[5])
{
int m;
float z=0;
for (m=0; m<5; m++)
z=z+x[m];
return (z);
}

main ( )
{
static float a[ ]= {2.5, 3.0, 1.5, 4.2, 5.0};
cout << "The value is equal to " << sum (a) << ".";
}
```

Program 5.23.

The output of the program is

```
The value is equal to 16.2.
```

The program is very straightforward. The next **Program 5.24** is similar to the previous one. It produces the same output. It shows, that you can define an array formal parameter as **float x[]** without specifying the number of array elements at all.

```
#include <iostream.h>

float sum (float x[ ])
{
int m=0;
float z=0;
while (x[m]!=0.0)
{
z=z+x[m];
m++;
}
return (z);
}

main ( )
{
static float a[ ]= {2.5, 3.0, 1.5, 4.2, 5.0, 0.0};
cout << "The value is equal to " << sum (a);
}
```

Program 5.24.

The program has the same output as the previous one. It uses the **while** loop to add up the array elements in the **sum()** function. The loop condition is **x[m]!=0.0**, since we know that the last array element is equal to zero. We increment **m** by 1 every loop cycle, so the next **x[m]** element can be accessed during the next loop cycle.

Handle a multi-dimensional array similar to one-dimensional. The function to which you pass a multi-dimensional array must contain the name of that array as its argument. You can use other arguments to stipulate the number of elements in each dimension. **Program 5.25** finds an average value of the elements of a multi-dimensional array.

```
#include <iostream.h>

float ave (int b[4][3]);

main ( )
{
static int a[4][3]={{2, 94, 3}, {33, 22, 11}, {20, 48,
                   10}, {1, 2, 3}};
cout << "The average is: " << ave (a) << ".";
```

```
}

float ave (int b[4][3])
{
int n, k;
float av=0;
for(n=0; n<4; n++)
for (k=0; k<3; k++)
av=av + b[n][k];
av=av/12;
return (av);
}
```

Program 5.25.

The output of this program is

```
The average is: 20.75.
```

 The program consists of two functions: **main()** and **ave()**. We use **main()** to declare the **a[4][3]** array, to call the **ave()** function, and to display the result. The actual calculation is performed by the **ave()** function. We add up all the **b[n][k]** elements by the double nested **for** loop. The sum is stored in the variable **av**. We divide it by the total number of elements 12 to find the average and return this value to **main()**. Here, the two-dimensional array is the formal parameter in the definition of the **ave()** function. We call the **ave()** function using the array name as an argument.

5.7. Function and argument data type.

 We have stated, the data type of every parameter in function definition and corresponding to it argument should be the same. For example, you define a function as

```
void function (int x, int y, int z)
```

This function should be called with all three arguments of type **int**. We insisted, the number and data types of the formal parameters and the arguments should be matched.

 C++ permits a data type mismatch between the parameters and the arguments. The passed arguments are never converted. A function modifies the values of their copies, that replace the formal parameters. It means, that the passed copies of the arguments will be converted to the required type. Many C++ compilers allow you to pass only **int** or **double**. Thus, **char** and **short** values are converted to **int** type. The **float** type is converted to **double**. Usually, if there is a mismatch in data types, the passed values are converted to the "upperprecision" type.

 You can cast a function argument to a desired type. For example, you declare

```
int m;
```

It can be type cast in a function as

```
function ( (float) m);
```

5.8. Recursive functions.

C++ and C permit a widely used feature called *recursive functions*. We will explain the recursive functions on an example. Let's assume, one wants to find a sum of first ten or more consecutive numbers. It is clear, the sum of 10 consecutive numbers is the sum of first nine of them plus the 10-th number. The sum of nine numbers is the sum of the first eight numbers plus one. We can go down further, until we come to zero plus another number. One can write an expression **sum(n)=sum(n-1)+n**. A *recursive function* is a function, that invokes itself. The recursive function feature is illustrated by **Program 5.26**. The program finds a sum of the first **n** numbers beginning from 1, where **n** is the number that you enter.

```
#include <iostream.h>

int sum (int m)
{
int value;
if (m<=0)
value=0;
else
value=m+sum (m-1);
return value;
}

main ( )
{
int n;
do
{
cout << "\nEnter the value.\n"
     << "To exit type value greater than 100.\n";
cin >> n;
if (n<=100)
cout << "The sum is equal to " << sum(n);
}
while (n<=100);
}
```

Program 5.26.

The output of this program is a message
```
    Enter the value.
    To exit type value greater than 100.
```
Then, you enter a value, for example, 4. The result is displayed on the screen
```
    The sum is equal to 10.
```
If you want to stop, enter the value greater than 100.

The program consists of two functions: **sum()** and **main()**. The **sum()** function computes the sum of consecutive integers from 1 up to a value that you enter. The **main()** function handles the input. It calls **sum()** function and displays its returned value by the **cout** object. One can find the sum of up to 100. It can be done many times, until the number greater than 100 is entered. This is achieved by putting the whole data input/output and call to the **sum()** function in the **do-while** loop. You should know by now how to call a function. It is the same for the recursive or any other functions. The difference is, that the recursive function returns the control to itself, or, to be precise, to a copy of itself.

Program 5.26 finds a sum using the recursive function feature. The line

```
value=m+sum(m-1);
```

calls **sum()** function from inside its own body and that is what makes it recursive. It works following way. When the value 4 is passed to the argument of the function, this line becomes

```
value=4+sum(3);
```

This line calls for **sum(3)**. The function **sum()** with the argument 3 becomes

```
value=3+sum(2);
```

It calls for the **sum()** function with the argument 2. The next expression is

```
value=2+sum(1);
```

and we finally come to

```
value=1+sum(0);
```

At last, the **sum()** function with 0 argument is called. The **if-else** statement selects zero to be returned by the function, if it is called with zero argument. It is important, that there is no recursion statement in this case. A recursive function should have a stop point. Otherwise, it might run forever.

The lowest **sum(0)=0**. This value will be plugged into the last expression to find **value**. Thus, the **sum(1)** is equal to **1+0=1**. Then, **value=2+sum(1)=2+1=3**. The next expression gives **value=3+sum(2)=3+3=6**. Finally, the last expression should be **value=4+sum(3)=4+6=10**. This is a sum of first four elements.

5.9. Inline functions.

Sometimes, when the same function is called a number of times, it results in execution time overhead. A function call requires some actions from a computer, such as loading the parameters into the stack and so on. This can result in some additional time for the program execution. C++ allows to use an **inline** qualifier in a function definition header. This causes a copy of the code of this function to be inserted in each place in a program, it is called from. It is like inserting the fragments into the program. Each fragment is the body of that function. So, the computer does not have to perform the actions needed for a function call, when a function is defined with **inline** qualifier. Loosely speaking, suppose, you declare a function as **inline** and call it in the program. That name of the function in any call to it in a program will be substituted by the body of that function from its definition. The computer will replace a call to this function with its code everywhere in the program. It decreases the operation time.

The trade-off of that procedure is the increase of the program size. Your computer can ignore the **inline** request. In general, we recommend to use this feature with very short frequently repeated functions. Consider following example.

```
#include <iostream.h>

inline float  square (float x)
{
return (x*x);
}

main ( )
{
float y1=6.2, y2=3.5;
cout << square (y1) << " " << square (y2);
}
```
                              Program 5.27.

The output of the program is
      38.44   12.25
We use the **inline** qualifier in the **square()** function definition. This will, hopefully, insert the copies of this function everywhere we call it from.

5.10. Default arguments.

A function can be called with passing the values to the arguments. It can be also called with the *default* arguments, or the arguments having preassigned values. A programmer can specify the default values of the arguments of the same function only once either in prototype or the function definition, whichever is coded first. So, if you write a function declaration first in the program, it must have the default values assigned to the parameters. When this function is called with the omitted argument, the default value is assigned to it. The default arguments must be the rightmost in a function parameters list. When that function is called, the omitted arguments must also be the rightmost. You cannot omit the second argument, for instance, and pass the third one. You would have to omit the third argument as well. Consider following example illustrating the default arguments.

```
#include <iostream.h>

int sum (int x, int y=1, int z=1, int q=1);

main ( )
{
cout << "Result with x=10 is: " << sum (10)
       << "\nResult with x=10, y=5 is: "
```

```
    << sum (10, 5) << "\nResult with x=10, y=5, z=3 "
    << "is: " << sum (10, 5, 3)
    << "\nResult with no default is: " << sum (10, 5, 3, 20);
}

int sum (int x, int y, int z, int q)
{   return (x+y+z+q); }
```
Program 5.28.

The output of the program is
```
    Result with x=10 is: 13
    Result with x=10, y=5 is: 17
    Result with x=10, y=5, z=3 is: 19
    Result with no default is: 38
```
The prototype **int sum (int x, int y=1, int z=1, int q=1)** is the first introduction of the **sum()** function. Therefore, it must contain the default parameter values **y=1**, **z=1**, **q=1**. As you see, we did not specify the default values of the parameters in the **sum()** function definition head, because we have already done it in its declaration. As you see, the default arguments should be the rightmost ones. If we do not assign the values to the function formal parameters, they assume the values assigned to them by default. If we do not pass three last arguments, they will be equal to 1 according to **sum()** function prototype. We could have assigned them different default values. We made **y** a parameter with default value, so we had to make all the rightmost parameters from **y** on to the right the default parameters. We call the function as **sum(10)** for the first time. This passes a value to **x**. The **y**, **z** and **q** parameters assume their default values. The call **sum(10, 5)** passes the values to **x** and **y**. **z** and **q** should get their default values. If we do not have a separate function declaration, the default parameter values must be specified in its definition header.

5.11. Function overloading.

Function overloading is a very important feature of C++. For example, you want to write one function that selects the least of two integers, another function that selects the least of two floating-point numbers. You would have to write two different functions in C. C++ permits the user to write those two functions using one name, for instance **comp()**. This is the *function overloading*, that uses the same function name for doing potentially different tasks on different data types. How will the compiler distinguish when to use which function. The functions under one name should have at least some of their formal parameters of different data types. The number of parameters can also be different in different functions with the same name. The programmers call it to distinguish the overloaded functions by the *signature*, which is the number and the types of their parameters. You cannot write two functions with the same name, same number and types of arguments, that differ only by the type of returned value. It will be considered as an error. Review an example, that compares two values, selects and prints the greater one.

```
#include <iostream.h>

int comp (int m, int k)
{
if (m>=k)    return (m);
else         return (k);
}

double comp (double p, double s)
{
if (p>=s)    return (p);
else         return (s);
}

main ( )
{
cout << "The greater floating-point number is "
     << comp (4.4, 7.8) << ".\nThe greater integer"
     << " number is " << comp (9, 2) << ".";
}
```

Program 5.29.

The output of the program is

```
The greater floating-point number is 7.8.
The greater integer number is 9.
```

We use **comp()** function, that is overloaded. We define it one time with the **int** type parameters. We define it for the second time with the **double** type parameters. When we call it as **comp(4.4, 7.8)**, it calls the function with the parameters of **double** type. We call it again with the integral arguments to call the function with **int** type formal parameters.

The compiler encodes each overloaded function in a way, that provides a type-safe linkage. The type-safe linkage means, that the computer calls only the correct version of an overloaded function with the parameters corresponding to the type and the number of passed arguments. If a function is heavily overloaded, the compiler tries to find the best suitable version of the overloaded function. If the match cannot be found, an error message is issued. The earlier C++ compilers versions required the overloaded functions to be preceded by the word **overload**. Modern compilers do not require any special keywords for the overloaded functions. The program below illustrates an overloaded function. Versions of that function have different number of parameters. We used the same argument types in two function versions. We could use different data types for similar parameters in each version of the overloaded function in our program.

```
#include <iostream.h>

int cube (int x, int y, int z)
```

```
{ return (x*y*z);   }
int cube (int s, int p)
{   return (s*p); }

main ( )
{
cout << cube (2, 3);
}
```

Program 5.30.

The output of the program is number 6.

5.12. Function templates.

Sometimes, one has to perform identical operations on different data types. This can be significantly simplified using *function templates*. They are also called template functions and functions with generic data types in different books. A programmer writes only one definition of a template function. When the function is called for execution, C++ auto-matically substitutes the fictional data type names used in templates with the needed data types. A function template is created in a following way:

1.Begin the template function definition with the line

```
template <class name1, class name2...>
```

Here, the **name1**, **name2** and so on are just any identifiers you wish to choose. Each of those chosen by you names will be used instead of the data type.

2. Write the normal function definition inserting **name1**, **name2** instead of data types for the return value and the formal parameters. Loosely speaking, you use those **name1**, **name2** and other names instead of the data types in the function definition. When this function is called, the computer will choose the data types appropriate for the passed arguments or the returned value instead of those funny ones. Those unspecified data types are called *generic data types*. They should become real data types, when the function is activated. A function definition with templates can have both regular and generic data types.

Let's assume, only one name, for instance, **name1** is used as a generic data type. It should be substituted by the same data type, or an error will be generated. Suppose, you use different identifiers (**name1**, **name2** ..) for the parameter types. It means that they can be substituted by the arguments of different data types. If you substitute them with the same data type arguments in this case, it will work on most compilers. Consider following example.

```
#include <iostream.h>

template <class DA, class DAA>
DAA multi (DAA x, DA y)
{ return (x*y); }
```

```
main ( )
{
int a=3;
double b=9.234;
cout << multi (b, a);
}
```

Program 5.31.

The output of this program is the number 27.702. The function **multi ()** is defined as a template. Its formal parameters and the returned value can have only two data types **DAA** and **DA**. Those two names are just the identifiers. You can substitute any data type instead of each of them. We use **DAA** and **DA** to specify, that we can call this function with the arguments of two data types.

Since we call **multi (b, a)** and **b** is of type **double**, the returned value shell be of **double** type. It is true, because we define the **multi ()** function with the returned value and the first parameter **x** to be of the same **DAA** data type. The computer understands, that the returned value has the same type as the first argument. It returns the result as **double**. If you call the function as **multi (a, b)**, the function will return the number 27, which is an integer value. This happens, because now the first argument **a** has **int** data type. This determines the data type of the returned value.

Consider another example, where we use only one generic data type arguments. Suppose, you draw a vector from the beginning of the coordinate system. Its length will be equal to $\sqrt{x^2 + y^2 + z^2}$ where **x**, **y**, **z** are the coordinates of its end. Program below finds the square of its length.

```
#include <iostream.h>

template <class DA>
DA ssum (DA x, DA y, DA z)
{ return (x*x+y*y+z*z);  }

main ( )
{
int a, b, c;
cout << "Enter coordinates of the vector\n";
cin >> a;
cin >> b;
cin >> c;
cout << "The square of the length is "
     << ssum (a, b, c) << ".";
  }
```

Program 5.32.

The program prompts the user to enter three coordinates. If we enter **2 3 4** ENTER, it displays

```
The square of the length is 29.
```
We used **DA** to substitute a data type. It can be any type, but all the arguments and the returned value shell be of the same data type. Try to use different data type arguments, and the error will be displayed.

What is the difference between the overloaded functions and the function templates? First, they are defined differently. Versions of the same overloaded function can perform potentially different absolutely non-related actions. Function template performs the same action for any data type. Its generic data types are substituted by the real data types.

This concluded the present chapter. You have learned many features of the functions. What makes them even more interesting is that you can combine some or all of them in one function. For instance, a function can use local and global variables. It can also be an overloaded function, or an inline function.

EXERCISES.

1. Run all the programs given in this chapter, if you have an access to a computer.
2. Write a program that finds a value of **x** to the power of **m**. It should have a separate function for input/output and a separate function for calculating the power. The data type of **x** is **double**, **m** has **int** type.
3. Write the function in the previous program as a template. It should have two generic data types.
4. Function **ln x** for **x>0** can be approximated by the series

$$\ln x = 2\left[\frac{x-1}{x+1} + \frac{(x-1)^3}{3(x+1)^3} + \frac{(x-1)^5}{5(x+1)^5} + ... + \frac{(x-1)^{2n+1}}{(2n+1)(x+1)^{2n+1}} + ...\right]$$

Write a program that computes this series. Make a decision how to split it on different functions. Use local and global variables.
5. Write two more programs to compute the series in the previous problem. The first program should use the overloaded function. The second program should use the function templates.
6. Write a function, that permits you to enter a polynomial, as for example, **y=3*x2+5*x−7**. Here, the numbers before the asterisk '*' are the coefficients, and the numbers after x are the powers. So, **3*x2** is "three times **x** to the power of 2". This function should recognize the coefficients and the powers. It should find the first and the second derivatives of the entered polynomial. Your function should be able to find the numeric values of the function and those derivatives in any given point. Use the formulas for the standard derivatives. Make a decision how to break the task on different functions. Use local and global variables. Use overloaded functions and inline functions where possible.
7. Write a program, that uses four different functions. One of the functions reads two fractions. Another function adds them up. In order to add them up, it should call the third function to find the common divisor. The fourth function organizes three others. Use local and global variables. Use inline functions where possible.
8. Write a program that consists of three functions. One organizes all the others. The second function reads two numbers. The third routine divides the smaller number by the

greater one. Write two versions with local and global variables. Use overloaded and inline functions.

9. Write your own small compiler. It should have three commands: *enter*, *add* and *out*. You compiler should be able to process a small program, written as

```
enter 20, 5:add:out:
```

The **enter** operator is used for entering as many values as needed. The end of input is the colon ":" sign. The entered values should be separated by a comma. When your computer encounters the **add** operator, it adds up all the numbers, that you have entered. This operator is separated from the **out** operator by the colon. The **out** operator provides the output to the screen. Your compiler should be able to check for the errors in writing the operators. Use the function templates, overloaded and inline functions, local and global variables if needed.

10. Write a few easy programs using functions:

a) A program that computes a so-called *golden mean*. A gold cut of value **a** is such a number **x** equal to $x = \sqrt{x(a-x)} \approx 0.618a$ The program must consist of two functions. One of them should be able to read a value. Another one has to calculate the gold cut and return it to the caller. Write two versions with local and global variables. Use inline functions.

b) A program that reads the number **x**, calculates its **1/x**, and returns it.

11. Write two programs that permit you to enter a 3*3 matrix and compute the sum of its diagonal elements. Make a decision how to structure the programs in functions. The first program uses regular functions. The second one uses a function template.

12. Write three programs that read an array and find the smallest array element. Make a decision how to structure the programs in functions for solving this problem. The first program uses the regular functions. The second one uses the overloaded functions. The third program should use the function templates.

13. Write a program to calculate a factorial of any number using recursive functions.

14. Write a program with a recursive function that prints all **n!** permutations of **n** elements **a[0] a[1]...a[n]**.

15. Write a program that solves the previous problem without the recursive functions.

16. Write a program that finds the Fibonacci series using recursive functions. The Fibonacci series are

```
0, 1, 1, 2, 3, 5, 8, 13, 21, 34, ...
```

They begin with 0 and 1. Each subsequent Fibonacci number is the sum of the two previous numbers. Therefore,

```
Fibonaccy(0)=0, Fibonaccy(1)=1,
Fibonaccy(2)= Fibonaccy(0)+Fibonaccy(1)=0+1=1,
Fibonaccy(3)= Fibonaccy(1)+Fibonaccy(2)=1+1=2,
Fibonaccy(4)= Fibonaccy(2)+Fibonaccy(3)=1+2=3.
```

We think you get an idea how to create a Fibonaccy number. Those numbers are famous, because they converge with the constant value 1.618.... This number often occurs in the nature. It has been called a *golden mean*. We used this number in problem 10 of this chapter.

17. Write a program that finds a square root of different numbers. The square root finding procedure should be a separate routine. We offer you following Newton-Ralphson algo-

rithm of doing that. Suppose, you want to find a square root of a number **a**. One more thing, - this method is an approximation. So, we also have to define a precision **q**, that specifies how close the obtained square root should be to the precise one. We will guess the square root using variable **tr**. The algorithm consists of three steps:

1. Set **tr** to any reasonable positive number, usually to 1.
2. If $\left| tr^2 - a \right| \prec q$ then stop the calculations. You have found the square root. Otherwise go to the next step.
3. Make the value of **tr** equal to **(a/tr+tr)/2** and go back to step 2.

18. Assume, you came to visit some abstract country Computer States. Their national currency is comflop. There are five most often used currency bills in this country: 1, 3, 5, 10, 25. Develop a program that first prompts the user to enter the amount he or she wants to pay. The program, then, displays all the possible ways of paying this amount with the national currency. Do not enter the numbers greater than 200 to avoid long calculation time.

19. A word that is read the same from the left to write or from the right to left is called a palindrome. For instance, "level", "rotor", "toot" and so on. Write two programs to detect those words. The first program should have a regular function for detection the palindromes. The second program should use a recursive function.

20. Write a program that will find all the solutions to the eight queen problem. It is a problem to place eight queens on a chessboard, so no queen is under attack from another one.

CHAPTER 6

STRUCTURES.

6.1. Introduction to structures.

Suppose, we want to create a database of personnel, which includes the first and the last names, age, and salary for each person working in a company. One can do it by grouping all this data in one entity characterizing one employee. It is convenient, because each employee will be characterized by one entity. It is easy to operate on one entity for changing the employee's data.

C++ as well as C allows you to do it using *structures*. A *structure* specifies a group of related data, that can have different types. They are addressed by one *structure* name. The meaning of that phrase will become clear soon.

We will first get acquainted with the foremost elements of structures and how to introduce a structure in the program. Then, we will see how to use the structures. So, be patient and we will just walk you step by step over this chapter.

The introduction of a structure to a program requires two steps. The first step is to declare a structure. The second step is to define a structure variable. The general way of declaring a structure is

```
struct name
{
...
};
```

One can see, the keyword **struct** should be followed by the name of the structure, which is an identifier. The name of the structure is called a *tag*. Then, one lists all the *members* of the structure inside the {} braces. The structure members can be variables, arrays, strings, even another structures and so on. They all are gathered under one tag name. The terminating brace }; should be followed by the semicolon. Let's consider an example of a structure declaration.

The structure given below implements a record keeping for an employee. That record has first and the last employee's names, his or her age and salary.

```
struct record
{
char firstname[10];
char lastname[15];
int age;
int yearsalary;
};
```

We have defined a structure named **record** in the above example. It includes two **char** type character arrays **firstname** and **lastname**, and two **int** type variables **age** and **yearsalary**.

We learned, a computer allocates sufficient storage for a variable, when it is declared. How does the computer know what size of storage to allocate? We declare the data type of any variable as **int**, **float** and so on. The words "**int**" or "**float**" in the declaration serve as the "templates". We use the word " template" here, that has no relation to the function templates studied in the previous chapter. We just want to point, that any of the words "**int**" or "**float**" tells the computer, what size of memory must be allocated to store one unit of data of this type. For example, a variable of type **int** would normally require two bytes of memory. The words "**int**", "**float**", etc. are called the data types. *In C++, once a structure is declared, it becomes a data type.*

Structure declaration does not allocate any memory cells for its storage in a computer. It creates a new data type with more less the same rights as **int** or **float**. It serves as a special data type. A structure declaration tells a computer, what size should be allocated for storing all the structure members. The structure **record** declaration in our example informs a computer that it needs 10 and 15 cells for two arrays (**firstname** and **lastname**) of the type **char** and two variables of type **int**. Thus, the words

```
struct record
```

become a name of the new data type. C++ even allows to use only one word

```
record
```

in a variable definition after the newly created structure data type has been declared. *A name of a structure (tag) will identify that particular structure data type.*

After the structure is declared, one can define a variable of that structure type (it is also called a structure variable). The definition of the structure variable allocates the physical memory sufficient to store one set of all the structure members. You define a structure variable in the form

```
struct tag  variable_name,...;
```

Thus, the structure variable definition can include the word "**struct**" and the **tag** (or, in other words, the name) of a particular structure. We can create two variables of type **struct record** to show the variable definition on an example

```
struct record employee1, employee2;
```

However, in C++ it is also legal and desirable to use only a name of a structure to specify the data type of a defined variable. Therefore, it is also possible and better to write the definition of the structure variables **employee1, employee2** as

```
record employee1, employee2;
```

You can omit the word **struct** only in a definition of a structure variable in C++. When you write a structure declaration, you still have to use the word **struct**. Here, we have defined two variables **employee1** and **employee2** of the **record** type. This definition shell allocate two memory cells, each capable of holding all the structure members. Therefore, each of the defined variables is a structure. The **employee1** consists of two strings **firstname[10]** and **lastname[15]**, and two variables **age** and **yearsalary**. The variable **employee2** has its own separate set of those two arrays and two variables. The structure members that belong to the second variable **employee2** have the same names as the structure members of the first variable **employee1**. However, they are different members. Each set of structure members that belongs to a particular variable is absolutely independent from another one. One can define any number of variables of the same structure type.

It is, sometimes, difficult to appreciate a notion of a variable of a structure type. Let's consider what does a value of a structure variable mean on an example. We declared structure **record** and defined two structure variables: **employee1** and **employee2**. For example, **employee1** is Patrick McCannon, 40 years old. His yearly income is $65000. The **employee2** is Charles Baker. He is 29 and his salary is $50000. The values of those two variables of a structure type are

employee1		**employee2**	
firstname	Patrick	**firstname**	Charles
lastname	McCanon	**lastname**	Baker
age	40	**age**	29
yearsalary	65000	**yearsalary**	50000

A value of a structure variable is a complete set of values of all the members of that structure. The value of the variable **employee1**, in our case, included the values of all the structure members: **firstname[10]**, **lastname[15]**, **yearsalary** and **age**. Thus, to assign a value to a variable **employee1** means to enter the values of the arrays and variables **firstname[10]**, **lastname[15]**, **age** and **yearsalary**. All those members are the content of the variable **employee1**. The same set of members is also the content of the variable **employee2**, which is another variable.

The advantage of using structures is that one, basically, can handle many values at once by referring to one name of a structure variable. It is convenient for databases, because all the data regarding one variable is combined together as a group. The structures are also the ancestors of the classes, that we will study later.

There is another way to declare a structure and its variables. It is given below.

```
record {
char firstname[10];
char lastname[15];
int age;
int yearsalary;
} employee1, employee2, employee3, employee4;
```

The structure and its variables can be declared and defined simultaneously in one statement as shown above. In this case, the variables should be placed in between the closing brace and the semicolon. A structure can be declared without a tag, using **struct** keyword to simultaneously declare the structure and define its variables. For example, the last example may be rewritten without a tag as

```
struct
{
char firstname[10];
char lastname[15];
int age;
int yearsalary;
}  employee1, employee2, employee3, employee4;
```

Here, we used just a few variables. Suppose, there are 200 employees working in a company. We would have a choice between using separate structure variables or an array of structure variables. C++ permits to use the arrays of structure variables. Let's introduce an array **employee[200]**. Those 200 variables would now be written in a compact form as a single array. The definition of an array of structures is the same as for the array of variables. In our case, it is

```
record employee[200];
```

This defines an *array containing structures*. In other words, every element of the **employee[200]** array is, in fact, a structure.

6.2. Operations on structures.

We now need to know, how to assign a value to a structure variable. Naturally, to assign a value to a structure variable means to assign the values to all the structure members. Remember, by the declaration of **employee1** variable, we have allocated a memory cell capable to hold two arrays and two integers. They are associated with that **employee1** variable. Now we have to learn how "to fill in" that empty memory cell.

To access a structure member corresponding to a particular variable one should write it in the form

```
variable.member
```

The name of the variable should be followed by the dot and the member name. For example, to access structure member **age** of the variable **employee1**, we should write **employee1.age**. One can assign a value to a structure member by means of an assignment operator

```
employee1.age = 40;
```

This expression assigns the value 40 to the member **age** of variable **employee1**. You should not confuse **employee1.age** and **employee2.age**. Both forms access the member **age** of the structure. Remember we mentioned, that each of the variables **employee1** and **employee2** has its own set of all the structure members. Even though the structure members **age** are called the same names, but they belong to the different structure variables **employee1** and **employee2**. So, the **employee1.age** and **employee2.age** represent two different memory cells. They are different and independent variables. When we assigned the value 40 to **employee1.age** it had nothing to do with the **employee2.age**.

To assign a value to a structure variable means to assign the values to some or every structure member of that variable. One can enter the data into the structure using input functions or objects, value assignment, and initialization. The input/output of the values to and from a structure variable is illustrated by the number of following programs.

The values of the structure members corresponding to any structure variable can be entered and displayed by means of input/output functions **scanf()**, **printf()**, etc., or objects **cout**, **cin** and so on. You learned some of them in the Chapter 2. You will learn most of them later in this book. An example is given in **Program 6.1**.

```
#include <stdio.h>
```

```
main( )
{

struct date
{
int month;
int day;
int year;
};

date tod;
printf("Type month, day and year as  m, d, y. \n");
scanf("%d, %d, %d", &tod.month,  &tod.day, &tod.year);
printf("Variable tod: %d.%d.%d\n", tod.month, tod.day,
        tod.year);
}
```

Program 6.1.

The program prompts a user.

    `Type month, day and year as  m, d, y.`

Suppose, we enter 5, 20, 96. The program displays

    `Variable tod: 5.20.96`

The program reads the month, day and the year. It places them in a structure type variable **tod** and displays in another form. We use **scanf()** function in **Program 6.1** to illustrate the input. Variable **tod** is entered by means of **scanf()** function as

    `scanf("%d, %d, %d", &tod.month,  &tod.day, &tod.year);`

To enter a value of variable **tod** means to read every member of structure **date**. We also display the value of variable **tod** by **printf()** function to see the results.

    `printf("Variable tod: %d.%d.%d\n", tod.month, tod.day,`
            `tod.year);`

We must output all the structure members to output the variable **tod**.

  Consider the I/O of the same structure performed by means of C++ I/O objects.

```
#include <iostream.h>

main( )

{
struct date
{
int month;
int day;
int year;
};
```

```
date tod;
cout << "Type month, day and year as m  d  y \n";
cin >> tod.month;
cin >> tod.day;
cin >> tod.year;
cout << "Variable tod: " << tod.month << "." << tod.day
     << "." << tod.year;
}
```

Program 6.2.

It prompts a user to enter the month, date and the year. We enter 5 15 96. It displays
    Variable tod: 5.15.96
One can assign the values to the structure variables. It is shown in the next program.

```
#include <stdio.h>

main( )
{

struct date
{
int month;
int day;
int year;
} test, fun;

test.month=5;
test.day=15;
test.year=1996;
printf("Variable test: %d.%d.%d\n", test.month, test.day,
        test.year);

fun.month = test.month;
fun.day = test.day;
fun.year = test.year;
printf("variable fun:%d.%d.%d\n", fun.month, fun.day,
        fun.year);
}
```

Program 6.3.

The output of the program is
    variable test: 5.15.1996
    variable fun: 5.15.1996
Here, we assign a value to **test** variable by assigning the values to **test.month**,
test.day, **test.year** separately. Those structure members belong or, in other words,

correspond to that variable.

Most of the operators and statements suitable for regular variables, that we have studied before or will study, are applicable to the structure variables. **Program 6.3** demonstrates regular assignment operator. It assigns the value of the variable **test** to the variable **fun**. We assign each structure member of **test** variable to corresponding structure member of **fun** as **fun.month = test.month** and so on. This requires three assignment statements. One can also do it in a shorter way. An assignment

```
fun=test;
```

can substitute all three of those assignments. It will assign the values of three members of variable **test** to the corresponding three members of the variable **fun**.

One can initialize a structure variable. To initialize a variable means to assign an initial value during that variable definition. The initialization is similar to the array initialization. A type and a name of a variable in the initialization are followed by the = operator and the initial values surrounded by the {} braces. Consider **Program 6.4**.

```
#include <iostream.h>

main( )
{
struct date
{
int month;
int day;
int year;
};
date check ={2, 9, 1996};
cout << "Variable check: " << check.month << "."
      << check.day << "." << check.year;
}
```

Program 6.4.

The output of the program is

```
Variable check: 2.9.1996
```

The structure variable **check** is initialized by

```
date check ={2, 9, 1996};
```

This line defines the structure variable **check** of structure **date** type and assigns the initial values to it. The initial values are written inside the {} braces separated by the commas. Our example contains three values inside the braces. Thus, all three structure members of variable **check** are initialized. The values are assigned to them in the order the members follow in the structure declaration. We have **check.month=2**, **check.day=9** and **check.year=1996**. Another way of structure initialization is

```
struct date {
int month;
int day;
int year;
```

```
} check ={10, 9, 1998};
```
One can initialize a structure variable with fewer values than are contained in the structure. For example,
```
date check1={12, 31}
```
This sets **check1.month** to 12 and **check1.day** to 31. It does not specify the value of **check1.year**. The initial value is set to zero by default (if not specified). Thus, **check1.year** is set to zero. Some old compilers might still require adding the word **static** to a structure initialization. It must precede all the other words. For example,
```
static date check ={2, 9, 1996};
```
It is the same as
```
date check ={2, 9, 1996};
```

6.3. Structures and arrays.

One can define an array of structures. We introduced an array **employee[200]**. Let's define now an array of variables **x[10]** of structure **date** type, that is written as
```
date x[10];
```
An array is just a set of variables, as we know. What we have learned about a structure variable is also applicable to the arrays of structrues. You can enter the data in each array element using the same means as for the variable. Just remember, that each such array element of a structure type consists of all the structure members. For example, to enter a value in **x[5]**, means to enter the values in **x[5].month**, **x[5].day** and **x[5].year**. Everything we have studied for the arrays is also applicable here. This means, that the index **n** has the same double meaning for an array of structures **x[n]**. It denotes the number of array elements during its definition. It specifies a particular structure array element, when used after definition. When an array is declared, **x[5]** specifies an array containing five elements. When you address to an array element **x[4]** later, index 4 refers to the fifth array element.

Program 6.5 illustrates how to use an array of structures. It allows us to enter five intervals **[x, y]**, and finds the smallest of them. Each interval is implemented as a structure **line** containing three members: **x**, **y** and **dif**. We define an array **a[5]** of structure **line** type.

```
#include <stdio.h>

main( )
{
struct line
{
int x;
int y;
int dif;
}a[5];
int m, z;
```

```
printf ("Enter five intervals as [x, y]. Press enter \
          after each.\n");
printf ("Use integers.\n");
for (m=0; m<5; m++)
{
scanf ("\n[%d, %d]", &a[m].x, &a[m].y);
z=a[m].x - a[m].y;
if (z<0)
a[m].dif=-z;
else
a[m].dif=z;
}
for (m=1; m<5; m++)
{
if (a[m].dif < a[0].dif)
a[0].dif = a[m].dif;
}
printf ("\nThe smallest interval: %d\n", a[0].dif);
}
```

Program 6.5.

The program first prompts the user

    Enter the interval as [x, y]. Press enter after each.
    Use integers.

We enter

    [-5,6] ENTER [3,-5] ENTER [4,6] ENTER [2,-4] ENTER
    [1,3] ENTER

The output of the program is

    The smallest interval: 2

The algorithm of solving this problem is following. You first have to provide a data input for all five array elements. To provide one array element input, means to enter **a[m].x**, **a[m].y** and **a[m].dif**. You have to do it for each of the five array elements. The members **a[m].x** and **a[m].y** stand for two ends of the interval. You enter only **a[m].x** and **a[m].y**. The member **a[m].dif** is the length of the interval found as the difference between the end coordinates. The computer calculates the length **a[m].dif**. The difference can be positive or negative. You want to compare positive quantities. Therefore, you program converts a negative value to a positive one.

When all the values are entered, you want to compare each of them and to select and print the smallest one. We can use the same algorithm that we used for sorting. We compare the length of the interval **a[m].dif** consecutively with **a[1].dif**, **a[2].dif** and so on. If any of **a[m].dif<a[0].dif**, they are swapped. This will yield the smallest value of the length stored in **a[0].dif**. This is a part of the sorting algorithm, that we have discussed earlier. Our algorithm messed up the lengths of the intervals for all the array elements. You can improve this algorithm by having a separate variable **q**, that will be assigned a value of **a[0].dif**. This value will be, then, compared with the **dif** member

of each array element **a[]**. If any of the values **a[m].dif** is less than the current value stored in **q**, it will be assigned to **q**. This will put the smallest value in the variable **q**, that will be displayed later.

We shell now review the code of **Program 6.5**. First ten program lines start the program and declare the structure **line**, array of structures **a[5]** and variables **m, z**. Next two lines display the messages inviting the user to enter the intervals. The first **for** loop reads all five array elements. It reads **a[m].x** and **a[m].y** directly by means of **scanf()** function. Their difference, which is the length of the interval, is assigned to **z**. The value of **z** is compared to zero in the **if-else** statement. The value of **z>=0** is assigned to **a[m].dif** directly. If **z** is less than zero, we assign **a[m].dif=-z**. The **if-else** statement is the last one in the first **for** loop.

Thus, we read two members for each array element **a[m]** directly and calculate the third one. You can see, the array containing structures is entered as a regular array by **for** loop. The only difference is, that we have to enter the structure members for each array element **a[m]** in every loop cycle.

We introduced the third structure member **a[m].dif** to store the difference. We did it for teaching purposes. In this particular problem, we could have used either **a[m].x** or **a[m].y** to store the difference. We could have assigned it to one of them by

```
a[m].x=z;
```

You could have used one variable less for solving this problem. However, let's go back to our program now.

After all the variables are entered, we should sort them and select the smallest. We achieve that by the second **for** loop. It performs the sorting procedure, as we have just discussed. The smallest value is displayed on the screen.

Initialization of the array containing structures can be studied on a following example.

```
date y[4] = {{1, 3, 1992}, {3, 10, 1984},
             {4, 2, 1922}, {7, 19, 1956}};
```

Here, each array element contains 3 structure members. We dealt with the structure **date** in **Program 6.4**. We use this structure again in the above line as an example. The above line defines an array **y[4]** consisting of structures containing 4 elements of structure **date** type. It also initializes that array by giving the initial values to its elements. As in the case of simple arrays, one can write it without the internal brackets

```
date y[4] = {1, 3, 1992, 3, 10, 1984, 4, 2, 1922,
             7, 19, 1956};
```

Compiler will take the first three values in the order and assign them to three structure members of the first array element. Second three values will be assigned to the second array element and so on.

We have discussed, how to handle the arrays of structures. C++ as well as C allows to have the arrays as the structure members, as we have seen. There is nothing special of handling those array members. We will consider a bit more complicated program. It will demonstrate the handling of arrays of structures. Each of those structures will also contain the arrays.

```
#include <iostream.h>                    /*line1*/
```

```
main( )                                    /*line2*/
{                                          /*line3*/
struct course                              /*line4*/
{                                          /*line5*/
char name[4];                              /*line6*/
int po;                                    /*line7*/
} temp;                                    /*line8*/

course stu[5]={{{'J', 'o', 'h', 'n'}, 60}, {{'J', 'a',
'c', 'k'},80}, {{'R', 'u', 't', 'h'}, 90}, {{'S', 'a',
'l', ' '}, 75}, {{'M', 'a', 'r', 'y'}, 70}}; /*line9*/

int m, k;                                  /*line10*/
for (m=0; m<4; m++)                        /*line11*/
for(k=m+1; k<=4; k++)                      /*line12*/
{                                          /*line13*/
if (stu[m].po<stu[k].po)                   /*line14*/
{                                          /*line15*/
temp=stu[m];                               /*line16*/
stu[m]=stu[k];                             /*line17*/
stu[k]=temp;                               /*line18*/
}}                                         /*line19*/
for (m=0; m<=4; m++)                       /*line20*/
{                                          /*line21*/
for (k=0; k<=3; k++)                       /*line22*/
cout << stu[m].name[k];                    /*line23*/
cout << " " << stu[m].po << "\n";          /*line24*/
}   }                                      /*line25*/
```

Program 6.6.

The program displays the students according to their scores. The output is

```
Ruth   90
Jack   80
Sal    75
Mary   70
John   60
```

This program declares the structure **course** at lines 4-8. This structure contains an array **name[4]** and the variable **po** as its members. The **name[4]** stands for the student name and **po** is his (her) score. There are five students in the class. We define and initialize an array of structures **stu[5]** at line 9 as having structure type **course**. Pay attention, how we initialize a structure member array **name[]**. For instance, let's take an element **stu[0]**. It is an element of the array of the structure **course** type. It gets its values from the braces

```
{{'J', 'o', 'h', 'n'}, 60},..
```

The part **{'J', 'o', 'h', 'n'}** initializes the structure member array **name[]**.

This is how you would initialize the arrays inside the structures. In general, you can enter the array elements by any means, that we described in the chapter on arrays. The score 60 is assigned to the member **po**.

The array of structures is sorted at lines 11-19. We use the same sorting algorithm as for the regular arrays. The criterion for sorting the array of structures in **Program 6.6** is that **stu[m].po** should be greater than **stu[k].po**. Otherwise, we swap the elements of the structure array **stu[]**. Thus, an array of structures can be sorted by the values of its members. We could sort this array of structures in an alphabetical order of its array members **name[]**. This way we can display the list of students in the alphabetical order of their names.

It is interesting to consider a simple assignment **temp=stu[m]** written at line 16. It is coded in one line. Let's rewrite this simple line to assign all the members of one structure variable to another. It will require following operations. We will have to write first

```
temp.po=stu[m].po;
```
Then, we must assign a member array **name[]** of the element **stu[m]** to the member array of variable **temp**. To assign a member array means to assign each of its elements to the corresponding elements of another member array. You would have to do it by

```
for (k=0; k<4; k++)
temp.name[k]=stu[m].name[k];
```

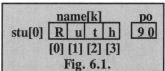

Fig. 6.1.

We use the **for** loop, because each of the **k** elements of **stu[m].name[k]** must be assigned to **temp.name[k]**. Is not it great, we could use only one line instead of three?

We display the sorted array at lines 20-25 of **Program 6.6**. It consists of two **for** loops. The outer **for** loop displays each of the structures **stu[m]**. The inner **for** loop displays all **k** elements of the member array **name[k]** for each structure type array element **stu[m]**. For example, **m=0** prints all **k** elements of **stu[0].name[k]** and **stu[0].po**. It is depicted in Fig. 6.1. We, in fact, display the first row of the output message for **m=0**

```
Ruth   90
```
The **m=1** should print all **k** elements of **stu[1].name[k]** and **stu[1].po** and so on until the last **m**.

6.4. Structures and functions.

As we learned, you should do two things before using a structure in a program: declare a structure and define a structure variable. When a program consists of a few functions, it can give you some problems. Let's consider some peculiarities of using a structure in a program with the functions.

When you declare a global variable of type **int**, compiler knows this data type. If you define a global variable

```
struct record x; or record x;
```
a computer might not understand the data type **record**. The structure type **record** is created by you. You create this data type by declaring this particular structure. If you

declare that data type inside a function, it will be visible only inside this function. If you want the computer to recognize this data type in any routine within the same source file or you want to define a global variable **x**, the **record** structure should be declared externally outside of any function. It will permit you to define a variable of that structure type in any function or globally. Consider a code fragment below.

```
struct day
{
int hour;
int minute;
};
day earlytime;
main( )
{
day time1;
...}

count( )
{
day latetime;
...
}
```

Structure **day** consists of members **hour** and **minute** in the above fragment. We declare **day** outside of any routine. It allows to define the variables of **day** type in either **main()** or **count()** functions. Thus, we can define the **day** type variables anywhere within the same source file. We define the **latetime** variable of **day** type inside **count()**, **time1** in **main()** routine and **earlytime** as a global variable. So, if a structure is declared globally, you can define external and internal variables of this type in any function of the same source file. If you declare a structure inside some function, you can define the variables of that structure type only inside that function. This structure data type as well as its variables can be only local in that function.

You can make a structure visible in a multi-source file program. In this case, the same structure should be declared in every source file, where it is used, with or without the word **extern** preceding the words **struct day**. Then, you can define an external variable of that structure type in each file. The definition of those variables in all but one file should be preceded by the word **extern**, as illustrated in **Program 6.7**. You already know, how to declare a multi-source file variable. The only addition to that required for the structures is to declare the structure type in each source file. An example is given in **Program 6.7**. We create a project, that consists of two source files **next.cpp** and **play.cpp**. This program introduces the structure **line** with two members **x** and **y**. It assigns them the values in the **main()** routine. The **length()** function changes a value of the variable **meas**. Since this is a structure variable, it has two members, as we have declared them.

We change the **meas.x** member of that variable. This value is then printed in **main()** routine to illustrate, that the actual change has happened. The program shows the communication between different source files. The structure **line** is declared in both source files. The multi-source file variable **meas** is defined in both files as having structure **line** type. We used word **extern** in the source file **next.cpp** for defining **meas** there. The content of the source file **C:\tcwin\bin\play.cpp** is

```
#include <iostream.h>

void length (void);

struct line
{
int x;
int y;
};
line meas;

main( )
{
meas.x=1;
meas.y=2;
length ( );
cout <<  meas.x;
}
```

The content of the source file **C:\tcwin\bin\next.cpp** is

```
struct line
{
int x;
int y;
};
extern line meas;

void length (void)
{
meas.x=meas.x-meas.y;
}
```

Program 6.7.

The output of the program is -1. The function **length()** does not take any arguments and does not return any values at all. We change the external structure variable, because it is accessible to all the functions of the program.

The C++ as well as C language allows to pass a structure as a function argument. A structure member can be also passed as an argument. The structures are passed by value as regular variables. The difference between a structure variable and a normal variable is that the first one consists of structure members. When you pass a structure as an argument of a function, the copies of the structure members are passed to the called function. Therefore, the original values of the variables passed to the called function cannot be changed. When the function execution is completed, all the changes to those arguments will be lost. Consider **Program 6.8** illustrating this concept.

```cpp
#include <iostream.h>

struct line
{
int x;
int y;
};

void length (line var);

main( )
{
struct line meas;
meas.x=1;
meas.y=2;
length (meas);
cout << meas.x << ", " << meas.y;
}

void length (line var)
{
var.x+=10;
var.y+=10;
}
```

Program 6.8.

The output of the program is **1, 2**. The program consists of two routines: **main()** and **length()**. We declare the structure **line** as global. We define the local variable **meas** inside **main()** of structure **line** type. It is passed as an argument to the function **length()**. The function **length()** increases the value of each structure member by 10. We print the members after function **length()** termination. It shows, that they have not changed. Another point of this program is important. If you pass the whole structure to a function, its parameters should have the structure type.

```cpp
void length (line var);
```

The function parameters can be of different structure types. This means, that you can use the variables of different structure types as function parameters.

One can pass a member as a function argument. The function parameter must have the data type of the structure member, that you intend to pass. It is shown in **Program 6.9**.

```cpp
#include <iostream.h>
```

```
void length (int var);

struct line
{
int x;
int y;
};

main( )
{
line meas;
meas.x=1;
meas.y=2;
length (meas.x);
cout << meas.x << ", " << meas.y;
}

void length (int var)
{
var+=10;
}
```

Program 6.9.

This program has the same output as the previous one. Here, we declare the parameter of the function **length()** as **int**.

```
void length (int var);
```

It has the same data type as the member **x**, that we pass to a function. The function **length()** handles this parameter as a regular variable. It accesses it by its name **var**.

A function can return a structure variable. In this case, its return data type must be of structure type. It is a very useful property. A function can return only one variable. By returning a structure variable, one can actually return a lot of information at once. **Program 6.10** demonstrates a return of the structure variable **test**.

```
#include <iostream.h>

struct line
{
int x;
int y;
};

line length (line val);

main( )
{
```

```
line meas;
meas.x=1;
meas.y=2;
meas=length (meas);
cout << meas.x << ", " << meas.y;
}

line length (line val)
{
line test;
test.x=val.x+10;
test.y=val.y+10;
return (test);
}
```

Program 6.10.

The output of this program is

```
11, 12
```

It consists of two functions: **main()** and **length()**. The **main()** function assigns the values to the members **meas.x** and **meas.y**. It calls the **length()** function by

```
meas=length (meas);
```

The **length()** function adds 10 to every structure member passed inside the argument variable **meas**. It assigns the result to the corresponding member of variable **test** by

```
test.x=val.x+10;
test.y=val.y+10;
```

The structure variable **test** is returned back to the caller. The **cout** object prints the returned structure members.

We want to point, that we did not have to introduce a new structure variable **test**. The assignments

```
val.x=val.x+10;
val.y=val.y+10;
```

are perfectly legitimate. The **val** is a formal parameter of the function **length()**. We could have returned this parameter. We introduced the variable **test** to show, that any variable not only the formal parameter can be returned.

Thus, a function can return a structure variable or its member. We know, a function returning a structure should be declared and defined as having the structure return type. In our example the **length()** function is declared as

```
line length (line val);
```

When a function returns a structure member, it is handled as a regular variable. The return type will be the same as the data type of the structure member. Loosely speaking, the function, that returns a structure member, "thinks" that it returns a regular variable, since no structure type is specified.

6.5. Structures containing structures.

The structures can have the members, that are the variables of the structure types. It is called the *nested structures*. Nested structures are the structures containing structures as their members, that can also contain member-structures and so on. Let's consider how to declare a nested structure on a following example.

```
struct date{
int month;
int day; };
struct hour_min {
int hour;
int min; };
struct moment
{
date todate;
hour_min a1;
int sec;
};
...
```

Here we have structure **moment**. It consists of two structure variables: **todate** of **date** type and **a1** of structure **hour_min** type. We also declare member **sec** inside the **moment** structure. The substructures **date** and **hour_min** are declared explicitly before the declaration of the structure **moment**. Only after that, we define the variables **todate** and **a1** as members of the structure **moment**. Therefore, the variables or arrays of a structure type can be members of a structure. The structure types of those variables should be declared earlier. One cannot write one structure declaration inside another structure declaration.

One defines a variable of the outer nested structure using the same form as for the regular structure variable. For example,

```
moment x;
```

The same syntax applies for accessing the members of structure types. For example, we access the member **todate** corresponding to outer structure variable **x** by

```
x.todate
```

To access one of the members of a structure type member, use a construction like

```
x.todate.year
```

Here, **x** is the variable that has a type of the external structure **moment**. The second variable **todate** has a type of the internal structure **date**. The **year** is the member of that internal structure. Thus, by writing

```
x.todate.year =1990;
```

we have assigned 1990 to the member **year** of the structure member **todate** of the external structure variable **x**. The first dot accesses a substructure-member of the external structure. The second dot accesses a member of that substructure. Number of dots is equal to a number of nested substructures.

6.6. Unions.

Union is a very sophisticated feature of C and C++. The form of writing them is similar to structures. However, the meaning of unions is quite different. A union as a structure requires two steps of its introduction to a program. It should be first declared. One can, then, define its variable. The union should be declared with the first word **union**. Let's consider following fragment.

```
union mysample {
int a;
float b;
char c; };
```

Our example declares a union with the name **mysample**, that is preceded by the word **union**. The name of the union **mysample** is called the *tag*. The union declaration does not allocate any space for its storage. It is like telling the computer, that the name **mysample** can be either an integer, floating-point number or a character. You, loosely speaking, "worn" the computer about it. The declaration of a union is similar to creation of a new data type. *Once declared, a union becomes a data type in C++.* To use the unions in the program, one has to define a variable. Defining a variable allocates a physical storage for a union type variable.

A union variable is defined using the same rules as for the structure variables. The definition of a variable actually allocates the physical memory. In our case we can write

```
union mysample x;
```

We defined the variable **x** of the union **mysample** data type. When a union is declared, its name alone can be used to specify the union type of any variable, array and so on. Therefore, the variable definition form that uses only a union name as

```
mysample x;
```

can and must be used by C++ programmer. A union type specifies only one variable, that depending on the circumstances can have different data type. All the possible data types a variable of that union type can have are specified as internal union members. Thus, the member **int a** of union type **mysample** specifies, that our variable **x** can have **int** type. The member **float b** indicates that our variable **x** can also have **float** data type, if needed. Our variable **x** of union type can be used to store either an integer (**int a**), or a floating-point number (**float b**), or a character (**char c**).

When a union is declared, the computer is worned , that the definition of a variable of this type would require to allocate a memory cell only for one of union members. The size of that cell is determined by the data type of the union member, that occupies the largest memory cell. The number of union members does not matter, because they all represent only different types of one variable. The union type variable, can have only one value and data type at a time. Each new value assignment cancels the previous value. So, the largest memory size in the above union **mysample** is of type **float**.

The ways to declare a union and to define its variables are similar to that of the structures. We just show one of a number of familiar to you ways below

```
union mysample
{
```

```
int a;
float b;
char c;
} x;
```
A union, as well as the structure, can be declared without a tag. The way to do it is similar for both of them.

   The union members can be accessed in the same manner as the structure members. An **int** type variable can be accessed as **x.a**. The floating point value is accessed through **x.b** member. For example, an assignment operator can be written as
```
x.b = 2.98;
```
To enter a character one could write
```
scanf ("%c \n", &x.c); or
cin >> x.c;
```
You can use unions to create the arrays, that store different data types. For example,
```
union test
{
int a;
float b;
} row[20];
```
creates an array **row[20]** capable of storing either **float** or **int** values. A union can contain a structure as its member. Unions can also be structure members. For instance,
```
struct data
{
int x;
float y;

union
{
char z;
int z1;
}mix;

} var;
```
This structure consists of three members **x**, **y** and **mix**. Its **mix** member is a union variable, which can be either of type **char** or **int**. The first closing **}** brace is the union brace. The name **mix** typed between the closing brace and semicolon belongs to the union. It is the name of the union variable. The second name **}var;** is the name of the structure variable. Consider a program illustrating unions.

```
#include <iostream.h>

main( )
{
union ent
{
```

```
int x;
char a;
};
ent look;
char z;
int m;
cout << "Enter one number or character.\n";
cin >> z;
if (z>='0' && z<='9')
{
look.x=z-48;
cout << "You entered a digit " << look.x;
}
else
cout << "You entered a character " << (look.a=z);
cout << "\nThe end.\n";
}
```

Program 6.11.

   The program prompts a user to enter any character from the keyboard. If you enter a
letter or a special character, it displays a message, that this is a character. The entered
character is also displayed on the screen. If you enter a digit, the program displays a
message, that this is a digit. The digit is displayed on the screen. Pay attention, that we
have declared the union first. We define the variable **look** by

   ent look;

It can be also defined as **union ent look**. We declare the union **ent**. It becomes a data
type in C++. Its name can be used alone to define the variables as we have done.

   The program uses the **if-else** statement with the condition **z>='0' && z<='9'** to
distinguish between the digits and other characters. If you enter either a digit or a character, it is read as a character. The character is stored as integer equal to its ASCII (or any
other standard) value. Since many computers use ASCII storage convention, the difference
between the ASCII digit value and the actual digit is 48. If we entered a digit, the code
subtracts 48 from **z** and assigns the resilt to the **int** member of the union **look** by the
expression **look.x=z-48**. If we enter a letter or a character, the code assigns it to the
char member **a** of the union **look** by **look.a=z**.

   A union that does not have a tag and is not used to declare a variable or any other object
(array and so on) of its type is called an *anonymous union*. An example is

   union
   {
   int x;
   char y;
   }

The members of this union can be accessed directly as **x** or **y** within the scope, where it is
visible. For example, a union declared in a function is visible inside that function.

6.7. The *typedef* construction.

C and C++ permit to call a data type by any other word. One can substitute any data type by another word using the **typedef** statement. It has a form.

    typedef *data_type* *user-provided_word;*

This allows to substitute the ***data_type*** by the ***user-provided_word*** anywhere in the program. For example,

    typedef int MY;

We can now write a program and declare a variable as

    MY x;

The computer will understand, that this variable **x** has **int** type. This is the result of **typedef** statement. The computer interprets the word **MY** as word **int**. Loosely speaking, you can now declare a variable with the type **MY**. The computer understands it as a word **int**. So, the computer will substitute the word **MY** everywhere with the word **int**. Thus, **MY x** becomes equivalent to **int x**.

The **typedef** is often used with structures and unions. For example,

    typedef struct measurement
    {
    int x;
    int y;
    } TRY ;

The **typedef** should precede the structure (union) declaration. The word **TRY** written between the closing brace and the semicolon becomes an equivalent of the structure type **measurement**. The **TRY z** can now be used to define a structure variable instead of **measurement z**. Consider a program that uses the **typedef** statement.

```
#include <stdio.h>

main( )
{
typedef struct
{
int x;
int y;
} TRY ;
typedef float F;
TRY var;
F res;
var.x=2;
var.y=3;
res=(var.x+var.y)/2.0;
printf ("%f\n", res);
}
```

Program 6.12.

This program finds an average of the values stored in members **var.x** and **var.y** and displays it. The output of the program is **2.500000**. The program is pretty understandable. Here, we substitute **float** data type by **F**. We also substitute the structure type by the word **TRY**. We do not use the tag "**measurement**" in the structure **typedef** statement.

Thus, the **typedef** construction only creates a synonym word for the data type. No new data type is created, no storage allocated. No variable can be used in this construct.

This statement can be used for better program portability. The portability is a property of the same code to be transferable to different systems. It is a very important factor in software development. The same C++ code might not run on different computer systems. The **typedef** statement makes it easier to go from one system to another.

For example, an **int** can be implemented as 32 bit cell and **short int** as 16 bit cell on system 1. Both of them are implemented as 16 bit cell on computer system 2. You write your program for the first system using

```
typedef  short int NUM;
```

The word **NUM** is used everywhere inside your code instead of **short int**. To go to the system 2, you will only need to change that line of code to

```
typedef  int  NUM;
```

6.8. Enumerated type.

The enumeration type is also called enumerated type. It specifies the values that the variables can accept by some user-provided names. Before one can use it in the program, two steps must be undertaken. An enumeration data type should be declared first. When an enumerated type is declared, it becomes a new data type for a particular program. Declaration of an enumeration type is similar to a structure declaration. It informs the computer, that a certain amount of storage can be required for an object of enumerated type. Declaration of an enumerated type should contain the word **enum** followed by the optional name of the type (called *tag*) and the list of the values. The list of the values is enclosed in **{}** braces and separated by the commas. The declaration is completed by a semicolon at the end. The tag is an identifier. Consider an example of enumerated type declaration

```
enum week
{
Monday, Tuesday, Wednesday, Thursday, Friday, Saturday,
Sunday
} ;
```

The next step is to define a variable of that type. We define variable **test** as

```
enum week test;
```

It is sufficient and more desirable in C++ to use only the tag without the word **enum** to define a variable of enumeration type. After an enumerated type is declared, the tag becomes a name of a new data type. Thus, **week** is a new data type. In our example we should use name **week** without the word **enum** to define the variable **test** as

```
week test;
```

If we write
```
test=Monday;
```
It will be the same as
```
test=0;
```
Each word in the brackets is called an *enumerator*. For instance, **Monday**, **Tuesday** are the enumerators. Each enumerator is a number. Sometimes, it is convenient to use a name instead of a number. An enumerator is a number for all practical purposes. C++ "thinks", that the first enumerator is 0, the second is 1, the third is 3 and so on. A value of each enumerator is by 1 greater than the value of the previous enumerator by default. Thus, **Monday** is 0, **Tuesday** is 1, **Wednesday** is 3 and so on. The value of each enumerator can be changed by a programmer. One assign any integer to a variable of enumerated type in C. In C++ you assign to a variable of enumerated type only one of its enumerators. For instance, variable **test** accepts only **Monday**, **Tuesday**, **Wednesday**, **Thursday**, **Friday**, **Saturday** and **Sunday** values.

```
#include <iostream.h>

main( )
{
enum numbers {one=20, two, three=5, four};
numbers var;
cout << (var=one) << ", " << (var=two) << ", "
     << (var=three) << ", " << (var=four);
}
```
Program 6.13.

We have declared an enumeration type and its variable **var**. We assigned the value 20 to **one** and 5 to **three**. The program assigns each of those words **one, ...four** to **var** and prints its values after each assignment. The output of this program is
```
20,   21,   5,   6
```
Notice, **two** and **four** are the incremented value of **one** and **three** respectively.
One can also use **typedef** statement as shown below.

```
#include <stdio.h>

main( )
{
typedef enum {one, two, three, four} NEW;
NEW var1=one;
printf ("%d\n", var1);
}
```
Program 6.14.

The output of this program is number 0. We declare the variable **var1** of **NEW** type. The word **NEW** is used in the **typedef** statement between the brace and the semicolon. We skipped the enumeration tag, although it can be used in the **typedef** statements.

6.9. Declaration and definition.

There is a certain amount of confusion between the declaration and definition used in a different way by different authors. The ANSI C Standard has resolved this confusion. Since it is given by the official document, we shell consider this subject. As you have noticed, we use the words "declaration" and "definition".

One declares a variable, an array, a function and so on. The declaration statement informs the computer about the required memory size for storing certain objects. It does not create a physical memory space, that will store those objects (variables, arrays, structures and so on). A declaration, that also creates a memory cell for an object is a definition.

The declaration of a variable or an array is also, typically, a definition, because the memory cells for the arrays and variables are created at the time they are declared. So, there is no difference between the declaration and definition of a variable or an array of variables. A structure, union, enumerated type, a class should be declared first. Only then, a variable of this type can be defined. A function declaration is its prototype. A function definition is, basically, the code of the function itself, consisting of a header and a body.

EXERCISES.

1. If you have an access to a computer facility run all the programs given in this chapter.
2. Write a program, that gives you the weekday for any date. You enter the month, day of the month and the year.
3. Rewrite program 20 to the Chapter 4 using a structure to hold all the part data. Another structure shell contain all the menu messages and a variable which should store your response to the menu messages.
4. Write a program that asks a user to enter a geometrical figure. The user can enter a circle, a triangle, a square, a cube. Depending on an entered figure, the program prompts the user to enter the sides necessary to calculate the area of the figure. The program calculates the area of the figure and displays it. For instance, if you enter a circle, the program should ask you to enter a diameter of this circle. It, then, calculates the area of the circle and displays it. Organize a name of a figure, its sides, area and all the messages related to that figure as a variable of a structure.
5. Write a program to simulate a card shuffling. Use an array of 36 structure variables. Each structure variable consists of two structure members to represent the card's suit and rank. You should use two random number selection functions to place randomly 4 suits and 9 ranks into 36 structure variables, that represent the cards. There cannot be more than one card having the same suit and rank among those 36. When all 36 structure variables are filled, this should represent the initial combination of cards. The initial combination should be stored and displayed at the end of the shuffling. The program, then, performs a shuffling swapping two randomly selected cards for 100 times. Read about random functions in Chapter 20 in the section about the **<stdlib.h>** header file.

CHAPTER 7

CHARACTER STRINGS.

7.1. Introduction to strings.

Sometimes, it is important to know, where is an end of a character array. **Program 7.1** elucidates this point to you.

```cpp
#include <iostream.h>

void add_end(char x[ ],char y[ ],int q,int p,char z[ ]);

main( )
{
static char row1[12]={'c','h','a','r','a','c','t',
                      'e','r', ' '};
static char row2[7]={'a','r','r','a','y'};
char row3[20];
int n=10, k=5;
add_end (row1, row2, n, k, row3);
for (n=0; n<15; n++)
cout << row3[n];
}

void add_end (char x[ ],char y[ ],int q,int p,char z[ ])
{
int m;
for(m=0; m<q; m++)
z[m]=x[m];
for (m=q; m<(q+p); m++)
z[m]=y[m-q];
}
```

Program 7.1.

The output of the program is
```
character array
```
This program consists of two functions: **main()** and **add_end()**. The **main()** function declares three arrays **row1**, **row2**, **row3** and two variables **n**, **k**. After that,

`main()` calls the `add_end()` function. It copies `n=10` positions of `row1` to `row3`. It then, copies `k=5` positions of `row2` to `row3` beginning from the 11th position of `row3`. As you can see, `row1` has 12 elements. We only need ten of them to copy the word 'character' and the blank space. We have to declare the variable `n` and use it for the maximum number of positions to be copied from `row1`. The `row2` has seven elements. We have to declare `k=5`, that should limit the number of copied from `row2` positions to five. We display `row3` in `main()` by means of `for` loop.

The `add_end()` function has five formal parameters: array `x[]`, array `y[]`, number of positions to be copied from the first array `q`, number of positions to be copied from the second array `p` and the array to which both arrays are copied `z[]`. Parameter `q` gets its value from `n` and the argument `k` is passed to the parameter `q`. Array `x[]` is copied to `z[]` by means of the first `for` loop.

```
for(m=0; m<q; m++)
z[m]=x[m];
```

It copies each `x[m]` element to the corresponding element of `z[m]`. The second array `y[m]` is copied after the first one by another `for` loop.

```
for (m=q; m<(q+p); m++)
z[m]=y[m-q];
```

Here `m` changes from `q` to `q+p`, because we want to start from the 11th position and fill in five elements of `z[]`. The second array `y[m-q]` must start from the first position. This is why we use `m-q` as its subscript.

We pass all three arrays as the arguments of the `add_end()` function by

```
add_end (row1, row2, n, k, row3);
```

After copying is completed, the control returns to `main()`. It prints new string `row3`.

This program needs variables `n` and `k` and corresponding two function parameters `q` and `p` to copy the parts of `row1` and `row2` containing only the characters. It can be inconvenient to keep track of a number of characters in each array. Imagine, we declared `row1[20]`, copied the word 'character' there, and did not keep track of a number of filled positions. We would not know, from which position of `row3` to begin to copy `row2`.

Thus, the old idea about putting a character at the end of each word in each array could be very promising. We can introduce a check for that character, as we did. This way we could know, when the end of the word has been reached. We can select any character we want. One condition, we have to be sure, that it will not be a part of any entered word. Putting this character at the end of both words 'character' and 'array' simplifies the program. Each array element will be copied, until that special character is encountered. This eliminates the need for the variables `n` and `k`. We do not need to know, how many positions each word occupies inside an array, because we check for a signal character on its end.

What character is it? We can use '0', that we already used, or any other character we want. The C++ and C languages make our lives even easier. They introduce a special kind of arrays called *strings* or *character strings*.

Character strings are one-dimensional type `char` arrays of characters, terminated by a null or end-of-string marker '\0'. They can contain any combination of characters, numbers and letters. The character '\0' turns to be better than our '0', because it is less likely to appear in the words or other data. It is called the *null-character*. Indeed, as you remember, the backslash \ character in C/C++ is not treated as a separate character in strings or character constants. Therefore, '\0' represents a single character. When one declares a string, one extra position should be allocated for this marker. This null-character is inserted automatically, when the computer "knows", that you deal with the string.

How to specify the strings in the program? You can do it by two means. You can declare them in the same manner as the arrays. The difference is how you initialize them. Strings are initialized delimited by double quote marks. For example,

```
static char x[ ]={"language"};
static char x[ ]="language";
```

Both forms will specify a null-terminated string. The number inside the [] brackets is optional. If there is no number inside the brackets, the computer creates an array that can accommodate all the characters inside the double quotation marks plus the null character. Again, the number inside the [] brackets, if you choose to write it, should be at least by 1 greater than the number of characters entered in " " double quotation marks. You should do it, because the null character is added automatically to the end of the string. The two above forms are equivalent to array initialization

```
char x[ ]={'l','a','n','g','u','a','g','e','\0'};
```

This way you initialize a regular character array and manually enter the null-character. The previous two forms are more convenient for writing.

You can wonder, where will the null-character be added, if you enter something like

```
char x[ ]={"C is great.\n"};
```

The null-character will be added after the newline character.

7.2. String input/output.

You can specify a character string by entering it using the **scanf()** function. The **scanf()** should use the **%s** format specification field for the strings. The **%s** field skips any leading white spaces (blank space, tab '**\t**', newline '**\n**', formfeed '**\f**' characters). It reads a group of characters from a standard input, until the next white space is encountered. For example, an input of the string **row3** can be achieved by

```
scanf ("%s", row3);
```

The character string **row3** should be declared before one can use it. The **scanf()** function reads the character array **row3** from the terminal and adds the null-character '\0' to the end. The character **&** is not used before **row3** in this function for reading the character arrays. We will explain it in the next chapter. Review **Program 7.2**.

```
#include <stdio.h>

main( )
{
char row3[20];
int n;
scanf ("%s", row3);
for (n=0; n<15; n++)
```

```
printf ("%c", row3[n]);
}
```

Program 7.2.

We enter from the keyboard
     one, two, three
After pressing **ENTER**, the program displays
     one,
There is a blank space between the comma and the word '**two**'. It terminates the input.

The program uses **scanf("%s", row3)** for the string input. The string is displayed by means of the **for** loop by **printf("%c", row3[n])** function as any array. We want to emphasize, again, that a string is an array. Thus, anything applicable to an array can be used for it as well. Loosely speaking, it is an array with one extra character on the end. This extra character permits the user to do some extras. Those extras are the subject of this chapter.

The format specification field **%s** can be used not only in the input function. It can be used in the **printf()** function as well. The **%s** displays the characters, until the end of string character is encountered. Consider how this can simplify the program.

```
#include <stdio.h>

main( )
{
char row3[20]= "one, two, three";
printf ("%s", row3);
}
```

Program 7.3.

The program displays
     one, two, three
This program displays the same word without any loops and additional variables. The **%s** format writes the character string to the output, until it encounters the null-character '**\0**'. The null character is not displayed. This form of output has certain advantages compare to the output of the previous program. Unfortunately, **%s** format can be used only for the null-terminated strings.

One can use the field width in the string format specification fields as, for example, **%10s** or **%3s**. The **scanf()** function will terminate the reading, when either or both events occur: the first white space character in the input is encountered, the number of the characters specified by the field width has been read. Review following example.

```
#include <stdio.h>

main( )
{
char row3[20];
```

```
printf ("Enter a word.\n");
scanf ("%5s", row3);
printf ("%s", row3);
}
```

Program 7.4.

We enter the word

    identification

The computer displays

    ident

The **printf()** function can use the precision to specify the number of characters to be displayed in the string. In this case, the output is terminated, when either or both of the events occur: the null-character is encountered, the number of characters specified by the precision has been printed. Try to run **Program 7.4** using

    printf ("%.6s", row3);

The program produces a six character output if **row3[20]="identification"**. In case if we declare **row3[ ]="one two three"**, the output is the word

    one tw

What if you enter a text, where the words are separated by the white spaces? In this case, use as many **scanf()** functions as needed. **Program 7.5** demonstrates a small word processor. One can enter up to 79 characters or one sentence. The input is terminated, if 79 characters have been read or characters '.' or '?' are encountered.

```
#include <stdio.h>                                    /*line1*/

void my_edit (char inp_dat[ ], char stor[ ]); /*line2*/

main( )                                               /*line3*/
{                                                     /*line4*/
char row[20],line[80];                                /*line5*/
my_edit(row, line);                                   /*line6*/
printf ("%s", line);                                  /*line7*/
}                                                     /*line8*/

void my_edit (char inp_dat[ ], char stor[ ]) /*line9*/
{                                                     /*line10*/
int n, m, k=0, p=20, fl=1;                            /*line11*/
while (fl && k<79)                                    /*line12*/
{                                                     /*line13*/
scanf ("%s", inp_dat);                                /*line14*/
for (m=0;  m<p; m++)                                  /*line15*/
{                                                     /*line16*/
stor[k+m]=inp_dat[m];                                 /*line17*/
if (inp_dat[m]=='.'||inp_dat[m]=='?')                 /*line18*/
fl=0;                                                 /*line19*/
```

```
if (inp_dat[m+1]=='\0')                    /*line20*/
{                                          /*line21*/
stor[k+m+1]=' ';                           /*line22*/
p=m-2;                                     /*line23*/
} }                                        /*line24*/
k=k+m+1;                                   /*line25*/
p=20;                                      /*line26*/
}                                          /*line27*/
stor[k]='\0';                              /*line28*/
}                                          /*line29*/
```

Program 7.5.

If you enter

    This is only a test.

The output is

    This is only a test.

The program consists of two functions: **main()** and **my_edit()**. The **main()** declares two character arrays, calls **my_edit()**, displays the result. The **my_edit()** function reads the input and puts it into an array.

Let's review the **my_edit()** function. It begins with the header and data declaration at lines 9-11. It reads the strings with the **scanf()** function at line 14. The **scanf()** terminates after every word. This is why it should be inside a loop. It is, indeed, written inside **while** loop with two conditions specified at line 12 as **(fl && k<79)**. Thus, **scanf()** will be called after each word, until we enter 79 character or end an entered sentence. Every time the string is read, it is stored in **inp_dat**. The new word is written over the old word. This is why we have to transfer its content into the bigger array **stor** after each reading. We copy a word from **inp_dat** string into **stor** by the expression **stor[k+m]=inp_dat[m]** inside the **for** loop at line 15-17. It is done on the element by element basis. The flag variable **fl** is set to zero, if a dot or a question mark are encountered in **inp_dat[m]**. It is handled by the **if** statement at lines 18, 19. It terminates the **while** loop and stops the data input. If the **if** statement recognizes the null-character in **inp_dat[m]**, it makes **p** less than **m** by making **p=m-2** and stops the **for** loop. **if** statement also places a blank space at the end of a word.

Every time we transfer a new word to **stor**, it starts from the end of the previous word plus one position. One position is needed for the white space to separate the words, when you read them. This is done by the expression at line 22. It is a part of the **if** statement at line 20. When the **scanf()** reads a word with the **%s** format and places it into an array, it is automatically terminated by the null-character. When the content of the small array is dumped into the big one, we do not want a null-character to be copied every time. We want it only once at the end of **stor**, so it can be displayed as a string.

Each **while** loop executes **k=k+m+1**. This assures that the next word will be placed in the big array **stor[k+m]** beginning from the end of the previous word plus one position. The end of each **while** loop cycle sets **p** back to 20 (line 26) to assure, that a 20 character word can be read again next time. Line 28 puts the null character at the last position entered in the **stor** array.

You can use more than one format specification field to enter strings, values, and to read them. When you use a few format specification fields, be cautious with the field width. Each format field will read specified number of characters, or it will stop reading when a white character occurs in the input. For instance, you can read

```
scanf("%6s %s %d", row1, row2, &x);
```

The input will be broken apart and stored in the strings **row1**, **row2** and the variable **x**.

One can enter a string using either **scanf()** with the **%c** format or **getchar()** functions. They will read the next incoming character, whatever it is. To read character strings, use those functions inside the loops and place a null-character at the end.

```
#include <stdio.h>

main ( )
{
char row[80];
int n, m=79;
printf ("enter any characters\n");
printf ("when done press ENTER\n");
for(n=0;n<m; n++)
{
scanf ("%c", &row[n]);
if (row[n]=='\n')
m=0;
}
row[n-1]='\0';
while (row[m]!='\0')
{
printf ("%c", row[m]);
m=m+1;
} }
```

Program 7.6.

The program reads any set of up to 79 characters and displays it. The input of characters is stopped, when either 79 of them have been read or a newline character has been encountered. This function illustrates a single character I/O of a string. The string is read by the **scanf()** with the **%c** format. The input is performed by the **for** loop as for a regular array. The only difference is that we add the null character as the last element by **row[n-1]='\0'**. The output is performed similar to a regular array by the **while** loop. The output stops, when the null-character is encountered.

7.3. C++ specific string input/output.

Here we will consider specific C++ I/O features for the character strings. A string input can be performed character by character from the standard input. Each character can be placed in an array of characters. One can use the loops for the repetitive inputs.

```
#include <iostream.h>

main ( )
{
char x[10];
int m;
for (m=0; m<9; m++)
cin >> x[m];
x[9]='\0';
cout << x;
}
```

Program 7.7.

You enter any number of any characters, for instance: **qwertyuioqwertyuio**. The output of the program is **qwertyuio**. The **cin** inside the **for** loop reads 9 characters one by one. The 10th character is the null character, added by the program. We display the whole string using **cout << x**. Here, **x** is the name of the character array to be displayed. *So, you display a string with the **cout** by using the string name to the right of the insertion operator. It is important - the **cout** object stops a string output, when it encounters the null-character.* Since **cin** ignores any leading white spaces before the entered characters, it will only read and display the characters. Therefore, if we enter **abc def ghi jkl**, the output will still be **abcdefghi**. We could have done the output on a character by character basis with **cout << x[n]** inside a loop.

One can enter a character string using the **get()** function, written as **cin.get()**. It is written after a dot in the construction **cin.get()**. It is called a *member-function*. The form of writing it is analogous to the structure members. We will study later why.

The **cin** object can read a character string at once. As usually, the **cin** object ignores any leading white spaces before the first character of the string. It reads a string, until the first white character is encountered. Consider following example illustrating it.

```
#include <iostream.h>

main ( )
{
char x[30];
cin >> x;
cout << x;
}
```

Program 7.8.

You enter any string, for instance,
```
How are you?
```
The output is

How

The **cin** reads the characters, until it encountered the white space between the words. This is why it reads only one word "**How**". How does the **cin** know, that the input is a character string? The extracted data is stored in a character array **x[]**. This tells the computer, that the input should be a character string. Pay attention, we use only the name of the character array, in which the data is stored, to enter the data with **cin**.

One can also use the member-function **get()** to enter the data. It can be written in three different ways. The **cin.get()** used with no arguments reads the first entered from a keyboard character (even a white character) and returns it. An expression **a=cin.get()** will assign a character to a **char** variable **a**. One can also use this member-function as **cin.get(a)**. In this case, the first white or non-white character read from the keyboard will be assigned to the **char** variable **a** in its argument.

One can also call **get()** with three arguments. Its prototype is

```
cin.get (char arr, int size, char del);
```

The first parameter of this function is a name of a character array **arr**. The second argument **size** is the number of the characters to be entered. The third argument **del** is some character. The function reads up to **size-1** number of characters (including white spaces) from the keyboard and places them into the array **arr**. It automatically adds a null-character to the end. Thus, the **size** cannot exceed the total number of the array elements. The **del** argument is some character. If it is entered, it would terminate an input even before the **size** number of characters is read. Let's say, we write **cin.get(arr, 30, 'a')**. The character input is terminated when one or both of the events are true: when the function has encountered the character **a**, when 29 characters have been read. If the function encounters that character **a**, it will not be placed into the array **arr**. One does not have to specify that special character. It is a default function parameter specified as the newline character. Consider an example.

```
#include <iostream.h>

main ( )
{
char x[20];
cin.get (x, 20);
cout << x;
}
```

Program 7.9.

You enter

How are you doing today? and press **ENTER**.

The output is

How are you doing t

One can also use the **getline()** member-function in **cin.getline()**. It has the same three parameters as **get()** member-function and operates in exactly same way.

One can use **write()** and **read()** member-functions for an unformatted I/O. Both functions have similar prototypes.

```
cout.write (char arr, int size);
cin.read (char arr, int size);
```
The **write()** function copies **size** number of characters from the character array **arr** to the monitor screen. The **read()** function copies **size** number of characters from the keyboard to character array **arr**. Consider an example.

```
#include <iostream.h>

main ( )
{
char x[20];
int m;
cin.read (x, 20);
for (m=0; m<20; m++)
cout << x[m];
}
```

Program 7.10.

You type in any number of characters. The program displays 20 of them. We display the characters one by one. The unformatted input does not add the null-character to the end of the string automatically. We could have displayed the content of the array **x** without any loops, simply by **cout.write(x, 20)**. One can also display a string using it directly as an argument. For instance,

```
cout.write ("How are you?", 12);
```
One can also use the member-function **width()**. Its argument in **cout.width(n)** or **cin.width(n)** specifies the maximum number of characters to be displayed or read respectively. The **cin.width(n)** terminates the data input, after **n** characters have been read from the keyboard, or the first white character after a non-white group of characters has been encountered. If **n** is set to 0, the **cin** reads the characters until it encounters the white space. The **cout.width(n)** terminates the data output, after it has displayed **n** characters on the screen, or the null-character has been encountered. If **n** is set to 0, the **cout** displays the characters, until it reaches a null-character. The width is set to 0 after each insertion or extraction on some compilers. Next program illustrates the string I/O with the specified width.

```
#include <iostream.h>

main ( )
{
char x[20];
cin.width (20);
cin >>x;
cout.width (20);
cout << x;
```

```
}
```

Program 7.11.

You enter any number of characters. The program displays up to 20 characters.

One can use the **setw(n)** manipulator for the character string I/O. The argument **n** specifies the number of the characters to be displayed. One should include additional **<iomanip.h>** header file in this case. Consider following example.

```
#include <iostream.h>
#include <iomanip.h>

main ( )
{
char x[20];
cin >> setw (10) >>x;
cout << setw(20) << x;
}
```

Program 7.12.

You enter any number of characters. The program displays up to 10 of the entered characters. The leading white characters are ignored. The input is terminated, if a white space following any of the characters have been encountered, or 9 characters have been read. This means, that if you enter

ababababababababababab

the output will be

ababababa

7.4. Standard library functions.

C++ inherited from C some standard library functions for actions on the character strings. We discuss them in Chapter 20. Here, we will consider only some functions for: copying strings (**strcpy**, **strncpy**), string concatenation (**strcat**, **strncat**). The **<string.h>** header file describes those functions. It must be included as

```
#include <string.h>
```

any time when any of those functions is called. Unfortunately, each function uses the pointers, that we do not know yet. This is why we will give the proper treatment to all the functions in Chapter 20, after we study the pointers in the next chapter.

The **strcpy()** function is written in the form

```
strcpy (line1, line2);
```

It copies the content of the character array **line2** to the array **line1**. The **line1** and **line2** are the array names. The **strncpy()** function is written in a form

```
strncpy (line1, line2, n);
```

The **strncpy()** function copies first **n** characters of **line2** to the array **line1**. The **strncpy()** function typically does not add the null-character to the end of the copied string. If you want to display the copied characters as a string, add the null-character. Following program illustrates **strcpy()** function.

```
#include <iostream.h>
#include <string.h>

main ( )
{
char x[40];
char y[40]="How are you?";
strcpy (x, y);
cout << y << endl;
}
```

Program 7.13.

The output of the program is

```
How are you?
```

The **strcat()** function is written in a form

```
strcat (line1, line2);
```

It appends the second string **line2** to the end of the first **line1**. The null-character of the first string is deleted. The null-character of the second string completes the new combined string. The **line2** string remains unchanged. The **strcat()** function is written in the form

```
strncat (line1, line2, n);
```

It appends first **n** characters of the string **line2** to the end of the string **line1**. Consider following example, illustrating **strcat()** function.

```
#include <iostream.h>
#include <string.h>

main ( )
{
char x[40]="How are you?";
char y[40]=" Thanks, I am fine.";
strcat (x, y);
cout << x << endl;
}
```

Program 7.14.

The output of the program is

```
How are you? Thanks, I am fine.
```

We now have enough knowledge to write the programs, that will perform the same operations as the described library function. Consider following program, that copies a content of one string into another one.

```
#include <iostream.h>

void mycopy (char a[], char b[])
{
int m=0;
while (b[m] !='\0')
{
a[m]=b[m];
m++;
}
a[m]='\0';
}

main ( )
{
char x[40];
char y[40]=" Thanks, I am fine.";
mycopy (x, y);
cout << x << endl;
}
```

Program 7.15.

The output of the program is

    Thanks, I am fine.

   The above program copies the content of the **y[]** string to **x[]**. It consists of two functions: **main()** and **mycopy()**. The **mycopy()** has two array parameters: **a[]** and **b[]**. It copies a content of the array **b[]** into **a[]**. It is equivalent to the **strcpy()** library function.

EXERCISES.

1. Run all the programs given in this chapter if you have an access to a computer.
2. Write two programs that perform the same task. They prompt the user to enter a string. After the string has been entered, they ask to select the number of the first and the last character to display. The program, then, displays a fragment of that string beginning and ending with the characters whose numbers were selected. For instance, you enter

    How are you?

and specify to display a fragment beginning from the 5th and ending with the 8th character. The program displays

    are

Both programs should check if a user specifies the character numbers that exist in the string. For instance, a program should generate an error message if for the above string you specify to display a fragment from the 6th to 20th character. Try to structure your programs in functions. The first program should use C I/O and the second one should use

C++ I/O tools.

3. Write a program that compares two strings. If both strings are identical, it displays a proper message. There is a standard library function that performs that action.

4. Write two programs that prompt a user to enter a string and looks for a certain character in the entered string. They display the number of times a specified character appears in the string and every position at which it appears. The first program should use C I/O and the second one should use C++ I/O tools.

5. Write two programs, both capable of storing a string of 40 characters long. Both should allow to delete and insert any character. Both programs should check, if an entered string has a length of no more than 40 characters (including null-termination character). The same check should be performed, when inserting a character into a string. Try to structure your programs in functions. The first program should use C I/O and the second one should use C++ I/O tools.

6. Write a program that permits to enter up to 10 words, each containing up to 20 characters. It then sorts and displays all the words in an alphabetical order.

7. Write a program that reads a string from an input and recognizes if it is an integer, floating- point number or a character sequence. For instance, if we enter 341, the program should display a message indicating that we have entered an integral number.

8. Write a program that reads a phrase and displays capitalized first letters of each word. For example, if we enter "How are you?", the program displays **HAY**.

9. Write a program that reads two strings and adds a certain number of characters from the second string to the end of the first one.

10. One of the first spy codes used numbers instead of letters. They were easy to break, because each language has certain rules. For instance, you read a number of pages in any book. Some alphabet letters appear in a text with certain average frequency. Knowing those frequencies allowed to assume that certain numbers correspond to certain letters. Then, the cryptologists tried to read simple words, identified other letters. It allowed to brake a code after code. Write a program that reads a string up to 40 characters and displays every letter appeared in that string and the number of times it has appeared.

11. Write a program that reads simple questions from a keyboard, like

        Do you go to school?

and replies on them. A positive or negative answer should be selected randomly. You can use a random number function from the chapter on standard library functions. It randomly selects numbers within a certain range. Half of the range can correspond to positive and half to the negative answer on a question. If a number generated by a random number function falls, for example, into a lower half of the range, the program responds negatively. If the function generates a number from another half of the interval, a positive answer on the entered question is given. The answer on the above question can be something like

        No I don't. I don't go to school.

12. Write a small word-processor program with a spell-check. It should contain a spelling of a few words. The program should permit a user to enter a phrase up to 80 characters long. It then should go over each word in the entered string and check each word spelling comparing them with the stored words. If no stored word matches the word in a string, a program should display a menu prompting a user to skip or to type in a correct version of

a word. Whatever an answer is, it should then ask a user, if this word should be added to the library of stored words in the word-processor. If the answer is "Yes", the word should be added to the library of stored words. If a word in the entered string matches any of the stored words and is written incorrectly, a user should be given an option whether he or she wants to correct the spelling. Since it is an exercise, do not use a library of more than 10-15 words up to 15 characters each. However, ask your class instructor about the size of that word processor.

CHAPTER 8

POINTERS.

8.1. Introduction to pointers.

You can be reached by mailing a letter to your home address. Each memory cell has an address in the computer. Your address can include the state, city, street, building and apartment number. Computer cell address is just a cell number. Each memory cell can be addressed by its number. A computer reaches its memory cells by their numbers.

Suppose, we have an **int** type variable **z** and we want to use it. We can easily access that variable just by calling it by name. This variable is just one cell in the computer memory among millions of others. When we declare a variable, this cell is allocated in the memory. We call a variable by name to operate with it. For example, we make an assignment simply by **z=5**. The computer finds the cell allocated for **z** and puts 5 in this location. You, as a programmer, do not have to worry, where to allocate a place for **z**. You do not have to worry, how much space to allocate. You even do not have to worry about the address in the memory, where to look for **z**. It is done by the computer. You just type in the name of the variable, the computer takes care of finding this variable. This is known as a direct call, or call by name.

C++ allows you to call a variable using the address of its cell. For instance, let's introduce another variable **ptr**. One can make the value of **ptr** equal to the *address* or cell number of any other variable. A variable holding an address is called a *pointer variable*, or simply a *pointer*. A pointer name is just an identifier. Pointer variable is a special kind of a variable. One should tell the computer, that the variable **ptr** is a pointer. Thus, a pointer variable should be declared a bit different. For instance,

```
int * ptr;
```

Here **ptr** is just a name of the variable. Asterisk ***** shows, that this variable will be a "pointer to" another object (which can be a variable, array, structure and so on). It is called an *indirection* operator. The data type **int** tells us, that it will be a pointer to a variable of type **int**. So, we can use **ptr**, as a pointer to any variable of type **int**. A pointer declaration indicates to what data type objects can that pointer point to. Since variable **z**, introduced earlier here, is of type **int**, we can use **ptr** as a pointer to **z**. If **z** were of type **float**, we could not use **ptr** pointer for **z**. If you declare a pointer to a certain data type, it can point only to the objects of this data type. To use **ptr** as a pointer to **float** type variable, it must be declared as a pointer to a **float** type as

```
float * ptr;
```

Thus, **float *** in the last declaration specifies, we declare a pointer to the **float** data type. We declare the variable **ptr** to be a pointer to the type **float** variables.

Let's introduce the operator " **&** ", that is called an *address operator*. You know, when a variable is declared a cell is allocated to hold it. You can call that variable by its name. But what if you need to know the address of that cell, that stores our variable? When **&** is used immediately before a variable, it implies to the address or the location of the cell, where the variable is contained. So, **&z** is the address of the cell, where the variable **z** is stored. This address is a number. We can assign it to a proper pointer. For instance, a pointer declared as a pointer to **int** type can hold an address of an **int** type variable. The address can be assigned to a pointer by the assignment operator

```
ptr=& z;
```

It assigns the address of the cell allocated for **z** to the variable **ptr**. Assume, **ptr** is a pointer to **int** and **z** has **int** data type. This assignment is shown in Fig. 8.1. We made up the address of the cell containing **z** as equal to 7845. The content of the cell **ptr** becomes the number 7845, which is the address of the cell containing **z**. Now, **ptr** "points" towards **z** cell. Cell **z** can be empty. It can also contain any integer, because **z** has **int** type. The pointer **ptr** just directs us to it. We can put a value into **z** cell. Let's assign a value to **z**.

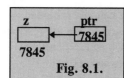

Fig. 8.1.

```
z=10;
```

This puts the value 10 inside **z** cell. It is done with the assignment operator, without any pointers. Same can be done with the pointers. The content of **z** cell can be accessed by its address stored in the pointer to it. One can just write

```
*ptr=10;
```

Here, the value 10 has been assigned to ***ptr**. The form ***ptr** accesses the cell, whose address (7845 in our case) is stored in the pointer **ptr** cell (Fig. 8.1). The computer accesses the cell with the address 7845, that belongs to the variable **z**, and puts the value 10 into it. We review it in **Program 8.1**.

```
#include <iostream.h>

main ( )
{
int x=5;
int * a;
a=&x;
cout << "x=" << x << ", " << "*a=" << *a << "\n"
     << "&x=" << &x << ", " << "a=" << a << "\n";
*a=10;
cout << "x=" << x << ", " << "*a=" << *a << "\n";
}
```

Program 8.1.

The output of the program is
```
x=5, *a=5
&x=0x1ae8, a=0x1ae8
x=10, *a=10
```

We declare the **int** type variable **x=5** and a pointer **a** to the type **int**. We assign the address of the variable **x** to **a** by **a=&x**. Since **a** points towards **x**, one can change the value of **x** by direct assignment **x=10** or by *de-reference* ***a=10**.

Program 8.1 displays the initial value of **x=5**. It is accessed as **x** and ***a** to show you the equivalence of two notations. We also show you the address of cell **x** by displaying **&x** and **a**. In our case it was 0x1ae8. That address might be different on your computer. It depends from where does your system allocate a cell for the variable **x**. We, then, change the value of **x** to 10 by ***a=10**. New value is displayed in the same two notations. We also caution you, never choose the address of the variable by yourself. This can crash the system or some software installed on your computer.

The indirection operator ***** has two different meanings in C. It specifies a pointer in the declarations. Remember, we have declared **int *ptr** in the beginning of the chapter or **int *a** in **Program 8.1**? The indirection operator ***** specified pointers **ptr** and **a** there. The indirection operator is also used to access an object anywhere else but the declaration. For example, we accessed the variable **x** as ***a** in **Program 8.1**. So, you can assign a value to **x** or display the value of **x** accessing it as ***a**.

There are some restrictions on using the address operator "**&**". It cannot be applied to a constant, i.e., something like **&125** is illegal. It cannot be applied to the expressions involving some operators, as for example, arithmetic operators such as **/**. Therefore, the reference **&(var/2-200)** is an error. The address operator cannot be applied to a register variable. Suppose, you have a declared register variable **x** and pointer **qo**. Then, **qo=&x** might cause an error. The register variables are stored not in the internal memory but rather in the CPU registers. Their storage has no address.

A pointer, as any variable, can be initialized in its declaration. We can call the pointer declaration as definition as well. It has no difference as in case of the regular variables. So far, when we defined a pointer **ptr** to an **int** variable **z**, we did it in two steps.

```
int *ptr;
ptr=&z;
```
If we initialize a pointer while declaring, it can be done in one line.
```
int * ptr =&z;
```
One can, sometimes, find a declaration
```
int **ptr;
```
which is perfectly legal. Each of the stars means "pointer to". It declares a pointer to a pointer to a variable of **int** type. One can use even *****ptr** and so on. If you intend to use a pointer to a pointer, it should be declared as such. We show it in **Program 8.2**.

```
#include <stdio.h>

main ( )
{
char var='A';
char * pt1, ** pt2, *** pt3;
pt1=&var;
pt2=&pt1;
pt3=&pt2;
```

```
printf ("%d, %d, %d\n", pt1, pt2, pt3);
printf ("%c, %d, %c, %c\n", *pt1, *pt2, **pt2, ***pt3);
}
```

Program 8.2.

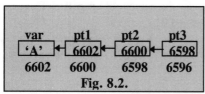

var   pt1   pt2   pt3

Fig. 8.2.

The output of the program is

    6602, 6600, 6598

    A, 6602, A, A

We have declared pointers to pointers in this program. Here **pt3** is a pointer to a pointer **pt2**, which is a pointer to pointer **pt1**. The **pt1** is a pointer to the **char** type variable **var**. The Fig. 8.2 shows, that **pt1** holds the address of the cell **var**, **pt2** stores the address of **pt1**, and **pt3** holds the address of **pt2**. All the pointers must have the same data type. The ***pt1** accesses the content of the cell **var**. Thus, the **printf("%c", *pt1)** will print **A**. It is called the first level of indirection. To access the content of **var** cell, you would have to address to it with ****pt2**. This will get **A** for you. It is called the second level of indirection. To access **var,** you would have to type *****pt3**. It is the third level of indirection.

We know, that the way of accessing a variable by its address using the pointer as ***pt** is call by de-reference. The number of stars, that have to be attached to the pointer to reference the value of a variable is called the *level of indirection*. We have considered three levels of indirection.

We will now describe a few examples of accessing different values with the pointers. Follow Fig. 8.2. The ***pt2** refers to the content of the cell **pt2**. It is the number 6600. The form ****pt3** is the same as ***(*pt3)**. It consists of the ***pt3**, that is the content of **pt3** cell. It is the number 6598. But this number is the address of the cell **pt2**. Thus, the ***(*pt3)** accesses the content of the cell **pt2** with the address 6598. This cell contains the number 6600. If we display ****pt3**, it will be the number 6600. You can run **Program 8.2**, and play with pointers to pointers. Do not expect to get the same pointer addresses as ours. Your data can be placed into different cells.

Next program gives you some additional experience in working with the pointers. It illustrates simple assignments with the pointers.

```
#include <iostream.h>

main ( )
{
int  m=5;
int *fr;
fr= &m;
*fr=m+1;
cout << m << ", " << (*fr+10);
}
```

Program 8.3.

The output of that program is

        6, 16

It should be easy for you to follow this program. It declares variable **m** and the pointer **fr**. It then makes **fr** to point to the cell **m**. We, then, perform an assignment **m=m+1** using the pointer instead of **m**. This assignment looks like ***fr=m+1**. The value of variable **m** is displayed after this assignment. This changes the content of the cell **m**. The **cout** displays the **(m+10)**. We have written it as **(*fr +10)**.

We wanted to emphasize following by this program. Once a pointer is assigned to point to a cell, it will point there until reassigned. You can access that cell, do assignments, arithmetical and other operations using that pointer.

8.2. Pointers and functions.

8.2.1. Passing and returning a pointer.

You can pass a pointer as an argument of a function. A function that accepts pointer arguments must have the parameters of the pointer types in its definition header and prototype. You pass a pointer argument by its name from the caller function.

It is called *cal- by-reference,* when an address and not a value is passes as a function argument. *When the pointer is passed as an argument, its value is copied into the corresponding formal parameter. Therefore, any operations on the formal parameter will not affect the passed to a function pointer. The value of that pointer cannot be changed. But the value of the cell this pointer points to can be changed by the called function. The change will retain, after the control is returned back to a caller.* You should remember that property. It is different from a call to a function, with passing a value of a variable as an argument, named a call-by-value and studied in Chapter 5.

Following program illustrates a call-by-reference. It takes a value, adds 10 to it, and displays the result.

```
#include <iostream.h>

void  ten_val(int *q);

main ( )
{
int n=10;
int *pr=&n;
ten_val (pr);
cout << *pr;
}

void ten_val (int *q)
{
*q=*q+10;
```

```
q=q+50;
}
```

Program 8.4.

The output of the program is

    20

It consists of two functions: **main()** and **ten_val()**. The **ten_val()** function has a pointer as its formal parameter in the definition header and prototype

```
void ten_val (int *q)
```

The **main()** calls **ten_val()** passing the pointer **pr** as an argument.

```
ten_val (pr);
```

Notice, we pass a pointer calling it by name. The pointer **pr** points to **n** in **main()** routine. It is passed as an argument to the **ten_val()** function. The value of the cell it points to is increased by 10 by the ***q=*q+10** expression. We also increase the value of the very pointer by 50 with **q=q+50**. You will learn later, one can subtract and add an integer to a pointer. Thus, the pointer **q** is now pointing to a different cell. When the control is given back to **main()**, the **cout << *pr** is executed. This displays the value of **n** increased by 10. As you see, the pointer **pr** still points to the same cell, even though its copy has been made pointing to a different cell in the **ten_val()** routine. The content of the **n** cell passed through the pointer **pr** to the **ten_val()** function has changed. You can see, call by reference, indeed, changes the content of the passed cell.

We could call the **ten_val()** function a bit differently. If a function is defined to have a pointer argument, it expects to receive an address. It does not matter whether we send the address as a pointer, or as an address operator. Thus, the function can be called as **ten_val(&n)** as well. It will produce the same effect.

We give you another example of pointers application. This program reads two values from a keyboard and prints ten folds the initial values following in the ascending order.

```
#include <iostream.h>

void swap_v (int *ptr1, int *ptr2);

main ( )
{
int min, max;
int *fq1=&min, *fq2=&max;
cin >> min;
cin >> max;
swap_v (fq1, fq2);
cout << "min*10=" << min << ", " << "max*10=" << max
     << "\n";
}
void swap_v (int *ptr1, int *ptr2)
{
int x;
if (*ptr1>*ptr2)
```

```
{
x= *ptr1;
*ptr1=*ptr2*10;
*ptr2=x*10;
}
else
{
*ptr1*=10;
*ptr2*=10;
} }
```

Program 8.5.

Enter two integers, for instance, 30 20 and press **ENTER**. The output of the program is
      min*10=200, max*10=300
If you enter 20 30, the numbers still go as 200, 300. Thus, the program swaps the entered numbers, if it is necessary to position them in the ascending order. The numbers are also multiplied by ten.

   The program consists of two functions: **main()** and **swap_v()**. The **main()** function declares two variables **min, max** and two pointers to them **fq1, fq2**. It reads two values from a keyboard, calls the **swap_v()** function, displays both numbers. The **swap_v()** function puts the numbers in ascending order and multiplies them by 10.

   The **swap_v()** function first compares the content of two cells corresponding to variables **min** and **max**. If ***ptr1>*ptr2**, the values of two variables are swapped by
      x= *ptr1;
      *ptr1=*ptr2*10;
      *ptr2=x*10;
The value contained inside a cell de-referenced by **ptr1** is assigned to the variable **x**. Then, the value of the cell pointed to by **ptr2** is multiplied by ten and placed into the cell pointed to by **ptr1**. After that, the initial value of **ptr1** stored by **x** is multiplied by 10 and placed into ***ptr2**. If the values are entered in the right order, they are just multiplied by 10. The new content of both cells is displayed by the **cout** in **main()**. Here, we passed the addresses of both cells **min** and **max** to the **swap_v()** function. The function was able to swap them and arrange in certain order.

   A function can also return a pointer. Following program illustrates that.

```
#include <iostream.h>

int *search(int a[ ], int p);

main ( )
{
static int row[5]={20, 10, 5, 40, 100};
int * pr;
pr=search(row, 5);
if (pr!=NULL)
```

```
cout << *pr;
else
cout << pr;
}

int *search (int a[ ], int p)
{
int k=1;
int *aq;
for (int m=0; m<p; m++)
{
if (a[m]==100)
{
aq=&a[m];
k=0;
p=m-2;
} }
if (k)
aq=NULL;
return (aq);
}
```

Program 8.6.

The output of the program is the value 100.

The program consists of two functions: **main()** and **search()**. The **search()** function is defined as returning a pointer.

```
int *search(int a[ ], int p)
```

It has **int** ***** type. Thus, it returns a pointer to **int** type value. The **main()** function declares and initializes an array **row[5]**. We also declare a pointer **pr**. **main()** calls the **search()** function and assigns the returned pointer to pointer **pr**. The **pr** pointer is compared to **NULL** pointer. If **pr** is not equal to **NULL**, the value it points to is printed. Otherwise, we print the **NULL** pointer, which is 0.

The **search()** function searches the passed array **row** for the value 100. If this array contains the value 100, then: it is assigned to the cell pointed to by the pointer **aq** as **aq=&a[m]**, variable **k** used as a flag is set to zero, the loop is terminated by making **p** less than **m** with **p=m-2**. In our case, 100 is at the end of the array. It is not necessary to terminate the loop by making **p** less than **m**. However, you can use it, when you have a long array. The value you search for can be in the middle or in the beginning of that array. So, it is a good idea to terminate the search, after it is found. If the value searched for has not been found, the **search()** function assigns a **NULL** value to the returned pointer **aq**. The way to check it is by comparing **k** to zero. If it is non-zero, the value has not been found.

8.2.2. Pointers to functions.

C++ allows to introduce a pointer to a function. In order to use a pointer to a function, one has to perform three step operation: to correctly declare a pointer to a function, to assign a pointer to a function, to call that function using the assigned pointer with the proper argument values.

Let's consider, how to declare a pointer to a function. A pointer cannot be used to point to any function. It should be declared to match a particular function, for which it will be used. In order to declare a pointer **fpt** to a function, one writes

```
return_ type (*fpt) (arg1_type, arg2_type, ... );
```

This statement declares a pointer to a function, that returns a value of **return_type** and has parameters of following data types: **arg1_type**, **arg2_type**, ... An example is

```
int (*fpt) (float, int, int);
```

Here, we declare the pointer **fpt** to some function. That yet unknown to us function must return an **int**. All the parentheses **int (*fpt)** in that pointer **fpt** declaration are necessary. Otherwise, this statement would be treated as a declaration of a function **fpt**, that returns a pointer to an **int**. We specify three data types in the brackets (**float, int, int**). This means, that the pointer will be applied to a function having three arguments: the first one of **float** type, the second and the third of **int** type.

After the pointer to a function has been declared, it can be assigned to a function. Before the assignment takes place, the function should be defined in the program. The pointer to the function should be of the same type as the returned by that function value. It should have the same number and types of parameters as they follow in that function prototype. If the function returns the value of type **int**, the pointer to that function must be declared as **int(*fpt)(...)**. If a function returns a **float** value, the pointer to that function should be declared as **float(*fpt)(...)**.

Let's show how to use a pointer to a function. Let's say, we have declared a pointer.

```
int (*fpt) (int);
```

The prototype of the function, to which pointer will be pointing to is

```
int play (int x);
```

The pointer can be assigned to the matching function by a simple assignment

```
fpt =play;
```

In order to call that function with the argument **x=4**, one writes

```
(*fpt) (x); or (*fpt) (4);
```

A pointer to a function without any arguments should look like

```
int (*fpt) ( );
```

It can be a pointer only to a function that does not have any parameters at all, because the pointer also has no parameters. A pointer to a function without parameters also has a form, that uses type **void** instead of the parameters as

```
int (*fpt) (void);
```

Consider following program, illustrating pointers to functions.

```
#include <iostream.h>
```

```
int sum(int x, int y);

main( )
{
int a=2, b=4, res;
int (*fp)(int, int);
fp=sum;
res= (*fp)(a, b);
cout << res;
}

int sum(int x, int y)
{
x=x+y;
return(x);
}
```

Program 8.7.

The output of the program is 6. It is a fairly straightforward program. It finds a sum of two arguments passed to the **sum()** function, and returns it to the caller. This program shows you how to create and use the pointer **fp** to the function **sum()**.

Following example shows an array of pointers to different functions.

```
#include <iostream.h>

void three (int x, int y);
void four (int x, int y);
void five (int x, int y);

main ( )
{
void (*qp[3])(int, int) = {three, four, five};
int m, k, r;
cout << " Enter two numbers to add.\n";
cin >> m;
cin >> k;
cout << "Enter 0 to multiply the sum by 3, "
     << "1 to multiply by 4, 2-by 5.\n";
cin >> r;
(*qp[r]) (m, k);
cout << "  end\n";
}

void three (int x, int y)
{  cout << (3*(x+y));  }
```

```
void four (int x, int y)
{   cout << (4*(x+y));   }

void five (int x, int y)
{   cout << (5*(x+y));   }
```
Program 8.8.

The program prompts the user to enter two numbers to calculate their sum.

```
Enter two numbers to add.
```

We enter 8 9 and press **ENTER**. One can press **ENTER** after entering each of them as well. We get

```
Enter 0 to multiply the sum by 3, 1 to multiply by 4,
2-by 5.
```

We enter 1. The program displays **68   end**

This program is not as difficult as it seems. It consists of four functions: **main()**, **three()**, **four()**, **five()**. The **three( )**, **four()** and **five()** functions are similar. Each of them has the return type **void**. Each of them accepts two arguments of **int** type, computes the sum, multiplies it by the corresponding number, and displays the result. The **main()** function provides the input of two values to be added and multiplied and asks the user to select by what number to multiply the sum. We shell concentrate on how do we create an array of pointers and assign them to the functions.

We introduce an array of pointers to functions and initialize it at once by

```
void (*qp[3])(int, int) = {three, four, five};
```

The **void(*qp[3])(int, int)** is a definition of an array of function pointers. We initialize this array and assign each function in **{}** braces to a pointer. It is the same as

```
qp[0]=three;   qp[1]=four; qp[2]=five;
```

Pointer **qp[0]** is assigned to the function **three()**, pointer **qp[1]** to the function **four()** and so on. Do not be afraid of the array elements **qp[0]**, **qp[1]**, **qp[2]**. Each of them is a pointer. They make a call of a particular function easy. It is done by

```
(*qp[r]) (m, k);
```

The arguments **m** and **k** will be passed to one of the functions. They are the numbers to be added. We select one of the array elements by choosing **r**. If we select **r=0**, the **(*qp[0])(m, k)** will be called. It points towards the **three()** function. This function will be called to execution. The "**end**" is displayed after function termination.

8.3. Pointers and arrays.

8.3.1. Introduction to pointers and arrays.

You must know, arrays and pointers are very closely related. *An array name is a constant. Its value determines the address of the first array element, i.e., an array name is, indeed, a pointer to the first element of that array.* Let's write

```
float s[200], *ptr;
```

It defines an array **s** and the pointer **ptr**. We can assign an address of the first array element to the variable **ptr** in two ways:

    ptr=s; or ptr=&s[0];

It is possible to write **ptr=s**, because the array name **s** is a pointer to the first array element **s[0]**. The **ptr=&s[0]** is equivalent to **ptr=s**, because it is the same thing. We assign the address of the first array element to the pointer **ptr**.

Look at the Fig. 8.3. Even though we made up the addresses on that figure, but it will help you to understand the idea of pointers and arrays. The **ptr** points to the first array element, e.g. to the memory cell with the address 8790. We know a property of any array, that its elements are placed in the order in the neighboring cells of the memory. If the first array element is located in the cell with address 8790, the second will be in the 8791 cell, third in 8792 cell and so on. When an array is declared, the computer allocates the cells in the memory, so, there is enough of them to hold all the array elements.

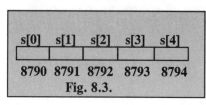

s[0] s[1] s[2] s[3] s[4]

8790 8791 8792 8793 8794

Fig. 8.3.

Pointers allow to do some operations with them. Let's consider a few examples of how to operate with the pointers. Let's assume, **ptr=s** in the beginning. If we write

    ptr=ptr+1;

It assigns a new value to **ptr**, and it is equal to **8790+1=8791**. Now ***ptr** accesses the content of the cell with the address 8791. It is the **s[1]** cell. If we add 1 again to the **ptr**, its value will become 8792. It will point to **s[2]**. So, we can refer to any **n** array element **s[n]**, by writing ***(ptr+n)**. Here, **s[0]** must be initially assigned to **ptr**, as we have discussed. For instance, to access the third array element, we write ***(ptr+2)**. Its value can be assigned to any variable. For example,

    x=*(ptr+2);

assigns the value of the third array element **s[2]** to the variable **x**.

One should be careful with the subscript **n** and the pointer **ptr**. If the pointer **ptr** was equal to **s**, then, **x=*(ptr+2)** must assign a value of **s[2]** to **x**. Suppose, you write **x=*(ptr+2)** again in a program. Then, the address before was 8792. You again add 2 to it. After that, it point to a cell **s[4]** with the address 8794. Subtracting 2 from the current value of the pointer

    ptr=ptr - 2;

will set it to point to **s[2]**. You can load any value in this cell. For example,

    *ptr=2.5;

The pointer was equal to 8794. The new value is **8794-2=8792**. That is an address of **s[2]**. The ***ptr=2.5** loads 2.5 into the cell, whose address the pointer **ptr** points to. Since it is the address of the element **s[2]**, 2.5 is assigned to **s[2]**.

The addresses of the adjacent cells of the array in Fig. 8.3 differ by 1. They might differ not only by one, but by two, for example. For instance, if the address of **s[0]** is 8790, the address of **s[1]** can be 8792. This should not bother you. Whenever you assign a pointer to an array element **ptr=s** and increase its value by one, it always points to the next array element. This means, that **ptr+1** in our case will point to the second array element **s[1]** and **ptr+n** shell point to **s[n]**. The computer will adjust the addresses in such a way, that if you increment a pointer by one, it will point towards the next array element up. Same is true for decreasing the pointer value.

We come to a conclusion. An array element can be accesses in the following ways:

1) It can be accessed by the index variable in its braces, as, for example, **s[n]**.

2) An array element can be accessed by a pointer. If we set a pointer to point to the first array element **ptr=s**, then, **ptr+n** is the address of array element **s[n]**. We can access any array element by regular indirection operator, as ***(ptr+n)**. Furthermore, a pointer has more flexibility. It can initially point to an address of any array element as **ptr=&s[n]**. You can subtract or add numbers to **ptr** in order to reach any array element. For instance, you make **ptr=s[2]**. You access **s[5]**, for example, by adding 3 to **ptr** pointer. It will be ***(ptr+3)**.

3) An array element **n** can be accessed by the ***(s+n)** expression, where **s** is the name of that array. We know, that the array name is the address of its first element. Therefore, adding **n** to it will reach its **s[n]** element.

Consider a program, that illustrates these three ways of accessing an array element.

```
#include <iostream.h>

main ( )
{
int arv[6]={10, 20, 30, 40, 50, 60};
int *w, m;
w=arv;
m=3;
cout << " We access arv[" << m << "]=" << (arv[m])
  << " We access *(w+2)=" << (*(w+2))
  << "\nWe access *(arv+1)=" << (*(arv+1));
}
```

Program 8.9.

The output of this program is

```
We access arv[3]=40 We access *(w+2)=30
We access *(arv+1)=20
```

8.3.2. Pointer arithmetic.

The pointers allow to perform some arithmetical and assignment operations on them. One can add or subtract the integral values from the pointers, as

```
ptr=ptr+2; or ptr=ptr-5;
```

One can use relational operators with pointers. Later you will learn, pointers can be used in the statements like **if(ptr1<=ptr2)**. A value of a pointer can be assigned to another one by the assignment operators, as for example, **ptr1=ptr2**. One can subtract or add two pointers and use increment and decrement operators with them. The

```
ptr ++; or ptr--;
```

subtract or add 1 to a pointer.

The pre- and post-increment operators have some peculiarities with the pointers. Look at the Fig. 8.3. We will introduce two pointers **ptr** and **qa** to the same data type. Let's assume, **ptr=s** and write an assignment

```
qa=ptr++;
```

This first assigns the address of **ptr** to **qa**. Thus, the value of **qa** is equal to 8790. After that, the value of the **ptr** is incremented by one. It should point to the address 8791 after that assignment. Thus **qa=8790** and **ptr=8791**. Pointer **qa** will point to **s[0]**, and **ptr** pointer will point to **s[1]**. Another assignment

```
qa=++ptr;
```

first increments **ptr** from 8790 to 8791. It, then, assigns this address to the **qa**. Both pointers should be equal to 8791 after the operation.

We will consider the assignments with **++*ptr** and ***++ptr**. To check them, let's presume, the pointer points to the address 8790 in Fig. 8.3. This is the array element **s[0]**. Its value we also assume to be 1.9. When ***++ptr** is executed, the **ptr** is set to the address **8790+1=8791**. It is **s[1]**. Then, the value of **s[1]** is accessed, so

```
x1=*++ptr;
```

assigns value of **s[1]** to **x**. If **s[1]** were equal to 20.5, then **x** becomes **20.5**.

Assume the same initial conditions, i.e., **ptr=s**. The expression

```
x1=++*ptr;
```

first accesses the content of **s[0]**, because nothing has happened with the address. Then, the value stored inside this cell, equal to 1.9, is increased by 1. The result of $1.9+1=2.9$ equals to 2.9. It is assigned to **x1**.

Let's perform the post-increment on the pointer **ptr**, which we presume pointing to the same array element **s[0]** with the address 8790.

```
*ptr++;
```

This expression would access the cell with the address 8790 first and then increment the value of **ptr** by one. Now we assign the value of that expression to another operand

```
x= *ptr++;
```

It assigns the value of **s[0]** to the variable **x**. Then, it increments the value of **ptr** by one. Consider **Program 8.10**.

```
#include <iostream.h>

main ( )
{
int arv[6]={10, 20, 30, 40, 50, 60};
int *w, m;
w=arv;
m=*w++;
cout << m << ", " << *w;
}
```

Program 8.10.

The output of the program is **10, 20**. It, indeed, assigns **arv[0]** to **m** and, then, increases **w** by 1, because the second array element is displayed, when we display ***w**. Use this program to check the pointer arithmetic explained above and given below in Table 8.1.

Just change the **m=*w++** line for each case.

Same is true for the decrement operator. The C++ language does not check, if you increment or decrement a pointer over the boundaries of an array. You can set a pointer to point to the array element before or after the last declared element. For example, you can refer to the cell before **s[0]** or after **s[4]** in Fig. 8.3. This might cause serious problems. Therefore, it is wise to check, if you refer to existing array element.

The pointer arithmetic is more applicable to the arrays, but can be used anywhere not only in applications with the arrays. Consider **Program 8.11**.

```
#include <stdio.h>

main ( )
{
int s[6];
int *ptr;
int n, m=0;
ptr=s;
for (n=0; n<6; ++n)
{
printf("Enter %d element\n", n);
scanf("%d", ptr);
++ ptr;
}
ptr=s;
while (m <6) {
printf ("What element to display? Enter number \
        greater than 5 to end.\n");
scanf("%d", &m);
ptr=ptr+m;
printf("The %d element is %d\n", m, *ptr);
ptr=ptr-m;
}}
```

Program 8.11.

This program allows to enter the **int** type array elements from the first to the last and to view them in the arbitrary order. It is done using pointers. We first declare an array **s[6]**, pointer **ptr**, variables **n** and **m**, and assign the address of the first array element to a pointer by **ptr=s**. All array elements are entered using **for** loop. The value of the **ptr** is increased by 1 each cycle using increment operator (**++ptr**). Thus, every new loop cycle increments **ptr** making it point to the next upper array element. The value of each array element is entered through the **scanf("%d", *ptr)** function. After the whole array has been entered, we can see its elements one by one in any order. It is implemented as the **while** loop. One can exit it by typing any number greater than 5.

The **ptr** is set to point to **s[0]** before the **while** loop. This is necessary, because the previous **for** loop has changed its value. We select any array element offsetting the value of the pointer **ptr** by **m** in **ptr=ptr+m**. Number **m** is added to the **ptr** each cycle. We select number **m** from 0 to 5, entering it through **scanf("%d \n", &m)**. An array element value is displayed by **printf()** function inside the **while** loop. The pointer is set to point to **s[0]** every time at the end of the cycle, by subtracting the very **m** number from the new value of the pointer. It is necessary to set the pointer to **s[0]** address before leaving loop cycle. We find **s[m]** by adding **m** to **ptr**. Hence, **ptr** should point to **s[0]** at the beginning of each **while** cycle.

We can achieve the same goal in the **while** loop, using the array name as a pointer.

```
while (m <6) {
printf ("what element to display? Enter number greater \
        than 5 to end.\n");
scanf("%d", &m);
ptr=s+m;
n=*(s+m);
printf("The %d element *(s+m)=%d, or *ptr=%d. \n",
       m, n, *ptr);    } }
```

Given loop can substitute the existing **while** loop in **Program 8.11**. The statement **ptr=s** before the **while** loop that sets **ptr** equal to **s** is not necessary, since we use **s** and **m** in **ptr=s+m** assignment. So, the expression **ptr=s+m** is quite legitimate. Because **ptr** pointer is a sum of **s**, that always points to the first array element, and **m**, the **ptr** does not need to be set to **s[0]** at the end of each loop.

Table 8.1. Pointer arithmetic.

Pointer notation	Explanation of the operation
p++	Post-increment: gets the value of p, then increments pointer by one p=p+1
p--	Post-decrement: gets the value of p, then decrements pointer by one as p=p-1
++p	Pre-increment: increments pointer by one p=p+1, then, gets the value of p
--p	Pre-decrement: decrements pointer by one p=p-1, then, gets the value of p
*(p++), *p++	Gets the value *p by de-reference, then increments p by one as p=p+1
++(*p), ++*p	Gets the value of *p, then increments that value by one as *p=*p+1
*(++p), *++p	Increments p, as p=p+1, then gets the value from the new address *(p+1)
*(p--), *p--	Gets the value of *p, then decrements p as p=p-1
*(--p), *--p	Decrements p, as p=p-1, then, gets the value at the new address *(p-1)
--(*p), --*p	Gets the value of *p, then decrements that value by one as *p=*p-1

To summarize we give you one more example. Let's assume, we need to access the fourth array element. It can be done referring to **s[3]**, or to ***(s+3)**. As an example, we assign the value 1000, to the fourth array element

```
s[3]=1000;
*(s+3) = 1000;
```

Those 2 assignment operators are identical, as you know.

8.3.3. An equivalence of arrays and pointers.

Previous sections have shown, that there is no practical difference in accessing the array elements using the regular notation **s[m]** or through the pointers. The array name is a pointer and can be used as such. We used **s** in **ptr=s+m** to access **s[m]** element in **Program 8.11**. It comes from a special deep relationship between the pointers and arrays in C and C++. Any array can be declared and handled by the pointers as well. The array and pointer syntax is interchangeable and can be mixed. We illustrate it in **Program 8.12**, that finds an array element with the greatest value.

```
#include <iostream.h>

int maxar ( int row[ ], int m)
{
int c1;
int *fp=row;
int *fpe=row+m-1;
c1=*fp;
for( ; fp<fpe; ++fp)
if (c1<*(fp+1))
c1=*(fp+1);
return (c1); }

main ( )
{
int ar[5];
int n;
for (n=0; n<5;++n)
{
cout << "enter integer element \n";
cin >> ar[n];
}
cout << "The maximum is " << maxar(ar, 5) << ".\n";
}
```

Program 8.12.

The program prompts a user to enter an integer array element. We enter an array of integral numbers

```
20   100   54   8   1
```

The output of the program is

```
The maximum is 100.
```

The program consists of two functions: **main()**, **maxar()**. The **main()** function declares an array **ar[5]** and performs an input of all array elements. It, then, prints the greatest numerical value of the array elements. The **maxar()** function finds the array element having a maximum value. It is plugged-in in **cout**.

The **maxar()** function takes two arguments - the array to be searched and the number of elements in this array. It uses a pointer notation. It declares two pointers. The first pointer ***fp=row** points towards the first array element of the parameter array **row**. The second pointer **fpe=row+m-1** points towards the last array element.

The function assigns the first array value to the variable **c1**. This value is compared consecutively to all other array elements. It is done by the **for** loop.

```
for( ; fp<fpe; ++fp)
if (c1<*(fp+1))
c1=*(fp+1);
```

This loop uses pointers as loop condition and loop expression. If any of the values compared to **c1** is greater, it will be assigned to **c1**. For instance, **row[2]>c1**. The **row[2]** value will be assigned to **c1**. The new value of **c1** is, then, compared with the rest of the array elements, starting from **row[3]**. If other value greater than the new **c1** value is found, it is assigned to **c1**. Let's presume, it is **row[3]>c1**. The value of **row[3]** is assigned to **c1**. The comparison goes on again starting from the next element after that, which is **row[4]**. The result of this search is the greatest numerical value in the array. It is returned to the caller and displayed. As you can see, we mix pointer and array notations in the program, and they work.

Next program triples the values of each **row[ ]** array element and displays them.

```
#include <iostream.h>

int *fill(int a[ ]);

main ( )
{
static int row[5]={20, 10, 5, 40, 100};
int * pr, k;
pr=fill(row);
for (k=0; k<5; k++)
cout << *(pr+k) << ", ";
}

int *fill(int a[ ])
{
int m;
```

```
static int arr[5];
for (m=0; m<5; m++)
arr[m]=3*a[m];
return (arr);
}
```

Program 8.13.

The output of this program is

```
60, 30, 15, 120, 300,
```

   You should be able to follow this program. We pass an array **row[]** as an argument of
the function **fill()**, that is called from **main()**. Function **fill()** triples each element of the passed array and stores their tripled values in another array **arr[]**. That
array is declared as **static** inside the **fill()** function. The **fill()** function returns
to the **main()** a pointer to the first element of its array **arr[]**. This array is, then,
handled from **main()** by the **pr** pointer. The array **arr[]** is not destroyed after the
fill() function terminates its execution, because it is declared as **static**.

8.3.4. Arrays of pointers.

   An array is known to be a group of variables of the same type. One can also use an array
of pointers. Each element of that array is a pointer. Those array elements can be the
pointers to other variables, structures, arrays, strings, unions and even pointers. An array
of pointers should be declared as such, for instance,

```
int *ptr[20];
```

Here, we have declared an array of twenty elements. Each of those elements is a pointer to
a variable of type **int**. The array of pointers can be initialized similarly to a regular array,
for instance,

```
char *word[10]={"abandon", "abase", "abash",
                         abate", "abbey"};
```

The above line declares and partially initializes an array of pointers to strings.

   Everything we have studied for the arrays is true for the arrays consisting of pointers. You
just have to get used to an idea, that each array element is, in fact, not a variable, but rather
a pointer to another object. That object can be a variable, string, another array, structure,
union, function and so on. This allows a tremendous flexibility in manipulating those
objects. **Program 8.14** illustrates the array of pointers.

```
#include <iostream.h>

main ( )
{
static char *word[]={"Programming ", "is ", "very ",
                     "interesting."};
for (int m=0; m<4; m++)
cout << word[m];
```

```
}
```
Program 8.14.

The output of the program is
```
Programming is very interesting.
```
The program declares and initializes the array of pointers ***word[]**. Each element of that array is a pointer to a string. The asterisk *****, used in the declaration of that array, specifies that it is a pointer. We display each array element using **for** loop. Since each element is a pointer, the **cout<<word[m]** displays a word in every loop.

8.4. Pointers and structures.

8.4.1. Pointers to structure members.

One can assign a pointer not only to a variable, or an array. A pointer can be assigned to a structure variable as well. Let's declare structure **number** and the variable **fn1** by
```
struct number
{
int x;
int y; };
number fn1;
```
We can assign a pointer **vp1** to that structure variable **fn1** in the same way as to any other variable. One has to declare **vp1** first as a pointer to a variable of **number** type. It should be, then, assigned to point to a structure variable, as shown below.
```
number * vp1;
vp1=&fn1;
```
Once we have made such a statement, any structure member can be accessed by writing
```
(*pointer).member
```
For example, we write **(*vp1).x** to access the member **x** of variable **fn1**. So, to assign, for example, the value 30 to that member, one writes
```
(*vp1).x=30;
```
Pointers are very often used with the structures. A special operator even was invented to simplify the addressing to the structure members. This operator is "**->**", that consists of dash or 'minus', followed by 'greater than' sign. To access any structure member by pointer, one writes
```
pointer->member
```
The **(*vp1).x** can be also rewritten as **vp->x**. Consider **Program 8.15**.

```
#include <stdio.h>

main ( )
{
struct number
{
```

```
int x;
int y;
};
number fn1, *vp;
vp=&fn1;
vp->x = 2;
(*vp).y =3;
vp->x = vp->x+vp->y;
vp->y= vp->x - vp->y;
printf("vp->x=%d, vp->y=%d.\n", vp->x, vp->y);
}
```

Program 8.15.

The output of the program is

    vp->x=5, vp->y=2.

Program 8.15 introduces the **number** structure, structure variable **fn1** and pointer **vp**. The **vp** pointer is assigned to point towards the variable **fn1**. After that, **fn1** can be accessed by pointing to it. Two structure members **x** and **y** of variable **fn1** are assigned values using the **vp** pointer. We access **x** and **y** members, using two different ways to access a member with pointers. **x** is accessed as **vp->x**, and **y** via **(*vp).y**. The program illustrates both ways of access. The new **x** is equal to **x=x+y=2+3=5**. The new **y** is equal **y=x-y=5-3=2**.

8.4.2. Structures containing pointers.

Pointer can also be a member of a structure **Program 8.16** illustrates that.

```
#include <iostream.h>

main( )
{

typedef struct num
{
int *x;
int *y;
} NUM;

NUM *pt, val;
int n=10, m=20;
pt=&val;
val.x=&n;
pt->y=&m;
cout << "*val.x=" << *val.x << ", " << "*pt->y="
```

```
          << *pt->y << "\n";
}
```

Program 8.16.

The output of this program is

```
    *val.x=10, *pt->y=20
```

The program declares the structure **num**, containing two pointers as its members: **x** and **y**. A structure containing pointers can also have variables, arrays, pointers and so on as its members. Our structure contains only pointers, because we wrote it just for pointer demonstration. We also declare a structure variable **var**, pointer to that structure **pt** and two variables **n** and **m**.

We assign the pointer **pt** to point towards the structure variable **var** by **pt=&var**. The structure members are assigned to point to variables **n** and **m** by

```
    val.x=&n;
    pt->y=&m;
```

Here, we wanted to show, that **x** and **y** can be accessed as any structure member by **val.x** or **pt->y**. You remember, that a structure variable accesses a structure member in a form **val.x**, and pointer accesses a structure member as **pt->y**. Again, the pointer structure members **x** and **y** should be accessed as the regular structure members. Both **x** and **y** are pointers. Therefore, both **val.x** and **pt->y** also represent pointers. This is why the assignments like **val.x=&n** are legitimate. We assign an address of the variable **n** to the pointer **val.x**. The address of **m** is assigned to **pt->y**. We also show how to dereference the member-pointer, when we print its value in **cout**. There we use those pointers with the asterisk operator as ***val.x** and ***pt->y**. This, as in case of a pointer to a simple variable, displays the values of the cells, to which those pointers point to. So, ***val.x** accesses the value of the variable **n**, the ***pt->y** accesses the value stored in **m**.

Therefore, *the pointers being the structure members are accessed as the regular structure members through the structure variable or a pointer to a structure.* Examples,

```
    var.x,  pt->x, (*pt).x
```

Since those constructions access the members-pointers, they are pointers. One can dereference those pointers in order to get a value they point to using the indirection operator *****. Examples are ***var.x**, ***pt->x**, ***(*pt).x**.

8.4.3. Passing a pointer to a structure as a function argument.

We have discussed a structure passed as a function argument in the chapter about the functions (Chapter 5). The C++ and C languages also allow to pass a pointer to a structure as a function argument. It is analogous to passing a pointer by "call-by-reference". Consider **Program 8.17**, illustrating that.

```
    #include <iostream.h>

    typedef struct num
```

```
{
int x;
int y;
} NUM;

void square (NUM *q);

main( )
{
NUM *pt;
pt->x=10;
pt->y=20;
square (pt);
cout << "pt->x=" << pt->x << ", " << "pt->y="
     << pt->y << "\n";
}

void square (NUM *q)
{
q->x = q->x*q->x;
q->y = q->y*q->y;
}
```

Program 8.17.

The output of the program is

```
pt->x=100, pt->y=400
```

This program calculates and prints squares of structure members **pt->x** and **pt->y**. Both members are assigned the values inside the **main()** routine. The **square()** function is called to square each of the members. The **square()** function has **void** type. It does not return a value. The values of each member are displayed in **main()** after getting the control back from **square()** function. The values of those members **pt->x** and **pt->y** have been changed by the **square()** function. They retain even after the control has been given back to the caller.

The expression **q->x = q->x*q->x** is a multiplication expression. Here, the asterisk is a multiplication sign. Do not confuse it with the indirection, although the same asterisk is used for both of them. We come to a conclusion.

When the structure is passed by its pointer, it can be changed by the called function. The pointer passed as the argument points to the structure location in the memory. Therefore, the called function performs the changes on the original structure members. The changes will retain even after the execution of called function is terminated.

You should not confuse this case with passing a structure variable as an argument of a function, that is known to be a "call-by-value". It operates on the copies of the original members. All the changes to the original values of the structure members in this case disappear after the termination of the called function.

8.5. Pointers and strings.

Using the pointers in strings is quite similar to arrays. **Program 8.18** handles the character strings in the pointer notation. It adds the second string to the end of the first.

```
#include <iostream.h>

main ( )
{
char str1[40]="This is the beginning.";
char str2[ ]=" And this is the end."  ;
char *add(char a[ ], char b[ ]);
cout << add(str1, str2);
}

char *add(char a[ ], char b[ ])
{
int n=0, m=0;
while (*(a+n)!='\0')
n=n+1;
while (*(b+m)!='\0')
{
*(a+n)=*(b+m);
n++;
m++;
}
*(a+n)='\0';
return (a);
}
```

Program 8.18.

The output of the program is the message on the screen

    This is the beginning. And this is the end.

It consists of two functions: **main()** and **add()**. The **main()** function declares two character strings **str1** and **str2**. It, then, displays concatenated string by **cout** with **add()** inserted in it. The **add()** function uses the first **while** loop to search for the end (null-character '**\0**') of the first string. It accesses each of its elements by de-referencing ***(a+n)**. When it encounters the end of the string, it copies each character from the second string to the first by ***(a+n)=*(b+m)**. A null-character is added to the end of the string. We need the null-character to display the string by **cout** object.

One of the peculiarities of using the pointers in strings is the pointer initialization. One can initialize a pointer to the string as

    char *ptr={"How are you?"};

Remember we printed a string by the **printf()** function using **%s** format? We typed the name of the character string as its argument

```
printf ("%s", a);
```

The name of the string **a[20]** is a pointer to the first element. Thus, we used a pointer to a string as an argument of **printf()** and in **cout** object. We read a string as

```
scanf ("%s", a);
```

The name of the string was used as an argument of **scanf()** function. It is a pointer to the string. We also used a pointer to a string in **cin**.

8.6. *const* declaration of pointers. Pointers of type *void*.

One can declare a pointer with the qualifier **const**. For instance, you declare

```
char *const pr=&var1;
```

This declares a **const** pointer **pr** pointing towards the variable **var1**. A pointer declared above cannot be redirected to point to another location in memory different from the one assigned during the initialization. However, the content of the memory cell, to which the pointer points to, can be changed. Let's explain what we just wrote in connection with the above code line. This notation allows the user to change the content of the variable, to which the pointer **pr** points to. One can assign a letter to the variable **var1** by ***pr='c'**. It can be changed to any other character as many times, as needed. *But one cannot modify the pointer itself, i.e., one cannot make it pointing to another variable*. If you attempt to reassign the pointer **pr** to another address **pr=&var2**, it will not work. We have given you an example of a pointer to a variable. In general, it can be a pointer to any object (structure, array, string and so on).

We will show an example of this pointer use in calling a function.

```
#include <iostream.h>

void ave (int *const );

main ( )
{
int x=20;
int  m;
ave (&x);
cout << x;
}

void ave (int *const aq)
{   *aq=*aq+2;   }
```
Program 8.19.

The output of the program is number 22. Here, we were able to modify the content of the cell, to which **aq** pointer points to. Try to introduce another variable **int y** inside the **ave()** function, and assign pointer **aq** to point towards it by **aq=&y**. You will get an error message, stating that the constant object cannot be modified.

One can declare a constant pointer slightly different. This will drastically change the way of how that pointer will operate. For example, we declare

```
const char *pr=&var1;
```

It is very close to the first form. Look more carefully. It is different. When a pointer is declared this way, one can make it pointing to any other variable. This means, that the pointer can be reassigned to point to a different address. But, the content of the variable, or, in general, any object the pointer points to, cannot be modified. Thus,

```
pr=&var2;
```

should work. It will reassign that pointer to point to another object. If you attempt to change the content of any object (in our case a string or a character variable) by ***pr='c'**, it will cause an error. The second case of **const** pointer would work for any type of object, as the first case. Therefore, the second pointer declaration permits to reassign the very pointer to another memory space, but it does not allow to change the content of the memory space that pointer points to. Consider an example.

```
#include <iostream.h>

int ave (const int *);

main ( )
{
int x[5]={10, 20, 30, 40, 50};
int  *apr, p;
apr=x;
p=ave (apr);
cout << p;
}

int ave (const int *aq)
{
int sum=0;
for (int k=0; k<5; k++)
sum=sum+ *(aq+k);
return sum;
}
```

Program 8.20.

The output of the program is the number 150. The program would not work, if you add a following line to the function **ave()**.

```
*(aq+k)=*(aq+k)+10;
```

The last case of **const** pointer is the declaration form

```
const char * const pr=&var;
```

Pointer declared this way cannot be reassigned to another location, once it is assigned for the first time. The content of the object it points to cannot be changed as well.

The pointers to type **void** are special type pointers. They can be cast to any other type of pointers. A pointer of **void** type is very useful for the functions, that have to return a pointer to any data type. One should use a pointer to **void** type there, and cast them to the required type for the return. We will study the functions having parameters and returning pointers to type **void**. We will deal with those functions studying the library functions and in the run-time allocation.

8.7. References.

8.7.1. Introduction to references.

Reference is a specific feature of C++. A reference can be interpreted as an alias for a variable. It can be interpreted as another name of a variable. When you initialize a reference, it becomes permanently associated with a variable. One cannot associate the same reference with another variable later on in the program code.

A reference is introduced by a simple procedure.

```
int x;
int &var=x;
```

We have declared a variable **x** and referenced it to a variable of the same data type **var** during its declaration. Thus, the declaration form **int &var=x** creates the variable **var** as a reference to **x**. Here, the **&** operator identifies the reference variable **var**. You have to specify a reference while declaring a variable. It "tells" the computer, that the variable **x** can be also called **var**. Those two identifiers are just two different names of the same variable. The same variable can be accessed by any of those two names. Suppose, you assign a value to the variable **var**

```
var=3;
```

Since variable **var** is aliased with **x**, the variable **x** should also become equal to 3. It is true vice versa. If we assign the value 5 to **x**, the variable **var** should also get the value 5. Hence, any operation on **var** produces the same effect on variable **x** and vice versa. **Program 8.21** illustrates the references.

```
#include <iostream.h>

main ( )
{
int one=200, &two=one;
cout << one << ", " << two << "\n";
two=two+40;
cout << one << ", " << two << "\n";
one=one+50;
cout << one << ", " << two << "\n";
}
```

Program 8.21.

The output of the program is

```
200, 200
240, 240
290, 290
```

This program declares and initializes variables **one=200** and **two** in one statement. It makes the variable **two** a reference to **one** by **&two=one**. The program illustrates, that by accessing any of the variables, you access both of them. By changing one variable, we change another one as well. We change **two** by **two=two+40** and this also changes the variable **one** to 240. The following change of **one** affects **two**.

We talked about de-referencing, when we discussed the pointers. You have even dealt with the **&** operator. The word "reference" here represents something completely different. It has no relation to pointers. It is a separate subject in C++. One should clearly understand, that the reference is neither a copy of nor a pointer to the same variable. It is, loosely speaking, just another name of the same variable. Thus, the storage is allocated only for one variable, which can be called by either of those identifiers. One can even print the addresses of both variables as shown below.

```
#include <iostream.h>

main ( )
{
int one=200, &two=one;
cout << hex << &one << ", " << &two;
}
```
Program 8.22.

The output of the program consists of two addresses

```
0x1ac8, 0x1ac8
```

Here, we print the addresses of both variables by

```
cout << hex << &one << ", " << &two;
```

The **&** operator here stands for the address operator. It gives an address of a variable.

```
int one=200, &two=one;
```

We can see, that reference variables **one** *and* **two** *have the same address, because they both are just two names of the same variable occupying the same memory cell.*

8.7.2. Initialization of references.

We saw, that a reference should be initialized. To initialize a reference means to associate it with another object, or variable. We did it, for instance, by **&var=x**. Here, we declared and initialized the reference simultaneously. In some cases the references do not require to be initialized, while you declare them:

• A reference does not need to be initialized while you declare it, when it is declared with the word **extern**. In this case it has been initialized elsewhere. For instance, it has been initialized in one source file. You just make it visible in another source file.

• A reference does not need to be initialized while you declare it, when it is a member of a class. In that case, it is initialized in the class's constructor function. We will study that when talking about classes.

• A reference does not need to be initialized while you declare it, when it is declared as a function parameter. It is assigned, when the function is called.

• A reference does not need to be initialized while you declare it, when it is declared as a function return type. It is assigned, when the function returns a value.
We will consider most of those cases below, so you will understand them.

8.7.3. Hidden anonymous objects.

The references have a peculiarity, that we should discuss. If the types of the reference and the object, used to initialize that reference, are different, the compiler cannot associate them correctly. In this case, the compiler builds a hidden anonymous object of the same type as the reference. The reference is tied to that anonymous object. Consider a program.

```
#include <iostream.h>

main ( )
{
int one=987;
long &two=one;
cout << "one=" << one << ", two=" << two << "\n";
two=5;
cout << "one=" << one << ", two=" << two << "\n";
one=10;
cout << "one=" << one << ", two=" << two << "\n";
}
```

Program 8.23.

The output of the program is
```
one=987, two=987
one=987, two=5
one=10, two=5
```
Program 8.23 declares and initializes **int** type variable **one=987**. It, then, declares a **long** type reference variable **two**, and initializes it as alias of **one**. The compiler creates a hidden variable of **long** type with the value 987. The variable **two** now refers to that nameless variable. When we display both variables **one** and **two** for the first time, they both have the same values. This happens, because **two** is now associated with an anonymous variable created by the computer of the same value as **one**. Both variables **one** and **two** are not referenced to each other after that declaration. In fact, they have no relation to

each other whatsoever. We show that in the program. When we change **two** to 5, the value of **one** remains unchanged and equal to 987. The vice versa is also true. When we change the value of **one** to 10, the value of **two** still remains equal to 5 from the previous setting.

Be aware of that effect, and never reference the variables of different data types to each other, unless you want them to work in a way described in **Program 8.23**. Sometimes, a reference is initialized with a constant. For example,

```
int &var=100;
```

The reference **var** does not have any named data to refer to. This generates a hidden anonymous object.

8.7.4. References and pointers. Restrictions on references.

There is the difference between the references and the pointers. However, both have something in common. Below we reference variable **var** to **x**.

```
int x, &var=x;
```

The same task can be achieved with the pointers. Below we declare the pointer **var** and make it pointing to the cell with the address **&x**.

```
int x;
int *const var=&x;
```

As you know, any assignment made to ***var** will affect **x** and vice versa. Because we have declared **var** with the qualifier **const**, you cannot make it pointing to another variable. Reference has this property also. A reference does not require * operator to access a value.

However, the references cannot be manipulated as flexible as pointers. One can distinguish between a pointer and a variable it points to by means of * operator. One cannot use * with references. Therefore, one manipulates only with the variables themselves using references. Thus, whatever you do to the reference **var** is, in fact, done to the variable **x**.

There are some restrictions, that you should remember while using them:

- You cannot create a reference to a reference variable.

- You cannot have an array of references.

- You cannot use a pointer to a reference.

- References cannot be used for the bit-fields.

8.7.5. References as function parameters.

Learning functions, we have learned, that there are two ways to pass a variable as an argument to a function:

- One can pass the variable by itself. It is "call-by-value". In this case, the function gets a copy of the variable, that it works on. All the modifications to that variable done by the function are discarded after the function execution is completed, if it is a local variable. One should also understand, that when the copy of the variable is created, it can be time consuming if, for example, this variable is a large structure.

• One can pass a pointer to a variable. It is "call-by-reference". In this case, the function receives the address of that actual variable. Some sources call that actual variable the "caller's copy". The function can access and modify that variable. The value will remain modified, after the control is given back to the caller. This way works much faster for large structures.

   C++ gives the user the third option to pass a variable: to pass a reference to a variable. So far, we have considered the references to give you an idea about their behavior. Now, we will talk about one of the possible ways of using them.

```
#include <iostream.h>
#include <string.h>

struct space
{
int x;
char sts[200];
};

void reffun (space &, int &);

main ( )
{
int a = 10;
space to={200, " the structure"};
reffun (to, a);
cout <<"The function has changed the values to:\n"
     <<"{" << to.x << ", " << to.sts << "},   "
     << "a=" << a;
}

void reffun (space &pass, int &k)
{
cout << "We passed:\n" <<"{" << pass.x << ",  "
     << pass.sts << "}" <<",   a="<< k << "\n";
pass.x=456;
strcpy (pass.sts, "We have changed the original.");
k=50;
}
```

Program 8.24.

The output of the program is
```
We passed:
{200, the structure}, a=10
The function has changed the values to:
```

```
{456, We have changed the original.}, a=50
```
This program illustrates how to use the references as the function parameters. The program first declares the structure **space** and the function with references as its parameters

```
void reffun (space &, int &);
```
This is a prototype of the function, that has two references as its formal parameters. The header in the function definition is

```
void reffun (space &pass, int &k)
```
The declaration and definition of the function with the reference parameters is almost identical to the function with the regular parameters. The only difference is the presence of **&** operator. A function parameter is a reference, if it is preceded by the **&** operator in the function prototype. Our function **reffun()** has two references as its parameters: **pass** and **k**. The parameter **pass** is the reference to structure **space** data type. The second parameter is a reference to the **int** type variable. Here, the references are not initialized. They are only declared. The form of writing a call of a function with the reference parameters is identical to a call-by-value form. In our example it is

```
reffun (to, a);
```
Pay attention, that no **&** is needed in a function call. We access the structure members as **pass.x** and **pass.sts** inside the **reffun()** routine. We do not need **->** to access the structure members. The variable is also accessed simply by its name **k**. We display the initial values of the structure members and the variable **k** in **reffun()** function. We, then, change the values of both structure members and the variable **k**. We display both members **to.x** and **to.sts**, when the control is resumed by **main()**. Their values have been changed during the **reffun()** function execution, and the changes are retained, even after **reffun()** is terminated.

We use **strcpy()** function in **Program 8.24** to copy the new string to **pass.sts** string. We included the **<string.h>** header file for using the **strcpy()** function.

Thus, when you use the references as the function parameters, you use the same syntax in calling and accessing them as for the call-by-value. But the called function operates on the caller's copy of the passed arguments. Therefore, the passed arguments will be changed and the changes will remain in effect after the caller resumes its execution.

We want to conclude this section with a number of practical advices. The use of references can, sometimes, lead to serious confusions. We advise to exercise caution in passing them as function arguments. In general, it is better to use the pointers, if the called function somehow modifies the passed parameters. It is a recommendation based on the common programming practices. The references to the constants should be passed as the arguments to the functions, that do not modify the parameters. The same function can have references, pointers, variables and any other kinds of arguments.

8.7.6. References as return values.

References can be used to return values from a function. Consider following program.

```
#include <iostream.h>
#include <string.h>
```

```
int var=2;

int &reffun (int x)
{
var=var*x;
return var;
}

main ( )
{
int m=10, k;
k=reffun (m);
cout << "k=" << k << ", var=" << var
     << " after assignment: var=";
reffun (m)=7;
cout << var;
}
```

Program 8.25.

The output of the program is

```
    k=20, var=20 after assignment: var=7
```

The above program demonstrates how to specify a reference as a return value. The function **reffun()** returns a reference. Its prototype and header in the definition specify the return value as a reference. Pay attention, how is it done

```
    int &reffun (int x)
```

The **int &** before the function name specifies, that the returned value is a reference to an **int** type variable.

Program 8.25 consists of functions **main()** and **reffun()**. The **main()** declares two **int** type variables: **m** and **k**. It passes **m** as an argument of the **reffun()** and assigns the returned by the function value to **k**. It then displays the values of **k** and the global variable **var**, which is used to return a value from **reffun()**. The program also uses an expression **reffun(m)=7**, that assigns a value 7 to the variable **var**.

The **reffun()** function returns the value of global variable **var**. We used a global variable, because our function **reffun()** returns a reference. A function cannot return a reference to a local auto variable. Suppose, we use a local variable **var** instead of global one in function **reffun()** in **Program 8.25**. Then, the local variable **var** goes out of scope, when the function returns. You would be returning a reference **var** to a variable, that is discarded after the termination of the **reffun()** function and no longer exists. In that case, the calling function would be referring to a value, that does not exist. Some compilers issue a warning, when the user tries to return the references to automatic variables. In some cases, a program appears to work, because the stack location that held that automatic variable is intact when one uses the reference. Many of those programs that appear to work will fail later due to some interrupts. Therefore, the results of such an error can be devastating.

You should use the references for passing and returning a reference to a function. All other operations can be done on the variable to which the reference refers to.

8.8. Arguments of *main()* function.

At this point we can discuss the **main()** function. You know, every program should have it. The computer begins the program execution from this function. So, it indicates to the computer the starting point of program execution. You cannot have more than one **main()** function in a program. You cannot call **main()** function from any other routine. When a program is called for an execution, the system calls the **main()** function. When the program execution is completed, the **main()** function terminates and gives the control back to the system. As any function, **main()** has parameters and the return value.

The parameters of **main()** function serve to a special purpose. There will be the programs, that might require some information, when you call them for execution. For example, you can develop a program, that computes areas of different geometrical figures. The program can find an area of a circle, or a square, or a triangle. You need to compute an area of a square. You can call that program and enter the figure whose area needs to be computed simultaneously. So, the program will start ready to compute an area of a particular figure, that you need. Notice, you can achieve the same result by different means. You can write a program, that starts its execution and then asks, an area of what geometrical figure do you want to compute. You just reply on a question displayed on the screen.

However, it is better in some cases to enter some data at the time of the program call. And this is what the parameters of the **main()** function are used for. The capability to supply the data at the time you call a program is provided by *command line arguments*. They are passed to **main()** function. The function has three parameters. The prototype of **main()** is

```
return_type main (int argc, char *argv[], char *env[])
```

The first parameter is the number of command line arguments passed to **main()**. It is called **argc** by convention. The conventional name **argv[]** is an array of pointers to character strings. The **env[]** is also an array of pointers to strings, that can handle the computer system issues.

You will understand **argc** and **argv[]** better after the following example. To execute a compiled program in DOS, you call it passing the command line arguments by the following statement.

```
C:\COMWIN\MYFOL\BOOK.EXE one 3 "how are you" 29 fine
```

It is a typical example of a call, that utilizes the command line arguments. Here, the **C:\COMWIN\MYFOL\BOOK.EXE** is the name of the file to be executed. It is followed by words, values and strings. We used six elements in this call including the name of the file. The **argc** is set by the system to the number of entered elements. In our case, it is 6. So, the **argc** value is set to 6. Each of those elements is placed in a memory cell. Each of the **argv[]** will point to one of those elements.

argv[0]	points towards	C:\COMWIN\MYFOL\BOOK.EXE
argv[1]	points towards	one
argv[2]	points towards	3
argv[3]	points towards	how are you

```
argv[4]        points towards        29
argv[5]        points towards        fine
```
Arguments are separated from each other by the blank spaces. To enter words separated by the white spaces as one argument, you must put them inside the double quotes " ".

You can ask, how to enter the command line arguments while you are still at the development stage. Each compiler permits to enter the command line arguments while you write a program and try to run it inside a compiler. You have to consult a compiler manual for doing it. You do not have to enter the name of the file on some compilers. You can enter all other arguments. But the **argv[0]** will still point to the file name.

Each of the **env[]** points towards some environmental strings. They help you to manipulate with the operating system. They are not a subject of our book. The **main()** function can be called with the first two arguments, or without arguments at all.

The **main()** function can return a value. It has a ***return_type***. The function can have **void** return type. It can have an **int** return type. In this case, the **main()** function must be terminated by a **return n** statement, where **n** is an integer. We did not write a return type for **main()** function up to this point, because we did not want to complicate things for you. From now on, we will use the return type for **main()** function. Consider a program illustrating the command line arguments of **main()**. It allows you to enter some English words as command line arguments, and gives a French translation of some of those words. The program implements an English-French dictionary. We give four words in this dictionary only for illustration purposes. This is why not all of the entered words will be translated. The dictionary skips the words that it "does not know".

```cpp
#include <iostream.h>
#include <string.h>

void main (int argc, char *argv[])
{
char *fr[]={"abricote", "accroc", "achat", "adieu" };
char *eng[]={"apricot", "tear", "buying", "farewell" };
char line[20], arr[20];
int k=0, qq=1, p=0, m=0, a, b;
for (m=0; m<argc; m++)
{
strcpy (line, argv[m]);
for (p=0; p<4; p++)
{
strcpy (arr, eng[p]);
while (k < 20 && arr[k]!='\0')
{
a=line[k];
b=arr[k];
if (a!=b)
qq=0;
k++;
```

```
    }
    k=0;
    if (qq > 0)
    cout << arr << "-" << fr[p] << endl;
    qq=1;
    } }    }
```

Program 8.26.

We enter following command line arguments

    `hello farewell apricot goodby`

The program displays

    `farewell-adieu`

    `apricot-abricote`

  The program declares four strings: **fr[]**, **eng[]**, **line[]** and **arr[]**. Two of those strings **fr[]** and **eng[]** store respectively French and English words. The first French word "**abricote**" in the string is translated to the first English word "**apricot**", the second French word corresponds to the second English word and so on. The program simply takes the command line arguments one by one and compares each of them to each of the English words stored in the **eng[]** string. If any of the typed in arguments matches any of this words, the computer displays this word and its French equivalent.

  The program consists of three nested loops. The most outer **for** loop selects the entered argument string **argv[m]** and copies it to the **line[]**. The inner **for** loop selects each of the words stored in **eng[p]** and copies it into **arr[]** string. It is more convenient to compare strings **line[]** and **arr[]** than **eng[p]** with **argv[m]**. The **while** compares each character in **line[]** with **arr[]**. If both are identical, the flag **qq** is set to zero. The **if** statement compares **qq** with zero. If **qq** is zero, the current **eng[p]** and corresponding to it **fr[p]** words are displayed.

EXERCISES.

1. If you have an access to a computer, run all the programs given in this chapter.
2. Write a pointer version of a function to sort three integers into ascending order. Do not use arrays.
3. Write your version of **strncat()** function using pointer notation.
4. Write your version of a function, that compares two strings if they are identical. Use pointer notation.
5. Write your version of **strncopy()** function using pointer notation.
6. Write a word processor described in exercise 12 of the previous chapter using pointer notation.
7. Write a program that reads 20 integers into an array and uses the selection sorting algorithm to sort the elements of that array into ascending order. The program should use the pointer notations to manipulate the array elements. The final array should be displayed on the screen. We will introduce you in nutshell to the selection sorting. Suppose, you are given an array of numbers **x[0]**, **x[1]**, **x[2]** ..., **x[n-1]**. The sorting is conducted in

three steps:

- Search for the smallest number among **x[0]**, **x[1]**, **x[2]** ..., **x[n-1]**. Say, the smallest number is the element **x[k]**, where **k** can be any element number. The **x[k]** is swapped with **x[0]**.

- Search for the smallest number among **x[1]**, **x[2]**, **x[3]** ..., **x[n-1]**. Say, the smallest number is the element **x[k]**, where **k** can be any element number. The **k** here and in the previous steps are not related in any way. It merely indicates an element number that stores the smallest value. The **x[k]** is swapped with **x[1]**.

- Repeat the previous step for **n-2** times starting each search from the next element number. The search proceeds, until the remaining unsearched array consists of 1 element. Thus, the third search will start from **x[2]**. Search after that search will start from **x[3]** and so on. Search ends, when only **x[n-1]** is left for the next search. This produces a sorted array.

We can give a following example. Suppose, we have to sort an array **a[6]**.

```
-3   69   10   -25   3   11
```

The first search starts from **a[0]=-3** and proceeds, until the smallest value is found. This value is -25. It is swapped with **a[0]**. After that the array looks like

```
-25   69   10   -3   3   11
```

The search then starts from **a[1]=69** and goes up. The smallest array element is now -3. It is swapped with **a[1]** to produce

```
-25   -3   10   69   3   11
```

The search starts from **a[2]=10** and goes up. The smallest element in the rest of the array is now equal to 3. It is swapped with **a[2]**. The array now reads

```
-25   -3   3   69   10   11
```

The search starts from **a[3]=69** and proceeds up. The smallest array element is now 10. The computer trades their places yielding

```
-25   -3   3   10   69   11
```

The last search starts from **a[4]**. It gives the final array

```
-25   -3   3   10   11   69
```

8. Write a program that reads 20 integers into an array and uses the bubble sorting algorithm to sort the elements of that array into ascending order. The program should use the pointer notations to manipulate the array elements. The final array should be displayed on the screen. We will introduce you to the bubble sorting. Suppose, you have an array of numbers **x[0]**, **x[1]**, **x[2]** ..., **x[n-1]**. You sort it in two steps:

- Compare each consecutive pair of elements from **x[0]** to **x[n-1]**. If an element on the right is smaller than the element on the left, swap them. The largest element should "bubble-up" to the right. In other words, you first compare **x[0]** to **x[1]** and swap them if **x[0]<x[1]**. You compare **x[1]** and **x[2]** and swap them if **x[1]<x[2]**. You, then, perform the same operation with **x[2]** and **x[3]**, **x[3]** and **x[4]** and so on. You end up comparing **x[n-2]** to **x[n-1]** and swapping them if **x[n-2]<x[n-1]**.

- Repeat the previous step, until no swapping occurs.

We give following example of how the bubble sorting is performed on an array. Suppose, you are given an array

```
-3   69   10   -25   3   11
```

It will be sorted by the bubble method producing following intermediate results after each step

```
 -3    10  -25    3    11    69
 -3   -25    3   10    11    69
-25    -3    3   10    11    69
```

9. Write a program that reads 20 integers into an array and uses the quicksort sorting algorithm to sort the elements of that array into ascending order. The program should use the pointer notations to manipulate the array elements. The final array should be displayed on the screen. We will introduce you in nutshell to the quicksort sorting. Suppose, you are given an array of numbers $x[0]$, $x[1]$, $x[2]$ ..., $x[n-1]$. The sorting is conducted in two steps:

- Select a value of an element in the array. Put all the elements with the values less than the chosen ones in one area. Put all the values equal or greater than the chosen value in another area. By "one area" and "another area" we mean just a location in the memory. You can declare 60 element array and use 20 of its cells for the entered data. Then, you can use 20 more cells to place the values less than the chosen one. The last 20 positions can be used for the chosen value and the value greater than it.

- Repeat the previous step with the array on the left and the array on the right. The "breaking down" procedure will make the sub-arrays from both left and the right arrays, then, the sub-arrays of those sub-arrays and so on, until the whole array is sorted.

10. Write a program that will calculate a square root of a number. Calculate the square root using Newton-Ralphson algorithm described in exercise 12 of Chapter 5. Structure your program into separate functions. Pass a reference to a function.

CHAPTER 9

MORE ABOUT OPERATORS.

Numbers are converted to the binary code and handled that way in a computer. We also discussed the concept of the information unit - a "bit". Computer processes a number of bits at once, this increases the speed. You know, the standard number of data lines, or bits processed at once are 8, 16, 32 for different processors. Eight bits represent a byte, a main unit, that a computer operates on. The rightmost byte's bit is called "least significant", and the leftmost is the "most significant" bit.

C and C++ allow to do operations on bits. The bit operators and their names are given in the Table 9.1. We will consider each of them in this chapter.

Table 9.1. Operations on bits.

Operator	Performed action
&	Bitwise AND
|	Bitwise inclusive OR
^	Bitwise exclusive OR
~	Complement
>>	Right shift
<<	Left shift

All the bit operations can be performed only on the data of **short**, **int**, **long** or **unsigned**, but not on **float** or **double** type.

9.1. Bitwise operators.

9.1.1. Bitwise AND operator.

Although modern computers more often use CPU designed for 32 bits, we will work with byte just for simplicity.

One can ask, what is the result of the AND operation on two bits. Let's assume, we compare only one bit of one number to one bit of another number. The result of this operation is stored in a separate bit. It is equal to "1", only when both of those bits are equal to "1". The resulting bit is equal to "0", if either, or each of two bits is "0".

We offer some simplified loose explanation to help to memorize this operator. The reason this operator is called AND is, that the result will be equal to "1", when both *the first and the second bits are equal to "1"*. A way to describe a logical operator is to introduce a *truth table*. It considers all possible combinations of those two input bits, and the result of a logical operation on them. Table 9.2 is a *truth table* for AND operator applied to two cells.

Table 9.2. AND truth table.

Bit A	Bit B	A&B
1	0	0
1	1	1
0	0	0
0	1	0

Now we can talk about the *Bitwise AND* operator. Bitwise AND operator is applied to two values **x** and **y** in the form

    x&y;

The '**&**' represents the bitwise AND operator. It acts on the binary representation of the values. The real numbers consist of more than one bit each. That (AND) operator compares corresponding bits of two values, and performs the AND operation on those two numbers bit by bit. How is it done? Imagine, that the AND operation is performed first on the least significant bits of both numbers, then on the next bit from the right of both numbers and so on through the most significant bit. Your computer does not necessarily do it in this order. Rather all the corresponding bits are compared at once. We just wanted you to understand, that the AND operation is performed on every bit of two entered numbers. The result will be a new binary number. Each of its bits is a result of AND logical operation on two corresponding bits. You can convert the result to decimal, octal or other base.

Consider performing AND operation on two numbers: **20&18**. Logical AND is applied bit by bit over those two numbers and the result is 16, or (00010000 in the binary number representation).

        20= 00010100
        18= 00010010
    20&18= 00010000=16;

In the above example, AND operation has been performed on two numbers 20 and 18. AND operation compares the least significant bits of these numbers. The result is "0". Then, AND is performed on the second bits of both numbers, and the result is "0" and so on. Only the fifth bit of both numbers is equal to "1". Therefore, only this bit gives "1" as a result. The final number after performing AND operation has "1" as its fifth bit. This binary number corresponds to the decimal number 16.

One can also write AND operator for three and more inputs, based on the behaviour of Bitwise AND described for two numbers. If writing a truth table for AND operator is a problem for you, simply group those values by two. For instance, one can group the expression **a & q & c** as **(a & q) & c** or as **a & (q & c)**. The **&** operation is first performed on **(a & q)** and, then, on the result of that operation and **c** for the **(a & q) & c** expression. The **a & (q & c)** expression first performs **(q & c)**, then, the AND operation on **a** and the result of **(q & c)**. We urge you to perform the AND operation on three values. You would, then, understand that it does not matter, where to put the parentheses. Two values inside the parentheses can be evaluated first using the truth table for two values, and the result of that AND operation can be subjected to AND operator with the third value. **Program 9.1** illustrates AND operator.

```
#include <iostream.h>

void main ( )
{
int xo1=037, xo2=026;
int xh1= 0xea9, xh2= 0xFC8;
int xd1= 89, xd2=53, xd3= 847;
int y;
cout << oct << (xo1  &  xo2) << ",  " << hex
      << (xh1  &  xh2) << ",  " << dec << (xd1  &  xd2)
      << ",  " << (xd1  &  xd2 & xd3);
}
```

                                  Program 9.1.

The output of the program is
          26, e88, 17, 1
   The operation performed by the program is pretty straightforward. It performs AND operation on variables, whose values are displayed as octal, hexadecimal and decimal numbers. It even performs AND operation on three variables. You can transfer each of those numbers into binary code, and apply AND to the binary numbers. Compare your results with the program output to check your understanding of this operator.
   One should understand, that the result of the bitwise AND operation is a number. Therefore, it can be assigned to a variable, or an array element, or a structure member and so on. For example, **y=a&b**.

9.1.2. Bitwise OR operators.

   The *Bitwise Inclusive OR* operator operates on binary representation of the values. The inclusive OR applied to two numbers performs its operation bit by bit on the corresponding bits of those two numbers. Thus, the OR operation is performed on least significant bits of both numbers, then on the next bits from the right and so on through the most significant bit.
   Two bits subjected to Inclusive OR operator will produce a resulting bit or output equal to "1", when one of the inputs, or both of them are equal to "1". Otherwise, it is equal to "0". The Inclusive OR operation on two variables **x1** and **x2** is written as
          x1 | x2;
One can describe this operator by the truth table for only two bits, given in Table 9.3. Consider applying this operator to the same two numbers as for **&** operator.
          20= 00010100
          18= 00010010
        20|18= 00010110=22;

One can see, the difference in bits that gives a different decimal number. The operator can also be applied to decimal, hexadecimal, octal, binary numbers, because they will be converted to a binary form anyway.

Table 9.3. Inclusive OR truth table.

Bit A	Bit B	A|B
1	1	1
1	0	1
0	1	1
0	0	0

The Bitwise Exclusive OR operator is often called XOR. It is equal to "1", only if one of the corresponding bits of two operands is equal to "1". The result is equal to "0", in case when both inputs are equal either to "1", or to "0".

Table 9.4. Exclusive OR truth table.

Bit A	Bit B	A^B
1	1	0
1	0	1
0	1	1
0	0	0

It also acts on the binary representations of the values. It processes two corresponding bits of two binary numbers bit by bit from the least to the most significant bit. Its action on two bits can be represented by the truth table, given in the Table 9.4. The operator has a format of writing

```
x1^x2;
```

Consider applying this operator to the same two numbers as before.

```
      20= 00010100
      18= 00010010
20^18= 00000110=6;
```

This operator produces a different decimal number. This operator can also be applied to decimal, hexadecimal, octal, binary numbers. Consider **Program 9.2**, that illustrates it.

```
#include <iostream.h>

void main ( )
{
int xo1=037, xo2=026;
int xh1= 0xEA9, xh2= 0xFC8;
int xd1= 89, xd2=53;
int y;
cout << oct << (xo1  |   xo2) << ", " << (xo1   ^ xo2)
        << ", " << hex << (xh1  |   xh2) << ", "
        << (xh1 ^   xh2) << ", " << dec << (xd1  |   xd2)
```

```
    << endl;
  xd1 ^= 11;
  xd2 |= 11;
  cout << xd1 << ", " << xd2;
  }
```
Program 9.2.

The output of the program is

```
  37, 11, fe9, 161, 125
  82, 63
```

The program is clear except two operators: **xd1 ^= 11** and **xd2 |= 11**. The first operator is equivalent to the expression

```
  xd1=xd1^11;
```

It performs following actions. First, exclusive bitwise OR operation is performed on number 11 and the variable **xd1**. The result value is assigned to the variable **xd1**. The second case (**xd2 |= 11**), is quite analogous to the first except that we perform an inclusive OR operation on number 11 and the variable **xd2**. It is equivalent to

```
  xd2= xd2 | 11;
```

The result of OR operation is assigned to the variable **xd2**. Both variables **xd1** and **xd2** are displayed later to indicate the change.

The results of OR operations can be assigned to another operand. For example,

```
  y=xd1 ^ xd2;
```

This assigns a result of Bitwise Exclusive OR operation to the variable **y**.

9.1.3. Complement operator.

The complement operator is a unary operator. It acts on one number in the binary representation. It acts on every bit of the binary number from the least significant bit up to the most significant bit. So, the bit equal to "1" becomes "0" and vice versa. Its action on a single bit is presented in the truth table, which is Table 9.5. Its format of writing is: **~x**. An example of complement operator action is

```
  x    0010101011001010
  ~x   1101010100110101
```

Table 9.5. Complement operator truth table.

Bit A	~A
1	0
0	1

One can use the complement operator along with AND, OR and other operators. Some examples of using the complement operator are given in **Program 9.3**.

```
  #include <stdio.h>
```

```
void main ( )
{
int xo1=037;
int xh1= 0xEA9, xh2= 0xFC8;
int xd1= 89, xd2=53;
printf("%o, ", ~xo1);
printf("%x, ", xh1 | ~xh2);
printf("%d, %d, ", ~xd1, ~xd1 & xd2);
xd1 &= ~11;
printf("%d. \n", xd1);
}
```
Program 9.3.

The output of the program is
```
177740, febf, -90, 36, 80
```
The given above program should be clear to you and does not need any explanations.

One should not confuse the logical and bitwise operators: logical **&&** AND operator and bitwise **&** AND operators, logical (||) OR and (|) bitwise Inclusive OR operators. The logical operator is used in the logical expression (we have discussed before) for producing TRUE/FALSE result. The bitwise operators perform bit by bit operations on operands.

As one of the applications of bitwise operators consider the **Program 9.4**, that tests for odd and even integers.

```
#include <iostream.h>

void main ( )
{
int odcheck=1, x;
cout << "Enter the number you want to check.\n";
cin >> x;
if (x & odcheck)
cout << "The number is odd.\n";
else
cout << "The number is even.\n";
}
```
Program 9.4.

The program first prompts the user to enter any integral number. If you enter any even number, it displays the message, that the number is even. If the number is odd, the program displays the message, that it is odd. The check for the oddness is the **if** statement condition

if (x&odcheck)

You will understand why the computer first does a bitwise AND on **x&odcheck** and only then compares the result to zero, after we learn the operator precedence in this chapter. The condition in **if** ANDs the entered number and number 1. Number 1 has only the least significant bit equal to one. All others are zeros. If the entered number **x** is odd, its last bit is 1. Therefore, the AND operation on any odd number **x** and 1 produces one. If the entered number is even, the AND operation on both numbers produces zero. This effect is used to test the entered number for oddness.

9.1.4. Shift Operators.

There are two shift operators used in C and C++: Left Shift Operator (**<<**) and Right Shift Operator (**>>**). They literally move bits left or right on certain number of positions. An example of writing the left shift operator is

```
x<<n;
```

This shifts the bits in the operand **x** to the left by **n** positions. An example of writing the right shift operator is

```
x>>n;
```

This shifts the bits in the operand **x** to the right by **n** positions. Let's consider some examples. For instance, review the expression **x<<2**, where **x** is equal to 3. This expression shifts the bits of the number 3 in binary representation two positions left. So, the execution of this command on the number 3 in the binary representation for 16 bit computer looks as

```
 3:        0000000000000011  (binary number 3 before shift);
 6:        0000000000000110  (first shift left leads to number 6);
12:        0000000000001100  (second shift left leads to number 12);
```

As one can see, two positions containing "1" moved left one position after the first shift and one more position after the second shift. This changed the binary numbers, from 3 to 6 for the first shift, and from 6 to 12 after the second. The empty positions are filled with "0".

Let's consider right shift by 3 positions of the binary number

```
208:        0000000011010000  (binary number 208 before shift);
104:        0000000001101000  (first shift left leads to number 104);
 52:        0000000000110100  (second shift left leads to number 52);
 26:        0000000000011010  (third shift left leads to number 26);
```

As can be seen, the sequence of "1" and "0" moves right one position during each right shift operation. It is appropriate to mention here, the right shift operator might differ from system to system except for operating on **unsigned** types of data. In this case the bit added at the left will be "0" on any system. Systems may pad differently for the other data types. Some systems always add "0" at the left (*logical shift*), when the positions move to the right. Others add "zeros" at the left positions only, when the pre-shifted integer is positive. Otherwise, only "ones" are added. Next program illustrates the shift operations.

```
#include <stdio.h>

void main ( )
{
int x=208, y=3, x1, y1;
```

```
x1=x>>2;
y1=y<<2;
printf ("%d, %d", x1, y1);
}
```
Program 9.5.

The output of this program is

```
    52, 12
```

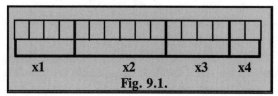

x1   x2   x3   x4

Fig. 9.1.

This program performs a shift of two positions to the right on the number 208, that we have discussed. It also performs a shift of two positions to the left on the number 3.

9.2. Bit fields.

Bit fields serve two purposes. They decrease the size of memory needed for program execution. They enable a programmer to access the individual bits of a machine word.

When a variable is declared, a standard number of bytes is allocated to store it. The size of the storage is standard for a data type. Sometimes, one does not need all the bits allocated for a value, because the values are expected to be not as big. So, fewer bits are needed. One can also use flags, which need one or two bits, and so on. If fewer bits are needed, one can put a number of variables in one machine word. This is achieved by using a bit-field variable. The bit-field variables are declared as structures as follows:

```
struct test
{
unsigned int x1 : 4;
unsigned int x2 : 6;
unsigned int x3 : 4;
unsigned int x4 : 2;
};
```

The only difference from the normal structures is the presence of colon (:) and the number after it. Number following the colon in those structures shows the length of the field for the variable. For instance,

```
unsigned int x1 : 4;
```

allocates 4 bits for the variable **x1**. Our structure corresponds to Fig. 9.1, that is just a pictorial representation of the **test** structure. Each structure member occupies certain number of bits. For instance, **x2** occupies 6 bits, 4 bits are allocated for **x3**, and **x4** is settled on two bit field. We have shown 16 bit word.

One accesses the bit fields in the same way as the structure members. You must declare a structure variable. For example, we declare the structure variable **trial** to the structure **test** by

```
test  trial;
```

Then, any structure member can be accessed in a familiar manner. For instance,

```
trial.x1
```

accesses the member **x1**. One can also use assignment operators for loading a number into the bit fields, or extracting it. The expression

```
trial.x2=10;
```

assigns a value of 10 to the structure member **x2**, that was introduced as bit field. The expression

```
y=trial.x2;
```

assigns the value 10 stored inside the bit field, corresponding to **x2** to a variable **y**. Bit fields can be used in the regular expressions, where they are automatically converted to **int** type. For example,

```
n=20 - trial.x2;
```

Use of **unsigned int** type of data with the bit fields provides portability, because data with signs can be handled differently for different systems. There are no rules of how many bit-field variables of what lengths are allowed in a program. Those bit field structures can also include a mix of regular data and bit fields. For instance,

```
struct inp_dat
{
unsigned int var1 : 9;
float var2;
unsigned int var3 : 4;
};
```

This structure has two bit field members **var1**, **var3** and a regular member variable **var2** of the type **float**. Bit fields are packed into words in the same order they follow in the structure. If one of them does not fit into the word, then free space would be left for the remainder of the word. For given above **inp_dat** structure, the first variable will occupy 9 positions of the 16 bit word. The rest of that word will be skipped. Second variable will be placed, beginning from the new word, because there is no space for it in the previous word. The third variable will be placed on 4 positions of the next word after **var2**.

If a structure has a bit field without a name, those bits inside the word are "skipped".

```
struct datstr
{
unsigned int qa1 :5;
unsigned int        :5;
unsigned int qb1 :6;
};
```

The first 5 bits of the word in the above structure are occupied by the member **qa1**. The following 5 bits are skipped. Next 6 bits are allocated for the variable **qb1**.

The operations on bit field are restricted. Some C/C++ compilers do not support bit fields larger than the size of the word. One can not have an array of bit fields. They can not be addressed via pointers. One cannot use references to the bit fields.

9.3. Operator precedence and associativity.

A number of C/C++ operators are presented in Table 9.6.

Table 9.6. Summary and description of C/C++ operators.

Operator	Description of the operator	Associativity
::	Scope resolution	Left to right
( ) [ ] . ->	Function call Array element Structure or union member Pointer to structure member	Left to right
-- ++	Decrement Increment	Right to left
! ~ - + & * sizeof (type)	Logical NOT One's complement Unary minus Unary plus Address Indirection Size in bytes Type cast	Right to left
new, delete	Allocate and free the memory	Left to right
->* .*	member pointer	Left to right
* / %	Multiply Divide Modulus	Left to right
+ -	Add Subtract	Left to right
<< >>	Left shift Right shift	Left to right
< <= > >=	Less than Less than or equal Greater than Greater than or equal	Left to right
== !=	Equal Not equal	Left to right
&	Bitwise AND	Left to right
^	Bitwise exclusive OR	Left to right
|	Bitwise OR	Left to right
&&	Logical AND	Left to right
||	Logical OR	Left to right
?:	Conditional expression	Right to left
=, *=, /=, %=, |=, +=, -=, <<=, &=, ^=,	Assignment operator Compound assignment operators.	Right to left
,	Comma	Left to right

The operators in Table 9.6 are listed in order of decreasing precedence from the top to the bottom. Higher precedence means, if there are two operators written together, the operator with the higher precedence will be evaluated and executed first. For instance, the increment $(++)$ operator has a higher precedence than the equality $(=)$ operator. Therefore, the increment operator will be executed before the equality.

Let's consider an example.

```
x + & y || z
```

Here, we have three operators: addition (+), address (&) and logical OR (||). The address operator has higher precedence than addition operator according to Table 9.6. Hence, the address operator will be executed first. The content of the cell pointed to by &y will be added to **x**. After that, the result of the operation will be ORed with **z**, because OR has lower precedence than any other operator in the expression.

Consider another example.

```
x=y*val.p;
```

Here, we multiply the structure member **val.p** by **y**, and assign the result to **x**. The structure member operator has higher precedence than any other. It is executed first. It is followed by the multiplication. The assignment has the lowest precedence according to our table. Therefore, it is executed last.

If there are the operators with the same precedence in an expression, then, the associativity controls the evaluation. The operators will be evaluated either from the left to the right or from the right to the left according to the operator associativity.

For example, according to the above table, the assignment operator has right to left associativity. This means, that in the expression **a=3**, the right side 3 is assigned to the left side **a**. For instance, review the expression **x=y=1**. Here, the value 1 is assigned to **y**. The value of **y=1** is, then, assigned to **x**. Finally, both **x** and **y** are set to 1.

EXERCISES.

1. Run all the programs of this chapter, if you have an access to a computer facility.
2. Write a program that adds two integral numbers by converting them into binary ones and doing the addition on two binary numbers bit by bit.
3. Write a program that alters a random bit of a number that an user enters.
4. Write a program that reads two numbers and converts them into binary ones. It, then, finds bitwise AND and OR of those two numbers. The program, then, restores the first of the numbers analyzing together bit by bit the results of AND, OR operations and the second entered number. Develop the algorithm for that procedure.
5. Write a program that multiplies two entered numbers. It converts both numbers to the binary format and multiplies as the binary ones. First develop an algorithm for multiplying two numbers in a binary format.
6. Write a program that divides two entered numbers. Both numbers are converted to the binary format and are divided as the binary ones. First develop an algorithm for dividing two numbers in a binary format.
7. Develop a program that reads a string from a keyboard and compresses it. The compressed version should be stored in other array. The program, then, restores the original string from the compressed version and displays it on the screen. (Hint: Use bit fields.).

Chapter 10

THE PREPROCESSOR DIRECTIVES.

Before any program in C++ is compiled and translated into object code, it goes through different stages of translation. One of those steps is the preprocessing. The preprocessor is a special program, that runs at the first stages of compilation. It does not compile the source code, but rather modifies it. The preprocessing is controlled by the preprocessor directives, that begin with the number (**#**) sign. That number sign should be the first non-blank character in the line on which it appears. It should be immediately followed by the preprocessor directive. You have dealt with one of those directives. It is **#include** directive.

Preprocessor directives can be coded anywhere in a program. The more conventional way is to write them at *the beginning of the program*, *outside of any function*. A preprocessor directive affects only the statements, that *follow it* in the *same source file*.

The preprocessor directives are discarded after they are executed. They do not get translated. They are not executable by the program. Those directives are just the commands to the preprocessor program to do some changes in the source code to be compiled, or, for example, to include some files. The code after preprocessing is called the *translation unit*. There are following preprocessor directives:

#define	**#elif**	**#else**	**#endif**
#error	**#if**	**#ifdef**	**#ifndef**
#include	**#line**	**#pragma**	**#undef**

10.1. The *#define* directive.

This command is written in the following format:
    #define *identifier expression*
This directive enables a user to replace the **identifier**, that appears anywhere in the program, by the **expression**. The **identifier** is just a name. It can be created using the usual rules for writing an identifier. The **identifier** in the **#define** directive is often called a *macro*. The **expression** can be a number, character, sign, operator, other statements, strings and string tokens of your choice. Sometimes, it is called a *replacement text* or *replacement list*. There is at least one blank space between **define**, **identifier** and **expression**. There is no semicolon after the **#define** directive. There is no white space between the **#** and **define**. The **#** must be the first non-white character in a line containing the preprocessor directive.

Let's consider how to use **#define**. It is used to assign symbolic names or macros:
1) to program constants;
2) to symbolic constants;

3) to an expression;

4) to a text;

5) to the macro instructions with and without parameters.

We will discuss all those cases and their specific features. This directive may improve extendibility and transportability of a program, which we will also discuss.

To call **#define** a "statement" is somewhat misleading. It is not an instruction that is executed, when the program is running. It is a directive to the preprocessor, which is a program that processes the source code before the compilation. If the preprocessor finds an **identifier** defined by **#define** directive in the program, it literally substitutes that **identifier** with its replacement text.

For example, we define

```
#define DOG 5
```

Value 5 is used as the **expression** (replacement text). **DOG** is the **identifier**. Loosely speaking, if the name **DOG** is found anywhere in the program, it would be replaced by the value 5. The computer performs a literal substitution of **DOG** by the number 5. The name **DOG** is not a variable. Therefore, one can not assign a value to it.

Again, one assigns a symbolic name to a program constant by writing, for instance:

```
#define INP_CONST 10
```

In this case, the identifier **INP_CONST** is a name of the constant. The expression part of the directive, that we want to assign to this name, is a constant 10. The name of the symbolic constant by convention is written with the uppercase letters.

Consider **Program 10.1**, that uses the **#define** with the TRUE and FALSE flags.

```cpp
#include <iostream.h>
#define    TRUE    1
#define    FALSE   0

int check (int a)
{
if (a>0)
a=TRUE;
else
a=FALSE;
return (a);
}

void main ( )
{
int x[10], k=0, n;
cout << "Enter 10 elements.\n";
for (n=0; n<10; ++n)
cin >> x[n];
cout << "Enter completed.\n";
for (n=0; n<10; ++n)
k=k+ check (x[n]);
```

```
cout << " There are " << k << " positive elements.\n";
}
```

Program 10.1.

You enter 10 integral numbers separated by spaces from each other and press **ENTER**. The program determines, how many of those ten entered values are positive. It displays a message on the screen, indicating the number of entered positive values.

The program consists of two functions: **main()** and **check()**. The **main()** routine declares an array **x[10]**. The **for** loop uses **cin** object to enter the values of array elements from the console. Another **for** loop is used to access each of the array elements again to check them for a sign. We use variable **k**, which is set to 0 initially, to count the number of positive array elements. It is done by the expression

```
k=k+ rowcheck (x[n]);
```

The function **check()** returns 1 during each cycle, when we access a positive array element. This increases the value of **k** by 1. It returns zero, when the negative array element is accessed. This does not increase **k**. The value of **k** is equal to the total number of positive array elements after completing the loop.

This program uses the **check()** function to determine whether a variable is positive. It is done by merely comparing the passed argument value to 0 in **if-else** statement. If **x[n]** is greater than zero, TRUE is returned to the caller. Otherwise, the function returns FALSE. Since both TRUE and FALSE have been defined to be equal to "1" or "0" respectively, either "1" or "0" value is returned by the **check()** to **main()**.

Another **#define** application is illustrated by **Program 10.2**. Here, we used a value of known to you constant $\pi = 3.14159265$. If one uses it too often in the program, it might be more convenient to define it in the beginning. It is also convenient, because the value of π is too long and difficult to remember every time. The program is just an illustration, because many compilers already have that value stored and easily available.

```
#include <stdio.h>
#define    P    3.14159265

double r, h;

double cylind_bas (void)
{
return( 2.0 * P * r * r);
};

double cyl_wal (void)
{
return ( 2 * P * r * h);
}

double cyl_vol (void)
{
```

```
return ( P * r * r * h);
}

void main ( )
{
printf("Enter  radius and height. \n");
scanf("%lf, %lf", &r, &h);
printf("area of top and bottom %.10f.\n",cylind_bas ( ));
printf ("area of the walls %.10f.\n", cyl_wal ( ));
printf ("volume of the cylinder %.10f.\n", cyl_vol ( ));
}
```
Program 10.2.

The program prompts to enter the radius and the height of a cylinder. We enter
```
2.5, 10
```
The program displays
```
area of top and bottom 39.2699081250.
area of the walls 157.07963250.
volume of the cylinder 196.3495406250.
```
This program is clear. It consists of four functions: **main()**, **cylind_bas()**, **cyl_wal()** and **cyl_vol()**. The variables (radius **r** and height **h**) are declared as global variables. The **main()** function reads the values of the global variables **r** and **h**. It calls **cylind_bas()**, **cyl_wal()** and **cyl_vol()**. The **cylind_bas()** function finds the area of the top and bottom circles of the cylinder. The **cyl_wal()** function finds the area of the walls. The **cyl_vol()** function finds the volume of the whole cylinder. Each of those function is used as an argument of the **printf()** in **main()**. The calculation results are displayed by the **printf()** functions inside the **main()** routine.

Three of those quantities are found from the following expressions. The area of the top and bottom circles of the cylinder is found from the expression **2 * P * r * r**. The area of the cylinder side wall is calculated by **2 * P * r * h**. The volume of the whole cylinder is equal to **P * r * r * h**.

This program uses the **#define** directive. Symbol **P** inside this program will be substituted by its value 3.141... during the preprocessing stage. No symbol **P** will exist in the program at the compilation stage. You will see letters **P** in the source file. But they all will be substituted by the number 3.14.. in the copy, that is processed by the compiler (translation unit). Thus, the compiler "sees" the expression **2.0 * P * r * r** as **2.0 * 3.14159265 * r * r** in the translation unit. From this point on, the program just calculates the value of the expression with the number instead of **P**.

Let's emphasize again, the **#define** statement is written without a semicolon (**;**).
```
#define    P    3.14159265
```
Suppose, you write the number with the semicolon as
```
#define    P    3.14159265;
```
The name **P** will be substituted by the number and semicolon. The **2*P*r*r** will look after substitution as

```
2.0 * 3.14159265; * r * r
```
Have you noticed a semicolon? Therefore, anything written after the second white space in **#define**, just blindly substitutes the identifier. If **3.14159265;** contains a semicolon, it will be substituted in the program along with the semicolon. Since the substitution is done before compilation, the preprocessor does not "care" what gets replaced. It just goes ahead and does it. At this point, it is just a set of characters. It does not have to be a valid C++ expression, because the compiler does not evaluate it at this stage. For instance,

```
#define CHECK     <=0
```
It contains **<=0**, which is not a valid C++ expression. When it is used inside the programs, it substitutes the fragments, that we would have to write explicitly, otherwise. Consider a code fragment.

```
#define CHECK     <=0
main ( )
{
...
if (x CHECK)
cout << x
...
}
```
When the word **CHECK** is found, it will be substituted. The **if** statement will look like

```
if (x <=0)
cout << x;
```

10.2. Additional features of *#define* directive.

Symbolic name can be assigned to a symbolic constant as follows

```
#define   AND        &&
#define   BITAND     &
#define   EQ         ==
```
Those are three examples of assigning a name to an operator or so called symbolic constant. One can define any other symbolic constant. Let's give an example of it.

```
#include <iostream.h>
#define   AND      &&

void main ( )
{
int x=2, y=-4;
if ( x>0 AND y>0)
cout << "They both are positive.\n";
else if (x>0)
cout << "x is positive.\n";
else
```

```
cout << "y is positive.\n";
}
```

Program 10.3.

The output of the program is

```
x is positive.
```

This program shows you an example of how to use **#define** to assign a symbolic name to a symbolic constant. We defined name **AND** to be used instead of the logical operator **&&**. We can write the program using the name **AND**. The compiler will change that name to the **&&** symbol at the preprocessing stage.

The program compares two numbers to 0 simultaneously using that **AND** operator. If both variables are greater than 0, then, the message stating that is displayed. If one of those numbers is less than 0, then **x** is compared with 0. If **x>0** is true, this number is the positive one. Otherwise, it is **y**.

Sometimes, the preprocessor directive is too long to fit into one line. In this case, a backslash (\) is used to inform the compiler, that the same preprocessor directive carries over to the next line. We discuss this feature on the **#define** example. But it is applicable to all the preprocessor directives. An example of such definition is

```
#define   LESS_OR_EQUAL   \
<=
```

Here, the symbolic constant **<=** is written from a new line. The first line ends with the backslash, that allowed us to write this definition on two lines.

One can define an expression using the preprocessor directive by writing

```
#define    P    3.14159265
#define    TWO_P_SQUARE        2*P*P
```

The second line defines an expression with **P**. One should also introduce the constant corresponding to **P** somewhere in the program, in order to be able to refer to it. We did it at the first line. The **TWO_P_SQUARE** is substituted by **2*P*P** anywhere in the program at the preprocessing stage. Every **P** in the last expression will be substituted by the number 3.14159265 according to the first definition.

One can substitute a text by **#define** directive. For example,

```
#define SPEAK3   n=0; n<10; \
n++
```

At least one space should separate the replacement text from the identifier. Everything up to the end of line is understood as a replacement text. It will be substituted inside the program. Do not forget, if the backslash is encountered, then the next line text will be included as well. Let's consider a simple program.

```
#include <iostream.h>
#define SPEAK3   n=0; n<10; \
n++

void main( )
{
int n, m=0;
```

```
for (SPEAK3)
m=m+n;
cout << m;
}
```

Program 10.4.

This is a familiar to you program, that calculates the sum. The **for** loop will look like
```
for (n=0; n<10; n++)
```
after the preprocessing stage. The output of this program is number 45.

There are two types of macros: *object-like* and *function-like*. An object-like macro defines an identifier and replaces it by the replacement text each time the identifier is encountered in the source file. We have discussed only this type of **#define** macros so far. We offer an example of object-like macros as the last point of our discussion.

```
#include <iostream.h>

#define NUM 100
void main( )
{
cout << NUM;
}
```

Program 10.5.

The output of this program is number 100. It is printed by the **cout** object.

We can now consider the function-like macros. Those macros remind functions. They can have the parameters. The purpose of writing the function-like macros is to create inline alternative of the short functions. They allow a user to avoid the usual function calls and returns. We will now discuss the examples of the function-like macro.

Consider the **#define** directive that is used for writing the macro instructions.
```
#define  DISPL_INVIT  cout << "How are you? \n"
```
The **cout** object should replace **DISPL_INVIT** in a program. It is illustrated below.

```
#include <iostream.h>

#define  DISPL_INVIT  cout << "How are you? \n"
void main( )
{
DISPL_INVIT;
}
```

Program 10.6.

The output of the program is
```
How are you?
```
There will be no **DISPL_INVIT** after the preprocessing. It will be changed to the **cout** object. Pay attention to the semicolon. It does not appear automatically. It should be either

written in **#define** or added after **DISPL_INVIT** inside **main()** routine.

The function-like macros can have arguments as well. In this case, the argument is attached to the identifier, for instance,

```
#define    CUBE(x)      x * x * x
```

An argument becomes an argument to the symbolic name **CUBE(x)**. The name **CUBE** has an argument **x** in the parentheses **(x)**. Consider following fragment.

```
#define    CUBE(x)      x * x * x
void main ( )
{
float y, z;
....
y=CUBE(z);
....      }
```

Wherever word **CUBE(..)** is encountered within the program, the variable inside the parentheses will be treated as an argument. The macro **CUBE(z)** will be replaced by its expression. The code fragment

```
y=CUBE(z);
```

will look like

```
y= z * z * z
```

after completing the preprocessor directive. The value of z^3 is assigned to **y**.

It is interesting to consider a possible program pitfall here. If instead of **CUBE(z)**, we would have **CUBE(z+2)**, then, one can expect the value $(z+2)^3$ to be assigned to **y**. But it is not a case, because the preprocessor performs a literal text replacement of the argument into the macro's definition. Hence, the assignment would look like

```
y= z+2 * z+2 * z+2;
```

Thus, new argument **z+2** literally replaces **x** in the expression **x * x * x** inside the **#define** directive. A directive, that can produce $(z+2)^3$ is

```
#define    CUBE(x)      (x) * (x) * (x)
```

The argument **z+2** substitutes every **x** in the expression **(x) * (x) * (x)** as before, but each **x** is now enclosed by the brackets as **(x)**. If the name **CUBE** is used now in a code as before, it produces

```
y=CUBE(z+2);
```

The result of preprocessor directive action is the assignment operator rewritten by it.

```
y= (z+2) * (z+2) * (z+2);
```

Consider a short program, that illustrates the use of function-like macros.

```
#include <iostream.h>

#define SQ(x) x*x

void main( )
{
int z=5;
z=SQ(z);
cout << z;
```

```
}
```

Program 10.7.

The output of the program is 25. It squares the value of **z** using **#define** macro.
Macros can have more than one argument, for instance,

```
#define  CONDIT(x, y, z)     x>=0 && y>2 || z-3 <5
void main ( )
{
. . . .
if (CONDIT(sa1, sb2, sc) )
. . . .
}
```

Here, the **#define** directive will change the content of **if** statement. The symbolic
word **CONDIT** with arguments **sa1**, **sb2** and **sc** will be substituted by

```
if (sa1>=0 && sb2>2 || sc-3 <5)
```

The arguments are passed in the order they go. The first argument **sa1** of **CONDIT** inside
the program is passed as the first argument **x** inside **define**, the second argument **sb2**
as **y** in **define** statement and so on.

ANSI C standard identifies five predefined macros, that have no arguments and cannot
be redefined. They begin and end with two underscores. We give them in Table 10.1. You
do not have to include any special files to access any of those macros. The commercial
compilers often also have some additional macros. You can find them in compiler manuals.

Table 10.1. The standard ANSI macros.

Macro	Description
__TIME__	Is equal to the current source file translation time in a format *hour:minutes:seconds*. If the operating system does not provide the time, the default is 17:00:00.
__DATE__	Represents the translation date of the current source file in the format *month day year*. When no date is provided by the operating system the dafault value is MAY 03 1957.
__FILE__	Is related to the name of the current source file. The file name is surrounded by the double quotation marks.
__LINE__	Gives the line number of a current source file. It can be altered with the **#line** directive.
__STDC__	It is defined and equal to 1, if compiler complies with ANSI C standard.

Following program displays the content of those standard macros.

```
#include <iostream.h>

void main( )
{
```

```
cout << "File " << __FILE__ << "\n" << "Current line is "
     << __LINE__ << "\n" << "Time: " << __TIME__ << "\n"
     << __DATE__;
}
```

Program 10.8.

The output of this program is

```
File play.cpp
Current line is 5
Time: 10:17:19
Jun 17 1996
```

10.3. The *#include* statement.

The **#include** statement, or *file-inclusion* directive is used to attach or to include different files in the programs. Those files usually have an extension **.h** in their names and are called the *header* files. Some of those inclusion files are standardized. Some are about to be standardized. Compiler vendors provide some additional header files. You must include the header files in the program, when they are needed. Your code might not be understood by the computer without including those files. You can also create the files by yourself, write some functions in them, and include those files in a source file. You should also use **.h** extensions to name those header files.

Suppose, one has to write a few programs which will contain the same definitions, like

```
#define   CM_IN_MET    100
#define   GM_IN_KG     1000
#define   MILLIVOLT    0.001
#define   KILLOVOLT    1000
...
```

One can write all those definitions every time for every new program, or to combine all those definitions in one file, called for instance **defunits.h**. If those definitions placed now in one file are needed, one can just include this file.

The **#include** statement has a format of writing

#include   "*filename.h*"   or
#include   <*filename.h*>

The **#include** directive causes the specified in it source file to be included in the current source file. The computer can use all the functions, written in that included source file for your current program. The difference in two forms of writing this directive is in the way in which the computer searches the directories for the specified file. Unfortunately, both ways are loosely specified by the standard. Therefore, they can change from a computer system to another computer system. Usually, the search for the file is conducted in the following way.

The double quotes around the name of the included file (**"*filename.h*"**) force the computer to look for the specified file first in the same file directory, that contains the source file. If the file specified inside those double quotes is not found there, the preprocessor will search other directories. Those other directories to search will be selected in accordance with how your operating system is configured or organized. If the (< >) characters are used to enclose the file name, those other directories will be searched in the same order as for the previous (" ") quotes. In this case, the file directory containing the source file will not be searched. If the file cannot be found in either of those cases, the error message will be displayed.

The file that you include with the **#include** directive can also include files using the **#include** command.

When **#include** is encountered, the preprocessor just inserts the content of the file named in this directive. The file is inserted beginning from the line in the program, where this **#include** directive is found. For instance,

```
#include "defunits.h"
void main
{
. . . . .
}
```

Here, the content of the **defunits.h** file will be inserted at the first line, where we wrote this **#include** directive. The translation unit looks after the replacement as

```
#define  CM_IN_MET    100
#include GM_IN_KG     1000
#include MILLIVOLT    0.001
#include KILLOVOLT    1000
void main
{
. . . . .
}
```

We want to emphasize, the file to be used with **#include** directive can contain any operators, statements and directives, not only **#define** statements. The action of pre-processor is just copying the content of that file into the place where you write the **#include** directive. It is the same, as you would just type it in. The **#include** statement is, typically, placed at the beginning of the program, outside any function or routine as any preprocessor directive. As any preprocessor directive, it acts inside the same source file, in which it is included.

Thus, there are three categories of files, that you can include in your program. First ones are the standard ANSI library files. We consider all of them in the last chapter. There are some C++ specific library files, that are about to become the standard files. We place them in the same category of the standard files. We will consider most of them later in this book. The second type files are the additional files created by the compiler vendors. Almost any commercial compiler has some extras. You have to read specific compiler manuals about them. The third category of files are the files, that you create and include in the program. Sometimes, you can write some specific drivers for some devices. The manufacturers of those devices can provide you with some other files to include. So, this can be another type of inclusion files.

10.4. The *#ifdef*, *#ifndef*, *#undef*, *#endif* directives.

The **#ifdef** directive is a conditional compilation directive. The **#ifdef** works in a way, that we consider on an example.

```
#ifdef      VOLUME
#define     LENGTH      10
#define     WIDTH       15
#define     HEIGHT      30
#endif
```

It instructs the preprocessor to define the constants **LENGTH**, **WIDTH**, **HEIGHT**, if the symbolic constant **VOLUME** has been already defined. So, here the line

```
#ifdef      VOLUME
```

instructs the preprocessor to check, if the constant **VOLUME** has been already defined. If it has, the preprocessor executes all the operators between the **#ifdef** and **#endif** directives. Again, the preprocessor checks, if the constant **VOLUME** is defined. It does not check, if this constant has a particular value.

Conditional directives can begin with **#if**, **#ifdef**, **#ifndef** and **#elif**. They all end with **#endif** directive. Next program illustrates some of those directives.

```
#include <iostream.h>
#define X

void main( )
{
cout << "Welcome to the program.\n";
#ifdef X
cout << "X is defined.\n";
#endif
cout << "You will always see it.\n";
}
```

Program 10.9.

The output of this program is

```
Welcome to the program.
X is defined
You will always see it.
```

It displays the statement, that **X** is defined, if it is so. And we, indeed, defined **X** earlier in the program. This program is an example of the **#ifdef-#endif** construction. Another example of this construction is given in **Program 10.10**.

```
#include <iostream.h>
#define X   2
#ifdef  X
#define Y   3
```

```
#endif

void main( )
{
int n;
n=X+Y;
cout << n;
}
```
Program 10.10.

This program defines **Y** if **X** has been defined. This allows us to find the sum **n=X+Y**. It is equal to 5. The number 5 is the output of the program.

The **#ifndef** directive is an opposite of **#ifdef**. Consider the code fragment.

```
#ifndef   VAR
#define   VAR 10
#endif
```

It will define the symbolic constant **var** to be 10, if it has not been defined. In other words, if the constant *constant_name*, whose name is contained in the line

```
#ifndef constant_name
```

has not been defined, then, the directives between **#ifndef** and **#endif** will work. Otherwise, the preprocesor will skip them all. We can rewrite the previous example.

```
#ifndef      VOLUME
#define      LENGTH        10
#define      WIDTH         15
#define      HEIGHT        30
#endif
```

It instructs the preprocessor to define the constants **LENGTH**, **WIDTH**, **HEIGHT**, if the symbolic constant **VOLUME** has *not* been already defined.

The **#undef** directive, as for instance,

```
#undef   X1
```

instructs the preprocessor to cancel any definition of **X1**, whether or not it has been defined before. When do you need to use it? Assume, you do not know, if the name **X1** has been defined before. But you want to define a constant or a variable named **X1** in your source file. In this case, you might type the **#undef X1** first as a precaution.

10.5. The *#if*, *#else*, *#elif*, *defined* directives.

The **#if** directive tells the preprocessor to discard a section of a source code, if a particular condition inside that **#if** does not hold. It is a conditional compilation directive. The format of writing that directive is

```
#if expression or constant
......
#endif
```

If the *expression* inside **#if** is not true or equal to zero, the source code between **#if** and **#endif** will be thrown away by the preprocessor. If the *expression* is true or not equal to zero, that fragment will be inserted into the program by the preprocessor in the same place, where it is written. Basically, the code fragment between **#if** and **#endif** would not move anywhere, if it is inserted. It would just be accessible for compilation. This is what we called "the fragment will be inserted". Condition inside **#if** can be a constant or an expression of integer type. For example,

```
#define NUMBER_A     1
#if NUMBER_A
#define  X      10
#define  Y      20
#endif
```

The **#if NUMBER_A** directive evaluates **NUMBER_A** constant, which we have defined to be 1. The source code up to **#endif** will be inserted into the program. If the **NUMBER_A** were defined as 0, then **#if NUMBER_A** would instruct the preprocessor to skip the code, contained between **#if** and **#endif**.

We can use the discussed property for debugging a program, as, for instance,

```
#include <stdio.h>
#define   TRACK   1

void main ( )
{
int n,m;
#if TRACK
printf("Enter two numbers to multiply.\n");
scanf("%d*%d", &n, &m);
n=n*m;
printf("n*m=%d\n", n);
#endif
printf("\nThe calculation is complete.\n");
}
```

Program 10.11.

Imagine, you are working in the environment, that has no debugging capabilities. Suppose, you want to skip the part of the code that works. You can write **#if** directive inside the routine, and make a constant inside it to be equal to zero. The **#endif** can be put to any location, so you can isolate any fragment and stop its execution. If you want to use it again, the constant inside **#if** can be changed to non-zero value. Review an example, given in the **Program 10.11**, that multiplies two integers **n** and **m**, entered by means of **scanf()** function. The symbolic constant **TRACK** has been defined at the beginning of the program. We have used **#if TRACK** and **#endif** to separate a fragment of the program between those lines. We have chosen a non-zero value for **TRACK**, so the fragment works. If we make **TRACK** equal to zero, by changing the **#define** directive at the first line, the chosen code fragment will not be compiled.

An example of a condition inside **#if** is

```
#if CALC>=3
....
#endif
```

One can use expressions inside **#if**, as we have used in **#if CALC>=3**. The symbolic constant **CALC** should be defined earlier using **#define** directive. If the conditional expression is true, the above fragment between **#if** and **#endif** will be compiled. Otherwise, it will be discarded. It is also possible to use multiple conditions, as, for instance,

```
#if defined(X1) || !defined(Y2)
....
#endif
```

A few ideas are presented in this fragment. The **#if** directive works in its usual way. If the condition is true, the code between **#if** and **#endif** is inserted and compiled. The given example shows, one can check for multiple conditions at once. We check here, whether **X1** has been defined or **Y2** has not been defined. The logical " **||** " (OR) operator is used to connect two conditions in the same manner, as in a regular **if** statement. The fragment will be substituted and compiled, when either the first, or the second, or both conditions inside **#if** are true.

Second interesting feature of the above example is the use of **defined(X1)**. That expression, called the **defined** operator, can be used in preprocessor directives to determine, if a macro (**X1**) has been defined. It has two alternative and equivalent formats of writing

> **defined(**_identifier_**)**
> **defined** _identifier_

The _identifier_ is called the argument of the preprocessor directive. The **defined** is TRUE or equal to 1, if its argument has been defined. It is FALSE or 0, otherwise. A name is viewed as defined, if it has been defined with **#define** and has not been undefined with **#undef**. In our example the **defined(X1)** is TRUE or equal to 1, if **X1** is currently defined as a macro. It is FALSE or equal to 0, if **X1** has never been defined before. It can also be 0, if **X1** has been **#undef** after the last definition.

Let's consider **#else** preprocessor directive. It plays virtually the same role, as for the regular **if-else** construction. It is used as a preprocessor conditional compilation directive and serves for the directive evaluation. The **#else** directive is used with **#if**, **#ifdef**, **#ifndef**. It works identical with all three conditional directives. Consider a code fragment, that will illustrate the **#else** directive.

```
#if  VARIABLE==1
#define SQU(x)  2*x
#else
#define SQU(x)  x*x
#endif
```

Here the condition is **#if VARIABLE==1**. The **VARIABLE** is defined earlier, and it is equal to 1. If the condition is true, the preprocessor will insert **#define SQU(x) 2*x**. Otherwise, **#define SQU(x) x*x** will be inserted. The end of each conditional compilation block is marked by **#endif**. One can use a number of directives between **#if** and **#else**, and between **#else** and **#endif**. So, if the condition is TRUE, the code between the **#if** (**#if**, **#ifdef**, **#ifndef**) and **#else** is inserted into a program by the preprocessor. Otherwise, the code between the **#else** and **#endif** will be inserted.

We would like to introduce the **#elif** directive, which is a short form of **else-if**. Consider following program.

```
#include <iostream.h>
#define A1
#if defined(A1)
#define INTRO   cout << " You defined A1. \n";
#elif defined(A2)
#define INTRO   cout << " You defined A2. \n";
#elif defined(A3)
#define INTRO   cout << " You defined A3. \n";
#endif

void main ( )
{
INTRO
}
```

Program 10.12.

This displays the message indicating what variable has been defined. You can define either of the variables named **A1**, **A2** or **A3** in the beginning of the program. If the first condition is true (if **A1** is defined), the first fragment

```
#define INTRO   cout << " You defined A1. \n";
```

will be inserted. All others will be discarded. If the first condition is not true, the preprocessor will evaluate the second condition. If the second condition is true, the second define will be left and all others skipped. If the second condition is not true as well, then the third condition is tested. If it is true, the third fragment should be inserted. All the other fragments will be skipped. The end of the block is as always the **#endif**. Our program should display the very first message.

```
You defined A1.
```

We will also show another example of the conditional compilation use.

```
...
void main ( )
{
#if defined(WAY1)
temp( );
#elif defined(WAY2)
voltage( );
#else
printend( );
#endif
...
}
```

This example calls function **temp()** to be compiled, if the macro **WAY1** has been defined. If **WAY2** has been defined, than the **voltage()** function should be compiled. If neither of identifiers **WAY1** nor **WAY2** has been defined, then the **printend()** function can be compiled. This example can be used in your source codes. Suppose, you have written a few functions in your program. You want only one of them to be compiled and work, depending on the conditions of the program. So, you can use this trick to choose the one you need.

10.6. The *#line*, *#error*, *#pragma* directives.

Suppose, you include one of your files in a program, as shown in the fragment below.

```
#include <myfile.h>
void main ( )
{
....
}
```

Suppose, **myfile.h** contains twenty lines, and you have made a mistake on the line 10 inside the **main()** routine. The compiler might indicate, that the error occurred at line 30, because the preprocessor has to add 20 lines of **myfile.h**. If you do not remember exactly the number of lines in **myfile.h**, you might not be able to find the line to be corrected. The problem of keeping truck of the lines would be more frustrating, if you include a few files in your source code. The way to overcome this is to use the **#line** directive. The format of using it is

#line   *number* " *filename"*

The *number* is an integer. It is the number of the line, on which this directive appears. For example, you write at some line of a program.

```
#line   5
```

That line will be assumed by the compiler to be the fifth line of code. The next line below will be the sixth one and so on. The filename contained in that directive is optional. It indicates the name of the current file, where it is used. Say, you work on your program source file called **hi.cpp**, and you write

```
#include <myfile.h>
#line 1
main ( )
{
....
}
```

Here, the line of code **#line 1** will now be the first line. The line containing **main()** is now the second and so on. We could have written

```
#line 1 "hi.cpp"
```

as well. It does not change anything.

The **#error** directive instructs the compiler to generate the error messages. It is used to indicate that some conditions are violated. Consider an example.

```
#if X==1 && X==3
```

```
#error Double macro definition
#endif
```

Here **#if** checks if the symbolic constant **x** has been defined to be 1 and 3 previously. If it is true, the **#error** directive will print its message.

```
Double macro definition
```

The format of writing **#error** is

#error *message*

It displays the **message**. The **message** is, sometimes, called a preprocessor-token.

The **#pragma** directive is a special one. Pragmas are compiler specific commands. Each compiler can have its own pragmas. If pragmas are not recognized by a specific compiler, they are ignored. You can find an information about the pragmas in compiler manuals. They perform very specific functions. We will not discuss them in this book.

10.7. Preprocessor operators.

We will consider following operators: the stringizing operator, the token-pasting operator, null directive.

The *stringizing* operator (**#**) converts macro parameter to the string constant. It is used only with the function-like macros taking arguments. Consider an example of writing this operator.

```
#define  phrase(row)  #row
```

If the macro **phrase()** is found in the program, it is substituted by its parameter. For example, a program line is **phrase(got it)**. This construction is substituted by the string "**got it**". Consider following program, that illustrates it.

```
#include <stdio.h>
#define  phrase(row) #row

void main ( )
{
printf ("%s\n", phrase(how are you));
printf (phrase (hello));
}
```

Program 10.13.

The output of this program is

```
how are you
hello
```

Here, both **printf()** functions should look after the preprocessing as

```
printf ("%s\n", "how are you");
printf ("hello");
```

You could achieve the same output as in **Program 10.13** by displaying the message with the **cout** object.

```
cout << phrase(how are you);
```

We want to demonstrate a more complex example.

```
#include <stdio.h>
#define  talk(row) printf ( #row "\n")

void main ( )
{
talk (knowing C is important);
talk ("knowing C is important");
}
```

Program 10.14.

The translation unit of this program can be

```
main ( )
{
printf ("knowing C is important" "\n");
printf ("\"knowing C is important\"" "\n");
}
```

The output of this program is

```
knowing C is important
"knowing C is important"
```

If the character contained in the argument needs an escape sequence, the **#** operator inserts it automatically. For instance, the second phrase

```
"\"knowing C is important\""
```

needed the backslash characters (\) for the double-quotation marks.

If a character **#** is present in a line by itself, it performs no operation at all. It is called *null* directive.

The *token-pasting* operator (**##**) can be considered on an example

```
#define  bend(x, y) x ## y
```

It is used in both object-like and function-like macros. It couples together different tokens, so they become one token. The resulting token should be a valid token. If a macro has the arguments, they are first replaced, then, pasted together. Consider **Program 10.15**.

```
#include <iostream.h>
#define  bend(x, y) x ## y

void main ( )
{
int a1=20;
cout << bend(a, 1 );
}
```

Program 10.15.

The output of the program is 20. We insert the **bend(a, 1)** function into the **cout** object. According to **#define**, the **bend(a, 1)** should be replaced by **a##1**. The token-pasting operator makes one word from **a** and **1**. It becomes **a1**, that is the name of the variable. Therefore, the preprocessing leads to the **cout** object looking like

```
cout << a1;
```

Since the value of **a1** is 20, that number is, in fact, displayed on the screen.

10.8. Expandability and transportability of a program.

The preprocessor directives can make a program easier to expand. Consider an example. You declare an array **a[20]** and write loops for the input and the output. They can look like

```
for (n=0; n<20; n++)
....
```

If you need to change the number of array elements, it will require to change all the loops and definitions. It can be more convenient to do it differently. We define some word, for instance **SIZE**. It can be used everywhere instead of the number 20. An array can be written as **a[SIZE]**. The loops will look like

```
for (n=0; n<SIZE; n++)
```

Now, to change the number of the elements, you should change the definition directive.

```
#define  SIZE  100
```

The transportability of the program can be improved, sometimes, by the preprocessor directives, although we will not discuss it in details. For example, you can improve the transportability of the operations on bits by the preprocessor directives.

EXERCISES.

1. Run all the examples of this chapter, if you have an access to a computer.
2. Write a program that uses macro **MYMAX** to find the greatest of three numbers.
3. Write a program that uses macro **MEPRINT** to print a string of characters that you enter.
4. Write a program that uses macro **AVARRAY** to find an average of an array of floating-point values. The macro should have an array and a number of elements in the array as its arguments.
5. Write a program that uses macro **MECALC** to calculate the biweekly gross earnings and the paycheck amount of an hourly paid employee. The macro takes an hourly wage and the number of hours worked as its arguments. If there are less then 80 hours worked for two weeks, the program displays the message, that the employee worked fewer hours than required. The tax rate is presumed to be flat 20%.
6. Write a program that uses a macro to sort an array. The program should read 20 numbers from the console, place them into an array, sort and display them.
7. Write a program that uses a macro to print your name on the screen.
8. Create a file in your project. This file must define the functions **st_read()** and **st_write()**. The first function reads the string up to 40 character long from a keyboard and places it in a string specified by its formal parameter. The second function writes the string stored in that array to the screen. Include the file as a header file in your

program. Use it to read a string from a keyboard and write it, then, to the screen.

9. Write a program code in a few source files combined in the same project. Investigate how your program can use the functions from the header file created in the previous program.

10. Create a program, that uses the stringizing and token-pasting operators.

11. Investigate if you can use a token-pasting operator inside the stringizing operator. How would you write this?

12. Write a program, that uses an **#error** directive.

CHAPTER 11

RUN-TIME ALLOCATION.

11.1. Essence of dynamic memory allocation.

The data or instruction you enter is placed in the memory and then processed. There are four regions in the memory, in which the computer organizes C/C++ program. According to Fig 11.1 they are: stack, free memory, global variable memory and the program memory. There is only fixed number of instructions in the program and fixed number of global variables. Therefore, the memory were the program and the global variables are placed remains unchanged during the program execution. The region between the stack and the global variables is called "heap" and is used for the dynamic memory allocation. Since the memory size is limited, there is a maximum number of bytes one can dynamically allocate. One can even run into a situation, when the stack and the heap can overlap. This is called a heap-stack collision and is considered a fatal run-time error.

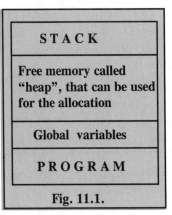

Fig. 11.1.

We are coming to a question what is the run-time or dynamic allocation? First, whenever you define a variable or an array in your program, a sufficient memory space is allocated for it. You have to declare a type of that variable, or array. For instance,

```
int m;
```

allocates a cell of memory capable of holding an integer number. This memory is allocated during program compilation and is called *compile-time allocation*.

In some cases a programmer does not know how many variables and what types will be entered into the program. Let's say, you want to write a program that keeps track of each part stored in a stock room. To keep track of one part means to have its name, model number, number of stored pieces, price, etc. For instance, a part is the screws. Their type is #6-32. You have 100 pieces. Their price is $1 for 20 pieces. The simplest solution would be to allocate an array of structures. Each element of the array will contain all this data for one part. But you do not know how many parts will be stored in the stock room. You can allocate some number, let's say, 1000 and hope, that this will be enough for all the parts. You can have more than 1000 parts. You can also have less than 1000 parts. In the last case, you will waist a lot of memory space.

This was just a very trivial example of what you have to deal with, if you declare the number and the type of all the variables explicitly while writing the code. The choice of the number and the type of the variables (or array elements and so on) and, therefore, the memory allocation for them could be postponed until running the program. It is called *dynamic* or *run-time allocation*. Dynamic allocation allows you to enter the variables as they are needed during the run, and the computer will still allocate a sufficient space for them. In this case, the total number of entered variables can be limited by the size of the heap memory. We will learn standard C functions used for the dynamic allocation: **calloc()**, **malloc()**, **realloc()** and **free()**. We will also study C++ style run-time allocation. Those are the tools for the run-time allocation. Another important skill is how to use them to actually create the program entities, that permit a user to enter needed number of variables at the time of the program run. We will study that in Chapter 19. The entities, such as linked lists, trees, stacks, queues, are used for entering the data at the run-time.

11.2. Standard C memory allocation functions.

11.2.1. The *sizeof* operator.

Before we discuss any of the memory allocation functions, let's consider the **sizeof** operator first. When one declares a variable to be of a specific data type, the computer allocates certain number of bytes for it. The number of bytes allocated for a data type might vary with the system. Sometimes, we have to tell the compiler, how many bytes of memory to allocate. We do it in **calloc()**, **malloc()** functions. If 2 bytes are reserved for a variable of **int** type by one system, it does not necessarily mean, that any other system reserves the same number of bytes for this type. It, sometimes, makes the programs not portable. The **sizeof** operator improves their portability.

The **sizeof** operator is written in the following format.

> **sizeof** (*argument*);

It computes and returns the size of its **argument** in bytes. The argument can be a variable, a pointer to an array, an object, a name of any data type. For instance,

```
#include <iostream.h>

void main(void)
{
float  x;
int m;
cout << sizeof(x) << ", " << sizeof(m) << ", "
     << sizeof(double);
}
```

Program 11.1.

The output of the program is: **4, 2, 8**. The sizes allocated for each of those data types can vary for your computer systems.

Let's declare a structure

```
struct test_data {
int q1;
int q2; }
```

The **sizeof(test_data)** will be equal to the size of the cell allocated to hold one variable of the structure **test_data** type.

Remember, the **sizeof** is an operator not a function even though it resembles a function. The computer simply calculates the size of the cell capable to hold the argument, and replaces the **sizeof** operator by the constant equal to that value. We get a value at the run-time. For instance, we will have 2 instead of **sizeof(int)** at run-time. One can assign this number to a variable. For instance, **y=sizeof(char)**. The value returned by the **sizeof** has **size_t** data type, so the variable it is assigned to should be of this type. The **size_t** data type is equivalent to any integer data type for many compilers. You can assign the values returned by the **sizeof** operator to the variables of the **unsigned long**, **long**, **int** data types. The **size_t** data type is described in a number of standard header files, for example, in the **<stddef.h>** file. One of those header files should be included, if you intend to use a variable of the **size_t** data type. The **size_t** is one of the safest data types for the integer data.

One can ask, how to find a size of a number of cells using the **sizeof** operator. Suppose, you need to find a size of three cells of type **int**. This is written as

   3*sizeof (int)

If you try to write it as **sizeof(3*int)**, it will be interpreted as an error. The size of an array **float arr[20]** can be found as

   sizeof (arr) which is equivalent to 20*sizeof (float)

Consider another example.

```
#include <iostream.h>

void main(void)
{
float  arr[30];
int m;
unsigned long s;
s=sizeof (arr);
cout << s << ",   ";
s=3*sizeof (int);
cout << s;
}
```

Program 11.2.

This program displays the sizes of two objects. The output is: **120,   6**.

11.2.2. The *calloc( )* function.

The synopsis of **calloc()** function is

```
void *calloc (size_t num, size_t size);
```
It allocates a memory block for an array consisting of **num** number of objects each of them occupying a cell of length **size**. The total size of an allocated memory block will be a equal to **num×size**. The first parameter **num** specifies the number of elements in an array. The second parameter, we called **size**, specifies how many bytes each of those arguments will occupy. Both arguments are specified by ANSI C standard to have **size_t** data type, although one can, in many cases, declare them as having any integer type.

The **calloc()** function returns a pointer to the first element of the array, if there is enough memory space. Otherwise, **NULL** pointer is returned. The **NULL** pointer is the address 0. It is used by a number of functions to stop their actions or to indicate an error. We have specified the value returned by the function to be a pointer to **void** type. We did it to indicate, it can be a pointer to any data type. Another important feature of the **calloc()** function is that, when the memory block is allocated, each byte of that block is set to zero. Unfortunately, the values are set to zero up to a floating-point on some compilers. So, you might not have to "clean" this memory block, if you intend to store integers or characters. You might have to call each cell of the memory and set it to zero.

The **calloc()** function is described in the **<stdlib.h>** ANSI C standard library file. In order to use the **calloc()** function, you must include this file in a program as
```
#include <stdlib.h>
```
Let's now consider some examples of writing this function. For instance, we write
```
char *ar;
...
ar= calloc (18, 5);
```
Here, both arguments are the constants. We allocated 18 places each 5 bytes long. One can use a mixture of the variables and constants as the arguments of the **calloc()** function. The values should be assigned to those variables prior to **calloc()** call. Examples are given below. For example, we declare
```
int m=15; k=10;
int *br;
```
The **calloc()** function can be called as
```
br=calloc (m, k);    or   br= calloc (15, k);    or
br= calloc (m, 10); or   br= calloc (15, 10);
```
One can also use **sizeof** operator to define the size of each allocated place in bytes.
```
br= calloc (30, sizeof (double) );
```
This function is, usually, written in another format. For example,
```
pr= (double *) calloc (30, sizeof (double) );
```
Here, the fragment **(double *)** is used to specifically *cast the type* of the returned pointer. Some compilers allow to write **calloc()** as well as **malloc()** functions with and without the type cast. We advise to use a format with the type cast for the **calloc()** function. It is illustrated in **Program 11.3**.

```
#include <iostream.h>
#include <stdlib.h>

void main (void)
```

```
{
int *pin, *out, n, coun=10;
pin=(int *)calloc (coun, sizeof (int));
if (pin==NULL )
{
cout << "unable to allocate memory\n";
exit (0);
}
for (n=0; n<coun; n++)
{
cout << "enter an integer number \n";
cin >> *(pin+n);
}
cout << "\n";
for (n=0; n<10; n++)
cout << *(pin+n) << ", ";
free (pin);
}
```
Program 11.3.

The program prompts us ten times to enter a number. We enter an integer number each time. They all are placed in the array pointed to by the **pin** pointer. We, then, display the content of the array.

The program uses **calloc()** function to specify the size of the array. The array pointed to by **pin** holds 10 integer elements. We conclude the program with **free()** function, which we will learn later in this chapter.

Program 11.3 uses the function **exit(0)**. It is described in the **<stdlib.h>** header file that should be included, if you intend to use the **exit()** function. The **exit()** function stops program execution in the point, where it is encountered. It takes an integral argument. It returns the value of its argument. Typically, you use 0 as an argument of **exit()** function for a normal program termination. You use other integer numbers for some serious errors that might occur or for abnormal program termination. We will study this function in the last chapter. Right now you can use this function for program termination.

11.2.3. The *malloc( )*, *realloc( )*, *free( )* functions.

The **malloc()** function prototype is
```
    void *malloc ( size_t size);
```
The parameter **size** has **size_t** data type according to ANSI C standard. You can pass an argument of any integer data type to **malloc()** on many compilers. The **malloc()** function allocates a block of memory. The argument **size** determines the physical size of memory in bytes that this block occupies. The function returns a pointer to the beginning of that memory block or the **NULL** pointer, in case of error. The function returns a pointer

to **void** type. The returned by the **malloc()** pointer can be cast to any data type. An example of writing the **malloc()** function is

```
p=malloc(100);
```

Here, the argument is a constant number. It allocates 100 bytes. Next example

```
zq=malloc(x);
```

has a variable as its argument. One must assign a value to that variable, prior to the call. One can also write

```
kl=malloc(30*sizeof(int) );
```

Above example uses an integer multiplier (30) and **sizeof** operator to define a size of the memory to be allocated. The multiplier can be 1, then

```
kl=malloc(sizeof(int) );
```

We can also write

```
ptr = (int *)malloc (30*sizeof(int) );
```

It is just another form of writing the same function. Here, we cast the type of the returned pointer. The function returns a pointer to **void** type. We use **(int *)** to cast the return type to a pointer to **int**. It is better to use this form of writing.

One can use **calloc()** to replace the **malloc()** function and vice versa. The lines

```
qp1=calloc (10, sizeof (int) );
qp2=calloc( 15, 1 );
```

can be substituted by

```
qp1=malloc (10* sizeof (int) );
qp2=malloc( 15 );
```

Following code fragment illustrates how to allocate a structure variable.

```
#include <stdlib.h>
#include <iostream.h>

void main(void)
{
struct test_data
{
int salary;
float weight;
char name[20];
};
struct test_data  *point_to;
point_to=( test_data  *) malloc (sizeof (test_data) );
if (point_to==NULL)
{
cout << "unable to allocate \n";
exit (1);
}
....
```

The **realloc()** function can mess up your data. Therefore, it should be used cautiously. The **realloc()** function prototype is

```
void *realloc (void *ptr1, size_t size);
```
It changes the size of the memory block pointed to by the first parameter **ptr1** to the size (in bytes) specified by its second parameter **size**. The function returns a pointer to a memory block, if it is successful. It returns **NULL** pointer in case of failure. The returned pointer is not necessarily equal to the first argument. Sometimes, there is not enough space to enlarge an object at a present place. So, that memory block is moved to another location. The returned by the function pointer as well as the first argument **ptr1** can be the pointers to any data type.

We will also study the **free()** function. Its synopsis is

```
void free (void ptr);
```
The parameter, we called **ptr**, is a pointer to a previously allocated memory block. The function releases back to the system the region of the memory pointed to by **ptr**. When we allocate a memory block, it is reserved for a particular entry. It cannot be used by the system for other purposes. But if it is not used, you want to "vacate" or to free it, so it becomes available to the system. The **free()** function does exactly that. It frees the previously occupied memory space pointed to by its parameter **ptr**. The **ptr** can be a pointer to any data type. The argument should be previously returned by one of the allocation functions. The **free()** function does not return any value, i.e., it has **void** type. We used it in **Program 11.3** to free the memory at the end.

A few rules to remember while working with the memory allocation functions. First, it is always wise to check, if the required memory can be allocated by simply comparing the returned pointer to **NULL**, as we did in **Program 11.3**. Second, the pointers returned by the **calloc()**, **malloc()** and **realloc()** should be rather saved in the static variables. The reasoning behind it is following. Let's say, you allocate a memory block while executing some function. If you execute this function and go to another routine, the memory is still allocated. But some other routine can discard a pointer to that memory. You lose control of the allocated memory, even though it can still exist. This can lead to a waste of memory space or an error. So, use the static variables, unless you know, that the memory block will be freed before the end of the routine.

Third, always try to free the memory, when you do not need it. The computer frees the memory, when your program completes the execution. Excessive memory slows the program execution. Besides, if you allocate a lot of memory, there might not be enough space for the program execution.

Fourth, try to avoid allocating small blocks of memory less than 25 or 50 bytes with **malloc()**. Also, **malloc()**, usually, allocates 16 or more bits over the requested size. The **malloc()** is typically used for the memory allocation. The last advice is to watch the **free()** function. Never call it with invalid argument, because this can potentially crash the system.

11.3. C++ style allocation. The *new* and *delete* operators.

C++ can use C dynamic allocation functions. But there are two additional operators for the run-time allocation in C++. They are: **new** and **delete**. The **new** operator is written in the form

```
ptr = new data_type;
```
It allocates memory to hold a value of **data_type** type and returns a pointer to it. We used an assignment statement showing that the operator returns a pointer. The returned pointer can be assigned to a pointer of the same data type. The **data_type** can be any valid data type. The **delete** operator is written in the form
```
delete ptr;
```
It frees the memory region pointed to by the pointer **ptr**. Consider following example illustrating the use of both operators.

```
#include <iostream.h>

void main ( )
{
int *q;
q=new int;
if (q==NULL)
{
cout << "Allocation was unsuccessfull" << endl;
return;
}
else
cout << " Memory allocated. Enter an integer number."
      << endl;
cin >> *q;
cout << "You have entered " << *q << endl;
delete q;
}
```

Program 11.4.

The program allocates a cell capable of storing an integer by **q=new int**. If the allocation was unsuccessful, it displays a failure message and stops the program execution. If the allocation was successful, the program prompts a user to enter an integer. If we enter, for instance 4, the program, then, displays
```
You have entered  4
```
Since a pointer to an allocated by **new** memory was assigned to **q**, we use it to place the entered by us value into that memory by **cin >> *q**. After the program displays the final message, the allocated memory is freed by **delete q**.

One can not only dynamically allocate a memory cell, but also initialize that memory at the run-time as well. To do this, one has to specify the initial value of that allocated memory inside the parentheses **( )** in the **new** operator. It is written in the form
```
q=new data_type (n);
```
This expression allocates the memory for storing one variable of the **data_type** type. It places the value **n** in this memory cell. Some examples of that are
```
ptr=new float (23.453); or  qp=new int (k); where k=10
```
Following program demonstrates the initialization.

```
#include <iostream.h>

void main ( )
{
int *q;
q=new int (123);
if (q==NULL)
{
cout << "Allocation was unsuccessfull" << endl;
return;
}
else
cout << " Memory allocated. " << "You have entered "
     << *q << "." << endl;
delete q;
}
```

Program 11.5.

The program displays

    `Memory allocated. You have entered 123.`

   The initialization of the dynamically allocated memory has been done by **q=new int (123)**. This expression placed the value 123 into the allocated memory cell.

   One can allocate and delete an array using **new** and **delete** operators. To allocate an array, the **new** operator should be written in the form

    ptr = new data_type [num];

This form allocates the space enough to hold a **data_type** type array of **num** number of elements. It also returns a pointer to that array. It is important to remember, you *cannot initialize dynamically allocated array*. The allocated space for an array can be freed by the **delete** operator, written in the form

    `delete [ ] ptr;`

It frees the memory area of an array pointed to by the pointer **ptr**. In some older C++ compiler versions you might have to specify the number of elements in that array. Therefore, you might have to write the **delete** operator in the form

    `delete [num] ptr;`

   Here, **num** is the number of elements in the array to be freed. Consider following program, that illustrates how to allocate an array dynamically.

```
#include <iostream.h>

void main ( )
{
float *q;
q=new float [5];
if (q==NULL)
{
```

```
cout << "Allocation was unsuccessfull" << endl;
return;
}
else
cout << "Memory allocated. "
      << "\nEnter 5 numbers separated by the blanks "
      << "and hit ENTER." << endl;
for (int k=0; k<5; k++)
cin >> q[k];
cout << "The numbers are: ";
for (k=0; k<5; k++)
cout << q[k] << ", ";
delete [ ] q;
}
```

Program 11.6.

The above program allocates memory for an array of 5 floating-point numbers using

```
q=new float [5];
```

If the memory is allocated successfully, it displays a proper message.

```
Memory allocated.
Enter 5 numbers separated by the blanks and hit ENTER.
```

Let's assume, we enter following five numbers: 1 2 3 4 5 and hit **ENTER**. The program displays

```
The numbers are: 1, 2, 3, 4, 5,
```

This concludes present chapter. We offer you some exercises for practicing.

EXERCISES.

1. Run all the programs of this chapter, if you have an access to a computer facility.
2. Write a program that displays the size of the memory required for allocating:
   a) an integer;
   b) a floating-point number;
   c) a character;
   d) a **unsigned long** variable;
   e) a **double** type variable;
3. Write short programs, that use **calloc()** and **malloc()** functions to allocate the memory for different types of data. Both functions should obtain the size required to allocate from the **sizeof** operator. The programs should allocate memory for the following entities:
   a) an array of 10 elements of type **int**;
   b) an array of 20 characters;
   c) an array of 5 floating-point numbers;
   d) an array of unions. Each union consists of a floating-point number and
      a character string of 20 elements;

     e) an array of 10 elements of a structure type. Each structure type consists of 2 integers and one character string. The character string can have up to 15 characters in it.

4. Write the same functions as required in exercise 3, but use the **new** and **delete** operators.

5. Write a program for a class of students. Each student must be represented as an array element of the structure data type. Each element should consist of two character strings. The first string is the first name. The second string is the last name of the student. There must be three more members in this structure type. The first one will store the age of a student. The second will store the number of attended years. The third member should store the GPA. A class consists of 20 students. Use the operators for the dynamic memory allocation to allocate the memory for all those students. Your program should be able to sort the students by their grades, number of attended years and the last names. Your program must display the size of each array element and the size of the whole array.

CHAPTER 12

CLASSES.

12.1. Introduction to objects.

Before talking about the classes and object-oriented programming, one shell first introduce the notion of objects. So far, we have occasionally called a variable, an array, a structure, a union and so on as an object. The notion of an object is much wider. The real life brings us the *objects*. Some of the object examples are: animals, buildings, people, cars, ships, TV, computers, plants, water and millions and millions more. Human thinking is organized in terms of objects. Human thinking can perform the *abstraction*, that enables us to create and describe some objects in a way, that can seem, sometimes, absolutely not related to the real world. We use the abstraction to describe the real world and to understand it better.

All the objects can be divided on two categories - animate and inanimate objects. The animate objects can change their state in time, i.e., they can move around, change their shape and color and so on. The inanimate objects do not change in time. They remain of the same shape, size and on the same position since creation. The examples of animate objects are people, animals, flowers, plants and so on. The inanimate objects are rocks, pictures and so on that are not moved or changed by people, animals and nature, although the rocks and pictures also change in time. Their change for our practical purposes can be considered very small and unrecognizable. One cannot separate animate and inanimate object only based on change of state. It is not necessarily true, in general. It is one of the criteria, that we used to separate those objects. It can hold for some types of objects for some duration of time.

All the objects have *attributes* like shape, color, size, weight and so on. All the objects can be characterized by their *behavior*, i.e., a car runs, turns, stops. An aircraft flies, goes up, goes down, crashes. A ball rolls, inflates, deflates, bounces. A human dies, lives, walks, lies, talks, cries, screams, eats and so on. People learn objects by studying their attributes and behavior. All the objects can be somehow divided on groups of similar objects, having some similar properties. One can separate plants, adults, babies, apes, tigers, cars and buses as different groups. The objects inside each group have a lot of similarities. Depending on the similar attributes we are looking for, the same groups can be rearranged. For instance, the tigers, apes and people can be separated in the group of alive objects.

The *object-oriented programming (OOP)* models the real world in a software. It creates the models for the groups with some similar characteristics. Those groups can be also called *classes*. Classes are *programmer-defined types*. To simplify the models, the OOP uses the *inheritance* and *multiple inheritance*, meaning that the newly created classes of objects inherit the characteristics of existing classes, adding to them some characteristics on their own.

The OOP also models the communications between the objects. The OOP encapsulates data (which are attributes) and the functions (representing the behavior) into entities called *objects*. Both the data and the functions are tied together inside an object. Objects can *hide the information*. This means, that even though the objects can communicate among themselves through *interfaces*, objects do not know how the other objects are implemented. It is possible, because in the real life, for instance, the car driver does not necessarily know all the details of how his car is built. It is considered a good programming practice in C++ to hide the content of the classes and to communicate through the class interfaces. In C++ the programming unit is the class, from which an object is created. Each class contains the data components called *data members* and the function components called *member functions*.

The content of the present chapter is broken on two chapters in a number of books, because of a significant size of the material on classes. We give it as one lengthy chapter, because we think, it logically belongs in the same place. We want you to see all the material given in this chapter as a whole. It is necessary for you, from our point of view, to see the logical unity of different class features, that we give here.

12.2. Introduction to classes.

12.2.1. Class example.

Classes permit the programmers to model objects. A class resembles a structure. It is an entity, that, like a structure, consists of other entities. Let's remind you, a structure, union, enumeration types, etc., we call derived data types. The data types such as **short**, **char**, **int**, **float**, etc., are called the fundamental data types. A class can consist of the variables, arrays, strings, and even other class objects of fundamental and derived data types as its members. They are called the *data members* of a class. Why? Because they contain the information or the data. A class can also have function as its members. They are called the *member functions*. They perform certain actions on the data members.

Classes have some similarities with the structures. Before one can use a class, it must be declared. Since a class contains the member functions, they all should be defined after the class declaration. *This creates a class data type.* You have learned, to be able to use a structure type, you should define a variable of that type. Same thing is true for classes. A variable of a class type is called an *object*. We just gave you an idea of how to introduce a class in a program. We must learn now how to do it practically. There are some peculiarities in doing it. Let's consider the classes on an example of the following program.

```
#include <iostream.h>

class Cat
{
```

```
private:
int x;
int y;
public:
int z;
Cat();
~Cat();
void gval (int, int);
void show ();
};

void Cat:: gval (int a, int b)
{
x=a;
y=b;
}

void Cat::show ()
{
cout << "x=" << x << ", " << "y=" << y << ", "
     << "z=" << z << endl;
}

Cat::Cat ( ) { }
Cat::~Cat ( ) { }

void main()
{
Cat obj1, obj2;
obj1.gval (1, 2);
obj1.z=3;
obj2.gval (20, 30);
obj2.z=50;
obj1.show ();
obj2.show ();
}
```

Program 12.1.

The output of the program is
```
x=1, y=2, z=3
x=20, x=30, z=50
```

12.2.2. Class declaration.

The above program declares a class, defines all its functions, defines the class objects, and, then, uses the class type through its objects. Let's first consider how does it declare a class. A class declaration begins with the keyword **class** followed by the *tag* (name of the class). The body of the class is contained inside the **{ }** braces. The closing brace **} ;** is terminated by a semicolon. **Program 12.1** declares the class **Cat**.

```
class Cat
{
private:
int x;
int y;
public:
int z;
Cat();
~Cat();
void gval (int, int);
void show ();
};
```

It contains the variables **x, y** as its members. It also contains four functions: **Cat()**, **~Cat()**, **gval()** and **show()**. Their prototypes are written inside the class. *Thus, you declare the data members and write the function prototypes for the function members in the class declaration.*

Our class also contains labels **public** and **private**, each followed by a colon (**:**). Those words specify the accessibility of the class members. All the members appearing after the word '**public:**' and down to the closing bracket **} ;** are called public members of the class. They are accessible to any member function inside the class. *They are accessible from the outside of the class via its objects.* The public class members will be manipulating the data inside the class for the outside needs. It is a class "interface" with the program. The public class members can serve to the parts of the program outside and inside the class. The outside parts of the program, that will use a class, are called *clients*. The clients can use a class through its interface (or public members). Again, the public class members can be used outside the class through its objects. We will see how to do it. The public members of our class are: **Cat()**, **gval()**, **~Cat()** and **show()** and **z**.

The private class members in our case are the ones grouped between the word '**private:**' and the '**public:**' label. They are **x** and **y**. The private class members can be used only by the class members and the special functions declared as 'friend'. We will study them later. *They cannot be accessed via class objects from the outside of the class.* When a class object is used by the clients, they do not necessarily have to know the internal members of that class. The private class members are intended for the internal use of a class. A class uses those private members to perform its external tasks. They are the hidden content of the class.

Usually, the member functions of a class are its public members, and the data members are the class private members. However, you may group the class members as required by a particular programming task. We have written the private part of the class first in **Program 12.1**. It is followed by the public class members. This order is not required. One can have public members of a class followed by the private. We could have written **public** label first. In this case, all the members from that label down to the closest

private label would have belonged to the public members. All the class members from the label **private** to the closing brace would have been the private class members. One can have any number of **private** and **public** labels in the same class. Many programmers prefer to group all the private members under one **private** label and all the public members under one **public** label.

In case of multiple labels, the private class members are contained between the word **private** and the first following below **public** label, or the closing **}** bracket. For the multiple labels, the public class members are contained between the word **public** and the first following below **private** label, or the closing **}** bracket. *The default access for the class members is* **private***. Therefore, if you do not specify the class members as public or private, they will be assumed to be* **private***.* We will begin to illustrate how to work with both **private** and **public** members later.

This concludes class declaration. The next step is to define the class member functions.

12.2.3. Member function definition.

Program 12.1 defines the member functions in a following way.

```
void Cat:: gval (int a, int b)
{
x=a;
y=b;
}

void Cat::show ()
{
cout << "x=" << x << ", " << "y=" << y << ", "
     << "z=" << z << endl;
}

Cat::Cat ( ) { }
Cat::~Cat ( ) { }
```

There are four member functions in the **Cat** class: **Cat()**, **~Cat()**, **gval()** and **show()**. The definitions of all class member functions are shown above. Those are just regular definitions, except two things. *First*, the definition header of every class member function begins with specifying its return type followed by the **Cat::** and the name of the function. An example is

```
void Cat::show( )
```

Here, the header begins with the **void** function return type followed by the **Cat::** and the name of the function **show()**. The **Cat::** is the name of the class in which the function has been declared (in our case **Cat**) followed by the **::** operator, called *binary scope resolution operator*. Why does one need this operator? Different classes can have the same member names. One uses the scope resolution operator to "bind" the member name, it is used with, to the class. The name declared with the **::** operator will have the *class scope*. Therefore, it will be visible and accessible only inside the class. Any other part of the program "does not know" about the existence of that name.

By declaring our internal class functions **Cat()**, **~Cat()**, **gval()** and **show()** as **Cat::**, we have made them invisible to any other part of the program but the class **Cat**. *Therefore, they can be used only via the objects of their class type.* You can declare other functions with any of those names (**check()** or **disp()**) anywhere in the program without any problems. The program will treat them as different functions. The member functions of the class **Cat** are accessible, usable and visible inside the class. They can become visible outside the class, only when you access them by means of the objects of that class.

Second, we have declared two functions with the names **Cat()** and **~Cat()**. They are special functions. The **Cat()** function is called a *constructor*. It has the same name as the class itself. It does not have a type of the return value. Hence, it does not return any value. Its definition contains only **Cat::** (class name and scope operator). It can be written with or without the parameters. You do not even have to declare and define the constructor. It will be automatically created by the compiler, if you do not specify a constructor function in your class. It is used to create the objects of a class. A constructor is executed, when an object is created. An object is created, when an object comes into a scope. It means that an object is created, when a function in which it is defined begins its execution. If an object is defined globally, it is created when the program execution begins. A class must have a constructor function. The constructor can be written by a user. Again, if omitted, it will be created by the computer.

We write a constructor, that has no statements in **Program 12.1**. There is nothing magic about the constructor. You do not write anything special that it needs to create an object. Loosely speaking, a constructor does it on its own. However, a constructor can be coded to perform some additional actions. For instance, you can assign the initial values to your object through the constructor. Furthermore, even that can be done by any other function.

The **~Cat()** function is called the *destructor*. It is called, when a class object goes out of scope. It does not have any parameters. It does not return a value. It just destroys an object of its class, when an object goes out of the scope. It means, when a function where an object is defined terminates, it needs to be discarded, as any variable. The variables are discarded by a computer. The objects of a class type are destroyed by the class destructor.

We will return to both destructor and constructor a bit later in this book. So, do not try to understand them now. Do not hurry to understand the classes now as well. Just read the book, and we will gradually walk you through them.

Our **Cat** class also contains two regular member functions. The **gval()** function has two parameters **a** and **b**. It assigns the arguments, passed to its parameters, to the class data members **x** and **y**. The **show()** function displays the values stored currently in the **x**, **y** and **z** data members. Both **gval()** and **show()** functions have **void** return type. It is not a rule. Class member functions can return a value of any data type.

One can ask, how can the **gval()** and **show()** functions access the class members **x**, **y**, **z**, that have not been declared in these functions. The variables **x**, **y**, **z** have been declared as the members of the class **Cat**. In C++, any member function of a class can use the data members of the same class without any redeclaration. So, the data members **x**, **y**, **z** are accessible to all the member functions of the same class. *Loosely speaking, class data members can be used by the member functions of the same class as their own* *variables. Each member function of a class can change them. The change remains in effect for the same object, until the value is changed again.*

12.2.4. Using classes.

Thus, a class is a user-defined data type. Once declared, it becomes a new data type. The name of that class will represent a new data type. How do you use this data type? In the same way you use a structure type - by defining a variable of structure type and using it. To use a class data type, you define a variable of a class type. The variables of class types are called the *objects*. Why do we call a variable of a class type an object? An object is a conventional name for a variable of a class type. It is called an object, because it can be used for describing the objects of a real world. An object of a class type can have the attributes. They can be stored in the data members. It can develop a behavior, that is described by the internal member functions. An object of a class type is a basis for the object-oriented programming. We will discuss how to use the class type on an example of the same **Program 12.1**.

```
void main()
{
Cat obj1, obj2;
obj1.gval (1, 2);
obj1.z=3;
obj2.gval (20, 30);
obj2.z=50;
obj1.show ();
obj2.show ();
}
```

The program defines two objects **obj1** and **obj2** of the class type **Cat**. We mentioned, the classes have some similarities with the structures. *The class members are accessed in the same manner as the structure members, using a dot.* The form to access a class member is

```
object.member
```

Here, the **object** is the name of an object of a class type. The **member** is a member of that class. An example of member function call is

```
obj1.gval (1, 2);
```

It calls member function **gval()** that belongs to the object **obj1** with the arguments 1 and 2. An example of accessing a data member with the object is

```
obj1.z=3;
```

The above form assigns the value 3 to the data member **z** of the object **obj1**.

Each structure variable consists of all the structure members. Each of the defined class type objects **obj1** and **obj2** "gets its own set" of all the **private** and **public** class members. In other words, the **obj1** comprises a set of class member variables **x**, **y**, **z**, and the functions **Cat()**, **~Cat()**, **gval()**, **show()**. The **obj2** contains a different set of variables **x**, **y**, **z**, and the functions **Cat()**, **~Cat()**, **gval()**, **show()**. Thus, **obj1.show()** and **obj2.show()** are two separate entities. In the first case, the **show()**

member function belongs to the object **obj1**. In the second case, the **show()** function belongs to the object **obj2**.

An object can call a member function of its class. An object can access only a data member of its class. Pay attention, the **obj1** accesses only the member **obj1.z** and two member functions **obj1.gval()**, **obj1.show()**. Same is true for the object **obj2**. Class members **z**, **gval()** and **show()** have been declared as **public**. This is why both objects can access only those members. We said, that the public members of a class can be used from the outside of the class via objects of that class data type. This is what we meant by that. A class object can use any of the public class members. It can access public data members, change their value. It can call any public member function. We have learned the form used to access the class members. This form should be used for doing that. So, the program operates with the public class members directly through the objects of that class.

An object of a class data type cannot access the private members of a class. If we have written **obj1.x=3**, that would have been considered as an error. The private class member **x** cannot be accessed via an external object even, if it is an object of the same class data type. This is what we meant by saying, that a program cannot directly access the private members of a class outside of that class. Notice, that the private class members can be accessed by the internal class member. The member **x** can be accessed by the **gval()** and **show()** functions. They both are the public functions and can be used by the objects of the class type. Hence, the private class members can be made accessible to the class objects through the public functions.

We want to conclude rephrasing one of our previous points. For instance, we call **obj1.gval()** function. The **gval()** member function, as we know, has a class **Cat** scope. It can be used from outside of the class only as a member function with the objects of **Cat** class. We call **gval()** or **show()** functions as **obj1.gval()** or **obj1.show()** from **main()**. Try to call them from **main()** simply as **show()** or **gval()**, for instance. You would get an error message. You can even declare and define a function with the same name **show()** or **gval()** in the same source file or even in another class and use it. They will be completely different functions. Only if **show()** appears with the object of **Cat** class, it will be understood as the function, that we have declared inside that class. This is why we define the member functions with the **Cat::** as having class scope.

12.3. Objects and initializers.

Consider following program.

```
#include <iostream.h>                    //line1

class Dat                                //line2
{                                        //line3
public :                                 //line4
Dat ( int mon, int day, int year);      //line5
```

```
void check ( );                              //line6
void disp ( );                               //line7
~Dat ( );                                    //line8
private :                                    //line9
int m, d, y;                                 //line10
};                                           //line11

Dat::Dat (int mon, int day, int year)        //line12
{                                            //line13
m=mon;                                       //line14
d=day;                                       //line15
y=year;                                      //line16
}                                            //line17

void Dat::check ( )                          //line18
{                                            //line19
static int per[ ]= {0, 31, 28, 31, 30, 31, 30, 31, 31,
               30, 31, 30, 31};              //line20
int k;                                       //line21
k=m;                                         //line22
if (per[k]<d)    d=0;                        //line23
}                                            //line24

void Dat::disp ( )                           //line25
{                                            //line26
static char *moname[ ]={"none", "Jan", "Feb", "Mar",
          "Apr", "May", "Jun", "Jul", "Aug", "Sep",
          "Oct", "Nov", "Dec"};              //line27
cout <<moname[m] <<", " << d << ", "<< y << "\n";//line28
}                                            //line29

Dat:: ~Dat( )                                //line30
{   }                                        //line31

void main ( )                                //line32
{                                            //line33
Dat test1 (2, 20, 1996);                     //line34
Dat test2 (3, 40, 1996);                     //line35
test1.disp ( );                              //line36
test2.check ( );                             //line37
test2.disp ( );                              //line38
}                                            //line39
```

Program 12.2.

The output of the program is

```
Feb, 20, 1996
Mar, 0, 1996
```

We declare the class **Dat** with all its members at lines 2-11. The class consists of **private** data members **m, d, y**, and **public** function members **Dat()**, **check()**, **disp()** and **~Dat()**. We intend to use this class for manipulations with time. As we saw earlier, all the data members and the member functions are declared inside the class. All the member functions are defined outside the class right after its declaration. The header in each function definition contains the return type followed by the class name and scope resolution operator. For example, **void Dat::check()**.

We have declared four public member functions in our class in **Program 12.2**. The first one is a constructor **Dat()**. We define it at lines 12-17. It has three parameters **mon, day, year** of **int** data type. The **Dat()** constructor creates an object of the class. It also assigns the values of its parameters **mon, day, year** to private class members **m, d** and **y** respectively.

We define the **check()** function at lines 18-24. The **check()** function declares and initializes an array **per[]**. Each element of the array is equal to the maximum possible number of days in each month. The first array element **per[0]** is made equal to zero. It is done, because the array begins from the **per[0]** element, but the month count begins from **m=1**. The **per[1]** corresponds to the number of days in January. The **per[2]** corresponds to the number of days in February and so on. The **check()** function checks, if the number of days stored in the class member **d** is not greater than the maximum number of days in a given month. It is done by **if** statement.

```
    if (per[m]<d)    d=0;
```

d is made equal to zero, if it is greater than the maximum number of days in a month.

The **disp()** member function is defined at lines 25-29. It just displays the name of the current month, day of the month and the year. Its implementation should be quite clear to you. The **disp()** function declares the **moname[]** array of strings. Each of the strings contains the name of the month. It is displayed by using the pointer to a string **moname[m]** in **cout**. The **disp()** function uses the member variables **m, d, y** in the **cout** object as

```
    cout <<moname[m] <<", " << d << ", "<< y << "\n";
```

The destructor **~Dat()** is defined at lines 30-31. It consists of no statements. It just destroys an object of the class. Let's discuss how do we use the class in **Program 12.2**. It is used inside the **main()** function at lines 32-39. We define two objects of the **Dat** class type. Let's consider how we operate with at least one of them. We define it as

```
    Dat test1 (2, 20, 1996);
```

This starts the constructor function, which creates an object. When we define an object **test1**, we create an object that contains all those private and public class members. The object **test1** has its own set of **private** members **m, d, y**, and **public** members **Dat(), check(), disp()** and **~Dat()**. The object **test2** has the same class type. It also contains a separate set of the same data and function members.

We wrote a class constructor, that has the parameters. When a class constructor has the parameters, the computer expects you to define and initialize an object of that class at the same time. The numeric values are passed to the constructor function during the object definition by the form

```
    class-name object (arg1, arg2, arg3....);
```

Here, the **class-name** is the name of the class. The **object** is the name of the object that you declare. It is followed by the list of parameters in the braces. The parameters **arg1**, **arg2**, **arg3**... are called *initializers*. We have passed the numerical values to the **Dat** class constructor in **Program 12.2** by the definitions

Dat test1 (2, 20, 1996); or Dat test2 (3, 40, 1996);

Those are the examples of the given above form. The constructor matches its first parameter with the first initializer, the second parameter with the second initializer and so on. In case of the object **test1**, the value 3 is passed to **mon**, 20 is passed to **day** and 1996 is passed to **year**. A constructor can have no parameters at all. In this case an object is defined without any initializers. We called **test1.disp()** to display the date corresponding to the first object.

We also declare another class object.

Dat test2 (3, 40, 1996);

The second number 40 stands for the number of days. We have selected an object with the silly number of days in a month to demonstrate you the **check()** function. We call **test2.check()** function to check the second object. It sets **d** class member to zero. When we call **test2.disp()** to display the second object, we get **Mar, 0, 1996**.

12.4. Member functions.

We want to emphasize again, that an object of a class can be defined without the initializers. We have rewritten **Program 12.2** to demonstrate it. The new version also demonstrates some other properties of classes.

```
#include <iostream.h>

class Dat
{
public :
Dat ( );
void check(int , int , int );
void disp (int , int , int );
~Dat ( );
private :
int m, d, y;
};

Dat::Dat ( )
{    m=d=y=0;      }

void Dat::check(int a, int b, int c)
{
m=a;
d=b;
```

```
y=c;
 static int per[ ]= {0, 31, 28, 31, 30, 31, 30, 31, 31,
                     30, 31, 30, 31};
if (per[m]<d)
{
d=0;
cout << "Date error.\n";
}}

void Dat::disp(int mon, int day, int year)
{
static char *moname[ ]={"none", "Jan", "Feb", "Mar",
        "Apr", "May", "Jun", "Jul", "Aug", "Sep", "Oct",
        "Nov", "Dec"};
check(mon, day, year);
cout <<moname[m] <<" " << d << ", "<< y << "\n";
}

Dat:: ~Dat( )
{   //no code
}

void main ( )
{
Dat test1, test2;
test1.disp(2, 20, 1996);
cout << "Beginning of test2.check( ) execution.\n";
test2.check(3, 40, 1996);
cout << "The end of test2.check( ) execution.\n";
test2.disp(3, 40, 1996);
}
```
Program 12.3.

The output of the program is
```
Feb 20, 1996
Beginning of test2.check( ) execution.
Date error.
The end of test2.check( ) execution.
Date error.
Mar 0, 1996.
```
The program is very similar to the previous, but has some significant differences. We declare class **Dat**, that has the same members as in **Program 12.2**. The difference of the present class comes in functions. Now **check()** and **disp()** member functions have formal parameters. The constructor does not have the formal parameters.

The **check()** function has three parameters **a, b, c** in **Program 12.3**. It assigns their values to the class member variables **m**, **d**, **y**. The function declares and initializes the **per[]** array. Each member of that array, as previously, corresponds to the number of days in each month. The first array element **per[0]** is made equal to zero. It is done, because the array begins with the **per[0]** element, but we want the **per[1]** to correspond to the number of days in January, **per[2]** to correspond to number of days in February and so on. The **check()** function, again, checks, if the entered day number is not greater than the maximum number of days in the entered month. If the number of days is greater, the function displays the message "**Date error**" and sets member **d** to zero.

Our class also contains the **disp()** function, that has three formal parameters: **mon**, **day**, **year**. The **disp()** function displays the date. It calls the **check()** function to inspect, if the entered number of days in a month does not exceed the maximum possible number of days. Pay attention, that the class member function **disp()** calls the member function **check()** of the same class as a regular function without any dots. It is a rule. The functions that belong to the same class can call each other as regular functions. The **disp()** function declares the **moname[]** array of strings. Each of the strings is the name of the month. It is displayed by **cout**. The **cout** object also displays the day of the month **d** and the year **y**.

We used the constructor function **Dat()** without parameters. It assigns zero values to all the class data members. We have also written the empty destructor **~Dat()**.

One can use any arguments in any member functions. Each member function behaves itself inside the class as an independent regular function. It can have its arguments. It can be called independently. It can call any other function and even another member function. In our **Program 12.3** member function **disp()** calls another member function **check()** of the same class. We stress it again, *the member functions of the same class can call each other without any dots just as the regular functions.*

Both functions **check()** and **disp()** are still declared of type **void** with respect to the return values. So, both of them do not return any values. But the member functions can return values of any data type. They can even return the values of the class members. They are just as regular functions. Do not be afraid of them. The member functions of the class are regular functions. Their difference from the regular functions is, that they must be called from the *outside of the class* in the structure member notation, as for example, **test2.check(3, 40, 1996)**. They also differ from the regular functions by the fact, that the class name and the (**::**) scope resolution operator must appear in the header of the member function definition. Their other differences are: they can freely use the data members of the same class without declaring them, they can call the same class member functions simply by names not in the structure member notation.

We use the class in our **Program 12.3** pretty straightforward. We declare two objects **test1** and **test2** of type **Dat** in the beginning of **main()**. Both objects are declared without the initializers, because the class constructor function does not have any parameters. We first display the date **test1.disp(2, 20, 1996)**. We, then, display a message, that we begin the **test2.check()**. Since the **test2.check(3, 40, 1996)** contains funny day argument 40, it should display an error message. The date error message is, in fact, displayed on the screen. We, then, display another message notifying the user, that the execution of **test2.check()** member function has been completed. The computer executes **test2.disp(3, 40, 1996)**. We call the **disp()** member function. You can see, it calls the **check()** member function. You see the second error message displayed by the **check()** function. Only after that, the entered date gets displayed.

One can declare so-called *utility functions* in a class. A utility function is usually declared as **private** in a class. It does some operations inside the class. The class clients do not have an access to them. For instance, we could declare the **check()** function as **private** class member. One would not be able to use it with the class objects. The call **test2.check(3, 40, 1996)**, for example, would be an error. But the **check()** function could still be used by any member of the class. We can leave it in the **disp()** function. This way, if the user calls the **disp()** function, the entered date will be first checked by the **check()** function.

You have seen, that the class serves as a data type for the objects. A class has some obvious similarities with the structures. Its declaration is quite similar to the structures. It consists of members. One accesses the class members in the same way as structure members, using the dot. A class and a structure can have **private** and **public** members. A structure variable comprises all the structure members. A class object consists of all the class members. But a class is not exactly a structure. A class differs from structures. A class declares member functions in it. A class has constructor and destructor. A class type is used for defining an object, that has a deeper meaning than a structure variable.

12.5. Constructors.

We have run into the constructor and destructor functions in the previous programs. Here, we should get closer acquainted with them. We first consider the constructor. Why do we need it at the first place? Let's return to our **Dat** class discussed above. It contains four member functions: **Dat()**, **check()**, **disp()** and **~Dat()**. It also contains three data members: **m, d, y**. C++ has following property. The class data members cannot be initialized in the class declaration. For instance, if you try to declare variable **m** in class **Dat** declaration, and initialize it, this will lead to an error.

Thus, if you write in the class declaration

```
private :
int m=1, d, y;
```

This will be interpreted as an error, because we initialized the variable **m** by making it equal to 1 as **m=1**. If you want to assign any initial value to any class member, you have to use the class constructor function. You can also use any other member function, that will take the external arguments from the class object and assign them to the class members. We did it in **Program 12.3** in **check()** member function. It had three formal parameters: **a, b, c**. Their values were assigned to the class members **m, d, y**.

Let's summarize what do we know about the constructors. First, the constructor has the same name as the class itself. It should be declared inside the class as a **public** member. It can be declared with or without the parameters. Second, one cannot specify the return type for the constructor function, not even **void**. The constructor does not contain **return** statement. Therefore, the constructor does not return any values. It creates an object of the class. You are not obligated to declare a constructor. If you do not declare a constructor, the compiler automatically creates one that does not have any statements or parameters. Its existence is necessary, because it is necessary to create an object. It is a good practice, if a programmer creates a constructor function, even if it consists only of the name and opening and closing braces.

Third, the constructor is executed, when an object of a class is initialized. The programmers do not write anything specific in the constructor for the object creation. The object creation by the constructor is administrated by the compiler. The programmers can use this function for performing any other action as well. One can use the constructor member function to assign the initial values to the class members, display messages and so on.

We wrote a constructor **Dat()** in **Program 12.2**, that had three parameters. It assigned the arguments, passed to those three parameters, to the data members of the class. This permitted us to declare the objects like **Dat test1(2, 20, 1996)** with the initial values, that have been passed to the class data members. The values inside the braces of **test1()** were passed to the constructor as the arguments.

Consider following program, that demonstrates some properties of a class constructor.

```
#include <iostream.h>

class Numb
{
public :
Numb ( );         // Constructor
int mult(int);
int sum (int);
~Numb ( );       // Destructor
private :
int x, y;
};

Numb::Numb ( )
{    x=y=1;      }

int Numb::mult(int val1)
{
x=x*val1;
return x;
}

int Numb::sum(int val2)
{
y=y+val2;
return y;
}

Numb:: ~Numb( )
```

```
{    }

void main ( )
{
Numb try1, try2;
int m, k, d=9;
for (int p=0; p<3; p++)
{
m=try1.mult (5);
k=try2.sum (d);
}
cout << "m=" << m << ", " << "k=" << k;
}
```

Program 12.4.

The output of the program is

  m=125, k=28

The program declares the class **Numb** containing two data members **x**, **y** and four functions **Numb()**, **mult()**, **sum()**, **~Numb()**. We again have four functions in our class. It is just a coincidence. One can declare any number of functions in a class. The class is declared by the rules you have learned. The word **class** precedes the name of the class. The data and the function members are declared between the **{}** braces. We, then, define all the class functions. The **Numb()** function is a constructor. It sets all the member variables in the class to 1. The **mult()** function has one parameter **val1**. It computes **x=x*val1** and returns the value of member **x** every time it is called. The **sum()** function has one parameter **var2**. The **sum()** function computes **y=y+val2** and returns the value of **y**. The class also includes a destructor function **~Numb()**.

We declare two objects of the **Numb** class **try1**, **try2** in **main()**. We, then, use the **for** loop to call the **try1.mult(5)** and **try2.sum(d)** member functions three times. The value of **d** is set to 9. The values returned by both functions are assigned to **m** and **k** respectively. We want to know the following: when the constructor function **Numb()** is called. Is it called only when the objects **try1** or **try2** are created when the function, in which they are defined, comes into a scope? Is it called every time when one uses either the class members or the objects of a class? The **Numb()** constructor sets **x** and **y** to 1. Therefore, if it is executed every time when an object is used, the values of **x** and **y** should be set to 1 every loop cycle. We should have **m** equal to 5 and **k** equal to 9 after three cycles. The values of **x** and **y** should increase each loop cycle, if the constructor is called only once during the construction of the object. We should have **m=125** and **k=28** after three loops. Since the last two values are the result of the program execution, we can make a conclusion: *the constructor is executed only when an object of class type is created, when a function, in which it is defined, comes into a scope.*

12.6. Constructor overloading. Default parameters.

One can declare more than one constructor for a class, if each constructor has a different parameter list. This means, that you can overload the constructor function. Consider following program, that should illustrate it.

```cpp
#include <iostream.h>

class N
{
int x, y, z;
public:
N ( );
N (int , int , int);
int mat (int, int, int), sum ( );
~N ( );
};

N::N ( )
{
cout << "The constructor without the parameters "
     << "is activated.\n";
}

N::N ( int n, int m, int k)
{
cout << "The constructor with the parameters "
     << "is activated.\n";
x=n;
y=m;
z=k;
}

int N::mat (int a, int b, int c )
{ return ((a+b)*c); }

int N::sum ( )
{ return (x+y+z);   }

N::~N( )
{    }

void main ( )
{
```

```
cout << "Declaring an object without initializers.\n";
N try1;
cout << "Declaring an object with initializers.\n";
N try2 (2, 3, 4);
cout << "mat( )=" << try1.mat (5, 7, 9) << "    "
     << "sum( )=" << try2.sum( );
}
```

Program 12.5.

The output of the program is

```
Declaring an object without initializers.
The constructor without the parameters is activated.
Declaring an object with initializers.
The constructor with the parameters is activated.
mat( )=108  sum( )=9
```

The above program declares class **N**, that contains three private data members **x**, **y**, **z** and five public member functions **N()**, **N()**, **mat()**, **sum()**, **~N()**. As you see, our class **N** contains two constructors. One of them **N()** does not have any parameters. The second constructor **N(int, int, int)** can accept three arguments. We also declared two mathematical functions **mat()**, **sum()**. They return the integral values. Those two functions perform simple mathematical calculations. You should not have any problems understanding them.

We declare two objects **try1** and **try2** in **main()** function. Before we declare the first object **try1**, we display the message

```
Declaring an object without any initializers.
```

Since the object **try1** does not have any initializers, the class constructor without the parameters is executed. That constructor displays its message

```
The constructor without the parameters is activated.
```

We, then, display a message, that we are about to declare an object with the initializers. And we, indeed, declare the object **try2(2, 3, 4)** with three initializers. Creation of this object starts the **N(int , int , int)** constructor. We get the message about it on the screen. We intentionally coded the messages into each constructor function. When they are executed, those messages will be displayed on the screen. This will allow us to see, which constructor is activated.

The **main()** function displays the results of the mathematical calculations, performed by **mat()** and **sum()** functions on different objects.

We learned, that we can write a constructor with or without the formal parameters. Treat an overloaded class constructor as a regular overloaded function. For instance, you can write overloaded constructors, as any overloaded functions, with the same number of parameters, that differ only by their types in each version. Then, the types of object initializers will determine what constructor version must be called.

One can also write a constructor function having the default parameters. It means, that some or all constructor parameters can have default values. We have reviewed functions with default parameters earlier in this book. The constructor obeys to all those rules for the default parameters. Program 12.6 illustrates constructors with default parameters.

```
#include <iostream.h>

class N
{
int x, y, z;
public:
N ( );
N (int, int =1, int =1);
int sum ( );
~N ( );
};

N::N ( )    { }

N::N ( int n, int m, int k)
{
x=n;
y=m;
z=k;
}

int N::sum ( )
{ return (x+y+z);   }

N::~N( )
{    }

void main ( )
{
N mine1 (2), mine2 (2, 3), mine3 (2, 3, 4);
cout << mine1.sum( ) << ", " << mine2.sum( ) << ", "
     << mine3.sum( ) ;
}
```
Program 12.6.

The output of the program is

     4, 6, 9

The program declares class **N** consisting of three functions and three data members. The first constructor **N()** of this class has two default parameters **m** and **k**. It takes three arguments and assigns them to the class members **x**, **y**, **z**. The class members are used by the **sum()** function, that returns the sum of **x+y+z**. We declare three objects **mine1(2)**, **mine2(2, 3)** and **mine3(2, 3, 4)**. The object **mine1** passes the first argument 2 and other two arguments are assumed to be equal to the default values. We specified them to be equal to 1 for each argument by default. The object **mine2** passes two arguments 2 and 3. The third argument is equal to its default value 1. The object **mine3** passes all three arguments. So, none of the arguments will have a default value. Our program displays the returned by the **sum()** value for each of those three cases.

A class can have either or both - overloaded constructors and constructors with some default arguments. **Program 12.6** demonstrates a class with an overloaded constructor. The first constructor version has three parameters with two default ones. The second version has no parameters at all. **Program 12.6** demonstrates a property of default constructors. Programmers, usually, call the *default* constructors those ones, that have the default values specified for all their parameters or do not have any parameters. A class can have only one default constructor in it. It is true for most modern compilers. Let's write

```
N ( );
N (int , int =5, int =2);
```

Class **N** can have the above two constructors. If a class has following two constructors

```
N ( );
N (int =1, int =2, int =3);
```

it will give an error. Here, the first constructor has no parameters. All the parameters of the second constructor have their default values. Therefore, both constructors are the default ones. And a class can have only one default constructor.

12.7. Constructors and destructors. Scope of an object.

We have learned about the constructors. Here, we will talk a bit about the destructor function, and try to give you an idea, when both functions are called.

The destructor function is required in a class. Its name repeats the name of the class. It is preceded by the tilt (~) character. Go back to **Program 12.6**. The destructor of class **N** in **Program 12.6** is declared inside the class as **~N()**. It is defined as

```
N::~N( )    {      }
```

It has no parameters and does not return any values. The destructor function does not have a return type, as you can see in any of the above programs. The destructor definition header consists of the name of the class followed by the **::** operator and the destructor name as **N::~N()**. This particular destructor does nothing. However, one can have a destructor performing some operations. Just do not forget, that the destructor cannot take any arguments. A class can have only one destructor member function. This means that the destructor function cannot be overloaded. The destructor is called, when a class object goes out of scope. In other words, the destructor is called when an object is destroyed. It prepares the object for the destruction.

So far, we talked about local, global and static variables. Everything remains the same for the object. In a sense, a class object is a variable. It is rather close to a structure variable. We have studied variables and functions. Everything studied for a variable is applicable for an object. The objects can also be local **auto**, global, **static** and **extern**. The objects are very close to the structure variables. As we know, a storage class for a structure variable is determined by two factors. The first factor is where do you declare a structure type. The second factor is where do you define a structure variable. Before you define an object, you have to declare its class data type. Typically, you declare class data type apart from any function in a source file. We will learn later, you can declare a class in a separate file, that can be included as your header file using the **#include** statement. Then, depending where and how you define an object of that class, it can become a **local**, **global**, **static** or **extern** object.

A local object is defined inside one of the program routines. It is visible and can be accessed only in the function, in which it has been defined in. The local **auto** object is created, when the function where it is defined, is executed. The local object is destroyed after that function termination.

The global object is defined outside any routine of the source file. It will be visible within the same source file, in which it has been defined. It will be created in the beginning of the program and destroyed at its end. An **extern** object is visible in different source files. It will be created at the beginning of the program and destroyed before the program termination. An object can also be defined with the word **static**, that precedes the class data type. A **static** object is created, when the function, where it is declared, is called. A **static** object is destroyed at the program termination.

Program 12.7 demonstrates how to define the local, global and **static** objects. It also illustrates when they are created and destroyed. We know, that the constructor member function is executed when an object is created, and the destructor runs when an object is destroyed. Thus, by establishing the order of constructor and destructor execution, one can see when an object is created or destroyed. The program below is an excellent example of doing it.

```
#include <iostream.h>
#include <string.h>

class Talk
{
public :
Talk (char *);
~Talk ( );
private :
char sym[25];
};

Talk::Talk (char *sts)
{
strcpy (sym, sts);
cout << "This is a constructor for " << sym
     << " object.\n";
}

Talk::~Talk ( )
{
cout << "This is a destructor for " << sym
     << " object.\n";
}
```

```
Talk glo ("global");

void fun ( )
{
static Talk fo1 ("static function");
Talk fo2 ("local function");
cout << "The function is about to be terminated.\n";
}

void main ( )
{
static Talk mo1 ("static in main( )");
Talk mo2 ("local in main( )");
cout << "We are about to call fun( ) from main( ).\n";
fun ( );
cout << " We are back in main( ).\n";
}
```

Program 12.7.

The output of the program is

```
This is a constructor for global object.
This is a constructor for static in main( ) object.
This is a constructor for local in main( ) object.
We are about to call fun( ) from main( ).
This is a constructor for static function object.
This is a constructor for local function object.
The function is about to be terminated.
This is a destructor for local function object.
We are back in main( ).
This is a destructor for local in main( ) object.
This is a destructor for static in main( ) object.
This is a destructor for static function object.
This is a destructor for global object.
```

The above program displays a sequence of messages. It will allow us to understand, when an object is created and destroyed. We have declared a class **Talk**, that consists of two **public** member functions: constructor **Talk()** and destructor **~Talk()**. It also consists of a string array **sym[]** as its private member. The constructor **Talk()** has a pointer to a string **sts** as its parameter. The constructor consists of two lines.

```
strcpy (sym, sts);
cout << "This is a constructor for " << sym
     << " object.\n";
```

The first line copies the content of the string **sts** to string **sym**. Next line displays a message, that "**This is a constructor for ... object.**". The dots between the words "**for**" and "**object**" are replaced by the content of the string **sym**.

For example, we declare static object **mo1("static in main()")**. It has a string

"static in main()" as its argument. This string is copied into **sym**. This is why, when an object is created, a constructor can display following message

```
This is a constructor for static in main( ) object.
```

Therefore, we can incorporate the name of an object into the constructor message. When the constructor is executed, it displays that message with the name of the object, that it creates. This permits us to see, which particular object has been created. So, we can see if the static in **main()** or any other objects have been created.

The destructor function takes no arguments. But it displays a message by

```
cout << "This is a destructor for " << sym
        << " object.\n";
```

The content of the character string **sym[]** is filled in by the constructor member function. And it contains the name of the object, that will be destroyed. The name of an object has been placed into string **sym** by the constructor of a particular object. This way we will know, when each of the objects in the program will be destroyed.

The program consists of two functions: **main()** and **fun()**. The program defines a global object **glo** of class **Talk** type. It is defined outside of any function. We also define one local object **mo2** and one static local object **mo1** both of **Talk** class type in **main()**. See how we define static object **mo1**. The word **static** is followed by the class name **Talk** and, then, by the name of the object **mo1**. Two other objects are defined in **fun()** function: local object **fo2** and local static object **fo1**.

The program should first create the global object. We get the first message from the constructor of the global object.

```
This is a constructor for global object.
```

This shows, that the global object **glo** has been created. The program starts the execution from the **main()** function. Both static **mo1** and auto local object **mo2** in **main()** get created. We get two messages from their constructors, that prove it. The program displays a message immediately before calling the **fun()** function. We, then, see two messages from the local auto and static object constructors. It signals, that both **fo1** and **fo2** have been created. This proves, that the local objects, defined in a function, are created whenever that function is called for execution. The function **fun()** displays the message before its termination. This indicates to us, that the function is about to be terminated. Now, we can observe, what happens with the local objects of that function upon its termination.

We see, that the destructor for the local function object **fo2** is activated. Therefore, the object **fo2** is destroyed after the function termination. And it is normal. The **fo2** is a local auto object in the **fun()** function. It should be destroyed, after the function "goes out of the scope" or, in other words, terminates its execution. The computer displays the message that the control is given back to **main()**, after the object is terminated. You can see, this concludes the **main()** execution. After that, the program destroys the local object **mo2** and the static object **mo1** in **main()**, the static object **fo1**, and the global object **glo**.

12.8. Inline member functions.

One can use **inline** functions as class members. Any member function including the constructor can be an **inline** function. Your request for an **inline** function might not be honored by the compiler. We would also recommend to write short and often used member functions as **inline** functions. There are two ways of writing **inline** functions. The first way is illustrated by **Program 12.8**.

```
#include <iostream.h>

class N
{
int x, y, z;
public:
N (int, int, int);
int mat ( )
{ return ((x+y)*z); }

int sum ( )
{ return (x+y+z);   }
~N ( );
};

N::N ( int n, int m, int k)
{
x=n;
y=m;
z=k;
}

N::~N( )
{    }

void main ( )
{
N mine (2, 3, 4);
cout << "mine.mat( )=" << mine.mat ( ) << "   "
     << "mine.sum( )=" << mine.sum( );
}
```

Program 12.8.

The output of the program is
    mine.mat ( )=20 mine.sum ( )=9
  The program declares class **N**, that has some similarities with the class discussed in

Program 12.5. Present class has three private data members **x**, **y**, **z**, and four member functions **N()**, **mat()**, **sum()** and **~N()**. Two of those functions **mat()** and **sum()** are the **inline** functions. They are defined inside the class declaration. For instance, consider the **mat()** function. It is completely defined inside the class **N**.

```
int mat ( )
{ return ((x+y)*z); }
```

*When a function is defined inside the class declaration, it becomes an **inline** member function.* A copy of its code will be squeezed in the program, where it is called. This is the same as for the regular inline functions. The **inline** function defined inside a class does not use the word **inline** or the name of the class and the **::** operator. You can see, that both **mat()** and **sum()** functions do not use **N::** in their headers. The word **inline** is not used with them as well. The fact, that they are defined inside the declaration of a class, tells the compiler, that they are **inline** functions. Any class member function, including the constructor, can be made an **inline** function.

Another way of writing an **inline** member function is illustrated below.

```
#include <iostream.h>

class N
{
int x, y, z;
public:
N (int, int, int);
int mat ( ), sum( );
~N ( );
};

N::N ( int n, int m, int k)
{
x=n;
y=m;
z=k;
}
inline int N::mat ( )
{ return ((x+y)*z); }

inline int N::sum ( )
{ return (x+y+z);   }

N::~N( )
{    }

void main ( )
{
N mine (2, 3, 4);
```

```
cout << "mine.mat( )=" << mine.mat ( ) << "   "
     << "mine.sum( )=" << mine.sum( );
}
```

Program 12.9.

The output of the program is

```
mine.mat( )=20   mine.sum( )=9
```

This program is similar to the previous one. Here, the class **N** is also similar to the class declared in the previous program. It also contains two **inline** class member functions: **mat()** and **sum()**. But here, we define both functions outside of the class declaration. The definition header of an inline function, defined outside the class declaration, begins with the word **inline** followed by the return type, name of the class, the scope resolution **::** operator, the name of the function and the list of its formal parameters. As an example we give the definition of a function from the above program.

```
inline int N::mat ( )
{ return ((x+y)*z); }
```

Review the definition header in our example. Here, the **inline** is followed by the return data type **int**, name of the class **N**, scope resolution operator **::**, name of the function **mat** and list of its formal parameters in the brackets **()**. Since the function does not have any formal parameters, the brackets are empty. We can write regular body of the inline function only after that.

12.9. Member access functions.

You have learned, that a class can contain the **private** and **public** members. One cannot access the private members from the outside of the class. However, private members can be accessed and used by the public class members. We learned how the constructor or any other function can get the data through their parameters and respectively set the values of the private members to any value. Sometimes, it is a good idea to use the member functions that do not perform any other action, but only access the individual class members and set them to specified values. Let's call them *access functions*. We offer following program illustrating an idea of an access function.

```
#include <iostream.h>

class Dat
{
public :
Dat ( );
void disp (), acmonth(int ), acday (int ), acyear (int );
~Dat ( );
private :
int m, d, y;
};
```

```
Dat::Dat ( )
{
m=d=y=0;
}

void Dat::disp( )
{
cout << "month is " << m << " " << "day is " << d
     << "  " << "year is " << y;
}

void Dat:: acmonth (int a)      { m=a;    }

void Dat::acday (int b)              {    d=b;    }

void Dat::acyear (int c)             {   y=c;   }

Dat:: ~Dat( )
{      }

void main ( )
{
Dat test;
int n, p, k;
cout <<"enter the month, then day and year.\n";
cin >> n;
cin >> p;
cin >>k;
test.acmonth (n);
test.acday (p);
test.acyear (k);
test.disp( );
}
```

Program 12.10.

The program prompts the user to enter the month, day and year. For instance, we enter
```
5 20 1998
```
The program displays the message
```
month is 5 day is 20 year is 1998
```
The program looks lengthy, but it is relatively easy to understand. We declare class **Dat** consisting of **private** data members **m**, **d**, **y**, and **public** functions **Dat ()**, **~Dat ()**, **disp ()**, **acmonth()**, **acday ()**, **acyear ()**. Constructor **Dat ()** sets all the class data members to zero. The **disp ()** function displays the current values of **m**, **d** and **y**. Each of the **acmonth ()**, **acday ()**, **acyear ()** functions is used to access the corresponding class data member and set its value. Each of those functions has a parameter.

The value of that parameter is acquired, when a member function is called. This value is assigned to a class data member. We want to store the month, day and year in the class members. This is why we picked the names of the access functions as **acmonth()**, **acday()**, **acyear()**. Function **acmonth()** assigns the value of its formal parameter **a** to the class data member **m**. The **acday()** function assigns the value of its formal parameter **b** to the class data member **d**. The **acyear()** sets the class member **y** to the value passed to its parameter **c**.

We use this class in the **main()** function. We declare the object **test** of the **Dat** class type. We enter the values of variables **n**, **p**, **k** from the keyboard. It is coded with three **cin** objects. The read values are passed as arguments to **test.acmonth(n)**, **test.acday(p)** and **test.acyear(k)**. We display the new values of **m**, **d** and **y** class members using **test.disp()**.

12.10. Pointers to objects.

You know, one can access a structure directly by name, or through a pointer to that structure. Similarly, a class members can be accessed directly by name, or through a pointer to that class. So far, we have discussed accessing class members directly by name. Here, we will discuss doing it using pointers. A class member can be accessed by a pointer to an object using the same **->** operator. The procedure of using the pointers to the objects is the same as for the pointers to the structure variables. One has to define a pointer to a class type. Then, the address of an object of that class type should be assigned to that pointer. It is like making a pointer to point to a variable. But here we make it pointing towards an object instead of a variable. Review following program illustrating it.

```
#include <iostream.h>

class Example
{
int val;
public:

void arr_val (int a)  { val=a;  }

void display ( )  {  cout << val << "  ";  }
} ;

void main ( )
{
Example name, *pr;
pr=&name;
name.arr_val (20);
pr->display ( );
```

```
pr->arr_val (39);
name.display ( );
}
```

Program 12.11.

The output of the program is

        20 39

We declare class **Example** consisting of **private** variable **val** and two member functions **arr_val()** and **display()**. We did not write the constructor and destructor. They will be created by the compiler. We use this class in **main()**. There, we declare an object **name** of an **Example** class type and pointer **pr**. We assign the address of the object **name** to the pointer **pr** by **pr=&name**. We, then, illustrate, that we can assign the value 20 using a name of an object, as **name.arr_val(20)**. We can display it by **pr->display()**. The opposite is true as well. We can assign the value 39 in pointer notation **pr->arr_val(39)** and display as **name.display()**. So, the pointer and direct notation of accessing the class members are interchangeable, and give the same results.

12.11. Object assignment.

We know, one variable can be assigned to another one. If we write **x=y**, the content of the variable **y** will be assigned to the variable **x**. Same can be applied to objects. The objects, that belong to the same class type can be assigned to each other. For instance,

        obj2=obj1;

When one object **obj1** is assigned to another one **obj2**, the second object gets a bitwise copy of the content of the first object. So, the content of both objects becomes identical. This means, that corresponding members of each object have the same values after the assignment. It is demonstrated by the following program.

```
#include <iostream.h>

class Example
{
int n, m;
public:
void arr_val (int x, int y) { n=x, m=y; }

void display ( )
{  cout << "n=" << n << " " << "m=" << m << "\n";   }

} ;

void main ( )
{
```

```
Example sm1, sm2;
sm1.arr_val (5, 7);
sm2.arr_val (1, 1);
sm1.display ( );
sm2.display ( );
sm2=sm1;
sm2.display ( );
sm2.arr_val (10, 20);
sm2.display ( );
}
```

Program 12.12.

The output of the program is

```
n=5  m=7
n=1  m=1
n=5  m=7
n=10  m=20
```

It uses the same class and function names, but they differ from the previous program. The program declares class **Example** containing **private** data members **n**, **m**, and functions **arr_val()**, **display()**. The **arr_val()** function has two parameters **x** and **y**. It assigns the values of **x** and **y** to the class data members **n** and **m** respectively. Both data members are displayed by the **display()** member function.

We use this class in **main()** function. We declare two objects **sm1** and **sm2** of **Example** class type. We assign the initial values to the data members of each object by **sm1.arr_val(5, 7)** and **sm2.arr_val(1, 1)**. We, then, display the initial values of each object. Their values are the first two lines of output. You can see, the data members of those two objects **sm1** and **sm2** have different values. After that, we assign the current values of all data members of **sm1** to **sm2** by **sm2=sm1**. We, then, display the object **sm2** by the **sm2.display()**. This gives us the third line of the output. Now, corresponding data members of two objects have identical values. The data members **n** of both objects **sm1** and **sm2** have equal values after the assignment. It is 5. The data members **m** of both objects are equal to 7 after the assignment. We alter the values of the **sm2** data members by **sm2.arr_val(10, 20)** and display them at the last output line. Two last code lines illustrate, that the values of the data members of an object can be changed anytime in the program.

12.12. Arrays of objects.

We have studied the arrays of variables. Similarly, the arrays of objects are legal in C++. An array of objects can be introduced in two steps. First, you declare a class type. Then, you define an array of objects of that class. Defining an array of objects is analogous to the regular arrays. In the program below, we define an array of objects by

```
Example sm[3];
```

Notation is the same as for the arrays of variables. Here, we have defined an array of objects of class **Example** containing 3 elements. The computer will allocate three cells, each capable of storing one full set of **Example** class data members. The index inside the [] braces has the same ambiguity. It shows the total number of array elements in the definition and addresses a particular array element later in the program.

When you declare an array of objects, the computer calls a constructor function one time for each array element. Thus, each array object requires personal constructor. It is reasonable. Each array element is a separate object. And as a separate object, it needs a constructor function for its creation. The same happens with the destructors. Each array element, as a separate object, needs a destructor function, when the array gets discarded. Thus, the destructor function is called once for each array element, when the array goes out of scope.

One can declare multidimensional arrays of objects. One can also use the pointers for handling the arrays of objects. **Program 12.13** illustrates the arrays of objects.

```
#include <iostream.h>
#include <stdio.h>

class Example
{
int n, m;
public:
void arr_val (int x, int y) { n=x, m=y; }

void display ( )
{   cout << "n=" << n << " " << "m=" << m << "\n";   }

} ;

void main ( )
{
Example sm[3];
int a, b;
cout << "Enter 3 pairs of numbers as a, b\n"
     << " Press ENTER after each pair.\n";
for (int p=0; p<3; p++)
{
scanf (" %d, %d", &a, &b);
sm[p].arr_val (a, b);
}
for (p=0; p<3; p++)
sm[p].display ( );
}
```

Program 12.13.

The program asks the user to enter three pairs of integer numbers separated by the comma.

Let's say, we enter
```
1, 2 ENTER   3, 4 ENTER   5, 6 ENTER
```
Each of those pairs has been assigned to the corresponding array element. The program then displays them by pairs. We place the data into the array and, then, display it to give you some feeling of how to work with an array of objects.

12.13. Passing objects to functions.

We have seen, that a variable, array, structure, union and so on can be passed as an argument to a function. One can pass an object to a function as well. An object is passed to a function using call-by-value. *In this case, the function parameter must have the class data type. You pass an object as an argument of the called function by name.* **Program 12.14** below introduces the function **fun()**. It takes an object as its argument. The formal parameter of this function has a class **Exa** type. Consider its prototype.
```
void fun (Exa k)
```
The object is passed to that function by value as
```
fun (sm);
```
Here, **sm** is the name of the object. The "call-by-value" means that the copy of an object will be passed as an argument of a function. The function will be able to use this copy of an object. All the changes made on the passed copy will not affect the original object. The content of the original object will remain unchanged and will be restored after the function termination. All the changes on the passed copy of an object will be discarded after the function, to which it was passed, is terminated. Passing an object is analogous to passing a structure by value. All the members of that object are passed to the function at once. We offer following program to illustrate it.

```cpp
#include <iostream.h>

class Exa
{
int n;
public:
void val (int a) {  n=a;  }

void display ( ) {  cout << "n=" << n << "   " ;  }

} ;

void fun (Exa k)
{
k.val (25);
k.display ( );
}
```

```
void main ( )
{
Exa sm;
sm.val (3);
fun (sm);
sm.display ( );
}
```

Program 12.14.

The output of the program is

    n=25   n=3

   The program declares class **Exa** containing **private** data member **n** and **public** functions **val()** and **display()**. Function **val()** has one parameter **a**. It assigns the value of that parameter to the data member **n**. The **display()** function displays the current value of **n** on the screen. The constructor and destructor functions of the **Exa** class will be created by the compiler automatically.

   Program 12.14 contains two functions: **main()** and **fun()**. We declare an object **sm** of class **Exa** type in **main()**. We set **sm** data member equal to 3 by calling the **sm.val(3)** member function. The next line calls **fun()** function with object **sm** as an argument. We also display the value of data member of the **sm** object after the function execution by **sm.display()**. The **fun()** function has an object of class **Exa** as its formal parameter. Call **fun(sm)** passes the data member of the object **sm** to the function **fun()**. The **fun()** function assigns a new value to the data member of the passed object by **k.val(25)**. It also displays the data member **n** of that object by **k.display()**. This yields **n=25**. When the control returns back to **main()**, the value of **n** is displayed again. It is equal to **n=3**. This indicates, that even though we have changed the value of **n** in the copy of the object, but the original remains unchanged. Passing simple objects is a pretty straightforward procedure. However, object constructor and destructor might cause some unexpected events. And you should understand them. Consider following program.

```
#include <iostream.h>

class See
{
int n;
public:
See (int a) {  n=a; cout << "Constructor running.\n";  }

void display ( )  {  cout << "n=" << n << "  " ;  }

~See ( ) { cout << "Destructor running.\n";  }

} ;

void fun (See k)
```

```
{
k.display ( );
}

void main ( )
{
See sm (5);
fun (sm);
cout << "The control is back to main( ).\n";
}
```
Program 12.15.

The output of the program is
```
Constructor running.
n=5 Destructor running.
The control is back to main( ).
Destructor running.
```
We declared class **See** containing one data member **n** and three functions: **See()**, **display()** and **~See()**. Here, we have explicitly written the constructor **See()** and destructor **~See()**. The constructor has a parameter. It assigns a value to the data member **n**. The constructor also displays a message "**Constructor running.**" when executed. The destructor also displays a message when executed. The messages allow us to see when the constructor and destructor are executed. The program consists of two functions: **main()** and **fun()**. The **main()** function declares an object **sm** of **See** class and calls the **fun()** functions. The **fun()** function takes an object **sm** as its argument and displays the value of its data member **n**.

The program reveals a peculiar behavior. The output of our program contains two messages from the destructor. It means, that a destructor of the object, passed to a function, runs twice. Why is it so? When an object is passed to a function, a copy of that object is created and passed. Therefore, one might think, it is like a creation of a new object. When a copy of an argument is made during the function call, it does not require an additional constructor. Why? A constructor has been called, when the object **sm** has been created. The constructor is not called, when a program creates a copy of an existing object. This is reasonable, because one can do any changes to an original object (in our case **sm**) in the program and only then pass it to a function. When you pass an object, you want to use the current state of an object, not its initial state. If the constructor have been called when you passed the **sm** object to a function, it would have created a new object. The initial values of the data members of that new object would not have been related to the data members of **sm** object. This is why a system does not call a constructor, creating a copy of the passed object.

When the function is terminated, its copy gets destroyed. This requires the destructor, because the object might require some operations on it. For instance, the object destruction might require to free the memory space, where it has been stored. The call to a destructor, in this case, displays the first "**Destructor running.**" message on the screen. We intentionally coded **cout** object in **main()**. When the control is returned back to **main()**, it displays a proper message. Now we can see, that the called function is terminated. This permits us to see, that the second message from the destructor is displayed only, when the whole program terminates. Therefore, the second destructor is executed, when the original object **sm** is destroyed.

One can pass an object using call-by-reference. In this case, a pointer to the object is used as a function argument. The original object address is passed to the called function. Therefore, it can change the passed object, and the change will remain in effect, even after the function is terminated. Consider following example.

```
#include <iostream.h>

class Exa
{
int n;
public:
void val (int a) {  n=a;  }
void display ( ) {  cout << "n=" << n << "  " ;  }
} ;

void fun (Exa *k)
{
k->display( );
k->val (25);
k->display ( );
}

void main ( )
{
Exa sm, *pr;
pr=&sm;
sm.val (3);
fun (pr);
sm.display ( );
}
```

Program 12.16.

The output of the program is
    n=3 n=25 n=25

Here, we declare an object **sm** of class **Exa** and the pointer **pr** of the same class inside **main()**. The pointer **pr** is made pointing towards **sm** by **pr=&sm**. We assign the value 3 to the member **sm.n** by **sm.val(3)** in **main()**. We, then, call **fun(pr)** function and pass pointer **pr** as its argument. *A function, taking a pointer to a class type as an argument, should be declared and defined as having a pointer parameter of that class.* And our function **fun()**, indeed, has a pointer to class **Exa** data type as its parameter. Its header is written as

```
         void fun (Exa *k)
```
The **fun()** function first displays the value of member **n** of the passed object. It is still equal to 3. The **fun()** function, then, changes it to 25 by **k->val(25)** and displays again. We confirm, that the function has changed the value of the member **n**. The control returns back to **main()**. We display the member **n** of the passed object **sm** again. It is still **n=25** after returning to **main()**. Thus, the passed object remains changed even after the **fun()** function termination.

One can pass a number of objects to a function. Each object can have any number of members. There might be some problems with passing the objects as the function arguments, related to the run-time or dynamic memory allocation.

12.14. Passing objects that allocate dynamic memory.

We will consider a case, when the objects are passed to the functions by means of the call-by-value. It assumes, that a copy of an object is created and passed as an argument to a function. As you know, creation of that copy object does not require a constructor function. Your computer simply duplicates an object to be passed as an argument. When a function goes out of the scope, that passed object is destroyed by a destructor function of its class. This minimizes, but does not eliminate possible damage, that a function might do to the object. For instance, assume that an object passed to a function allocates dynamic memory and frees it when destroyed. The destructor of its local copy inside a function will free the memory that belongs to the original object, when the copy object is destroyed. This might damage the original object making it impossible to use. Consider a program that illustrates it.

```cpp
#include <iostream.h>

class mytry
{
int *pr;
public:
mytry ( );
~mytry ( );
void myassign (int m) { *pr=m; }
int myshow ( ) { return *pr; }
} ;

mytry::mytry ( )
{
cout << "Memory allocation begins." << endl;
pr = new int;
if (!pr)
{
cout << "Cannot allocate." << endl;
```

```
return;
} }

mytry::~mytry ( )
{
cout << "Freeing the allocated memory." << endl;
delete pr;
}

void disp ( mytry x)
{
cout << x.myshow ( ) << endl;
}

void main ( )
{
mytry ob;
ob.myassign (5);
disp (ob);
}
```

Program 12.17.

The output of the program is

```
Memory allocation begins.
5
Freeing the allocated memory.
Freeing the allocated memory.
```

Some compilers display an extra line stating "**Null statement assignment**". Even if you do not see this error message, the error has occurred in this program.

The program declares class **mytry**, that consists of a pointer **pr** and member functions: constructor, destructor, **myassign()** and **myshow()**. The **myassign()** function assigns an integral value to the cell pointed to by the data member pointer **pr**. The **myshow()** function returns the value currently contained in the cell pointed to by **pr**. The constructor **mytry()** allocates dynamic memory for a data member and creates an object of the class. The destructor **~mytry()** is defined next. It destroys an object of the class and frees the allocated for its member memory.

Program 12.17 declares and defines the function **disp()**, that displays the content of the cell pointed to by the **pr** data member. The **mytry** class is used in **main()** routine. There we declare object **ob** and assign the value 5 to its data member. We, then, call the **disp()** function to display that value. The program performs a simple action. However, the program illustrates some interesting effects related to passing an object to the function, in which the destructor frees the dynamically allocated memory.

The above program produces an error. Why does the error happen? When we create the object **ob** in **main()** routine, the memory that stores a data member of this object is dynamically allocated by the class constructor. An address of that memory cell is assigned to **ob.pr**. We pass **ob** as an argument of the **disp(ob)** function. The **ob** object is copied into the object **x**, which is a parameter of the **disp()** function. Therefore, **x.pr** stores the same address as **ob.pr**, when the **disp()** function is activated. When the **disp()** function completes its execution, the copy object, passed to it, is destroyed by the class destructor **~mytry()**. The destructor frees the memory pointed to by **x.pr**. Consequently, it can free and destroy the data member of the original object, that occupies a memory cell with the same address. We have a case, when a copy object can destroy a memory cell, that is still used by the original object **ob**. It is a serious problem.

We have considered only one side of the problem. Here is another side. When the whole program terminates, the data member of the **ob** object is destroyed again. This causes the same memory cell to be freed again. Freeing the same memory cell twice can affect the whole dynamic allocation system causing some abnormal effects along with the displayed error messages. As you can see, the destructor message is displayed twice. That tells us, that the destructor runs twice in the above program.

Now, we have to consider the ways to avoid this problem, when destructor function destroys the copy object destroying the original object as well. A way to do it is to pass to a function a pointer or a reference to an object, rather than an object itself. Following program is almost identical to the previous one. But it passes a reference to an object to the function **void disp(mytry &x)**.

```cpp
#include <iostream.h>

class mytry
{
int *pr;
public:
mytry ( );
~mytry ( );
void myassign (int m) { *pr=m; }
int myshow ( ) { return *pr; }
} ;
mytry::mytry ( )
{
cout << "Memory allocation begins." << endl;
pr = new int;
if (!pr)
{
cout << "Cannot allocate." << endl;
return;
} }

mytry::~mytry ( )
{
cout << "Freeing the allocated memory." << endl;
delete pr;
```

```
        }
        void disp ( mytry &x)
        {
        cout << x.myshow ( ) << endl;
        }

        void main ( )
        {
        mytry ob;
        ob.myassign (5);
        disp (ob);
        }
```

Program 12.18.

The output of the program is

```
        Memory allocation begins.
        5
        Freeing the allocated memory.
```

The destructor in the above program runs only once. It does eliminate the error of the **Program 12.17.**

12.15. Returning objects.

We have seen, that the objects can be passed to a function. An object can be returned by a function as well. *The function returning an object should be declared and defined as having a class type return value.* We use the function **func ( )**, that returns an object of class **See** in **Program 12.19** below. Its prototype is

```
        See fun ( )
```

Thus, the function prototype should indicate a class return type. In our case, it is class **See**. A function returns an object by means of the **return** statement. In our program below, function **fun ( )** returns an object by means of **return ob** statement. The **ob** object is defined as having class **See** type.

```
        #include <iostream.h>
        #include <string.h>

        class See
        {
        char sym[20];
        public:
        void val (char *a) {  strcpy (sym, a);  }
        void display ( )    {  cout << sym;  }
        } ;
```

```
See fun ( )
{
char sts[20];
See ob;
cout << "Enter any word and hit ENTER.\n";
cin >> sts;
ob.val (sts);
return ob;
}

void main ( )
{
See sm ;
sm=fun ( );
sm.display( );
}
```
                    Program 12.19.

The program prompts the user to enter any word. We enter **object**. It displays
```
object
```
This program consists of two functions: **main()** and **fun()**. The **fun()** function creates an object **ob**. The **fun()** function also prompts a user to enter any word from the keyboard and reads it. The word is placed into the string **sts**, that is used as an argument in **ob.val(sts)**. The member function **val()** copies the content of the **sts** string into the object **ob** data member string **ob.sym**. The object **ob** is, then, returned by the **fun()** function and assigned to the object **sm**. We display the content of the object **sm** member string **sm.sym** by the **sm.display()**. This indicates, that object **ob** was, indeed, returned by the **fun()** function and assigned to the object **sm**.

12.16. Returning objects that allocate dynamic memory.

Returning an object can be tricky. When a function returns an object, a temporary object is created automatically. That temporary object holds the returned value. In other words, that object is, in fact, returned by the function. After a function returns the object, it gets destroyed. Imagine, that the returned object has a destructor, that frees dynamically allocated memory. That memory can be freed despite the fact, the object that is assigned the return value can still use it. Following program illustrates that.

```
#include <iostream.h>

class mytry
{
int *pr;
```

```
public:
mytry ( ) { cout << "Constructor is running." << endl; };

~mytry ( )
{ cout << "Deleting an object." << endl; delete pr; };

void myassign (int m) { *pr=m; }

int myshow ( ) { return *pr; }

} ;

mytry func ( )
{
mytry a;
a.myassign (20);
return a;
}

void main ( )
{
mytry ob;
ob=func ( );
cout << ob.myshow ( )<< endl;
}
```

Program 12.20.

The ouptut of the program is

```
Constructor is running.
Constructor is running.
Deleting an object.
Deleting an object.
20
Deleting an object.
```

Above program declares class **mytry**, that consists of a pointer to an integer **pr** and four member functions: constructor, destructor, **myassign()** and **myshow()**. The **myassign()** function assigns a value passed to its parameter to a cell pointed to by the **pr**. The **myshow()** function returns a value stored in the cell pointed to by the **pr** pointer. The constructor function creates an object of the class and displays its message on the screen. The destructor function destroys a data member of class type object, displays its message on the screen, and frees the memory cell pointed to by **pr**. The program also declares and defines the **func()** function, that assigns the value 20 to the data member of its object **a**. The object **a** is returned by the function. An object **ob** of the class **mytry** is declared in **main()** function. The **ob=func()** in **main()** assigns the object returned by the **func()** function to **ob**.

If you look at the program output, the class destructor is called three times. It is called for the first time, when the **func()** function completes the execution and its local object **a** goes out of scope. The second call to the destructor is made, when the temporary object returned by the **func()** is destroyed. We remember, that when a function returns an object, the computer automatically creates a temporary object to hold the returned value. That temporary object is just a copy of the returned object. This temporary object is destroyed after the function has returned its value. This is why you see the second message from a destructor function. The class destructor **~mytry()** is called for the third and the last time when the program terminates and **ob** object inside **main()** function gets destroyed.

The first call to the destructor releases the memory allocated for the cell pointed to by the **pr** pointer. Two subsequent calls to the destructor **~mytry()** try to free the memory cell, that has been released already. This can damage the whole dynamic memory allocation system. Some compilers display the error messages in those cases.

So, try to avoid returning an object, that can screw the allocation system. Couple more solutions are to return a pointer or a reference to an object or use a copy constructor and an overloaded assignment operator. We will discuss them.

12.17. Classes and references.

We have seen in the previous sections, that a reference to a class type object can be passed to a program function. We have given you an example of doing it. A reference to an object can be returned by a program function. Next program demonstrates it.

```cpp
#include <iostream.h>

class Cat
{
private:
int x, y;
public:
Cat (int a, int b) { x=a, y=b; }
Cat () { x=0, y=0; }
~Cat () { }

void show ()
{ cout << "x=" << x << ", " << "y=" << y << endl; }

};

Cat q (1, 2);

Cat & obchange ( )
{  return q;  }
```

```
void main()
{
Cat ob1, ob2 (3, 4);
ob1=obchange ();
ob1.show ();
obchange ()=ob2;
q.show ();
}
```

Program 12.21.

The output of the program is

```
x=1, y=2
x=3, y=4
```

The program declares class **Cat** and defines three objects of this class: global object **q**, local objects **ob1** and **ob2** in **main()**. The program consists of functions **main()** and **obchange()**. The **obchange()** function returns a reference to a global object **q**. How do we know, that the **obchange()** function returns a reference to an oject of **Cat** class type? Its return type is specified as **Cat &** in the definition header. We illustrate how to handle a function returning a reference to an object in **main()**. We assign the returned by **obchange()** object by **ob1=obchange()** and display the content of **ob1**. We, then, write **obchange()=ob2**. It illustrates, that the function **obchange()** became a reference to the object **q**. It can be assigned a value of an object. We display the altered data members of object **q** by **q.show()**. Remember, you cannot return a reference to a local object, because a local object of a function is discarded after the function termination.

We will now review classes containing functions returning references. Typically, a public member function is used to return a reference to a private data member.

```
#include <iostream.h>

class Dat
{
int mon, day, year;
public:
Dat (int a, int b, int c) { mon=a, day=b, year=c; }

int &refmonth ( );

void disp ( )
{ cout << mon << "/" << day << "/" << year << "\n"; }

} ;

int & Dat:: refmonth ( )
{
if (mon>=12)
```

```
cout << "Wrong month number.\n";
return mon;
}

void main ( )
{
Dat mine (4, 20, 1996);
int m=mine.refmonth ( );
cout << m <<"\n";
mine.disp ( );
mine.refmonth ( )=12;
mine.disp ( );
mine.refmonth ( )++ ;
mine.disp ( );
}
```

Program 12.22.

The otuput of the program is

```
4
4/20/1996
12/20/1996
Wrong month number
13/20/1996
```

We have declared class **Dat**. The **refmonth()** function is one of the members of that class. It returns a reference to the private data member **mon**. We use this function in **main()** to get a value of the variable **mon** in the assignment

```
int m=mine.refmonth ( );
```

We also use this function to assign the value 12 to the member **mon**.

```
mine.refmonth ( )=12;
```

So, the member function can be treated as a variable. We even increment the value of class member **mon** to 13 using the **refmonth()** function by

```
mine.refmonth ( )++ ;
```

You should not use the function returning a reference as a variable for a number of reasons. First, is that the syntax of that assignment can be confusing. Second, the function checks the range every time the assignment is made. This requires some additional time making the program not efficient. The third reason is, that you, actually, make the private data member public. You defeat the purpose of making it private at the first place.

12.18. Copy constructors.

We know, that a class constructor can be overloaded. One can also create and use a copy class constructor. When do you need it? It is used when: an object is passed as a parameter to a function, or returned by a function, or a copy of an object has been made, or, in general, when an object is used to initialize another one. You will not always write the copy constructors in those cases. You will do it only under special circumstances. For instance, you will use a copy constructor, when the objects use run-time allocation.

For instance, an object is passed to a function. The computer makes a copy of that object and passes it to the function. We have learned, there are cases when passing an exact copy of an object is highly undesirable. For instance, a class constructor allocates the memory cells for some object members. Then, the copy will point to the place, in the memory in which the original object is stored. Thus, if you change the values stored in this location, you will make the changes of the original object as well. When the function terminates, the destructor of that copy object will be called. It can damage or alter the original object. Here you might need to use a copy constructor.

Another case is when an object is returned by a function. Usually, a computer creates a temporary object just to hold the copy of the returned by the function value. This temporary object is destroyed once the value is returned back to the caller. The destruction of that object is performed by its class destructor. That destructor can free the dynamically allocated memory of that object. This might lead to some peculiar effects. It is better, if you use a copy constructor in this situation as well.

A copy constructor acts on an object only when it is initialized. It does not act, when the assignments are made. A copy constructor is written in a general form as

```
Cat (const Cat &one)
{
```
constructor statements
```
}
```

The **Cat** is the name of the class. The **& one** is the reference to an object that is used to create another object. We want you to distinguish between an overloaded constructor and a copy constructor. A copy constructor should not be confused with overloading a constructor function. A copy constructor is a specific form of a class constructor, that creates a copy of an object. Below we give you examples, when a copy constructor use might be beneficial. Here we use the object **ob** of the **trial** class type.

```
trial w = ob; // here object ob explicitly initializes w
fun (ob); // object ob is passed as a parameter
ob=fun ( ); // object ob is returned by a function
```

We will now consider how to apply a copy constructor to each of those three cases.

12.18.1. Copy constructors for objects-arguments.

We have discussed, that when an object is passed as a function argument, its copy is created and passed to the function. When a copy of that object is created, a constructor is not called. If you specify a copy constructor in a class, it will be called to create that copy object. In other words, if you specify a copy constructor, the computer will call this copy constructor, when a copy object needs to be created. We illustrate how to pass an argument to a function, using copy constructor, by the following program.

```
#include <iostream.h>
```

```
class mytry
{
int *pr;
public:
mytry ( );
mytry (const mytry &myob);
~mytry ( );
void myassign (int m) { *pr=m; }
int myshow ( ) { return *pr; }
  } ;

mytry::mytry (const mytry &myob)
{
 cout << "Copy constructor memory allocation begins."
      << endl;
pr = new int;
if (!pr)
{
cout << "Cannot allocate." << endl;
return;
}
*pr=*myob.pr;
}

mytry::mytry ( )
{
cout << "Memory allocation begins." << endl;
pr = new int;
if (!pr)
{
cout << "Cannot allocate." << endl;
return;
} }

mytry::~mytry ( )
{
cout << "Freeing the allocated memory." << endl;
delete pr;
}

void disp (mytry x)
{   cout << x.myshow ( ) << endl;   }

void main ( )
{
```

```
mytry ob;
ob.myassign (5);
disp (ob);
}
```

Program 12.23.

The output of the program is

```
Memory allocation begins.
Copy constructor memory allocation begins.
5
Freeing the allocated memory.
Freeing the allocated memory.
```

The above program declares class **mytry**, that contains pointer **pr** and five member functions: constructor, copy constructor, destructor, **myassign()** and **myshow()**. The **myassign()** member function assigns a value to the cell pointed to by the **pr** pointer. The **myshow()** member function returns the content of the cell pointed to by the **pr**. The regular constructor and the **disp()** functions are defined in the specified order right after the copy constructor.

Look at the **main()** function. We first define the object **ob** of the **mytry** class. We assign the value 5 to the data member of that object by **ob.myassign(5)**. This member function simply places number 5 in the cell pointed to by **pr**. This cell is a part of the **ob** object. It has been dynamically allocated by the class constructor, when the **ob** object was created. We, then, pass object **ob** as an argument of the **disp(ob)** function to display the content of its data member. It is the place, where the copy constructor will come to action.

The regular class constructor, among other things, allocates a memory cell for an integer and stores its address in **ob.p** pointer, when we create **ob** object in **main()**. A copy constructor is called, when we pass **ob** to the object **x** of **disp()** function. The copy constructor creates another cell to store an integer and passes the address of that cell to the **pr** pointer. But it is another **pr** pointer. It points to a different cell. It is associated with the copy object passed to **x**. Hence, the **ob.pr** and **x.pr** point to different locations in the computer memory.

Let's rephrase our point again to make it more comprehensible. When there is no copy constructor, object **ob** is simply copied and passed to the **disp()** function. No constructor is called to create a copy. So, **ob.pr** and **x.pr** contain the same address. If you free the memory pointed to by **x.pr**, it is in the same location as specified by **ob.pr**. If you specify a copy constructor, it will be executed when a copy of the object is created.

The copy constructor definition begins with

```
mytry::mytry (const mytry &myob)
```

When you pass an object to the **disp()** function, a copy constructor is called. The copy constructor gets the data from the object **ob**, that becomes associated with its parameter object **myob**. The copy constructor contains **new** operator. It creates another object, that has its own memory cell pointed to by **pr**. The copy constructor places the value stored by the original object into the copy object by the ***pr=*myob.pr** expression. Thus, the copy constructor creates another object, that is passed to **disp()** function. So, both **ob** and **x** are now different objects. The addresses of the **ob.pr** and **x.pr** are now different. They are two different pointers. But the number stored in both cells is the same. When **x** object goes out of the scope and the cell pointed to by its **pr** pointer is destroyed, it does not affect the pointer **pr** of the object **ob**. Therefore, a copy destructor eliminates the effects of passing an object with the run-time allocation to a function.

A regular constructor displays the first message in **Program 12.23**. It creates the **ob** object. A copy constructor is called, when this object is passed to the **disp()** function and a copy object is created. The copy constructor displays the second message on the screen. The **disp()** function displays the value 5. The next line is written by the destructor function, that destroys the object after the **disp()** termination. The last line belongs to the class destructor, that destroys the **ob** object at program termination.

12.18.2. Copy constructors for objects initializing objects.

Let's now consider a situation, when one object initializes another one. If a class contains a copy constructor, it will be called in this case. Consider following example.

```
#include <iostream.h>

class mytry
{
int *pr;
public:
mytry ( );
mytry (const mytry &myob);
~mytry ( );
void myassign (int m) { *pr=m; }
int myshow ( ) { return *pr; }
} ;

mytry::mytry (const mytry &myob)
{
cout << "Copy constructor memory allocation begins."
       << endl;
pr = new int;
if (!pr)
{
cout << "Cannot allocate." << endl;
return;
}
*pr=*myob.pr;
}

mytry::mytry ( )
```

```
{
cout << "Memory allocation begins." << endl;
pr = new int;
if (!pr)
{
cout << "Cannot allocate." << endl;
return;
} }

mytry::~mytry ( )
{
cout << "Freeing the allocated memory." << endl;
delete pr;
}

void main ( )
{
mytry ob;
ob.myassign (5);
mytry another = ob;
cout << another.myshow ( )<< endl;
}
```

Program 12.24.

The program has the same output as the previous one. The above program is similar to the previous one. Our **mytry** class has two constructors. One of them is a copy constructor. We declare two objects **ob** and **another** of the **mytry** class type in **main()**. The regular constructor creates the **ob** object. The copy constructor is called, when we define and initialize **another** object by **mytry another=ob**. The copy constructor allocates a separate memory for the object **another**. If a copy constructor has not existed in this case, the object **another** would have been an exact copy of object **ob**, and **ob.pr** would have pointed to the same cell as **another.pr**. Copy constructor makes **ob.pr** and **another.pr** pointing to different memory cells. However, the contents of both cells are identical.

You also have to understand, a copy constructor acts only when an object is initialized. A copy constructor would have not been called, if we would have done following
```
mytry another;
another = ob;
```
Here, the **another = ob** is not an initialization. It is an assignment.

12.18.3. Copy constructors for returned objects.

If you write a copy constructor in a class, the computer calls it to create a temporary object in cases of the functions returning an object. We illustrate it in a program below.

```
#include <iostream.h>

class dummy
{
public:
dummy ( ) { cout << " This is a constructor." << endl; }

dummy (const dummy &tr)
{ cout << "This is a copy constructor." << endl; }

~dummy ( ) { cout << "Destroying object." << endl; }

} ;

dummy see (char *x)
{
dummy mo;
cout << x;
return mo;
}

void main ( )
{
dummy ob;
ob=see ("Started function.\n");
}
```

Program 12.25.

The output of the program is
```
This is a constructor.
This is a constructor.
Started function.
This is a copy constructor.
Destroying object.
Destroying object.
Destroying object.
```
  The output messages of the above program can be interpreted as follows. The first two messages are posted by two calls to the constructor functions. The first call creates the **ob** object inside **main()** function. The second call to the constructor creates the **mo** object inside the **see()** function. The third message belongs to the **see()** function. It informs, that the function has been invoked. It is followed by the copy constructor message. A copy constructor is called, when a temporary object is created as a return value of the function **see()**. Next three messages notify, that the destructor has been called three times to destroy the object **mo**, the temporary return and the **ob** objects respectively.

12.19. Friend functions and friend classes.

We know, that the **private** class members are accessible only for the same class members. It is also possible for a non-member function to access the private class members. To do it, a prototype of that non-member function should be included as a **public** member in the class declaration. The prototype of that function should begin with the word **friend**. The outside functions, that can access the private and public class members are called *friend functions*. Any program function can be made a friend function of any class. Even a member function of some class can be made a member function of any other classes. A function can be a friend of any number of classes. Consider following example.

```
#include <iostream.h>

class mine
{
int x, y;
public:
mine (int a, int b) { x=a, y=b;  }
friend float ave (mine z);
} ;

float ave (mine z) {  return ( (z.x+z.y)/2.0);    }

void main ( )
{
mine sm (2, 3);
cout << ave (sm);
}
```

Program 12.26.

The output of the program is the number 2.5.

This program declares class **mine** consisting of two private data members **x, y**. We have written the constructor **mine()** explicitly. The destructor will be generated by the compiler. The class **mine** has a friend function **ave()**, that finds an average value of its data members. The **ave()** function does not belong to class **mine**. It is not a member function. It is a regular program function. Since it is declared as a friend of the class **mine**, it can access any class members, and even the private ones. The function **ave()** has an object of the class as its argument. In general, it can have the parameters of any type. If you want to operate on the class, the function should have an object of a class type as its parameter. The **ave()** function finds an average of two private data members of the class using the expression **(z.x+z.y)/2.0**.

We declare and initialize the object **sm** of class **mine** type in **main()**. This object is passed as an argument of **ave()** function, that accesses **x** and **y** private data members and finds their average for the **sm** object.

The friend function **ave()** does not do anything special in the above program. You might even ask, what would one gain by using friend functions. Friend functions are useful in a number of circumstances. They are used for overloading some operators, simplifying the creation of some types of I/O functions. Another way of using friend functions is suggested by **Program 12.27**. Think about two different classes having one of the data members, that represents the same entity. For instance, you have two houses A and B. One family lives in each house. You group the family name, the price paid for the house, the house age in a class. Let's assume, those houses can get the power outage, or, in other words, lose the electricity for some time. You want to know, if the electricity is OK in each house. One can declare an additional data member in each class, that represents the power conditions. If that variable is HIGH, then, there is light in a house. If it is LOW, the power is OFF. Suppose, you want to check this variable in both houses (or classes) at once. To do that, you declare a variable in each class and write a friend function, that checks both power states and displays a proper message.

Program 12.27 demonstrates that idea. We did not set each class as a house with all the data. We used some fictional classes. We wanted to illustrate the friend function **test()**, that checks two class members of two different classes and displays certain messages, depending on the states of those class members.

```
#include <iostream.h>                      //line 1
#include <stdio.h>                         //line 2

const int HIGH=1;                          //line 3
const int LOW=0;                           //line 4

class one;                                 //line 5
class two                                  //line 6
{                                          //line 7
int x;                                     //line 8
public:                                    //line 9
void val(int );                            //line 10
friend int test (one p1, two p2);          //line 11
} ;                                        //line 12

class one                                  //line 13
{                                          //line 14
int x, y, z;                               //line 15
public:                                    //line 16
void val(int );                            //line 17

void giv (int p1, int p2, int p3) { x=p1, y=p2, z=p3; }
                                           //line 18
int sum ( ) { return (x+y+z); }            //line 19
friend int test (one p1, two p2);          //line 20
```

```
} ;                                      //line 21
void one:: val(int a) { x=a;   }         //line 22
void two:: val(int a) { x=a;   }         //line 23

int test (one p1, two p2)                //line 24
{                                        //line 25
if (p1.x == HIGH && p2.x == HIGH)        //line 26
return HIGH;                             //line 27
else                                     //line 28
return LOW;                              //line 29
}                                        //line 30

void main ( )                            //line 31
{                                        //line 32
one ob1;                                 //line 33
two ob2;                                 //line 34
int k, q;                                //line 35
cout <<" 1 corresponds to HIGH state and 0 to LOW.\n"
     <<" Enter two states separated by a comma."
     << " For instance 1, 0.\n";         //line 36
scanf ("%d, %d", &k, &q);                //line 37
ob1.val (k);                             //line 38
ob2.val (q);                             //line 39
if(test(ob1, ob2))cout << "Objects are in high state.\n";
                                         //line 40
else cout << "State failure.\n";         //line 41
}                                        //line 42
```

Program 12.27.

The program displays the message

    1 corresponds to HIGH state and 0 to LOW.
    Enter two states separated by a comma. For instance 1, 0.
If you enter a combination of numbers other than **1, 1**, it displays
    State failure.
If you enter **1,1**, it displays a message
    Objects are in high state.

The program begins with defining two constants HIGH and LOW at lines 3, 4. Line 5 contains a **class one** statement. This statement declares a class type **one** before we actually define the very class **one**. It is called a *forward reference*. A class name can be referenced with the word **class** even before it is defined. One can, then, use this name (in our case **one**) to define the objects of that class. The referenced class **one** can even be declared after we define its objects. Look at our program. We declare the **test ()** function as a friend of both classes **one** and **two**. That function has objects of both classes as its parameters. Therefore, we had to reference the class **one** before defining it, in order to be able to declare the **test ()** function with the parameters of classes **one** and **two** data types. We declare class **two** at lines 6-12. It is followed by the class **one** declaration at lines 13-21.

As you see, both classes differ by data members and member functions. However, one can find the data member **x** in both classes. It is technically the same name. But you know, that the class members have class scope. Therefore, it is a completely different variable in each class. We will use the friend function **test()** to examine the variables with that name in both classes, but they are different variables. We have chosen the same name for both variables to indicate, that each of those variables will be used for characterizing the same quantity. One more example, both classes have the function **val()**, that performs analogous task. But it is an absolutely different function in each class. We define both **val()** functions at lines 22, 23.

The function **test()** is defined at lines 24-30. It has the objects of both classes as its parameters. The function compares the member **x** of each class and returns HIGH value, if both members are in HIGH state. We define objects **ob1** and **ob2** at lines 33, 34 in **main()**, that have class types **one** and **two** respectively. The program prompts the user to enter a combination of two digits, each of which can be either 1 or 0. Those values are, then, assigned to the **x** data members of each class object by **ob1.val(k)** and **ob2.val(q)** at lines 38, 39. After that, the program compares both values to 0.

```
if(test(ob1, ob2))cout << "Objects are in high state.\n";
else cout << "State failure.\n";        //line 41
```

This should give you an idea about the above program.

One can declare a friend class. In this case, the class declared as a friend, is able to access all the private and public members of the class, for which it is a friend. To declare class B as a friend of class A, one has to include the name of class B preceded by the word **friend** in the class A declaration. Suppose, you declare class A.

```
class A
{
int x, y, z....
.....
friend B;
}
```

The line **friend B** makes class B a friend of class A. The friendship works in an interesting way. Let's assume, class B is a friend of class A, and class C is a friend of class B. This does not make class C a friend of class A. The friendship is neither transitive nor symmetric. Class A is not a friend of class B, if class B is a friend of A.

12.20. Keyword *this*.

Each time a member function is called, the compiler automatically generates a pointer called **this**. That pointer points towards the object that calls a member function. For instance, one can assign a value to the member **x** of class **one** in **Program 12.28** below by writing **x=10** or **this->x=10** in a class member function. So, pointer **this** can be used inside any member function to refer to the invoking object.

```
#include <iostream.h>

class one
{
int x;
public:
void val(int a) { this->x=a;   }
void disp ( ) { cout << this->x;}
} ;

void main ( )
{
one ob1;
ob1.val (5);
ob1.disp ( );
}
```

Program 12.28.

The output of the program is the number 5. Here we use **this->x** form to assign a value to the data member **x** of the object **ob1**. We can do it inside **val()** member function, because **ob1** calls it. Present example is trivial. You will learn some other more important cases where pointer **this** is quite useful in the next chapter.

12.21. Using header files.

It is a common practice in C++ to divide your source file when dealing with classes. You should place class declaration in a header file. The definition of all the class member functions is usually placed in a source file. The program can be written in the same source file or in a different source file, that belongs to the same project. The header files have **.h** and the source files, usually, have **.cpp** extensions.

The inline member functions are, usually, placed in the header file along with the class declaration. The **#include** statements must be put in the source files. If you deal with large classes, each class declaration should be placed in a separate header file. In this case, the member function definitions should be placed in different source files for separate classes. Consider following program, that illustrates that approach. It is a copy of **Program 12.3**, that has been placed in three files. All three files were a part of a project **C:\MSVC\MYPR\MSBOOK.DEF**.

This is the content of **C:\MSVC\MYPR\ mine.h** file.

```
#include <iostream.h>
#ifndef mine_h
#define mine_h
class Dat
{
```

```
public :
Dat ( );
void check(int , int , int );
void disp (int , int , int );
~Dat ( );
private :
int m, d, y;
};
#endif
```

This is the content of **C:\MSVC\MYPR\msone.cpp** file.

```
#include "mine.h"

Dat::Dat ( )    {    m=d=y=0;      }

void Dat::check(int a, int b, int c)
{
m=a;
d=b;
y=c;
static int per[ ]= {0, 31, 28, 31, 30, 31, 30, 31, 31,
                    30, 31, 30, 31};
if (per[m]<d)
{
d=0;
cout << "Date error.\n";
}}

void Dat::disp(int mon, int day, int year)
{
static char *moname[ ]={"none", "Jan", "Feb", "Mar",
              "Apr", "May", "Jun", "Jul", "Aug", "Sep",
              "Oct", "Nov", "Dec"};
check(mon, day, year);
cout <<moname[m] <<" " << d << ", "<< y << "\n";
}

Dat:: ~Dat( )
{   }
```

This is the content of **C:\MSVC\MYPR\mstwo.cpp** file.

```
#include "mine.h"
```

```
void main ( )
{
Dat test1, test2;
test1.disp(2, 20, 1996);
cout << "Beginning of test2.check( ) execution.\n";
test2.check(3, 40, 1996);
cout << "The end of test2.check( ) execution.\n";
test2.disp(3, 40, 1996);
}
```

Program 12.29.

This program has the same output as **Program 12.3**. The only thing that needs our clarification consists of two lines at the beginning of the header file

```
#ifndef mine_h
#define mine_h
```

These two lines provide the conditional compilation. It is used to prevent multiple inclusion of the header files in the multi-source file programs. The header file is terminated by the **#endif** directive.

12.22. *const* objects, member functions and data members.

12.22.1. *const* objects and member functions.

One can declare a **const** object, member function, or a data member of a class. Let's consider each of those three class entities separately.

One can define a **const** object similar to a regular object. For instance,

```
const Dat myday (04, 28, 1900);
```

Here, we have defined and initialized a **const** object **myday** of **Dat** class data type. A **const** object cannot be modified by an assignment. The initial values of its members cannot be changed. Hence, one should define and initialize a **const** object at the same time, as shown. Any attempt to change any member of **myday(04, 28, 1900)** object is impossible. One can assign a **const** object to a non-constant object of the same class. The expressions like

```
yourday=myday;
```

where the object **yourday** is a non-constant object of class **Dat**, are quite legitimate. We just assign the content of the constant object **myday** to the **yourday** object.

When an object is defined as **const**, C++ does not allow you to call a class member function with that object. Let's assume, function **disp()** is a member function of the same class **Dat**. Object **myday** has the same class type. If we call **myday.disp()**, the computer will generate an error message. Why is it so? You know, that a **const** object cannot be modified. An object, in general, can be modified by the member functions of a class. When we initialized our object **myday**, three numbers 4, 28, 1900 were just the initial values of that object. One can, potentially, attempt to modify them using the class member functions. The compiler does not try to determine, which class member function can change an object and which will just read the data. It prevents any **const** class type object from calling any class member function. If one cannot use any function with an object, it cannot be modified. This is the best assurance, that nothing can go wrong.

One can use a **const** object to call the **const** class member functions only. The **const** member functions cannot modify any object, not only **const** one. The **const** class member functions are read-only functions. They just display the content of an object. The **const** member functions cannot call a non-**const** function. This is why they can be used with the **const** objects. The compiler "is not afraid" of them, because they cannot modify an object. The **const** member functions are written slightly differently from the regular member functions. This is why the compiler recognizes them and allows calls to them with the constant objects. A **const** member function should be specified as **const** in both declaration and definition. The word **const** is added after the function's parameter list. Consider following example.

```
#include <iostream.h>

class Time
{
int mon, day, year;
public:

Time ( int a, int b, int c ) { mon=a, day=b, year=c;   }
int showmonth ( ) const;
int showdate ( ) const { return day;   }
int showyear ( ) const;

void displ ( ) const
{ cout << mon << "/" << day << "/" << year; }

void setmonth (int m) { mon=m;   }
void setdate (int d)  { day=d;   }
void setyear (int y)  { year=y; }
~Time ( );
} ;

int Time :: showmonth ( ) const { return mon; }
int Time :: showyear ( ) const { return year; }
Time :: ~Time ( ) {    }

void main ( )
{
const Time obc (04, 10, 1996);
Time obn (05, 12, 1997);
int k;
k=obc.showmonth ( );
```

```
        cout << k << " ";
        obn.setmonth (10);
        cout << "     " << obn.showmonth ( ) << "     ";
        obn.displ( );
    }
```

Program 12.30.

The output of the program is

        4   10   10/12/1997

This program declares the class **Time**. It consists of three private data members: **mon**, **day**, **year** and a set of member functions. The **const** functions are: **showmonth()**, **showdate()**, **showyear()**, **displ()**. The non-**const** member functions are: **Time()**, **~Time()**, **setmonth()**, **setdate()**, **setyear()**. The **setmonth()**, **setdate()**, **setyear()** member functions are used to set the values of the class data members **mon**, **day**, **year** respectively. The **const** functions **showmonth()**, **showdate()** and **showyear()** are used to display **mon**, **day**, **year** respectively. The **displ()** function displays **mon**, **day**, **year** simultaneously as a date.

We wrote the **showdate()** and **displ()** functions as **inline**. Their definitions are given inside the class. As you see, the headers of both functions contain the word **const** after the list of parameters.

```
        int showdate ( ) const { return day;   }
        void displ ( ) const
        { cout << mon << "/" << day << "/" << year; }
```

In general, **const** functions can be inline or not inline functions. Our **const** member functions do not have any parameters. It is just a coincidence. In general, a **const** function can have formal parameters. The **showmonth()** and **showyear()** member functions are **const** functions as well. But they are not **inline** functions. We have written their prototypes inside the class with the word **const** after the parameter list. For example,

```
        int showyear ( ) const;
```

Their definition headers also contain the word **const** following the parameter list. For example,

```
        int Time :: showyear ( ) const { return year; }
```

Thus, a **const** member function should be specified with the word **const** after the parameter list in *both* the declaration and definition. If a **const** function is an **inline** function, it is defined inside the class. In this case, the word **const** is used only ones in a header of that definition.

We use our member functions to operate on different objects. We define and initialize two objects **obc** and **obn** in **main()**. The **obc** is a **const** object of a class. We show, that we can, in fact, call a constant member function **obc.showmonth()** with that object, and display the current value of the variable **mon**. We also show, we can call and modify a non-**const** object by **obn.setmonth(10)**. You can try to see for yourself, that the call **obc.setmonth(10)** gives an error. It happens, because you call a non-**const** member function **setmonth()** for the **const** object **obc**. Our program also shows, that the call **obn.displ()** is possible. One can use a **const** function to read the current state of a non-**const** object. We just print the content of the data members of the object **obn** when calling **obn.displ()**.

It is a good programming practice to declare the member functions that only display or read the data as **const** functions. This gives a user a possibility to declare **const** objects later in the program.

12.22.2. *const* data members.

One can declare class data members as **const**. Those **const** data members must get their initial values at the time they are initialized. A number of current C++ versions do not permit to do it by a simple assignment. In this case, special *member initializers* should be used to provide the constructor with the initial values of the **const** data members. You will apprehend this material better after following program.

```
#include <iostream.h>

class Num
{
int val;
const int mul;
public:
Num (int a, int b);
int mures ( ) {return (val*mul); }
void disp ( ) { cout << val << " " << mul << "\n"; }
};

Num::Num (int a, int b)
: mul (b)
{ val=a; }
void main ( )
{
Num x (2, 3);
x.disp ( );
cout << x.mures ( );
}
```

Program 12.31.

The output of the program is

2   3
6

Here, we declare class **Num** containing two private data members **val** and **mul** and three functions: **Num()**, **mures()**, **disp()**. The **mul** data member is declared as **const**. The destructor function will be created automatically. There is nothing magic about a class containing a **const** data member. The very class containing the **const** data members and all its member functions can be used as the regular class. Just do not attempt to modify the **const** data member by any member functions. As you can see, there is another subtlety in how we assign the initial value to the **const** data member. For example, if our class did not have any **const** data members, one would initialize the data members of our class **Num** by the very simple constructor function.

```
Num::Num (int a, int b)    { val=a, mul=b; }
```

This would assign the initial values to the class private data members, if they were the regular non-**const** members. If we defined an object as **Num x (2, 3)**, constructor **Num** would assign 2 to **val** and 3 to **mul** of object **x**. Unfortunately, we have a **const** data member **mul** as a class member. If you try to use the above constructor function in **Program 12.31** instead of the one written in it, you will get an error message. Initialization of **const** member requires a special trick with the initializers. You can ask why is it so? It is just the way C++ was created. If you look at **Program 12.31**, the constructor of the class is written as

```
Num::Num (int a, int b)
: mul (b)
{ val=a; }
```

A value stored in parameter **a** is assigned to the data member **val**. A value stored in parameter **b** is copied to the **const** data member **mul**. The assignment form is

```
:mul (b)
```

This is a special form of initialization for the **const** class data member. This form begins with the colon **:** followed by the name of the **const** data member (in our case **mul**) and the corresponding parameter inside the **()** braces. The assignment is written after the constructor function parameters list and before the opening bracket **{**. That form of assignment should not be terminated by the semicolon.

12.23. Classes containing member objects.

12.23.1. Classes and member objects without initializers.

A class can contain objects of another classes as its members. It is called *composition*. Therefore, the objects of a class type can be the members of their class or other classes. Consider following program.

```
#include <iostream.h>                    //line 1
#include <string.h>                      //line 2

class Dat                                //line 3
{                                        //line 4
int mon, day, year;                      //line 5
public:                                  //line 6
Dat ( ) {    }                           //line 7
void set (int a, int b, int c) { mon=a, day=b, year=c; }
                                         //line 8
```

```
    void disp ( ) { cout << mon << "/" << day << "/"
                   << year << "\n"; }  //line 9

    };                                      //line 10

    class Student                           //line 11
    {                                       //line 12
    char firstname[20], lastname[30];       //line 13
    Dat birth;                              //line 14
    public:                                 //line 15
    void first(char *n1) { strcpy (firstname, n1); }//line 16
    void last(char *n2) {  strcpy (lastname, n2); }//line 17
    void born (int x, int y, int z) { birth.set (x, y, z); }
//line 18
    void show ( );                          //line 19
    };                                      //line 20
    void Student::show ( )                  //line 21
    {                                       //line 22
    cout << firstname << " " << lastname << " "; //line 23
    birth.disp ( );                         //line 24
    }                                       //line 25

    void main ( )                           //line 26
    {                                       //line 27
    Student one;                            //line 28
    char arr[ ]="Collins";                  //line 29
    one.first ("John");                     //line 30
    one.last (arr);                         //line 31
    one.born (11, 24, 1962);                //line 32
    one.show ( );                           //line 33
    }                                       //line 34
```
Program 12.32.

The otuput of the program is
```
    John Collins 11/24/1962
```
We declare two classes in this program. The class **Dat** is supposed to be a date of birth of a student. It consists of private data members **mon**, **day**, **year** and public member functions **set()**, **disp()**.The program declares class **Dat** at lines 3-10. The **set()** member function sets the data members to the values passed as its arguments. The **disp()** member function displays current values of all three data members for a particular object.

Student's first and last names are stored by the class **Student**. The **Student** class also stores the date of birth. We declare class **Student** at lines 11-20. It consists of three data members. Two of them are the character strings **firstname** and **lastname**. The third data member is the object **birth** of the **Dat** class type. Class **Student** consists of a few member functions. The **first()** member function copies the content of its string parameter **n1** into the **firstname** member at line 16. Member function **last()** copies the content of its string parameter **n2** into the **lastname** member string at line 17. Member function **born()** has three parameters. It passes them as the arguments to the **birth.set()** member function of class **Dat** at line 18.

We use the member functions of external **Student** class to call member functions of the internal object class **Dat**. The **birth.set()** member function used in **born()** sets the values of **birth** object.

We display a content of the data members of the **Student** class by **show()** member function at lines 21-25. The contents of both **lastname** and **firstname** are displayed by the **cout** object. The content of object **birth** is displayed by the member function **birth.disp()** of class **Dat**.

We show how to operate with this composition class in **main()** function at lines 26-34. We declare an object **one** of the **Student** class. The program run starts the constructor and creates the objects **birth** and **one**. We do not assign any initial values to them. Their constructors do not have any parameters. But we can assign the values to one or both objects later. The **firstname** gets its string by **one.first("John")**. Member string **lastname** is loaded by the **one.last(arr)** member function. And the object **birth** is assigned its values by the **one.born(11, 24, 1962)** member function. The content of **one** is, then, displayed by **one.show()** member function.

The above program has shown following. *Suppose, class A contains an object of class B as its member. One can call member functions of class B from the member functions of class A to assign the values to the member object of class A. Both the external object of class A type and the member object of A class can be initialized without any values. You, then, can use the member functions to assign the values to the objects of classes A and B.* A class can have any number of member objects of different class types.

12.23.2. Classes and member objects with initializers.

One can assign the initial values to an object of a class containing a member object, while creating it. A class constructor is, usually, used for that. Following program demonstrates how to initialize classes containing objects by a constructor.

```
#include <iostream.h>              //line 1
#include <string.h>                //line 2

class Dat                          //line 3
{                                  //line 4
int mon, day, year;                //line 5
public:                            //line 6
Dat (int w, int e, int r) { mon=w, day=e, year=r;    }
                                   //line 7
void disp ( ) { cout << mon << "/" << day << "/" << year
                 << "\n"; }  //line 8
};                                 //line 9
```

```
class Student                  //line 10
{                              //line 11
char firstname[20], lastname[30];//line 12
Dat birth;                     //line 13
public:                        //line 14
Student (char *, char *, int, int, int );    //line 15
void show ( );                 //line 16
};                             //line 17

Student::Student (char *st1, char *st2, int a, int b,
                  int c)       //line 18
:birth (a, b, c)              //line 19
{                              //line 20
strcpy (firstname, st1);      //line 21
strcpy (lastname, st2);       //line 22
}                              //line 23

void Student::show ( )         //line 24
{                              //line 25
cout << firstname << " " << lastname << " "; //line 26
birth.disp ( );                //line 27
}                              //line 28

void main ( )                  //line 29
{                              //line 30
char arr1[ ]="John", arr2[ ]="Collins";       //line 31
Student one (arr1, arr2, 11, 24, 62);  //line 32
one.show ( );                  //line 33
}                              //line 34
```
Program 12.33.

This program has the same output as the previous one. **Program 12.33** is similar to the previous one, but there are some differences. We also declare class **Dat** at lines 3-9. It consists of the same three private data members **mon**, **day**, **year**. We wrote two public functions: the constructor **Dat()** and the **disp()** function. The destructor will be created by the compiler. Now, the constructor of that class has three parameters: **w**, **e**, **r**. It assigns the initial values to the **Dat** class private members **mon**, **day**, **year**. You already know, if a constructor has parameters, the object must be defined with the parentheses and initializers. Let's see, how it is implemented, when a class has an object as its member.

To do that, look at the declaration of the **Student** class at lines 10-17. It contains the data members **firstname**, **lastname**, **birth**, and two functions - constructor **Student()** and **show()** function. We could have left all the functions from the previous program. However, we left only the functions necessary for this discussion. The constructor **Student()** in our program has the parameters. It is declared as

```
Student (char *, char *, int, int, int );    //line 15
```

The constructor of class **Student** initializes the members of this class. It also passes three arguments to its member object **birth**. The object **birth** is initialized by the constructor of its class **Dat()**. The definition of the **Student()** constructor function is given at lines 18-23. Its parameters **a**, **b** and **c** are used to call the object **birth** with the initializers as

```
    :birth (a, b, c)                      //line 19
```

This form starts the constructor **Dat()** of class **Dat**, that has 3 parameters. This form initializes a member object of a class. The form consists of a colon **:** followed by the name of the member object (in our case **birth**) and the list of initializers. The number of initilaizers should be equal to the number of parameters in the corresponding class constructor. In our case, the **Dat()** constructor, that creates the **birth** object, has three parameters. This form is used in the constructor of the class, that contains an object member. The form immediately follows the list of parameters in the definition header of the constructor.

Two other arguments **st1** and **st2** of **Student()** function are used to initialize the data members of the **Student** class. The constructor simply copies the content of its parameters into corresponding data member by **strcpy()** function at lines 21, 22.

The object **one** is created in **main()** by

```
    Student one (arr1, arr2, 11, 24, 62);        //line 32
```

We display the content of that object by the **one.show()** member function at line 33.

We have learned following. An object of class A type containing an object of class B type as its member can be initialized by the constructors. The constructor of A class has to provide a sufficient number of parameters for its own data members and for the data members of the object of class B. The constructor of class A must have a special initialization form for the object of class B. In our case it is **:birth(a, b, c)**. *The number of initializers in this form should be equal to the number of parameters in the constructor function of class B. Even though we have shown only one member object of class A, but a class can contain any number of objects of any other classes. This can add the arguments to the constructor function of class A.*

The way of initializing a member object presented by **Program 12.33** becomes vital, when that member object is declared with the **const** keyword. You cannot call any functions but the constructor to perform the **const** object initialization.

Following program illustrates one more way of initializing an object of a class containing a member object. **Program 12.34** is very similar to the previous program.

```
#include <iostream.h>
#include <string.h>

class Dat
{
int mon, day, year;
public:
Dat ( ) {  }
void set (int a, int b, int c) { mon=a, day=b, year=c; }
```

```
void disp ( )
{ cout << mon << "/" << day << "/" << year << "\n"; }
};

class Student
{
char firstname[20], lastname[30];
Dat birth;
public:
Student (char *, char *, int, int, int );
void show ( );
};

Student::Student (char *st1, char *st2, int x, int y,
                  int z)
{
strcpy (firstname, st1);
strcpy (lastname, st2);
birth.set (x, y, z);
}

void Student::show ( )
{
cout << firstname << " " << lastname << " ";
birth.disp ( );
}

void main ( )
{
char arr1[20]="John", arr2[20]="Collins";
Student one (arr1, arr2, 11, 24, 62);
one.show ( );
}
```

Program 12.34.

The output of this program is the same as in the previous two programs. Here, the object **birth** of class **Dat** is a member of class **Student**. But the constructor **Dat()** does not have any parameters. The constructor of class **Student()**, however, has the same five parameters. It uses the **strcpy()** function to pass the initial strings to the **firstname** and **lastname** members. It calls the function **birth.set(x, y, z)** of **Dat** class to set the initial values of the object **birth**. The above example demonstrates the way to initialize an object of a class type with a member object. *An object of the class B type being a member of a class A can be initialized by the constructor of that class A, that starts constructor of class B. That constructor of class A can call the member functions of class B and pass its parameters as the arguments to those member functions.*

We offer you last program, that is just a modification of **Program 12.33**. It illustrates the initialization of an object of a class containing member objects. It also illustrates how to modify that object later. The program initializes an object **one** by **Student one(arr1, arr2, 11, 24, 62)** statement and displays it. It, then, prompts a user, if anything in the displayed sequence should be changed. One can change the content of the string **firstname**, or **lastname**, or the date of **birth** of a student using the member functions of the class **Student**.

```
#include <iostream.h>
#include <string.h>

class Dat
{
int mon, day, year;
public:
Dat (int w, int e, int r) { mon=w, day=e, year=r;    }
void set (int a, int b, int c) { mon=a, day=b, year=c; }

void disp ( )
{ cout << mon << "/" << day << "/" << year << "\n"; }

};

class Student
{
char firstname[20], lastname[30];
Dat birth;
public:
Student (char *, char *, int, int, int );
void first (char *n1) { strcpy (firstname, n1); }
void last (char *n2) {  strcpy (lastname, n2); }
void born (int x, int y, int z) { birth.set (x, y, z); }
void show ( );
};

Student::Student (char *st1, char *st2, int mon, int day,
                  int year)
:birth (mon, day, year)
{
strcpy (firstname, st1);
strcpy (lastname, st2);
}

void Student::show ( )
{
```

```
cout << firstname << " " << lastname << " ";
birth.disp ( );
}

void main ( )
{
char arr1[20]="John", arr2[20]="Collins";
int n, n1, n2, n3;
Student one (arr1, arr2, 11, 24, 62);
one.show ( );
cout << "Press 0 if it is right, 1 to correct the first"
     << " name, 2 to \ncorrect the second name, "
     << "3 for the month day or year\n";
cin >> n;
switch (n)
{
case 1:
cout << "Correct the first name\n";
cin >> arr1;
one.first (arr1);
one.show ( );
break;
case 2:
cout << "Correct the last name\n";
cin >> arr2;
one.last (arr2);
one.show ( );
break;
case 3:
cout << " Enter month, day and year of birth separated"
     << " by space, press ENTER\n";
cin >> n1;
cin >> n2;
cin >> n3;
one.born (n1, n2, n3);
one.show ( );
break;
default:
break;
} }
```

Program 12.35.

We have demonstrated in all the programs of this paragraph how to handle a class containing an object as its member. The member objects of the class are created, when an object of that class enters the scope. Loosely speaking, the inner member object of a class is created, at the same time when the outer object of the class is created.

12.24. *static* **class members.**

A class can have **static** data members and member functions. A class can contain a number of **static** members. Both public and private class members can be declared as **static**. The **static** member functions are, usually, used to handle **static** data members. They do not have **this** pointer. Therefore, no **this** pointer can be used with them. You remember, when you create an object, a new copy of all class members is created. By declaring a class member as **static**, you tell the computer, that whatever number of objects of that class you create, there will be only one copy of that **static** class member. This means that only one copy of the **static** class member exists. All the objects of the class will share that one copy among each other. If an object changes the value of the **static** class member, it will remain changed for all other objects. Consider following program.

```
#include <iostream.h>                        //line 1

class Test                                   //line 2
{                                            //line 3
int x;                                       //line 4
public:                                      //line 5
static int y;                                //line 6
void set (int a, int b) { x=a, y=b; }        //line 7
void static stset (int c) { y=c ; }          //line 8
void noset (int d) { x=d; }                  //line 9
void show ( ) { cout << x << " " << y; }//line 10
};                                           //line 11

int Test::y=0;                               //line 12

void main ( )                                //line 13
{                                            //line 14
Test ob, see;                                //line 15
Test::stset(2);                              //line 16
ob.noset (3);                                //line 17
ob.show ( );                                 //line 18
see.set (10, 15);                            //line 19
cout << "after static change  ";             //line 20
ob.show ( );                                 //line 21
}                                            //line 22
```

Program 12.36.

The output of the program is

```
   3 2 after static change   3   15
```
Above program declares **Test** class at lines 2-11. It contains private data member **x** and public **static** data member **y**. The class also consists of six functions: **set()**, **stset()**, **noset()**, **show()**, constructor and destructor. The **stset()** function is declared as **static**. The **set()**, **stset()**, **noset()** functions, basically, set all or some of the class data members to some values. The **show()** function displays them.

This program illustrates an important property of a **static** data member. We declare **static** class member **y** at line 6. This is only a declaration of the static member, not its definition. A **static** data member cannot be handled by the class constructor function, because the **static** member should be initialized once but the constructor runs every time a class type object is created. This is why you need to define the static class data member globally in the source file outside the class. We define it by

```
   int Test::y=0;                          //line 12
```
The definition begins with the data type followed by the class name, scope resolution operator **::** and the name of the data member. You can also assign it an initial value, as we did at line 12. This definition tells the computer to which class the **static** data member belongs and allocates the storage for it.

We demonstrate you how to use the static data member in **main()** function at lines 13-22. We define two objects **ob** and **see** of the **Test** class. The class data members including the **static** one can be handled in a usual way by the member functions. The **static** member functions and member objects exist independently of the class objects. They can be used, accessed and changed without using any object. It is done by

```
   Test::stset(2);                         //line 16
```
Here, we use the **static** function **stset()** to set an object. It is used in a special notation. The name of the class and the **::** operator should precede the static function. We can also set the **static** member **y** directly by

```
   Test::y=2;
```
Try to substitute it instead of line 16 and run the above program. It will run without any problems.

We set the **x** data member of the object **ob** to 3 by the **ob.noset(3)** at line 17 and display both data members by **ob.show()** at line 18. The result is 3 2. We, then, set both data members of the object **see** to 10 and 15 by **see.set(10, 15)**. You know, that there is only one copy of the **static** member. We just changed it using the **see** object. It should remain changed. We prove it by displaying the content of the object **ob** again by **ob.show()**. The new values are 3 and 15. The value of **static** data member **y** has been changed from 2 to 15.

We want to add couple more ideas. A **static** data member can be both public and private. Static member functions can access *only* **static** class members. They cannot call non-**static** member functions. They cannot have the pointer **this** assosiated with them. We have made the **static** function **stset()** an **inline** function. Let's now review how to write it with the word **static** as a regular function. We offer you an answer. Its declaration at line 8 should have the word **static** in it as

```
   void static stset  (int c);
```
But the definition of that function should be written without the word **static** as

```
   void  Test ::stset (int c) { y=c ; }
```

12.25. Operators .* and ->*.

We would like to introduce so-called *pointer-to-member* **.*** and **->*** operators. You can specify a pointer to a class member. Those two operators allow you to access class members via pointers to them. Following program illustrates the use of those operators in accessing a member **x** and the member function **res()** of class **Exa**.

```
#include <iostream.h>

class Exa
{
public:
int x;
void res (int );
};

void Exa::res (int a)
{
int k, m=1;
for (k=1; k<=x; k++)
m=m*k;
cout << (a*m) << endl;
}

void main()
{
Exa ob;
int Exa::*pd; //declare a pointer to a data member
void (Exa::*pf)(int a) ; //declare a pointer to a
                         //function member
pd=&Exa::x;  //directing a pointer to data member
pf=&Exa::res; //directing a pointer to member function
ob.*pd=3; //accessing data member x
(ob.*pf)(3); //accessing member function
cout << "The x member is: " << ob.x;
}
```

Program 12.37.

The output of the program is
```
18
The x member is: 3
```
The program declares class **Exa**, that consists of data member **x**, member function **res()**. The **res()** member function finds a factorial of numbers from 1 to that stored in **x** and multiplies the factorial by the value passed to its parameter **a**. We use the class type

in **main()**. We create two member pointers there. The **pd** is a pointer to the data member **x**. The **pf** is a pointer to the member function **res()**. We make **pd** pointing towards the member **x** by **pd=&Exa::x**. Pointer **pf** is directed towards function **res()** by **pf=&Exa::res** assignment. We also define the **ob** object. We, then, access both members of object **ob** using the pointer-to-member operators.

We used object **ob** in the above program. We accessed the members of that object by **.*** operator. One also uses the **->*** operator, when dealing with a pointer to an object of class type. The program, illustrating it, is given below.

```
#include <iostream.h>

class Exa
{
public:
int x;
void gval (int b) { x=b; }
void res (int );
};

void Exa::res (int a)
{
int k, m=1;
for (k=1; k<=x; k++)
m=m*k;
cout << (a*m) << endl;
}

void main()
{
Exa ob, *clpr;
int Exa::*pd;
void (Exa::*pf)(int a) ;
pd=&Exa::x;
pf=&Exa::res;
clpr=&ob;
clpr->*pd=3;
(clpr->*pf)(3);
cout << "The x member is: " << clpr->x;
}
```

Program 12.38.

The program has the same output as the previous one. It is also very similar to the previous program.

EXERCISES.

1. Run all the examples of this chapter, if you have an access to a computer facility.

2. Compare classes, structures and unions. What do they have in common? What is the difference between them?

3. Write a class, that stores day, month and the year. It should perform following actions:
    1) it permits to enter two dates;
    2) it displays the day of the week, and the week of the year for any entered date;
    3) it displays the number of days between two dates;
    4) it checks if the date is correct;
    5) it displays the date, when you enter the week of a year and the day of a week;
Write a program with that class, that performs all those actions.

4. Write a class that is able to
    1) read two complex numbers, that consist of a real and imaginary parts. The imaginary part begins with the symbol **i**;
    2) add two complex numbers. To add two complex numbers means to add their real parts, and, then, separately add their imaginary parts;
       (1+i3) + (5-i10) = 6 - i7
    3) subtract two complex numbers. To subtract two complex numbers means to subtract their real parts, and, then, to subtract their imaginary parts separately;
    4) multiply two complex numbers. You multiply two complex numbers, as two brackets. For instance,
       (2+i3)*(1-i5)=2*(1-i5)+i3*(1-i5)=2-i10+i3+15=17-i7
    The multiplication obeys to the following rules. Multiplication of two real parts produces a real part. Multiplication of a real an imaginary parts produces an imaginary part. Multiplication of two imaginary parts produces a real part multiplied by (-1);
    5) display the complex values and the results on the screen.
Write a program, that uses the above class and performs all the above operations.

5. Write a class that is able to store two fractions. It can also perform addition, subtraction, multiplication and division of those fractions. Write a program that uses the described class and performs all those actions.

6. Write a class, that finds and displays the areas of a circle, square, triangle, trapezoid. Write a program that performs all those actions.

7. Write programs, that perform some useful actions with the classes utilizing one and more of the following features:
    1) classes with the constructors with and without the parameters;
    2) dynamic memory allocation;
    3) passing and returning the objects to and from a function;
    4) references to objects;
    5) objects as class members;
    6) **const** and **static** class members and objects;
    7) friend and inline functions;
    8) copy constructors;

CHAPTER 13

OPERATOR OVERLOADING.

13.1. Introduction to operator overloading.

Operator overloading is an important feature of C++. You have learned how to create and use a class. You use a class by means of its member functions. They perform certain tasks. One can perform some of those tasks creating new operators, using the existing notations of those operators. For instance, C++ allows you to create an operator doing some fancy arithmetical operation and call it + sign. If you write + sign, it can do a simple addition, or it can do that fancy arithmetic operation depending on circumstances. This is called *operator overloading*. You create a new operator action from existing operators by means of the *operator functions*. In other words, you write a function, specifying another action, that can be performed by the same operator.

You have dealt with the overloaded operators. For instance, the stream insertion operator << is also a left-shift operator. An ability to create those operators is a very powerful tool of C++. However, not all the operators can be overloaded. Table 13.1 gives us the operators, that can be overloaded.

Table 13.1. The operators that can be overloaded.

+	^	>	,	*=	^=	&&	()
-	&	<	++	/=	&=	||	->
*	|	<=	--	%=	|=	<<	->*
/	~	>=	+=	==	<<=	>>	new
%	!	=	-=	!=	>>=	[]	delete

We will teach you how to create and use the overloaded operators. Now we want to consider some general rules. There are some restrictions on operator overloading.

• You cannot create your own operators. You have to use only the operators given in Table 13.1. For instance, you create an operator using @&* characters. It will be interpreted as an error by the compiler, because this operator is not in the table.

• You cannot change the number of operands the initial operator operates on. For example, logical NOT operator (~) operates only on one operand. It is a unary operator. So, you cannot use it to perform an operation on more than one operand. Whatever operation you write with (~), the expression like x=~y is possible, while x=z~y will lead to an error. We will give you another example. The + operator acts on two operands. You can use it to do the operations on two variables or objects, for instance. You cannot use it to perform operations on more than two operands.

- You can change neither the operator precedence nor associativity. The addition operator + and multiplication operator * can do a number of operations. But the * operator will be evaluated earlier than +. Since the + and – operators have left to right associativity, they will be evaluated in this order.

    x=y-z+k; is equal to x=(y-z)+k;

- You cannot change the way in which an operator performs its action on the built-in data types. The built-in data types are the fundamental data types, such as **int**, **float**, etc. For instance, you cannot change the way the addition operator performs an addition of two integers.

- Following operators given in Table 13.2 cannot be overloaded.

    We give you a few advices on how to overload the operators. We would advise you to overload an operator, when the meaning of that operator is obvious. For example, the arithmetic operators like +, –, * and / are meaningful when used for the numbers. So, a sum or multiplication of two numbers is a normal operation. Imagine, we add two objects **one** and **two** of **Student** class described in Chapter 12. One can hardly understand the result produced by such an action. However, you can use it wisely. For instance,

    three=one+two;

Table 13.2. Non-overloadable operators.

Operator	Operator's name
.	Class member operator
.*	Pointer to member operator
::	Scope resolution operator
?:	Conditional expression operator

Do not use too many overloaded operators. They can make your program very difficult to read. Other programmers may have to maintain your program, and they might have difficulties of understanding it. You can have difficulties even with your own program later on.

13.2. Operator overloading with member functions.

In order to be able to use an existing operator in a new way, you have to create an operator function. This function will specify the new action of the operator. This function can be a member of a class. It can be a non-member function, typically, a friend of a class. Each of those two cases slightly changes the implementation of that operator function. We will discuss both of them. Here we will show how to create a binary operator function, that is a member of a class.

In general, you decide whether to make an operator function a member or a friend of the class. However, if you ever decide to overload (), [], ->, =, the operator overloading function should always be a class member.

Let's now show how to create a member operator function. It has a declaration (prototype) and a definition form, as any function. It is declared inside a class as

    type operator ... (type par1);

Here, the **type** is the data type of the returned value. It can be any of the fundamental data types. It can have any of the derived data types, for example, a structure or class type. It is followed by the keyword **operator**. The presence of that word indicates, that an operator function will be created. The sequence of dots **. . .** succeeds that word in our form. This is the place for an actual operator. This is the name of the operator, that you would call to perform the action coded in your operator function. If you put **+** sign and write the operator overloading function, then, **+** beside its normal addition action will be able to perform another action. You also specify the types and the names of the function parameters in the **( )** braces. The prototype should be terminated by the semicolon.

The operator function definition has the form

```
type classname :: operator ... (type par1)
{
body of the function
}
```

As you see, it is similar to the regular functions. It has a header and the body of the function contained between the **{ }** braces. The header contains two additional features compare to the declaration: the name of the class *classname* and the **: :** operator, indicating the class scope of the operator function. The operator function definition, typically, follows class declaration and is written outside of the class. Following example illustrates operator overloading using operator member functions.

```
#include <iostream.h>                    //line 1

class dim {                               //line 2
int x, y, z;                              //line 3
public:                                   //line 4
dim ( ) { x=y=z=0; }                      //line 5
dim (int a, int b, int c) { x=a, y=b, z=c; } //line 6
dim operator - (dim r);                   //line 7

void disp ( ) { cout << x <<", " << y << ", " << z
                     << "\n"; }            //line 8
} ;                                        //line 9

dim dim::operator - (dim r)               //line 10
{                                         //line 11
dim one;                                  //line 12
one.x=x-r.x;                              //line 13
one.y=y-r.y;                              //line 14
one.z=z-r.z;                              //line 15
return one;                               //line 16
}                                         //line 17

void main ( )                             //line 18
{                                         //line 19
```

```
dim k (2, 4, 6), m (10, 20, 30), n;      //line 20
n=k-m;                                   //line 21
n.disp ( );                              //line 22
n=m-k-n;                                 //line 23
n.disp ( );                              //line 24
}                                        //line 25
```

Program 13.1.

The output of the program is
```
-8, -16, -24
16, 32, 48
```

We will briefly describe the program and, then, explain some vital points. The program declares **dim** class at lines 2-9. We want to use this class to operate on the coordinates in three-dimensional space. The class consists of three private data members **x, y, z**, function **disp()**, operator function **operator-()**. Thus, the **dim** class has one overloaded – operator. We write two constructor functions, one with parameters and another one without them. We overload the constructor just for our convenience, so we can declare objects of that class with and without the braces. We declare objects **k, m** and **n** of **dim** class type and perform the subtraction operations on them by the **n=m-k-n** or **n=k-m** expressions in **main()** function at lines 18-25. The result of each operation is displayed on the screen.

We will consider the – operator function now. The operator function, that determines the new operation of the – operator, is declared within the class at line 7. It is defined at lines 10-17. The – is a binary operator. By "binary" we mean here, that it acts between two operands (for instance, two variables or objects). Let us clarify first how the operator function is called. When we write **n=k-m** in **main()** routine, the **k-m** expression requires the overloaded minus operator. Both **k** and **m** are the objects of class **dim** type. Regular minus does not subtract two objects. This is why we have to write a minus operator function, that subtracts two objects. When the compiler "sees" **k-m**, it starts the operator overloading function.

How do you call a regular function? You call it by name. The operator function is also called by its name. The "**-**" is the name of the minus function. If the compiler cannot perform a regular minus operation, it will look for minus operator function. The operator function will be started. The operator function is called by the object to the left of it. Hence, **k-** calls the minus operator function in **Program 13.1**. The expression **k-m**, loosely speaking, is the full form of the call to the binary operator member function. You call a regular function by name, as for example, **func()**. A call to an operator binary function contains the operands on the left and the right, and the symbol of that operator in the middle. Thus, the **k-m** form is just a call to an operator function. The operator function will perform its action. The **k-m** form will cause an action of that operator function. If that function returns a value, the **k-m** form will be replaced by a value or an object.

One can ask how the arguments are passed to a binary operator function. For example, the operator function **operator-()** has only one parameter **r** in **Program 13.1**. It is possible, because our operator function is a class member function. The rule is, when you write a binary operator overloading as a member function, only one argument is explicitly passed to that function. The other argument is implicitly passed by means of **this** pointer. *In binary operators (such as -, +, etc.,) the left object causes the call to the operator function. It is passed by means of* **this** *pointer. The operand on the right of its operator symbol is passed as an argument to the operator function. A binary member function is called by an object on the left of its operator symbol. Thus, the left operand of a binary member function can be only an object of its class type.*

We subtract two objects **k-m** at line 21 in **Program 13.1**. According to the above rule, object **k** is passed by means of **this** pointer, the object **m** is passed as an argument of - operator function. An operand on the left can be only an object of class **dim** in our case. It is, indeed, an object **k** of class **dim**. An operand **m** on the right of - sign is another object **m** of the same class type. It can be an operand of any data type.

Now a question is how to write an operator function. You write it as a regular function. The only difference you have to keep in mind, is how this function gets its arguments. We have discussed how the values or objects are passed to an operator function. Our operator function specifies a fairly simple action for the - operator. It subtracts corresponding coordinates of two objects. It computes the difference for each coordinate in an unusual fashion. For example,

```
    one.y=y - r.y;                          //line 14
```
Here, we have the difference **y-r.y**. This difference is, in fact, nothing else but

```
    this->y - r.y;
```
The single **y** is **this->y**, because it will be the corresponding data member of the object on the left. The - operator function stores the result of the subtraction of each data member in the object **one**. Object **one** is returned by that function.

Now let us summarize how to write binary operator functions as class member functions. They can return an object or any other type. They can even have **void** return type. Those functions are written as regular ones. They can consist of different statements and operators just as regular functions. They have two major differences from the regular functions. First, when you write those expressions be aware, that the members of the object on the left will be accessed through **this** pointer. Therefore, if you write a class member by name, it is considered as a member of the object on the left. An operand on the right is accessed through the function parameter. An operand on the right can be a variable, object, etc. Second, you call this function just by the operator symbol. The compiler will determine, which meaning of the overloaded operator to use based on evaluation of the operands on both sides. For example, the lines of code in **Program 13.1**

```
    n=k-m;                                  //line 21
    n=m-k-n;                                //line 23
```
will call our operator function. The - operator will subtract the respective coordinates of **k** and **m** at line 21. The result of the operation will be returned by the operator function and assigned to the object **n**. The values of its members -8, -16, -24 are displayed as the first output line.

There are two subtraction operations at line 23. The first one will subtract **m-k**. Here, the operand on the left is **m**, on the right is **k**. The result of this operation will interact with object **n**, and produce the second subtraction procedure. The result of that second subtraction will be assigned to the object **n** and displayed on the screen.

13.3. Addition to overloading with member function.

Program 13.1 changes neither the object on the right nor the object on the left. Your operator function can change an operand that is passed through its pointer. It means, that an object on the left of the operator can be changed by the operator, because it is passed by its **this** pointer. You know, when an argument is passed via a pointer, its content can be changed. An object on the right is passed by call-by-value. Hence, only its copy is passed, and the original cannot be altered. Consider following program, that does change the object on the left.

```
#include <iostream.h>                      //line 1

class dim {                                //line 2
int x, y, z;                               //line 3
public:                                    //line 4
dim ( ) { x=y=z=0; }                       //line 5
dim (int a, int b, int c) { x=a, y=b, z=c; } //line 6
dim operator - (dim r);                    //line 7

void disp ( ) { cout << x <<", " << y << ", " << z
                     << "\n"; }            //line 8
} ;                                        //line 9

dim dim::operator - (dim r)                //line 10
{                                          //line 11
x=x-r.x;                                   //line 12
y=y-r.y;                                   //line 13
z=z-r.z;                                   //line 14
return *this;                              //line 15
}                                          //line 16

void main ( )                              //line 17
{                                          //line 18
dim k (2, 4, 6), m (10, 20, 30), n;       //line 19
n=k-m;                                     //line 20
n.disp ( );                                //line 21
k.disp ( );                                //line 22
m.disp ( );                                //line 23
}                                          //line 24
```

Program 13.2.

The output of the program is
```
-8, -16, -24
-8, -16, -24
```

```
10, 20, 30
```
This program is quite analogous to the previous one. However, the – operator function
is written a bit different than before. Look at its definition at lines 10-16. The – operator
function also subtracts the corresponding coordinates of two objects. Instead of declaring
the third object and assigning the results of the subtraction to its members, it assigns the
results to the object on the left. It is done by the assignment statements like

```
    x=x-r.x;                                    //line 12
```
The function returns the content of the object **k** pointed to by **this** pointer.

```
    return *this;                               //line 15
```
The result of the **k-m** operation is stored in the object **k**. It is assigned to the object **n** of
dim class by the **n=k-m** expression. We display the content of the objects **n**, **k** and **m** to
show, that the member values of objects **n** and **k** are equal.

We mentioned, the overloaded operator does not necessarily have to return an object as
its action. This depends on the type of the value returned by the operator function. Following program introduces – operator function, that returns an integer as a result of its
operation. It also operates on two objects. But it finds the result of the expression

```
    one=(x-r.x)+(y-r.y)+(z-r.z);
```
That integer is returned by the operator function.

```
    #include <iostream.h>                    //line 1

    class dim {                              //line 2
    int x, y, z;                             //line 3
    public:                                  //line 4
    dim (int a, int b, int c) { x=a, y=b, z=c; } //line 5
    int operator - (dim r);                  //line 6
    } ;                                      //line 7

    int dim::operator - (dim r)              //line 8
    {                                        //line 9
    int one;                                 //line 10
    one=(x-r.x)+(y-r.y)+(z-r.z);             //line 11
    return one;                              //line 12
    }                                        //line 13

    void main ( )                            //line 14
    {                                        //line 15
    dim k (2, 4, 6), m (10, 20, 30);
    int n;                                   //line 16
    n=k-m;                                   //line 17
    cout << n;                               //line 18
    }                                        //line 19
```
                              Program 13.3.

The output of the program is the number -48. It is very similar to **Program 13.1**.

We illustrated how to write a binary operator overloading function as a class member. We want to illustrate binary operator overloading on an example of another operator. Let's consider an assignment operator overloading. Following program illustrates it.

```
#include <iostream.h>                    //line 1

class dim {                              //line 2
int x, y, z;                             //line 3
public:                                  //line 4
dim ( ) { x=y=z=0; }                     //line 5
dim (int a, int b, int c) { x=a, y=b, z=c; } //line 6
dim operator = (dim w);                  //line 7

void disp ( ) { cout << x <<", " << y << ", " << z
                    << "\n"; }           //line 8

} ;                                      //line 9

dim dim :: operator =(dim w)             //line 10
{                                        //line 11
x=w.x;                                   //line 12
y=w.y;                                   //line 13
z=w.z;                                   //line 14
return *this;                            //line 15
}                                        //line 16

void main ( )                            //line 17
{                                        //line 18
dim k (2, 4, 6), m (10, 20, 30), n;      //line 19
n=k=m;                                   //line 20
n.disp ( );                              //line 21
k.disp ( );                              //line 22
}                                        //line 23
```
Program 13.4.

The output of the program is
```
10, 20, 30
10, 20, 30
```
The program declares class **dim** at lines 1-9, consisting of three private data members **x**, **y**, **z**, member function **disp()** and assignment (**=**) operator function. The class also has an overloaded constructor. The class is just a modification of the class we have used in a few previous programs of this chapter. We will concentrate on considering the assignment operator function in this example. It is declared as a class member inside the class at line 7. It is defined at lines 10-16.

The **=** operator, as we know, is a binary one. It obeys to the rules of the binary operator overloading. Thus, the operator function shell have only one parameter. Our = operator function operates on objects. Its parameter is an object. It returns an object of **dim** type. What it does? You call this function for two objects **a** and **b** of class **dim** as **a=b**. It makes all the data members of the object **b** on the right equal to the corresponding data members of the object **a** on the left. How can one write it? Think about it. One has to assign all the data members of the object on the right to the respective data members of the object on the left. An object on the left must be returned. Our object of **dim** class has three data members. So, we write three assignments like

```
    x=w.x;                                    //line 12
```

Here, the **x** on the left is nothing else, but **this->x**. This accesses **x** member of the object on the left. The object on the right is passed as the argument. So, we access its data member as **w.x**. Our operator function consists of three of those assignments, one for each data members. It returns the content of the object on the left

```
    return *this;                             //line 15
```

We use our class in the **main()** function. We declare objects **k, m, n** at line 19. We use our assignment operator in the expression

```
    n=k=m;                                    //line 20
```

Here, the assignment is first performed on the objects **k=m**. The assignment returns the content of the pointer **this**, which is a content of the object **k**. The content of the object **k** is equal to that of object **m**. The next assignment is **n=k**. It assigns the content of the object **k**, that has been returned by the pointer **this**, to the object **n**. The pointer **this** makes possible the assignments like **m=n=k**. There was no need to write an assignment operator function for the objects, as we did it. Our operator function produces the result, that we could achieve using the regular assignment operator for the objects. We just wanted to illustrate our point.

The order of operands in an operation is essential in many cases. For instance, you add or multiply two operands. For simplicity you can thing about the variables being those operands. Then, **x+y** is equal to **y+x**. The same is true for **x*y** and **y*x**. But **x-y** and **y-x** will produce different results. For instance, 3-2=1 and 2-3=-1. When change in the order of two operands affects the result of operation, those operators are called *non-commutative*. The subtraction and division are non-commutative operators. You must pay attention to which operator is on the left and which is on the right. The addition operation is a commutative operation.

13.4. Unary operators overloading with member functions.

We will review how to write the operator overloading functions for the unary operators. The operator function will still be a class member. When you use a class member operator function to overload a unary operator, it does not need any parameters at all. No object is passed to that operator explicitly. The operation will be performed on the object, that generates the call. The object will be passed to that function by means of **this** pointer. Using that mechanism, one can overload such unary operators, as, for instance, increment **++**, decrement **--**, or unary minus **-**. Consider following program illustrating unary operators.

```
#include <iostream.h>

class dim {
int x, y, z;
public:
dim ( ) { x=y=z=0; }
dim (int a, int b, int c) { x=a, y=b, z=c; }
dim  operator ++ ( );

void disp ( )
{ cout << x <<", " << y << ", " << z << "\n"; }

} ;

dim  dim :: operator ++( )
{
x++;
y++;
z++;
return *this;
}

void main ( )
{
dim  m (10, 20, 30);
++m;
m.disp ( );
}
```

Program 13.5.

The output of the program is

     11, 21, 31

   This program declares class **dim** consisting of three private data members **x, y, z**, function **disp()** and increment **++** operator overloading function. The constructor of this class is overloaded. Overloaded constructor is, again, not a requirement for writing operator functions. We just did it for our convenience. That way we can declare the class objects with and without the initial parameters. We did not write the destructor function. It will be created by the compiler.

   The increment operator function is declared without any parameters. It does not need them. The object that calls the function will be passed by means of **this** pointer.

     dim operator ++( )

Our increment operator function increases the values stored in class members **x, y** and **z** by 1. It is done by means of the statements like **x++**, that is, in fact, **this->x++** operation on the data members. The operator function returns **this** pointer. We use this overloaded operator to perform an action on the object **++m** of **dim** class type in **main()**.

The result is displayed by the program.

As you know, there are pre- and post-increment operators. The above program is written for the object pre-increment **++m**. Some compilers, especially the older versions, will be able to perform both **++m** and **m++** as a pre-increment operation using our operator function. You can get a warning message during the program compilation on some modern compilers. One can write a unary post-increment operator function on the most recent C++ compilers. Consider following program.

```
#include <iostream.h>

class dim {
int x, y, z;
public:
dim ( ) { x=y=z=0; }
dim (int a, int b, int c) { x=a, y=b, z=c; }
dim  operator ++ (int mine);

void disp ( )
{ cout << x <<", " << y << ", " << z << "\n"; }
} ;

dim  dim :: operator ++(int mine)
{
dim obj=*this;
x++;
y++;
z++;
return obj;
}

void main ( )
{
dim  m (10, 20, 30), k;
k=m++;
m.disp ( );
k.disp ( );
}
```

Program 13.6.

The output of the program is
```
11, 21, 31
10, 20, 30
```

This program is very similar to the previous one. Except, the increment operator function now has a parameter. It is written slightly different. The prototype of the operator function is

```
dim operator ++(int mine)
```
The presence of the parameter tells the compiler, that the operator will follow an object, when you use it. So, if you want your increment operator **++** to follow the object as in **m++**, write a parameter of type **int** in the argument function. That parameter will not be used. It is just a way to indicate to the compiler, that the object passed to the function precedes the operator.

We write our post-increment function differently. As you remember, the assignment **a=b++** first assigns the value of **b** to **a** and only then increments the value of **b**. Same was true for the variables. It is true for the objects. This is why our operator function first assigns to the object **obj** the current values of the data members of the object ***this** that called it.

```
dim obj=*this.
```
It, then, increments all the data members of the original object pointed to by **this** by the expressions like **x++**. The function returns object **obj**, that stores the original values of the object passed to it. Thus, the post-increment operator function returns the original values of the data members of the object passed to it. It also increments the values of the data members of that object.

The examples of writing and using the overloaded increment operator can be generalized for any unary operator, because that operator is a unary one. Unary operator overloading function can be a class member. In this case it does not need any parameters. If you use an operator after the object that calls it, the operator function needs a dummy parameter, that is not used.

13.5. Binary operators and friend functions.

The binary operator overloading function can be an outside function. But it normally is a friend of a class. In this case, it should have two parameters, because the friend functions do not have **this** pointer. Therefore, one cannot pass an argument by **this** pointer implicitly. This is why one needs additional parameter in the binary operator function to pass the argument explicitly. The first parameter is the operand on the left of the operator. The second parameter takes a value from an operand on the right. Next program is very similar to **Program 13.1**, but features the friend operator function.

```
#include <iostream.h>                    //line 1

class dim {                              //line 2
int x, y, z;                             //line 3
public:                                  //line 4
dim ( ) { x=y=z=0; }                     //line 5
dim (int a, int b, int c) { x=a, y=b, z=c; } //line 6
friend dim operator - (dim left, dim right); //line 7

void disp ( ) { cout << x <<", " << y << ", " << z
                << "\n"; }               //line 8
```

```
} ;                                     //line 9

dim operator - (dim left, dim right)    //line 10
{                                       //line 11
dim one;                                //line 12
one.x=left.x-right.x;                   //line 13
one.y=left.y-right.y;                   //line 14
one.z=left.z-right.z;                   //line 15
return one;                             //line 16
}                                       //line 17

void main ( )                           //line 18
{                                       //line 19
dim k (2, 4, 6), m (10, 20, 30), n;     //line 20
n=k-m;                                  //line 21
n.disp ( );                             //line 22
n=m-k-n;                                //line 23
n.disp ( );                             //line 24
}                                       //line 25
```
Program 13.7.

The output of the program is
```
 -8, -16, -24
 16, 32, 48
```
The above program declares class **dim** at lines 2-9. The subtraction operator function is a friend of that class. It is declared as
```
friend dim operator - (dim left, dim right); //line 7
```
As you see, it has two parameters **left** and **right**. The operator function is written at lines 10-17. It subtracts corresponding object data members using the statements like
```
one.x=left.x-right.x;                   //line 13
```
Two arguments are needed for the subtraction.

The parameters of the friend operator function as well as the return value can have any data type. The friend function does not have to be called by an object on the left of the operator. One can code any reasonable operation performed by the binary operators. For example, following program allows to subtract "an object from an integer".

```
#include <iostream.h>                   //line 1

class dim {                             //line 2
int x, y, z;                            //line 3
public:                                 //line 4
dim ( ) { x=y=z=0; }                    //line 5
dim (int a, int b, int c) { x=a, y=b, z=c; } //line 6
friend dim operator - (int left, dim right); //line 7
```

```
void disp ( ) { cout << x <<", " << y << ", " << z
                    << "\n"; }            //line 8

} ;                                       //line 9

dim operator - (int left, dim right)      //line 10
{                                         //line 11
dim one;                                  //line 12
one.x=left-right.x;                       //line 13
one.y=left-right.y;                       //line 14
one.z=left-right.z;                       //line 15
return one;                               //line 16
}                                         //line 17

void main ( )                             //line 18
{                                         //line 19
dim m (10, 20, 30), n;                    //line 20
int k=5;                                  //line 21
n=k-m;                                    //line 22
n.disp ( );                               //line 23
}                                         //line 24
```

Program 13.8.

The output of the program is
```
-5, -15, -25
```
This program declares familiar to us **dim** class. That class has a friend function.
```
friend dim operator - (int left, dim right);  //line 7
```
The overloading function of the subtraction operator has two parameters. One of them is the integer **left**, another one is the object **right** of the **dim** class. The operator function is implemented at lines 10-17. It declares object **one** of class **dim**. It subtracts **right.x** member of an object **right** from the number **left** on the left side.
```
one.x=left-right.x;                       //line 13
```
The new modified object **one** is returned by the operator function. We use subtraction operator in **main()** function in the expression **n=k-m** at line 22.

The above program is a typical example of when you have to use only a friend function. When binary operator function is implemented as class member function, the object on the left is passed by means of **this** pointer. It means, that if your operator function is a class member, the left operand passed to that function can be only an object of the same class. Thus, the operator coded by the member operator functions cannot perform operations like
```
25+obj;
```
Here an operand on the left is an integer. The operator member function "expects" to get an object of its class. So, you cannot code that operation with the operator member functions. You need to use the outside friend operator functions, because they accept two arguments. You can make those arguments of any data type. Only the expressions like

```
obj+25;
```
can be coded by the operator member function, presuming that **obj** has same class type to which the overloaded **+** operator belongs. One has to also write that function, so it can add an object and an integer.

One can ask, how to make a program to perform any of the operations **25+obj** or **obj+25**? Since we were discussing the minus operation, we want our program to be able to perform the operations like **25-obj** and **obj-25**. Thus, we want to create a minus operator capable to either subtract an object from an integer or an integer from an object. In this case, we write two minus operator overloading functions as class friends. It is shown in the program below.

```
#include <iostream.h>                    //line 1

class dim {                              //line 2
int x, y, z;                             //line 3
public:                                  //line 4
dim ( ) { x=y=z=0; }                     //line 5
dim (int a, int b, int c) { x=a, y=b, z=c; } //line 6
friend dim operator - (int left, dim right); //line 7
friend dim operator - (dim left, int right); //line 8

void disp ( ) { cout << x <<", " << y << ", " << z
                << "\n"; }               //line 9

} ;                                      //line 10

dim operator - (int left, dim right)     //line 11
{                                        //line 12
dim one;                                 //line 13
one.x=left-right.x;                      //line 14
one.y=left-right.y;                      //line 15
one.z=left-right.z;                      //line 16
return one;                              //line 17
}                                        //line 18

dim operator - (dim left, int right)     //line 19
{                                        //line 20
dim one;                                 //line 21
one.x=left.x-right;                      //line 22
one.y=left.y-right;                      //line 23
one.z=left.z-right;                      //line 24
return one;                              //line 25
}                                        //line 26

void main ( )                            //line 27
```

```
{                                          //line 28
dim m (10, 20, 30), n;                     //line 29
int k=5;
n=m-k;                                     //line 30
n.disp ( );                                //line 31
}                                          //line 32
```

Program 13.9.

The output of the program is

```
5, 15, 25
```

Above program declares class **dim** at lines 2-10. That class has two friend minus operator functions.

```
friend dim operator - (int left, dim right); //line 7
friend dim operator - (dim left, int right); //line 8
```

The minus operator function declared at line 7 expects an integral number on the left and the object on the right. The operator function declared at line 8 expects an object on the left and an integer on the right. We do nothing else, but overloading of the operator function. And it is possible to overload the operator function, as any other function in C++. When you call the minus operator function with the object on the left and an integer on the right, the function declared at line 8 will do the job. When an object is on the right and the integer number is on the left, the function declared at line 7 will be called with the minus operator. Both functions are absolutely independent. They are just as regular functions and can perform the tasks of the regular functions. So, do not be afraid of them. Our program, then, defines both functions at lines 11-26 and uses one of them in **main()**.

We can generalize how to use outside friend operator functions for the operator overloading. Any friend binary operator function has two parameters. The first one is expected to be passed from an operand to the left from the operator. The second parameter will accept the data from the operand on the right. Both parameters can be of the same and different data type. This way gives more flexibility in writing operator overloading functions compare to writing binary operator functions as class members. When a binary operator function is a class member, the left operand is expected to be an object of the same class. This is a limitation of operator member functions.

13.6. Unary operators and friend functions.

One can use a friend function to overload a unary operator. You remember, when a unary operator function is implemented as class member function, it does not need any arguments. The object is passed by means of **this** pointer. You remember, when an argument of a function is a pointer, the content of the cell, its argument points to, can be permanently changed by that function. The changes will retain after the function execution is terminated. When an object is passed by means of **this** pointer, it can be changed. A friend function does not have **this** pointer. An argument should be passed to it explicitly. What happens, if we pass a regular argument to a unary operator friend function as

```
test operator ++ (test ob)
{
ob.x++;
ob.y++;
ob.z++;
return ob;
   }
```

The copy of the object will be passed to the parameter **ob** of the unary **++** operator function. All the changes made on that copy will be discarded after the function terminates its execution. So, the original object will not be changed after the function completes its execution. This is why, when you need the changes made by the unary operator function on the object to retain, you should use a reference parameter. In case of **++** and **−** operators, we want the changes to retain after the operator function completes its action. Therefore, we use unary operator function with a reference parameter. It is implemented in the program below.

```
#include <iostream.h>              //line 1

class test                         //line 2
{                                  //line 3
int x, y, z;                       //line 4
public:                            //line 5
test ( ) { x=y=z=0; }              //line 6
test (int a, int b, int c) { x=a, y=b, z=c; }//line 7
friend test operator ++ (test &ob);     //line 8

void disp ( ) {cout << x << ", " << y << ", " << z
                 << "\n"; }        //line 9

} ;                                //line 10

test operator ++ (test &ob)        //line 11
{                                  //line 12
ob.x++;                            //line 13
ob.y++;                            //line 14
ob.z++;                            //line 15
return ob;                         //line 16
}                                  //line 17

void main ( )                      //line 18
{                                  //line 19
test m (2, 4, 6), k;               //line 20
++m;                               //line 21
m.disp ( );                        //line 22
k=++m;                             //line 23
```

```
m.disp ( );                                    //line 24
k.disp ( );                                    //line 25
}                                              //line 26
```
Program 13.10.

The output of the program is
```
3, 5, 7
4, 6, 8
4, 6, 8
```
The program declares class **test** at lines 2-10. The increment operator function is a friend of this class. It is declared as such by
```
friend test operator ++ (test &ob);       //line 8
```
The function has a reference to the object of class **test** as its parameter. The very function is defined at lines 11-17. We use the overloaded increment operator in the **main()** function at lines 18-26. We define objects **m** and **k** of that class in **main()** function. We, then, increment **m** by **++m** and display it. The values of its members change to 3, 5, 7. We, then, show an assignment and increment operator working together at line 23. We assign **k=++m**, and display both objects **m** and **k**.

Here, we implemented a pre-increment operator, i.e., when the operand (in our case an object) follows the **++** operator. Some older compilers do not distinguish between the post- and pre-increment operators. Some current compiler versions distinguish between the different unary operator forms. They might generate the warning messages, if you try to use a pre-increment operator function for the post-increment operation. You write the post-increment operator function using two parameters. Its second dummy parameter can be of type **int**. Review following program, utilizing that idea.

```
#include <iostream.h>

class test
{
int x, y, z;
public:
test ( ) { x=y=z=0; }
test (int a, int b, int c) { x=a, y=b, z=c; }
friend test operator ++ (test &ob);
friend test operator ++ (test &ob, int mine);

void disp ( ) {cout << x << ", " << y << ", " << z
                << "\n"; }
} ;

test operator ++ (test &ob)
{
ob.x++;
ob.y++;
```

```
  ob.z++;
  return ob;
  }

  test operator ++ (test &ob, int mine)
  {
  test one=ob;
  ob.x++;
  ob.y++;
  ob.z++;
  return one;
  }

  void main ( )
  {
  test m (2, 4, 6), k;
  cout << "pre-increment\n";
  k=++m;
  m.disp ( );
  k.disp ( );
  cout << "post-increment\n";
  k=m++;
  m.disp ( );
  k.disp ( );
  }
```

Program 13.11.

The output of the program is

```
  pre-increment
  3, 5, 7
  3, 5, 7
  post-increment
  4, 6, 8
  3, 5, 7
```

This program is very similar to the previous one. But here, the class has two friend increment operator functions

```
  friend test operator ++ (test &ob);
  friend test operator ++ (test &ob, int mine);
```

The second function declaration has two parameters. The second parameter **int mine** is a dummy parameter. It merely informs the compiler, that the operator function is written for use an object that precedes the operator. This post-increment operator function will work in the cases like **m++**. We have written this function slightly different, as you see. It returns the initial values of the object's data members. Then, it increments those data members.

The program also demonstrates, that we can overload an operator function. We have written two increment functions. The compiler will decide which one to use, when the operator is applied to the objects. We use both functions in **main()** on the objects of **test** class. You should not have any problems understanding that program.

Let's summarize the information. A unary member operator function has a dummy parameter only when an operand is expected to precede the operator in a call to it. Otherwise, it has no parameters. It gets its argument by means of **this** pointer. The argument is expected to be an object of the class in which it is declared. One has to write a friend unary operator function with the argument. Friend operator function uses two arguments only when the operator is expected to follow the operand, that calls it. The second argument is a dummy argument. It is not used in the operator function. The friend operator function has one parameter, otherwise.

13.7. Overloading other operators.

Here, we will demonstrate how to overload some of the operators, so you can get better feeling of how to do it.

13.7.1. Overloading the relational operators.

The relational operators (such as **>**, **<=**, **==**, etc.) are typical binary operators. Therefore, you can overload them using the rules described for the binary operators. You have to write the operator function in order to overload any relational operator. That operator function can be a class member or a non-member friend of a class. When writing an operator function for relational operators, one has to keep in mind, that the function has to return only one of two values. It should return 1, if the condition is true, or 0 otherwise. Consider following program.

```
#include <iostream.h>

class test
{
int x, y, z;
public:
test (int a, int b, int c) { x=a, y=b, z=c; }
int operator == (test ob);

void disp ( )
{cout << x << ", " << y << ", " << z << "\n"; }

} ;

int test:: operator == (test ob)
{
```

```
if (x==ob.x && y==ob.y && z==ob.z)
return 1;
else
return 0;
}

void main ( )
{
test m (2, 4, 6), k (2, 4, 7);
if (m==k) cout << "Two objects are equal.\n";
else cout << "Two objects are different.\n";
}
```

Program 13.12.

The output of the program is

    Two objects are different.

The program declares class **test** containing **==** operator function

    int operator == (test ob);

The relational operators are the binary ones. We already know how to write the binary operator functions as class members. They have one parameter. Our function has one parameter **ob**. This is the operand to the right of the operator. The left operand should be an object of a class type. This class type must contain our relational operator function as its member. The object will be passed by means of **this** pointer.

Our **==** operator function returns 1, if the condition

    if (x==ob.x && y==ob.y && z==ob.z)

is true. Otherwise, it returns zero. The condition compares corresponding data members of the objects on the left and right. This version of **==** operator is used in **main()** function in **if-else** statement.

    if (m==k) cout << "Two objects are equal.\n";
    else cout << "Two objects are different.\n";

The expression **m==k** produces 1, if two objects are equal, and 0 otherwise. Thus, the statement takes one of familiar to us forms. It can be either **if(0)** or **if(1)**.

13.7.2. Overloading [ ].

We will overload now the **[]** array subscription operator. It is considered a binary operator, when overloaded. The **[]** operator can be overloaded relative to a class. Its operator function can be only a class member. Consider following program, illustrating the use of **[]** operator.

```
#include <iostream.h>                      //line 1

const int N=4;                             //line 2
class test                                 //line 3
```

```
{                                        //line 4
int x[N];                                //line 5
public:                                  //line 6
test ();                                 //line 7
void set ( );                            //line 8
int operator [ ](int p);                 //line 9
} ;                                      //line 10

test::test ()                            //line 11
{                                        //line 12
for (int k=0; k<N; k++)                  //line 13
x[k]=0;                                  //line 14
}                                        //line 15

void test:: set( )                       //line 16
{                                        //line 17
cout << "Enter all four array elements of the object.\n";
                                         //line 18
for (int n=0; n<N; n++)                  //line 19
cin >> x[n];                             //line 20
}                                        //line 21

int test:: operator [ ] (int p) { return x[p]; }//line 22

void main ( )                            //line 23
{                                        //line 24
test aq;                                 //line 25
int s;                                   //line 26
aq.set ( );                              //line 27
cout << "Enter array element of that object to"
     << " display.\n";                   //line 28
cin >> s;                                //line 29
cout << aq[s-1];                         //line 30
}                                        //line 31
```

Program 13.13.

The program displays the message

```
Enter all four array elements of the object.
```

For instance, we enter **2 4 6 8** and press **ENTER**. The program prompts us to enter the number of the array element to display. If we enter 2, it displays the number 4. It is the second array element.

The program declares class **test** at lines 2-10 consisting of array **x[N]** private data member. The array consists of **N=4** members. The class also includes the member function **set()** and **[]** operator function. The constructor function **test()** is defined explicitly outside the class at lines 11-15. It sets each array element of an object to zero.

However, it is not required to set to zero all the array elements. The **set()** member function displays the message, prompting the user to enter all the array elements.

```
cout << "Enter all four array elements of the object.\n";
```

It reads all 4 array elements of a given object. That function is defined at lines 16-21.

Pay attention to how we declare the **[]** operator function

```
int operator [ ] (int p);                    //line 9
```

The declaration contains the word **operator** and the name of the overloaded operator **[]**, as it should. It has one parameter **p** of **int** type. The declaration of the operator function also specifies the returned value type. The parameter and the returned value can be of any type. Furthermore, their data types can be different. It depends on the operation, that you want to perform with overloaded **[]** operator. The **[]** operator function definition is

```
int test:: operator [ ] (int p) { return x[p]; }//line 22
```

We use the operator function in **main()**, after all array elements of object **aq** are entered by the **aq.set()** function. We enter the number of element, that we want to display on the screen. The program, then, asks what element to display. We enter the number of the element. It is displayed it by

```
cout << aq[s-1];                             //line 30
```

So, we call the **[]** operator function in the program by the object to the left of it at line 30. Call **aq[2]** is the same as **operator[](2)**. The operator function returns a value stored in the member array element **x[2]** of object **aq**. The **x[2]** is the form **this->x[2]**.

An object like **aq[s-1]** with our **[]** overloaded operator can be only on the right side of any assignment, because the operator function returns a value. So, **aq[s-1]** form is just a number. The **aq** object calls the operator function. The function returns a value, that replaces **aq[s-1]**. This value is passed to the output object **cout** in our program. We could assign it to a variable. The object **aq[s-1]** with our overloaded **[]** operator can assign a value to another operand. One cannot assign a value to an object like **aq[s-1]=55**, that uses our operator. We can rewrite our operator function for doing that. If the **[]** operator function returns a reference to any data type, it will allow us to assign a value to an object like **aq[s-1]**. Program below illustrates it.

```
#include <iostream.h>

const int N=4;
class test
{
int x[N];
public:
test ();
void set ( );
int & operator [ ](int p);
} ;

test::test ()
```

```
{
for (int k=0; k<N; k++)
x[k]=0;
}

void test:: set( )
{
cout << "Enter all four array elements of the object.\n";
for (int n=0; n<N; n++)
cin >> x[n];
}

int & test:: operator [ ] (int p) { return x[p]; }

void main ( )
{
test aq;
int s;
aq.set ( );
cout <<"Enter array element of that object to change.\n";
cin >> s;
aq[s-1]=55;
cout << aq[s-1];
}
```
Program 13.14.

The program first prompts the user
    Enter all four array elements of the object.
Let's assume, we enter the same four values
    2 ENTER 4 ENTER 6 ENTER 8 ENTER
Here we hit the **ENTER** after each number. In the previous program we pressed **ENTER** after entering all four values. Both ways are correct. This reminds you, that you can hit **ENTER** after each number, or after all the entered values, when entering numeric values. The program, then, displays.
    Enter array element of that object to change.
We enter the number of an element to change, for instance, 2. The second array element of the array will be changed to 55 and displayed.
   Now the objects like **aq[s-1]**, that use **[]** operator, can assign their values to **int** variables as well as accept the values from the variables. The returned value is a reference to the **int** data type, so it returns or accepts an integral number. **Program 13.14** is very similar to **Program 13.13**. Our operator function now returns a reference to an integer instead of just an integer. The function definition is written as
    int & test:: operator [ ] (int p) { return x[p]; }
This allowed us to assign the value 55 to **aq[s-1]** in **main()** function.
   We know, that neither C nor C++ checks for possible overrun of an array boundary.

This means, that you can declare an array consisting of 10 elements, try to do an operation on the 15th element, for example, and not even get a warning, that element does not exist. You can write a check for an array boundary overrun in the [] operator function. Following program illustrates it.

```cpp
#include <iostream.h>
#include <stdlib.h>

const int N=4;
class test
{
int x[N];
public:
test ();
void set ( );
int & operator [ ](int p);
} ;

test::test ()
{
for (int k=0; k<N; k++)
x[k]=0;
}

void test:: set( )
{
cout << "Enter all four array elements of the object.\n";
for (int n=0; n<N; n++)
cin >> x[n];
}

int & test::  operator [ ] (int p)
{
if (p<0 || p>=N)
{
cout << "error in array element number\n";
exit (0);
}
return x[p];
}

void main ( )
{
test aq;
int s;
```

```
aq.set ( );
cout <<"Enter array element of that object to change.\n";
cin >> s;
aq[s-1]=55;
cout << aq[s-1];
}
```

Program 13.15.

The output of the program is similar to the previous one. The program reads four array elements into the member array of the object **aq**. You have to enter the numbers separated by at least one space and press **ENTER** after the last entry. However, you can enter the data pressing **ENTER** after each entry as well. When the program prompts to enter the number of the element to be changed, we enter the number of the array element to be changed. Its value is read and stored in the variable **s**. It is assigned the value 55 and displayed. If **s** is a less than zero or greater than 3, an error message is displayed and the program execution is stopped.

This program differs from the previous one only by the content of **[]** operator function. The operator function checks, if the subscript **p** is a positive integer and does not exceed the number of array elements. If **if(p<0 || p>=N)** is true, the error message is displayed and the program is terminated by the library function **exit(0)**. We include **<stdlib.h>** file to be able to use the **exit()** library function.

13.7.3. Overloading + Operators for a String Class.

We have considered how to overload minus operator to subtract two objects. We could have considered how to add two objects as well. Here, we review another meaning of the arithmetic operators. Our next example demonstrates another way of thinking. The overloaded operators can, sometimes, perform very unusual actions. You should not be afraid to think, what operator can substitute what action. Just do not get carried away. We used arithmetic operators to subtract corresponding members of two objects. How about using plus operator to concatenate the strings? We demonstrate this idea on the following example.

```
#include <iostream.h>
#include <string.h>

class sttest
{
char st[40];
public:
sttest (char *let) { strcpy (st, let); }
sttest ( ) { };
sttest operator + (sttest ob);
sttest operator + (char *row);
```

```
void disp ( ) { cout << st << "\n"; }
} ;

sttest sttest :: operator + (sttest ob)
{
sttest mine;
strcpy (mine.st, st);
strcat (mine.st, ob.st);
return mine;
}

sttest sttest :: operator + (char *row)
{
sttest mine;
strcpy (mine.st, st);
strcat (mine.st, row);
return mine;
}

void main ( )
{
sttest one ("How are "), two ("you?"), three;
char a[ ]="we doing?";
three=one+two;
three.disp( );
three=one+a;
three.disp( );
three=one + "you means nothing.";
three.disp( );
}
```

Program 13.16.

The output of the program is

```
How are you?
How are we doing?
How are you means nothing.
```

The above program declared class **sttest** consisting of a string **st** data member, **disp()** function and two **+** operator functions. Our class has overloaded constructor function **sttest()**. You can see, the **+** operator function is overloaded in our class. The two prototypes of the operator functions are

```
sttest operator + (sttest ob);
sttest operator + (char *row);
```

The first one adds two objects of class **sttest**. The second one adds an object on the left to the character string on the right.

The first operator function has an object **ob** of class **sttest** as its parameter. Its definition starts with declaring the object **mine** of class **sttest**. It copies the content of the string member **this->st** of the object, that calls the **+** operator function, into the string **mine.st** of **mine** object by

```
strcpy (mine.st, st);
```

It, then, concatenates the content of the object on the left with the content of its parameter string **ob.st** by

```
strcat (mine.st, ob.st);
```

The function returns concatenated **mine** object. We use that operator in **main()** function to add two objects like

```
three=one+two;
```

The function is called by the object **one**, which is passed by means of **this** pointer. The object **two** on the right will be passed to the parameter **ob**. The concatenation is performed and the result is assigned to the object **three**.

The **sttest operator + (char *row)** operator function adds a string to an object string member. It receives two arguments. The first one is an object to the left of the **+** operator, that calls the function for execution. The second argument is the string on the right passed to parameter **row**. The operator function declares the **mine** object. It copies the content of the string member of the object on the left to **mine.st** by

```
strcpy (mine.st, st);
```

The **st** is a short notation of **this->st**. The operator function, then, concatenates that string with the string, that should be passed on the right by

```
strcat (mine.st, row);
```

The **mine** object is returned. We illustrate how to use this function in **main()**.

13.7.4. Overloading *new* and *delete* operators.

One can overload **new** and **delete** operators. Why would you want to overloaded those operators? You might want to allocate the memory in some non-standard operations. For example, you might want to write the data to a disk file when the heap memory is not sufficient. You have to know how to overload those operators. Overloaded **new** and **delete** operators have compiler specific forms. In order to write an overloaded **new** and **delete** operators, you have to consult your compiler manuals. However, there are operator overloading forms that will work on a number of compilers. We give them below.

You can write **new** operator function in a form specified below

```
void *operator new (size_t  size)
{
statements performing allocation
return ptr;
}
```

The **new** operator function must be declared as returning a pointer to a generic **void** data type, or to the data type for which it allocates the memory. It has the parameter **size** of the **size_t** data type. The **size_t** type is discussed in Chapter 20. A **long** type can be used instead of **size_t**. The operator function must return a pointer to the allocated memory. There are no other constraints on how to overload the **new** operator.

The **delete** operator function can be written in a following format

```
void operator delete (void *ptr)
{
```
statements to free the memory
```
}
```

The function has a pointer **ptr** to the memory to be freed as its parameter. We offer you a program to illustrate those operators. They use **malloc()** and **free()** standard C library functions to respectively allocate and free the memory space.

```cpp
#include <iostream.h>
#include <string.h>
#include <stdlib.h>

class student
{
char *name;
float gpa;
int year;
public:
void stload (char *pr, float x, int m);
void disp ( );
void * operator new (size_t size);
void operator delete (void * q);
};

void * student:: operator new (size_t size)
{
cout << "Object allocation is being performed." << endl;
return malloc (size);
}

void student::operator delete (void * q)
{
cout << "An object is about to be destroyed." << endl;
free (q);
}

void student::stload (char *pr, float x, int m)
{
strcpy (name, pr);
gpa=x;
year=m;
}
```

```
void student::disp ( )
{
cout << name << " GPA: " << gpa << " year: " << year
     << endl;
}

void main ( )
{
student *s1;
s1 = new student ( );
s1->stload ("John", 3.3, 2);
s1->disp ( );
delete s1;
}
```
Program 13.17.

The output of the program is

```
Object allocation is being performed.
John GPA: 3.3 year: 2
An object is about to be destroyed.
```

Our **delete** and **new** overloaded operators are the members of the class **student**. They are used to allocate and free the memory space for an object of the class.

13.7.5. Overloading ( ) operator.

One can overload the ( ) operator. It can be used in different applications. This operator can have a number of parameters. One of the arguments comes from an object to the left of the parentheses. Other arguments are written inside the parentheses. The program below demonstrates one of the applications of ( ) operator.

```
#include <iostream.h>

class Exa
{
int arr[3][2];
public:
Exa ( ){ };
void assigval ( );
int operator () (int a, int b) { return arr[a][b]; }
};

void Exa :: assigval ( )
{
int k, m;
```

```
cout << "Enter six array elements of this object.\n";
for (k=0; k<3; k++)
for (m=0; m<2; m++)
cin >> arr[k][m];
}

void main()
{
Exa ob;
ob.assigval ( );
cout << " Displaying arr[1][1] of this object: "
    << ob (1, 1);
}
```

Program 13.18.

The program prompts a user to enter six array elements. Let's assume, we enter
```
10 20 30 40 50 60
```
and press **ENTER**. The output of the program is
```
Displaying arr[1][1] of this object: 40
```
  The program declares class **Exa**, that consists of an array **arr[3][2]** data member,
function **assigval()**, operator function **operator()(int ,int)**. The function
assigval() prompts a user to enter six array elements, reads them and places into the
member array. The **()** operator function displays the **arr[1][1]** array element for a
given object. We use both functions in **main()**. There, we define an object **ob** of the
class **Exa**. We assign the values to all the array elements **arr[][]** of that object by the
ob.assigval(). We display the **arr[1][1]** array element by means of the **ob(1,
1)**. The **ob(1, 1)** uses the overloaded **()** operator function.
  Let's now consider **()** operator overloading function. We wrote it as inline function
inside the class just for simplicity.
```
    int operator () (int a, int b) { return arr[a][b]; }
```
The function returns an integer. It can return any data type, in general. However, an
overloaded **()** operator function does not have to return anything. You can declare it with
void return type. Member **arr** of our class is a multi-dimensional array. It requires two
subscripts. When we need to display member array element **arr[][]**, it can be called by
means of that member function. The function has two parameters. Two arguments must
be written inside the **()** parentheses, when we call the function. We called it as **ob(1,
1)**. Both arguments will be passed to the parameters **a** and **b**. First argument substitutes
the first subscript **a** in the **arr[a][b]**. The second argument is the second array subscript **b**. There will be more than two arguments inside the parentheses, if you specify
more parameters.
  The **()** operator function also gets an extra hidden **argument**, because it is a member
function of a class. That hidden argument is the **object** that precedes the **()** brackets. It
calls the operator function for execution. It is passed by means of its **this** pointer. Our
operator function returns **arr[a][b]**. It is **this->arr[a][b]** of the object **ob**.
  If we have written the **()** operator function not as **inline** version, we would have had

to declare it inside the class as
```
    int operator ()(int, int);
```
We would have had to define it, then, outside of the class as
```
    int Exa :: operator ()(int a, int b){ return arr[a][b]; }
```

13.8. Converting between types.

You already know how to deal with conversions of the fundamental data types, such as **int**, **float**, **double**, etc. When you assign a value of one type to a variable of another data type, the compiler converts the assigned data type. For example, if a variable **x** of **long** data type gets assigned to **int** type variable **y** (**y=x**), the value passed to **y** gets converted to **int**. When you add the variables with different data types, all but one data types are converted. Data type conversion can occur, when you pass an argument to a function. For example it occurs, when you pass an integer argument to a function, that has **float** parameter. Data type conversion can occur, when a function returns a value. You can cast the types of data to any other types. You, should understand the rules of conversion by now.

The conversion can be done on class objects. The compiler cannot do it on its own in case of objects. You should specify that conversion by the conversion function or constructor conversion function. Let's study how to convert objects in more details.

13.8.1. Constructor conversion function.

A constructor function with one parameter can perform a conversion. *The constructor function can convert to its own class a type used as a constructor parameter.* In other words, you write a constructor function with one parameter in a class. The computer will be able to convert the data type specified for a constructor parameter to a class type, if it is necessary. It will occur, when you, for instance, assign an integer to an object of the class, to which the constructor belongs.

If any other parameters are present in such type converting constructor, they all must be the default parameters. The parameter, that will be converted, can have any fundamental data type, such as **int**, **float**, **double**. It can have a structure, union and even class type. In this section we will consider conversion from fundamental data types. Following program illustrates such conversion constructor.

```
    #include <iostream.h>

    class num
    {
    int x, y, z;
    public:
    num(int a, int b=1, int c=1) { x=a, y=b, z=c; }
    void disp ( )
    { cout << x << ", " << y << ", " << z << "\n"; }
```

```
} ;

void main ( )
{
num one=7, two (5, 5, 5);
one.disp( );
int k=2, m=20;
one=k;
one.disp( );
two=num (m);
two.disp ( );
}
```

Program 13.19.

The output of the program is

```
7, 1, 1
2, 1, 1
20, 1, 1
```

The above program declares class **num**, consisting of three variables and **disp()** member function. Our class has a constructor function

```
num(int a, int b=1, int c=1) { x=a, y=b, z=c; }
```

The function has one regular and two default arguments. It is a regular constructor function. Since it has only one regular argument, it can perform a data type conversion. Its first parameter has **int** data type. The constructor function belongs to **num** class. It will convert an integer of type **int** to the class **num** type, if needed. As you see, **num()** is a regular class constructor. It has only one regular parameter. The very presence of a constructor with only one parameter in a class permits a type conversion. Why? It is the rule of C++.

We use this property of our constructor function in **main()**. The data conversion occurs, when we assign an integer to an object of **num** class. There are two ways of doing it. One of them is to assign an integer to an object directly, as we did in the program by **one=7** and **one=k**, where **k=2**. When we display the object **one** after each of those assignments, the output is 7, 1, 1 and 2, 1, 1 for the first and the second assignments respectively. The numbers 7 and 2 are converted into the objects.

The second way is to write an assignment like **two=num(m)**. Here, the number **m** in the brackets gets assigned to the object **two**. You assign an integer using it as an argument of the constructor function explicitly. The constructor does not return any values. The meaningless, at the first glance, form of assignment **two=num(m)** tells the computer, that the value **m** in the brackets gets assigned to the object. The value **m** must have the same data type as the first constructor parameter.

Therefore, a constructor with one parameter can convert the data of its argument to the data type of the class, in which that constructor is declared. If the type conversion constructor has a few parameters, it can still convert only one. The others should be default parameters. They do not accept any values in case of conversion. They just pass their default values.

13.8.2. Conversion functions.

One can use special conversion functions to convert an object of a class to any other data type. The conversion functions remind the operator functions. The conversion functions are typically used as class members. As any functions, they must be declared and defined. Their definition form is

```
classname :: operator type ( )
{
type value;
...
return value;
}
```

Here, the **type** is the data type to which your object will be converted to. The member conversion function converts the objects of its class to the data type specified by **type**. The function returns an object (or variable) **value**. The returned **value** is a converted value of the class. The conversion functions are declared inside the class. The functions can be defined inside the class, as **inline** or regular functions. Their declaration form (or the prototype) is

```
operator type ( );
```

There is almost no limitation on what can you code in a conversion function. Treat them as regular functions. We illustrate them in the following example.

```
#include <iostream.h>

class Test
{
int x, y;
public:

Test (int a, int b) { x=a, y=b; }

operator int ( );

} ;

Test::operator int ( )
{
int z=y+x;
return z;
}

void main ( )
{
Test one (5, 7);
```

```
int k=one;
cout << "Converted value is " << k;
}
```
Program 13.20.

The output of the program is
```
Converted value is 12
```
Program 13.20 declares class **Test**, that among other members consists of the conversion function
```
operator int ( );
```
This function converts any object of the class **Test** to the **int** data type, if necessary. The conversion function does not just convert the class to any data type. It performs the conversion, if it is necessary. For instance, you assign an object of this class to an integer. In this case, the object needs to be converted to **int** data type. Since the conversion function is, in fact, a function, it can perform any action on the object before returning an integer.

Our conversion function adds two data members of the class **int z=y+x** and returns their sum **z**. We use the conversion function in **main()** in the assignment
```
int k=one;
```
Here, the object **one** of class **Test** data type gets assigned to the integer **k**. We, then, display the value of **k** to show, that the assignment has gone successfully. We have shown you how to convert an object to an integer. One can convert an object to any other data types, including structures and even other class types.

Thus, the class conversion functions are the members of the class. They can convert the objects of their class to any other data type.

13.8.3. Class conversions.

So far, we have shown how to convert classes to and from fundamental data types. Now, we intend to show how to convert from one class type to another one. It can be done by the constructor functions, as well as by means of the conversion functions. We illustrate both ways in the following program.

```
#include <iostream.h>                   //line 1

class Event                             //line 2
{                                       //line 3
public:                                 //line 4
int m, d;                               //line 5
Event ( ) { };                          //line 6
Event (int x, int y) { m=x, d=y; }      //line 7
void disp ( ) { cout << m << "-" << d << "\n"; }//line 8
} ;                                     //line 9
```

```
class Dat                                        //line 10
{                                                //line 11
int mon, day, year;                              //line 12
public:                                          //line 13
Dat ( ) { }                                      //line 14
Dat (int a, int b, int c) { mon=a, day=b, year=c; }
                                                 //line 15
Dat (Event);                                     //line 16
operator Event ( );                              //line 17

void disp ( ) { cout << mon << "/" << day << "/"
                   << year << "\n"; } //line 18

} ;                                              //line 19

Dat::Dat (Event po)                              //line 20
{                                                //line 21
mon=po.m;                                        //line 22
day=po.d;                                        //line 23
year =1996;                                      //line 24
}                                                //line 25

Dat::operator Event ( )                          //line 26
{                                                //line 27
Event tr;                                        //line 28
tr.m=mon;                                        //line 29
tr.d=day;                                        //line 30
return tr;                                       //line 31
}                                                //line 32

void main ( )                                    //line 33
{                                                //line 34
Dat one (6, 12, 1990), tes;                      //line 35
Event two (5, 10), mine;                         //line 36
mine=one;                                        //line 37
mine.disp ( );                                   //line 38
tes=two;                                         //line 39
tes.disp( );                                     //line 40
}                                                //line 41
```

Program 13.21.

The output of the program is

```
6-12
5/10/1996
```

The program declares classes **Event** and **Dat**. The **Event** class is declared at lines 2-

9. It consists of public data members **m**, **d**, and the member function **disp()**. It has two constructors. The **Dat** class is declared at lines 10-19. It has private data members **mon**, **day**, **year**, function **disp()**, conversion function **operator Event()**. The **Dat** class comprises three constructors. The **Dat (Event)** constructor performs class conversion from **Event** to the **Dat** class type. The **operator Event()** conversion function converts from the **Dat** class type to the **Event** class type.

We will not stop on how did we write regular constructor and other functions of each class. They are pretty explicit. We will discuss the conversion constructor and the conversion function. The conversion constructor is a member of the **Dat** class. It is declared as

```
   Dat (Event);                                    //line 16
```

The constructor is defined at lines 20-25. It assigns the data members of **Event** class to the corresponding data members of the **Dat** class. As you have guessed, we intended to use **mon** for the month, **day** for the day of the month, and **year** for the year in class **Dat**. Class **Event** has only two data members: **m** and **d**. We intended to use them to store respectively a month and a day of a month.

The **Event** class has two and the **Dat** class has three data members. The **Dat()** constructor converts an object of the **Event** class to an object of **Dat** class. Since the **year** member of **Dat** class does not get its value from the converted object, we can assign a value to it by any other means. We have chosen to assign a value of 1996 to it in the constructor function. We could have done any operation on the data members of the object **tes** by this constructor. Remember, that a conversion constructor is similar to a regular constructor. The conversion constructor runs, in case of an assignment, like

```
   tes=two;                                        //line 39
```

It assigns an object **two** of the **Event** class to the object **tes** of **Dat** class. Since this assignment has objects of different classes at both ends, one of the objects is converted to the data type of another one. In the assignment statements the data passed from the operand on the right is converted to the data type of the operand on the left.

In order to make this assignment work, we wrote the constructor conversion function. This is the case, when it is needed. We display the object **tes.disp()**to see, if the conversion has been successful. The output of this assignment is 5/10/1996. *You should use the constructor function to convert to its class an object of another class.*

The **operator Event()** conversion function is defined at lines 26-32. It, basically, assigns two data members of **Dat** class to the corresponding data members of **Event** class. The function returns an object **tr** of **Event** class type. The computer uses this conversion function in the assignment statement

```
   mine=one;                                       //line 37
```

It assigns the object **one** of the **Dat** class to the object **mine** of **Event** class type. This is the case, when the conversion takes place. The conversion is outlined by the conversion function. If you do not specify the conversion by the constructor or the conversion function, the program will generate an error, when a conversion is needed. *A member conversion function usually converts an object of its class to another class.* One does not have to use both of them in one program. We use the conversion constructor and the conversion function in the same program just to illustrate both features. A class can have a number of conversion functions and constructors.

We want to emphasize a very important point. Our conversion constructor and **opera-**

tor Event () conversion function are the members of **Dat** class. They operate with **m** and **d** data members of the **Event** class. We access those data members from the functions, that do not belong to the **Event** class. To make them accessible, the data members of the **Event** class should be public members. You can have them as private data members only if you write the access functions and use those functions in the constructor and **operator Event ()** conversion function.

The conversion function is called, when a conversion is needed. It is an implicit conversion. So far we have dealt with an implicit conversion. One can use a conversion via cast and reverse cast. This is an explicit conversion. The same conversion function can be used in all three cases. Next program illustrates all the ways of type conversion.

```
#include <iostream.h>

class Event
{
public:
int m, d;
Event ( ) { };
Event (int x, int y) { m=x, d=y; }
void disp ( ) { cout << m << "-" << d << "\n"; }
} ;

class Dat
{
int mon, day, year;
public:
Dat ( ) { }
Dat (int a, int b, int c) { mon=a, day=b, year=c; }
operator Event ( );
} ;

Dat::operator Event ( )
{
Event tr;
tr.m=mon;
tr.d=day;
return tr;
}

void main ( )
{
Dat one (6, 12, 1990), two (3, 3, 1800), three (8, 25,
                                                1989);
Event mine1, mine2, mine3;
mine1=one;                      // implicit conversion
```

```
mine1.disp( );
mine2= (Event) two;          // conversion via type cast
mine2.disp( );
mine3= Event (three);        // conversion via reverse cast
mine3.disp( );
}
```

Program 13.22.

The output of the program is
```
6-12
3-3
8-25
```

The program is similar to the previous one. It does not use the conversion constructor function for simplicity. The **operator Event ()** function is the same as in the previous program. **Program 13.22** shows the implicit conversion activated by the assignment operator. It also illustrates the conversion via data cast and reverse cast. Look at the comments to see, where in the program this is implemented.

EXERCISES.

1. Run all examples of the present chapter, if you have an access to a computer facility.
2. Write two programs containing a class with an operator overloading function. It overloads the **/=** operator. The operator divides a sum of two class members by any floating-point number. The operator function should be a class member in the first program, and a friend of a class in the second program.
3. Write two programs containing a class with an operator overloading function. It overloads the **!** operator. The operator changes a sign of a sum of two class members. The operator function should be a class member in the first program, and a friend of a class in the second program.
4. Write two programs containing a class with an operator overloading function. It overloads the **,** operator. The operator concatenates two strings and separates them by a comma. A string is a data member of a class. The operator function should be a class member in the first program, and a friend of a class in the second program.
5. Write a program containing a class with an operator overloading function. It overloads the **[]** operator. The operator returns the smallest number in a member array of floating-point numbers.
6. Write a program containing a class with an operator overloading function. The **!=** operator compares integers in the array members of two objects. The operator returns the smallest number of both arrays. The operator also displays a message, which object contains that smallest value.
7. Write a program containing a class with the operator overloading functions. The class represents a complex number. The operators should perform multiplication, addition, subtraction and comparison of two objects of that class. The operators should also perform an increment and decrement of a real part of a complex number. The operators

should also allow to add an object and a real part of a complex number.

8. Write a program, that converts a union into a class.

9. Write a program, that converts a string into a class.

10. Write a few programs containing classes with overloading operator functions.

11. Write a program, that converts class **Myfirst** consistsing of an array and two floating-point numbers into the class **Mysec**. The **Mysec** class consists of three integers. The average of an array member in **Myfirst** class should be assigned to one of the **Mysec** class members.

CHAPTER 14

INHERITANCE.

14.1. Introduction to inheritance.

The subject of this chapter is a very important feature of object-oriented programming - *inheritance*. C++ supports the inheritance, which is a way to incorporate one class into another one. You can declare class **A** and make it a part of another class **B**. Then, class **B**

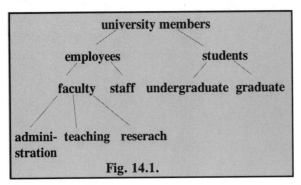

Fig. 14.1.

will be able to use the data members and the member functions of class **A**. Loosely speaking, class **B** "inherits" the content of class **A**. This is called the *inheritance*. Class **A** is called the *base class*. Class **B** is called the *derived class*.

The inheritance produces new classes, that have more features than the base classes.

Inheritance forms tree-like hierarchical structures. A base class is a part of a derived class. The derived class can also be a base class for another class derived from it and so on. Consider, for instance, a very simple example of hierarchy. A university is a pretty large organization. It consists of people associated with it, or its members. All those people can be divided on employees and the students. The employees can also be divided on faculty members and staff. The faculty can also be divided on the administrators

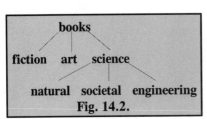

Fig. 14.2.

(deans, department chairs), teaching faculty. There also are the research faculty members in some universities. The students can be divided on undergraduate and graduate students. This simple hierarchy is given in Fig. 14.1.

We can give you another example of hierarchy. Take a book. Books can be: fiction, science, art and so on. The science books can be

divided on books in natural science (physics, chemistry), societal science (history, economics, philosophy) and engineering. This hierarchy is shown on Fig. 14.2.

One can ask, why do we need to talk about the hierarchy at all? The answer is, that it helps us to understand not only the nature of the inheritance, but the whole object-oriented programming. How? Imagine, you have to create the classes describing the university depicted on Fig. 14.1. Each of the university groups (such as students, faculty, staff and so on) will become a separate class. A university in your particular model will be represented by that number of classes. You will first write class **member**. This class can include the first and last name, social security and the address of every university member. It also can include some functions as well. This is something, that any university member should have. When you write the **student** class, it will include all the data from the **member** class. It will also require some more specific details to include. For instance, it will also have the number of years the student has spent in school, GPA and so on. Thus, class **member** will be a base class for the derived class **student**. Another way to say it, is that the class **member** will be inherited by the class **student**.

The **undergraduate** and **graduate** student classes might require some additional details and so on. Therefore, each of them will include the **student** class plus some additional data members and, possibly, member functions. This is the way you can describe all the university community, by creating new classes based on the old ones plus some specific features. The top level of the hierarchy represents the most common classes used by the classes at the lower levels. So, the upper levels in Fig. 14.1 are the base classes for the next level down. The lines illustrate which class is inherited by which. For instance, a line connects the **employees** and the **staff** categories in Fig. 14.1. The **employees** are located at the upper level. If we declare them as classes, the **employees** will be a base class for **staff**. The second class will include all the members of the first one. The **employees** will be a part of the **staff** class. It is reasonable, because the **staff** class must have more characteristics than **employees**.

Now we shell consider, how to incorporate one class into another one, how to use it, and what advantages can it give.

14.2. Base classes and derived classes.

We will illustrate how to create the classes using inheritance and how to operate with them. We will start from the following example.

```
#include <iostream.h>

class num
{
int x, y;
public:
void set(int a, int b) { x=a, y=b; }

void disp ( )
{ cout << "x=" << x << ", " << "y=" << y << "\n"; }

} ;

class dernum : public num
```

```
{
int z;
public:
void setd (int c) { z=c; }
void show ( ) { cout << "z=" << z << "\n"; }
} ;

void main( )
{
dernum one;
one.setd (5);
one.set (1, 2);
one.disp ( );
one.show ( );
}
```

Program 14.1.

The output of the program is
```
x=1, y=2
z=5
```

We declare two classes in **Program 14.1**. Class **num** consists of two private data members **x**, **y**, functions **set()** and **disp()**. The second class **dernum** consists of class **num**, one public data member **z**, functions **setd()** and **show()**. We have not shown the constructors and destructors for both classes. They will be created by the compiler. The class **dernum** consists of class **num**. The way to write it is
```
class dernum : public num
{   .....
}
```
The above lines declare class **dernum**, consisting of class **num** among other things. The declaration form is analogous to the regular form. However, there are some differences. As you see, the tag **num** before the { opening bracket is preceded by the colon (:) and the word **public**. The colon should separate the names of two classes. The word **public** is called an *access* or *access specifier*. One can use either **public**, **private** or **protected** to specify an access. The access stipulates how accessible will be the members of the **num** class to the **dernum** class. Sometimes, the access specifier is called a type of inheritance. We will discuss it soon. Class **dernum** consists of class **num** along with some other members. Therefore, class **num** is called a base class and class **dernum** is called a derived class.

Thus, the general form for declaring classes, that inherit other classes is
```
class derived-classname : access_specifier base-classname
{ body of the class }
```
Program 14.1 illustrates the inheritance. There, the *derived-classname* is the class name **dernum**, *access_specifier* is **public** and the *base-classname* is the class name **num**.

We made both base and derived classes easy to read in **Program 14.1**. All the member functions are quite explicit, so you should understand them. We use both classes in the **main()** function. We define object **one** of the **dernum** class there and manipulate with it. Our object **one** consists of data member **z** and two inherited from the class **num** data members **x**, **y**. We set those data members using functions **one.setd(5)** and **one.set(1, 2)** of both classes. We display the content of all three data members of the object **one** by **one.disp()** and **one.show()** functions of both classes. Thus, the object **one** of class **dernum** data type has, in fact, inherited all the data members and function members of the class **num**.

14.3. Type of inheritance.

14.3.1. The *private* and *public* base class access.

Program 14.1 has a catch. You can see, even though the object **one** has inherited members of class **num**, but we set the members **x**, **y** of class **num** by its own member function **one.set(1, 2)**. Here, we come to the issue of access between the base and derived classes. Our program has declared **public** access of the base class by the line

```
class dernum : public num
```

The word **public** is called an *access specifier* or simply an *access*. There are three access specifiers used in inheritance: **public**, **private** and **protected**.

When a base class has **public** access, all its **public** members become **public** members of the derived class. This means, that all the **public** members of the class **num**, become a supplement to the **public** members of the class **dernum**. This is why object **one** of class **dernum** uses **one.set(1, 2)** and **one.disp()** member functions as the functions of its own class.

The **private** members of the base class **num** are not accessible to any members of the derived class **dernum** in *any case for any type of inheritance*. It does not matter how you declare the base class access to the derived class, but the **private** members of the base class can be accessed only by its own members. You can access the **private** members of the base class only through its own **public** members. This is why we set and display the data members **x**, **y** of **num** class only by means of its **one.set(1, 2)** and **one.disp()** member functions. If we try to assign a value to a **private** member of class **num**, as

```
one.x=3;
```

the computer will give an error. Again, the **private** members of the base class are not accessible to any members of the derived class. Thus, even though the **public** members of the base class are treated by the derived class as its own, but an access to the **private** base class members is possible only via base class **public** members.

So far, we have discussed the case, when the base class is specified with the **public** access to the derived class. Now, change one line of code. The line

```
class dernum : public num
```

is to be rewritten as

```
class dernum : private num
```

You can now try to run **Program 14.1** after changing only one line of code. It will not run. You will get an error message stating, that **set()** and **disp()** functions are not accessible. What has gone wrong? You have just changed an access of the base class to **private**. Now, **public** members of the base class will become **private** members of the derived class. Therefore, the **public** members of the base class are inaccessible from outside the derived class. So, you cannot access them via objects of the derived class. But they are accessible to the members of the derived class, because they became now the **private** members of the derived class.

In our case, the calls **one.set(1, 2)** and **one.disp()** will generate an error, because the **set()** and **disp()** functions are now **private** members of **dernum** class, and they are called from the **main()** function by the object of the class. The **set()** and **disp()** functions can still be used by the members of **dernum** class. We now have to change **Program 13.1** slightly, in order to be able to run it using the **private** base class access to the derived class. It is implemented in **Program 14.2**.

```cpp
#include <iostream.h>

class num
{
int x, y;
public:
void set(int a, int b) { x=a, y=b; }

void disp ( )
{ cout << "x=" << x << ", " << "y=" << y << "\n"; }

} ;

class dernum : private num
{
int z;
public:
void setd (int, int, int );
void show ( );
} ;

void dernum::setd (int n, int m, int k)
{
set (n, m);
z=k;
}

void dernum::show ( )
{
disp( );
cout << "z=" << z << "\n";
```

```
}

void main( )
{
dernum one;
one.setd (1, 2, 5);
one.show ( );
}
```

Program 14.2.

The output of the program is
```
x=1, y=2
z=5
```

The program is very similar to the previous one. It also declares two classes. The **dernum** class is a derived class. The **num** class is a base class. But the base class **num** has **private** access in this program. All its **public** members become **private** members of the **dernum** class. Therefore, we cannot use them via the objects of the derived class. This is why we incorporate them into the member functions of the **dernum** class. Consider how we wrote the **setd()** member function, for example,

```
void dernum::setd (int n, int m, int k)
{
set (n, m);
z=k;
}
```

It is a **public** member of the **dernum** class. And it calls the **set()** member function of the base class **num** to set the values of class **num** data members **x** and **y**. Since **z** is a member of **dernum** class, it can be assigned a value directly by **z=k**. We use the same approach for displaying all three data members on the screen by the **show()** member function. Both functions are used in **main()**. They illustrate how to use an inherited class with the **private** access.

We have discussed the **public** and **private** access of the base class. If you do not specify the access of the base class, then, it is **private** by default if a derived class is a **class**. If a derived class is a structure, the access will be **public** by default.

14.3.2. The *protected* members and base class.

To complete the subject of accessibility, we have to discuss the **protected** access. What can we declare as **protected**? You can declare class members as **protected**. One can also specify a base class access as **protected**. This gives us a new type of inheritance. We could have considered **protected** class members in Chapter 12, when we talked about classes. The reason why we talk about them in this chapter is following. The **protected** members reveal their true meaning only in inheritance.

14.3.2.1. The *protected* class members.

When we talked about class members, we learned that they can be declared either **private** or **public**. Class members can be also declared as **protected**. The specifier **protected** can occur anywhere in the class declaration. For example,

```
class Look
{
int a, b;
char x[10];
protected:
float c;
int d, r;
public:
Look( );
void set (int s, int p, float q, char row[10]);
void screen ( );
}
```

The **protected** class members are written between the access specifier **protected:** terminated by a colon down to the end of the class or next access specifier. A class can have any number of **protected** members. In our example, the protected members are

```
float c;
int d, r;
```

The **protected** class members normally behave themselves as **private** class members. They are accessible to all non-static member and friend functions of the class, where they have been declared. But they are not accessible from the outside of the class and via objects. The difference occurs, when a class containing **protected** members is inherited by another class.

There can be three cases of inheritance. A base class can be inherited as **public** (or with the access specifier **public**). In this case, the **protected** members of the base class become **protected** members of the derived class as well. It means, the **protected** members of the base class can be used by the derived class members. We demonstrate it in **Program 14.3**.

A base class can be inherited as **private**. In this case, **protected** members of the base class become **private** members of the derived class. They can be accessed by the non-static member functions and friend functions of the derived class. They cannot be accessed from the outside of the derived class via objects. A base class can be inherited as **protected**. Then, **protected** members of the base class become **protected** members of the derived class.

Why do we need to inherit a class with **protected** members using different inheritance types? Let's assume, class **A** is the base for the class **B**. Class **C** inherits class **B** as its base. If both classes are inherited as **public**, then, the **protected** members of class **A** will be **protected** members of both classes **B** and **C** as well as any other class, that will inherit any of them publicly. If class **B** inherits class **A** as **private**, **protected** members of **A** become **private** members of **B**. Hence, class **B** will not be able to pass an access to them to class C.

```
#include <iostream.h>

class num
{
protected:
int x, y;
public:
void set(int a, int b) { x=a, y=b; }

void disp ( ) { cout << "x=" << x << ", " << "y="
                        << y << "\n"; }

} ;

class dernum : public num
{
int z;
public:
void setd (int q, int w, int c) { x=q, y=w, z=c; }

void show ( ) { cout << "x=" << x << ", " << "y="
                        << y << ", " << "z=" << z << "\n"; }

} ;

void main( )
{
dernum one;
one.setd (3, 4, 5);
one.show ( );
one.set (1, 2);
one.show ( );
}
```

Program 14.3.

The output of the program is
```
x=3, y=4, z=5
x=1, y=2, z=5
```

The above program declares two familiar to us classes: **num** and **dernum**. The second class inherits the first one as **public**. The base class **num** has **protected** members **x** and **y**. The protected members of the base class **num** become protected members of the derived class **dernum**. The derived class **dernum** can access the **protected** members **x** and **y** of the **num** class as well as its own member **z** by

```
        void setd (int q, int w, int c) { x=q, y=w, z=c; }
```
The **show()** member function also accesses members **x, y, z** of class **dernum**.
```
        void show ( ) { cout << "x=" << x << ", " << "y=" << y
                             << ", " << "z=" << z << "\n"; }
```
Both functions access the **protected** members **x** and **y** as the members of their own class. We use both functions in **main()**. We assign the values to all the members by **one.setd(3, 4, 5)**, and display them using the **one.show()** member function. We, then, use **one.set(1, 2)** to reset the values of **x** and **y**.

If you call any of **protected** members of the **num** class by a statement like
```
        one.x=10;
```
it will lead to an error. This happens, because, as we stated, a **protected** class member behaves like a **private** one for the outside of the class access.

The **protected** specifier can be used for the structure members. It cannot be used for the unions, because a union can neither be inherited nor inherit another class. Some compilers will allow you to use the **protected** specifiers in unions, but since the unions are not used in inheritance, **protected** becomes **private** for unions.

14.3.2.2. The *protected* specifier in inherited base class.

One can use **protected** access specifier for a base class, when it is inherited by another class. In this case, all the **public** and **protected** members of the base class become **protected** members of the derived class. If you change one line in the class **dernum** declaration in **Program 14.3** from
```
        class dernum : public num
```
to
```
        class dernum : protected num
```
it will give you an error message. The problem is, that now **one.set(1, 2)** member function of **num** class becomes a **protected** member of class **dernum**. So, if you use it with the object **one** of **dernum** class type, it will not be accessible. However, the base class function **set()** is still accessible to its own objects, for which it is still a **public** member.

The fact, that the base class **A** is inherited by any other class, does not affect class **A**. The members and objects of class **A** type act as they "do not know", that this class has been inherited. So, for objects of class **A** type and its members it is still an independent class. The inheritance rules specify how the members of a base class will behave in a derived class. The base class is still an independent class, and can be used by itself. We illustrate it in the following program.

```
        #include <iostream.h>

        class num
        {
        protected:
        int x, y;
```

```
public:
void set(int a, int b) { x=a, y=b; }

void disp ( ) { cout << "x=" << x << ", " << "y="
                         << y << "\n"; }
} ;

class dernum : protected num
{
int z;
public:
void setd (int q, int w, int c) { x=q, y=w, z=c; }

void show ( ) { cout << "x=" << x << ", " << "y=" << y
                         << ", " << "z=" << z << "\n"; }
} ;

void main( )
{
dernum one;
num two;
one.setd (3, 4, 5);
one.show ( );
two.set (1, 2);
two.disp ( );
}
```

Program 14.4.

The output of the program is
```
x=3, y=4, z=5
x=1, y=2
```

Program 14.4 is very similar to Program 14.3. The members of the derived class **dernum** access the **protected** and **public** members of the base class, as we have discussed. We declare two objects in Program 14.4: the object **one** of **dernum** class and the object **two** of **num** class. This is why Program 14.4 is different. We wanted to show, that even though the base class **num** is inherited by the derived class **dernum**, but the objects of **num** class "do not know anything" about **dernum** class. Thus, the inheritance works one way - from the base class to the derived class. The objects of the base class do not share the members of the derived class. Try to call **two.show()**. You will get an error. It happens, because the object **two** of class **num** type calls the member function **show()** of the **dernum** class. The member function **show()** has the **dernum** class visibility scope.

The program will run fine, if we rewrite some of its functions. For instance,
```
void setd (int q, int w, int c) { x=q, y=w, z=c; }
```

can be rewritten as

```
void setd (int q, int w, int c) { set (q, w), z=c; }
```

14.3.3. Generalization of types of inheritance.

The inheritance of different class members is summarized in Table 14.1. It is a condensed essence of our discussion on inheritance types.

Table 14.1. Accessibility of a base class member in a derived class.

Base class member access	Base is inherited as `public`	Base is inherited as `private`	Base is inherited as `protected`
Base class member is specified as `public`	The base member is `public` member of derived class. It can be accessed directly by any non-static member function, friend function, outside function. It can be accessed via an object of the derived class in the program outside the class.	The base member is `private` member of derived class. It is accessible to all non-static member functions and friend functions of the derived class. Cannot be accessed via derived class objects and outside functions.	The base member is `protected` member of derived class. It can be accessed directly by any non-static member function, friend function of derived class. Cannot be accessed via derived class objects.
Base class member is specified as `private`	The base member is hidden in the base class. It can be accessed by the non-static member functions and friends of its own class. Inaccessible to derived class.	The base member is hidden in the base class. It can be accessed by the non-static member functions and friends of its own class. Inaccessible to derived class.	The base member is hidden in the base class. It can be accessed by the non-static member functions and friends of its own class. Inaccessible to derived class.
Base class member is specified as `protected`	The base member is `protected` member of derived class. It can be accessed directly by any non-static member function, friend function of derived class. Cannot be accessed via derived class objects.	The base member is `private` member of derived class. It is accessible to all non-static member functions and friend functions of the derived class. Cannot be accessed via derived class objects.	The base member is `protected` member of derived class. It can be accessed directly by any non-static member function, friend function of derived class. Cannot be accessed via derived class objects.

We review what happens with the access to **public, protected** and **private** members of the base class from the derived class point of view, when the base is inherited by the derived class.

The access specifier, with which the derived class inherits the base, changes the access of base class members for the derived class. If a base class is inherited as **public**, it does not change the access to the base class members from the derived class. If a base class is inherited as **private**, all its members become private members of the derived class. If a class is inherited as **protected**, its members will also change their access accordingly.

14.4. Inheritance and objects with initializers.

So far, you have been dealing with classes, that have constructors without any parameters. Here, we will teach you how to handle the inheritance, when the base class constructor has the parameters. Consider following example.

```
#include <iostream.h>              //line 1
#include <string.h>                //line 2

class member                       //line 3
{                                  //line 4
char first[20], last[20];          //line 5
int age;                           //line 6
public:                            //line 7
member ( char *,  char *);         //line 8
void set (int c) { age=c; }        //line 9

void disp ( ) { cout << first << " " << last << " age: "
             << age << "\n"; }      //line 10

~member ( ) { };                   //line 11
} ;                                //line 12


class student : public member      //line 13
{                                  //line 14
int year;                          //line 15
float gpa;                         //line 16
public:                            //line 17
student (char *one, char *two);    //line 18
~student ( ) { }                   //line 19
void sety (int a) { year=a; }      //line 20
void setg (float b) { gpa=b; }     //line 21

void show ( ) { cout << "student of the " << year
```

```
                  << " year, GPA " << gpa << "\n"; }//line 22

    } ;                                    //line 23


    member::member (char *row1, char *row2)//line 24
    {                                      //line 25
    strcpy (first, row1);                  //line 26
    strcpy (last, row2);                   //line 27
    }                                      //line 28

    student::student (char *one, char *two)//line 29
    :member (one, two)                     //line 30
    {    }                                 //line 31


    void main ( )                          //line 32
    {                                      //line 33
    student mike("Mike", "Johnson");       //line 34
    mike.set (20);                         //line 35
    mike.sety (2);                         //line 36
    mike.setg (3.7);                       //line 37
    mike.disp ( );                         //line 38
    mike.show ( );                         //line 39
    member pete ("Jack", "Wilson");        //line 40
    pete.set (25);                         //line 41
    pete.disp ( );                         //line 42
    }                                      //line 43
```
Program 14.5.

The output of the program is
```
    Mike Johnson age: 20
    student of the 2 year, GPA 3.7
    Jack Wilson age: 25
```
Remember, we have discussed a university community, and how to build classes corresponding to university members, students, employees, etc. We try to build two classes in the above program: the base class **member** and the derived class **student**. We use these classes in **main()** routine to show simple actions, that can be done using the objects of those classes. We, basically, just enter and display the data using the objects of those two classes.

Class **member** is declared at lines 3-12. It consists of three private data members: two character arrays **first**, **last**, and the integer **age**. We intended to store the first name of the university member in the string **first**, the last name in the string **last**, and the member's age in the variable **age**. The class also contains two public function members: **set()** and **disp()**. We explicitly write constructor **member()** and destructor **~mem-**

ber() for that class.

We declare class **student** at lines 13-23. It is a derived class. It inherits base class **member** with the **public** access specifier as shown at line 13

```
class student : public member            //line 13
```

Our derived class has some additional members. It has two data members: **year** and **gpa**. The first variable stands for the number of years that a student has spent in the university. The second variable is student's grade point average (GPA). The **student** class also consists of member functions **sety()**, **setg()** and **show()**.

We manipulate with the objects of both classes in **main()** at lines 32-43. Pay attention, that the object **mike** assigns the values to the private member of the base class **member** by means of its own **mike.set()** member function. Same happens during the display. It is familiar to us from the previous programs.

We also do some simple manipulations on the object **pete** of **member** class type. The **member** class is an independent class. The derived class cannot change the way how the **member** class interacts with its own type objects. Also, the base class object can not access the derived class members in any case. Loosely speaking, it just does not know about them. If we write something like **pete.sety(4)** in our program, it will give an error, because **pete** object has class **member** type and the function **sety()** is a member of class **student**. Thus, an object of the derived class can use the members of its base class, but the base class cannot use the members of the derived class. It is reasonable, because class **member** is a part of class **student**, but there is nothing from the class **student** inside the **member** class.

This example illustrates classes, in which the constructor functions have parameters. The base class constructor has two parameters **row1** and **row2**. It copies its first and the second parameter strings into **first** and **last** data members of class **member**. It is implemented at lines 24-28. The **student()** constructor has two parameters in our case. It has to pass two parameter strings to the **member()** constructor, because only that constructor can initiate the string members of **member** class. Pay attention, how **student()** constructor passes two of its parameters to the constructor **member()**.

```
student::student (char *one, char *two)//line 29
   :member (one, two)                    //line 30
```

We have seen this form already, when a class member was an object of a class type. The form **:member(one, two)** is a part of the derived class constructor header. It should precede the opening brace **{** of the derived class constructor **student()**. It begins with the **:** colon operator. The argument with the name **one** inside the constructor **student()** is also a name of the argument in **:member(one, two)**. Hence, the argument **one** in the derived class constructor **student()** will be passed to the constructor **:member (one, two)** of the base class. String **two** is a parameter in both constructors. It will be also passed to the base class constructor.

14.5. Addition to inheritance and objects with initializers.

In general, when a base class constructor has parameters, the derived class constructor must have the parameters too. The object of the derived class is initialized with the initializers to be passed to the base class. The values are passed through the constructor of derived class. You write a derived class constructor with parameters as follows.

```
derived_constructor (type1 arg1, type2 arg2...)
:base_constructor (type1 arg1, ...)
{
body of the derived class constructor;
}
```

The **derived_constructor()** function has a list of parameters **arg1, arg2,...** of different types (**type1, type2**) in the above form. Some of them will be passed to **base_constructor**, using **:base constructor (type1 arg1, ...)** form. The form for passing the arguments must precede constructor's body opening bracket.

In general, a number of parameters in the derived class constructor does not have to be equal to the number of parameters in the base class constructor. The derived class constructor can use any or all of its parameters for itself and/or pass all or some of its parameters to the base class constructor. Even the parameters of the derived class constructor, that must be passed to the base class constructor as arguments, can be used by the derived class constructor. We can rewrite previous program to illustrate it.

```
#include <iostream.h>
#include <string.h>

class member
{
char first[20], last[20];
int age;
public:
member ( char *,  char *);
void set (int c) { age=c; }

void disp ( ) { cout << first << " " << last << " age: "
                    << age << "\n"; }

~member ( ) { };
} ;

class student : public member
{
int year;
float gpa;
public:
student (char *, char *, int );
~student ( ) { }
void sety (int a) { year=a; }
void setg (float b) { gpa=b; }
```

```
void show ( ) { cout << "student of the " << year
                     << " year, GPA " << gpa << "\n"; }
} ;

member::member (char *row1, char *row2)
{
strcpy (first, row1);
strcpy (last, row2);
}


student::student (char *one, char *two, int dur)
:member (one, two)
{
char st1[20], st2[20];
strcpy (st1, one);
strcpy (st2, two);
cout << "An object " << st1 << " " << st2
    << " has been created.\n";
year=dur;
}


void main ( )
{
student mike("Mike", "Johnson", 3);
mike.set (21);
mike.setg (3.7);
mike.disp ( );
mike.show ( );
}
```

Program 14.6.

The output of the program is

```
An object Mike Johnson has been created.
Mike Johnson age: 21
student of the 3 year, GPA 3.7
```

The constructor **student()** of the derived class has three parameters in the above program. Two of them **one** and **two** are passed as the arguments to the base class constructor **member()**. Those parameters are also used in **student()** constructor to display a message, that an object has been created. Both parameters are used to display the name of that object. The third parameter **dur** assigns a value to the **year** member of the derived class. Object **mike("Mike", "Johnson", 3)** of the **student** class type is defined with three initializers in **main()** function. The **mike.set(21)** and **mike.setg(3.7)** functions are used to assign a value to the base class member **age** and the derived class member **gpa** respectively. The content of the whole object **mike** is, then, displayed. The above program illustrates constructors with parameters in the base and derived classes.

   One can ask, what happens if a derived class constructor has the parameters and the base class constructor does not? You do not use the the base class constructor form in the derived class constructor in this case. The derived class constructor assigns the initial values to the members of derived class.

   The above two programs have illustrated the inheritance with the **public** access of the base class. We will review **private** base access next. **Program 14.6** needs to be modified, if you change the access of the base class to **private**. It is shown below.

```cpp
#include <iostream.h>
#include <string.h>

class member
{
char first[20], last[20];
int age;
public:
member ( char *,  char *);
void set (int c) { age=c; }

void disp ( ) { cout << first << " " << last
                     << " age: " << age << "\n"; }

~member ( ) { };
} ;

class student : private member
{
int year;
float gpa;
public:
student (char *one, char *two);
~student ( ) { }
void sets (int, float, int);
void show ( );
} ;

member::member (char *row1, char *row2)
{
strcpy (first, row1);
strcpy (last, row2);
}

student::student (char *one, char *two)
:member (one, two)
```

```
{     }
void student::show( )
{
disp( );
cout << "student of the " << year << " year, GPA "
     << gpa << "\n";
}

void student::sets (int a, float b, int q)
{
set (q);
year =a;
gpa=b;
}

void main ( )
{
student mike("Mike", "Johnson");
mike.sets(2, 3.5, 24);
mike.show ( );
}
```

Program 14.7.

The output of the program is

```
Mike Johnson age: 24
student of the 2 year, GPA 3.5
```

This program differs from the previous by the implementation of member functions **sets()** and **show()**. Here, the base class has a **private** access. However, the program will work fine, if we change the base class access to **public**.

We offer you an interactive version of **Program 14.7** below. We read the class members from the keyboard in this program.

```
#include <iostream.h>
#include <string.h>

class member
{
char first[20], last[20];
int age;
public:
member ( char *,  char *);
void set (int c) { age=c; }

void disp ( ) { cout << first << " " << last << " age: "
                 << age << "\n"; }
```

```
~member ( ) { };
} ;

class student : public member
{
int year;
float gpa;
public:
student (char *one, char *two);
~student ( ) { }
void sety (int a) { year=a; }
void setg (float b) { gpa=b; }
void show ( ) { cout << "student of the " << year
                     << " year, GPA " << gpa << "\n"; }
} ;

member::member (char *row1, char *row2)
{
strcpy (first, row1);
strcpy (last, row2);
}

student::student (char *one, char *two)
:member (one, two)
{      }

void main ( )
{
int n, k;
float m;
char na1[20], na2[20];
cout << "Enter student's first and last names."
     << "Press ENTER.\n";
cin >> na1;
cin >> na2;
student mike(na1, na2);
cout << "Enter student's age, number of years in school,"
     << " GPA separated by spaces. Press ENTER.\n";
cin >> n;
cin >> k;
cin >> m;
mike.set(n);
mike.sety (k);
mike.setg (m);
mike.disp ( );
```

```
mike.show ( );
}
```

Program 14.8.

You enter all the data regarding a student and the program displays it.

14.6. Conversion between base and derived classes.

An object of publicly derived class can be converted and used as an object of the base class. In other words, if a class inherits its base class as public, an object of derived class type can be converted to the base class type. A base class object, however, cannot be treated as a derived class object. Doing that, can lead to an error. There are different ways of converting the objects from a derived to a base class. One of the ways is a direct assignment. Consider following program.

```
#include <iostream.h>

class num
{
protected:
int x, y;
public:
void set(int a, int b) { x=a, y=b; }

void disp ( ) { cout << "x=" << x << ", " << "y="
                     << y << "\n"; }
} ;

class dernum : public num
{
int z;
public:
void setd (int q, int w, int c) { x=q, y=w, z=c; }

void show ( ) { cout << "x=" << x << ", " << "y=" << y
                     << ", " << "z=" << z << "\n"; }

} ;

void main( )
{
dernum one;
num two;
one.setd (3, 4, 5);
```

```
one.show ( );
two=one;
two.disp( );
}
```

Program 14.9.

The output of the program is

```
x=3, y=4, z=5
x=3, y=4
```

The program declares class **num**, which becomes a base class for the derived class **dernum**. An object **one** of the **dernum** class is assigned to the object **two** of the base class **num** type in **main()** by

```
two=one;
```

We display the content of both objects **one** and **two** to show, that the assignment has taken place. If you try to run this program, changing the assignment to

```
one=two;
```

it must give an error. An object of the base class type cannot be converted to derived class type.

One can use pointers to convert base and derived classes between each other. Program below illustrates a few ways of pointer conversions between the classes.

```cpp
#include <iostream.h>

class num
{
protected:
int x, y;
public:
void set(int a, int b) { x=a, y=b; }

void disp ( ) { cout << "x=" << x << ", " << "y="
                     << y << "\n"; }
} ;

class dernum : public num
{
int z;
public:
void setd (int q, int w, int c) { x=q, y=w, z=c; }

void show ( ) { cout << "x=" << x << ", " << "y=" << y
                     << ", " << "z=" << z << "\n"; }

} ;
```

```
void main( )
{
dernum one, *prd;
num *np, two;
one.setd (3, 4, 5);
two.set (1, 10);
one.show ( );
cout << "Assigning the address of the derived class"
     << " object to the base class pointer.\n";
np=&one;
np->disp( );
cout << "Casting base class pointer to the derived"
     << " class.\nThe base class pointer still points to"
     << " the derived class object.\n";
prd=(dernum *)np;
prd->show( );
cout << "Casting base class pointer to the derived"
     << " class.\nThe base class pointer points to the"
     << " base class object.\n";
np=&two;
prd= (dernum *) np;
prd->show( );
}
```

Program 14.10.

The output of the program is

```
x=3, y=4, z=5
Assigning the address of the derived class object to the
base class pointer.
x=3, y=4,
Casting base class pointer to the derived class.
The base class pointer points to the derived class
object.
x=3, y=4, z=5
Casting base class pointer to the derived class.
The base class pointer points to the base class object.
x=1, y=10, z=3
```

The program declares two classes. The **num** class becomes a base class for the derived **dernum** class. The program illustrates three ways of pointer conversion between the base and derived classes. Each conversion type is separated by the **cout** object carrying the message of how the conversion has been performed. We believe, you will be able to follow this program without our help.

14.7. Derived class constructors and destructors.

We know, that derived class consists of one or more base classes. When a derived class object is initiated, the derived and the base class constructors are called. It takes both the derived and the base class destructor functions to destroy a derived class object. It might be important to know, whether the base or the derived class constructor or destructor runs first to create or destroy an object respectively. Following program illustrates the creation and destruction of a derived class object.

```cpp
#include <iostream.h>

class Bas
{
public:

Bas ( )
{ cout << "Base class constructor is running.\n"; }

~Bas ( )
{ cout << "Base class dectructor is running.\n"; }

} ;

class derlow : public Bas
{
public:

derlow ( )
{ cout << "Derived class constructor is running.\n"; }

~derlow ( )
{ cout << "Derived class destructor is running.\n"; }

} ;

void main ( )
{
derlow obdl;
}
```
Program 14.11.

The output of the program is
```
Base class constructor is running.
Derived class constructor is running.
```

```
Derived class destructor is running.
Base class dectructor is running.
```

You see, when an object is created the base class constructor runs first. The derived class constructor runs the second. When an object is destroyed, the derived class destructor runs first, and the base class destructor second.

In what order do the constructors and destructors run, if a derived class becomes a base class of another class? It is illustrated by the following program.

```cpp
#include <iostream.h>

class Bas
{
public:

Bas ( )
{ cout << "Base class constructor is running.\n"; }

~Bas ( )
{ cout << "Base class dectructor is running.\n"; }

} ;

class derlow : public Bas
{
public:

derlow ( ) { cout << "Simple derived class constructor"
                  << " is running.\n"; }

~derlow ( ){ cout << "Simple derived class destructor is"
                  << " running.\n"; }

} ;

class derhigh : public derlow
{
public:

derhigh ( ) { cout << "Complex derived class constructor"
                   << " is running.\n"; }

~derhigh ( ){ cout << "Complex derived class destructor"
                   << " is running.\n"; }

} ;
```

```
void main ( )
{
derhigh obdh;
}
```

Program 14.12.

The output of the program is

```
Base class constructor is running.
Simple derived class constructor is running.
Complex derived class constructor is running.
Complex derived class destructor is running.
Simple derived class destructor is running.
Base class dectructor is running.
```

The program illustrates following. Let's assume, we declare three classes. Class **A** becomes a base class of the derived class **B**. We make class **B** a base class of class **C**. When an object of class **C** is initiated, three constructors are called. The first one is the **A** class constructor, the second is **B** class constructor, the third is **C** class constructor. Thus, the constructors are called in the order from the lowest base class to the highest derived class. The destructors are called in the opposite order. First runs the destructor of **C** class, then, **B** class destructor, then, **A** class destructor.

14.8. Redefinition of base class members.

Derived class inherits the base class with a specified access. Sometimes, you want to change the access status for some of the base class members. C++ permits you to do that. To change the access of a base class member, it should be redeclared inside the derived class, as **private**, **public** or **protected** member using following form

    base-class_name::*member;*

Here, the ***base-class_name*** is the name of the base class. It is followed by the **::** operator. The ***member*** is just a name of a base class member. This form should be written among **public** members of the derived class to make it **public**. It must be written among **private** or **protected** members of the derived class to make the base class member **private** or **protected** respectively.

You cannot change a member access specified in the base class declaration. You can change the access of inherited base class member only to its original access. We will explain it. For example, base class member **x** has been declared as **public** and the base class has been inherited as **private**. You can redeclare **x** in the derived class only as **public**. Consider following program, illustrating access redeclaration.

```
#include <iostream.h>

class num
{
public:
```

```
int x, y;
void set1(int a) { x=a; }
void set2(int b) { y=b; }

void disp ( )
{ cout << "x=" << x << ", " << "y=" << y << "\n"; }


} ;

class dernum :private num
{
int z;
public:
num::x;
void setd (int q, int w, int c) { x=q, y=w, z=c; }

void show ( ) { cout << "x=" << x << ", " << "y=" << y
                     << ", " << "z=" << z << "\n"; }


} ;

void main( )
{
dernum one;
one.setd (3, 4, 5);
one.show ( );
one.x=10;
one.show ( );
}
```

Program 14.13.

The output of the program is

```
x=3, y=4, z=5
x=10, y=4, z=5
```

This program declares two classes **num** and **dernum**. The **num** class is inherited as a base class with the **private** access by the **dernum** class.

```
class dernum :private num
```

All the members of the base class **num** become **private** members of the **dernum** class, and, therefore, cannot be used outside of the derived class. But we redeclare member **x** of the **num** class in the **dernum** class by

```
num::x;
```

Look at the **dernum** class declaration. Member **x** is redeclared among the **public** members of class **dernum**. This makes it **public**.

Since member **x** is now a **public** member, it can be called from the outside of the class. We demonstrate it by changing its value through the object **one** in **main()** function. All data members of object **one** are set to some values by **one.setd(3, 4, 5)** and displayed. The assignment

```
one.x=10;
```

changes the value of **x** to 10. We demonstrate that, by displaying the new content of object **one** by **one.show()**. If you try to assign **one.y=20**, it will lead to an error. The member **y** is still a **private** member of the derived class. You changed an access only for **x** member of the base class.

If you try to redefine member **x** as protected, i.e., among protected members of the **dernum** class, it will give an error. You can only restore the initial member access status, that it has in the base class. You cannot change that access status.

14.9. Multiple inheritance.

A class can inherit more than one base class. It is called *multiple inheritance*. Consider following program, illustrating the multiple inheritance.

```cpp
#include <iostream.h>

class num1
{
int x;
public:
void set1(int a) { x=a; }
void disp1 ( ) { cout << "x=" << x << ", "; }
} ;

class num2
{
int y;
public:
void set2(int b) { y=b; }
void disp2 ( ) { cout << "y=" << y << ", "; }
} ;

class dernum :public num1, public num2
{
int z;
public:

void setd (int q, int w, int c)
{ set1(q), set2 (w), z=c; }

void show ( ) { disp1( ), disp2( ), cout << "z=" << z
                                       << "\n"; }
```

```
} ;

void main( )
{
dernum one;
one.setd (3, 4, 5);
one.show ( );
one.set1 (10);
one.set2 (20);
one.show ( );
}
```

Program 14.14.

The output of the program is
```
x=3,  y=4,  z=5
x=10,  y=20,  z=5
```
The program declares three classes: **num1**, **num2** and **dernum**. The **dernum** inherits two other classes **num1**, **num2** as its base classes. It is arranged by the line
```
class dernum :public num1, public num2
```
The multiple bases are specified in the same way as for the one base inheritance. The name of the derived class should be followed by the colon operator **:** and the list of the base classes. The base classes are separated by the commas from each other. Each base class has its own access specifier. We specified both base classes to be inherited as **public**. It is a pure coincidence. The access of each class is independent of the others. Thus, the access specifiers of the base classes can differ from each other.

The above program illustrates, that the derived classes with multiple bases are handled in the same way as one base classes. Each base is independent. An access specifier of each base determines an access only for that class. **Program 14.14** illustrates multiple base classes, where the constructors do not have any parameters. Next program illustrates multiple inheritance, when class constructors have the parameters.

```
#include <iostream.h>

class num1
{
int x;
public:
num1 (int p) {x=p; }
void set1(int a) { x=a; }
void disp1 ( ) { cout << "x=" << x << ", "; }
} ;

class num2
{
int y;
```

```
public:
num2 (int k) { y=k; }
void set2(int b) { y=b; }
void disp2 ( ) { cout << "y=" << y << ", "; }
} ;

class dernum :public num1, public num2
{
int z;
public:
dernum (int , int, int);

void setd (int q, int w, int c)
{ set1(q), set2 (w), z=c; }

void show ( ) { disp1( ), disp2( ), cout <<"z=" << z
                                          << "\n"; }


} ;



dernum::dernum (int t, int r, int u)
:num1 (t), num2 (r)
{
z=u;
}

void main( )
{
dernum one (1, 2, 3);
one.show ( );
}
```
Program 14.15.

The output of the program is

    x=1, y=2, z=3

The program declares three classes: **num1**, **num2** and **dernum**. The **dernum** inherits two other classes **num1**, **num2** as its base classes. Each of the base classes has a constructor function with the arguments. The derived class constructor has three arguments in our program. Two of them are passed to the base classes. This is achieved by the same construction used for one base class. In our example it is

    dernum::dernum (int t, int r, int u)
    :num1 (t), num2 (r)

The definition of derived class constructor should contain the calls to the constructors of the base classes in its header. Our header contains **num1(t)** and **num2(r)**. The calls to base class constructors must be preceded by the colon **:**. Base class constructors should be separated from each other by the commas. The parameters of the derived class constructor are passed as the arguments to the base class constructors. We passed the first parameter of **dernum()** constructor to the first base class. It is not a rule. You can pass any arguments in any order to the base class constructors from a derived class constructor.

Even though the derived class constructor passes some of its parameters to the base classes, but it still can use all or any of its parameters. Our derived class constructor uses only the third parameter in it. It assigns the value of that parameter to class member **z**. Derived class constructors can even use those parameters, that have been passed to the base class constructors. Therefore, a constructor fragment shown below is quite legitimate.

```
dernum::dernum (int t, int r, int u)
:num1 (t), num2 (r)
{
z=u+t+r;
}
```

This concludes the material we wanted to give you on the multiple inheritance.

14.10. Hierarchical inheritance.

We have mentioned and have even given you some examples of hierarchical inheritance. Here, we will consider it briefly, so you can get more familiar with it. The meaning of the hierarchical inheritance is, that the derived class can become a base class for another class. That other class can, in turn, become a base class for the third class and so on. Thus, we can have a case, when class **A** is a base of the class **B**, class **B** is the base of the class **C**, class **C** is the base class of the class **D** and so on. Classes **A, B, C, D** can be inherited with any (**public, private, protected**) access specifier. The access specifiers for classes **A, B** and **C** in the hierarchical inheritance are independent from each other and should be chosen based on your need.

Following example introduces the hierarchical inheritance of the classes, in which the constructors do not have the parameters.

```
#include <iostream.h>

class num1
{
int x;
public:
void set1(int a) { x=a; }
void disp1 ( ) { cout << "x=" << x << ", "; }
} ;

class num2 : private num1
{
```

```
int y;
public:
void set2 (int b1, int b2) { set1 (b1), y=b2; }

void disp2 ( ) { disp1( ), cout << "y=" << y << ", "; }

} ;

class dernum :public num2
{
int z;
public:
void setd (int c) { z=c; }
void show ( ) { cout <<"z=" << z << "\n"; }
} ;

void main ( )
{
dernum one;
one.set2 (1, 2);
one.setd (3);
one.disp2 ( );
one.show ( );
}
```

Program 14.16.

The output of the program is

    x=1, y=2, z=3

The program declares three classes: **num1**, **num2** and **dernum**. The **num1** class becomes a base class for the **num2** class, which is a base for the **dernum** class. The **num1** class is inherited as **private**, while the **num2** class is inherited as **public**. We used different access specifiers to illustrate different hierarchical inheritance.

Since the **num1** class is inherited by the **num2** with **private** access specifier, its members become **private** members of **num2**. As you know, the **private** members of the derived class are accessible only inside that derived class. This is why we had to write the **public** member functions of **num2** class in the following way.

    void set2 (int b1, int b2) { set1 (b1), y=b2; }
    void disp2 ( ) { disp1( ), cout << "y=" << y << ", "; }

The **set2()** member function of the **num2** class calls **set1()** member function of the **num1** class, and **disp2()** calls **disp1()**. We would not be able to call any of the **num1** members from the outside of the **num2** class. Therefore, the derived class **num2** must contain the access functions for its base class member. This way, when we call **set2()**, for example, we would be able to change the data members of the derived class **num2** and the base class **num1**.

The **num2** class is inherited by the **dernum** class as **public**. The **public** members of

num2 become **public** members of the **dernum** class. If the **num1** class has been inherited by **num2** class as **public**, the **dernum** class would have been able to access **public** members of both classes in our program. **Program 14.16** defines and uses the object **one** of the **dernum** class in **main()** function. We show there, how to assign and display the data members of all classes using the member functions **one.show()** and **one.setd()** of class **dernum** and the functions **one.set2()**, **one.disp()** of base class **num2**.

Everything learned for the hierarchical inheritance for the classes, in which the constructors do not have parameters, is true for the classes, having the constructors with the parameters. We demonstrate it below.

```
#include <iostream.h>                    //line 1

class num1                               //line 2
{                                        //line 3
int x;                                   //line 4
public:                                  //line 5
num1 (int p) {x=p; }                     //line 6
void set1(int a) { x=a; }                //line 7
void disp1 ( ) { cout << "x=" << x << ", "; }//line 8
} ;                                      //line 9

class num2 : private num1                //line 10
{                                        //line 11
int y;                                   //line 12
public:                                  //line 13
num2 (int , int );                       //line 14
void set2(int b1, int b2) { set1(b1), y=b2; }//line 15

void disp2 ( ) { disp1( ), cout << "y=" << y << ", "; }
                                         //line 16

} ;                                      //line 17

class dernum :public num2                //line 18
{                                        //line 19
int z;                                   //line 20
public:                                  //line 21
dernum (int , int, int);                 //line 22
void setd (int c) { z=c; }               //line 23
void show ( ) { cout <<"z=" << z << "\n"; }  //line 24
} ;                                      //line 25

num2::num2 (int k1, int k2)              //line 26
 :num1(k1)                               //line 27
```

```
{                                       //line 28
y=k2;                                   //line 29
}                                       //line 30

dernum::dernum(int q, int w, int e)     //line 31
:num2 (q, w)                            //line 32
{                                       //line 33
z=e;                                    //line 34
}                                       //line 35

void main( )                            //line 36
{                                       //line 37
dernum one (2, 4, 6);                   //line 38
one.disp2 ( );                          //line 39
one.show ( );                           //line 40
one.set2 (1, 3);                        //line 41
one.setd (5);                           //line 42
one.disp2 ( );                          //line 43
one.show ( );                           //line 44
}                                       //line 45
```
Program 14.17.

The output of the program is
```
x=2, y=4, z=6
x=1, y=3, z=5
```
We declare class **num1** at lines 2-9. Its constructor is defined explicitly with the parameter **p** at line 5. This class becomes a base class of the **num2** class. The **num2** class is declared at lines 10-17. Its constructor with the parameters is declared explicitly at line 14. Otherwise, **num2** declaration is quite similar to its declaration in the previous program. Class **dernum** is declared at lines 18-25. It is declared similar to the previous program, except, here, the constructor is declared explicitly with the parameters at line 22. Compare the definition of **num1()** constructor and the declarations of the **num2()** and **dernum()** constructors in **Program 14.17**. We have combined them together below.
```
num1 (int p) {x=p; }                    //line 6
num2 (int , int );                      //line 14
dernum (int , int, int);                //line 22
```
When an object of **dernum** class is created, it will have the initializers. Each of the classes in our program has one member, that it initializes. The **dernum()** function uses one argument to set its own member **z** to its initial value. It passes two other arguments to the **num2()** constructor. The **dernum()** constructor header contains
```
dernum::dernum(int q, int w, int e)     //line 31
:num2 (q, w)                            //line 32
```
The special form **:num2(q, w)** is used in **dernum()** constructor definition. This passes two arguments to **num2()**. The **num2()** constructor definition also contains

```
num2::num2 (int k1, int k2)                    //line 26
 :num1(k1)                                     //line 27
```

The **num2()** constructor uses one of the passed arguments for its class member **y**. The form **:num1(k1)** passes another argument to the **num1()** constructor function. That argument is used to set the value of **num1()** class member **x**.

A constructor that passes its arguments to another constructor can use any or all of those arguments. For example, the **dernum()** constructor can be changed to

```
dernum::dernum(int q, int w, int e)
 :num2 (q, w)
{
z=e*w+2*q;
}
```

The **num2()** has two parameters and the **dernum()** constructor has three parameters in our program. It does not mean, that the derived class constructor should have the same or greater number of parameters than the base class. The program below is similar to the one above. However, the **dernum()** constructor has only one parameter in the program below. It is not treated as an error by the compiler for as long as it passes the correct number of arguments to the base class constructor. Pay attention, that **dernum()** not only passes the same argument twice to **num2()** constructor function, but it also uses that argument to assign a value to class member **z**.

```
#include <iostream.h>

class num1
{
int x;
public:
num1 (int p) {x=p; }
void set1(int a) { x=a; }
void disp1 ( ) { cout << "x=" << x << ", "; }
} ;

class num2 : private num1
{
int y;
public:
num2 (int , int );
void set2(int b1, int b2) { set1(b1), y=b2; }
void disp2 ( ) { disp1( ), cout << "y=" << y << ", "; }


} ;

class dernum :public num2
{
int z;
```

```
public:
dernum (int );
void setd (int c) { z=c; }
void show ( ) { cout <<"z=" << z << "\n"; }
} ;

num2::num2 (int k1, int k2)
:num1(k1)
{
y=k2;
}

dernum::dernum(int q)
:num2 (q, q)
{
z=q;
}

void main( )
{
dernum one (2);
one.disp2 ( );
one.show ( );
}
```

Program 14.18.

The output of the program is
```
x=2, y=2, z=2
```

14.11. Virtual base classes.

When a class inherits a number of classes, it might lead to some problems. Let's assume, we have two derived classes **B1** and **B2**. Each of them has inherited the base class **A**. We now create class **C**, that inherits both classes **B1** and **B2**. Since each of the classes **B1** and **B2** contains a copy of class **A**, an object of class **C** type should consist of two copies of class **A** members. And this can be a problem.

```
class A
{
public:
int x;
} ;

class B1 : public A
{
```

```
public:
int y;
};

class B2 : public A
{
public:
int z;
};

class C : public B1, public B2
{
public:
int q;
};
```

The above fragment illustrates our classes. Let's declare an object of class **C**.

```
C ob;
```

If we now write an assignment **ob.z=5**, it will become ambiguous. We assign the value 5 to the member **x**. But member **x** exists in both derived classes **B1** and **B2**. The compiler does not know to which one to assign that value. This can give an error.

The situation has two solutions. The first one is to use the scope resolution operator **::**. It permits you to select to which **x** to assign the value. **Program 14.19** illustrates this solution.

```
#include <iostream.h>

class foun
{
public:
int x;
void set(int a) { x=a; }
void disp ( ) { cout << "x=" << x << ", "; }
} ;

class num1 : public foun
{
public:
int y;
void set1(int b1) { y=b1; }
void disp1 ( ) { disp( ), cout << "y=" << y << ", "; }
} ;

class num2 : public foun
{
public:
```

```
int z;
void set2 (int b2) { z=b2; }
void disp2 ( ) { cout << "z=" << z << ", "; }
} ;

class dernum :public num1, public num2
{
public:
int s;
void setd (int c) { s=c; }
void show ( ) { cout << "s=" << s << "\n"; }
} ;

void main( )
{
dernum one;
one.num1::set (1);
one.num2::x=2;
one.num1::disp ( );
one.num2::disp ( );
one.set1 (3);
one.set2 (4);
one.s=one.num1::x + one.num2::x + one.y + one.z;
one.show ( );
}
```

Program 14.19.

The output of the program is

    x=1, x=2, s=10

The program declares four classes: **foun**, **num1**, **num2** and **dernum**. The **foun** class is inherited as a base class by both **num1** and **num2** classes. The **dernum** class inherits both **num1** and **num2** as its base classes. Therefore, there are two copies of **foun** in an object of **dernum** class type. We illustrate how to select the right copy in **main()**. We declare the object **one** of class **dernum** and assign the values to both of its **x** members by

    one.num1::set (1);
    one.num2::x=2;

The **num1::** indicates, that the copy of the base class inherited by the **num1** class is selected. You can see, the first line assigns the value using the **set()** member function and the second line accesses **x** of **num2** class directly. This illustrates how to access a member function or a data member of a class using scope resolution operator. We display those two values using the same trick with the scope resolution operator.

There are cases, when two copies of the same base are not needed in the derived class. Imagine a situation. Each of the classes **num1** and **num2** inherits the base **foun**. Both of the classes **num1** and **num2** are inherited by the **dernum** class. But only one copy of the **foun** base class should be present in the **dernum** class. How to achieve it? The solution is - *virtual base classes*. When two or more classes are derived from a common base, there can be only one copy of that common base in a class derived from those derived classes. And this is achieved by adding word **virtual** to that common base, when it is inherited. The word **virtual** should precede the access specifier of the inherited class. Consider following program.

```cpp
#include <iostream.h>

class foun
{
public:
int x;
void set(int a) { x=a; }
void disp ( ) { cout << "x=" << x << ", "; }
} ;

class num1 : virtual public foun
{
public:
int y;
void set1(int b1) { y=b1; }
void disp1 ( ) { disp( ), cout << "y=" << y << ", "; }
} ;

class num2 : virtual public foun
{
public:
int z;
void set2(int b2) { z=b2; }
void disp2 ( ) { cout << "z=" << z << ", "; }
} ;

class dernum :public num1, public num2
{
public:
int s;
void setd (int c) { s=c; }
void show ( ) { cout <<"s=" << s << "\n"; }
} ;

void main( )
{
dernum one;
one.set (1);
one.disp ( );
```

```
one.set1 (3);
one.set2 (4);
one.s=one.x + one.y + one.z;
one.show ( );
}
```

Program 14.20.

The output of the program is

```
x=1,  s=8
```

That program should be pretty self-explanatory for you. The common base class is inherited by both derived classes as

```
class num1 : virtual public foun
```

and

```
class num2 : virtual public foun
```

The word **virtual** does not make any difference for the objects of either **num1** or **num2**. If only one of the classes **num1** or **num2** is inherited by the **dernum** class, their virtual base makes no difference. Only one copy of the class **foun** would be present in **dernum** in this case. If both classes **num1** and **num2** are inherited by the **dernum** class, only one **foun** class copy must be present in the **dernum** class anyway.

EXERCISES.

1. Run all the examples of this chapter, if you have an access to a computer facility.

2. Write a program containing some of the classes described in Fig. 14.1. The program should model a university. The university has 20 students. Some of them pay tuition (about $10000 a year), some receive the tuition waivers. Only the students with GPA 3.6 and higher receive a tuition waiver. There are 6 graduate students among them. They do not pay tuition. They receive stipends about $5000 a year. The university has 5 faculties. Three of them make $30000 a year. Two of them make $50000 a year. The university has a staff of 3 people, and a president. The staff makes $20000, $20000, $25000 a year respectively. The president makes $80000 a year. Make up the names of students, faculty and staff. The university pays $20000 a year for outside services.

Your program must calculate the optimal budget of the university. This might include even cutting on the aid to the graduate students and laying off the faculty and staff. Your budget also depends on how many students will get GPA of 3.6 and higher. You can also rise the tuition. But each percent of tuition increase will scare away a percent of under-graduate students. You can lay off some of the faculty, but it can increase the population of unsatisfied graduate and undergraduate students. They can leave the school. Besides, you cannot lay off 2 faculty members, because they have tenure. If a body of graduate students becomes less than a quarter of all the students, the university becomes a college. You want to avoid that. You can borrow money, but the interest rates can sooner or later destroy the school.

3. Write a program with a class, that describes geometrical figures. It should inherit some geometrical classes. It should be able to find the areas and the volumes of those geometri-

cal figures. The class should be organized as a separate header file.

4. Write a program with a class describing a stock room. It should inherit other classes. It should use virtual base.

5. Write a program, that converts a pointer of derived class to a base class.

6. Make up a few classes, that inherit others and write the programs with them. Each of those classes should represent some practical life entity.

CHAPTER 15

VIRTUAL FUNCTIONS AND POLYMORPHISM.

Polymorphism is one of the tools of the object-oriented programming. It means, loosely speaking, using different implementations of the same function, or when one statement can call different forms of the same function. The word "polymorphism" means the property "to assume many forms". Many authors identify two types of polymorphism: run-time and compile-time. Some controversy does exist about the polymorphism definition. Some authors define the polymorphism as only run-time process. We will not take a side on this issue. Our purpose is to teach you as many features of C++, as you might need, but not to argue about the definition of polymorphism. The compile-time polymorphism is represented by the operator and function overloading. The run-time polymorphism is achieved through the use of derived classes and, so-called *virtual functions*, which are the subject of this chapter.

15.1. Pointers to base and derived classes.

The pointers to the derived and base classes are the foundation of the polymorphism. Let's consider them. We know, that a pointer to one data type cannot point to another data type. It is true in C as well as in C++. In C++ a pointer to an object of the base class can be used to point to an object of any class derived from that base. Thus, if we have a base class **Bas** and derived class **Der**

```
    Bas *pr, obb;
    Der obd;
```

then, the pointer **pr** can point to the base class object **obb** as well as to the derived class object **obd**. So, any of the following assignments is possible

```
    pr=&obb;
    pr=&obd;
```

When the pointer to the base class type **pr** points to the derived class object **obd**, it can access only the members of the base class in the derived class. It cannot access the members specific for the derived class. Consider following program.

```
    #include <iostream.h>
    #include <string.h>

    class eng
    {
```

```
char line[20];
public:
void ent (char *row) { strcpy (line, row); }
void disp ( ) { cout << line << " - "; }
} ;

class fren : public eng
{
char fline[20];
public:
void fr_ent (char *frow) { strcpy (fline, frow); }
void fr_disp ( ) { disp ( ), cout << fline <<"\n"; }
} ;

void main ( )
{
eng *pr;
fren obd;
pr=&obd;
obd.fr_ent ("chat");
pr->ent("cat");
obd.fr_disp( );
}
```

Program 15.1.

The output of the program is

```
cat-chat
```

We wrote a program, that displays an English word and corresponding to it French word. You can use it as a foundation for writing some dictionary programs. It declares two classes: **eng** and **fren**. The **fren** class inherits **eng** as its base class with the **public** access. We use both classes in **main()** routine. We declare an object of **fren** class type and the pointer **pr** to the **eng** class. We make pointer **pr** pointing towards the object **obd** by **pr=&obd** statement. This statements assigns the address of the derived class object **obd** to the pointer **pr**. The **ent()** function is a member of the base class **eng**. It becomes a **public** member of the class **fren** by inheritance. We access this function through the pointer **pr**. It accesses the base class part of the object **obd**. If we tried to use **pr->fr_disp()**, or **pr->fr_ent()**, it would give an error. Both **fr_disp()** and **pr->fr_ent()** functions are the members of the derived class **fren** only. They cannot be accessed via **pr** pointer to the base class type.

The **pr->ent("cat")** copies the string "**cat**" to the member **line[]**. It is the English word to be displayed. The **obd.fr_ent("chat")** copies the string "**chat**" to the member **fline[]**. This is the French equivalent of the English word. We display both words by **obd.fr_disp()** in **Program 15.1**.

In general, you can access the derived class objects by the base class pointer, if you cast its data type to the derived class. If you substitute the line

```
      obd.fr_disp();
```
by the line
```
      ((fren *)pr)->fr_disp( );
```
the program should run fine, because you change the data type of the base class pointer to
the derived class.

15.2. Introduction to virtual functions.

The polymorphism is achieved by means of the virtual function and the inheritance. A
virtual function is declared in a base class as **virtual** and redefined in at least one
derived class. It can be redefined again in any derived class and in more than one derived
class. Different derived classes can redefine absolutely different versions of the same
virtual function. The original and the redefined versions must have the same type and
number of parameters, and the same returned value type. The polymorphism describes the
events occurring, when a virtual function is accessed via a base class pointer. When a
virtual function is accessed through the base class pointer, C++ chooses which version
of that function to call. The determination of which function version is executed is made
at a run-time. It is based upon the type of an object, that the base class pointer points to.
So, if the pointer points to different object types, different versions of a function with the
same name are executed. It will become more obvious to you after going over the following program.

```
      #include <iostream.h>

      class Bas
      {
      public:

      virtual void disp ( )
      { cout << "This is the base function.\n"; }

      } ;

      class Der1 : public Bas
      {
      public:

      void disp ( ) { cout << "This is the first derived class"
                           << " function.\n"; }

      } ;

      class Der2 : public Bas
      {
```

```
public:

void disp ( ) { cout << "This is the second derived"
                     << " class function.\n"; }

} ;

void main ( )
{
Bas *pr, obb;
Der1 obd1;
Der2 obd2;
pr=&obb; //assigning the pointer to the base object
pr->disp ( );
pr=&obd1;   //assigning the pointer to the Der1 object
pr->disp ( );
pr=&obd2;   //assigning the pointer to the Der2 object
pr->disp ( );
}
```
Program 15.2.

The output of the program is
```
This is the base function.
This is the first derived class function.
This is the second derived class function.
```
The program declares three classes: **Bas**, **Der1** and **Der2**. The **Bas** class becomes a base class for both **Der1** and **Der2**. To make the understanding of our program easier, each class consists of only one member - **disp()** function. It is a virtual function. Why? We declare it with the word **virtual**, that precedes the function declaration in the base class **Bas**. Consider it.
```
virtual void disp ( )
{ cout << "This is the base function.\n";
```
Thus, the word **virtual** should be the first word in the function declaration. The function declaration and definition are combined in our example. We have written it as **inline** function for the sake of simplicity. One can ask, what happens if you have to write the function, where the declaration and definition are separate? We rewrite the same function to show, how to be in that case.
```
class Bas
{
public:
virtual void disp ( );
} ;

void Bas:: disp ( )
{
```

```
    cout << "This is the base function.\n";
    }
```

We have changed only the part of the program, that declares and defines the **disp()** function in the base class. As you see, the word **virtual** is used *only in the declaration not definition* of the virtual function. It is used only inside the base class. Now, let's return to our **Program 15.2**. We define and declare **disp()** function as **virtual** only inside the base class. Function **disp()** is redeclared and redefined in other two derived classes. Again, we could have declared that function in **Der1** and **Der2** and could have defined the function in each of the classes separately outside of the class, as regular member function.

We have chosen to redeclare and redefine the member functions at once in each of the **Der1** and **Der2** classes for the only reason - to make the program shorter and better readable. The virtual functions are declared and defined as regular functions. The only difference is the presence of the word **virtual** in the declaration of such a function in the base class. You can use the word **virtual**, when redeclaring (not redefining) the virtual function in other derived classes. But it is not necessary.

Now we can explain you how to use the virtual functions. We define the objects inside **main()** in **Program 15.2**. The object **obb** and the pointer **pr** are an object and a pointer to the base class **Bas** type. We also define the object **obd1** of the class **Der1** type and the object **obd2** having class **Der2** data type. We make the **pr** pointer pointing towards the **obb** object of the same class **Bas** by

```
    pr=&obb; //assigning the pointer to the base object
```

We, then, call the **disp()** virtual function using the pointer as

```
    pr->disp ( );
```

Remember, C++ determines which version of the virtual function to call based on what object the base class pointer points to at the run-time. The term "at the run-time" means when the program is executed. It is called *dynamic binding*. Our pointer first points to the object of its own class. Therefore, the **disp()** member function of the **Bas** class is executed. This yields the message on the screen

```
    This is the base function.
```

We, then, reassign our pointer **pr** by

```
    pr=&obd1;    //assigning the pointer to the Der1 object
```

Since it now points to the **Der1** class object, the **disp()** member function of that class is executed now, when we call

```
    pr->disp ( );
```

The above version displays the second message on the screen. We also write the third assignment of the **pr** pointer.

```
    pr=&obd2;    //assigning the pointer to the Der2 object
```

The pointer points towards the object of the **Der2** class after that assignment. The third call **pr->disp()** starts the version of the **disp()** function, that is the member of the **Der2** class. This happens because the pointer **pr** points towards the object of the **Der2** class, and C++ selects the version of the virtual function depending to what class object the base class pointer points to.

A corresponding version of the **disp()** member function could have been called by **obb.disp()**, **obd1.disp()** and **obd2.disp()** respectively in those three cases.

Each of the objects would have accessed its own copy named **disp()** function, because each of those member functions has a class scope visibility. That would have been a regular way. We are now studying a new feature of C++ - polymorphism. It allows to access different functions by the same base pointer during program run-time. We will see later in this book, why the virtual functions are important.

The virtual functions are connected to inheritance. If we talk about a base class pointer, this tells us, that there should be an inheritance involved. The virtual functions are first declared as such in the base class and redefined in other derived classes, as you know. Redefinition of the virtual function in the derived classes is called *overriding*. Do not be afraid of this word. It is just a term. A class that has a virtual function as its member is called a *polymorphic class*. This notion applies to the base as well as derived classes, that inherit the base classes containing virtual functions.

One can mix the redefinition of the virtual function with the function overloading. A virtual function is a fundamentally different feature. The overloaded function versions are known to differ by the types and/or number of parameters. At the other hand, the redefined virtual function must have exactly the same number and the types of its parameters. Furthermore, the prototypes for a virtual function and its redefinitions must be the same. If those prototypes for the virtual function are different, then it is considered to be an overloaded function. Another important property of a virtual function - it cannot be a friend of the class in which it is used. However, it can be a friend of any other class. Last feature - the class constructors cannot be virtual, while the destructors can.

15.3. Virtual functions and inheritance.

Here we want to emphasize a few points about the virtual functions and inheritance. We will begin with following. What happens, if a virtual function is not redefined in the derived class? Consider following program.

```
#include <iostream.h>

class Bas
{
public:
virtual void disp ( );
} ;

void Bas:: disp ( )
{
cout << "This is the base function.\n";
}

class Der1 : public Bas
{
public:
```

```
void disp ( ) { cout << "This is the first derived class"
                    << " function.\n"; }


} ;

class Der2 : public Bas
{
} ;

void main ( )
{
Bas *pr, obb;
Der1 obd1;
Der2 obd2;
pr=&obb; //assigning the pointer to the base object
pr->disp ( );
pr=&obd1;    //assigning the pointer to the Der1 object
pr->disp ( );
pr=&obd2;    //assigning the pointer to the Der2 object
pr->disp ( );
}
```

Program 15.3.

The output of the program is

```
This is the base function.
This is the first derived class function.
This is the base function.
```

Program 15.3 is similar to the previous one. It declares three classes: **Bas, Der1** and **Der2**. Both classes **Der1** and **Der2** inherit **Bas** as the base class. The virtual function **disp()** is declared as such in the base class. The function is redefined only in the **Der1** class. We do not redefine it in the derived class **Der2**. We, again, use the virtual function in **main()** function. There, we define the same three objects and the pointer **pr** to the base class type. We assign that pointer to the address of the base class object **obb** first. The call **pr->disp()** calls the base class version of **disp()** function. This displays the first message on the screen.

We reassign the pointer to the object **obd1** and call **pr->disp()** again. It calls the **Der1** class version of **disp()** function and displays the second message. So far, the program has been behaving as the previous one. The difference occurs in the third assignment. There, we assign the address of the **obd2** object to the pointer **pr**, and call **pr->disp()**. But we do not redefine function **disp()** in the **Der2** class. Therefore, the **pr->disp()** call calls the base class version of that function. This is why the first and the third messages displayed on the screen are identical to each other. One can derive a conclusion. *Assume, that you do not redefine the base class virtual function in the derived class **A**. Then, the base class version of that function will be called, when accessed via base class pointer pointing toward an object of class **A**.*

Let's assume, class **A** is inherited as a base by the class **B**. Class **B** is inherited as a base by the class **C**. Class **C** is inherited by the class **D** and so on. If we declare a virtual function in class **A**, then, any other derived class in the hierarchy still acquires this function as virtual. In other words, if a virtual function is declared in class **A**, it is inherited by any other derived class (**B**, **C**, **D**, etc.) in the hierarchy. You can redefine that virtual function in any hierarchically derived class. For instance, if you declare a virtual function in class **A** and do not redefine it in class **B**, you can still redefine it in class **C**. Consider following program.

```
#include <iostream.h>

class Bas
{
public:
virtual void disp ( );
} ;

void Bas:: disp ( )
{
cout << "This is the base function.\n";
}

class Der1 : public Bas
{
} ;

class Der2 : public Der1
{
} ;

void main ( )
{
Bas *pr, obb;
Der1 obd1;
Der2 obd2;
pr=&obb; //assigning the pointer to the base object
pr->disp ( );
pr=&obd1;   //assigning the pointer to the Der1 object
pr->disp ( );
pr=&obd2;   //assigning the pointer to the Der2 object
pr->disp ( );
}
```

Program 15.4.

The output of the program is

```
This is the base function.
This is the base function.
This is the base function.
```

As you see, the virtual function **disp( )** of the base class is inherited by the **Der1** class, which is, in turn, inherited as the base class by the **Der2** class. Since, the **disp( )** function has not been redefined in any other derived class, it is called by the **pr->disp( )** statement does not matter, whether **pr** points to **obb**, **obd1**, or **obd2**.

We will consider one more case of interaction between the virtual functions and inheritance. Assume, that class **A** is inherited as a base class by class **B**, class **B** is inherited as a base by class **C** and so on. We declare a virtual function in class **A**. It is redefined in class **B**. We assign an address of an object of class **C** to the base class **A** pointer. We, then, call that virtual function by the base class pointer. Which version **A** or **B** of the virtual function is called? Consider following program.

```cpp
#include <iostream.h>

class Bas
{
public:
virtual void disp ( );
} ;

void Bas:: disp ( )
{
cout << "This is the base function.\n";
}

class Der1 : public Bas
{
public:
void disp ( ) { cout << "This is the first derived class"
                     << " function.\n"; }
} ;

class Der2 : public Der1
{
} ;

void main ( )
{
Bas *pr, obb;
Der1 obd1;
Der2 obd2;
pr=&obb; //assigning the pointer to the base object
pr->disp ( );
```

```
pr=&obd1;    //assigning the pointer to the Der1 object
pr->disp ( );
pr=&obd2;    //assigning the pointer to the Der2 object
pr->disp ( );
}
```

Program 15.5.

The output of the program is

```
This is the base function.
This is the first derived class function.
This is the first derived class function.
```

The above program declares three classes: **Bas**, **Der1**, **Der2**. Class **Bas** is inherited by **Der1**, and the **Der1** class is inherited by **Der2**. The virtual function **disp()** is declared in class **Bas**. We redefine it in class **Der1**. We use those classes in **main()**, where we define objects **obb**, **obd1**, and **obd2** and a pointer to an object. We, then, assign the pointer **pr** to point towards the objects **obb**, **obd1**, and **obd2**, and observe which version of the virtual function is called by **pr->disp()** in each of those cases. The output message shows us, which member function has been called. The **pr=&obb** assignment calls the base class version. The first derived class version is called after **pr=&obd1** assignment. The third assignment **pr=&obd2** assigns the address of the **Der2** class object **obd2** to the base class pointer **pr**. The **pr->disp()** line after that statement calls the **Der1** version of the virtual function.

Why? The virtual function defined in **Bas** was later redefined in the derived class **Der1**. That class along with its version of the virtual function was inherited by the derived class **Der2**. That version of the virtual function will run, when you call it through a pointer to an object of the **Der2** class type. It produces the third displayed message line.

15.4. Use of virtual functions.

We will show you, how to use the virtual functions in the programs. To start, let's solve a simple problem in physics. We will first introduce the *acceleration* **a**, *speed* **v** and distance **s**. The acceleration of a body is, loosely speaking, the rate of its velocity change per unit time. We take from the physics books following formula for finding the velocity of accelerating body, that starts from its rest position: **v=at**. Here, **t** is the time in seconds. The distance, that body will travel during time **t** is equal to $s = v \times t^2 / 2$. Now, let's create a program, that will calculate it for us.

```
#include <iostream.h>

class Mov
{
public:
virtual float moving (float , float);
void disp ( ) { cout << "Nothing to display.\n"; }
```

```
} ;

float Mov::moving (float x, float y)
{
cout << "No problem has been specified.\n";
return 0.0;
}

class Speed : public Mov
{
float sp;
public:
float moving (float , float );
void show_sp ( )
{ cout << "The speed is " << sp << "\n"; }
} ;

float Speed :: moving (float a1, float t1)
{
return (sp=a1*t1);
}

class Dist : public Mov
{
float d;
public:
float moving (float, float);

void show_dis ( ) { cout << "The distance gone by the"
                         << " body is " << d <<"\n"; }

} ;

float Dist::moving ( float a2, float t2)
{
return (d=a2*t2*t2/2);
}

void main ( )
{
Mov *pr, obb;
Speed obd1;
Dist obd2;
pr=&obb; //assigning the pointer to the base object
cout << pr->moving (2.5, 3.0) <<"\n";
```

```
pr=&obd1;    //assigning the pointer to the Speed object
cout << pr->moving (2.5, 3.0) << "   ";
obd1.show_sp ( );
pr=&obd2;    //assigning the pointer to the Dist object
cout << pr->moving (2.5, 3.0) << "\n";
}
```

Program 15.6.

The output of the program is

```
No problem has been specified.
0
7.5   The speed is 7.5
11.25
```

The program declares three classes: **Mov**, **Speed**, **Dist**. Both **Speed** and **Dist** classes inherit **Mov** as the base class. We also declare the **moving()** function as a virtual one. It is redefined in each of two derived classes **Speed**, **Dist**. The function **moving()** of class **Speed** finds the speed of an object moving with the constant acceleration. The same member function of class **Dist** finds the distance that an object has traveled. We also introduce additional displaying function in each class, although we do not use all of them in our program. A real class can contain a number of data and function members along with a number of virtual functions.

We want to offer you another example of virtual function application. It finds the volumes of simple geometrical figures.

```
#include <iostream.h>

class volume
{
protected:
float x, y, z;
public:
void set (float a, float b, float c) {x=a, y=b, z=c; }

virtual void disp_vol ( ) { cout << "No calculation has"
                     << " been performed yet.\n";}

} ;



class paral: public volume
{
public:

void disp_vol ( )
{ cout << "The volume of the parallelipiped "
```

```
            << "with the sides " << "\n"
            << x << ", " << y << ", " << z << " is equal to "
            << x*y*z << ".\n"; }


    } ;



    class pyramid : public volume
    {
    public:

    void disp_vol ( ) { cout << "Volume of the pyramid "
            << "with the right angle triangular base " << x
            << ", " << y << "\n" << " and the height " << z
            << " is equal to " << x*y*z/2 << ". ";}


    } ;



    void main ( )
    {
    volume *pt, ob1;
    paral ob2;
    pyramid ob3;
    pt=&ob1;    //pointer assignment to the base class object
    pt->set (2.0, 3.0, 4.0);
    pt->disp_vol ( );
    pt=&ob2;  //pointer assignment to the paral class object
    pt->set (2.0, 3.0, 4.0);
    pt->disp_vol ( );
    pt=&ob3; //pointer assignment to the pyramid class object
    pt->set (2.0, 3.0, 4.0);
    pt->disp_vol ( );
    }
```

Program 15.7.

The output of the program is

```
    No calculation has been performed yet.
    The volume of the parallelipiped with the sides
    2, 3, 4 is equal to 24.
    Volume of the pyramid with the right angle triangular
    base 2, 3
    and the height 4 is equal to 12.
```

The program declares three classes: **volume, paral, pyramid**. The **volume** class is inherited by both **paral** and **pyramid** classes. The virtual function **disp_vol()** is declared in the base class **volume**. The **paral** and **pyramid** classes redefine that function, so it calculates the volumes of a parallelepiped and pyramid respectively. The virtual function is called by means of the base class pointer **pt**. The sides of each figure are entered by means of the **set()** member function. It belongs to the base class, and is accessed by the base class pointer in all three cases.

The **set()** is a regular member function. It performs an operation common for all the derived classes. It assigns passed to it arguments to the corresponding data members **x**, **y** and **z**. The **disp_vol()** function is declared as virtual, because the formulas for computing the volumes of different geometrical figures are different. So, each of the figures is represented by its own class **paral** or **pyramid**. Each of the classes inherits the **volume** class. Pay attention, how do we handle an object of each class in **main()**. We pass the lengths of all the sides and get the calculated volumes for different figures by the same statements

```
pt->set (2.0, 3.0, 4.0);
pt->disp_vol ( );
```

Which figure will be selected depends on a particular assignment of the base class pointer **pt** prior to those two statements.

15.5. Continuation on use of virtual functions.

We have been dealing with the classes representing different geometrical figures in the above program. Our classes in that program could compute and display the volumes of three different dimensional figures. What if we want to find a volume of a sphere, or a cylinder? We would need to use only one or two parameters of the virtual function, and it has three of them. Can we use the virtual functions when we need only some of their parameters? Yes, we can. We illustrate it in following program. It is similar to the above program, but has an additional class, displaying a volume of a sphere.

```
#include <iostream.h>

class volume
{
protected:
float x, y, z;
public:

void set (float a, float b=1, float c=1){x=a, y=b, z=c;}

virtual void disp_vol ( ) { cout << "No calculation has"
                            << " been performed yet.\n"; }

} ;
```

```cpp
class paral: public volume
{
public:

void disp_vol ( )
 {cout << "The volume of the parallelipiped "
       << "with the sides " << "\n" << x << ", " << y
       << ", " << z << " is equal to " << x*y*z << "\n";}


} ;

class pyramid : public volume
{
public:

void disp_vol ( ) {
cout << "Volume of the pyramid " << "with the right"
<< " angle triangle base " << x << ", " << y << "\n"
<< " and the height " << z << " is equal to "
<< x*y*z/2 << "\n";
}
} ;


class sphere: public volume
{
public:

void disp_vol ( )
{
cout << "Volume of the sphere " << "with radius "
    << x << " is " << 4*x*x*x/3 << ". ";
}
} ;


void main ( )
{
volume *pt, ob1;
paral ob2;
pyramid ob3;
sphere ob4;

pt=&ob1;    //pointer assignment to the base class object
pt->set (2.0, 3.0, 4.0);
```

```
pt->disp_vol ( );
pt=&ob2;  //pointer assignment to the paral class object
pt->set (2.0, 3.0, 4.0);
pt->disp_vol ( );

pt=&ob3; //pointer assignment to the pyramid class object
pt->set (2.0, 3.0, 4.0);
pt->disp_vol ( );

pt=&ob4; //pointer assignment to the sphere class object
pt->set (2.0);
pt->disp_vol ( );
}
```

Program 15.8.

The output of the program is
```
No calculation has been performed yet.
The volume of the parallelipiped with the sides
2, 3, 4 is equal to 24.
Volume of the pyramid with the right angle triangular
base 2, 3
and the height 4 is equal to 12.
Volume of the sphere with radius 2 is 10.666667.
```
How to write a virtual function for classes that use different number of its parameters? Our **set ( )** member function of **sphere** class takes only one argument, while the **set ( )** member function of the other classes needs three. The first solution is to enter some dummy values for two additional arguments in **set ( )** member function, when it is used for the **sphere** class. **Program 15.8** illustrates a better way. It declares the **set ( )** member function as having two default parameters.

```
void set(float a, float b=1, float c=1) {x=a, y=b, z=c; }
```
So, one can call it with three, two or even one argument, as we did in the above program. And the general way of building the base and inherited classes is preserved.

This program illustrates the idea of polymorphism and virtual functions. The polymorphism is an important tool of the object-oriented programming (OOP). Why? It allows the generalized base class to introduce the functions that will be common to all the derived classes. At the same time they permit the derived classes to define other specific actions, that will be performed by those functions. This idea is, sometimes, interpreted slightly different. The base class determines the general *interface* (or set of functions) that any object derived from that class must have. The derived class can redefine the actual way (or method) in which that interface would work.

One can ask, why having one interface is important. It helps to handle very difficult programs. Imagine, you know that all the objects are accessed in the same way, when you develop a program. You can vary your interface, but you will have to remember only one interface. The separation of interface and implementation, as we studied in the previous chapters, permits the creation of class libraries. They can be written by the third party, or by other vendor. They will save you time on developing the programs.

15.6. Pure virtual functions and abstract classes.

You know, if a base class virtual function is not overridden in the derived classes, its base class version will be used in those derived classes. Sometimes, the base class version has no meaning. For example, the base class version of the **disp_vol()** function in two previous programs was simply a place holder. It could not display any areas at all, because no figure was specified. So, we used that version to display a warning. If you do not need the base class version, use so-called *pure virtual functions*.

A pure virtual function is declared in a base class in the form

    virtual *type function-name* **(***list of parameters***)=0;**

The **=0** tells the compiler, that it is a pure virtual function. All other declaration components are the same as for the regular virtual function. A pure virtual function has no definition in its base class. This is why all derived classes must define their own version of a pure virtual function. Otherwise, the computer reports an error. A class having at least one pure virtual function is called an *abstract*. If you declare a pure virtual member function in a class, there can be no objects of that class. This means, you cannot define any objects of that class. That class can be used only as a base class for the derived classes. It is logically reasonable, because you cannot have an object of a class, in which one or more functions have no definitions. However, one can still declare the pointers to that abstract class data type. Those pointers are needed to support run-time polymorphism. Consider following program.

```
#include <iostream.h>

class Bas
{
public:
virtual void disp ( ) =0;
} ;

class Der1 : public Bas
{
public:

void disp ( ) { cout << "This is the first derived class"
                    << " function.\n"; }

} ;

class Der2 : public Bas
{
public:
```

```
void disp ( ) { cout << "This is the second derived"
                     << " class function.\n"; }

} ;


void main ( )
{
Bas *pr;
Der1 obd1;
Der2 obd2;
pr=&obd1;    //assigning the pointer to the Der1 object
pr->disp ( );
pr=&obd2;    //assigning the pointer to the Der2 object
pr->disp ( );
}
```

Program 15.9.

The output of the program is

    This is the first derived class function.
    This is the second derived class function.

We declare pure virtual function **disp()** in the base class **Bas**. As you know, it has to be defined in every derived class, that inherits the class containing pure virtual function. We define that pure virtual function **disp()** in both classes **Der1** and **Der2**. We do not define any object of **Bas** class. Doing so could lead to an error, because one cannot declare an object of an abstract class. The **Bas** class is an abstract class, because it contains the pure virtual function without definition. The **Der1** and **Der2** classes declare and define their versions of the virtual function **disp()**. We, however, declare pointer **pr** of the **Bas** class.

15.7. Virtual destructors.

A class hierarchy and polymorphism can lead to some problems, when dealing with the objects, that allocate dynamic memory. When you destroy an object in the hierarchy by applying the **delete** operator to a base class pointer, the destructor function of the base class is called. Unfortunately, it happens regardless to which derived class object the base class pointer points to at that moment. This can cause an error.

The way to go in this case is to declare the destructor of a base class as virtual. It is a rule in C++: if a base class destructor is virtual, all the derived class destructors become virtual as well. Now, when you destroy an object in the hierarchy by applying the **delete** operator to a base class pointer that points to a derived class objects, the computer calls a derived class destructor for that object. The base class destructor runs right after that class destructor. Why? Because the base class part of the derived class is still destroyed by its own destructor.

EXERCISES.

1. Run all examples of this chapter, if you have an access to a computer facility.
2. Write a program described in exercise 2 of previous chapter. Use virtual functions.
3. Write a program described in exercise 3 of previous chapter. Use virtual functions.
4. A company has different employees. The engineers receive their salary. The technicians are paid hourly. The sales people are paid their salary, plus they receive a commission from the sold product. Develop classes for those employees. Use inheritance and polymorphism. Your program should compute bi-weekly income of each employee.
5. Develop a program, that controls electric energy, heat and water distribution on a plant. A plant has four departments. The heat consumption by each department is proportional to a temperature outside the plant and the size of the department. The electric energy consumption is proportional to the number of working machine-tools in each department. Besides, part of the electric energy is consumed by the lights. The consumption of the electricity by the lights is proportional to a size of a particular department. The water consumption is proportional to the number of working machine-tools, and the number of working people in each department. Use inheritance and polymorphism in this program. You can complete the missing details and write the program in the most suitable for you way.
6. Write a program that processes the measurements and estimates an error. There will be following classes in the program. Class **Measur** reads 5 measuremtns x_n of the same physical quantity **x**. The class **Ave** computes and displays the average of those measurements equal to

$$= \sum_{n=1}^{5} \frac{x_n}{5} .$$

The class **RMS** computes

$$\sigma = \sqrt{\frac{\sum_{n=1}^{5} (x_n - \mu)^2}{5}} .$$

It is very important in error estimation. Use inheritance and virtual functions.
7. Write a program that uses inheritance and polymorphism on some practical example.

CHAPTER 16

TEMPLATES AND EXCEPTION HANDLING.

16.1. Function templates.

Sometimes, one has to perform identical operations on different data types. This can be significantly simplified using *function templates*, that have recently been introduced to C++. It might not be supported by some older compilers. Sometimes, the function templates are called *generic functions*. Those functions perform the same operation on different data types. The data types on which those functions will operate in a program depend on the data types of the arguments passed to them during invocation. For instance, you want to sort an array. You can use the same algorithm. You can have the arrays of different data types. So, you can write a sorting function. What data type gets sorted would depend on what type of an array is passed to the sorting function, when it is called. This chapter finalizes your knowledge of templates introduced in Chapter 5.

You know, that one must define the data types of the returned values and the formal parameters in any function prototype. A function template uses chosen by you words instead of the data types. When that function is called to carry out its action, C++ automatically generates a function with the arguments of the needed type. One cannot declare and, then, define a template function. It can only be defined. Naturally, as for the regular functions, the definition header is treated as its declaration. To create a function template you must do following two steps.

The first step is to begin the function template definition with the line

```
template <class name1, class name2...>
```

Here, the **name1**, **name2** and so on are just any identifiers you wish to choose. Each of those chosen by you names will be used instead of the data type. Those names are just the placeholders for the data type. The actual data types will replace those names, when a function is invoked. The second step is to write the normal function definition inserting **name1**, **name2** instead of the data types for the return value and the formal parameters. Those **name1**, **name2** and so on are called *generic data types*.

One can face two cases in writing the function templates. First, all the formal parameters and returned by the function value can have the same data type. Second, the data types of the returned value and/or the formal parameters can be different. This means, that, in general, the function parameters can have different data types. Also, the returned by the generic function value can have the same data type as one or more of its parameters. The data type of the returned value can differ from the data types of any function's parameters.

Let's consider the first case, when the returned value and the formal parameters of a function have the same data type. You write the function definition inserting only one name for the types of the returned value and the parameters. If you put only one name (identifier) before each parameter and before the function name, this should tell the computer, that they all have the same data type. For example,

```
template <class mine>
mine func (mine x1, mine x2, mine x3)
  {  /* function definition */ }
```

We defined the function **func()** with three parameters in the above fragment. We have chosen the name **mine** for the generic data type. It is inserted in the places, where you would expect to find the data types. The word **mine** used before the function name **func** specifies the type of the returned value. The word **mine** preceding each of the parameters **x1**, **x2**, **x3** specifies their data types. Since it is only one word, this signals to computer, that they all should have the same data type. Those templates are called *the functions with one generic type*. What data type? It will be determined by the computer at the time, when you call this function for execution. When this function is called to perform an action on the integers, for instance, your computer would substitute the word **mine** by the data type **int**. So, if you call this function as

```
func (10, 20);
```

it will perform an action on the integers and return an integer value. But if you call it as

```
func (10, 20.5);
```

it will generate an error. Why? The first argument is an integer, but the second one is a floating-point value. The types of the arguments are different. And we used one word to specify all the arguments. The mismatch in the argument types confuses the computer and leads to an error message.

Consider a practical example, where we use only one data type. From the geometry, if you draw a vector from the beginning of the coordinate system, its length will be equal to

$\sqrt{x^2 + y^2 + z^2}$, where **x**, **y** and **z** are the coordinates of its end. We present a program, that finds a square of its length.

```
#include <iostream.h>
template <class DA>
DA ssum (DA x, DA y, DA z)
{ return (x*x+y*y+z*z);   }

void main ( )
{
int a, b, c;
float q=2.5, w=3.5, e=4.5;
cout << "Enter integral coordinates of the vector\n";
cin >> a;
cin >> b;
cin >> c;
cout << "The result for the int coordinates is "
```

```
    << ssum (a, b, c) << ".\n" << "The result for the float"
    << " coordinates is " << ssum (q, w, e) << ".\n";
 }
```

Program 16.1.

The program prompts a user to enter coordinates. We enter **2 3 4 ENTER**, it displays
```
    The result for the int coordinates is 29.
    The result for the float coordinates is 38.75.
```
Pay attention, how we begin the function template definition
```
    template <class DA>
```
This form specifies the beginning of the template for the computer. It also introduces an identifier **DA**, that will be used as a placeholder. We use **DA** to substitute a data type. It can be any type, but all the arguments and the returned value shell be of the same data type. We call generic function **ssum()** twice. First time the parameters of the template function **ssum()** and its returned value have **int** data type, because we invoke it with the integral arguments **ssum(a, b, c)**. Second time we invoke it with the floating-point arguments. The results of both calculations are displayed by the program. Try to call it with different data type arguments, and the error message will be displayed.

Now, we can consider the case, when there are different data types in one template. The template functions of that type are called the functions with *multiple generic types*. You handle them very simple. You define the template with the different data types in the same way as a template with one data type. You use dissimilar words for different data types. For instance,
```
    template <class mine, class yours, class another>
    another func (mine x1, another x2, yours x3)
    {  /* function definition */ }
```
Each of the words still remains a placeholder for a data type. But we have three different type identifiers here: **mine**, **yours**, **another**. This signals to the computer, that there will possibly be three distinct data types in the **func()** function. You can invoke this function with the arguments
```
    func (3, 2.51, 'p');
```
The computer will "assume", that **mine** corresponds to **int**, **another** to **float**, and **yours** to **char**. Since the types of the returned by the function value and the second parameter **x2** have the same placeholder **another**, they are assumed to have the same data type. The second parameter accepts the **float** type value in our example. Therefore, the returned by the function value will also have **float** data type.

A case of function template with different data types has one interesting feature. It is supported by a number of compilers. Remember, you could not use different data types in the templates with one generic type. But you can use the same data type in the functions with multiple generic data types. Let's return to our **func()** function above. It can be called with the arguments
```
    func ( 3, 5, 'p');
```
Here, the first and the second parameters are substituted by the values of **int** data type, even though different generic types **mine** and **another** are used for the first and the second parameter. When a generic function is called, any instance of the same generic

word inside the function is substituted by the same data type. For example, type **int** replaces the word **another** of the parameter **x2**. The word **another** will be replaced by the **int** type everywhere in the function **func()**. So, if that function returns a value of **another** generic type, it will now have an **int** type. One can even call the function with multiple generic parameters passing the arguments of one data type to it, as

```
    func (2, 3, 4);
```
Consider following example of templates with multiple generic types.

```
    #include <iostream.h>
    template <class DA, class DAA>
    DAA multi (DAA x, DA y)
    { return (x*y); }

    void main ( )
    {
    int a=3;
    double b=9.234;
    cout << multi (b, a);
    }
```
Program 16.2.

The output of this program is the number 27.702. The function **multi()** has been defined as a template. Its formal parameters and the returned value can have up to two data types **DAA** and **DA**. Those two names are just the identifiers. They can be replaced by any data type. We use **DAA** and **DA** to specify to the compiler, that we can call this function with the arguments of two different data types.

  Since we call **multi(b, a)** and **b** is of type **double**, the returned value shell be of **double** type. This happens, because we define the **multi()** function with the returned value and the first parameter **x** to be of the same **DAA** data type. The compiler understands, that the returned value has the same type as the first argument, and returns the result as **double**. If you call the function as **multi(a, b)**, the function will return the number 27, which is an integer value. This happens, because now the first argument **a** has **int** data type. This determines the data type of the returned value.

16.2. Generic function overloading.

  Is it possible to overload a generic function? The answer is - yes. One can overload it in a few ways. One can overload generic function by writing its versions with different number of parameters. It is illustrated below.

```
    #include <iostream.h>
    template <class DA>
    DA ssum (DA x, DA y, DA z)
    { return (x*x+y*y+z*z);   }
```

```
template <class DA>
DA ssum (DA x, DA y)
{ return (x*x+y*y);   }

void main ( )
{
int a, b, c;
cout << "Enter coordinates of the vector\n";
cin >> a;
cin >> b;
cin >> c;
cout << "The result for three int coordinates is "
     << ssum (a, b, c) << ".\n"
     << "The result for two int coordinates is "
     << ssum (a, b) << ".\n";
}
```

Program 16.3.

The program prompts the user to enter the coordinates of a vector. We enter **2 3 4**. The output of the program is

```
The result for three int coordinates is 29.
The result for two int coordinates is 13.
```

We have overloaded the generic function **ssum()**. One version has three parameters. Another one has two parameters. We call the function twice in the above program. The first call passes three arguments to the function. The compiler invokes a three parameter version of the template function. We also demonstrate the two parameter version by calling **ssum(a, b)** with two arguments.

One can overload a generic function in another way. The definition of the generic function includes the placeholders, that become the data types, when the function is called. One can overload a template function by writing one of its versions for some particular argument types. Consider following program.

```
#include <iostream.h>
template <class DA>
DA ssum (DA x, DA y, DA z)
{ return (x*x+y*y+z*z);   }

float ssum (float x, float y, float z)
{
cout << "\nThis is the floating-point version. "
     << " The result is: " ;
return (x*x+y*y+z*z);
}

void main ( )
```

```
{
int a=3, b=4, c=5, d;
float q=5.5, w=6.4, e=7.2;
d=ssum (a, b, c);
cout << "The result for int is: ";
cout << d;
cout << ssum (q, w, e) << ".\n";
}
```

Program 16.4.

The output of the program is

```
The result for int is:  50.
This is the floating-point version. The result is:
123.049995
```

Here, the generic function **ssum()** has been defined for a generic data type. But we have also rewritten it for the **float** data type arguments and returned value. The **ssum()** version for the **float** type arguments contains the message, that identifies it

```
cout << "\nThis is the floating-point version. "
         << " The result is: " ;
```

This is how we can determine, when this particular version is invoked. We call the **ssum()** function twice from **main()** routine. The first call **ssum(a, b, c)** passes the integers to the function. It invokes a regular template function. We call the same function with the floating-point arguments by the **ssum(q, w, e)**. If you look at the second output message, it belongs to the floating-point version of the **ssum()** function. Hence, both function versions can be called, depending on the type of parameters, if you redefine the template function for any particular parameter data type.

16.3. Generic classes.

So far, we have discussed the generic functions, also called the template functions. C++ permits to define a generic class (sometimes called template class). Imagine an array of any data type. It can be an aray of characters, or an array of integers, or floating-point values. You specify the operations on that array, arranging those operations and the array as the members of a class. The data type of some of the class members can be determined when a class object is used. It will depend on what data type elements will be placed in that array. The operations on that array can be performed by the template classes, or, in other words, by the generic classes.

The generic class declaration begins with the following form:

```
template <class name1, class name2...> class class-name
{
class declaration
}
```

The **name1**, **name2**, etc., are the identifiers. As in the case of a function template, they are the placeholders for the data types for generic classes. The very data types will be assigned during the call. Here, the ***class-name*** stands for the name of the declared class. You define an object of a generic class using form

```
class-name <type1, type2, type3...> object;
```

Regularly you define an object specifying its ***class-name***. In the case of generic classes, one should also specify the actual data types to substitute the placeholders. And those data types are listed in the <>, as we illustrated in the above form.

16.3.1. Classes with one generic data type.

There can be generic (or so called template) classes with one data type and multiple data types. We will first consider the generic classes with one data type. They are illustrated by the following program. The program declares a class, that provides an I/O for a generic array. The type of the array elements is determined by the data type of the read array. The program simply assigns the values to the member array elements, and, then, displays them. We illustrate two cases of I/O. First time, the character array is placed into a member array and read from it. We also place into a member array and display the floating-point numbers. This illustrates, that any data type elements can be handled by a generic class. The program also shows how to write the generic functions, that are generic class members. Although **Program 16.5** seems too long, but it is pretty easy. We will go over its code right after the program.

```
#include <iostream.h>                      //line 1
template <class mine> class Data           //line 2
{                                          //line 3
mine arr[10];                              //line 4
int n, m;                                  //line 5
public:                                    //line 6
Data ( ) { n=-1, m=0; }                    //line 7
void d_ent( mine q);                       //line 8
mine disp ( );                             //line 9
void show ( );                             //line 10
} ;                                        //line 11

template <class mine > void Data <mine> :: d_ent( mine q)
                                           //line 12
{                                          //line 13
if  (n<10)                                 //line 14
{                                          //line 15
n++;                                       //line 16
arr[n]=q;                                  //line 17
}                                          //line 18
else                                       //line 19
cout << "Array element is out of array space.\n" ;//line 20
}                                          //line 21
```

```
template <class mine > void Data <mine> :: show( )//line 22
{                                       //line 23
while (m<=n && arr[m] != '\0')          //line 24
{                                       //line 25
m++;                                    //line 26
cout << arr[m-1] << ", ";               //line 27
}                                       //line 28
cout << "\n";                           //line 29
m=0;                                    //line 30
};                                      //line 31

template <class mine > mine Data <mine> :: disp( )
                                        //line 32
{                                       //line 33
if (m<=n && arr[m] != '\0')             //line 34
{                                       //line 35
m++;                                    //line 36
return arr[m-1];                        //line 37
}   }                                   //line 38

void main ( )                           //line 39
{                                       //line 40
char row[ ]="testing";                  //line 41
float el[ ]={1, 3, 5, 7, 9};            //line 42
Data <float> ob1;                       //line 43
Data <char> ob2;                        //line 44
for (int dig=0; dig<5; dig++)           //line 45
ob1.d_ent (el[dig]);                    //line 46
for (dig=0; dig<8; dig++)               //line 47
ob2.d_ent (row[dig]);                   //line 48
ob1.show ( );                           //line 49
ob2.show ( );                           //line 50
for (dig=0; dig<5; dig++)               //line 51
cout << ob1.disp ( ) ;                  //line 52
cout <<"\n";                            //line 53
for (dig=0; dig<8; dig++)               //line 54
cout << ob2.disp ( );                   //line 55
}                                       //line 56
```

Program 16.5.

The output of the program is
```
1, 3, 5, 7, 9
t, e, s, t, i, n, g
13579
testing
```

The program declares generic class **Data** at lines 2-11. We use the word **mine** for the generic data type. That class contains generic type array **arr[10]** and integers **n, m**, as its data members. There are three member functions in the **Data** class. They are: **d_ent()**, **disp()** and **show()**. The **disp()** function returns a generic data type. The **d_ent()** function has a generic parameter. Therefore, a generic class can contain regular and generic members. The type of the generic class members will be specified by an object of that class type. The generic class declaration is similar to a regular one. You just use the word specified for a generic type to declare generic members of the class. After template class declaration, one must define its member functions.

Our program demonstrates how to write regular and generic member function for a generic class. The **d_ent()** function has generic type parameter **q**. It is declared inside the class as

```
    void d_ent( mine q);                    //line 8
```
The definition of that function is written at lines 12-21. It simply places the value passed to its parameter into the corresponding member array element by

```
    arr[n]=q;                               //line 17
```
The function uses the class data member **n** to access the array elements. Every time you call **d_ent( )**, it increments the value of **n** accessing the next array element. If you call this function 10 times, it will assign the values to all 10 array elements. It also checks, if the accessed array element is within the boundaries of the array. In other words, it simply checks, if one does not try to access the 11-th and greater elements. The function returns no value, because it has **void** return type. It definition header is

```
    template <class mine > void Data <mine> :: d_ent( mine q)
```
Definition of any class template function should begin with the form

```
    template <class ...>
```
In our case it is

```
    template <class mine>
```
This form is followed by the function return type. Our **d_ent()** function has **void** returned value data type. The type of the returned value should be followed by the class name and the generic types list in the **<>** braces. Our function definition header has **Data <mine>**. It is followed by the scope resolution operator **::**, the function name and the list of its parameters with the data types. Our function is **d_ent(mine q)**. All these elements are necessary, when you define a member function of the template class outside of that class. But, as you know, one can combine a declaration and a definition of a member function. If **d_ent()** function body were shorter, we could have declared and defined it at line 8. It could have looked as

```
    void d_ent( mine q) {........}          //line 8
```
The **show()** member function of **Data** class is declared at line 10 and defined at lines 22-31. It simply displays all the elements of the **arr** member array on the screen. Its definition header should be clear to us at this point. The function has no parameters and **void** return type.

```
    template <class mine > void Data <mine> :: show( )
```
The **disp()** function of our **Data** class is declared at line 9 and defined at lines 32-38. It accesses an array element and returns its value. Therefore, it must have a generic data return type **mine**.

```
template <class mine > mine Data <mine> :: disp( )
```
Our class **Data** is used in **main()** function at lines 39-56. We declare two arrays at lines 41, 42. The **row[]** is a character string, and **el[]** is an array of floating-point values. We also define two objects of class **Data** type.

```
Data <float> ob1;                           //line 43
Data <char> ob2;                            //line 44
```
Each of them will have a different data type generic class members. Object **ob1** has the **<float>** type generic class members. This means, that the word **mine** will represent a **float** data type. It will be substituted as a data type for the **arr[]** class data member and the functions **disp()**, **d_ent()**. The **ob2** object will handle **char** data type. It will become the type of all the template members of this object.

You can see, the objects of the template classes have a special declaration form. The objects of the template classes can be declared with or without initializers, as regular class objects. They should specify the data type, that will substitute the generic data type. This substitution is specified in the **<>**.

Lines 45-56 of **Program 16.5** code perform the input/output of different data types. We use the loops to enter the floating-point numbers by **ob1.d_ent(el[dig])**. The characters are entered by means of **ob2.d_ent(row[dig])**. Depending on an object, the same class functions are used to enter the characters and floating-point values. We, then, illustrate the output of different data types.

We offer you below a version of the same program, that determines what data type to enter by communicating with a user. It asks the user, whether the entered data will be the floating-point values or the characters. Based on the user's response, it selects between the **ob1** and **ob2**, that handle floating-point values and the characters respectively. Each of those objects can read and display corresponding to it data type. A user selects, which of these objects to put to work. The program below differs from the previous program only by some parts of the **main()** function. It should not be a problem for you to go over it.

```
#include <iostream.h>
template <class mine> class Data
{
mine arr[10];
int n, m;
public:
Data ( ) { n=-1, m=0; }
void d_ent( mine q);
mine disp ( );
void show ( );
} ;

template <class mine > void Data <mine> :: d_ent( mine q)
{
if (n<10)
{
n++;
```

```
arr[n]=q;
}
else
cout << "Array element is out of array space.\n" ;
}

template <class mine > void Data <mine> :: show( )
{
while (m<=n && arr[m] != '\0')
{
m++;
cout << arr[m-1] << ", ";
}
cout << "\n";
m=0;
};

template <class mine > mine Data <mine> :: disp( )
{
if (m<=n && arr[m] != '\0')
{
m++;
return arr[m-1];
}  }

void main ( )
{
char row[10];
float el[10];
int choice, p;
Data <float> ob1;
Data <char> ob2;
cout << "For floating-point numbers"
     << " type 0" << " for characters type 1.\n";
cin >>choice;
if (choice==0)
{
cout << "How many numbers to enter? Maximum is 9.\n";
cin >>p;
cout << "Enter " << p << " numbers and hit ENTER, or "
     << "hit ENTER after each entry.\n";
for (int k=0; k<p; k++)
cin >> el[k];
for (int dig=0; dig<k; dig++)
ob1.d_ent (el[dig]);
```

```
ob1.show ( );
for (dig=0; dig<k; dig++)
cout << ob1.disp ( ) << ", " ;
cout <<"\n";
}
else
{
cout << " Enter a word up to 10 characters.\n";
cin >>row;
for (int dig=0; dig<9; dig++)
ob2.d_ent (row[dig]);
ob2.show ( );
} }
```

Program 16.6.

The program first prompts the user

For floating-point numbers type 0 for characters type 1.
Depending on what number you enter, it, then, asks you to enter either the numbers or the characters. Whatever you enter gets displayed on the screen.

16.3.2. Classes with a number of generic data types.

A template class can contain a number of generic types. You declare the classes with multiple generic types and their members similar to the classes with one generic data type. All the generic data types are listed in **<>**, separated by the comma. The program below demonstrates it.

```
#include <iostream.h>
template <class My1, class My2> class Data
{
My1 x;
My2 y;
public:
Data (My1 a, My2 b) { x=a, y=b; }
void show ( );
} ;
template <class My1, class My2>
void Data <class My1, class My2> :: show ( )
{
cout << "x is - " << x << ", y is - " << y << "\n";
}

void main ( )
{
```

```
Data <char, float> ob1 ('q', 2.123);
Data < int, char *> ob2 (100, " it's unbelievable");
ob1.show ( );
ob2.show ( );
}
```

Program 16.7.

The output of the program is

```
x is -q, y is - 2.123
x is - 100, y is - it's unbelievable
```

The program declares class **Data**, that contains two data members **x**, **y**, and one function member **show()**. The constructor function is defined explicitly. Each of the data members has its own generic data type. The template class has two generic data types - **My1** and **My2**. The **show()** member function definition header must look familiar to you

```
template <class My1, class My2>
void Data <class My1, class My2> :: show ( )
```

It contains the same fragments as the functions in template classes with one generic type. We have two generic data types in the braces **<class My1, class My2>**.

We use that template class in the **main()** function. There, we define two objects **ob1** and **ob2**, that specify a real type of each generic type. Since the class constructor has the parameters, each object should be defined with the initializers. The object definition form is also familiar to us. For instance,

```
Data <char, float> ob1 ('q', 2.123);
```

specifies the **My1** to be a **char** data type. The **My2** becomes **float**. Each of them can be of any data type. They can even be the character strings. It is illustrated in the definition of the second object.

```
Data < int, char *> ob2 (100, " it's unbelievable");
```

Here, the second data type was specified as **char***. It indicates a string of characters.

Our particular example presents to you the objects, that must have the initializers in their definition. For example, **ob1('q', 2.123)**. You can create template classes, in which the constructor does not have the parameters. Their objects do not require the initializers when you define them.

16.4. Exception handling.

The exception handling is a recent feature introduced to C++. Some of your compilers might not have it. It is a very powerful tool, that allows you to catch the problems in the programs. We will first consider the form of exception throwing. We will, then, consider how to use it, and what does it do.

The exception handling construction consists of a few parts. It looks similar to

```
try {
//try block code fragment
}
catch (type1 name1)
```

```
{
//catch code fragment
}
...
catch (typeN   nameN)
{
//catch code fragment
}
```

The exception handling construction consists of one **try** block followed by any number of **catch** blocks. The **try** block can contain any code fragment. That block begins with the word **try** and an opening **{** bracket. It is terminated by the closing **}** bracket. The **try** block is followed by one or more **catch** blocks. Those **catch** blocks belong to that **try** block. Each **catch** block has an optional parameter. The body of each **catch** block is surrounded by the **{}** brackets. Block **try** contains a special **throw** statement. The **throw** statement is written in the form

```
throw exception;
```

The **try** block, usually, contains a **throw** statement. Keep in mind, each **try** block is followed by a number of **catch** blocks each having an optional parameter. When **throw** statement is executed, the program leaves the **try** block and looks for associated **catch** block with the parameter type matching the *exception* type in **throw**. If the program finds a **catch** block with the parameter type matching the data type of the *exception*, that **catch** block gets executed completely. The **catch** block parameter receives its value from the *exception*. Programmers say, that the **throw** statement throws an exception, that is caught by the proper exception handler. The **catch** blocks are called the *exception handlers* or *exception catchers*. What can be an *exception*? It can be an object, a variable, an array, a string and so on.

After the proper **catch** block is executed, the program continues its execution with the first statement after all the **catch** blocks, that are associated with the same **try** block. If the thrown exception does not match the data types of the parameters in any of the associated with it **catch** blocks, the program looks for any other **catch** blocks, even if they are associated with another **try**. If no match if found in the program, the program calls **terminate**, that calls **abort()** function. It terminates the program.

We will illustrate the exception handling by the following program.

```
#include <iostream.h>
void main ( )
{
int m, k;
cout << "Enter two integers a and b, that can divide a:b"
     << " without a remainder.\n";
cin >> m;
cin >> k;
char word[ ]="You have made an error.\n";
try
{
```

```
if (m%k>0)
throw word;
cout << "You have entered right numbers.\n";
}
catch ( char *rec)
{
cout << "An exception catcher has been activated.\n"
     << rec;
}
cout << "The execution of the program proceeds.\n";
}
```
Program 16.8.

The program first prompts the user to enter two numbers displaying the message
```
Enter two integers a and b, that can divide a:b without a
remainder.
```
For example, we enter the numbers 6 and 3. The output of the program is
```
You have entered right numbers.
The execution of the program proceeds.
```
If we enter 6 and 4, the output is
```
An exception catcher has been activated.
You have made an error.
The execution of the program proceeds.
```
Our **Program 16.8** has one **try** and one **catch** block inside the **main()** function. The **catch** block is associated with that **try** block, because it immediately follows the **try** block. The program activates the exception thrower, when the first of two entered by the user values cannot be evenly divided by the second value.
```
if (m%k>0)        throw word;
```
You, as a programmer, decide when to throw an exception. Therefore, you can impose any condition. When we enter 6 and 3, everything goes fine. The **try** block gets executed completely. Its **throw** statement is not executed. The computer skips the **catch** block, and executes the first statement after it. It happens to be a **cout** object, that displays the message
```
The execution of the program proceeds.
```
Now, we enter 6 and 4. They cannot be divided without a remainder. The **throw** statement is executed. Now the program looks for the **catch** block, that has a parameter of the same data type as the thrown exception. Our exception is a character string **word**. Our **catch** block has a parameter
```
catch ( char *rec)
```
Hence, it will be executed. The content of the **word** is passed to that parameter. Our **catch** block displays the error message.

An exception can be also thrown from a statement outside the **try** block. But that **throw** function should be a statement in a function, that is called from a **try** block. We have rewritten our program to demonstrate this case of exception throwing.

```cpp
#include <iostream.h>

void test (float s, float p)
{
char word[ ]="You have made an error.\n";
if (s%p>0)
throw word;
}

void main ( )
{
float m, k;
cout << "Enter two values a and b, that can divide a:b"
     << " without a remainder.\n";
cin >> m;
cin >> k;
try
{
test (m, k);
cout << "You have entered right numbers.\n";
}
catch ( char *rec)
{
cout << "An exception catcher has been activated.\n"
     << rec;
}
cout << "The execution of the program proceeds.\n";
}
```

Program 16.9.

This program has the same output as the previous one. The condition in the **try** block is now performed by the **test()** function, which is called from within that **try** block. Now, the **test()** function throws an exception.

The exception handling can be a separate function. In this case, every time that function is called, a new exception can be thrown. It is illustrated by the following program.

```cpp
#include <iostream.h>

void test (int s, int p)
{
char word[ ]="You have made an error.\n";
try
{
if (s%p>0)
throw word;
```

```
cout << "You have entered right numbers.\n";
}

catch ( char *rec)
{
cout << "An exception catcher has been activated.\n"
     << rec;
} }

void main ( )
{
float m, k;
cout << "Enter two values a and b, that can divide a:b"
     << " without a remainder.\n";
cin >> m;
cin >> k;
test (m, k);
cout << "The execution of the program proceeds.\n";
}
```

Program 16.10.

This program has the same output as previous two programs. Here, the exception handling is done by the **test()** function, called when the exception handling is needed.

16.5. Exception handling options.

Sometimes, a programmer wants a catcher to catch any exceptions rather than a certain data type. In this case, the exception handler must contain the ellipsis as its parameter.

```
catch (...)
{
//catcher's body
}
```

will catch any thrown data type exception. The ellipsis would tell the computer, that any data type exception can be handled by this catcher. And the exception will start the execution of the **catch** block with ellipsis. Consider following program.

```
#include <iostream.h>

void test (int s, int p)
{
char word[ ]="You have made an error.\n";
try
{
if (s%p==0) throw 1;
```

```
if (s%p>0 && s%p <5) throw word;
if (s%p>5) throw 5.123;
cout << "You have entered right numbers.\n";
}

catch ( char *rec)
{
cout << "A character exception catcher has been"
     << " activated.\n" << rec;
}

catch (...)
{
cout << "A general catcher has been activated.\n";
}

void main ( )
{
float m, k;
cout << "Enter two values a and b, I will divide a:b.\n";
cin >> m;
cin >> k;
test (m, k);
cout << "The execution of the program proceeds.\n";
}
```
Program 16.11.

This program prompts you to enter two numbers. The exception handler is implemented as the **test()** function. Depending on the remainder, different data types are thrown to the catcher. There are two catchers in the program. The first one **catch(char *rec)** catches only the character strings. The second one **catch(...)** catches any data types. Since the character string catcher precedes the all type catcher, the thrown string exception will be caught by the **catch(char *rec)** exception handler. The other exceptions will be handled by the second handler.

An exception handler can perform any operation you need. There is one limitation. You cannot use the objects defined in the **try** block in an exception handler. Those objects are destroyed, when the program leaves the **try** block to go to the catcher.

16.6. Exception restrictions.

If you call a function from the **try** block, the types of thrown exceptions can be limited. You can prevent that function from throwing certain exception types and even from throwing the exceptions at all. The general form of that function definition is

   return-type function-name (*parameters*) **throw** (*types*)

```
{
//body of the function
}
```

The form is called an *exception specification*. It contains the **throw** used with the parentheses. We wrote *types* inside the parentheses. One can write any number of different data types inside these parentheses. Only one condition - each data type must be separated by a comma, as the regular parameters in a regular function.

But this form is not a regular function. And it serves to a different purpose. The parameters inside the parentheses denote the data types, that can be thrown as an exception from the function, whose name is specified. In our case, it is *function-name()*. It is, sometimes, called a *throw (or exception) list*. For instance, you specify

```
int fun(int a, float b) throw (float, mine, char);
```

The throw list of the **fun()** function is **(float, mine, char)**. Let's say, you intend to throw an exception in the **fun()** function. That exception will be thrown only if it has **float**, **mine** or **char** data types. The **mine** data type is obviously some derived data type. For instance, it can be a structure or class. Our function can throw an exception of this type and *the types derived from it*.

If you write a function without any exception specification, it can throw any exception. To write a function without an exception specification means to declare it regularly without the word **throw()**. We have done it in the previous sections of this chapter. But if you declare a function as is specified in this section, you introduce the exception specification. If you specify the parameters in **throw()**, those will be the types of exceptions, that can be thrown. If you write an exception specification with an empty exception list, that function can throw no exceptions at all. So, the function

```
int fun(int a, float b) throw ( );
```

can throw no exceptions. What if you write an exception specification and throw an unspecified exception. You would expect it to be treated as an error. However, it is not likely to be treated as an error by your compiler. If an unspecified exception is thrown, a compiler is more likely to generate a call to its **unexpected()** function.

To illustrate exception specifications, we will consider following program.

```
#include <iostream.h>

void test (int s, int p) throw (int, char*, float)
{
char word[ ]="You have made an error.\n";
if (s%p==0) throw 1;
if (s%p>0 && s%p <5) throw word;
if (s%p>5) throw 5.123;
}

void main ( )
{
float m, k;
cout << "Enter two values a and b, that can divide a:b"
```

```
                << " without a remainder.\n";
    cin >> m;
    cin >> k;
    try
    {
    test (m, k);
    cout << "You have entered right numbers.\n";
    }

    catch ( char *rec)
    {
    cout << "A character exception catcher has been"
            << " activated.\n" << rec;
    }

    catch (int w)
    {
    cout << "An int catcher has been activated.\n";
    }

    catch (float c)
    {
    cout << "An int catcher has been activated.\n";
    }

    cout << "The execution of the program proceeds.\n";
    }
```

Program 16.12.

The **test()** function called from the **try** block can throw the exceptions of only **int**, **char***, and **float** data types, because the definition header of that function is

```
    void test (float s, float p) throw (int, char float)
```

16.7. Exception rethrowing. Applications of exceptions.

Sometimes, when an exception is caught by the catcher, it is necessary to throw an exception again. It happens, when we want another catcher to do some other action. In this case, the **catch** block should contain the **throw** statement without any exceptions. It is called to *rethrow an exception*. The call from the **try** block activates the corresponding exception handler. The exception handler may, in turn, throw another exception. The rethrown exception cannot be handled by the same catcher. It is handled by the first **catch** block of the next **try**.

An exception throwing can be used, if some error is detected in a constructor. For instance, a constructor tries to allocate a space for an object, and it fails. A constructor cannot return a value. Therefore, it cannot inform a program about occurred problem. There are ways around it. One of the logical ways to warn about an error would be to throw an exception. The exception can tell the program, that an error has occurred in a constructor. It is also possible to throw an exception from a destructor.

Inheritance can bring more capabilities to the exception throwing. It can also cause the problems. If **catch** can catch an exception of a base class type, it is capable to catch an exception of a class derived from that base class or its derived classes.

EXERCISES.

1. Run all the programs of this chapter, if you have an access to a computer facility.

2. Write the programs, that verify the following statements:
 - all the objects created in the block, from which an exception is thrown, are destroyed when an exception is thrown from that block;
  - the order in which the exception handlers are written is important, because the first matching handler will be executed;

3. Write a program that reads a line of characters and throws an exception, when it encounters the words "**do it**". The exception handler displays the message
```
Can't handle it. Have a nice day.
```

4. Write a program that creates an object. The object contains a data member, that stores a floating-point number. It can be only positive. An object is created with the initializers. The program must throw an exception, when an object with a negative data member is created. It should display a message and terminate the program execution.

5. Write a program that rethrows an exception.

6. Write a program, that throws an exception. Invent a case, when an exception is thrown. The program contains a function, that specifies what exceptions can be thrown.

7. Write a program that leads to an error caused by inheritance. You program must catch an exception of some base class. This should make the program to throw an exception erroneously because of an object of a derived class.

8. Write a program, that throws an exception from a destructor of an object used in a deeply nested function call.

CHAPTER 17

C STYLE INPUT AND OUTPUT.

C++ inherited a rich Standard Library from C. Here, we will study the input/output capabilities that have come from C. They are implemented in C standard library. We will discuss most of the following macros in this chapter:

BUFSIZ	**clearerr**	**EOF**	**fclose**
fflush	**feof**	**ferror**	**fgetc**
fgetpos	**fgets**	**FILE**	**FILENAME_MAX**
fopen	**FOPEN_MAX**	**fpos_t**	**fprintf**
fputc	**fputs**	**fread**	**freopen**
fscanf	**fseek**	**fsetpos**	**ftell**
fwrite	**getc**	**getchar**	**gets**
_IOLBF	**_IOFBF**	**_IONBF**	**L_tmpnam**
NULL	**perror**	**printf**	**putc**
putchar	**puts**	**remove**	**rename**
rewind	**scanf**	**SEEK_CUR**	**SEEK_END**
SEEK_SET	**setbuf**	**setvbuf**	**size_t**
sprintf	**sscanf**	**stderr**	**stdin**
stdout	**tmpfile**	**TMP_MAX**	**tmpnam**
ungetc	**vfprintf**	**vprintf**	**vsprintf**

They are specified in the **stdio.h** standard library file. In order to use any of given in those columns macros or functions, one should include **stdio.h** standard library file

```
#include <stdio.h>
```

It is better to do it in the beginning of the program outside of any given routine, as we have discussed. The file **<stdio.h>** will act within the source file, in which it is included. Almost all of those macros are used in the input/output operations.

The input/output is conducted in two distinct ways: buffered file input/output called formatted or high-level, unbuffered file input/output called unformatted or binary. The first way is used to read or write ASCII character files, for instance, texts. The second way is used for handling binary data. The ANSI standard, however, does not define the unbuffered file I/O expanding instead the definition of the buffered systems. We will discuss all the features of those two systems, because of their widespread use. Some C compilers might provide additional I/O routines, that are compiler specific and are not discussed in this book.

17.1. Introduction to file input/output.

So, far we have dealt with the input/output from the console, i.e., keyboard and the screen. Here, we introduce the disk filing system functions, which allow to create, read and write the information to/from the files on a hard disk. The console functions are a special case of input/output functions. We will begin with the file input/output and proceed to other input/output operations. Functions, handling those disk files are divided into two levels: *high-level* and *low-level* functions.

High-level functions provide a more manageable access to the disk files than low-level functions. High-level functions call low-level functions during execution. High-level functions are easier to use, and portable (computer system independent). Files accessed with the high-level functions are sometimes called *streams*. Most of the high-level I/O functions are specified in the ANSI C Standard library. The high-level functions are:

file handling functions: `fsopen()`, `fclose()`, `fcloseall()`, `fdopen()`, `fflush()`, `fopen()`, `freopen()`, `setbuf()`, `setvbuf()`, `remove()`, `rename()`, `tmpnam()`, `tmpfile()`.

character I/O functions: `fgetc()`, `fgetchar()`, `fgets()`, `fputchar()`, `fputc()`, `fputs()`, `fread()`, `fwrite()`, `getc()`, `getchar()`, `gets()`, `putc()`, `putchar()`, `puts()`, `ungetc()`.

formatted I/O functions: `printf()`, `scanf()`, `sprintf()`, `sscanf()`, `vfprintf()`, `vprintf()`, `vsprintf()`.

file positioning and error functions: `clearerr()`, `feof()`, `ferror()`, `perror()`, `fgetpos()`, `fseek()`, `fsetpos()`, `ftell()`, `rewind()`.

The low-level functions are operating-system-dependent. They are not specified in the standard library. However, they are pretty much similar from a compiler to a compiler. They typically access a disk sector at a time. Low-level files are manipulated with a number called *file descriptor*. Some of the low-level functions are `close`, `creat`, `dup`, `dup2`, `eof`, `lseek`, `open`, `read`, `sopen`, `tell`, `unlink`, `write`.

One cannot use high- and low-level functions together. For instance, if you open a file with high-level function, you can not use low-level functions on this file. If you want to use low-level functions on it, close it and open it again using low-level function.

Before continuing our discussion, we want to introduce a concept of a *stream*. It is associated with a sequence of bytes flowing into (input) or flowing out (output) of the program. Your data can be coming from the keyboard, disk file, a modem or some peripheral (interface) device. You can send the data to the screen, disk file, printer or a modem. So, peripherals and files are called streams in C and C++. A stream, therefore, can be understood as a logical device with which a program performs input/output. If you read a book, the information is transferred from the book to your head. Similarly, the I/O should be to or from a file or some other logical device. Therefore, a stream is always associated with that device or file. All devices or files, to which the information is transferred, might differ in their properties, but the streams have similar properties. What does it mean? The streams handle the ways of accessing different files and devices. Some files might be accessed differently, but the user does not have to know that. A programmer just writes some similar commands, and does not worry about those differences. The stream should provide the input/output.

Sometimes, as we mentioned, the disk files are called the streams as well. It is somewhat misleading, but many authors use this term in relation to a file. The stream is, again, a logical device for performing I/O. When a file is opened, it is linked to a stream. Thus, it is ready for performing input/output operation. The file is severed from a stream, when it is closed. We will use the term stream calling the files, sometimes. But you should understand, what is really a stream.

There are two types of streams: text and binary. A text stream is used to handle a text, i.e., a textual information. It is just a sequence of characters, that might be ordered somehow. You can also change an order. They can be organized into lines, terminated by the newline character. Characters could be added, altered or deleted during input/output on different computer systems. This happens, because different computers write or read the data to or from the stream somewhat different. How a character would be entered into a file is implementation specific, i.e., it depends from a particular computer system. For instance, a newline character may get converted into a carriage return or line feed sequence.

Therefore, there might not be a one-to-one correspondence or mapping between the external and stream characters. The data inside and outside a stream can be equal, only if one tries to obey certain rules. Some of them are implementation dependent. But C standard specifies the conditions, under which the data would not be changed. They are: the data should consist only of printable characters, the control characters (such as horizontal tab, newline character and so on) should be immediately followed by a space character, the last character should be a newline character. Sometimes, the spaces after control characters get zapped. It depends on a particular computer.

The binary streams store the characters in the form of "1" and "0". Each character is transferred into its binary representation and stored that way. The characteristic feature of a binary file is, that it does not perform any character translations. It maps the characters one-to-one. Binary stream, however, can add some numbers of null ('\0') characters. It depends on a particular system.

One might not see any difference between the text and binary files. The characters are presented as "0" and "1" in the computer memory in both types of files. What is the difference? The text file might be structured as lines terminated by the new-line character. There is no maximum line length limitation for a stream. The last line does not have to be terminated by the newline character. Text files can change some characters. Binary files do not change any characters. There is an internal difference in accessing a file. You open a binary file as such. If you want to read a binary file, you should access it as a binary. A binary file can be opened and read by a text stream and vice versa, text file can be opened and read by a binary stream. We will study, how to open, manipulate and close each type of files.

17.2. Stream opening.

A file is linked to a stream, when it is opened. This link ends when it is closed. Before you can do anything with a file, it should be opened. One has to remember to close all the opened files at the end of program execution. The file opening procedure comes to writing two lines, for example,

```
FILE   *pointername;
....
pointername=fopen("filename", "mode");
```

Those two lines do not have to follow each other immediately, but the first line must precede the second one in a program.

The first line is a declaration of a pointer called *file pointer*. It is as if we declare a pointer to the data type **FILE**. The **pointername** in the first line stands for the name of that pointer. It can be any identifier. The **FILE** is just a special data type. It is sometimes called a *pseudo* type. A file can be accessed and manipulated by a pointer of that type. A pointer to **FILE** type is designated to hold a pointer to a file. Thus, you should use only pointers to **FILE** type to open, close and access the files.

The second line

```
pointername=fopen("filename", "mode");
```

opens that file. The function, that is used to open a file is called **fopen()**. It opens or in, some cases, creates the files. Each file is associated with a file pointer. The file pointer is the address of the file. It is also an address of the first character inside the file. The **fopen()** function opens or creates a file. It also returns a pointer to that file.

Why does it return a pointer? If a file is opened, you want to have a way to address this file. You want to call it somehow, so the compiler knows, when you want to access this file. C creators decided, that it should be done through the file pointers. And the **fopen()** function that opens a file, should return the address of that file. Therefore, **fopen()** function returns a pointer to **FILE** type to the opened or created file. If a file cannot be opened or created, it returns a special **NULL** pointer, whose value is defined in **<stdio.h>** file. The **NULL** pointer or zero address is reserved by the computer for some special circumstances. You will see throughout this book, it is widely used for signaling errors occurring during various function executions. It is used in different algorithms, to signal an end of something. The **NULL** pointer is described not only in **<stdio.h>** header file. It is also described in some other standard header files. You can write **NULL** pointer as 0.

We assigned returned by **fopen()** function pointer to a pointer to type **FILE** by

```
pointername=fopen("filename", "mode");
```

You will see soon, the **FILE** type is also used for *end-of-file* (**EOF**) character, that indicates the end of file (no more characters). The **FILE** type can represent an *error indicator* and *file position indicator*. The *file position indicator*, as you will see, allows you to move inside a file to read and write the characters at any position inside the file.

The **fopen()** function has two parameters: **filename** and **mode**. The **filename** is the name of the file to be opened. You can create a file to hold the data. Data file can be called any name. We prefer to use the extensions "**.d**" or "**.dat**". The compiler, usually, places this file in the same directory, where your project is, if you do not particularly specify the directory. An example of a file name is "**info.dat**". One can use a name of a file to be opened directly in the function, as "**info.dat**", for example. One can place a name of a file to be opened in a separate character string, and use a pointer to that string as the first argument for opening a file.

A file cannot be accessed without opening it. To open a file, you should specify, if it is opened for reading, writing, reading and writing, or appending data to the end. That is set by the **mode** argument. A file must be opened in a correct mode. For example, if a file is opened in *read* mode, you would not be able to write in it. The *write* mode might destroy any previous information, contained inside the file and write new data over the old information. If you want to append something to a file, choosing *write* mode could be crucial. The **mode** argument, in a sense, instructs the computer, what do you want to do with the opened file. The Table 17.1 contains the possible modes to be used to access the text files.

Table 17.1. Modes for opening a text file.

MODE	FILE OPENING ACTION
"r"	Opens a file accessible for reading. The data can only be read from this file. If the file does not exist, gives an error.
"w"	Opens a file accessible only for writing the data into it. If the file does not exist, creates a new file.
"a"	Opens a file only for appending information to its end. The data can be only added to the end. If the file does not exist, a new file is created.
"r+"	Opens a file accessible for both reading and writing. Shows an error in case, if the file does not exist.
"w+"	Opens a file accessible for both reading and writing. If the file does not exist, creates a new file.
"a+"	Opens a file for both appending information to the end of the file and reading from it. The data can be only added to the end of the file. If the file does not exist, a new file is created.

The same modes are applicable for accessing binary files. In case of binary files, letter **b** should be added to the mode. It becomes: "**rb**", "**wb**", "**ab**", "**r+b**" or "**rb+**", "**w+b**" or "**wb+**", "**a+b**" or "**ab+**". Here, the first letter shows the mode according to the Table 17.1. The letter **b** only specifies that it is a binary file. For instance, the mode **wb** opens a binary file accessible only for writing the data into it. If the file does not exist, a new file is created.

The synopsis of the **fopen()** function is

```
FILE *fopen (const char *filename, const char *mode);
```

We introduced the **fopen()** function to you at the beginning of the section. The function prototype demonstrates the data types of all the arguments. You can also see the type of returned data. We will give you the prototypes of all standard functions.

The file is closed with **fclose()** function. When one opens a file, its content is often copied to the RAM memory buffer. The **fclose()** function causes the data from this buffer to be written to the hard disk, and, then, closes the stream file. If one wants to access this file next time, it should be opened again. How does the computer find a file when it is opened again? The answer is - by its name. But when a file is opened, it is accessed by its pointer. The argument of the **fclose()** function is a file pointer returned by the **fopen()** function. This pointer indicates the address of the file to be closed. When you open a file with the **fopen()** function, it returns a pointer to that file. When you call the **fclose()** function with that pointer, it closes the file associated with its argument pointer. In other words, the computer closes the file associated with the location, specified by the argument of **fclose()** function. The **fclose()** function returns 0, if the file is properly closed, and -1 (or **EOF**) in case of any error. Its synopsis is

```
int    fclose (FILE *ptr)
```

Many computer systems do not require a file to be necessarily closed, because they close it automatically after program termination. But one should try to close unused files, to save the memory space. Besides, the maximum number of files, that could be opened at any time is limited. Also, if a file is not closed properly, you can lose the data. For instance, the data can be lost, if the power goes off, or one of the applications freezes and so on. Next program illustrates a file opening/closing procedure.

```
#include <stdio.h>

void main (void)
{
FILE *ptr;
if ((ptr = fopen( "info.dat","r") ) == NULL)
printf ("The file info.dat can't be opened.\n");
else
printf("The file info.dat has been opened.\n");
fclose (ptr);
}
```

Program 17.1.

The output of the program is

```
The file info.dat can't be opened.
```

Here we have demonstrated the procedure of opening the **info.dat** file. We introduced the **if-else** statement to check, if the file can be opened. The **if-else** statement checks, if the **fopen()** function returns the **NULL** value, which signals the failure to open a file. It is always a good idea to check for that. You should remember from the Table 17.1, that **"r"** and **"r+"** modes cannot create a new file, if it does not exist. We have not created a file with the name **info.dat** previously. Therefore, it cannot be opened by our program. All other options will create a new file if the file with the specified name is not found.

Consider another program illustrating the file opening and closure.

```
#include <stdio.h>

void main (void)
{
FILE *ptr;
static char name[ ]= "info.dat";
static char mo[ ]= "w";
int m;
if (( ptr = fopen( name, mo ) ) == NULL)
printf ("The file info.dat can't be opened.\n");
```

```
else
printf("The file info.dat has been opened.\n");
m=fclose (ptr);
if ( m==EOF)
printf("An error has occurred during the closure.\n");
else
printf("The file has been successully closed.\n");
}
```

Program 17.2.

The output of this program is

```
The file info.dat has been opened.
The file has been successully closed.
```

Program 17.2 is pretty much identical to the previous one, except couple features. Look at the opening of the file, that we called **info.dat**.

```
if (( ptr = fopen( name, mo ) ) == NULL)
```

The first argument of **fopen()** is not a name of that file. It is a pointer to a character string **name[]**, in which we placed the file's name.

```
static char name[ ]= "info.dat";
```

The second argument is the pointer to the character string **mo[]**, in which we placed the string specifying the opening mode. We wanted to demonstrate, that each or both of the arguments of the **fopen()** function can be the pointers to the character strings, containing the file name and the opening mode. We have chosen "**w**" opening mode. So, the file, specified by us, can be created.

We also demonstrated the closure of the file by the **fclose()** function. A file can be closed and checked, if the closure is completed. We perform it by

```
m=fclose (ptr);
if ( m==EOF)
printf("An error has occurred during the closure.\n");
else
printf("The file has been successully closed.\n");
```

In case, if any error has occurred during the closure procedure, the value of -1 will be returned by the **fclose()** function. The **if-else** statement will detect it, and the first message about the closure failure will be displayed. In case of successful closure, the second message will be displayed.

17.3. Additional information for file opening.

When you deal with the files, it is important to know, how many characters can one use for its name. This information is contained in **<stdio.h>** header file. The macro **FILENAME_MAX**, described in this header file, specifies the maximum size of an array of type **char** capable to hold the longest file name. In other words, the **FILENAME_MAX** is a constant number. This number tells, how many characters maximum (including string null-termination character) can one use to name a file. One can not change this number. It is given by the compiler. The constant just displays it for you. You could use it to specify the size of the string **name[FILENAME_MAX]**, in order to prevent using more characters for the file name than is allowed. To read this number one can write following.

```
#include <stdio.h>

main ( )
{
printf ("%d \n", FILENAME_MAX);
}
```

Program 17.3.

The output of this program was **80** for one of the compilers, that we have tried. Hence, we can use up to 80 characters to name a file. However, you can get another number.

Another feature is the macro **FOPEN_MAX**, which is also a number. This number shows the maximum number of files, that can be opened simultaneously. This number includes three standard I/O streams.

Three additional standard streams (files) are opened automatically by the computer, when you run a program. They can be addressed by the standard file pointers. Their names are also standard, and must be addressed, when needed.

```
FILE *stdin, *stdout, *stderr
```

Those three standard files are used: to input the data from the keyboard (**stdin**), to output the data to the screen (**stdout**) and to display an error (**stderr**). For instance, when we enter the characters from the keyboard, they are placed in the memory and, then, read from there. This place in memory or this stream is accessed by the standard pointer called **stdin**. Known to you **scanf()** function reads the data from the **stdin** stream. The **printf()** function displays the data to the **stdout** stream. There are some other standard streams. Table 17.2 shows five standard streams always open and available for input/output operation and the pointers to them. We will show you later in this chapter, how to handle some of them.

Table 17.2. Standard I/O streams.

POINTER NAME	DATA FLOW DEVICE
stdin	Standard input from the keyboard
stdout	Standard output to the screen
stderr	Standard error output coming to the screen
stdprn	Standard printer parallel port
stdaux	Standard auxiliary device serial port

One can also use **freopen()** function for stream opening. An example of writing it

```
pointername=freopen("filename", "mode", pr); where
FILE   * pointername;
```

The function synopsis is

```
FILE *freopen(const char *filename, const char *mode,
              FILE *pr);
```

It has three parameters. Two parameters **filename** and **mode** are the same as for the **fopen()** function. The third parameter **pr** is another stream pointer, or, as you have guessed, a pointer to some other stream file. This second file can be any of the five standard files or any other file, opened prior to call to the **reopen()** function. The **freopen()** function opens the file, whose name and mode are specified by the first two arguments, and associates it with that other stream file, pointed to by the third argument. Before opening any file, **freopen()** tries to close any file, that is currently associated or connected somehow with that other file, pointed to by **pr**. In given below example the second file is **stdout**. However, if **freopen()** cannot close any file associated with **stdout**, that failure is not reported, and the function proceeds with opening a file. The **freopen()** returns **NULL** in case, if a file cannot be opened. The function returns stream pointer **pr**, if it is successful. For instance, consider a program.

```
#include  <stdio.h>

void main (void)
{
FILE  *fpr;
printf ("You will see this message.\n");
if ((fpr=freopen ("info.dat", "w+", stdout)) == NULL)
printf ("Cannot open file.\n");
else
printf ("This phrase is put in your file.");
fclose (fpr);
printf ("The file is closed.\n");
   }
```

Program 17.4.

The output of the program on the screen is
    You will see this message.
We have created file **info.dat** previously, as you remember. If you open this file, you will see the message
    This phrase is put in your file.
  The program opens **info.dat** file by
    if ((fpr=freopen ("info.dat", "w+", stdout)) == NULL)
There are three arguments in this function call. The first two specify the file **info.dat** to be opened. The third argument is **stdout**, i.e., the file **info.dat** will be associated with the standard output **stdout**. We also check, if the file can be opened. If **fpr** is **NULL**, the function cannot open the file. The computer displays
    Cannot open file.
If the above message does not appear on the screen, everything has gone OK.
  This program explains the meaning of the association of **info.dat** with **stdout**. If the **info.dat** file is opened, the following line of code is executed
    printf ("This phrase is put in your file.");
One would expect to see this message on the screen. It is not displayed on the standard

output. Instead, it is written to the **info.dat** file. Thus, the I/O to or from the **stdout** is, in fact, performed on the **info.dat** file. This is what the **freopen()** does. The I/O to or from the file pointed to by the third argument is redirected to the file specified by the first two arguments. In other words, we access the file pointed to by the third argument. In our case it is **stdout**. We try to display a message using **printf()** function. But, instead of that, the **freopen()** function accesses the file specified in the first two arguments. In our case, the **printf()** function, instead of writing on the screen, wrote the message to the **info.dat** file. This is why we cannot see on the screen the message

```
    This phrase is put in your file.
```

It is written to the file. Our **freopen()** function redirected the standard stream.

We close the **info.dat** file. It is interesting, we do not see the message, that should be displayed by the next **printf()** function.

```
    fclose (fpr);
    printf ("The file is closed.\n");
```

The redirection specified by **freopen()** ends, when the program terminates. Here, we have closed the **info.dat** file, but the redirection still holds to the end of the program. We cannot write the message on the screen. It cannot be written to the file as well, because the file has been closed.

17.4. Character input/output functions.

Individual characters can be read from a file using following functions: **fgetc()**, **getc()**. One should remember to open the file to be read from in the correct mode, before any data could be accessed.

Before we consider any of those functions, we should dedicate couple words to a special character - **EOF**, called end-of-file. When the data is read from a file, we sooner or later come to the end of data, or to the last number or character in this file. There is nothing else in the file after that. If we attempt to go ahead and read the data beyond the last character, it might cause an error. This is why C and C++ have a capability to inform us about it, by putting a special flag at the end. Most of the I/O functions reading the data will return this special flag called **EOF** to indicate, when the end of a file is reached. The value of **EOF** is defined to be negative by the standard. It is equal to -1, although different compilers can use different values for that value.

We have introduced a notion of a *file position indicator*, sometimes, called *cursor*. The file pointer returned by the opening function points to the beginning of the file. The file position indicator is used to operate inside the file. It indicates the number of a position inside a file to be filled in or read.

Let's read a string

```
    " I want to understand C language. "
```

Read it helping yourself by moving your finger along this string from the beginning to the end. Now choose the letter "**w**" from the word "**want**". Move your finger to this letter. Something like that happens in the computer. Computer reads and writes a file letter by letter from the beginning to the end. Each letter is located at a certain position. For instance, the very "**w**" letter is located at the 4-th position from the beginning in our string above. Count it including spaces.

A stream is opened with a file pointer, which points to the beginning of a file. When you read or write to a file, it is like a computer follows for you with its "finger" position by position. This magic "finger" we called cursor or *file position indicator* or cursor. It is, loosely speaking, an offset in memory cells from a place in the memory, pointed to by your file pointer. A file pointer indicates the beginning of a file, which is its first cell. All other characters are accessed with respect to this point. If we set the cursor to the beginning of the string " **I want to understand C language.** ", and, then, increase it by 4, it would point to the letter "**w**" . Add 7 to the first position, for example, and it will be set to point to "**t**" in word "**want**" and so on.

Let's consider the **fgetc()** function. It reads a single character located at the current cursor position of an input stream file specified by the function's argument and advances the cursor by one position. Suppose, somebody read or wrote characters to the first five positions inside a file. Next **fgetc()** will read a character from the sixth position, and the file position indicator will be advanced by one position. It will be set to the seventh position. An example of writing the function is

```
a=fgetc (FILE *ptr);
```

Its parameter is a pointer to a file, from which the data must be read. Its synopsis is

```
int fgetc (FILE *ptr);
```

The **fgetc()** returns a character read from the file or **EOF**, if it reaches the end-of-file. The character is returned by the **fgetc()** without an extended sign, as a positive integer of **int** type. The **fgetc()** function is used to read the files, if the lines must be called a byte at a time, or for binary data files with variable length data records.

The **getc()** function reads a single character from a stream file pointed to by its argument, and returns it as an integer number without a sign. So, the type of returned value is an **int** as well. An example of writing the function is

```
a=getc (FILE  *ptr);
```

Its synopsis is

```
int  getc (FILE  *ptr);
```

Both **fgetc()** and **getc()** are two identical functions from the user's point of view. Although **getc()** is more likely to be implemented as a macro rather than a function in the standard library. Its argument should not be an expression.

The similar functions **fputc()** and **putc()** are used for writing a single character to a stream file. We will consider **fputc()** and everything written about it would be identical to **putc()**. It returns the character output as an unsigned integer. If the error is detected, **EOF** is returned. An example of writing the function is

```
a=fputc(z, pr); or fputc(z, pr);
```

It has two parameters. First one is **z** of **int** or **char** type. It is the variable, that stores a character to be written to a file. The first argument is the integer corresponding to a character. We already know, the characters are stored in the memory as binary numbers. You can enter a character as **char** variable. It can be an **int** variable. The **fputc()** function will write to a file a character corresponding to the integral value of its first argument. The **pr** is a pointer to a file to which the data is written. The synopsis of the function is

```
int fputc (int x, FILE  *ptr);
```

The **fputc()** writes the character stored in its first parameter to the current cursor position to the file specified by the second parameter **pr**. The function also advances the cursor to the next position. The **fputc()** returns the written character as an **int** type. Hence, we can get the integral value of the character. It can be converted to a character by printing it in **%c** format by **printf()** or **putchar()** functions. If any writing error occurs, the **EOF** is returned.

The **putc()** function is equivalent to **fputc()**, except it is rather implemented as a macro. Its argument should not be an expression.

Consider a program illustrating the use of character I/O functions.

```
#include  <stdio.h>                       /*line1*/

void main (void)                          /*line2*/
{                                         /*line3*/
int my_in, xa, n;                         /*line4*/
FILE *pq;                                 /*line5*/
pq= fopen("info.dat", "w");               /*line6*/
printf ("Enter 5 characters.\n");         /*line7*/
for (n=0; n<5; n++)                       /*line8*/
{                                         /*line9*/
my_in=getchar( );                         /*line10*/
xa = fputc( my_in, pq);                   /*line11*/
if(xa==EOF)                               /*line12*/
{                                         /*line13*/
printf("The error has occured.\n");       /*line14*/
n=5;                                      /*line15*/
}}                                        /*line16*/
fclose (pq);                              /*line17*/
pq= fopen("info.dat", "r");               /*line18*/
for (n=0; n<=5; n++)                      /*line19*/
{                                         /*line20*/
my_in= fgetc(pq);                         /*line21*/
if (my_in == EOF)                         /*line22*/
printf("\nThe end of file is reached.\n");   /*line23*/
else                                      /*line24*/
printf ("  %c  ", my_in);                 /*line25*/
}                                         /*line26*/
fclose (pq);                              /*line27*/
}                                         /*line28*/
```
Program 17.5.

The program prompts you to enter five characters. We enter **abcde**. Pay attention, that you have to enter all the characters and press **ENTER**. The output is
```
a   b   c   d   e
The end of file is reached.
```

This program, basically, opens the **info.dat** file, writes five characters to it, and closes that file. The file is opened again to read the characters from it. The read characters are displayed on the screen. The first five code lines begin the program, introduce all the variables and the file pointer. The **info.dat** file is opened by the code at line 6. The character input is performed by the **for** loop at lines 8-16.

A character is entered from the keyboard during each loop cycle using the assignment **my_in=getchar()** at line 10. Then, **my_in** is used in the **fputc(my_in, pq)** function at line 11. As you can see, the **fputc()** has two arguments, one is the variable **my_in** of **int** type, the second one is the file pointer **pq**. The **my_in** can have the **char** type. One can also take an advantage of function **fputc()**, returning a value, by assigning it to a variable

        xa = fputc(my_in, pq);
The value returned by **fputc()** is checked for the **EOF** by **if** statement at line 12. If we are getting back the **EOF**, this signals about an error and corresponding message is displayed by the **printf()** function at line 14. Line 15 sets the value of **n** to 5. We want to terminate the loop, if an error has occurred. We close our file with **fclose()** function at line 17. Why do we need to close the file? We want to start reading the file from the very first character, when we open it again. If we do not close the file and use the **fgetc()** function, it will read the sixth character. However, there are no other characters in the file after the fifth one.

We open the file again by the **fopen()** function at line 18. The content of the file is read by the **fgetc()** function inside the **for** loop.

        my_in= fgetc(pq);   /*line21*/
The returned by the function value is assigned to **my_in** and compared to the end of file. When there are no characters in the file, or a last character has been read, the **EOF** will be returned. We want to check for the end of file while reading the data. It is done by the **if-else** statement at lines 22-25. If **EOF** has not been reached, the computer displays the character read from the file. When the **EOF** is reached, the message about it is displayed by the **printf()** function at the line 23. After reading all the characters, the file is closed.

17.5. Continuation on character input/output.

Consider following program, which is very similar to the previous, and performs the same character I/O to and from the same file. It just operates with the string **my_in** and the pointer notation, while entering the characters into our file. We will not describe this program in details, because it is quite similar to the previous. We believe, it will be helpful, if you observe the data input performed in pointer notation.

```
#include  <stdio.h>

void main (void)
{
int  xa, n;
```

```
static char *my_in="abcde", *wq;
FILE *pq;
pq= fopen ("info.dat", "w");
printf ("Enter 5 characters.\n");
for (n=0; n<5; n++)
{
wq=&my_in[n];
xa = fputc(*(my_in+n), pq);
if(xa==EOF)
{
printf("The error has occured.\n");
n=5;
}}
fclose (pq);
pq= fopen("info.dat", "r");
for (n=0; n<=5; n++)
{
xa= fgetc(pq);
if (xa == EOF)
printf("\nThe end of file has been reached.\n");
else
printf (" %c ", xa);
}
fclose (pq);
}
```

Program 17.6.

This program has the same output as the previous one. Review the following **Program 17.7**. It shows, that the **putc()** function adds the characters to the end of the file, when it is opened in the "**a**" or "append" mode. If you open a file in the regular reading or writing mode, the cursor starts from the first position. If a file is opened in the append mode, the characters get added to the last character in the file.

```
#include  <stdio.h>

void main (void)
{
int my_in,xa, n;
FILE *pq;
pq= fopen("info.dat", "w");
printf ("Enter 10 characters.\n");
for (n=0; n<5; n++)
{
my_in=getchar( );
xa=fputc( my_in, pq);
```

```
}
fclose (pq);
pq= fopen("info.dat", "a");
for (n=0; n<5; n++)
{
my_in=getchar( );
xa=fputc( my_in, pq);
}
fclose (pq);
pq= fopen("info.dat", "r");
for (n=0; n<=10; n++)
{
my_in= fgetc(pq);
if (my_in == EOF)
printf("\nThe end of file is reached.\n");
else
printf ("  %c  ", my_in);
}
fclose (pq);
}
```

Program 17.7.

The program prompts to enter 10 characters. We enter **abcdeqwert**. The output is

```
a b c d e q w e r t
The end of the file is reached.
```

This program is very similar to **Program 17.5**, except here we open the same file three times. The file is opened in the writing mode for first time. Five characters are read from the keyboard and placed into the file. The file is, then, closed. The second time the file is opened in the "append" mode. Five more characters are written to the file. They are placed right after the last character, contained in this file. The file is closed again. The **info.dat** file is opened for the third time to read all ten characters.

We want to show how to write the characters to a file. Characters can be transferred from one file to another one by

```
test_in = fgetc (pq)
fputc (test_in, ga);
```

The first line gets a character from the file with the file pointer **pq** and assigns it to the **int** type variable **test_in**. The second line writes the value of this variable into the file with other file pointer **ga**. You can also use **x=fputc(test_in, ga)** format, if you want to check for **EOF** later. Both files should be opened and all the variables and pointers must be defined prior to that.

You can enter a character in a file directly. For instance, you enter a character in a file using a variable as

```
char ya='h';
...
fputc( ya, ga);   or another form is x= fputc( ya, ga);
```

Here, the variable **ya** is first declared and initialized. Then, its value is entered into the file with the file pointer **ga**. You can use a character as an argument of **fputc()** as

```
fputc( 'l', ga);
```

Let's also briefly generalize, what we know about **getchar()** and **putchar()** functions. Since we now understand the functions in general, we can talk about the returned values. We could not talk about them freely before.

The example of writing the **getchar()** function is

```
getchar (void); or getchar()
```

We can also use the returned value

x=getchar( ), where **c** is declared to have the **int** or **char** data types.

The synopsis of the function is

```
int getchar (void);
```

The function reads a character from the standard input (or the keyboard) at the current cursor position. It, then, advances the cursor by one position. The **getchar()** function returns the corresponding integral value of the read character or the **EOF** in case of errors.

The **getchar()** is similar to **fgetc()**. But it reads a character from the keyboard, i. e., from the **stdin** file. One could write **getchar()** as **fgetc(stdin)**.

An example of calling the **putchar()** function is

```
x=putchar (m); or putchar(m);
```

Where the argument **m** has **int** or **char** types. The function synopsis is

```
int putchar (int x);
```

It writes the character stored in the argument to the standard output (to the screen). The function returns the written character, or **EOF**, in case of error. The **putchar()** is equivalent to **fputc()** with **stdout** pointer as its second argument.

Consider following program as a short demonstration of both functions.

```
#include  <stdio.h>

void main (void)
{
int my_in, x='a';
my_in=putchar(x);
printf(" %c\n", my_in);
printf ("enter a character.\n");
my_in=getchar( );
printf("%c\n", my_in);
}
```

Program 17.8.

The program displays

    a a

It, then, prompts a user to enter a character. We enter **b**, it is displayed

    b

We will not discuss this program, because you shell be familiar with those functions by now.

17.6. String input/output functions.

Sometimes, it is more desirable to operate with larger portions of data, rather than individual characters. We shell consider the functions allowing to handle those text pieces.

The **fgets()** function prototype is

```
char  *fgets (char *row, int m, FILE *ptr);
```

The **fgets()** function reads a string from a stream file specified by the third parameter **ptr**, until either a '**\n**' or **EOF** character are encountered, or **m-1** characters have been read. The read characters are stored in the array, pointed to by the **row** parameter. A '**\0**' character is placed at the end of the string, as an end-of-string indicator. If you specify to read 10 characters, **fgets()** will read 9 and add '**\0**' to the end. So, the total will be 10 characters, as specified. Even though '**\n**' character terminates string reading, but it is retained in the string. So, the newline character '**\n**' is also included in the array. The newline character '**\n**' is not generated by the function automatically. It depends on the user to enter it. If no characters are read or the error is encountered, **fgets()** returns **NULL**. Otherwise, it returns the address of the array, which is its first argument. This returned pointer can be used to detect, if something went wrong.

Let's consider an example of **fgets()** function application.

```
#include <stdio.h>                    /*line1*/

void main (void)                      /*line2*/
{                                     /*line3*/
FILE    *pq;                          /*line4*/
char elem[20], *val;                  /*line5*/
int n, my_in;                         /*line6*/
pq= fopen ("info.dat", "w");          /*line7*/
printf ("Enter 37 characters.\n");    /*line8*/
for (n=0; n<37; n++)                  /*line9*/
{                                     /*line10*/
my_in=getchar( );                     /*line11*/
fputc( my_in, pq);                    /*line12*/
}                                     /*line13*/
fclose (pq);                          /*line14*/
pq=fopen("info.dat", "r");            /*line15*/
val=fgets(elem, 10, pq);              /*line16*/
if ( val ==NULL)                      /*line17*/
printf("reading error\n");            /*line18*/
else                                  /*line19*/
printf("string is : %s \n", elem);    /*line20*/
fclose ( pq );                        /*line21*/
}                                     /*line22*/
```

Program 17.9.

The program first prompts the user to enter 37 characters. We enter

```
A group consists of twenty students.
```

This phrase will be written to the **info.dat** file. The file will be closed and accessed again. Ten characters of that file will be displayed on the screen as

```
A group c
```

The first 14 lines of the code must be clear to you. They begin the program, introduce all the variables, array and the pointers. This code allows you to write a string to a file and close this file. We open the file again in the reading mode by the **fopen()** function at line 15. First 10 characters are read from the file by **fgets()** as

```
val =fgets(elem, 10, pq);
```

It has three arguments as one would expect: the array address **elem**, the number of characters to be read 10, and the file pointer **pq**. We took an advantage of assigning a pointer, returned by the **fgets()** function, to pointer **val** to the **char** type. The returned pointer is checked for **NULL** condition by the **if-else** statement at lines 17-20. If 10 characters have been placed into **elem** array, they will be displayed by

```
printf("string is : %s \n", elem);      /*line20*/
```

We close the file after that. We could have also written

```
fgets(elem, 10, pq);
```

This can also do the job, but you would not be able to check for an error.

The function **gets()** is analogous to **fgets()**, but has a few differences. The string is still read from a file and stored in an array. But **gets()** reads the data from the standard input, i.e., from **stdin** file. The **gets()** function reads the whole string, until the newline character '**\n**' or **EOF** are encountered. But it throws out the newline character. However, it automatically adds '**\0**' to the end of the copied to the array string. The **gets()** returns the address of that array or **NULL**, if an error occurred or no characters are stored in the file. Its synopsis is

```
char *gets (char *row);
```

Since the string is read from a standard file and no number of characters should be specified, the **gets()** function has only one parameter **row**. It is the address of the array, in which the string must be stored. Consider an example of how to use the function **gets()**.

```
char elem[40], *val;
val=gets(elem_array);
```

Here, we did not show the file opening procedure. You can see, the first line declares an array **elem[40]** of type **char** and pointer **val** to the same type. Second line shows the use of **gets()** function having one argument **elem** - the address of the array. We assigned the returned value to a pointer **val**. We can use its value, for instance, to check for **NULL** condition. One can also write the second line just as

```
fgets(elem_array);
```

However, this would prevent you from checking for an error.

We shell now consider how to write a string to a file. The **fputs()** performs this task. Its prototype is

```
int fputs (const char *row, FILE  *ptr);
```

The **fputs()** function writes a string of characters pointed to by **row** to a stream file pointed to by the file pointer **ptr**. It returns the last character written or **EOF** in case of error. The function does not add a newline character to the end of the string. If you need '**\n**' at the end, it should be entered into the array by you. Even though the **row** must be a null-terminated string, the '**\0**' character at its end is not put into the file.

The **puts()** function prototype is

```
int puts (const char *row);
```

It writes the string pointed to by its parameter **row** to the standard output (screen) file pointed to by **stdout**. It returns the last character or **EOF**, in case of error. It does not write '**\0**'. This character gets discarded. The character '**\n**' is appended to the end. An example of functions use is given in **Program 17.10**.

```
#include <stdio.h>

void main (void)
{
int n=12;
char row1[30], row2 [40];
FILE *ptr;
printf( "Enter up to 10 characters and press ENTER.\n");
scanf("%s", row1);
ptr = fopen ("info.dat", "w");
fputs (row1, ptr);
fclose (ptr);
ptr = fopen ("info.dat", "r");
fgets ( row2, n, ptr );
puts ( row2 ) ;
fclose ( ptr ) ;
}
```

Program 17.10.

The program prompts a user to enter up to ten characters. We enter **abcdefghij**. It will be read from the keyboard by the **scanf("%s", row1)** function and placed into the array **row1**. As you know, the **%s** adds the null-character to the end of the input.

We, then, open the **info.dat** file in the writing mode. The **fputs(row1, ptr)** function places the characters from the array **row1** into that file. The file is closed and opened, in order to access the first position inside it. The **fgets(row2, n, ptr)** function reads the string from the file and stores it in the array **row2**. The next line **puts(row2)** writes a string contained in **row2** array to the screen. Therefore, the same **abcdefghij** string gets displayed on the terminal screen.

The **ungetc()** function is written in the form

```
n=ungetc (x, ptr); or ungetc (x, ptr);
```

The function pushes back the character specified by its first parameter **x** to the file pointed to by its second parameter **ptr**. The function synopsis is

```
int  ungetc (int x, FILE *ptr);
```

The **ungetc()** function returns the character pushed back after conversion or **EOF** in the case of failure. We will review this function on the following example.

```
#include <stdio.h>                      /*line1*/

void main(void)                         /*line2*/
{                                       /*line3*/
static char row[ ]="abracadabra.";      /*line4*/
FILE *ptr;                              /*line5*/
int x;                                  /*line6*/
ptr = fopen ("info.dat", "w");          /*line7*/
fputs (row, ptr);                       /*line8*/
fclose (ptr);                           /*line9*/
ptr = fopen ("info.dat", "r");          /*line10*/
x=fgetc(ptr);                           /*line11*/
x=fgetc(ptr);                           /*line12*/
printf ("%c ", x);                      /*line13*/
x=fgetc(ptr);                           /*line14*/
printf ("%c ", x);                      /*line15*/
ungetc('w', ptr);                       /*line16*/
x='y';                                  /*line17*/
ungetc(x, ptr);                         /*line18*/
x=fgetc(ptr);                           /*line19*/
printf ("%c ", x);                      /*line20*/
x=fgetc(ptr);                           /*line21*/
printf ("%c ", x);                      /*line22*/
x=fgetc(ptr);                           /*line23*/
printf ("%c ", x);                      /*line24*/
fclose (ptr);                           /*line25*/
}                                       /*line26*/
```
Program 17.11.

The output of the program is

 b r y w a

Besides, the word **abrakadabra** is written to the file **info.dat**.

First nine lines of this program introduce all the variables, arrays and a file pointer. They open the **info.dat** file, write the word "**abracadabra**" to it, and close it. We open the **info.dat** file in the reading mode by the **fopen()** function at line 10.

We get three first characters from the file using **fgetc(ptr)** function and display the second and the third of those characters. Those two characters are "**b r**". This part of the code is implemented at the lines 11-15. From this point on, our program reviews the behaviour of the **ungetc()** function. Next three lines are

```
    ungetc('w', ptr);                       /*line16*/
    x='y';                                  /*line17*/
    ungetc(x, ptr);                         /*line18*/
```

Those three lines should push back two characters: '**w**' and '**y**'. One can push back a character, that is read from a file. The pushed-back character is not necessarily the one that we read. The standard requires any compiler to be able to do only one pushing back.

Many compilers perform more than one operation. We use three identical blocks

```
x=fgetc(ptr);                          /*line19*/
printf ("%c ", x);                     /*line20*/
```

to read the characters from the file and display them on the screen. As you remember, we have read 3 characters of the word "**abrakadabra**", before calling **ungetc()**. The file position indicator, therefore, has stopped at the fourth position. We have done two **ungetc( )** returning back two characters. When we read the file now, we get

```
y w a
```

We used this function two times to push back **w**, then **y**, and **x**. We can read those two characters only in the reversed order: first **y** and, then, **x**. Therefore, the characters, pushed back by the **ungetc()** function, are read in the order opposite to the order they have been pushed back. Only after we read those two pushed back characters, we can start reading again from the fourth position. This fourth character 'a' is read by the last **fgetc()** function. The function does not push back the **EOF**. An attempt to use any of the file positioning functions, such as studied later **fseek()**, **fsetpos()**, **rewind()**, undoes **ungetc()** operation and discards the character, that you have just pushed into the file.

17.7. Formatted input/output functions.

To format an input/output means to convert it to the desired type (**int**, **float**, **double** and so on) and present the data in the desired manner. Sometimes, the term *formatted I/O* is applied to the functions, that handle "human readable data". The formatted I/O is performed on an ASCII based text, rather than on binary files. We have learned **printf()** and **scanf()** as formatted console I/O functions. Here, we briefly repeat them again, and review some other functions. The input functions to be considered are **fscanf()**, **scanf()** and **sscanf()**. The output functions are **fprintf()** **sprintf()**, **vfprintf()**, **vprintf()**, and **vsprintf()**.

17.7.1. Formatted input functions.

The formatted input functions have a lot in common with each other. Consider it for yourself. The prototypes of all three functions are

```
int fscanf (FILE *ptr, const char *form, void *arg1,
            void *arg2...);
int sscanf (const char *row, const char *form,
            void *arg1, void *arg2...);
int  scanf (const char *form, void *arg1, void *arg2...);
```

All those three functions have in common is, that they read the data from some place and store it in their arguments (**void *arg1, void *arg2...**). Let's call any of those parameters **arg1, arg2...** a *storing argument*. They are the pointers to the buffers in the memory, where this read data should be placed. A buffer can be a variable, an array, a structure variable, etc. An input function can have a number of arguments. We have discussed it in connection with the **scanf()** function. For instance, **scanf("%d",**

&x) will store the read integral value in the cell with the address **&x**. We have shown, that the arguments are the pointers to type **void** in the prototypes of all three functions. You can cast those pointers to any data type. When the last storing argument gets the data, the functions terminate their action.

All three functions have the *format string* parameter, which is the pointer **form**. It describes the types and the formats of the data to be read. We will discuss it in a moment.

The functions differ by the places, from which they read the data. The **fscanf()** reads the data from a file (or stream). Its first parameter is a pointer **ptr** to that file. The **sscanf()** reads the data from another location (buffer) in memory. This buffer is a string array of type **char** for many compilers. Therefore, the **sscanf()** has a pointer to that **char** type array **row**, as its first parameter. The **scanf()** function, discussed earlier in this book, reads the data from the standard input file (keyboard). This file is accessed by the standard file pointer **stdin**. Since **stdin** is a standard file pointer, it can be skipped. This is why **scanf()** has two parameters. The **scanf()** can be also implemented using **fscanf()** as

```
fscanf (stdin,  form,  arg1, arg2);
```

Consider an example of writing the functions.

```
fscanf (ptr, "%d", &x); or n=fscanf (ptr, "%s", arr1);
sscanf (row, "%d", &x); or m=sscanf (row, "%s", arr1);
scanf ("%s", arr1); or k=scanf ("%d %s", &x, arr1);
```

We can assign the returned by each function value to some variable of **int** data type. We can do it, because each of those functions returns an integral number of input items. In case of failure, the **EOF**, zero or number less than the number of assigned input items is returned. One can use the returned value to check, if a function has succeeded. One can also check how many arguments have gotten their data if there are any doubts.

The *format string* **form** describes the way of reading the data from the input. Our discussion of a format string is applicable to all three input functions. A format string is a sequence of characters enclosed in the double quotation marks (**" "**). It can contain:

● White space characters, which might be any combinations of newlines, tabs and white spaces. They are ignored by the all three input scanning functions unless they are included inside square brackets.

● Letters, digits, and characters other than white space or **%**. It is called a *non-input format specification* and we will discuss it soon.

● A conversion code or so-called *input format specification* or *conversion specification field*. It specifies what data type will be read and what would be the format of the read data. The format specification field consists of a number of characters immediately following the **%** sign. We will study all possible format specifications below.

We have discussed the format strings and the format specification fields, when we studied the **printf()** and **scanf()** functions earlier in this book. Here, we will make our knowledge systematic. Now we can talk about **%** sign and all that follows it. It is the *input format specification field*. It consists of following parts:

```
%* [width] [conversion modifier] [conversion specifier]
```

Even though you see the braces in this notation, but we used them just to identify each component of *input format specification*. The symbols follow each other without the braces in the program. For example: **%*4s** or **%d**. Separate input format specification is used for each *argument*(*input field*). Each argument gets its own chunk of data. The data, that will be placed into one argument, is called an input field. In other words, separate **%*** [*width*][*conversion modifier*][*conversion specifier*] are used for each storing argument **arg1**, **arg2...**, in which the data is placed.

The percent sign **%** indicates the beginning of a format specification. It is followed by the optional assignment suppression operator *****. If this operator is present, the input field is skipped. In other words, the corresponding storing argument **arg1**, **arg2...** (array, variable, etc.) will not get its piece of the input string.

The number of the *input format specifications* should be equal to the number of storing arguments. If there are more storing arguments than format specifications in an input function, the extra storing arguments are ignored. If one used less arguments than *format specifications*, the situation might lead to an error. The *width* is just an integer number. It is optional and indicates a maximum number of characters, that will be read for corresponding storage argument. The *conversion modifiers* are also optional and are given in the Table 17.3. The conversion specifiers are given in the Table 17.4.

Table 17.3. The conversion modifiers.

Character	Description
h	Letter **h** can be used with **d**, **o**, **x** conversion specifiers described below. If used it specifies, that the corresponding storing argument is a pointer to a short decimal (**hd**), octal (**ho**) or hexadecimal (**hx**) data type variable.
l	When this character is used with the **d**, **o**, **x** conversion specifiers, it indicates, that the corresponding storing argument is a pointer to **long** type variable. If **l** is used with **e**, **f**, **g** conversion specifiers, the argument is a pointer to a **double** type variable.

17.7.2. Examples with formatted input functions.

We will consider a few examples.

```
#include <stdio.h>

void main (void)
{
static char a[ ]="Object-oriented programming.";
char b[20];
sscanf(a, "%s", b);
printf ("%s", b);
}
```

Program 17.12.

The output of this program is

```
Object-oriented
```
We used the **sscanf()** function with the **%s** format in **Program 17.12**. It reads a string, until the first white-space character is encountered. Hence, the **sscanf()** function reads only one word "**Object-oriented**" from the string array **a[]** and places it in **b[]**. We display the content of array **b[]** on the screen by the **printf()** function.

Table 17.4. The conversion specifiers.

Character	Used for following data type
d	Used for a decimal integer. Corresponding storing argument is a pointer to an **int**. Sometimes, an **i** character is used instead of **d**. It has same meaning as **d**.
u	The read data can be a signed decimal integer. Corresponding storing argument will be a pointer to **unsigned int** and it will be read as an unsigned. Can cause an error.
o	The data is an optionally signed octal integer (8 is the base). Corresponding storing argument is a pointer to **unsigned int**.
x	The data is an optionally signed hexadecimal integer. Its storing argument must be a pointer to an **unsigned int** variable.
e, f, g	The data is a floating-point value. Corresponding storing argument shell be a pointer to a **float** type variable.
F, G	Equivalent to **lf** and **le**. Corresponding storing argument is a pointer to a **double** type variable. Some compilers do not have those specifiers.
c	The value read is a character even if it is a white space character. Corresponding storing argument is a pointer to a **char** type variable.
s	Used for a character string. Reading begins with the first non-white space character and ends with the first white space character. A null (**\0**) character is added to the end of a string. Corresponding storing argument is a pointer to an array (string) of **char** type. It must have enough cells to accommodate the string plus null character.
p	Used to read a pointer to **void**. A storing argument shell be a pointer to a pointer to **void**. You might not have this option, and how does it work differs from compiler to compiler.
n	This option presumes no input data to be read. Corresponding storing argument shell be a pointer to an integer. The number of characters read from an input stream prior to function call with this specifier will be written to the corresponding storing argument.

Following example is similar to **Program 17.12**. It uses the width in the format specification field.

```
#include <stdio.h>

void main (void)
 {
```

```
static char a[ ]="Object-oriented programming.";
char b[20];
sscanf(a, "%6s", b);
printf ("%s", b);
}
```

Program 17.13.

The output of the program is
```
Object
```
We have specified to read only 6 characters by **%6s** in the format string of **sscanf()**
function. Therefore, only six first characters must be read from the output.
  We offer you another example.

```
#include <stdio.h>

void main (void)
{
static char a[ ]="it was 6";
int x;
sscanf(a, "it was %d", &x);
printf ("%d", x);
}
```

Program 17.14.

The output of this program is number 6. Here, we read an integral number from the string
a[] and place it into the cell, corresponding to the variable **x**.
  Program 17.14 demonstrates so-called *non-input format specification*. The format string
can contain some other characters, beside the format specification fields. Those other
characters are called *non-input format specification*. When the input function, that contains a set of characters in its format string, reads the data, it expects to read this set from
an input. For instance, the above program reads the data by the function
```
sscanf(a, "it was %d", &x);
```
The format string **"it was %d"** contains the words "**it was**". This is an example of
a non-input format specification. The computer expects to read those letters in exact order
from the input, before it gets to **%d**. The input stops and the input function terminates its
reading at the position, at which a first discrepancy occurs between the actual input and
the non-input format specification. The correspondence of the number of the white-space
characters in the input and the non-input format specification is ignored. Suppose, we
specify our string in **Program 17.14** as
```
static char a[ ]="it is 6";
```
  The input function will terminate, when it encounters letter "**i**" in the word "**is**",
because there is no such a letter in the format string **"it was %d"** of **sscanf()**. Our
function will never read the number. The read characters specified in non-input format
specification cannot be placed in a storing argument. They are used just to specify in what
part of the input string to expect a value to be read and stored. We specified, that the

integer to read will be at the very end by the format specification **%d** in our example. That character is recognized, the number is read and displayed.

One can have a number of the format specification fields in the same function, as well as a number of storing arguments. The data is assigned to the arguments in the order they follow. The first format specification field places the data into the first storing argument, the second format specification field copies the data to the second storing argument, the third format specification field - to the third storing argument and so on. When the data is copied to the last storing argument, an input function terminates its action at all. Now we know, the data input also stops, when a format string differs from an input string. The reading is terminated at the first position, on which the discrepancy occurs. It is illustrated by the couple additional examples.

```
#include <stdio.h>

void main (void)
{
static char a[]="First is 106, second is 49, third 9";
int x, y, z, k;
static char b[]="First is %d, second is %d, third is %d";
k=sscanf(a, b, &x, &y, &z);
printf ("%d, %d, %d, %d", x, y, z, k);
}
```
Program 17.15.

The output of the program is
    106, 49, 1794, 2.

Take a look at two strings **a[]** and **b[]**. The format string of **sscanf()** function is the string **b[]**. You see, it differs from the string **a[]** by the word '**is**' before the third number 9. The string **b[]** has it. The **a[]** string does not have it. When the first letter '**i**' of that word is encountered, the input will be terminated. This is why the function reads only two values 106 and 49. The third value 9 will not be read. This is what it means, that the input is terminated, when the first discrepancy between the input and the format strings occurs. The third output is just some meaningless number.

Program 17.15 also illustrates the returned by the **sscanf()** function value. It is assigned to **k** and displayed by the **printf()** function. Since, only two values were read and stored, it is equal to 2.

Following program illustrates the **fscanf()** and the non-input format specification.

```
#include <stdio.h>

void main (void)
{
static char a[ ]="The number 1234567891234";
int x;
FILE *pt;
```

```
pt=fopen("info.dat", "w");
fputs (a, pt);
fclose (pt);
pt=fopen("info.dat", "r");
fscanf(pt, "The number %4d", &x);
printf ("%d", x);
fclose (pt);
}
```

Program 17.16.

The output of the program is
```
1234
```
Besides, it writes the string
```
The number 1234567891234
```
to the file **info.dat**. We open the file **info.dat** twice. First time we write the string from the character string **a[]** to the file. The **info.dat** is opened for the second time in the reading mode. We read the integral value from the file by the
```
fscanf(pt, "The number %4d", &x);
```
The format string in the **fscanf()** looks very similar to the string inside the file. It has **%4d** format specification field. Here, the width is 4. It reads only four digits of the integral number **1234567891234**. We display **x** by the **printf()** function.

17.7.3. Exploring input functions.

Following program illustrates reading of the data type **double** from a file.

```
#include <stdio.h>

void main (void)
{
static char a[ ]="The number 12.345678912346789";
double x;
FILE *pt;
pt=fopen("my.dat", "w");
fputs (a, pt);
fclose (pt);
pt=fopen("my.dat", "r");
fscanf(pt, "The number %lf", &x);
printf ("%.14f", x);
fclose (pt);
}
```

Program 17.17.

The output is 12.345678912346789. The program also writes to **my.dat** file a string

```
    The number 12.345678912346789
```
Following program demonstrates the assignment suppression operator *.

```
#include <stdio.h>

void main (void)
{
static char a[ ]="The number 12345678912346789";
int x, y;
FILE *pt;
pt=fopen("my.dat", "w");
fputs (a, pt);
fclose (pt);
pt=fopen("my.dat", "r");
fscanf(pt, "The number %*4d %4d", &x, &y);
printf ("%d, %d", x, y);
fclose (pt);
}
```

Program 17.18.

The program output is
```
    5678, 0
```
If we have not used * operator in the first format specification, the value 1234 would have been assigned to **x**. The **y** would have gotten 5678. The output would have been
```
    1234, 5678
```
But the first format specification contains the assignment suppression operator *. This cases the value of **5678** to be assigned to **x**. The **y** does not receive any value at all.

We hope, you got the feeling of how to operate with the formatted input functions. You should expect, what type of data will be read. You should select the arguments of scanning functions to be the pointers to the same type. Do not be afraid of format specification fields. You should also select the conversion specifier, according to the type of the corresponding pointer argument and the data type to be read. If you intend to read **long**, **double** or **short** types, select the corresponding conversion modifier as well. When only a few positions should be read, select corresponding width.

The data input into each storing argument is stopped: when the number of positions corresponding to the widths for a particular argument is read, when the white space character following the data is encountered (except **%c** format), or when a different from a specified data type input is encountered.

If a width is not specified for a particular argument, the data is read, until a white space character or the data type different from specified by that format specification are encountered. A white space character always terminates the data input. Review next program.

```
#include <stdio.h>

void main (void)
```

```
{
static char a[ ]="The number 123   ";
int x;
sscanf(a, "The number %d", &x);
printf ("%d", x);
}
```
Program 17.19.

The output of the program is the number 123.

Here, the **sscanf(a, "The number %d", &x)** function reads the number 123. The **sscanf()** function recognizes the end of the number 123 by the white space character after it. One should be cautious in dealing with **%c** scanning format, which will read any character including a white space character. It will be terminated only after reading that one character.

An input is stopped, when a data type different from the one, specified by the format specification, is encountered. For example, consider the following program.

```
#include <stdio.h>

void main (void)
{
char a[ ]="The number 123end";
int x;
sscanf(a, "The number %d", &x);
printf ("%d", x);
}
```
Program 17.20.

The output of the program is the number 123. When this number is read, the letter 'e' is recognized as a different data type. Therefore, the data reading stops before this letter. This is why you read only the number 123 and nothing else. You should also remember, that any number of leading white spaces is ignored. The string **a[]** could have any number of any white spaces between "**number**" and "**123**" in **Program 17.20**. This would not prevent the **sscanf()** function from reading the value 123.

Following **Program 17.21** is similar to the previous. We just wanted to show, that the format string can be written according to its synopsis as
    sscanf(a, b, &x);
Here, **b** is a pointer to a string array, that contains the content of that format string.

```
#include <stdio.h>

void main (void)
{
static char a[ ]="The number 123end";
int x;
static char b[ ]="The number %d";
```

```
sscanf(a, b, &x);
printf ("%d", x);
}
```

Program 17.21.

The program output is the number 123.

17.7.4. Formatted output functions.

Functions **frintf()**, **printf()**, **sprintf()**, **vfprintf()**, **vprintf()** and
vsprintf() are used for the formatted output. The prototypes of all six functions are

```
int fprintf (FILE *ptr, const char *form, void arg1,
             void arg2...);
int printf (const char *form, void arg1, void arg2...);
int sprintf (char *row, const char *form, void arg1,
             void arg2...);
int vfprintf (FILE *ptr, const char *form, va_list arg);
int vprintf (const char *form, va_list arg);
int vsprintf (char *row, const char *form, va_list arg);
```

The second parameter of each function is the *format string* ***form**. The way in which the
data is written and its type is controlled by the format string. The **void arg1, void
arg2...** are called the *writing arguments*. They are the names of the variables and array
elements, although a pointer argument is used for the **%s** format specification.

The output functions perform following actions. The **fprintf()** function writes the
content of its writing arguments to the stream pointed to by the file pointer **ptr**. The
printf() function writes the content of its writing arguments to the standard output
file, (the monitor screen). Since the standard output stream is pointed to by **stdout**, one
can replace it by the **fprintf()** function written as

```
fprintf ( stdout," format string", arg1, arg2);
```

The **sprintf()** function writes the content of its writing arguments to a location in a
memory (buffer) pointed to by its first parameter **row**. That buffer is rather a string array
of type **char**. An extra null character is added to the end of a set of characters written to
that array.

Other three functions are equivalent to the first three except they use pointer to the
variable-length list of arguments as their writing arguments. You might want to skip those
functions, until you study **<stdarg.h>** header file of the Standard ANSI C library
functions. We will not discuss them in details.

A format string is pretty much analogous to that of the formatted input functions. It can
contain any characters and white spaces, that will be copied to the output. The white
spaces are not ignored. The output functions write the format string as is, except that the
escape characters will perform their actions and the format specification fields will be
substituted by the data. A format string also contains the *format specification fields*, as you
know. They, in fact, define how the data will be written. Each of those fields, for instance, **%4d** has the same general format

`%[`*conversion modifier*`][`*conversion specifier*`]`

It consists of:

- percentage sign **%**;

- optional *conversion modifiers*, that can follow the **%** sign. Modifiers provide some additional control on the data output. Table 17.5 gives them. One can use a few *conversion modifiers*, but they must be placed only in the order they follow in Table 17.5.

- the *conversion specifiers* that follow the *conversion modifiers*. The *conversion specifiers* are not optional. They determine, what is the type of data to be written. The *conversion specifiers* are given in Table 17.6.

Table 17.5. The conversion modifiers.

Modifier	Action caused by that conversion modifier
-	The data will be written as left-justified.
+	The values will be always written with the plus or minus sign.
#	Displays **0** or **0x** before octal and hexadecimal numbers respectively. For instance, **075** (octal), **0xc94** (hexadecimal). It displays floating-point numbers with the point, even if the fractional part is 0.
blank	No modifier specified.
0	The '**0**' should be placed before the field width. It displays the values written to the output with leading zeros and without blank spaces.
field width or *	The field width is an integer. For instance, in **%4d** the field width is 4. It specifies a number of characters to be written by a writing argument. If the converted value has fewer characters than the field width, the spaces will be added to the left to bring it to specified field width. If * is used instead of number, the width is contained in the argument.
. precision or *	Precision is an integer. It is preceded by a dot. For example, **.6**. One can use field width and precision for the same argument in one function. Precision shows the maximum number of characters to be copied to the output for the strings, when used with **s** conversion specifier. It also specifies the number of digits to appear after the decimal point, even if they are zeros for the **e**, **E**, **g**, **G** and **f** conversion specifiers. When used with **d**, **i**, **o**, **u**, **x** and **X**, precision indicates the number of digits to appear. Those values are padded with zeros to a specified precision. An asterisk * indicates, that the precision is specified in the argument.
h	Can be used with **d**, **i**, **o**, **u**, **x**, **X** specifiers. Indicates the argument and the copied data is converted to **short int** or **short unsigned int**.
L or **l**	Used for a **long** integer or **long double** writing argument.

Table 17.6. The conversion specifiers.

Character	Output format specified by that conversion character
c	Used for copying a single character to an output. Its writing argument is a variable name or an array element of **char**, **short** or **int** data type.
s	Used for a character string output. Terminates an output, when either **\0** is reached, or the number of characters specified by the precision has been written. An argument is a pointer to an array of **char** type.
d or i	Used to copy a signed **int** decimal number to an output. Writing argument is a variable name or array element of type **char** or **int**. With modifier **h** writing argument is converted to a **short int** type. If used with modifier **l** (as in **ld** or **li**) the argument must be **long**.
o	Used to copy a signed **int** octal number to an output. Writing argument is a variable or array element of type char or **int**. With modifier h the argument is converted to a **short int** octal number.
x	Used to copy a signed **int** hexadecimal number to an output. Writing argument is a variable or array element of type **char** or **int**. With modifier **h** the argument is **short int** type hexadecimal number.
u	Used to write an **unsigned int** decimal number to the output. The corresponding argument should be of the type **unsigned char**, or **unsigned int**, **unsigned short** when used with **h** (**hu**), **unsigned long int** when used with **l** (**lu**). The writing argument can be a name (not an address) of a variable or an array element.
e or E	Used to copy **float** or **double** value to an output as m.nnnnnne(-)xx. If no precision is specified, it writes up to 6 digits after a decimal point. Precision can change the number of digits after the decimal point. The part e(±)xx is the exponent. It means $10^{\pm xx}$. For instance, 986.92 is $9.869200 * 10^2$, or .00358 is $3.58 * 10^{-3}$ and so on. Writing argument is a variable or array element of type **float** or **double**.
f	Used for **float** or **double** decimal value. Writes them as m.nnnnnn. If no precision is specified, it writes only up to 6 digits after a decimal point. The writing argument is a variable or array element of type **float** or **double**. To write a number (for instance, 6) as a floating-point, you should add at least one digit after the point as 6.0. If precision is 0 and **#** flag is not specified, no decimal point is to appear.
g or G	It copies a value to the output in **f** or **e**, whichever format is shorter. Argument is a variable or array element of type **float** or **double**.
p	It is different from all the others. It is used to copy a pointer to **void** to an output. The writing argument is a pointer to **void**. The value of that pointer could be converted to a sequence of printable characters.
n	It displays the number of characters written to the output by the function containing this **%n**, prior to encountering this specifier. The writing argument is a pointer to an integer.
%	Used to copy the **%** to an output. An example of writing is **%%**.

17.7.5. Examples of formatted output functions.

Let's now consider a few examples of writing and reading functions. They will demonstrate how to use all those options given in the tables.

```
#include <stdio.h>

void main (void)
{
static char a[ ]="The average number is 30.45.";
char arr[50];
FILE *pt;
pt=fopen("my.dat", "w");
fprintf (pt, " It will be written:%s\n", a);
fclose (pt);
pt=fopen("my.dat", "r");
while ((fscanf(pt, "%s", arr)) !=EOF)
{
printf ("%s", arr);
printf (" ");
}
fclose (pt);
}
```

Program 17.22.

The output of the program is
    It will be written: The average number is 30.45.
   The program writes a formatted data into a file and reads it from that file. The file
my.dat is first opened in the writing mode. The **fprintf()** function writes its format
string **"It will be written:%s\n"** to the file. The format specification field gets
substituted by the string array **a[]**. Therefore, the message written to the file is: "**It
will be written: The average number is 30.45.**".
   The file is closed and opened again in the reading mode. We did it, because we want to
begin to read the string from the first cursor position. The string is read from the file by
the **fscanf()** function. There are white spaces after each word. We know, that the
white space character terminates the reading. Therefore, in order to read the whole phrase,
we set a **while** loop. The **fscanf()** function will read a new word every cycle, until
the end-of-file is encountered. And we check for the end-of-file using the returned value
of the **fscanf()** function. This value is the loop condition.
   The formatted input functions read and write the data to and from a file beginning from
the current cursor position. Consider following program.

```
#include <stdio.h>
```

```
void main (void)

{
static int a[ ]={30, 20, 10, 59, 43};
int x, y, z;
FILE *pt;
int n;
pt=fopen("my.dat", "w+");
for (n=0; n<5; n++)
{
fprintf (pt, "%d", a[n]);
fprintf (pt, "%c", ' ');
}
fclose (pt);
pt=fopen ("my.dat", "r");
fscanf(pt, "%d", &x);
printf ("%d ", x);
fscanf(pt, "%d", &y);
printf (" %d ", y);
fscanf(pt, "%d ", &z);
printf (" %d", z);
fclose (pt);
}
```

Program 17.23.

The output of the program is

    30 20 10

Besides, following sequence will be written to the **my.dat** file

    30 20 10 59 43

The program opens the **my.dat** file twice. First time it writes the array of integers **a[]** to it using **fprintf()** function inside the **for** loop. This part of the program is shown below

```
for (n=0; n<5; n++)
{
fprintf (pt, "%d", a[n]);
fprintf (pt, "%c", ' ');
}
```

There are two **fprintf()** functions inside the loop body. Each loop cycle writes one array element **a[n]** and one blank character. If we do not write a blank character every loop cycle, the numbers would be placed inside the file without any spaces between them. It would look like **3020105943**, and it would be impossible to read the values without a space between them with **fscanf(pt, "%d", &x)**. We would not be able to read the values, because one of the ways a scanning function determines the end of the read value is by the white space character. There are no white spaces between the values. In this case, we would have to specify the filed width, or the number of positions to be read per one value, as **fscanf(pt, "%2d", &x)**. Even though it will work in our case, but you might not know the correct number width in a real life. This is why we add white spaces between the numbers, while entering them.

   We reopen the file to read the data from it, because we intend to start from the first position. We use three **fscanf()** functions to read three values from the file. Pay attention, that the first function reads the first value, the second reads the second value and so on. You can see, the data is written and read to and from a file, beginning from the current cursor position. First **fscanf()** function reads the first value 30 and advances the cursor to the next value. This is why the second reading begins from the second value 20 and so on. We could have written a loop to output any number of values from the file. Following program demonstrates the string I/O.

```
#include <stdio.h>

void main (void)
{
static char a[ ]="abc";
char row[20] ;
int  n;
char x;
sprintf (row, "%s", a);
for (n=1; n<4; n++)
{
sscanf(row, "%c", &x);
printf ("%c ", x);
}
printf ("\n%s", row);
}
```
Program 17.24.

The output of the program is
```
   a a a
   abc
```
   The **sprintf(row, "%s", a)** function writes **a[]** to the string **row[]**. We, then, read characters from **row[]** three times by means of **sscanf(row, "%c", &x)** and display them on the screen. We get the character 'a' displayed three times. It is the first character of the string. We wanted to show, the reading with **sscanf()** always begins from the beginning of the strings. If we read a file with **fscanf()**, we would read consecutive characters. The strings are a bit different from the files in reading and writing the data. It is quite conceivable. The **sscanf()** and **sprintf()** functions use a pointer to an array as their first parameter. The pointer is the address of the first array element. Therefore, the reading and writing should begin from its first element.

17.8. Inside file manipulation functions.

Sometimes, one needs to select the data located on certain positions inside a file. For instance, we want to retrieve only the fifth, tenth and twelfth characters of some string inside a file. This is why one might need the tools to switch to different positions inside the file. So far, we have studied I/O functions, that can only read consecutive characters, i.e., following each other. After the data has been written to a file, we had to close and open it again to start reading from the first character. But there are functions, that allow to move to any position inside the file. Those functions are: **fseek()**, **fgetpos()**, **fsetpos()**, **ftell()** and **rewind()**.

The **fseek()** function moves the file position indicator to any location within a file. For instance, you have just read 20 positions inside the file, and you want to begin the next reading or writing from the 50-th position. This is done using **fseek()** function. This function sets the cursor to the required position and any writing or reading operation will begin from this position. The **fseek()** function prototype is

```
int fseek (FILE *ptr, long num, int start);
```

It has three parameters. The first parameter is a file pointer **ptr**, that is a pointer to the file for which the **fseek()** function will be used. The second parameter **num** is the offset. It tells how many positions the file position indicator should move from the starting point. The **num** can be a positive or negative number of **long** type. The starting point, or from where the offset will be counted, is determined by the third parameter **start**, which is the starting position. There are three standard starting points, and, therefore, the starting position can assume three states **SEEK_SET**, **SEEK_CUR** or **SEEK_END**. Each of the macros is just a number. Usually, **SEEK_SET**, **SEEK_CUR** or **SEEK_END** are equal to 0, 1, 2 respectively. Table 17.7 gives the starting point for each of those three macros.

Table 17.7. Starting positions for the **fseek()** function.

Starting position	The point from which the offset will be performed
SEEK_SET or **0**	beginning of the file
SEEK_CUR or **1**	current position
SEEK_END or **2**	the end of the file

The **fseek()** function sets the cursor of the file pointed to by its first parameter **ptr** to **num** position offset from the position specified by **start**. The next reading or writing from/to the file will start from a cursor position set by **fseek()**. One can write, for instance, two identical functions

```
fseek ( ptr, 20, SEEK_SET);   or   fseek ( ptr, 20, 0)
```

This will set the cursor to the 20th position from the beginning of the file. The function also returns 0 if successful, or a non-zero **int** value (often -1) or **EOF** in case of error.

This function can act differently on binary and text files. For a binary stream an offset can have any value, but some compilers do not support the **SEEK_END** value of the third argument. Before using **SEEK_END** as the third argument value check, if it works for your compiler. Create a binary file, fill it in with the data and see, if you can read this data correctly using this option. Text files can, sometimes, use the offset argument either equal

to 0 or equal to the value returned by the previously used on this stream **ftell()**
function. The third parameter of the **fseek()** function for the text files can accept only
SEEK_SET value on some compilers. Check your program for that to avoid crucial
errors. The **fseek()** clears the **EOF** for the stream, and undoes any action done by the
ungetc() function on the same stream. One can perform an input or output after
fseek(). Let's consider a few examples of using **fseek()**.

```
#include <stdio.h>

void main (void)
{
FILE  *qa;
static char line[ ]="This is a test.";
char x;
qa=fopen("my.dat", "w+");
fprintf(qa, "%s", line);
if ((fseek(qa, -4L, SEEK_END))!=EOF)
{
x=fgetc(qa);
printf ("%c", x);
}
else
printf ("error\n");
}
```

Program 17.25.

The output of the program is the letter **e**. It also writes a string of characters

  This is a test.

to the **my.dat** file. We begin the program with opening the **my.dat** file and writing the
line[] string into it. We, then, use the **fseek()** function to move 4 positions from the
end of the file. This will be the letter 'e' in the word '**test**'.

 Let's consider a few more examples.

  fseek (ptr, 3L, 0);

This will move the cursor to the third character after the first file character which is $1+3$
= 4th character. So, the next reading or writing to file following **fseek()** will start its
action from the 4-th character. It will be the letter '**s**' in the string '**This is a test.**'.
Consider next example.

  fseek (ptr, -10L, 2);

This will move the cursor to the tenth character before the end-of-file character. So, there
are 11 more positions including the **EOF** character in this file still to be read or written.
You should remember, the last byte of any file is followed by an extra **EOF** character for
the end-of-file indication. Thus, the next reading or writing function following **fseek()**,
will start its action from the 11-th character before the end. A call

  fseek (ptr, 0L, 2);

sets the file pointer to the **EOF** character, because the shift from **EOF** is 0.

The **rewind()** function resets the file position indicator (called shorter as cursor or file pointer) to the beginning of the file. The synopsis of the function is

```
void rewind (FILE  *ptr);
```

Its parameter **ptr** is a pointer to that file. Any writing or reading operation after that function will begin from the very first character. This function action is equivalent to

```
fseek ( ptr, 0L, 0);
```

The **rewind()** function has **void** return type. It returns no value. We demonstrate the application of this function in the program below.

```
#include <stdio.h>

void main (void)
{
FILE  *qa;
static char line[ ]="This is a test.";
char x;
qa=fopen("my.dat", "w+");
fprintf(qa, "%s", line);
rewind (qa);
x=fgetc(qa);
printf ("%c", x);
}
```

Program 17.26.

The output of the program is the letter **T**. We copy **line[]** string to the file **my.dat**. We use **rewind()**, and, then, read a character by the **fgetc()** function. It reads the first character '**T**'. Therefore, the cursor inside the file had been set to the first position by the **rewind()** function.

Let's talk about the **ftell()** function. Its synopsis is

```
long ftell (FILE *ptr);
```

The **ftell()** function acquires the current position of the file position indicator for the stream pointed to by its parameter **ptr**. It returns that current location of the file position indicator. So, one can assign it to any variable and get the data. This function can be used, if, for instance, you moved a lot inside a file, and do not know the current cursor position. The **ftell()** function returns a location of the file pointer as an offset in bytes from the beginning of the file. However, some systems do not give the offset in bytes. It can potentially cause portability problems. For a binary file the function returns the number of the characters from the beginning of the file. This is implemented in most compilers. The value returned by the **ftell()** function can be used as the second argument of **fseek()**. We demonstrate the use of the **ftell()** function on the following example.

```
#include <stdio.h>

void main (void)
{
```

```
FILE  *qa;
static char line[ ]="This is a test.";
long int x;
qa=fopen("my.dat", "w+");
fprintf(qa, "%s", line);
x=ftell(qa);
printf ("%ld", x);
}
```

Program 17.27.

The output of the program is 15. This is the number of characters from the beginning of the file returned by the **ftell()** function.

The **fgetpos()** function prototype is

```
int fgetpos (FILE *ptr, fpos_t  *ind);
```

The **fgetpos()** function places the current value under the cursor in the file pointed to by its first argument **ptr** in an object pointed to by its second argument **ind**.

As you see, the second argument is specified as a pointer to the data type **fpos_t**. The **fpos_t** is a special type of data. It is an integral number used with the variables, pointers and other objects, that specify a position within a file. One can copy the value defined by this type and pass it as an argument of a function, but no arithmetic operation can be performed on it.

The value stored in the **ind** argument of **fgetpos()** is used to set the **fsetpos()** function. The **fseek()** and **ftell()** can do pretty much the same job, but they might not be as reliable for some files, particularly large ones.

The **fgetpos()** returns zero, if successful. Non-zero is returned on failure and some implementation-defined positive value is stored in **errno**. You can read about **errno** in the next section.

The **fsetpos()** function prototype is

```
int  fsetpos (FILE *ptr, const fpos_t  *ind);
```

The **fsetpos()** sets the cursor of the stream pointed to by its first parameter **ptr** to a position specified by the value, retrieved from the object pointed to by its second parameter **ind**. One can not freely choose the value of the second argument. It should be obtained from the prior **fgetpos()** call for the same stream. Both **fgetpos()** and **fsetpos()** are meant to be used together. One should first use **fgetpos()** on a file. Current cursor position will be stored in a cell pointed to by its second argument.

17.9. Error functions.

Let's study standard error-handling functions: **clearerr()**, **feof()**, **ferror()**, **perror()**. C also uses a conventional variable **errno** for reporting the errors. It should be declared externally at the beginning of the program as

```
extern int errno;
```

This variable is called an *error indicator*. You do not have to assign any values to this variable. You just have to declare it. The compiler assigns values to this variable automatically. If an error occurres during the operations on a file, the error indicator **errno** will be set to ON and will remain ON. Once an error is encountered in a stream, all functions will return an error, until calls to **clearerr()** or **rewind()** are executed. This will reset the error flag to OFF, and will allow the program to proceed. The **clearerr()** function synopsis is

```
void  clearerr (FILE  *ptr);
```

Here, the **ptr** is a pointer to a file, in which an error has occurred. The **clearerr()** function has **void** return type. Therefore, it does not return any value.

The **feof()** function synopsis is

```
int  feof (FILE  *ptr);
```

where **ptr** is a file pointer. The **feof()** function tests for the **EOF** in a file pointed to by the **ptr**. The returned value has the **int** type. The **feof()** function returns a non-zero value, if **EOF** has been reached. Otherwise, 0 is returned. The **feof()** function is particularly useful, when working with binary files, because the **EOF** is a valid binary integer and can be misinterpreted. We advised you to use the returned values by some file I/O functions to test for the end-of-file. One should explicitly use **feof()** rather than test the return values of reading functions. For instance, it can be used instead of testing the **fgetc()** function to determine, when the **EOF** has been reached. The test for the **EOF** using **feof()** function can be written like

```
while (!feof (ptr) )
fgetc(ptr);...
```

The **ferror()** function synopsis is

```
int  ferror (FILE  *ptr);
```

Here, **ptr** is a file pointer. The **ferror()** function checks for any errors associated with the file, pointed to by its parameter **ptr**. If no error has occurred, 0 is returned. A nonzero value indicates an error. Just to remind, **ferror()** only tests for an error indicator, that stays ON, until **clearerr()** or, sometimes, **rewind()** are executed.

The **perror()** function synopsis is

```
void perror (const char *stpr);
```

Here, the **stpr** is a pointer to a string. The **perror()** function maps the error number of the **errno** expression to an error message. If **stpr** is not a null pointer and a character it points to is not a null character, then, the string pointed to by **stpr** is written to the standard error stream. That string will be concluded by a colon (**:**) and a space followed by the system error message and a newline character. The content of the system error message is implementation defined. Same message will be returned by the **strerror()** function with the **errno** argument.

Consider following program, that illustrates the use of some error functions.

```
#include <stdio.h>

extern int errno;
void main(void)
{
FILE *qw;
char mes[ ]="opening error\n";
```

```
if ((qw=fopen ("try.dat", "r"))==NULL)
{
perror (mes);
clearerr (qw);
}
else
printf ("opening completed\n");
printf ("errno value:%d", errno);
}
```

Program 17.28.

The output of the program is the following message

```
opening error
: No such file or directory
errno value:2
```

We tried to open in the reading mode a file, that does not exist. This, as you know, leads to an error. We used two error functions: **clearerr()** to clear the error and **perror()** to display the error message. We have also declared the **errno** variable. We have not assigned any value to this variable. It was assigned the value 2, when the file opening failed. Try to open a file, that can be open. The value of **errno** will be zero on most compilers. Your computer can produce a different error message, because the error messages are implementation-specific.

17.10. Miscellaneous file handling functions.

We also want to introduce two file access functions: **setbuf()** and **setvbuf()**. The **setvbuf()** function synopsis is

```
void setvbuf (FILE *ptr, char *buf, int mode,
              size_t size);
```

The first parameter **ptr** is a pointer to an opened file. The **buf** is a pointer to a character array. The last parameter **size** of data type **size_t** specifies the size of that buffer. The buffer is rather an array. The **size_t** is used for unsigned long integers. We discuss this data type in chapter about the Standard ANSI C Library Functions, when talking about the **<stddef.h>** header file. You can look it up right now. You would be able to understand everything written about this data type there. Just use this type, when you write the fourth argument of the **setvbuf()** function.

The **mode** parameter determines how the buffering of a file pointed to by **ptr** will be performed. There are three standard ways of buffering and three standard macros or names used for that: **_IOFBF**, **_IOLBF**, **_IONBF**.

The **_IOFBF** is used for the full buffering, i.e., the buffer reads or writes to the whole stream at once. The **_IOLBF** is used to indicate line buffering, when the stream is read or written line by line. Every time when a newline character is written or read, the buffer is flushed or cleared and, then, the next line is handled by the same buffer. The **_IONBF** is used for no buffering at all.

The **setvbuf()** function specifies the I/O buffer from the file, or how the file will communicate with the outside world. The **setvbuf()** function requests to perform the I/O to the file pointed to by **ptr** through the buffer pointed to by the pointer **buf** of size specified by its last parameter **size**. The I/O will be performed according to the **mode** argument.

The way in which the file would be buffered (or how would you write or read the data during I/O) is usually determined by the compiler. You should rely on it when you can. If you want to specify to the system how the file should be accessed during I/O, use the **setbuf()** and **setvbuf()** functions. When the **setvbuf()** function is used, it, basically, tells the computer, that the data I/O to and from a stream should go through a given size buffer. The function also tells the computer, how to get the data from the file: line by line, as the whole or the data should go directly to the file. Same stands for writing the data to a stream via buffer.

The **setvbuf()** function can be used only after the file pointed to by the file pointer **ptr** has been opened and before any other operation has been performed on that file. Almost any operation on the stream will preempt your choice of buffering. The content of that buffer should not be altered while the stream is still open. The content of the array buffer at any time is indeterminate, so you cannot use it for anything else. The **setvbuf()** and **setbuf()** requests for buffering can be ignored by the compiler. Consider a fragment of code illustrating, how to write a file buffering.

```
#include <stdio.h>
main ( )    {
char *row[300];
FILE *abc;
int md=_IOLBF;
abc=fopen ("test.dat", "w+");
setvbuf (abc, row, md, 300);....}
```

The **setvbuf()** function returns zero if successful. It returns a non-zero value, if **mode** has an invalid value or the request for buffering is not honored by the computer.

The **setbuf()** is identical to the **setvbuf()** function except, **setbuf()** does not return any value (it has **void** type), and it has only two parameters. Its synopsis is

```
void setbuf(FILE *ptr, char *buf);
```

It corresponds to the **setvbuf()** invoked with the parameter **mode** having value **_IOFBF** (or **_IONBF** if **buf** is a null pointer) and parameter **size** equal to **BUFSIZ**. The **BUFSIZ** is just a standard macro. It represents the size equal to preferred size of a buffer. It can range from couple hundred to a few thousand-odd bytes.

One can also do some operations on files. A file can be removed i.e., deleted by using the **remove()** function. Its prototype is

```
int remove (const char *name);
```

The examples are

```
n=remove (row); or  remove ("my.dat");
```

The name of the file to be erased is included in the double quotation marks. It can be also stored in a string pointed to by the argument **row**. This function is implementation defined. The file, whose name is specified in **remove()**, becomes not accessible after the function execution. Before you delete a file, it should be closed. Otherwise, the behavior of the function is not certain. The **remove()** function returns zero, if it was successful and non-zero otherwise.

A file can be renamed, i.e., a new name can be assigned to it using **rename()** function. The function synopsis is

```
int rename (const char *oldname, const char *newname);
```

It has two parameters. The **rename()** function assigns a new name pointed to by its second parameter **newname** to the file, that presently has the name pointed to by its first parameter **oldname**. Each parameter of this function is a pointer to a string containing the file name. One can write a string with the name of the file directly in the function as an argument. It should be surrounded with the double quotes. The **rename()** function returns zero, if a file name is changed and non-zero for a failure. In the last case, the name of the file remains unchanged. Consider an example.

```
#include <stdio.h>

void main (void)
{
FILE  *pt;
if ((pt=fopen ("info.dat", "r"))==NULL)
printf ("opening fail\n");
else
printf ("opening OK\n");
fclose (pt);
rename ("info.dat", "newna.dat");
if ((pt=fopen ("newna.dat", "r"))==NULL)
printf ("opening fail");
else
printf ("opening OK");
fclose (pt);
}
```

Program 17.29.

The output of the program is

```
opening OK
opening OK
```

We open the **info.dat** file and close it to show, that it exists. It is open in the reading mode. Therefore, it should be created before running the program. After we open and close the same file, it is renamed to the **newna.dat**. We also open the new file to show, that we renamed the old file and the file with the new name exists. As you see, we used the file names directly in the function, as **rename("info.dat", "newna.dat")**. Hence, you can put the strings directly as **rename()** function arguments, or use the pointers to the string arrays containing either or both file names.

The **tmpfile()** function creates a temporary binary file. This file will be automatically removed and the data placed in it will be lost, when it is closed or the program is terminated. You can use this file as a temporary data storage, while your program is in progress. The standard does not specify what happens, if the program is terminated abnormally while this file is still open. Therefore, it can be removed along with its data on some systems and might be saved on others. Since the file is binary, it is opened in "**wb+**" mode by the computer. The **tmpfile()** returns a pointer to the created stream or a null pointer in case, if the file cannot be created. Its synopsis is

```
FILE  *tmpfile (void);
```

All the operations normally performed on binary files can be performed on the files created by this function. Program below demonstrates the **tmpfile()** function.

```
#include <stdio.h>

void main (void)
{
FILE  *pt;
if ((pt=tmpfile( ))==NULL)
printf ("opening fail\n");
else
printf ("opening OK\n");
fclose (pt);
}
```

Program 17.30.

This program illustrates how to open a temporary file using the **tmpfile()** function. It also displays a message to indicate whether the opening was successful or not.

Suppose, you have a huge file directory and want to open a new file. But you do not remember, if a name of a new file to be created has not been used previously. C gives us a capability of creating new files without worrying, that their names could repeat the already existing ones. The **tmpname()** function is used in this case. Its synopsis is

```
char *tmpname (char *row);
```

It generates a valid file name, that differs from already existing file names, and places it in the array pointed to by **row**. Every time you call this function, it generates a new temporary file name. The **tmpname()** and **tmpfile()** can be called up to **TMP_MAX** times for all the subsequently executed programs. Both functions can be called more than **TMP_MAX** number of times on some systems. You can use this temporary name to create a new temporary file. You will have to delete this file manually. The **TMP_MAX** is a macro, that stores a maximum number of temporary files, that can be opened on your computer.

The name created by the **tmpfile()** function cannot consist of more characters, than the maximum number of characters allowed by the compiler. The **L_tmpname** is just a macro that, in fact, stores that maximum number of characters. One can declare the buffer large enough to hold that temporary file name as **char row[L_tmpname]**. That number can be hundreds of bytes long for some systems.

The last function we have to discuss is the **fflush()** function. Its synopsis is

```
int  fflush (FILE *ptr);
```

If a file pointed to by **ptr** is opened in a writing mode, the **fflush()** function writes the content of the output buffer to that file. If **ptr** points to a file opened in a reading mode, the **fflush()** clears the content of an input buffer. In both cases the file remains open. If **ptr** is a null pointer, the flushing action is performed on all streams. The **fflush()** function returns **EOF** in case of error. Otherwise, zero is returned.

The **fflush()** is used for protection from losing the data from a buffer due to some unexpected events, such as power failure or some abnormal program termination and so on. The flushing operation is performed automatically by the program after executing the **exit()** function or completing **main()**. The closure of an output file will also automatically flush the output stream associated with it.

17.11. Direct input/output functions.

The **fread()** function reads the data from a file and places it in a memory buffer. For example, the buffer can be an array or a variable of **int**, **float**, **char** type. The synopsis of the function is

```
size_t  fread (void *row, size_t size, size_t count,
                   FILE *ptr);
```
The first parameter **row** is a pointer to a memory buffer, that will receive the data from a stream file. The **size** is a **size_t** (or **int**) type number, and it stands for the size of each data unit to be read in bytes. The size of one variable can be determined by its data type. A size of a group of characters is a sum of the sizes needed to hold each character. Assume, one has a file containing, for example, seven character groups.

```
ps9em3i riuw201 eiro49d r93j12j 203o39s .......
```
If each character is specified to occupy two bytes, then, the **size** of each group is equal to 14. We will call each of those read at once data units a *record*.

Two last parameters are **count** and **ptr**. The **count** specifies the number of records to read, and the **ptr** is a pointer to a file, from which the data will be read. The **fread()** function reads up to **count** number of records, each of length **size**, from the file pointed to by **ptr** and places them in the buffer pointed to by **row**. An example of calling this function is

```
fread ( row, 20, 3, ptr );
```
Here, **fread()** function reads 3 pieces of data each 20 bytes long into an array pointed to by **row** from the stream pointed to by **ptr**. The **fread()** begins the reading from the current cursor position inside the file. The cursor just moves along with reading the characters. The function returns the number of elements successfully read. It returns number less than the number of elements successfully read, if an error or **EOF** is encountered. It returns zero, if the **size** or **count** is zero. In this case, the content of the array and the state of the stream remain unchanged.

The **fwrite()** function writes data from a memory buffer to a file. Its synopsis is

```
size_t  fread (void *row, size_t size, size_t count,
                   FILE *ptr);
```
Those arguments have the same meaning as for **fread()**. The difference is, that up to **count** number of records each of length **size** will be copied to the file specified by the **ptr** from the array pointed to by **row**. One can write

```
fwrite ( arr, 20, 3, qp );
```
For our particular example **fwrite()** function writes 3 pieces of data each 20 bytes long from an array pointed to by the **arr** pointer to the stream pointed to by **qp**. The **fwrite()** function also returns a number of elements successfully copied or the number less than that, if an error is encountered.

One can use those functions for reading and writing the structures. For instance,
```
struct mine
{
int x;
char z;
float ar[20];
} var;
```
One can write the content of **var** to the file pointed to by file pointer **fa** by
```
fwrite ( &var, sizeof (mine), 1, fa);
```
As you can see, the third argument here is equal to 1, that is, usually, used for a structure. The **sizeof(mine)** allocates enough memory to hold one variable of structure **mine** data type.

Both functions are used for performing I/O on binary rather, than on textual files. Consider following example illustrating the use of those functions.

```
#include <stdio.h>                        /*line1*/
#include <stdlib.h>                       /*line2*/
#define MAX 100                           /*line3*/

void main (int argc, char *argv[ ])       /*line4*/
{                                         /*line5*/
FILE *pin, *ptwo;                         /*line6*/
int in=1, num=34, n=0;                    /*line7*/
char a[MAX], line[50];                    /*line8*/
static char com[ ]="place";               /*line9*/
static char cont[ ]="This will be a content of the file";
                                          /*line10*/
pin=fopen ("onemy.dat", "w");             /*line11*/
fputs (cont, pin);                        /*line12*/
fclose(pin);                              /*line13*/
if (argc<4 || argc >4)                    /*line14*/
{                                         /*line15*/
fprintf (stderr, "command error\n");      /*line16*/
exit (0);                                 /*line17*/
}                                         /*line18*/
sprintf (line, "%s", argv[1]);            /*line19*/
while (line[n]!='\0' && com[n]!='\0' && n<20) /*line20*/
{                                         /*line21*/
if (line[n]!=com[n])                      /*line22*/
{                                         /*line23*/
```

```
fprintf (stderr, "bad statement\n");    /*line24*/
exit (0);                               /*line25*/
}                                       /*line26*/
n=n++;}                                 /*line27*/
if ((pin=fopen(argv[2], "rb"))==NULL)   /*line28*/
{                                       /*line29*/
fprintf (stderr, "No such a file\n");   /*line30*/
exit (0);                               /*line31*/
}                                       /*line32*/
ptwo=fopen (argv[3], "wb+");            /*line33*/
fread (a, in, num, pin);               /*line34*/
fwrite (a, 1, num, ptwo);              /*line35*/
rewind (ptwo);                          /*line36*/
fscanf(ptwo, "%s", line);              /*line37*/
printf ("%s\n", line);                 /*line38*/
fclose (pin);                           /*line39*/
fclose(ptwo);                           /*line40*/
}                                       /*line41*/
```
Program 17.31.

You run the program using three arguments for the **main()**

    place onemy.dat twomy.dat
The output of the program is

    This
Besides, it writes the phrase

    This will be a content of the file
to the **onemy.dat** file, and copies the content of that file to the **twomy.dat** file. The content of both files is not human readable. It contains a set of strange characters, which is rather a binary representation of the entered characters.

   The first ten code lines of **Program 17.31** write the preprocessor directives, declare all the variables, pointers and arrays. We open the **onemy.dat** file, copy into it the content of the string **cont[]**, and close it. It is done by the code at lines 11-13.

   Following lines make use of the **main()** arguments. Those arguments can provide us with the way of writing our own commands. We create a command

    place onemy.dat twomy.dat
that will copy the content of **onemy.dat** to the **twomy.dat** file. The above program provides the code, that will allow the computer to "understand" us and to fulfill it.

   We want to make the first word "**place**" in our command the symbolic word for the copy request. The second word is a name of a source file, from which the data will be copied. The third word is a name of the destination file. We use three words. You know, the very first argument of **main()** is the name of your source file. We did not show it. Our program performs the checking, that allows it to recognize the command. It, then, executes the command. We first check, if there are four arguments by the **if** statement at line 14. If **main()** does not have exactly four arguments, the message is displayed and the program is terminated. This is implemented at lines 16, 17.

After we checked for the correct number of words, we can check if the words are correct. We copy the word "**place**" into the array **line**. We compare each element of the array **line** to the corresponding element of the array **com** at lines 20-27. We initially put the word "**place**" in the array **com**. If the command entered as **main()** argument is "**place**", then each **line[n]** element must be equal to **com[n]**.

We open both files in the binary modes using **fopen()** at lines 28-33. We use a checking procedure for opening the **onemy.dat** file. The **argv[2]** and **argv[3]** point to the strings containing the third and the fourth entered words. The third word is the name of the **onemy.dat** file. The fourth word is the name of the **twomy.dat** file. Therefore, they are used as the arguments of **fopen()** function for opening both files. We copy the content of the first file to the second one by two lines

```
fread (a, in, num, pin);                        /*line34*/
fwrite (a, 1, num, ptwo);                       /*line35*/
```

The first line copies the content of the first file into the **a** array. The second line writes the content of that array to the second file. We, then, set the cursor to the beginning by the **rewind()** function at line 36, and read the second file by the **fscanf()** function at line 37. The string is placed into the **line** array and displayed on the screen by the **printf()** function at line 38. Since **fscanf()** is used with the format **%s** , the input stops when the first white space character is encountered. So, only word "**This**" will be placed in **line**. This is why only one word "**This**" gets displayed on the screen.

Following example illustrates direct read/write functions.

```c
#include <stdio.h>
#include <stdlib.h>

void main (void)
{
FILE *fap;
static float row[ ]={4.92, 5.1, 1.3, 94.22, 8.29, 7.1};
float new[6];
int n;
if ( (fap= fopen ("onemy.dat", "w+"))==NULL)
{
printf ("opening error\n");
exit (0);
}
fwrite (row, 2*sizeof (float), 3, fap);
rewind (fap);
fread (new, 3*sizeof (float), 2, fap);
for (n=0; n<6; n++)
printf (" %.2f ", new[n]);
fclose (fap);
}
```

Program 17.32.

The output of the program is

```
4.92   5.10   1.30   94.22   8.29   7.10
```

The program copies the string **row** to the file **onemy.dat** using the **fwrite()** function. It copies the content of that file to the array **new**. The array gets displayed on the
screen by the **printf()** function inside the **for** loop. The loop is needed, because we
display all six array elements. We opened the **onemy.dat** in a regular mode, although
you must use **fread()** and **fwrite()** mainly for binary files.

17.12. Binary file handling.

Binary files are very useful for numeric data for several reasons. First, they save the
memory space. For instance, the number 3928.47 in a text mode will occupy 6 bytes for
six numbers, one byte for the decimal point and, probably, two more bytes for spaces
before and after the whole value to separate it from the others. To understand why, recall
that each number, the decimal point and a space correspond to certain numerical values in
ASCII code. Each of them occupies a byte. The value 3928.47 would be treated as a set of
seven ASCII characters. Do not forget two spaces: one before and one after that value as
additional two ASCII characters. The floating-point number uses standard four bytes in
the binary format. So, it will, indeed, save some memory space.

Binary format saves computer time as well. For instance, when you use **fscanf()** or
fprintf() functions to handle the data for the text file, the ASCII value of each character is translated into binary format and only then transferred to or from the file. In case
of a binary file, you do not have to deal with those translations.

Binary format preserves the precision of the floating-point numbers, because it does not
perform the translation from binary to decimal ASCII and back to binary. It is also faster
to handle the structures in binary files using **fread()** or **fwrite()** functions.

There is nothing special about handling binary files. They are opened as regular files,
but in the binary modes. We have indicated those options for the **fopen()** function. One
can use almost all the functions discussed above for the binary files.

One of the pitfalls of operating with the binary files is the **EOF** character. When a file is
read in a binary mode, there is a possibility that an integer value equal to the **EOF** could be
read. This can be interpreted by the reading function as an end-of-file. The reading can be
terminated before the end-of-file is reached. This problem is solved by using **feof()** to
check for the **EOF** mark. We illustrate it in **Program 17.33**.

```
#include <stdio.h>
#define ROW 6

void main (void)
{
FILE *aq;
char name_f[ ]="onemy.dat";
char val[ROW]={1, 2, 3, -1, 4, 5};
char n;
```

```
aq=fopen (name_f, "wb+");
fwrite (val, sizeof(val), 1, aq);
rewind(aq);
while ((n=fgetc (aq))!= EOF)
printf (" %d ", n);
}
```

Program 17.33.

The output of the program is

   1   2   3

The output consists of only three numbers here? It is just an artifact of the way we have set up the I/O. We have placed an array **val[ROW]={1, 2, 3, -1, 4, 5}** into the file **onemy.dat**. We read from the file using **fgetc()** function in the **while** loop. The important thing is, that the program terminates before reading -1 from the file. It happens, because the file is opened in the binary mode. The returned by the **fgetc(aq)** value will stop the loop. This function interprets -1, found in the file, as the **EOF**. One must assign returned by the **fgetc()** value to a variable of type **char**.

In order to avoid this problem, the **while** loop should be rewritten as

```
while (!feof(aq))
{
n=fgetc (aq);
printf (" %d ", n);
}
```

17.13. Low-level input/output functions.

We have considered the high-level file handling functions, although they use low-level functions. One can use low-level functions directly in C++, keeping in mind, that they work directly with the operating system. This can make your programs less portable. At the other hand, it can give you more flexibility. Those functions are not defined in the ANSI C standard. Therefore, they might not be described in the standard header files. To use the low-level functions, one must include in a program some other header files. They are compiler specific. You must consult the compiler manuals. Many compilers describe low-level functions in all or some of the following header files: **<stdio.h>**, **<fcntl.h>**, **<sys\types.h>**, **<sys\stat.h>**, **<io.h>**, **<IO.H>**.

You must find out, which function is described in which file from your compiler manual or from the on-line help. Besides, some argument values of those functions can be described in some other files. For example, function **open()** is described in the files **<io.h>** or **<IO.H>** on some compilers. One of these files should be included. But some of its arguments can be described in **<fcntl.h>** and **<sys\stat.h>**. They must also be included.

You can easily find the required files by trials. First, you need to know exactly, which header files handle I/O of low-level functions. You include all those header files. If a function or its arguments are not described in a header file you included, the compiler will reply with an error message. You eliminate the files one by one and try to run the program. If an elimination of a file does not cause an error message during the run, this file can be excluded.

17.13.1. File opening and closure.

We will study **open()**, **creat()** and **close()** functions. The **open()** function opens a file in a certain mode. Its prototype is

```
int open (char *fname, int mode);
```

Here, the **fname** is a pointer to a string, containing a name of a file to be opened. You can put the name of your file directly in the **open()** function as its first argument. The name of the file must be surrounded by the double quotes, in that case. For some compilers it could be a complete name, that includes all the higher directories, as for instance in **DOS C:\...\myfile.d**. The second argument **mode** is a number, that determines what action can you perform on the opened file. It is chosen according to following Table 17.8.

Table 17.8. Second argument of the **open()** function.

Value of the argument	File is opened for following operations
0	open only for reading
1	open only for writing
2	open to read and write

The **open()** returns a positive integer if successful. It returns -1 in case of failure to open a file. The returned integer is called a *file descriptor*. It must be assigned to an **int** variable. This number or *file descriptor* is used to access the opened file at any time during the program run. You will need it, for instance, for I/O into this file and later for closing it. The file descriptor is different for each file. If you open a few files, each of the returned values would be different. When you try to open a file using the **open()** function, some compilers do not create a new file, if a file with that name has not been created before. In this case, the **open()** can fail and give an opening error.

Some compilers specify another prototype of the **open()** function, although just described above prototype of this function might work with them as well. Another function prototype form is

```
int open (char *fname, int flag [, int mode]);
```

It has three parameters. The **fname** is a pointer to a string containing a file name. One can write the string enclosed by the double quotes directly in the function, as we have discussed previously. The second parameter **flag** specifies the file access mode, that the file opens in. For some compilers its values are specified in the **<fcntl.h>** header file. We give some of those values in Table 17.9.

The third parameter **mode** specifies the mode, in which newly created file should be opened. The third argument is optional. It is used only, when the **open()** function creates a new file. The function creates a new file, when the **flag** parameter is equal to O_CREATE. The values of that parameter are specified in **<sys\stat.h>** file for some compilers. Some of those values are given in Table 17.10.

Table 17.9. Values of the **flag** argument of the **open()** function.

Argument	Specified by it file access mode
	Read/write flags
O_RDONLY	File is opened only for reading.
O_WRONLY	File is opened only for writing.
_RDWR	File is opened for both reading and writing.
	Binary/text flags
O_BINARY	File is opened in a binary mode.
O_TEXT	File is opened in the text mode.
	Other flags
O_APPEND	File is opened in append mode. The new data can be only appended to the end of the file.
O_CREAT	Creates and opens a new file.
O_TRUNC	File is opened with truncation. If it already exists, its length will be truncated to zero. All other file attributes remain unchanged.

Table 17.10. Values of the **mode** argument of the **open()** function.

Argument	Specified by it file opening mode
S_IREAD	The opened file can be read.
S_IWRITE	The data can be written to opened file.
S_IREAD|S_IWRITE	One can read and write the data to and from a file.

One **open()** function can have a few **flag** arguments. They are separated by the '|' mark. If an error occurs during the opening, the function not only returns -1. It also writes a corresponding error message to **errno**. We give those error messages written to the **errno** in Table 17.11. In general, the parameters of **open()** function can accept some other values as well. We recommend to consult your compiler manual.

To create a new file and open it, use the **creat()** function. Its prototype is

```
int creat (char *filename, int mode);
```

The **filename** is a pointer to a string, containing the name of the file to be opened. It can also be included directly in the function surrounded by the double quotation marks. The second parameter **mode** is the accessing mode similar to the one specified for the **open()** function. You can use the values of the **mode** parameter given in Table 17.8.

You can also use the values of **mode** parameter specified in Table 17.10. Look up your compiler User's Manual for more details. The **creat()** returns a positive integer if successful and -1 in case of failure. It can also set the **errno** to **EACCES**, **EMFILE** or **ENOENT**. The error messages are given in Table 17.11. Both the **open()** and **create()** functions are very similar. An example of writing **create()** function is

```
m=create ("myone.dat", S_IREAD);
m=create (row, 1);
```

The first form uses the file name "**myone.dat**" as the first argument. The second argument corresponds to Table 17.8. The second form shows, that you can place a name of a file into a string pointed to by the **row**, and include it in the first argument. The second argument is specified according to Table 17.10.

Table 17.11. Some error messages written to the **errno** by the **open()** function.

Error message	The error it indicates
ENOENT	Indicates that there is no such a file or directory. You are trying to open a file, that does not exists. Create it first.
EMFILE	Indicates that there are too many open files. Close some of them. The system cannot handle so many files at once.
EACCES	Request to open a file is denied by the system.
EINVACC	An invalid access code has been used. Check the arguments

The **close()** function closes the previously opened file. Its prototype is

```
int close (int n);
```

where **n** number is a file descriptor that has been returned by one of the opening functions. **Program 17.34** demonstrates the **open()** and **close()** functions.

```
#include <stdio.h>
#include <IO.H>

void main(void)
{
int ret;
ret=open ("onemy.dat", 1);
if (ret==-1)
printf ("cannot open\n");
else
printf ("opened\n");
close (ret);
}
```

Program 17.34.

The program opens the **onemy.dat** file in the writing mode with the **open()** function. If the opening is successful, it displays the message

```
opened
```

The file is, then, closed by means of the **close()** function. If the opening cannot be performed, the proper failure message

```
cannot open
```

is displayed. This form of the **open()** function cannot create new files. An error will appear, if the file does not exist already. Consider the next example.

```
#include <stdio.h>
#include <io.h>
#include <fcntl.h>
#include <sys\stat.h>
```

```
void main(void)
{
int ret;
ret=open ("see.dat", O_TEXT | O_WRONLY | O_CREAT,
          S_IWRITE );
if (ret==-1)
printf ("cannot open\n");
else
printf ("opened\n");
close (ret);
}
```

Program 17.35.

This program is analogous to the previous. It opens and closes a file and displays the same messages. It differs by the number of included header files and the form of writing the **open()** function as

```
ret=open ("see.dat", O_TEXT | O_WRONLY | O_CREAT,
          S_IWRITE );
```

It uses a few **flag** arguments, such as **O_TEXT**, **O_WRONLY**, **O_CREAT**. They are separated by the '|' mark. It also has the third argument equal to **S_IWRITE**. The set of second arguments is separated from the third argument by the comma.

17.13.2. Reading and writing functions.

We will study functions: **read()**, **write()**, **unlink()**, **lseek()**, **tell()**.
The **read()** function synopsis is

```
int read (int n , char *buf , int num);
```

Here, **n** is the file descriptor showing from which file to read the data. The second parameter called by us **buf** is a pointer to a location in memory reserved for pulling this data. This buffer could be an array or a variable, for example. The third parameter **num** is a number of characters to be read from the file. In case, if **buf** is a variable the **num** should be equal to 1. The **read()** function copies **num** number of characters from the file specified by the file descriptor **n** into the buffer pointed to by **buf**. So, the **read()** function "reads" the data from a file. If **read()** function is successful, it returns the number of read bytes or, sometimes, zero. It returns -1, in case of failure. The **errno** will be set to **EACCES** or **EBADF** (bad file number), in case of any error. Maximum 65534 bytes can be read by this function at once.

The **write()** function prototype is

```
int write (int n , char *buf , int num);
```

All the arguments have the same meaning as in **read()** function. The **write()**, however, copies **num** number of characters from the memory buffer **buf** to the disk file, specified by the file descriptor **n**. It returns the number of written bytes if successful or -1 in case of error. The **errno** will be set to **EACCES** or **EBADF** in case of error. Maximum 65534 bytes can be written by this function at once.

If you wish to delete a file, use the **unlink()** function. Its synopsis is

```
int unlink (const char *filename);
```

Here, the **filename** is a pointer to a string array containing the name of the file to be deleted. One can write the name of the file to be deleted directly into the function surrounded by the double quotes as

```
m=unlink ("onemy.dat");
```

The **unlink()** function deletes the file specified by its argument. You might have to write the name of the file with all the directory paths for some computer systems. The file should be closed, before using this function. A call to **unlink()** function cannot delete the files used in the read only mode on some compilers. The function returns zero, if successful. In case of error, it returns a non-zero value and sets **errno** to **EACCES** or **ENOENT** values.

Unbuffered random-access file I/O can be performed by **lseek()**. Its prototype is

```
long int lseek (int fd, long offset, int start);
```

The first parameter **fd** is a file descriptor, that indicates to which file you apply the **lseek()** function. The second parameter is the **offset**. It has a **long** type. The **start** is the starting point of the file position indicator. Its values are given in Table 17.12. The **lseek()** moves the cursor of the file specified by **fd** from the position indicated by **start** argument to another position shifted by **offset** number of bytes from the **start**. It normally returns a new cursor position in bytes from the beginning of the file or -1L upon failure.

Table 17.12. Values of the **start** argument of the **lseek()** function.

Argument	Meaning of the argument
0 or **SEEK_SET**	Starting point is the beginning of the file.
1 or **SEEK_CUR**	Starting point is the current cursor position.
2 or **SEEK_END**	Starting point is the end of the file.

When the data is read from the file, it is, sometimes, important to know if the end of the file **EOF** is reached. The low-level function **eof()** tests whether the **EOF** has been reached. Its synopsis is

```
int oef (int fd);
```

Here, number **fd** is the file descriptor of the file, on which this function will be acting. The **eof()** returns 1, if the file position indicator is at **EOF**. Otherwise, 0 is returned. If -1 is returned, the **errno** is set to the **EBADF** or **EINVAL**(invalid argument) values.

The **tell()** function gets the current cursor position inside the file specified by its parameter **fd**. Its synopsis is

```
long tell (int fd);
```

The function returns that current cursor position, if it is successful or -1L in case of error. The **errno** is set to the **EBADF**, in case of error.

Program 17.36 demonstrates the use of some of those functions. To run this program you better create a file **myfile.d** prior to running this program.

```
#include <stdio.h>                          /*line1*/
#include <io.h>                             /*line2*/
```

```
#include <fcntl.h>                                /*line3*/
#include <sys\stat.h>                             /*line4*/
#include <stdlib.h>                               /*line5*/
extern int errno;                                 /*line6*/

void main(void)                                   /*line7*/
{                                                 /*line8*/
int  ret;                                         /*line9*/
static char addr[ ]="Boston, Massachusetts."; /*line10*/
char r[23];                                       /*line11*/
long a=0, k;                                      /*line12*/
ret=open ("onemy.dat", O_TEXT | O_RDWR);     /*line13*/
if (ret==-1)                                      /*line14*/
printf ("cannot open\n");                         /*line15*/
else                                              /*line16*/
printf ("opened\n");                              /*line17*/
write (ret, addr, 22);                            /*line18*/
if (errno!=0)                                     /*line19*/
{                                                 /*line20*/
printf ("writing error\n");                       /*line21*/
exit (0);                                         /*line22*/
}                                                 /*line23*/
if  ((k=lseek(ret, a, SEEK_SET))==-1L)       /*line24*/
{                                                 /*line25*/
printf ("setting error.\n");                      /*line26*/
exit (0);                                         /*line27*/
}                                                 /*line28*/
read (ret, r, 22);                                /*line29*/
printf ("%s", r);                                 /*line30*/
close (ret);                                      /*line31*/
printf ("\nerrno=%d, k=%ld",errno, k);       /*line32*/
}                                                 /*line33*/
```

Program 17.36.

The output of the program is
```
opened
Boston, Massachusetts.
errno=0, k=0
```
The program opens the file **myone.dat** using the **open()** function at line 13. It writes the content of the string **addr** to this file by means of **write()** function at line 18. The file cursor is set to the beginning of the file by the **lseek()** function at line 24, so we can read this file from the beginning. Then, the content of the file is copied to the string **r** by the **read()** function at line 29. The file is closed by the **close()** function at line 31. The content of string **r** is displayed by the **printf()** at line 32.

Table 17.13. Standard I/O streams.

Pointer name	File descriptor	What does the file provide
stdin	0	Standard input from the keyboard
stdout	1	Standard output to the screen
stderr	2	Standard error output to the screen
stdaux	3	Standard auxiliary device serial port
stdprn	4	Standard printer parallel port

Program 17.36 introduces various ways of checking, if some of those file handling functions were successful. We check, if **open()** was successful by checking its returned value **ret**. It is done by the **if-else** statement at lines 14-17. Since the file was opened successfully, the message "**opened**" is displayed by the program. We check, if the **write()** function was successful by checking the **errno** variable at line 19 right after the function call. The **lseek()** function is checked by its returned value **k**. We display the values of **errno** and **k** on the screen as well.

One can ask how to access the standard files by means of the low-level I/O functions. The standard files have standard file pointers pointing to them. You address them by those pointer names, that you know. Each of the standard files can be accessed by the low-level I/O functions. Each of the standard files has its standard file descriptor. Typical file descriptors for the standard files are given in Table 17.13.

17.14. Standard input/output streams.

The standard streams were mentioned in the beginning of this chapter. They all are opened automatically by the operating system. They are given in Table 17.2. Here, we will briefly review them.

The **stdin** file is your keyboard and is used whenever the data is to be read from the keyboard. To "be read" means to be copied from the keyboard to some other location. The following functions input the data from **stdin**: **getchar()**, **getc()**, **gets()** and **scanf()**. The **stdout** denotes the screen stream. It is used, when the data must be displayed on the screen. The following functions output the data to the **stdout**: **printf()**, **putchar()**, **putc()**, **puts()**, **vprintf()**.

The **stderr** file is used for displaying error messages on the screen. This file cannot be I/O redirected. There is no function that uses **stderr** directly, although one can write to that file, for instance, by

```
fprintf ( stderr, "just checking the error file.\n");
```
The **stderr** ought to be used for the banner messages (i.e., the messages for the user about the program copyright, author and so on) and error messages.

The **stdaux** file is the main serial communication port. Since it is defined as **COM1** on a PC, the **stdaux** writes to that port. An example of writing to this port is

```
fprintf ( stdaux, "just checking the file.\n");
```
The **stdprn** denotes the system printer. This file should be used for the data to be printed out. The **stdprn** file cannot be redirected. It has to be used only for printing out the data. For instance,

```
fprintf ( stdprn, "just checking the file.\n");
```
Everything, we said about file I/O, will be applicable to those standard files. You can apply many of the file handling functions using the name of the standard file as an argument wherever a file name is required.

EXERCISES.

1. Run all the programs of this chapter, if you have an access to a computer facility.

2. Write a program, that opens and closes a file in the:
   - writing mode;
   - reading mode;
   - appending mode;
   - binary reading and writing mode.

3. Write a program, that opens a file in a writing mode, writes a text into it and closes that file. The program, then, opens the file again and searches for a specified by you word in the file. If the word is found, a proper message is displayed. The program must use the character I/O functions only.

4. Write a program, that copies a message from one file to another one. A message can contain some arithmetic operations like 2+10, or 30×15. Those operations must be identified, when your program reads the data from a file. The operations must be performed. The results should be displayed on the screen.

5. Write a program, that writes numeric data to a file. That program must read the data from that file and display it on the screen. You must use only formatted I/O functions.

6. Write a program, that reads a name of an employee, his (her) position, salary and writes them to some file in the form of a table. You can design any form of that table.

7. Write a program, that reads the data from a keyboard, places it in a file, copies the data to another file. The program, then, reads the data from the second file and displays it on the screen. Use only formatted I/O functions for doing all the operations.

8. Write a small word processor. A user should be able to type in a text. The program puts it in a file. It, then, asks a user, if the text is to be edited. The editing is done by parts. The computer reads a line of characters from the file and displays it on the screen. The user can change it. It will be written back to the file beginning from the same place, where it was before the editing. The program, then, reads another line of characters and lets the user edit it. The edited line is returned back to the file. The program reads the next chunk of data and lets you edit it. This continues, until all the text, initially contained inside the file, is edited. The edited file is, then, displayed. We leave you a freedom in a way how your program will edit the lines. The main requirement of the program is that the file is read and edited part by part. The edited parts are returned to the positions inside the file where they were initially.

9. Write a program, that places an array {25, -100, 421, 20, -98, -278, 5} in a binary file. The array is, then, read to a memory, sorted and displayed on the screen.

10. Write a program, that reads a sequence of characters from a standard input using the **scanf()** function inside the **for** loop.

11. Write a program that reads octal numbers from a keyboard and places them as the

hexadecimal numbers in a file. The file is, then, read and the numbers are displayed as decimal ones on the screen.

12. Write a program, that reads a sequence of either floating-point values or the characters from a keyboard. If the floating-point values have been entered, the program displays the proper message and finds their average. If you enter a sequence of characters, the program displays them on the screen accompanied by the corresponding message.

13. Write a program, that performs a file I/O and checks for all the discussed in this chapter errors.

14. Write a program, that writes and reads the data respectively to and from a file. Use only low-level I/O functions.

15. Write a program that creates a file, renames and deletes it.

CHAPTER 18

C++ STYLE INPUT AND OUTPUT.

18.1. Introduction to C++ input/output.

We will discuss C++ stream and file I/O in this chapter. You know, that C does not have its own I/O statements. This is why the library of I/O functions has been created. Just include corresponding header file in the program, and you can perform the data input/ output by simply writing a proper function. C++ does not have its own I/O statements as well. C++ uses the standard C library as well as its own I/O library. The C++ I/O library is called *iostream library*. We have learned some of the tools for I/O in C++. We will study the C++ style I/O thoroughly in this chapter.

Unfortunatelly, the **iostream** library used by C++ is not standardized yet. The draft of C++ standard library, which includes **iostream** library, has been already created. But it has not been approved yet. So, it is not an ANSI standard nor has it been an ISO standardized. This permits some differences from a vendor to a vendor. And even when the standard is approved, the contemporary compilers will be still used for a while. This is why we give you most important functions for the C++ I/O currently used on a number of compilers and from the C++ Standard Draft.

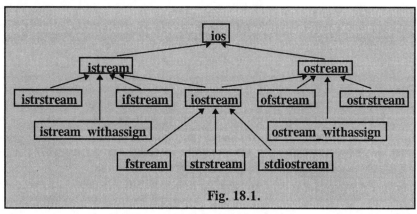

Fig. 18.1.

In C++, the input/output is performed by means of classes. The classes are written in the header files. So, you would have to include proper header files in order to be able to perform the I/O. We will teach you which header files to include for using certain classes. We will also teach you how to use the member functions and data members of those classes to perform the input or output. Again, you have used some of those member functions. Here, we just have to give you the whole picture.

The I/O in C++ is performed by the objects of different classes. The I/O classes are not untouchable. You can create new classes from those standard ones using inheritance. This is why it is important that you know which library classes are derived from which. We give you one concept of the **iostream** library in Fig. 18.1. For now it is only a picture for you. But we will discuss most of its classes. You will understand this figure after reading this chapter.

Why is it important to have this picture? You look at the picture and see which classes are inherited from which. Just by looking at the Fig. 18.1 one can say what are the base classes for any class presented there. We will go with you over the most important, from our point of view, member functions of each class. If you know member functions in the base classes, you know which functions are inherited by the derived classes. So, you can use more features of each class in the programs. Those classes can be used as the bases for your own derived classes. And you want to know, what members those classes can bring into the derived classes. Some of those classes are used for an input, some are used for the output. Some of those classes work for both input and output. You use some of those classes to operate with streams. Some of the classes are used for the disk file I/O. We will study which classes and how can be used for what operations.

Fig.18.1 illustrates a part of the **iostream** library implemented on some compilers. Each word in the rectangle stands for a class name. We want to point, the **iostream** library on your compiler can differ a bit from the one described here. You will be able to use any **iostream** library after reading this book. But you should not be afraid to contact the manuals or "Help" keys on your compilers.

Do not ask yourself, what this diagram has to do with the input or the output. Just try to look at it and understand which class is inherited by which for now. The top line **ios** class in Fig. 18.1 is the most basic class. It is inherited as virtual class by each of the classes at the second from the top line. For example, classes **ostream** and **istream** inherit class **ios**. You go by the arrows. The top class is the most basic. It will be inherited by the down level classes. The down level classes will be inherited by the classes even further down and so on.

So, how do you determine which class is inherited by which in Fig. 18.1? The answer is: by the arrow. The line with the arrow goes from the derived class to the base class. An arrow points towards the base from the derived class. Look at the Fig 18.1. You see the arrow line going from the **istream** class towards the **ios** class. The **ios** class is at the end of the arrow. It is a base for the **istream** class. There are four arrow lines going towards the **istream** class. It means, that the **istream** is inherited directly by classes: **istream_withassign**, **istrstream**, **ifstream**, **iostream**.

You can go over Fig. 18.1 and trace which class is derived from which. You see, many different classes inherit the same base classes. Therefore, many classes should have a number of identical member functions and data members. Furthermore, those I/O classes are put in separate header files. At the first glance, there is too much confusion about it. You should have no confusion on a lot of things after reading this chapter.

When we considered C type I/O, you had to know which functions are used for the input or output for files, strings and so on. You also had to remember, which header files to include with them. It is slightly different with C++ I/O. You have to remember what classes are used for what purposes. You also have to know the base classes for the classes you choose. Then, you would have an idea what functions are in your disposal. Any class you use is described in a certain header file. So, you need to remember that header file. When we talk about each class, we will give the name of the header file, in which every particular class is described. That header file should be included in your program. It would not work without it. So, if you need to know, which header file to include for which class, you can always look it up in this chapter. For instance, the **ios** class requires the inclusion of the **<iostream.h>** header file. We did not want to scare you with this information. It is not as difficult, as you think. Just follow us.

18.2. Stream input/output.

The C++ stream I/O functions "are spread" around different classes. The most basic one is the **ios** class. It consists of different data and function members. The data members specify different formatting modes, stream and file opening modes. They will be used by the functions of **ios** and other classes for handling and formatting the I/O. Those data and function members are inherited by the **istream** and **ostream** classes, that perform stream input and output respectively. The **istream** and **ostream** classes are inherited by the **iostream** class. We will discuss the other classes later.

18.2.1. Stream output.

We will consider the output first. So far, we have been using **cout** object a lot, and got acquainted with it. Here, we might repeat some of the facts known to you. But we will also expand your knowledge of the stream output.

The **cout**, **cerr**, **clog** are the objects of the **ostream** class type according to the standard draft. However, some compilers define them as **ostream_withassign** class type objects. But there is a little difference between both classes. In many cases you would not even see the difference. The **ostream** class also defines an overloaded stream insertion operator **<<**. We can use the **cout** object and the extraction operator for the output. The **cout** object is set up in a way, that it writes the data to the standard output stream - screen (**stdout**). The **ios** class is a base class for the **ostream**. We can use any of **ios** members with the **cout** object. The members of the **ios** class are given in the reference section of this chapter. We discuss them in the present and other sections of this chapter. Using **ios** members along with the **ostream** class members and objects gives us much flexibility for the output. The **cerr** is a predefined class object, that you can use to report a standard error. It performs an output with the limited buffering. The **clog** is also a predefined object for error reporting. It is fully buffered. The **ostream** class is typically described in the **<iostream.h>** header file. It must be included in a program, if you intend to use any of **ostream** class members.

We do not demonstrate you any programs, where the output is implemented by the **cout** object. You have had enough of them. But we will begin with review of two output member functions of the **ostream** class: **put()** and **write()**. The first one is used for a single character output. Its prototype is

```
ostream& put (char x);
```
It copies a character stored in its parameter **x** to the stream. A character to be copied can be also placed in the **put()** function directly surrounded by the single quotes, as shown in **Program 18.1**. **Program 18.1** uses the **cout** object of the **ostream** class, so the character is written to the standard output stream - the screen.

```
#include <iostream.h>

void main ( )
{
cout.put ('a');
cout.put ('b').put('1').put (' ').put('2');
}
```

Program 18.1.

The output of the program is
```
    ab1 2
```
One can use one **put()** member function or a number of **put()** functions with one object as **cout.put('b').put('1').put(' ').put('2')**. They will be executed in the order they follow.

The **write()** is a member function of the **ostream** class. It is used for an unformatted output of a sequence of characters (and even for one character). The **write()** function is also often used for a binary output. It is an overloaded function. Its prototypes are
```
ostream& write (const char* arr, int num);
ostream& write (const unsigned char* arr, int num);
ostream& write (const signed char* arr, int num);
```
The first parameter **arr** is a pointer to a character array to be copied to a stream. The second parameter **num** is a number of characters to be written. The function copies **num** number of characters from an array pointed to by **arr** to the stream. The stream is determined by the object of the **ostream** class, with which the function is used. **Program 18.2** demonstrates the **write()** function. Since it uses the **cout** object, the data is copied to the standard output - the screen.

```
#include <iostream.h>

void main ( )
{
char q[ ]="How are you doing?";
char ab[8]={'c', 'o', 'm', 'p', 'u', 't', 'e', 'r'};

cout.write (q, 7);
cout.put (' ');
cout.write ("This is another one.", 20);
cout.put (' ');
cout.write (ab, 4);
```

```
}
```
Program 18.2.

The output of the program is
```
How are This is another one. comp
```
The program illustrates an output of string **q**, array of characters **ab** using **write()** function. It also illustrates an output to the screen, when a character string is incorporated as an argument into the **write()** function as
```
cout.write ("This is another one.", 20);
```
We have discussed a notion of a cursor in the previous chapter. In this chapter we discuss the *get* and *put* pointers. Think about typing a document on a type writer. Each time you type a new letter, the carriage (or cursor) of that writer is moved to the next position. So, the next letter can be typed only to the following position. We can say, that the cursor moves to the next position within the stream, when you output every single character. If you perform stream output the cursor is called a put pointer in C++. Respectively, programmers call the input stream cursor a get pointer.

18.2.2. Additional features of an output.

The **ostream** class inherits the **ios** class as its base. Therefore, the members of the **ios** class can be used with the objects of the **ostream** class. The **ios** class declares a number of so called *format flags*. Their data type is **fmtflags**, according to the standard library draft. However, many compilers use **long** data type for them. So, we use the **long** data type instead of the **fmtflags** in the function prototypes below. The format flags can be used to change the appearance and representation of the data I/O. We will later review how they affect the output. The **flags()**, **unsetf()** and **setf()** member functions of the **ios** class can set and unset those flags.

The first function is overloaded. It has two prototypes.
```
long flags (long flag_arg);
long flags ( ) const;
```
The first version of **flags()** function sets the stream internal flag to the value stored in the parameter **flag_arg**. The **flag_arg** name was made up by us and is just an identifier. You can use any name for it. The first version returns the flag of the previous stream state. The second version of the **flags()** function produces no active action. It just reads and returns the current stream flag. It can be used in some conditions, checking or inquiring about the current stream format.

The **setf()** is also an overloaded function. It also has two prototypes.
```
long setf (long flag_arg);
long setf (long flag_arg1, long flag_arg2);
```
The first version of the **setf()** function sets the stream internal flag to the value specified by the **flag_arg**. It returns the previous value of the flag. The second version of this function has two parameters. Both of them are the flags of the same type as in the first function. But the second parameter **flag_arg2** will be changed by the function. It will accept the flag value of the first **flag_arg1** parameter. It returns the previous flag.

The **unsetf()** function prototype is

```
long unsetf (long flag_arg);
```

The function clears (or unsets) the flag stored in its parameter **fl_arg**.

We have indicated, **unsetf()**, **flags()** and **setf()** member functions return a value of the **long** type. These functions accept the arguments and return the values of the **long** type. Once again, these functions accept **ios** class format flags as their arguments and return them. The format flags have **fmtflags** data type, according to the C++ Standard Library Draft. However, a number of modern compilers still use the **long** data type for them. The data type **long** is equivalent to **fmtflags**. A format flag can be implemented as just a bit of memory in some location. Each flag has its own bit. This is how a computer recognizes different flags. If a bit corresponding to a particular flag is set to one, this flag is considered to be set on. If the bit is set to zero, it is cleared. The flag is set off. A number of flags is limited. All the flags are declared in the **ios** class and are given below. We review in this section how the flags and the flag handling functions work with the **ostream** class objects. But they can work with the objects of any other class, that inherits **ios** directly or indirectly. The arguments and returned values of **unsetf()**, **flags()** and **setf()** member functions can accept only following flags of the **ios** class:

- **dec**, **oct** or **hex** flags are used to convert an integer input or to generate an integer output in decimal, octal or hexadecimal bases respectively;

- **fixed** flag is used to produce a floating-point output in a fixed-point notation;

- **internal** flag adds fill characters at some internal positions in some outputs;

- **left** and **right** flags are used to add fill characters respectively to the left or right of certain output;

- **scientific** flag is used to generate floating-point output in scientific notation;

- **showbase** is used to produce a prefix, showing the numeric base of integer output;

- **showpoint** flag produces a decimal point in generated floating-point output;

- **showpos** flag is used to display a + sign in non-negative numeric output;

- **skipws** flag skips some leading white spaces before some input operations;

- **unitbuf** flag flushes the output after completing it;

- **uppercase** flag replaces the lowercase letters with their uppercase equivalent;

The **fmtflags** type also defines three constants: **adjustfield**, **basefield**, **floatfield**. The **adjustfield** can accept either **left**, **right** or **internal** values. The **basefield** can be equal to **dec**, **oct** or **hex**. The **floatfield** mask can have one of two flag values: **scientific** and **fixed**. Each of the flags can be accessed using the **::** scope resolution operator. For example, we can write **ios::showpos** or **ios::dec**. We will now show you how to use the members of **ios** class with **ostream** class objects.

18.2.2.1. Changing a base of a stream.

First three flags are: **dec**, **hex**, **oct**. If any of those flags is set on, it changes the base of the integers, written to the output. If **hex** is on, the integers will be represented as hexadecimal numbers. The **oct** or **dec** flags can display the integers as octal or decimal values respectively. The default flag is **dec**. The numbers are written (read) as decimal, until **oct** or **hex** flag is set on. If any of the flags is set on, it will stay on until you change it to another one. Consider following programs.

```
#include <iostream.h>

void main ( )
{
int x=20;
cout.setf(ios::oct);
cout << x;
}
```
Program 18.3.

The output of the program is the octal number 24. It is displayed on the screen in the octal base, because we used the **cout** object. The stream, associated with the **cout** object, is set to the octal mode in **Program 18.3**. This stream is known to be the standard output (the screen). Review another program.

```
#include <iostream.h>

void main ( )
{
int x=20;
cout.flags(ios::hex);
cout << x;
}
```
Program 18.4.

The program output is the hexadecimal number 14. Both programs 18.3 and 18.4 change the base of the number. They demonstrate the **setf()** and **flags()** member functions of the **ios** class. The flags are written as **ios::hex** and **ios::oct**.

The **ios** class also offers so-called *stream manipulators*. They can be inserted into an object. They can set the format flags on. You can look up, how does the standard draft specify the stream manipulators later in this chapter. In some modern compiler versions the stream manipulators are used a bit differently. They have the same names as the format flags of **fmtflags** data type. A manipulator is inserted into an object that performs an output using extraction operator. Following program demonstrates two of them with the **cout** object.

```
#include <iostream.h>

void main ( )
{
int x=59;
cout << x << hex << " " << x << oct << " " << x;
}
```

Program 18.5.

The output of the program is
```
59    3b    73
```

18.2.2.2. Output termination.

Sometimes, it is desirable to terminate an output with a newline character. So, the next output can start from a new line. One can do it by simply adding the newline character into an output string. For instance,
```
cout << "How are you.\n" << "I am fine.";
```
As you know, this will produce a two line output
```
How are you?
I am fine.
```
There are stream manipulators, that allow to do this operation as well. For example, the **endl**. You use it by inserting it into an output stream. It inserts a newline character and flashes the buffer. For example,
```
cout << "How are you?" << endl;
```
Another useful manipulator is the **ends**. You use it by inserting it into an output stream. It inserts a null character '**\0**'. It can be useful when dealing with the strings.

18.2.2.3. Floating-point values formatting.

Normally, the **cout** object displays only meaningful floating-point value digits. This means, that the trailing zeros get truncated and no exponent is shown. So, the normal way of displaying such a value would be, for example, 1.94, 29.8, 495.81 and so on. The **scientific**, **fixed**, **showpoint** flags can change the appearance of an output of a floating-point value. The **scientific** flag converts a floating-point value to the scientific notation. The **fixed** flag is used to output a floating-point number with the specified number of digits. We will show you later how to specify a number of digits in a floating-point value. Assume for now, the number of digits in a floating-point value is set by the computer. It is called a default number of digits. The **showpoint** also causes a number like 50.0 to be written with the trailing zeros after a point. In other words, the **showpoint** flag will display a value with the decimal point and the trailing zeros. Consider a program below, that illustrates all these flags.

```
#include <iostream.h>
```

```
void main ( )
{
float x=20.1234, y=30.0;
cout << x << "   ";
cout.flags(ios::fixed);
cout << x << " ";
cout.setf(ios::scientific);
cout << x <<endl;
cout.flags(ios::showpoint);
cout << y <<endl;
}
```

Program 18.6.

The output of the program is

```
20.1234   20.123400   2.012340e+001
30.0000
```

The program also presents **endl** manipulator of **ostream** class. It inserts a newline character and flushes the buffer. It can be used with any kind of data for ending the output operation.

One can also set a precision of a floating-point value, that is a number of digits after a point. The precision can be set by the **precision()** member function of the **ios** class. It is an overloaded function. The prototypes of the **precision()** function are

```
int precision (int num);
int precision ( ) const;
```

The argument **num** of that function is an integer. Its value corresponds to a number of digits after the point, with which the floating-point values will be written. However, some compilers understand the value of **num** as a total number of digits in a floating-point value. The first overloaded **precision()** function returns the previous precision. The second **precision()** function does not do any action. It just returns the current precision setting. **Program 18.7** demonstrates this function.

```
#include <iostream.h>

void main ( )
{
double x=20.11111111;
cout << x << "   ";
cout.precision (3);
cout << x << "   ";
cout.precision(7);
cout << x << "\nargument 7 sets the precision to "
     << cout.precision ( ) << endl;
}
```

Program 18.7.

The output of the program on our compiler is

```
20.1111  20.1  20.11111
argument 7 sets the precision to 7
```

The program displays the same floating-point value with the default precision, and two other precisions set by the user. It also uses the **precision()** function without an argument. The returned by it value is inserted into the **cout** object.

18.2.2.4. Width of the fields.

The objects of the **ostream** class, as well as any object of any other derived from the **ios** class, can use the **width()** member function of the **ios** class. The function is overloaded. Its prototypes are

```
int width (int wn);
int width ( ) const;
```

The **wn** parameter is the minimum field width in characters. The first overloaded **width()** function sets the width of output (input) field to a specified by **wn** number. What does it mean? Suppose, we display a number and specify the minimum number of characters per each input/output. Suppose, we indicate **width(5)** and display the numbers 10000, 10 and 8. Each of those numbers will be padded from the left to the specified width **wn** by the stream fill characters. The numbers will be padded by the spaces by default. We will show, how to choose the fill characters soon. The output is

```
10000    10     8
```

There are three spaces between 10000 and 10. There are four spaces between 10 and 8. You can specify to pad the streams with **x** character. In this case, the output should be

```
10000xxx10xxxx8
```

What happens, if the number of digits in a value or the length of a string is greater than the specified width? That field is displayed in full, because the **wn** specifies the *minimum* width of a field. So, the number 2000000 will get displayed in full, even if the specified width is 5. If the parameter **wn** is 0, the width is set by default, i.e., the field width is equal to the length of each output. So, the exact number of positions needed for the output of the 10000, 10, 8 numbers will be provided by default or when **wn=0**. The width is set to the default value after completing each input/output. The first version of the **width()** function returns the previous width. Our second version of the overloaded **width()** function does not set the width. It just reads and returns the current width. We demonstrate the **width()** function in the following program.

```
#include <iostream.h>

void main ( )
{
for (int m=0; m<6; m++)
{
cout.width (4);
cout << m;
```

```
}   }
```
Program 18.8.

The output of the program on the screen is

   0   1   2   3   4   5

Here, the width has been set to 4 by **cout.width(4)**. So, any value or a character will be displayed on 4 positions. You can see, each of the numbers from 0 to 5 is displayed on 4 positions. Each of the numbers is a separate output called *output field*, as you know. We have included **cout.width()** in the **for** loop. It will be repeated every time before the **cout** object performs an output. Why did we do it? A width is set to a default every time, after an object performs an I/O operation. To set a non-default width, you should call the **width()** function every time before using an object for I/O. We wanted to set the width of the output for the **cout** object. We set it by calling **cout.width(4)**. We had to include this function in the loop, because the output width was reset to the default each time after using the **cout** object. One can use the **width()** function for different formatting features. You have seen some of them earlier in this book. We have demonstrated how to create a table. We can give you another simple example of doing it.

```cpp
#include <iostream.h>
#include <string.h>

class stu
{
private:
char name[8];
int gpa;
public:
stu (char *line, int num);
void disp ( );
};

stu::stu (char *line, int num)
{
strcpy (name, line);
gpa=num;
}

void stu::disp ( )
{
cout.width (8);
cout << name << "|";
cout.width (6);
cout << gpa << " |" << endl;
}
```

```
void main ( )
{
stu one ("John ", 30), two ("Pete ", 25),
    three ("Ann ", 75);
cout << "Student | Grade |" << endl;
one.disp ( );
two.disp ( );
three.disp ( );
}
```

Program 18.9.

The output of the program is simply a table.

```
Student | Grade |
   John |    30 |
   Pete |    25 |
    Ann |    75 |
```

18.2.2.5. Justification of the fields.

We discussed, that C++ permits you to display a number or a character on a certain number of positions. We called it a field, and set its width by the **width()** function. Let's assume, you display a value, for instance 5, on a field with 3 position width. The computer will fill two leading positions with the filling characters (so far empty spaces) and write the number 5 at the third position. You can change it. You can ask the computer to write the number first and only then fill two additional spaces with fill characters (blanks). This is done by means of familiar to us format flags of the **ios** class. We have studied some of those flags. Here we offer three additional flags. They specify how a value or a character ought to be aligned inside its field. They are: **left**, **right** and **internal**. Those three flags are mutually exclusive. It means, that if one of them is on, the two remaining flags are off. For instance, if you set the **left** flag, both the **right** and **internal** flags will be set to off automatically by the computer. The default flag set by the system is **right**. **Program 18.10** demonstrates each of those flags.

```
#include <iostream.h>

void main ( )
{
cout << "The default alignment is right justified."
    << endl;
cout.width (6);
cout << "**" << endl;
cout << "Demonstrating left justified output." << endl;
cout.setf (ios::left);
cout.width (6);
```

```
    cout << "**" << endl;
    cout << "Demonstrating internal justified output."
        << endl;
    cout.setf (ios::internal, ios::adjustfield);
    cout.width (6);
    cout << "**" << endl;
    }
```

Program 18.10.

The output of the program is

```
The default alignment is right justified.
    **
Demonstrating left justified output.
**
Demonstrating internal justified output.
    **
```

We set the field width to 6 positions every time before displaying two stars. The first time we do not specify how it will be displayed. The computer displays four filling characters, which are the blank spaces, in our case. Two remaining positions are filled by two stars **. We, then, reset the field justification to the left by **cout.setf (ios::left)**. You can use any of the flag setting functions or manipulators to set the flags. We display two stars at the next line after making the output left justified. You can see, the stars precede the blank spaces. We, then, set the third flag on by **cout.setf(ios::internal, ios::adjustfield)**. We use the other form of the **setf()** function.

18.2.2.6. Padding (filling) characters.

So far, we have been displaying the characters or the values on the fields of specified width. The computer filled the unoccupied positions with the blank spaces. Those characters that fill the unoccupied positions are also called the *padding characters*. A blank space is a default filling character. In general, you can specify what characters can be used to fill unoccupied spaces. It can be done using the **fill()** overloaded member function of the **ios** class. Its prototypes are

```
    char fill (char arg);
    char fill ( ) const;
```

The first function has **char** type parameter, we called **arg**. It can be any letter, digit, character, white space and so on. This is a new fill character to be used for the padding between the fields. The first version of the **fill()** function sets stream's padding character to that stored in its argument. After calling the first **fill()** function, the computer pads the fields between the characters or values with the characters specified by that function. The default character is the space. The first **fill()** function returns the previous fill value. The second **fill()** function has no parameters. It just reads and returns stream's current fill character. It can be used in some conditions or to inform the program about current fill character. We used type **char** for the parameter and the returned value of the **fill()** function. This data type is used for that function by the number of modern compilers. However, the C++ Standard Library Draft specifies this type as **int**. **Program 18.11** demonstrates the **fill()** function.

```
#include <iostream.h>

void main ( )
{
char y;
cout << "Padding character is blank by default." << endl;
cout.width (6);
cout << "**" << endl;
cout << "The padding character is 0." << endl;
cout.fill ('0');
cout.width (6);
cout << "**" << endl;
cout << "The padding character is ?." << endl;
y='?';
cout.fill (y);
cout.width (6);
cout << "**" << endl;
cout << "Output has same padding characters until you"
     << " reset it." << endl;
cout.width (6);
cout <<"**";
}
```
Program 18.11.

The output of the program is
```
Padding character is blank by default.
    **
The padding character is 0.
0000**
The padding character is ?.
?????**
Output has same padding characters until you reset it.
  ?????**
```
 The program demonstrates four settings. We first display two stars using a default character for padding the unoccupied position of the field of 8 characters. We, then, change the padding (or filling character) to '0'. We display the field again, and you see four zeros preceding two stars. The filling character is, then, set to '?'. We present an output again. We repeat the output one more time with the same setting of filling character ('?'). It illustrates, that once you change a padding character, it stays this way until altered. The above program illustrates, that a padding character can be also used as an argument of

fill() function directly. In that case, it should be surrounded by the single quote marks as **cout.fill('0')**. A padding character can be also set by the **cout.fill(z)**, where the argument can store any character. In our case, we called the argument **y** and made it equal to **?**.

18.2.2.7. Lower/uppercase characters.

One can also convert to the uppercase the exponent **E** of the floating-point value and the letters in the hexadecimal numbers. It requires the use of familiar to us **uppercase** flag of the **ios** class. We give a short example of its use below.

```
#include <iostream.h>

void main ( )
{
cout.setf (ios::uppercase);
cout << " You should see following in the uppercase. "
     << "\n" << 2.15e15 << "   " << hex << 9899976
     << endl;
}
```

Program 18.12.

The output of this program is

```
You should see following in the uppercase.
2.15E15   970FC8
```

18.2.3. Parametrized manipulators.

We have discussed some of those parametrized manipulators earlier. The parametrized manipulators, described in this section, can perform the same tasks as some **ios** class member functions. You can set the flags, width, precision, using those parameterized manipulators. They can be used for both input and output streams. They all are described in the **<iomanip.h>** header file. It should be included in the program as

```
#include <iomanip.h>
```

if any of following manipulators are used: **setiosflags()**, **resetiosflags()**, **setfill()**, **setw()**, **setprecision()**. Since those manipulators usually go with the other **ios** class functions, the **<iostream.h>** header must be usually included as

```
#include <iostream.h>
```

There are a few more manipulators, that we will not discuss. Some of the manipulators, like insertion (>>) and extraction (<<) operators, are redefined in other classes. So, they can be used without the inclusion of the **<iomanip.h>** header file. In this section we will talk only about those manipulators, that are specific for **<iomanip.h>**, and cannot be used without that header file.

The **<iomanip.h>** defines three template classes: **smanip<T>**, **imanip<T>**,

omanip<T>. Here, the **<T>** is the template data type of the template class. You will hardly use this information in the programs. We give it just for a general knowledge. The manipulators are used for the same purposes as the member functions discussed previously. The **setiosflags()** and **resetiosflags()** manipulators are used to set a flag specified by their arguments on and off respectively. They are analogous to **setf()** and **unsetf()** member functions. The **setfill()** manipulator is similar to the **fill()** member function of the **ios** class. It allows to choose a padding character. The **setw()** is analogous to the **width()** function. It sets the field width. The **setprecision()** manipulator acts similarly to **precision()** member function. It sets the precision of the field.

We begin with the **setiosflags()**. Its prototype looks difficult but is easy to use

```
smanip<ios::fmtflags> setiosflags (ios::fmtflags fl_arg);
```

The **fmtflags** type can be substituted by **long**, leading to another form of prototype

```
smanip( long ) setiosflags (long fl_arg);
```

The **fl_arg** parameter can be any format flag of the **ios** class. The manipulator sets on specified by its parameter format flag. These flags in the manipulator parameter can be combined using the OR (|) operator. The setting holds until the next change.

The **resetioflag()** manipulator has following prototypes.

```
smanip<ios::fmtflags>resetiosflags(ios::fmtflags fl_arg);
smanip ( long ) resetiosflags (long flag_arg);
```

The **fl_arg** parameter can be any format flag of the **ios** class. The manipulator clears (or sets off) the specified by **fl_arg** parameter format flag. Its parameter flags can be combined by using OR (|) operator. The clear setting holds until the next change. Consider following example.

```
#include <iostream.h>
#include <iomanip.h>

void main ( )
{
cout << "decimal: " << 999 << " is set to hexadecimal "
     << setiosflags (ios::hex) << 999 << endl;
cout << "it still holds giving hexadecimal of 8883 as "
     << 8883 << resetiosflags (ios::hex)
     << "\nis reset, now 8883 is " << 8883 << endl;
}
```

Program 18.13.

The output of the program is

```
decimal: 999 is set to hexadecimal 3e7
it still holds giving hexadecimal of 8883 as 22b3
is reset, now 8883 is 8883
```

The program shows how the **hex** format flag of the **ios** class has been set on by the **setiosflag()** and reset to off by the **resetiosflag()** manipulators. The **hex** flag is used along with the class name **ios** and scope resolution operator (::) as **ios::hex**.

Pay attention, how we use the parametrized manipulators **setiosflags()** and **resetiosflags()**. They are *inserted* into the **cout** object by the **<<** operator. You cannot use any parametrized manipulator as a member function. For instance,

```
cout.setiosflag (ios::hex);
```

must generate an error. You have to insert them into an object as shown in **Program 18.13**. This is how they differ from the member functions.

The third manipulator is **setfill()**. Its synopsis is

```
smanip <int> setfill (int x);
```

The parameter **x** contains new stream's fill character. The **setfill()** manipulator sets the filling characters of any output filed to the one contained in its parameters **x**. The default character is the space. The setting holds, until you change it.

The **setw()** manipulator has following synopsis

```
smanip < int > setw (int num);
```

The manipulator sets the width of the I/O field to the value **num** specified by its parameter. The setting holds, until you change it. Below, we review an example demonstrating both **setfill()** and **setw()** manipulators.

```
#include <iostream.h>
#include <iomanip.h>

void main ( )
{
char line[ ]="hello";
cout << "You will see padding and changing field width."
      << setfill ('-') << endl;
for (int m=6; m<9; m++)
cout << setw (m) << line << "\n";
}
```

Program 18.14.

The output of the program is

```
-hello
--hello
---hello
```

The **setprecision()** parametrized manipulator has a format of writing

```
smanip<int>setprecision (int num);
```

Its parameter **num** is the number of significant digits or the number of decimal digits after a decimal point. The **setprecision()** manipulator sets the stream precision to the number specified by its parameter **num**. The default precision is six digits. A precision indicates the number of digits after the decimal point, if the display format is **scientific** or **fixed**. If the format is neither floating-point nor fixed, then, the precision indicates the number of significant digits in a value. The setting imposed by **setprecision()** remains in effect, until you change it. Review following example.

```
#include <iostream.h>
```

```
#include <iomanip.h>

void main ( )
{
cout << setprecision (4) << 20.123456;
}
```

Program 18.15.

The output of the program is number 20.1235, when we ran it on the Borland Turbo
C++ compiler. It was 20.12 on Microsoft Visual C++ compiler.

18.2.4. Stream input.

A standard stream input (from the keyboard) C++ style is performed by the **istream**
class object **cin**. In general, an object of **istream** class uses the members of this class
to perform an input from any general stream. Some compilers define the **cin** object as
having **istream_withassign** class data type, which is not a standard type. Since the
istream is inherited by the **istream_withassign** class, all the functions reviewed
below must work fine with this object. Besides, there is little difference between two
classes. We study some members of **istream** class in this section. The **istream** class
declares a number of functions and the overloaded **>>** stream extraction operator function. You must know by now, how to use the **cin** object and the extraction operator. The
described below functions must work similar for providing an input for any stream with
any object of the **istream** class. We illustrate the input class on the example of the **cin**
object, because an input from the keyboard is easier to comprehend.

   The **istream** class is described in the **<iostream.h>** header file. That header file
must be included in a program, if you intend to use the **istream** class members or
objects. Look at Fig 18.1. It tells you, that the **istream** class inherited the **ios** class as
a base. We will first discuss some of the member functions of the **istream** class, that are
used for an unformatted stream input. Later we will discuss, how the **istream** class uses
the members of the inherited **ios** class. We start with **get()**, **getline()** and **read()**
member functions of **istream** class.

   The **get()** function is heavily overloaded. One can use **get()** function version without the arguments. The prototype of this function is
```
    int get ( );
```
You use it through its return value. The function extracts a first character from a stream
and returns it. It can even be a white space character. If no character is extracted, it can
return the **EOF** and call the **setstate(failbit)** function to report an error. You can
assign that character to a **char** or an **unsigned char** variable, for example,
```
    x=obj.get ( );  here x has char or unsigned char type.
```
Other three prototypes of the function are
```
    istream& get (char* arr, int num, char st = '\n');
    istream& get (unsigned char* arr, int num,
                char st = '\n');
```

```
istream& get (signed char* arr, int num,
              char st = '\n');
```
The **arr** in all three versions of the function is a pointer to a character array. The **num** is the number of stored characters, including the null-terminating character. The **st** stores so-called delimiter character, equal to the newline by the default. All three above functions copy the characters from a stream and store them in an array pointed to by **arr**. Each of those three functions reads the characters from the stream, until any or a combination of the following events occurs:
- the **num-1** number of input characters has been read. Each of the versions adds the null character, if it cannot be found in the input;
- the **EOF** character occurs in the input sequence;
- the character specified by the parameter **st** occurs in the input sequence

Neither of those functions extracts the delimiter from the stream or returns it. Each of the functions returns a reference to **istream** class **this** pointer. If a function does not get any characters, it calls **setstate(failbit)** to inform about an error. Why there are three prototypes? Because you can place read characters into three types of strings. The **get()** function is an **istream** class member function. Therefore, it cannot be used by itself. It should be called with an object of **istream** class or its derived classes. The object of the **istream** class is associated with the input stream, from which the **get()** function performs an input. Consider a few examples.

```
#include <iostream.h>

void main ( )
{
char q;
cout << "Enter a letter." <<endl;
q=cin.get ( );
cout << q << endl;
}
```
Program 18.16.

The program displays a message on the screen
```
Enter a letter
```
Let's assume, we enter letter **a** from a keyboard. The program types **a** on the screen. Here we use a version of the **get()** function with no parameters. It reads a letter and returns it. This letter can be assigned to a character variable, in our case **q**. The program reads the character from the keyboard (standard input), because the **get()** function is used with the **cin** object. Let's review next example.

```
#include <iostream.h>

void main ( )
{
char  q[20];
```

```
char x=',';
cout << "Enter a phrase." << endl;
cin.get (q, 40, x);
cout << q << endl;
}
```

Program 18.17.

The program prompts the user to enter a phrase. Let's assume, we type

```
The weather is good, isn't it?
```

The program will display the phrase up to the comma

```
The weather is good
```

because the comma is stored in the delimiter **x**. This is where the reading stops. If you write **get()** function in **Program 18.17** as **cin.get(q, 10, x)**, the program prints

```
The weath
```

In the last case, the computer reads 10 first characters. The delimiter character can be also entered directly as the third argument of **get()** function. For example,

```
cin.get (q, 40, ',');
```

You can use **cin.get(q, 40)**. Then, the delimiter is by default a newline character.

One can use other three forms of the **get()** function. All they do is read a character from a stream and store it in a variable specified by **get()** function argument. The prototypes differ by the types, that their argument can have. The prototypes are

```
istream& get (char& ent);
istream& get (unsigned char& ent);
istream& get (signed char& ent);
```

The **ent** parameter is a reference to a character. Each of the functions reads a character from a stream and stores it as specified by the reference argument. If the functions do not get any characters, they call **setstate(failbit)** to inform about an error. We offer you a program below. It shows how to use these versions of **get()** function.

```
#include <iostream.h>

void main ( )
{
char   q ;
cout << "Enter a character." << endl;
cin.get (q);
cout << q << endl;
   }
```

Program 18.18.

The program prompts the user to enter a letter. We enter a letter, for instance **b**. The entered letter **b** is read by **cin.get(q)**. It gets stored in the variable **q**, which is an argument of the **get()** function. We, then, display the letter by the **cout** object. You can also see another obvious thing. The **get()** is an **istream** class member function. Therefore, it can be used only in association with an object of **istream** or derived from it classes. We use it as a member function of the **cin** object. There exists one more version of this function. We will study it later.

The unformatted input is also performed by the overloaded **getline()** member function of the **istream** class. Its prototypes are

```
istream& getline (char* arr, int num, char st = '\n');
istream& getline (unsigned char* arr, int num,
                  char st = '\n');
istream& getline (signed char* arr, int num,
                  char st = '\n');
```

The **arr** in all three functions is a pointer to a character array. The **num** is the number of stored characters, including the null-terminating character. The **st** is a delimiter character, equal to the newline by default. Each of these three versions copies the characters from the stream to the array pointed to by the pointer **arr**, until any or combination of the following events occurs:

- the **num-1** number of characters has been read. The function stops the input and calls the **setstate(failbit)**;
- the **EOF** character occurs in the input sequence. In this case, the function stops the input and calls the **setstate(eofbit)** to warn the computer, that the **EOF** has been reached;
- the character specified by the parameter **st** occurs in the input sequence;

Each of those functions extracts the delimiter from the stream but does not store it. Each version returns a reference to **istream** class **this** pointer. If the function does not get any characters, it calls **setstate(failbit)** to inform about an error. The function is quite analogous to some versions of the **get()** function. You can run **Program 18.17** to investigate the **getline()** function. Substitute **cin.get()** by **cin.getline(q, 40, x)**. Both functions must work identically.

Let's discuss another unformatted input function. It is the overloaded **read()** function of the **istream** class. Its prototypes are

```
istream& read (char* arr, int num);
istream& read (unsigned char* arr, int num);
istream& read (signed char* arr, int num);
```

Each of the function versions copies the characters from an input stream to an array pointed to by **arr**, until **num** characters are read or **EOF** occurs in the input sequence. There are three prototypes of this function, because there are three types that the **arr** array can have. The stream is a standard input (keyboard), if the function is used with **cin** object. The function returns a reference to **istream** class **this** pointer. If the **EOF** is encountered in the input, the functions warn the computer by calling **setstate(failbit)** function. Typically, one uses the **read()** function for the binary stream input. Review following example.

```
#include <iostream.h>

void main ( )
{
char  q[20];
```

```
cout << "Enter a phrase." << endl;
cin.read (q, 20);
cout << "Read " << cin.gcount ( ) << " characters."
     << endl;
cout.write (q, 20);
}
```
Program 18.19.

The program prompts a user to enter a phrase. Let's assume, we enter
```
The weather is good today, isn't it?
```
The program displays
```
Read 20 characters
The weather is good
```
The **read()** member function reads from the keyboard 20 characters specified by its second argument and stores them in the array **q**. We, then, display the content of this array by the **write()** member function of the class **ostream** used with the object **cout**. Since **read()** is an **istream** class member function, it can be used only in association with an object of the same or derived class. We use it with **cin** as **cin.read(q, 20)**.

The program also illustrates a use of another function. It is the **gcount()** member function of the **istream** class. It does not have any parameters. Its prototype is
```
    int gcount ( ) const;
```
It returns a number of read characters. We used it as **cin.gcount()**, so it returned the latest number of characters read by the **cin** object. We specified 20 characters to be read. This is why the **gcount()** function returned number 20.

18.2.5. Additional features of the stream input.

We have indicated, that **istream** inherited the **ios** class. Therefore, an object of **istream** class can use the members of **ios** class. We have discussed some members of the **ios** class in connection with the **ostream** class. They can be used in the same way by the objects of **istream** class. This section illustrates how to use some of the members of **ios** class.

One can also use the **ios** class format flags with the input stream objects. Familiar format setting functions can be used to set on and off different flags. For instance, **setf()**, **flags()**, **unsetf()** and so on. The **dec, oct, hex** flags can be set for the input of the integral values. Then, the input values will be treated as decimal, octal and hexadecimal numbers. Although almost any flag can be set for the input objects, but there is no point in using some of those flags. For instance, the **uppercase** flag can be meaningless for an input. Not all the member functions of **ios** class are useful for the input, even though technically you can use **ios** class member functions with the input stream objects. So, always use your common sense in determining which function or data member of the **ios** class to use with an I/O stream. We give you an example below.

```
#include <iostream.h>

void main ( )
{
int x;
cin.setf (ios::hex);
cin >> x;
cout << x << endl;
}
```

Program 18.20.

For example, we enter letter **c** from a keyboard and press **ENTER**. Letter **c** is a hex number that corresponds to the decimal number 12. The program indeed displays the value 12 on the screen. The program reads the number as a hexadecimal, because we have associated **hex** flag with the **cin** object by writing **cin.setf(ios::hex)**. The output object **cout** "does not know" about the **hex** flag being on, because a flag was set for the object **cin**. So, **cout** displays the decimal value of **x** by default.

You can also set the field width and the precision for the input. The field width can be very useful, when there is a line of characters or number, and you have to read only a few characters or digits. It can be also helpful, when a line of characters should be read and stored in a few variables, where each variable is supposed to read only a number of characters. You set the field width by **width(m)** function, that has been discussed before. Again, the parameter **m** stores the number of positions in one field. This number of positions will be stored in one variable or array. We give you an example of that.

```
#include <iostream.h>

void main ( )
{
char x[8];
cin.width (4);
cin >> x;
cout << x;
}
```

Program 18.21.

We type **qwertyuiopqwertyuio**. The program displays

qwe

The **cin.width(4)** sets the number of characters to be read by one variable (or the field width) to 4. You enter a sequence of characters. Only 3 of them will be read. The null character becomes the fourth character of the string. You can also set a precision for reading a value using the **precision()** member function of the **ios** class.

18.2.6. Stream error reporting.

The **ios** class is inherited by all the I/O classes. Therefore, the members of the **ios** class can be used with the objects of other classes. The **ios** class has an error checking capability. It can be used by all the I/O classes. Let's discuss it in details.

The **ios** class has another bitmask type members. They are the **iostate** bitmask type members. They are just the flags that are set on, if an error occurs due to the manipulations with the I/O streams. There are four flags of that data type in the **ios** class: **badbit**, **eofbit**, **failbit** and **goodbit**. The **badbit** flag is set on to signal about the loss of some bits in an input or output sequences. When some of the bits are not what they should be, the information can be distorted or lost. The **eofbit** is used to signal, that the input operation has reached the end of the input information. An example of setting such a bit on can be when one reads the data from a file and reaches an end-of-file (**EOF**). The **failbit** is used to indicate that the input or output of one or more characters has failed. The **goodbit** is on when all other error bits are off, i.e., it is on when there is no error in an I/O stream.

The **ios** class even declares four functions, that can check if any of those bits is on. None of those functions has a parameter. Each of them returns an integral number.

The **good()** function. Its prototype is

```
int good ( ) const;
```

The function is used for checking the stream's status. If all stream error bits are clear, it will return a non-zero value. Otherwise, it will return zero. You can use it to check for I/O stream error status.

The **bad()** function. Its prototype is

```
int bad ( ) const;
```

The function returns a non-zero value in case of a serious I/O problem. Usually, the error detected by this function sets the **badbit** flag on. If the **bad()** function detects an error, all the I/O operations should be stopped immediately.

The **eof()** function. Its prototype is

```
int eof ( ) const;
```

This function is usually used, when I/O is performed on a file. The function returns a nonzero value if the end of file has been reached. Reaching the end of file sets the **eofbit** flag on. The **eof()** function returns a non-zero value, when the **eofbit** flag is set on.

The **fail()** function. Its prototype is

```
int fail ( ) const;
```

The function returns a nonzero value when any I/O error occurs. The error detected by this function also sets either **badbit** or **failbit** flags on. One might want to know, if an error detected by the **fail()** function is fatal. In this case, one should also call the **bad()** function. If **bad()** returns 0, the error condition can be assumed to be nonfatal. The I/O can be resumed after clearing all the error flags. The **fail()** function does not detect the end of file.

The error bits can be obtained directly. The **rdstate()** function returns a value that corresponds to a flag (**goodbit**, **eofbit**, **failbit** or **badbit**) that is currently on. The prototype of that function is

```
    int rdstate ( ) const;
```
One can impose the conditions on the returned value to check which flags are on.
```
    if (rdstate ( ) ==goodbit).... or
    if (rdstate ( ) & badbit)...
```
If a failure bit has been set on, it can be cleared or, in other words, set off by the **clear( )** function. Its prototype is
```
    void clear (int stat);
```
The **stat** parameter can accept any of the values: **goodbit**, **badbit**, **eofbit** or **failbit**. The **clear( )** function clears the error state flag specified by its parameter. If parameter **stat** is set to 0, all the error bits are cleared. For example,
```
    clear (goodbit);
    clear (badbit | eofbit );
```
One can use the bitwise OR (|) operator to include the bits to be cleared.

Following program illustrates the error flags and the functions that check for them.

```
    #include <iostream.h>

    void main( )
    {
    float k;
    cout << "Flags are OK if no I/O error is detected."
        << endl << "cin.bad( ) reads " << cin.bad ( )
        << endl << "cin.fail( ) reads " << cin.fail ( )
        << endl << "cin.eof( ) reads " << cin.eof ( ) << endl
         << "cin.good( ) reads " << cin.good ( ) << endl
         << "cin.rdstate( ) reads " << cin.rdstate( ) << endl
         << "Now perform an erroneous operation."
        << " Enter a character." << endl;
    cin >> k;
      cout << "Now an error has been detected." << endl
            << "cin.bad( ) reads " << cin.bad ( ) << endl
            << "cin.fail( ) reads " << cin.fail ( ) << endl
            << "cin.eof( ) reads " << cin.eof ( ) << endl
             << "cin.good( ) reads " << cin.good ( ) << endl
            << "cin.rdstate( ) reads " << cin.rdstate ( )
            << endl << " We now clear the error state."
            << endl;
    cin.clear ( );
    cout << "The flags that were on has been reset." << endl
           << "cin.bad( ) reads " << cin.bad ( ) << endl
          << "cin.fail( ) reads " << cin.fail ( ) << endl
          << "cin.eof( ) reads " << cin.eof ( ) << endl
           << "cin.good( ) reads " << cin.good ( ) << endl
           << "cin.rdstate( ) reads " << cin.rdstate ( )
           << endl;
```

```
}
```
Program 18.22.

We first display the returned values by all the error checking functions in the above program. Since we did not do anything wrong, no error is likely to occur. And the first **cout** should display

```
Flags are OK if no I/O error is detected.
cin.bad( ) reads 0
cin.fail( ) reads 0
cin.eof( ) reads 0
cin.good( ) reads 0
cin.rdstate( ) reads 1
Now perform an erroneous operation. Enter a character.
```
The program prompts a user to make an error by entering a character. The program waits for a floating-point number to be entered as a value of **x**. If you enter a character, it will be considered as an abnormal input. The program warns a user, that an error has been detected and, then, displays the status of each error flag.

```
Now an error has been detected.
cin.bad( ) reads 0
cin.fail( ) reads 2
cin.eof( ) reads 0
cin.good( ) reads 0
cin.rdstate( ) reads 2
```
The **cin.fail()** member function reports an error caused by the **cin** object. Therefore, the **failbit** flag should be on at that time. The **cin.rdstate()** function also reports, that this flag has gone on. We use **cin.clear()** to clear the error flags associated with the **cin** object. The output of the program shows, the **cin** related error flags are set off again.

```
We now clear the error state.
cin.bad( ) reads 0
cin.fail( ) reads 0
cin.eof( ) reads 0
cin.good( ) reads 1
cin.rdstate( ) reads 0
```
You can use those functions in conditional statements to check if no error has occurred during stream I/O. You will see some of them acting for a file input/output.

18.2.7. *streambuf* object.

Let's discuss a very important point in stream I/O. The **istream** and **ostream** classes perform the stream input and output respectively. They can perform the I/O for a general stream. The **cin** and **cout** objects are just two standard objects, designed to perform an I/O to/from a standard stream. You can create other objects for performing the I/O operations with any other stream. Now, look at the following constructors

```
ios (streambuf *pr);
istream (streambuf *pr);
ostream (streambuf *pr);
```

They create an object of the **ios**, **istream** and **ostream** classes respectively. They all accept a pointer to a **streambuf** object as their argument. An object of the **streambuf** class controls an input/output to a stream. It is called the *stream buffer*. It provides an interface for the I/O operations. For instance, the objects of the **ostream** class that perform an output, such as **cout**, etc., call on member functions of that class to insert the characters into an output sequence. The **cin** object, for instance, calls on the members of this class to extract the characters from the input sequence. Whenever an object of any of those classes is created, an object of the **streambuf** class is also attached to it by the compiler. A **streambuf**-derived class object will be attached to an object of any class derived from these classes. You can use the **streambuf** object in those classes without ever having to define it explicitly. You do not have to know anything about this object at all. We were able to do all above I/O operations without even mentioning that object.

We do not advise to try to define the **streambuf** objects and work with them directly. However, we give the member functions of that class in the reference section of this chapter. Detailed operations with the **streambuf** objects are beyond the scope of this book. You must get a lot more exprerienced with C++ to be able even to understand them. This will come to you, after you do some programming in C++. You can read some specific information about the I/O streams only after that. This book offers a good quality introductory and intermediate professional level of C++.

So, the **istream** class extracts (or copies) the characters from a stream. We associate that object with the stream. Loosely speaking, it writes the data from a stream to "some place" else. This is called an input. The **ostream** class writes (copies) the characters from "some place" to a stream. The **ios** class members determine I/O formatting, status, etc. The **streambuf** object controls the I/O to a stream.

18.3. File input/output.

So far, we have dealt with the general stream data I/O. To illustrate the stream I/O, we used the **cout** and **cin** objects for the I/O from the keyboard or to the monitor. You realize, you need a way to store the data. As you know from the previous chapters, the data can be placed in the disk files and stored there. You just have to learn how to open and close disk files, and how to write and read the information to and from them in C++. You already know how to do it using C. It is still valid and can be used in C++. Nevertheless, C++ offers additional tools, which are implemented in the **iostream** library. There are two ways of accessing a file: sequential and random file access. We will study how to access a file using both ways.

In general, we advise you not to be afraid to operate with the disk files, or any files. If you ask how to handle the files, the answer is very simple. First you open a file. Then, you read or write the data respectively from or to that file. After the I/O is completed, a file should be closed. We will first study how to open and close a file. Then, we will study how to read and write the data. After you are familiar with those two steps, it should not be too difficult to handle the files at all.

18.3.1. Opening and closing a file.

In general, a file in C++ can be understood as a sequential stream of bytes. A file ends with the end-of-file **EOF** character. It tells the computer when to stop reading the data. There are three classes that handle disk files. The **ifstream** class objects can open and handle a file only for an input. The **ofstream** class objects open and handle a file only for an output. The **fstream** class is used for both input and output. How do you use those objects? First you define an object of a class type. Then, you use the member functions of its and its base classes to open and manipulate a file. When an object opens a file, it becomes associated with that file. We will explain the meaning of that. When you create an object of any of those three file handling classes and open a file, the computer attaches an object of the **filebuf** class to it. The **filebuf** class object, attached to a file, controls how the data will be read and written to a file. You will communicate with a file through some buffer in the memory. If you write a data to a file, it might be placed in this buffer before copying it to the file. If you read the data from a file, it might be copied from the file to this buffer. It will be, then, copied to the screen or any other file or device. The **filebuf** class has been derived from the **streambuf** class. Include **<fstream.h>** header, when dealing with **ifstream**, **ofstream**, **fstream** classes. These classes are described in **<fstream.h>** header.

To open a file, you first have to know whether it will be used for the data input, output, or for both input and output. That is something you should determine according to a particular problem. Depending on that, define an object of **ifstream**, **ofstream**, **fstream** classes.

The C++ Library Draft does not specify the **fstream** class. However, modern C++ compilers have this class in their **<fstream.h>** header. C++ Library Draft specifies 6 classes in this header: **filebuf**, **ifstream**, **ofstream**, **stdiobuf**, **istdiostream**, **ostdiostream**. We will not study last two classes. They assist with extracting and inserting into a stream

18.3.1.1. Opening and closing a file for reading only.

To open a file for the input only, you should use **ifstream** class object. The **ifstream** is derived from the **istream** class according to Fig. 18.1. Therefore, it inherited the **istream** and **ios** class members. We will begin with the constructors. The **ifstream** class declares a number of constructors. Its most used prototypes are

```
ifstream ( );
ifstream (const char* pr, int Mode = ios::in,
          int PBuf = filebuf::openprot);
ifstream (filedesc fd);
ifstream (filedesc fd, char* q, int num);
```
We also want to confront you with two more member function prototypes
```
void open (const char* pr, int Mode = ios::in,
```

```
                    int PBuf = filebuf::openprot );
     void close ( );
```

The third and the fourth constructors from the above four are not specified in the C++ Standard Draft. However, they are used by a number of compilers. This is why we give them. The **open()** and the **close()** functions are used for opening and closing a file respectively. Sometimes, a constructor can open a file. It depends on which of the four constructor forms you use. Sometimes, after you construct an object, the **open()** function should be used with that object for opening a file. An opened file should be always closed by the **close()** function. Even though it might seem to you too much information to have four constructors and two functions at once, do not get scared. We will introduce you very gradually to each of them.

Let's first study the meaning of the parameters in each of those functions. Some of those functions have the parameters with the same names. The same name parameters have the same meaning, even though they appear in different functions. So, we just give you a meaning of each of them.

The **pr** is a pointer to a string containing a name of the file to be opened. The name of the file can contain even the path of that file, i.e., the name of a subdirectory in which the file will be placed by the computer. For instance, you open the file **mine.dat** with the path **C:\tcwin\bin\mine.dat**. You can place it in a character string pointed to by **pr**. The parameter we called **Mode** specifies in which mode a file should be opened, i.e., whether it will be opened for input, for output, or for adding the data to it, or as a binary one and so on. The **Mode** parameter can have a value, which is selected from a group of values. This group is specified as the flags of the **openmode** bitmask type in the **ios** class. So, it is another example of using the base class **ios** by the derived class objects. The **ifstream** class objects can use the **ios** class members to specify an opening mode of a file.

We discuss those members of the **ios** class in this section. They are the flags of the **openmode** data type. They are specified by proposed C++ Standard Draft. Most modern compilers still use the **int** data type instead of the **openmode**. The flags are given in Table 18.1. **ifstream** class object can use some of them. We will discuss them soon.

You can use more than one flag as **Mode** argument. In this case, different flags should be combined by the OR (|) operator. We will show it later.

The **PBuf** parameter determines a protection mode for buffered files. Disregard it at this point. It is a default parameter anyway, so you do not have to specify it at this point. Besides, C++ Standard Draft does not specify this parameter. Nevertheless, this parameter is specified by the number of compilers.

The **fd** is a file descriptor. When a file is opened by a low-level function, it is assigned a file descriptor. So, some of the constructors use that **fd** as their parameter. The **filedesc** data type is just an equivalent of **int**. Many compilers use **int** data type instead of **filedesc**, that is specified by the standard draft. The other two parameters **q** and **num** are the pointer and the length of the previously allocated reserve area. I/O to and from a file can be performed directly. It can be also performed through an intermediate step. The data can be copied to some memory array first. It can, then, be transferred to another device or another location. This intermediate memory space, through which an I/O is performed, is called a buffer, as you know. We called this memory buffer a reserve area.

The I/O performed through that intermediate step is called a buffered I/O.

Table 18.1. Opening mode flags.

Flag	Used for following action
ios::app	File is opened for appending. You can add data to it. If any data existed before, it does not get truncated. If the file does not exist, it is created.
ios::ate	File is opened and the cursor moves to its end.
ios::binary	File is opened in binary mode. By deault a file is opened in **ios::text** mode.
ios::in	File is opened for an input or for reading from it. If the file does not exist, the opening usually fails. However, some compilers can create a file, even if you open it in this mode.
ios::out	File is opened for an output or for writing. Any previous data will be truncated. If the file does not exist, it is created.
ios::trunc	File is opened. Its previous content is deleted.
ios::nocreate	It specifies, a file should be opened only if it already exists. If it does not exist, the opening fails.
ios::noreplace	It specifies, that a file should be opened, if it does not exist yet. Otherwise, an opening will fail.

We can now review each function in the beginning of this section. The constructor
```
ifstream ( );
```
simply creates an object of the **ifstream** class. If your object is created by the first constructor, you need to use the **open()** member function to open a file. The function
```
open (const char* pr, int Mode = ios::in,
        int PBuf = filebuf::openprot);
```
opens a file whose name is stored in a string pointed to by **pr** in a mode specified by **Mode** parameter. The protection mode of that file is specified by the **PBuf** parameter. The **open()** function has **void** return type. It does not return any value. It sets the **ios::failbit** flag on, if any opening error has occurred. Review an example.

```
#include <iostream.h>
#include <fstream.h>

void main ( )
{
ifstream mine;
mine.open ("mytry.dat", ios::in);
if ( mine.fail( ) == 0)
cout << "An opening was successful.";
else
cout <<"An opening error has occured.";
mine.close ( );
mine.clear (ios::badbit | ios::failbit);
```

}

Program 18.23.

The program opens and closes a file with the name **mytry.dat**. Even though it works on some compilers, but the reading object cannot open a file that does not exist. And it is true for many compilers. You have to use an **ofstream** or **fstream** class object to open a non-existing file, in general. As you see, we have used file name in the **open()** function directly as an argument. A file name can be plugged-in as the first argument of the **open()** function directly. It should be surrounded by the double quotes " ", when used this way. In our case, we wrote

```
mine.open ("mytry.dat", ios::in);
```

It would be the same as placing **mytry.dat** string into some character array and using a pointer to that array as an argument

```
char line[ ]= " mytry.dat"
mine.open (line, ios::in);
```

We have mentioned, when an object opens a file it becomes associated with that file. Here, we demonstrated what does it mean. You declare an object. In this section we speak about **ifstream** class. So, it will be an object of that class. We have defined the object **mine** of the **ifstream** class. We used **open()** function with **mine** object as **mine.open()**. The file opened by the member function used with the object **mine** became associated with this object. If you use **mine.close()**, the computer will know that you intend to close the **mytry.dat** file. The **close()** member function does not have any parameters. It does not need them. *Thus, when an **ifstream** class object opens a file, it becomes associated with that object. If you call class member functions with this object, they will operate on the file opened by this object.*

The second argument of the **open()** function in the above example was **ios::in**. We give you all possible values of that second parameter for all three file handling classes in Table 18.1. You will learn later, this parameter is used in similar functions in other classes. However, you should realize, here we are discussing how to open a file using an object of the **ifstream** class. The **ifstream** class provides a file input. So, you cannot open a file with the **ifstream** class object for an output. Thus, the second parameter of the **open()** function of the **ifstream** class cannot accept **ios::out** and **ios::app** values.

Program 18.23 uses the condition **if(mine.fail()==0)** to check if the file opening was successful. This is an example of error checking functions in action.

When you define an object, that can be created by the second constructor

```
ifstream (const char* pr, int Mode = ios::in,
               int PBuf = filebuf::openprot);
```

it automatically opens a file. So, you do not have to use the **open()** function. The name of that file is contained in a string pointed to by the pointer **pr**. That file is opened in the mode specified by the **Mode** parameter. The protection of that file is specified by the third parameter, that we will discuss later. Again, the third parameter does not exist in the standard draft. But it does exist in many compilers currently on the market. You do not have to specify the last argument, since it is a default argument. Review another example.

```
#include <iostream.h>
#include <fstream.h>

void main ( )
{
char line[ ]="mytry.dat";
ifstream mine (line, ios::in);
if (!mine)
cerr << "An opening was not successful.";
else
cout <<"An opening was successful.";
mine.close ( );
}
```

Program 18.24.

The above program opens a file with a given name. It will not open a new file for all compilers. Some compilers do not allow to open a non-existing file for reading. We define the object **mine** using the second overloaded version of the constructor

```
ifstream mine (line, ios::in);
```

This opens the file **mytry.dat** and associates the object **mine** with this file. Our program has a new feature. It uses the overloaded **!** operator of the **ios** class. This operator can be used with an object of **ios** and any class derived from it. We used it with the **mine** object as **if(!mine)**. The **!** operator returns a nonzero value, if either **failbit** or **badbit** are set on during file opening. We know, those bits are set on in case of an error. So, if a file opens normally, the operator should return zero. The error message will be skipped. The opening message will be displayed. In case of an error, a failure message will be displayed.

One can define the objects, that are created by the third and the fourth constructors.

```
ifstream (filedesc fd);
ifstream (filedesc fd, char* q, int num);
```

Here, **fd** is the file descriptor. We know the file descriptors from the previous chapter. Just to remind you, the **fd** is an integer. The **int** type is used instead of **filedesc** type for the **fd** parameter on many compilers. Both **int** and **filedesc** types are used for the integers. It is a value returned by the C low-level **open()** function. For instance, a file has been opened by the low-level C **open()** function as follows

```
a = open ("myfile.dat", mode);
```

File descriptor **a** became associated with **myfile.dat** file. We can create an object

```
ifstream see1 ( a );
```

This object **see1** is created by the **ifstream(filedesc a)** constructor. This constructor creates an object that becomes associated with *an opened buffered disk file*, described by the file descriptor stored in the variable **a**. The buffer for that file is created by the computer by default.

You can also create the objects, that will not only be associated with an *existing opened file*, but will also specify explicitly the name and the size of the buffer to use for the I/O of that particular file. Those objects are created by **ifstream(filedesc fd, char***

q, int num) constructor. This constructor creates an object, that becomes associated with an existing opened file specified by the file descriptor **fd**. This constructor also associates with that file an input buffer based on an array. That array buffer is pointed to by the pointer **q** and has a size of **num** bytes or characters. For example,

```
ifstream one (x, arr, 20);
```

This definition will create the object **one**. That object will handle the file, whose file descriptor is stored in variable **x**. The file input will be performed through the reserve area 20 bytes long pointed to by the pointer **arr**. You can make that file unbuffered, using **NULL** pointer as the second argument, or 0 as the third one. For example,

```
ifstream one (x, NULL, 0);
```

This, basically, covers the opening of a file with an object of **ifstream** class.

Many compilers handle the file input as follows. When an object of **ifstream** class opens a file, the computer attaches another object to that file as well. That object, as we said, handles the I/O buffering of the file. It is an object of the **filebuf** class. We will review this class later in the reference section of this chapter. The last **ifstream** class constructor version allows you to select the size and location of that buffer area. You can even make a choice whether that buffer will exist at all. All other constructors and the class member function **open()** do not allow you to configure that buffer. It is performed by the system. However, you have some control on the buffer. We will study how to do it later. We will not discuss the **filebuf** objects specifically for the **ofstream** and **fstream** classes. However, a **filebuf** object is attached to an object of any of these classes. As you will see, almost all the functions in all these three classes are called and act similarly. The difference between them is, that **ifstream** class functions handle only file input, while **ofstream** class is used for only output and **fstream** for both input and output. Therefore, the **filebuf** class object will be attached to an object of any of those three classes to provide I/O from and to a file.

18.3.1.2. Opening and closing a file for writing only.

An object of the **ofstream** class is used to open a disk file for an output only. The **ofstream** is derived from the **ostream** class according to Fig. 18.1. Hence, it inherits the **ostream** and **ios** class members. In order to open a disk file for an output only, you need to define an object of the **ofstream** class. That object will open a file, and will become associated with it. The **ofstream** class declares four constructors. The third and the fourth constructors are not specified in C++ Standard Library Draft. However, they are used by a number of compilers.

```
ofstream ( );
ofstream (const char* pr, int Mode = ios::out,
          int PBuf = filebuf::openprot);
ofstream (filedesc fd );
ofstream (filedesc fd, char* q, int num);
```

The disk file opening and closing member functions of the **ostream** class are

```
void open (const char* pr, int Mode = ios::out,
           int PBuf = filebuf::openprot);
```

```
void close ( );
```

All these functions look the same and have the same parameters as the functions of the **ifstream** class from the previous section. The difference is that here you create an object of the **ofstream** class and open a file only for writing data into it. Previous section dealt with the **ifstream** class and the files opened for reading only. So, we will go very briefly over how to open a file for writing only.

You can define an object that will be created by the constructor

```
ofstream ( );
```

That object must use the **open()** member function of the **ofstream** class to open a file for writing only, and will become associated with the opened file. The **open()** function will open a file, whose name is contained inside the string pointed to by **pr** in the mode specified by the second parameter **Mode**. The possible values of the **Mode** parameter are specified in Table 18.1. You have to exclude the **ios::in** value, because the file is not opened for reading. The third parameter of the **open()** function specifies the protection mode of the file to be opened. The third parameter is not specified in C++ Standard Draft. However, it is used on some compilers. The **open()** function does not return any value. But it sets the **ios::failbit** or **ios::badbit** flags on, if the file cannot be opened. Consider an example.

```
#include <iostream.h>
#include <fstream.h>

void main ( )
{
char line[ ]="mytry.dat";
ofstream mine;
mine.open(line, ios::out);
if (!mine)
cerr << "An opening was not successful.";
else
cout <<"An opening was successful.";
mine.close ( );
}
```

Program 18.25.

If this program opens the file **mytry.dat**, it displays the message

```
An opening was successful.
```

This program should be quite clear to you. It defines an object **mine** of the **ofstream** class. This object uses the **open()** member function of the **ofstream** class to open the **mytry.dat** file. After the file is opened, the **mine** object becomes associated with the **mytry.dat** file. The **mine.close()** closes that **mytry.dat** file. You can close that file and associate the **mine** object with another file after that.

Other **ofstream** constructors do not need the **open()** function. The

```
ofstream (const char* pr, int Mode = ios::out,
          int PBuf = filebuf::openprot);
```

constructor creates an object and opens a file, that becomes "attached" or associated with that object. The name of that file to be opened is stored in a character array pointed to by the pointer **pr**. The file is opened in the mode determined by the value of the **Mode** parameter in Table 18.1. The third parameter **PBuf** specifies the protection mode. If a file cannot be opened by a constructor, it will set on **ios::failbit** flag. You can always check, if the error flags have not been set up. We offer you another program that demonstrates a file opening in the writing mode by this constructor.

```
#include <iostream.h>
#include <fstream.h>

void main ( )
{
char line[ ]="mytry.dat";
ofstream mine (line, ios::out);
if (!mine)
cerr << "An opening was not successful.";
else
cout <<"An opening was successful.";
mine.close ( );
}
```
Program 18.26.

The program opens the **mytry.dat** file and displays a message about it.

One can also create and attach an object to an opened file. To do that, you must define an object, that will be constructed by the third and the fourth constructors

```
ofstream (filedesc fd);
ofstream (filedesc fd, char* q, int num);
```

Both constructors are not specified by the C++ Standard Draft. They contain the **filedesc** type parameter. It is, in fact, an **int** data type. It is used instead of **filedesc** type in a number of compilers. The **fd** stands for the file descriptor of the file, that has been created and opened before by the low-level C opening function. The **q** and **num** parameters specify the pointer and the length of the buffer to be used for the disk file buffering. The third constructor creates an object, associates it with an *opened* file specified by the file descriptor stored in **fd**. It uses computer-specified buffer for the file I/O.

The last constructor creates an object, associates it with an opened file specified by the file descriptor stored in **fd**. It uses a user-specified I/O buffer. In the last case, the buffered I/O will be performed through an existing array of size **num** pointed to by the pointer **q**. This buffer is called a reserve area by some sources. If you want to open an unbuffered file by the last constructor, use **NULL** pointer as the second argument or 0 as the third one. Again, both constructors do not need the **open()** member function to open a file, because they create the objects associated with the opened files. Following program illustrates an opening of a file.

```
#include <iostream.h>
```

```
#include <fstream.h>
#include <IO.H>

void main(void)
{
int ret;
ret=open ("mytry.dat", 1);
if (ret==-1)
cout << "cannot open\n";
else
cout << "opened\n";

ofstream mine (ret);
mine.close ( );
}
```

Program 18.27.

The program opens and closes the **mytry.dat** file. It displays the message.

```
opened
```

The message informs, that the file is opened by the C low-level **open()** function. Do not confuse C low-level **open()** function with the **ofstream** class **open()** member function. They are different functions. We included **<io.h>** file to be able to use the low-level **open()** function. It returns the **mytry.dat** file descriptor, which we assign to the variable **ret**. We, then, define the object **mine** of **ofstream** class by **ofstream mine(ret)**. This statement creates the object **mine** and associates it with the opened **mytry.dat** file. The file is closed by **mine.close()**.

18.3.1.3. Opening and closing a file for I/O.

One can open a file for both reading and writing. A file can be opened for I/O by means of the **fstream** class objects and member functions. The **fstream** class is a class derived from the **iostream** class. The **iostream** class inherits the **istream** and **ostream** classes. Hence, the **fstream** class indirectly inherits the **istream**, **ostream** and **ios** classes. It means, an object of **fstream** class can use members of any of these classes. To open a file for I/O, you define an object of the **fstream** class. A file can be opened by the **fstream** constructor, while an object is constructed. A file can be also opened using **open()** member function of the **fstream** class. An object of the **fstream** class can be created by one of four following constructors

```
fstream ( );
fstream (const char* pr, int Mode,
         int PBuf = filebuf::openprot);
fstream (filedesc fd);
fstream (filedesc fd, char* q, int num);
```

To open and close a file, one might use following **fstream** member functions

```
    void open (const char* pr, int Mode,
              int PBuf = filebuf::openprot);
    void close ( );
```

All these functions work similarly to the **ifstream** or **ofstream** classes. The only difference is that **ifstream** class object opens a file only for reading and **ofstream** object only for writing to it. The **fstream** class object can open a file either for reading or writing, or for both. The **Mode** parameter specifies in which mode your file will be opened. The **Mode** parameter values can be found in Table 18.1. One can use a few values combined with the OR operator as **Mode** argument.

You know from the previous chapter, a file can be opened in one of the following modes: **w**, **r**, **a**, **wb**, **rb**, **ab**, **a+**, **w+**, **r+**, **a+b**, **w+b**, **r+b**. These modes denote a file to be opened for: **w** - for writing only, **r** - for reading only and so on. Now consider how a file opening mode can be specified by the **ios** class enumerators used for the **Mode** argument. The

ios::in corresponds to **"r"**;

ios::out | ios::trunc corresponds to **"w"**, because for writing to the file you want to open it in the output mode. The opened file must also be truncated if opened in writing mode. This means, that all the previous data inside this file should be deleted;

ios::out | ios::app corresponds to **"a"**, because this opens a file for an output;

ios::in | ios::binary corresponds to reading in the binary mode **"rb"**;

ios::out | ios::trunc | ios::binary is writing in the binary mode **"wb"**;

ios::out | ios::app | ios::binary corresponds to appending in the binary mode **"ab"**;

ios::in | ios::out corresponds to opening file for reading and writing **"r+"**;

ios::in | ios::out | ios::trunc corresponds to **"w+"**;

ios::in | ios::out | ios::app corresponds to **"a+"**;

ios::in | ios::out | ios::binary corresponds to **"r+b"**;

ios::in | ios::out | ios::trunc | ios::binary corresponds to **"w+b"**;

ios::in | ios::out | ios::app | ios::binary corresponds to **"a+b"**.

We offer you following program just as a demonstration of one of those modes.

```
    #include <fstream.h>

    void main(void)
    {
    int ret;
    char line[20]="mytry.dat";
    ofstream mine;
    mine.open (line, ios::in | ios::out | ios::trunc
               | ios::binary) ;
    if (!mine)
    cerr << "An opening was not successful.";
    else
    cout << "An opening was successful.";
    mine.close ( );
```

}

Program 18.28.

The program opens the **mytry.dat** file and displays a message that the opening was successful. If file cannot be opened or an error occurs, the error message is displayed.

18.3.2. Sequential file input and output.

We have talked about a cursor, that is also called a file position indicator. We have to say couple more words about it. It can be better appreciated as a typewriter cursor, that shows a precise place at which a character will be typed in. After a typewriter types a character, the cursor is advanced to a next position. Same can be applied to reading. You read a letter at the cursor, and, then, that cursor moves to the next position. In C++ we also introduced the get and put pointers. When you read a character from a certain position inside a file (stream), the cursor advances by one position. In this case, one can say that this is a get pointer. When you write a letter to a file (stream), one speaks about a put pointer that moves.

Both put and get pointers belong to the different streams. We will learn, that the disk file input (or reading the data from a disk file) is performed by the objects of the **ifstream** class. An **ifstream** class has no reading functions on its own. It can open and close a file. It can perform some other operations. How can its objects perform an input from a file? The **ifstream** class is derived from the **istream** class. An object of the **ifstream** class can, therefore, use the member functions of the **istream** and **ios** classes. Thus, an object of the **ifstream** class can use known to us **get()**, **read()** and other functions. But this time they perform an input from a disk file associated with that object. Do not try to understand how it is done yet. We will show it to you.

The data output (or writing a data to a disk file) is provided by the **ofstream** class objects. The **ofstream** class has directly inherited the **ostream** and indirectly **ios** class. This is why an object of the **ofstream** class can use the member functions of the **ostream** and **ios** classes. This is why we can use the **put()**, **write()** and other functions, that, in this case, operate on a file associated with a particular object.

The **fstream** class objects can perform both input and output. The **fstream** class has been derived from the **iostream** class, which is derived from the **istream** and **ostream** classes. So, the **fstream** class has indirectly inherited the **ios** class as well. An object of this class can use the member functions of any of those classes for performing an I/O for a disk file.

The get pointer inside a file is related to an input streams and **ifstream** class objects, while the put pointer is tied to the output and **ofstream** class objects. The **fstream** class objects establish two streams - one for an output and another one for an input. Both pointers must be independent in theory. On a number of compilers only one of the pointers is active any time. When a get pointer of the **fstream** object moves to a certain position and reading switches to writing, the put pointer starts from the last position of the get pointer. It is true for a number of compilers. The same is true vice versa. We, sometimes, use the word cursor without specifying whether it is a get or put pointer, because we want to indicate an I/O position inside a file rather than talking about a particular pointer.

The sequential file I/O is performed sequentially position by position. This means, that the put or get pointers do not jump over a position. They go gradually from position to the next position performing respectively output or input. Now consider how to perform a sequential file I/O.

18.3.2.1. Reading and writing text from and to a file.

Both **<<** and **>>** operators can be used to read the data from a file or to write it to a file respectively. Remember, we have been using the **<<** operator with the **cout** object for displaying the data on the screen. The screen is nothing else but a standard file. So, the **ofstream** or **fstream** class objects can write the data to any other file, that they opened. And the data they write to a file can be passed to those objects by the stream insertion operators (**<<**) described in the **ostream** class. The **ifstream** or **fstream** class objects can read the data from a file. That data can be extracted from the files by the stream extraction operators (**>>**) declared in the **istream** class. Following program illustrates that.

```
#include <fstream.h>

void main(void)
{
char line[20]="mytry.dat";
ofstream mine;
mine.open (line, ios::out) ;
if (!mine)
cerr << "An opening was not successful.";
else
cout <<"An opening was successful.";
mine << 73 << " " << 5.5 << " delitescent";
mine.close ( );
}
```
Program 18.29.

If successful, the program displays a message
```
An opening was successful.
```
It also opens a file, and writes
```
73 5.5 delitescent
```
to it. The file is, then, closed. If you open the **mytry.dat** file after the program run, it will contain the numbers and the word written to it. The data is written to the file by the **mine** object, that gets the data through the insertion operator (**<<**). The program should also work, if **mine** is declared as an object of the **fstream** class. The data written to the **mytry.dat** file can be read by the next program.

```
#include <fstream.h>

void main(void)
{
char line[20]="mytry.dat";
char arr[40];
int x;
float y;
ifstream next;
next.open (line, ios::in) ;
if (!next)
cerr << "An opening was not successful.";
else
cout <<"An opening was successful.\n"
      << "We are getting a message from a file.\n";
next >> x;
next >> y;
next >> arr;
cout << x << " " << y << " " << arr;
next.close ( );
}
```

Program 18.30.

The program opens the **mytry.dat** file and reads the data from it. It displays following messages

```
An opening was successful.
We are getting a message from a file.
73 5.5 delitescent
```

The object **next** and extraction operator (**>>**) extract the data from the **mytry.dat** and pass it to the **int** type variable **x**, **float** variable **y** and character string **arr**. They all are displayed on the screen by the **cout** object. The program must also work, if we make **next** an object of the **fstream** class.

Program 18.31 reads and writes the data to the same file.

```
#include <fstream.h>

void main(void)
{
char line[20]="mytry.dat";
char arr[40];
int x;
float y;
ofstream mine;
ifstream next;
mine.open (line, ios::out) ;
```

```
if (!mine)
cerr << "An opening was not successful.";
else
cout <<"An opening was successful.\n";
mine << 73 << " " << 5.5 << " impressive";
mine.close ( );
next.open (line, ios::in) ;
if (!next)
cerr << "An opening was not successful.";
else
cout <<"An opening was successful.\n"
     << "We are getting a message from a file.\n";
next >> x;
next >> y;
next >> arr;
cout << x << " " << y << " " << arr;
next.close ( );
}
```
Program 18.31.

The output of the program is

```
An opening was successful.
An opening was successful.
We are getting a message from a file.
73  5.5  impressive
```

The program opens a file, writes the data to it, and closes it. The file is, then, opened again for reading. The data is read and displayed on the screen. One can ask why do we have to close the file and to open it again. Remember, we talk about a sequential file I/O in this section. When you write the data to a file and want to read the whole file, the get pointer must be placed at the beginning of the file. If you move the cursor to the beginning of the file, it can be hardly called a sequential file access. However, we have another option - to close a file. When a file is opened again for reading, the get pointer is located at the very first position, that will be read next.

18.3.2.2. Unformatted file I/O.

What does it mean to perform a data output to a file? It means to copy the data into that file. An unformatted file output can be performed by the **put()** member function of the **ostream** class. Data input from a file means to copy the data from a file. An unformatted data input is performed by the **get()** and **getline()** member functions of the **istream** class. We have discussed all the prototypes of those functions, when talking about stream I/O. There is nothing special about a file I/O. Since **ofstream** has inherited **ostream** class and the **ifstream** class has been derived from the **istream**, one can use **get()**, **getline()**, **put()** to perform file I/O. Just use **get()** with the **ifstream** and

fstream objects. The **put()** member function must be used with the **ofstream** or **fstream** objects. Review the following program.

```
#include <fstream.h>

void main( )
{
char *arr="How are you?";
ofstream mewrite;
mewrite.open ("mytry.dat", ios::out | ios::binary) ;
if (!mewrite)
cerr << "An opening was not successful.";
else
cout <<"An opening was successful.";
while (*arr !='\0' )
mewrite.put (*arr++);
mewrite.close ( );
}
```

Program 18.32.

The program opens the file **mytry.dat** for an output as a binary one. If the opening is successful, it displays a message

    An opening was successful.

The message "**How are you?**" gets written to the **mytry.dat** file as well.

Object **mewrite** has opened the **mytry.dat** file. Therefore, it is now associated with this file. We write the content of the string **arr** to the file using **while** loop as

    while (*arr !='\0')
    mewrite.put (*arr++);

We know, that every time **put()** function places a character stored in its argument into a file or a stream, it advances a cursor by one. Thus, the next character will be placed at the next position inside a file or a stream. It is like an analogy with the typewriter, as we have mentioned. You type a character and the cursor moves to the next position on a paper. Each time we use **put()** function, it writes to a position inside the file a content of the cell pointed to by current value of the pointer **arr**. Then, the pointer is incremented by **arr++** to point to the next array element. Next loop writes that next array element to a new position inside a file. The looping ends when the end of the **arr** string is reached, or when the condition ***arr !='\0'** becomes false. We know, that any character string is terminated by a null character. And our **arr** string is also terminated by this character. The program works, if you make **mewrite** an object of the **fstream** class.

You can use the **get()** member function of the **istream** class for reading from a file. We will not discuss this function and all its prototypes again. We have discussed them earlier. Here, we just give the prototypes and show how to use the **get()** function to read the data from a file. Some of the **get()** function prototypes are

```
int get ( );
istream& get (char* arr, int num, char st = '\n');
```

```
istream& get (unsigned char* arr, int num,
                char st = '\n');
istream& get (signed char* arr, int num,
                char st = '\n');
```

You can get the information about the parameters of this function from the previous sections of this chapter or from the reference section. Review following example that illustrates how to use one of those **get()** functions.

```
#include <fstream.h>

void main( )
{
ifstream meread;
char line[15];
meread.open ("mytry.dat", ios::in | ios::binary) ;
if (!meread)
{
cerr << "An opening was not successful.";
return;
}
else
cout <<" An opening was successful.\n"
      << "We are getting a message from a file.\n";
meread.get (line, 14);
cout << line;
meread.close( );
}
```

Program 18.33.

The program opens the same **mytry.dat** file and reads its content. Recall, that we have written a string to a file in **Program 18.32**. Above program should read the same phrase from our file. If the opening and reading is successful, the program displays following messages

```
An opening was successful.
We are getting a message from a file.
How are you?
```

The program declares and uses the **meread** object of the **ifstream** class to read the data from a file. It will also run, if we make **meread** an object of the **fstream** class.

We also remind you three more prototypes.

```
istream& get (char& ent);
istream& get (unsigned char& ent);
istream& get (signed char& ent);
```

We illustrate the use of those three **get()** function prototypes for the file input by the following program.

```
#include <fstream.h>

void main( )
{
ifstream meread;
char a;
meread.open ("mytry.dat", ios::in | ios::binary) ;
if (!meread)
{
cerr << "An opening was not successful.";
return;
}
else
cout <<" An opening was successful.\n"
     << "We are getting a message from a file.\n";
while (meread.get(a))
cout << a;
}
```

Program 18.34.

This program also reads the phrase from the same **mytry.dat** file, that has been written
by **Program 18.32**. Since it performs exactly the same action as the previous program,
both programs have the same output.

To perform an input/output in the same program, write **Program 18.32** and **Program
18.34** as one source file. One can perform I/O in the same program using even the same
object for both input and output. It is shown in the program below.

```
#include <fstream.h>

void main( )
{
char *arr="How are you?";
char a;
fstream me;
me.open ("mytry.dat", ios::out | ios::binary) ;
if (!me)
cerr << "An opening was not successful.";
else
cout <<"An opening was successful.";
while (*arr !='\0' )
me.put(*arr++);
me.close ( );
me.open ("mytry.dat", ios::in | ios::binary) ;
if (!me)
{
```

```
cerr << "An opening was not successful.";
return;
}
else
cout <<" An opening was successful.\n"
       << "We are getting a message from a file.\n";
me.get (a);
while (!me.eof( ))
{
cout << a;
me.get(a);
}
me.close( );
}
```

Program 18.35.

This program is combined from the previous ones. You should not have any problems with it. It opens file **mytry.dat**, writes data into it. It, then, closes the file and opens it again. The data is read from the file and displayed on the screen. The file is, then, closed. The program terminates. This program uses the same **fstream** class object **me** for all the operations. The program also uses the **eof()** member function of the **ios** class as a condition in **while(!me.eof())** loop. The function returns a non-zero value, when the end-of-file has been reached. This stops the reading from the file. The **EOF** checking is important to prevent the cursor going over the end of the file.

The **getline()** function is used for reading the data from a file. The prototypes of the function are

```
istream& getline (char* arr, int num,
                  char st = '\n');
istream& getline (unsigned char* arr, int num,
                  char st = '\n');
istream& getline (signed char* arr, int num,
                  char st = '\n');
```

We have discussed this function. Furthermore, it is analogous to some of the **get()** function prototypes. This is why we do not offer any examples to illustrate this function in this section.

18.3.2.3. *read( )* and *write( )* functions.

The familiar to us **read()** and **write()** member functions are used for the file input and output. We have learned how to use them for a stream I/O. Now, we will give you a very sketchy look on how to use them for the file I/O. It is pretty similar. We will briefly remind you both function prototypes. The **write()** is an overloaded function. It has following prototypes

```
ostream& write (const char* arr, int num);
```

```
ostream& write (const unsigned char* arr, int num);
ostream& write (const signed char* arr, int num);
```
It writes to a stream (or to a file) **num** number of characters from the array pointed to by **arr**. The **read()** is an overloaded function. It has following prototypes
```
istream& read (char* arr, int num);
istream& read (unsigned char* arr, int num);
istream& read (signed char* arr, int num);
```
 The function reads the data from a stream and places it into the array pointed to by **arr**. For more detailed information about **read()** and **write()** functions please refer to the reference section or previous sections of this chapter. Let's consider an example to illustrate both **read()** and **write()** functions.

```
#include <fstream.h>

void main( )
{
int a[6]= {10, 20, 30, 40, 50, 60};
int x[6];
ofstream mewrite;
ifstream meread;
mewrite.open ("mytry.dat", ios::out | ios::binary) ;
if (!mewrite)
cerr << "An opening was not successful.";
else
cout <<"An opening was successful.";
mewrite.write ( (unsigned char *) &a, 12);
mewrite.close ( );
meread.open ("mytry.dat", ios::in | ios::binary) ;
if (!meread)
{
cerr << "An opening was not successful.";
return;
}
else
cout <<" An opening was successful.\n"
        << "We are getting a message from a file.\n";
meread.read ((unsigned char *) &x, 12);
for (int m=0; m<6; m++)
cout << x[m] << "   ";
meread.close( );
}
```

Program 18.36.

  The program opens the **mytry.dat** file and writes an array of numbers **a[]** to it. We use an object **mewrite** of **ofstream** class type. The data is written to the file by

```
mewrite.write ( (unsigned char *) &a, 12);
```
We used **&a** in the statement, but it would work as simply **a**. We had to cast the data type of the parameter **&a** to **unsigned char *** in order to be able to use it in the **write()** function. The file is closed and opened again by the **meread** object of the **ifstream** class. The object reads the data from a file by means of **read()** function.
```
meread.read ((unsigned char *) &x, 12);
```
The numbers read from the file are placed into array **x[]**. The content of this array is, then, displayed on the screen.

If the program is successful, you should see following messages on your screen
```
An opening was successful. An opening was successful.
We are getting a message from a file.
10  20  30  40  50  60
```
We used **read()** and **write()** for the I/O of the numbers. The program must work, if we use the same object of **fstream** class. The **read()** and **write()** functions typically perform I/O for the binary streams or files.

Sometimes, it is necessary to change the opening mode of an open file. Suppose, you opened a file in a text mode and want to change it to a binary for using **read()** and **write()** functions. You can use the **setmode()** member function. Each of the file handling classes (**ifstream**, **ofstream** and **fstream**) has its own **setmode()** member function. The function prototype is the same in every class.
```
int setmode (int Mode = filebuf::text);
```
It sets the file handling mode to the one specified by its parameter **Mode**. The parameter sets the file to the text mode by default. The **Mode** values are specified in Table 18.1. The function returns -1, if unsuccessful or any error has occurred. So, if you open a file in a text mode using the object **meread**, the file mode can be changed to a binary by following expression
```
meread.setmode (filebuf::binary);
```

18.3.3. Random file input/output.

We have returned to the notion of the typewriter a few times in this book. So far, we have read and written the data in the order of position by position, as if you would type a page on a typewriter, or read it by eyes letter by letter. This was a sequential input and output. The random file I/O uses the same **get()** and **put()** functions. It also uses some other functions to move to a needed position inside a stream (or a file in our case). Loosely speaking, if you read or write the data position by position, it is a sequential file I/O. If you read and write a data using the same functions, but also use couple additional functions to move around the file cursor, it is called a random access. For instance, you read a word. Cursor stops at some position. You, then, use some function to move that cursor 100 positions ahead, and read next word. This is a random input. You already know how to read and write the data. We just have to acquaint you with the functions that permit to move the cursor around a file.

The first is the **seekg()** function. It moves the get pointer (or cursor) to a specified position inside a file or a stream. It is an overloaded function, that has two prototypes

```
istream& seekg (streampos pos);
istream& seekg (streamoff dif, ios::seek_dir qq);
```

The first version simply moves get pointer to position **pos** from the beginning of a file. The second function moves the cursor **dif** number of bytes from a position within a stream (file) specified by its second parameter **qq**. The **streampos** and **streamoff** are the data types equivalent to **long**. Many modern compilers use **long** data type instead of them. The **qq** is a parameter of an enumerated data type **seek_dir** declared in the **ios** class. The **qq** can accept only the values specified in Table 18.2.

Table 18.2. Allowable values of the **ios::seek_dir** type enumerators.

Alternative argument value	Argument value	Denotes the starting point
SEEK_SET	**ios::beg**	to the beginning of a stream (file)
SEEK_CUR	**ios::cur**	to the the current position in a stream (file)
SEEK_END	**ios::end**	to the end of a stream (file)

So, if **qq** is **ios::beg** (or **SEEK_SET**) and **dif** is 5, the get pointer will be set to the fifth position from the first position inside the file.

You should also use the **seekp()** function to move the put pointer (or cursor) to a required position within a stream (file). The function is overloaded and has two prototypes

```
ostream& seekp (streampos pos);
ostream& seekp (streamoff dif, ios::seek_dir qq);
```

Both prototypes of the **seekp()** function are analogous to those of the **seekg()** function. Furthermore, as you see, all the parameters of both functions are similar. The difference between them is, that the **seekp()** is a member function of the **ostream** class. Therefore, it must be used for moving the put pointer. The **seekg()** is a member of the **istream** class and must be used to move to the get pointer to a specified position. However, any of those functions would move both pointers when used on a number of compilers. **Program 18.37** illustrates those functions.

```
#include <fstream.h>

void main( )
{
char *arr="How are you?";
char a;
int m=0;
fstream me;
me.open ("mytry.dat", ios::out | ios::in | ios::binary) ;
if (!me)
cerr << "An opening was not successful.";
else
cout <<"An opening was successful.\n";
while (*arr !='\0' )
me.put(*arr++);
```

```
me.seekg (4, ios::beg);
me.put ('x');
me.get (a);
while (!me.eof( ) && m<20)
{
cout << a;
m++;
me.get(a);
}
me.close( );
}
```

Program 18.37.

The program opens the **mytry.dat** file and displays a message

An opening was successful.

It writes "**How are you?**" string to it. We, then, use **me.seekg(4, ios::beg)** function and expect to move the cursor to the fourth position from the beginning of the file. We write the letter **x** to the next position by the **me.put('x')**. The content of the file is, then, displayed by the **while** loop that uses **me.get(a)**.

If you open the **mytry.dat** file, it should contain a message

How xre you?

So, the **me.seekg(4, ios::beg)** moved the put pointer to the fourth position. Following **me.put('x')** placed **x** on the fifth position. And it will be the case for a number of compilers. But the output on the screen read by the **while** loop will begin from the sixth position. You should read

re you?

on your screen. Therefore, the get pointer was also moved to the fourth position by the **seekg()** member function, and, then, advanced by one more position, when **x** was written to a file. Thus, the **seekg()** member function also moved the get pointer as well. It is true for a number of compilers. The program must run and produce the same results, if you replace **me.seekg(4, ios::beg)** by **me.seekp(4, ios::beg)**.

There are no **seekg()** or **seekp()** functions in the **istream**, **ostream** classes in C++ Standard Draft. However, those functions are used and will, probably, be widely used. So, you must know them. The C++ Standard Library Draft specifies substitute functions **seekpos()**, **seekoff()** and others of the **filebuf** class. They can be used for moving inside a file, since that object is associated with any **ifstream** or **ofstream** class object. They are reviewed in the next section and in the reference section in this chapter.

18.3.4. Addition to file input/output.

Unfortunately, the C++ Standard Library Draft does not specify the **seekp()** and **seekg()** member functions. It does not specify the **fstream** class. We believe, those functions and the **fstream** class will be around for a long time to come. One can ask, how to perform a sequential file I/O using the tools provided by C++ Standard Draft. How to read and write to the same file in this case. The answer is simple. You have to use the member functions of the **streambuf** and **filebuf** classes. The most important functions of those classes are described in the reference section of this chapter. Here, we will show you how to use some of them on the streams.

 The **filebuf** class declares a number of functions. The **open()** and **close()** functions of that class can be used respectively for opening and closing a file. The prototypes of those functions are

```
filebuf * open (const char* pr, ios::openmode Mode);
void close ( );
```

The **open()** function opens the file, whose name is stored in the array pointed to by the pointer **pr**, in the mode specified by the parameter **Mode**. The second parameter can accept the values specified in the **ios** class and given in Table 18.1. So, an object of **filebuf** class can open and close a file. When that object opens a file, it becomes associated with that file.

 Now we have to find a way to read and write the data to that file. We can use the objects of **istream** and **ostream** classes for that. Remember we wrote the constructors of those classes in section 18.2.7? They all had a pointer to a **streambuf** class object as their parameter. The **streambuf** class is inherited by the **filebuf** class as public. Therefore, we can open a file for I/O if we define three objects

```
filebuf cont;
ostream meout (&cont);
istream mein (&cont);
```

The **cont.open()** can open a file. The **meout** and **mein** will perform the output and input. The **meout** object can use the members of the **ostream** and **ios** classes. The **mein** can use the members of the **istream** and **ios** classes. Review an example.

```
#include <fstream.h>

void main( )
{
char *arr="How are you?";
char a;
int m=0;
filebuf cont;
ostream meout (&cont);
istream mein (&cont);
if (cont.open ("mytry.dat", ios::out | ios::in |
               ios::binary) )
cout <<"An opening was successful.\n";
else
cerr << "An opening was not successful.";
while (*arr !='\0' )
meout.put(*arr++);
```

```
cont.seekoff (4, ios::beg, ios::in | ios::out);
meout.put ('x');
mein.get (a);
while (!mein.eof( ) && m<20)
{
cout << a;
m++;
mein.get(a);
}
cont.close( );
}
```
Program 18.38.

The ouptut of **Program 18.38** is similar to **Program 18.37**. The previous program has been rewritten in a new style explained above. We use the **cont** object of the **filebuf** class to open and close our file. As you see, the **meout** object uses the **put()** member function of **ostream** class. The **mein** object of **istream** class uses the member function of that class.

We use the **seekoff()** member function of the **filebuf/** (**streambuf**) class to move the cursor inside the file. The prototype of the function is

```
virtual streampos seekoff (streamoff dif, ios::seekdir qq,
                    ios::openmode Mode = ios::in | ios::out);
```
The function moves the cursor **diff** number of positions from the point inside the stream specified by the **qq** parameter. The **Mode** parameter specifies the stream opening mode. It can accept the values specified in Table 18.1. The second argument **qq** can accept the values specified in Table 18.2.

Following program illustrates another way of handling files using the tools of C++ Standard Library Draft.

```
#include <fstream.h>

void main( )
{
char *arr="How are you?";
char a;
int m=0;
ofstream me;
me.open ("mytry.dat", ios::out | ios::in | ios::binary) ;
istream see (me.rdbuf ());
if (!me)
cerr << "An opening was not successful.";
else
cout <<"An opening was successful.\n";
see.get (a);
while (!see.eof( ) && m<20)
```

```
{
cout << a;
m++;
see.get(a);
}
me.close( );
}
```

Program 18.39.

The program has the same output as the previous two programs. Here, we use the object **me** of the **ofstream** class to open the **mytry.dat** file. We assume, the previous program has written something to that file. We want to read the data from the file. We use the **see** object of the **istream** class to read the data. That object is associated with the file by the following code line

```
istream see (me.rdbuf( ));
```

That line creates the object **see**. We know, the **istream** class constructor has a pointer to a **streambuf** object as its parameter. Therefore, the initializer of the **see** object must be a pointer to a **streambuf**-derived class type object. The **rdbuf()** member function of the **ofstream** class is used with **me** object as **me.rdbuf()**. It returns a pointer to the **filebuf** object associated with **me**. The **see** object becomes associated with the same stream as **me**. So, it can read the content of **mytry.dat** file.

We could have done an opposite thing, by defining an object of **ifstream** class

```
ifstream me;
me.open ("mytry.dat", ios::out | ios::in | ios::binary) ;
ostream see (me.rdbuf( ));
```

The **filebuf** class also has a **rdbuf()** member function. It is a separate function. It returns a pointer to a filebuf object. You can use it to associate the objects of **ifstream** and **ofstream** classes with the same file.

18.4. String stream I/O.

We have learned the console and file I/O streams. C++ also permits an array-based I/O. An array-based I/O means, that the data will be written or read respectively to or from an array in the RAM. The objects of three classes are used to handle the string streams: **istrstream** (string input), **ostrstream** (string output), **strstream** (both string input and output). All those three classes are typically described in the **<strstrea.h>** or **<strstream.h>** header file. Whenever any of those classes is used, you must include **<strstrea.h>** header file in a program. The **ostrstream** is derived from the **ostream** class. The **istrstream** is derived from the **istream** class. The **strstream** inherits the **iostream** class as its base.

The stream input is performed by the objects of the **istrstream** class. The **istrstream** is derived from the **istream** class, which is derived from the **ios** class. Therefore, the string input class can use the members of those classes. Remember, you have all the richness of **ios** flags, general and flag setting functions plus all the **istream** class members. To use any of those functions, you just have to define an object of **istrstream** class first. The **istrstream** class has four constructors according to C++ Standard Draft. Two of them are used more often

```
istrstream (char* narr);
istrstream (char* arr, int num);
```

The first constructor creates an object of the class, and associates it with the null termi- nated string pointed to by the pointer **narr**. The second constructor creates an object of the class and associates it with the string that is **num** bytes long and is pointed to by the pointer **arr**. After an object of the class is created, you can use the members of **istream** and **ios** classes to perform an input. Review following program.

```
#include <strstream.h>

void main( )
{
char q[ ]= " vivacious 20.25 0xa";
char row[24];
istrstream ob (q);
float a;
int b;
ob >> row;
ob >> a;
ob >> b;
cout << row << " " << a << " "  << b << endl;
}
```

Program 18.40.

The output of the program is

```
vivacious  20.25  10
```

The program creates the object **ob** of class **istrstream** and associates it with the string **q**. We use the string extraction operators from the **istream** class to read the content of the string **q**. The content is placed in the string **arr** and variables **a** and **b**. You can use the **get()**, **getline()**, **read()** member functions of the **istream** class to copy the data from a string associated with an object of **istrstream** class. All the member functions must be used with the **istrstream** class type objects. Where can you copy a string (or perform a string input) that is associated with an object of **istrstream** class? You can copy it to other locations in the memory, for instance.

A string stream output is performed by the **ostrstream** class object. Now, we shell review how to create such an object. We, therefore, should take a look on the class constructors. The class has two overloaded constructors.

```
ostrstream ( );
ostrstream (char* pr, int num, int Mode = ios::out);
```

Here, the **pr** is a pointer to the array to which the stream will write the characters. The stream is associated with the object of this class. The total number of written characters cannot exceed **num**. You can also specify a mode for which the stream is opened, or leave the default in place. An example of string stream output is given below.

```
#include <strstream.h>

void main( )
{
char q[40];
ostrstream ob (q, 40);
char x;
ob << "How are you? " << hex << 999 << ends;
cout << q;
}
```
Program 18.41.

The output of the program is
```
How are you? 3e7
```
We create the object **ob**, that performs the string stream operation. The data is inserted into that stream by the insertion operator (**<<**). The data is written to the character array **q** associated with the string output object **ob**.

The string stream output copies the data to a string associated with the **ostrstream** class object from any other location in the memory. The **ostrstream** has inherited the **ostream** and indirectly **ios** class. Therefore, an object of the **ostrstream** class type can use the member functions of both base classes.

The **strstream** class is used for a string I/O. It can perform both input and output from and to a string, associated with the class object. Since we have illustrated how to do it on the examples for the **istrstream** and **ostrstream** class objects, we do not offer a program with a **strstream** class object. The **strstream** class object will be able to perform both actions illustrated in the last two programs. The **strstream** class is widely used. However, it is not specified by the C++ Standard Draft.

18.5. User-created streams and manipulators.

18.5.1. Stream manipulators.

We have discussed the manipulators earlier in this book. You can create your own manipulator functions. They can be useful in a number of cases. First, there might be a case in a program, when you have to repeat the same sequence of operations many times during an I/O. You can combine all those operations in one manipulator, and use it as needed. Second, they can be useful, when you perform an I/O operation to the device for which none of the standard manipulators works. You can create your own manipulator and use it as needed.

One can create the manipulators that do not take the arguments, and the manipulators that do take the arguments. We will not teach you how to create the parametrized manipulators (or the manipulators having the parameters). They are compiler specific, and can be found in the compiler manuals. We will, however, discuss the manipulators that do not take arguments. The body of such a manipulator consists of some basic parts, that we will study on the following half-empirical example.

```
ostream &name ( ostream &another_name)
{
manipulator statements
return another_name;
}
```

We begin writing the above manipulator function with specifying its returned value type **ostream**. This type can be different. We have chosen to return an object of the **ostream** class. Our function indeed returns the object **another_name**, that has **ostream** type. We could have chosen any other object type. The **name** is the name of the manipulator. It goes with the **&** character, as **&name**. The manipulator function does have a parameter. In our case, it is an object of the same class **ostream**. We called it **&another_name**. It is used with the **&** character. You have to understand, even though our manipulator function has a parameter, but that manipulator is used without any arguments in the program. Review an example.

```
#include <iostream.h>

ostream &see (ostream &obj)
{
obj.fill ('@');
obj.width (8);
return obj;
}
void main ( )
{
cout << 35 << "," << see << 35;
}
```

Program 18.42.

The output of the program is
```
35,@@@@@@35
```
The program creates the **see** manipulator, that sets the width of a displayed number to 8, and sets the fill character to **@**. Pay attention, how do we use that manipulator. We insert it into the **ostream** object **cout**. We illustrate the use of the **istream** type manipulator in the next program.

```
#include <iostream.h>

istream &see (istream &obj)
{
cout << "It is a manipulator. Enter an integer.\n";
return obj;
```

```
}
void main ( )
{
int k;
cin >> see >> k;
cout << " The value is: " << k << endl;
}
```

Program 18.43.

The program displays a message
```
It is a manipulator. Enter an integer.
```
After you enter a number, for instance 8, it displays
```
The value is: 8
```
The above program creates an **istream** manipulator **see**, that displays a message on the screen. It extracts and returns the content of the input stream **cin**.

18.5.2. User-defined types of input and output.

C++ permits the I/O operations of the standard data types. But an user can also create customary data types. Those data types can be processed by overloading the insetion and extraction operators (**<<** and **>>**), for example. The examples of standard types are numbers, arrays and so on. You must know how to perform their I/O. But what if you have to perform an I/O of an object of some created by you class data type? C++ permits you to do it, as we said. It is illustrated by the following program.

```
#include <iostream.h>                        //line 1

class acquaint                                //line 2
{                                             //line 3
friend ostream &operator << ( ostream &, acquaint & );
                                              //line 4
friend istream &operator >> ( istream &, acquaint & );
                                              //line 5
private:                                      //line 6
char phone[16];                               //line 7
char name[7];                                 //line 8
} ;                                           //line 9

ostream &operator << (ostream &out, acquaint &rec)
                                              //line 10
{                                             //line 11
out << "tel." << rec.phone << " name: " << rec.name;
                                              //line 12
return out;                                   //line 13
```

```
}                                           //line 14

istream &operator >>(istream &in, acquaint &rec)//line 15
{                                           //line 16
in.get (rec.phone, 15);                     //line 17
rec.phone[15]='\0';                         //line 18
in.ignore (1);                              //line 19
in.get (rec.name, 6);                       //line 20
rec.name[6]='\0';                           //line 21
return in;                                  //line 22
}                                           //line 23

void main ( )                               //line 24
{                                           //line 25
acquaint oneentry;                          //line 26
cout << "Enter phone number area code first "
     << "as (111)-111-1111"                 //line 27
     << "\n followed by space and five letter name."
     << endl;                               //line 28
cin >> oneentry;                            //line 29
cout << oneentry <<endl;                    //line 30
}                                           //line 31
```

Program 18.44.

The program displays a message

    Enter phone number area code first as (111)-111-1111
    followed by space and five letter name.

We enter

    (800)-111-1111 Mary

The computer displays

    tel. (800)-111-1111 name: Mary

  The program declares class **acquaint** at lines 2-9, that contains two string members **phone** and **name**. An object of this class will hold a phone number and a name of a person, to whom that number belongs. The **acquaint** class has two friend operator functions, declared at lines 4, 5. Those two operator functions permit to insert into an output or to extract from an input an object of class **acquaint**. In other words, those operators will allow to output and to input the content of a created by us object. Our

    ostream &operator << (ostream &out, acquaint &rec)

function is defined at lines 10-14. The **<<** operator inserts the content of the **phone** and **name** strings of the **acquaint** class into an output stream object, that we called **out**. It, then, returns an object **out** of the **ostream** class. Our

    istream &operator >> (istream &in, acquaint &rec)

operator function is defined at lines 15-23. It reads each of the data members of class **acquaint**. The data members are copied to **in** object of input class **istream**.

  The **acquaint** class object is used inside the **main()** routine at lines 24-31. We called this object as **oneentry**. We illustrate an input and output respectively to and from that object. The line

```
    cin >> oneentry;                                    //line 29
```

uses the overloaded extraction operator specified by its prototype

```
    istream &operator >> (istream &in, acquaint &rec)
```

As you see, it accepts an object of the **istream** class on the left and an object of the **acquaint** class on the right. This is exactly the expression **cin >>oneentry**. So, this expression must perform an input of the **acquaint** class object. The output is performed by the

```
    cout << oneentry <<endl;                            //line 30
```

Compare **cout << oneentry** with the operator function

```
    ostream &operator << (ostream &out, acquaint &rec)
```

It accepts an object of the **ostream** class on the left and the object of the **acquaint** class on the right. This operator performs an output of the **acquaint** class object.

18.6. Brief C++ I/O reference with some explanations.

This reference section describes the most important functions of **iostream** library from our point of view. We give the suggested standard functions along with the functions used in modern compilers, that might be different from the standard ones.

18.6.1. *ios* class.

The **ios** class is the most general class. It serves as a base class for almost all others. You will use this class rarely by itself. It means, you would hardly construct the objects of this class, or use it as a base for your own classes. But since this class is inherited by a number of others, you will use its member functions. The **ios** class is described in the **<iostream.h>** header file on many compilers. However, C++ Standard Library Draft places it in a **<ios>** header file. So, you can try to include each of those headers when using **ios** class objects and see which one would work. We must mention a very important point. Suppose, you use **ios** class member function with an object of, let's say, **ifstream** class. The **ifstream** class is described in the **<fstream.h>** header file. When you use **ios** class members with the **ifstream** class object, you must include the header file of the derived class. That is the **<fstream.h>** header. So you do not include the **<iostream>**. Why? Because the **ios** class is an indirect base for the **ifstream** class. The **<iostream.h>** (**<ios>**) header will be included only if you intend to use an object of the **ios** class type.

The **ios** class inherited some other classes, which we will not talk about. Its data members are the **static** bitmask data type flags. The **ios** class data members are typically **protected** members. They do not perform any operations. Each of the flags corresponds to a certain operation. Each flag, loosely speaking, "tells" through a member function, how the computer must do an operation specified by some other functions, or what it must expect. We will first give you the **fmtflags** data type members. They are called the *format flags* and are given below:

- **dec**, **oct** or **hex** convert an integer I/O to decimal, octal or hexadecimal base respectively;

- **fixed** is used to produce a floating-point output in a fixed-point notation;

- **internal** is used to add fill characters at some internal point in some outputs;

- **left** and **right** add fill characters respectively to the left or right of an output;

- **scientific** generates floating-point output in a scientific notation;

- **showbase** produces a prefix, that shows the numeric base of the integer output;

- **showpoint** produces a decimal point in generated floating-point output;

- **showpos** displays a + sign in non-negative numeric output;

- **skipws** skips some leading white spaces before some input operations;

- **unitbuf** flushes the output after completing it;

- **uppercase** replaces some lowercase letters with their uppercase equivalent;

The **fmtflags** type defines constants called masks: **adjustfield**, **basefield**, **floatfield**. The **adjustfield** accepts **left**, **right** or **internal** values. The **basefield** accepts **dec**, **oct**, **hex** values. **floatfield** accepts **scientific** and **fixed** values. Each flag is accessed through the **::** scope resolution operator. For example, we can write **ios::showpos** or **ios::dec**. One can ask, how are the flags of that data type declared within the class. Review their declaration example.

```
static const fmtflag oct;
static const fmtflag unitbuf;
static const fmtflag adjustfield;
```

The C++ Standard Draft specifies those data members as **fmtflag**. Many compilers use **long** data type instead of **fmtflag**. The above flags can be specified using **long** as, for example,

```
static const long adjustfield;
```

The **ios** class also declares the **iostate** bitmask data type member flags. The flags are set on, when an action corresponding to Table 18.3 occurs.

Table 18.3. Failure flags meaning.

Flag	Failure it indicates
badbit	loss of some bits in an input or output sequences
eofbit	input operation has reached the end of the input information
failbit	the input or output of one or more characters has failed
goodbit	is on, when all other failure bits are off

The **openmode** is another protected bitmask data type. There are following flags of that type: **app**, **ate**, **ate**, **binary**, **in**, **out**, **trunc**, **text**. Each flag name is used in the functions to tell them to perform a certain operation. The **openmode** flags tell to the opening functions in what mode to open a file. Each flag action is specified in Table 18.1

earlier in this chapter.

The class also consists of following **static** data members of enumerated **seekdir** data type: **beg**, **cur** and **end**. They are used in the member functions of different classes to move the cursor (or put/get pointers) to some position inside a stream. Their action is specified in Table 18.2 earlier in this chapter.

The **ios** class consists of a number of function members. They can be divided on groups with respect to the performed tasks. Again, the member functions of the class are declared one by one within the class. The class does not divide them on groups or anything else. We separate those member functions into groups just for making them easier to apprehend. Let's first consider the class constructor and destructor.

```
ios (streambuf *pr); //private
ios ( );  //protected
virtual ~ios()  //public
```

Here, the **pr** is a pointer to an existing **streambuf** class type object. The constructor creates an object of the class. The virtual destructor destroys it.

The first group of functions deals with the flags and a format access. It consists of following functions:

• Two overloaded **flags()** functions. The prototypes of both of them are

```
long flags (long flag_arg);
long flags ( ) const;
```

The first function sets the stream internal flag to the value specified by its parameter **flag_arg**. The **flag_arg** can accept the values of the flag class members of **fmtflags** (**long**) data type. The first function version returns a flag of the previous stream state. The second function produces no active action. It just reads and returns the current stream flag.

• Two overloaded **setf()** functions. The prototypes of both functions are

```
long setf (long flag_arg);
long setf (long flag_arg1, long flag_arg2);
```

The first function sets the stream internal flag to the one specified by the **flag_arg**. The **flag_arg** can accept the values of the flag class members of **fmtflags** (**long**) data type. The function returns the previous value of the flag of **fmtflags** or (**long**) type. The second function version has two parameters. Its second parameter **flag_arg2** will be changed by the function. It accepts the flag value of the first **flag_arg1** parameter. It returns the previous flag of **fmtflags** or (**long**) type.

The **unsetf()** function prototype for a number of compilers is

```
long unsetf (long flag_arg);
```

It clears the flag passed as an argument to **flag_arg** and returns the previous flag of **fmtflags** or (**long**) type. However, according to C++ Standard Draft the function prototype is

```
void unsetf (fmtflags flag_arg);
```

• Two overloaded **fill()** functions. Their prototypes are

```
char fill (char arg);
char fill ( ) const;
```

The first **fill()** functions sets stream's padding character to that given in its argument. The default character is the space. The first **fill()** function returns the previous fill value. The second overloaded **fill()** function has no parameters. It just reads and returns stream's current fill character.

- Two overloaded **precision()** functions. Their prototypes are

```
int precision (int num);
int precision ( ) const;
```

The first overloaded **precision()** function sets the stream's precision to **num**. It means, that any output of the floating-point value after use of this function will have **num** number of significant digits or the digits after the decimal point. The default number of digits for an output of a floating-point value is seven. If a format flag is set to **scientific** or **fixed** prior to call to this function, the first version of **precision()** sets to **num** the number of digits after the decimal point for the floating-point output. If the format flag is neither **scientific** nor **fixed**, the function sets to **num** the total number of digits after a decimal point. The first overloaded **precision()** function returns the previous precision. The second overloaded **precision()** function produces no action. It just returns the current precision value of the stream.

- Two overloaded **width()** functions. Their prototypes are:

```
int width (int wn);
int width ( ) const;
```

The first overloaded **width()** function sets the width of the output field to the number specified by **wn**. The first **width()** function returns the previous width. The second **width()** function does not set the width. It just reads and returns the current width.

Another group of **ios** member function are the status testing functions. Prototypes of four of those functions are given below. Their actions are specified in Table 18.4.

```
int good ( ) const;
int bad ( ) const;
int eof ( ) const;
int fail ( ) const;
```

Table 18.4. Error checking **ios** class member functions.

Function	Action performed by the function
good()	Returns a non-zero, if all error bits are off. Otherwise, it returns zero.
bad()	Returns a non-zero value, if **badbit** is on. Otherwise, it returns zero.
eof()	Returns a non-zero value, if **eofbit** is on. Otherwise, it returns zero.
fail()	Returns a non-zero value, if **badbit** or **failbit** are set on. Otherwise, it returns zero.

Couple more functions of this group are presented below.

- The **rdstate()** function. Its prototype for a number of compilers looks like

```
int rdstate ( ) const;
```

The function returns the current error state. The error state is one of the specified by the discussed before mask data members: **goodbit**, **eofbit**, **failbit** or **badbit**. The C++ Standard Draft specifies the prototype as

```
iostate rdstate ( ) const;
```

- The **clear()** function. Its prototype is

```
void clear (int stat); // used by a number of compilers
```

```
void clear (iostate stat); // used by C++ Standard Draft
```
The **stat** parameter can be set to any of the values: **goodbit**, **badbit**, **eofbit** or **failbit**. The **clear()** function clears the error state flag specified by its parameter. If parameter **stat** is set to 0, all the error bits are cleared. Examples of its use are

```
clear (goodbit);
clear (badbit | eofbit );
```
One can use the bitwise OR (|) operator to include the bits to be cleared.

A number of functions can be combined in so called user defined format flags. This group includes following functions:

- The **bitalloc()** function. Its prototype is

```
static long bitalloc ( );
```
The **ios** class defines 15 format flag bits. They are accessible via flags and some other member functions. Each flag corresponds to one bit. These bits are, usually, located in a 32-bit private **ios** data member. They are accessible via enumerators such as **ios::left**, **ios::dec** and so on. The **bitalloc()** member function allows you to get a previously unused bit. You can, then, use its return value as a new flag. You can set or test a custom flag built from that bit. You can use other functions of the class to access, set and test that bit. The function is used, but is not specified in C++ standard.

- The **xalloc()** function. Its prototype is

```
static int xalloc ( );
```
The function produces some extra object state variables without deriving them through the class. It is capable of doing it by returning an index to an unused 32-bit word. It is done internally. The **iword()** or **pword()** member functions can convert that index to a reference or a pointer. Each new call to **xalloc()** nullifies the values returned by previous calls to **iword()** and **pword()**.

- The **iword()** function. Its prototype is

```
long& iword (int ind) const;
```
The **ind** is an index returned by the **xalloc()** function. The **iword()** function returns a reference to a special purpose 32-bit word. You can use that word as an additional variable associated with an object of **ios** class.

- The **pword()** function. Its prototype is

```
void*& pword (int ind) const;
```
The **ind** is an index returned by the **xalloc()** function. The **iword()** function returns a reference to a pointer to a special purpose 32-bit word. Use that word as an additional variable associated with an object of **ios** class.

The next group consists of miscellaneous functions. They are:

- Two overloaded **delbuf()** functions. Their prototypes are

```
void delbuf (int nflag);
int delbuf ( ) const;
```
Those functions can be potentially inherited and used with the functions of the **streambuf** class. The first overloaded **delbuf()** function assigns a value of its parameter **nflag** to the stream's buffer-deletion flag. A nonzero value specifies, that the destructor **~ios()** must delete the attached to the stream object of **streambuf** class. A zero value precludes the deletion. The second overloaded **delbuf()** function just reads and returns the current value of the flag.

- The **rdbuf()** function. Its prototype is

```
streambuf* rdbuf ( ) const;
streambuf* rdbuf (streambuf * pr);
```

The first function has no parameters. It only reads and returns a pointer to an object of the **streambuf** class type. The second version assigns the pointer **pr** to a **streambuf** class object associated with the stream.

- The **sync_with_stdio()** function. Its prototype is

```
static void sync_with_stdio ( );
```

The function synchronizes the C++ streams with the standard C I/O routines. After call to this function, the **cin**, **cout**, **cerr**, **clog** streams are set to use with the **stdin**, **stdout**, and **stderr** standard streams. Unfortunately, it should lead to some performance deterioration, because there is a buffering in C++ streams and the standard C input/output. The **cin**, **cout**, **cerr**, **clog** streams can be now used with the **stdiobuf** class objects rather than with the **filebuf** object. We want to point, the **sync_with_stdio()** function belongs to the **ios** class. And **cin**, **cout**, **cerr**, **clog** streams belong to other classes. Therefore, our function becomes useful, when **ios** class is inherited and used for the classes, which declare those **cin**, **cout**, **cerr**, **clog** streams. Call to that function sets the **ios::stdio** for all the streams.

- Two overloaded **tie()** functions. Their prototypes are

```
ostream* tie (ostream* ptr);
ostream* tie ( ) const;
```

The **ptr** is a pointer to the **ostream** class object. The functions must be used with the **ostream** objects. The first version of the **tie()** function ties a stream to a specified **ostream** object. It returns the value of the previous pointer, or **NULL** if a stream has not been tied before. A stream **tie()** enables automatic stream flushing when needed during I/O. By default, **cin**, **cerr** and **clog** are tied to **cout**. The second version returns the value of the latest tie pointer or **NULL** if this stream has not been tied yet.

The **ios** class declares some overloaded operators. They are:

- The overloaded **void*** operator. The operator function prototype is

```
operator void* ( ) const;
```

That operator returns a non-null pointer if **failbit** or **badbit** is set on in a stream.

- The **!** operator. The operator function prototype is

```
int operator !( ) const;
```

It returns a nonzero value if either **failbit** or **badbit** is set on in a stream.

The **ios** class also includes a manipulation function group. Each function returns its parameter **arg**. We give their prototypes according to C++ Standard Draft below.

- **ios&dec(ios & arg); ios&oct(ios & arg);** or **ios&hex(ios & arg);**

Call to each of the functions causes the I/O of a data field after the call to be interpreted as a decimal, octal or hexadecimal value respectively. The actions of those functions are equivalent to the respective calls to

```
arg.setf (ios::dec, ios::basefield); or arg.setf (ios::dec,
ios::basefield); or arg.setf (ios::dec, ios::basefield);
```

- **ios & fixed(ios & arg);** or **ios & scientific(ios & arg);**

Functions set the I/O of the floating-point data field to **fixed** or **scientific** notation respectively. Those functions are equivalent to

```
arg.setf (ios::fixed, ios::floatfield);
arg.setf (ios::scientific, ios::floatfield);
```

- **ios & internal(ios & arg);**

It adds the padding fill characters to some I/O data fields. It is equivalent to

```
arg.setf (ios::internal, ios::adjustfield);
```

- **ios & left(ios & arg);** or **ios & right(ios & arg);**

Each function sets a stream so it adds the padding characters to the left or right respectively for the data I/O. Those functions are equivalent to

```
arg.setf (ios::left, ios::adjustfield); or
arg.setf (ios::right, ios::adjustfield);
```

- **ios & showbase(ios & arg);** or **ios & noshowbase(ios & arg);**

The functions show or prohibit the showing of the base of the subsequent integer fields. The functions are equivalent to respectively

```
arg.setf (ios::showbase); or arg.unsetf (ios::showbase);
```

- **ios & showpoint(ios & arg);** or **ios & noshowpoint(ios & arg);**

The functions set a stream so it generates or does not generate the decimal point respectively. The actions of the functions are equivalent to respectively

```
arg.setf (ios::showpoint); or arg.unsetf (ios::showpoint);
```

- **ios & showpos(ios & arg);** and **ios & noshowpos(ios & arg);**

The functions set a stream so it respectively generates or does not generate a **+** sign in the non-negative output. It is equivalent to respectively

```
arg.setf (ios::showpos); or arg.unsetf (ios::showpos);
```

- **ios & skipws(ios & arg);** and **ios & noskipws(ios & arg);**

Those functions respectively set the stream to skip or not to skip the leading white spaces in some input operations. The functions are equivalent to respectively

```
arg.setf (ios::skipws); or arg.unsetf (ios::skipws);
```

- **ios & uppercase(ios & arg);** or **ios & nouppercase(ios & arg);**

The functions respectively substitute or do not substitute some lowercase letters with the uppercase ones. The actions of both functions can be also achieved by respectively

```
arg.setf (ios::uppercase); or arg.unsetf (ios::uppercase);
```

Many compilers still do not offer the above manipulator functions. They might do it in the future, because those manipulators can become a part of the C++ library. Some manipulators are offered by a number of compilers. They are inserted in the streams. They have the same form as the format flags. Some are given in Table 18.5.

Table 18.5. Stream manipulators and their effect on the streams.

Manipulator	Causes the subsequent I/O fields to be interpreted
dec	The subsequent I/O fields are interpreted as decimal numbers.
oct	The subsequent I/O fields are interpreted as octal values.
hex	The subsequent I/O fields are interpreted as hexadecimal values.
binary	Sets the stream mode to binary.
text	Sets the stream mode to text.

For instance, you want to use the **ios & oct(ios & obj)** function to set the I/O field for the integers to be interpreted as the octal numbers. You also must understand, that you hardly use the **ios** class objects by themselves. You would deal with the **ios** class members as inherited by other classes. For instance, if you want the output to be interpreted as the octal numbers, write the **ostream** class object **cout** as

```
cout << oct;  or
oct (cout);
```

Both forms perform the same action. The form **oct(cout)** might not work on all the compilers yet.

18.6.2. Input stream classes.

There are four most often used input stream classes in C++: **istream**, **ifstream**, **istrstream**, **istream_withassign**. The **istream** class contains a number of members useful for all other input streams. This is why it is a base class for all other input stream classes. The **ifstream** class is used for the file input. The **istream_withassign** class is used for the **cin** object and for reassigning the objects. It is specified for some compilers. It has very minor differences from the **istream** class. Furthermore, object **cin** can be treated as an object of **istream** class in many cases. So, you even do not have to know about the very existence of **istream_withassign** class. The class **istrstream** is used for the string input.

18.6.2.1. *istream* class.

The **istream** class is commonly used for the input from the standard input stream. In C, such standard stream is known to be **stdin**. One of the most known objects of that class is the object **cin** according to C++ Standard Library Draft, although you can create other objects. The object **cin** is a member of the **istream_withassign** class on some compilers. Yet, it can be treated as a member of the **istream** class, because both classes have very little difference. The **istream** class is derived from the virtual public base class **ios**. A majority of member functions of the **istream** class are used for the formatted and unformatted input. All the member functions of this class are declared as **public**. You must include the **iostream.h** header file, when dealing with that class objects, as

```
#include <iostream.h>
```

C++ Standard Library Draft specifies this class in the **<istream>** header file. You can try to include each of those two headers separately to determine which one would work on your system. Now, we shell discuss the members of the class.

The standard constructor of the class is overloaded. Its prototypes are

```
istream ( );//not specified by C++ Standard Library Draft
istream (streambuf* pr);
```

Parameter **pr** is a pointer to an existing object of a **streambuf**-derived class. The constructor constructs an object of **istream** data type. The destructor synopsis is

```
virtual ~istream ( );
```

The virtual destructor destroys an object of **istream** class.

We will now discuss the prefix and postfix functions.
- The first function is **ipfx()**.
  ```
  int ipfx (int prep = 0);
  ```
The function is called by the input functions right before extracting the data from the stream. The **ipfx()** function prepares the stream for formatted or unformatted input. The **ipfx(0)** is called for the formatted input. The unformatted input functions usually call **ipfx(1)**. The **prep** parameter for the unformatted functions should be equal to the number of characters to be read. The **ipfx()** calls **tie()** and **flush()** to tie up the input and synchronize the output sequence with associated external C streams. The **ipfx()** function does not necessary call the **flush()** function.

An **ios** class object tied to this stream can be flushed if **prep** is 0 or, if **prep** specifies more characters than there are in the input buffer. The **ipfx()** function can extract leading white spaces if **ios::skipws** is set on. The function returns a nonzero value, if its action is successful, or 0 in case of a stream error. If some error is detected in the stream, the **ipfx()** function does nothing.
- The synopsis of the **isfx()** function is
  ```
  void isfx ( );
  ```
The function is called at the very end of every extraction. If you write an input, that uses an object of the **istream** class, use both **ob.ipfx(prep)** and **ob.isfx()**. Here, the **ob** is the name of the object.

All following functions are used for the input.
- The **get()** overloaded function is used for an unformatted input. Its prototypes are
  ```
  int get ( );
  ```
This function extracts a single character (even white space) from a stream and returns it as **unsigned char**. If no character is extracted the function returns the **EOF**.
```
istream& get (char* arr, int num, char st = '\n');
istream& get (unsigned char* arr, int num,
              char st = '\n');
istream& get (signed char* arr, int num,
              char st = '\n');
```
All three above functions extract the characters from a stream and store them in the array pointed to by **arr**. The extraction stops, when:
- the **num-1** characters have been read (it adds the null character, if not found);
- the **EOF** character occurs in the input sequence;
- the character specified by the parameter **st** occurs in the input sequence;
Neither of those three functions extracts the delimiter from the stream or returns it. Each of the functions returns a reference to **this** pointer of the **istream** class. If no characters are read, the **setstate(failbit)** is called to inform about an error.
```
istream& get (char& ent);
istream& get (unsigned char& ent);
istream& get (signed char& ent);
```
Each of the functions reads a character from a stream and stores it as specified in the reference parameter **ent**. The **setstate(failbit)** is called in case of no input.
```
istream& get (streambuf& rob, char  st = '\n');
```
Parameter **rob** in the above prototype is a reference to an object of a **streambuf-**

derived class. The **st** is a delimiter character, equal to the newline by the default. The function reads the characters from a stream and stores them in the **streambuf** object referenced by **rob**. The reading of a sequence of characters stops when:
- **EOF** or error is encountered;
- the specified by the **st** character occured in the input sequence;
- an exception occurs;

The function does not extract the delimiter from the stream or returns it. Above version returns a reference to **this** pointer of the **istream** class. If the function does not get any characters, it calls **setstate(failbit)** to inform about an error.

- The overloaded **getline()** function is used for an unformatted input.

```
istream& getline (char* arr, int num, char st = '\n');
istream& getline (unsigned char* arr, int num,
                  char st = '\n');
istream& getline (signed char* arr, int num,
                  char st = '\n');
```

Each of three functions reads the characters from the stream and stores them in the array pointed to by **arr**. The input stops, when
- **num-1** characters are read (then stops input, calls **setstate(failbit)**);
- the **EOF** occurs in the input sequence (the function calls **setstate(eofbit)**);
- the character specified by the parameter **st** occurs in the input sequence;

Each of those three functions extracts the delimiter from the stream but does not store it. Each function returns a reference to **istream** class **this** pointer. If the functions do not get any characters, they call **setstate(failbit)** to inform about an error.

- An overloaded **read()** function is used for an unformatted input. Its prototypes are

```
istream& read (char* arr, int num);
istream& read (unsigned char* arr, int num);
istream& read (signed char* arr, int num);
```

The function reads the characters from a stream and stores them in an array pointed to by the **arr** pointer. Each of the functions reads the input characters, until **n** characters are read or **EOF** occurs in the input sequence. In the second case, each function warns the computer calling **setstate(failbit)** function. The functions return a reference to **this** pointer of **istream** class.

- The **ignore()** function has following synopsis

```
istream& ignore (int num = 1, int st = EOF);
```

The function reads and discards the characters from a stream, until:
- the **num** number of characters has been read;
- **EOF** is encountered in the input (it warns the computer by **setstate(eofbit)**);
- the character corresponding to the one stored in the **st** parameter is encountered;

The **st** parameter is **EOF** by default. The delimiter character is extracted. The function returns a reference to **this** pointer of the **istream** class.

- The **peek()** function has following synopsis:

```
int peek ( );
```

It returns the next character or **EOF**, if the stream is at the last file position or **ipfx()** function issued an error warning. The character is not extracted from the stream.

- The **gcount()** function prototype is

```
int gcount ( ) const;
```
It returns the number of extracted characters by the last unformatted input function.
- The **eatwhite()** function synopsis is
```
void eatwhite ( );
```
This function is not a part of a C++ Standard Library Draft, although some compilers
make it a part of **istream** class. It will eat any white spaces in a subsequent attempt to
read a stream. So any white space in a stream input will be ignored.

The following group represents miscellaneous functions, used for different purposes.
- The **putmfc()** function, specified by some compilers, has a synopsis
```
istream& putmfc (char x);
```
The function puts a character stored in its parameter **x** back into the input stream. The
result is unspecified, if the character does not match to the previously extracted one. The
standard draft uses the name **putback()** for the same function.
- The **sync()** function synopsis is
```
int sync ( );
```
The function synchronizes the internal buffer of the stream with the external character
source. You will hardly use this function. It returns **EOF** in case of error.
- The **seekg()** overloaded function has two prototypes
```
istream& seekg (streampos pos);
istream& seekg (streamoff dif, ios::seek_dir qq);
```
The first overloaded function sets the cursor position (or the get pointer) inside a stream,
associated with **istream** or derived class object, to a position specified by the **pos**
parameter. The positions are counted from the beginning of the stream. The second overloaded **seekg()** function offsets the cursor of a stream, associated with an object of
istream or derived class, by the **dif** number of positions counted from the position
qq. The **streampos** is a data type equivalent to **long** on some compilers. It is used for
the cursor positioning within a file or a stream. The **streamoff** data type is also equivalent to **long**. The point with respect to which the offset is measured is given by the **qq**
parameter of the **seek_dir** or equivalent to it **seekdir** data type. The **qq** parameter
can accept only the following flag values, specified in the **ios** class: **ios::beg**,
ios::cur, **ios::end**. They are specified in Table 18.2 in this chapter. The function
is not specified by the C++ Standard Library Draft. Nevertheless, it is widely used by
many compilers.
- The **tellg()** function is not a standard stream function, although used by a number
of compilers. Its synopsis is
```
streampos tellg ( );
```
It gets the current cursor position inside a stream and returns it as **streampos** type.

The **istream** class defines an overloaded extraction operator. It extracts its argument
from the stream. We give you all the prototypes of the overloaded **>>** operator member
function just for the information. You know what action it performs already.
```
istream& operator >> (char* arr);
istream& operator >> (unsigned char* arr);
istream& operator >> (signed char* arr);
istream& operator >> (char& var);
istream& operator >> (unsigned char& var);
```

```
istream& operator >> (signed char& var);
istream& operator >> (short& var);
istream& operator >> (unsigned short& var);
istream& operator >> (int& var);
istream& operator >> (unsigned int& var);
istream& operator >> (long& var);
istream& operator >> (unsigned long& var);
istream& operator >> (float& var);
istream& operator >> (double& var);
istream& operator >> (long double& var); (16-bit only)
istream& operator >> (streambuf* row);
istream& operator >> (istream& (*fp)(istream&) );
istream& operator >> (ios& (*fp)(ios&) );
```

You can use manipulators of both **istream** and **ios** classes with last two operators. The same goal achieved by the **eatwhite()** function can be reached by the **ws** manipulator. It extracts the leading white spaces from a stream. Its synopsis is

```
ws
```

18.6.2.2. *ifstream* class.

The **ifstream** is derived from the **istream** class. Some compilers can use the **istream** and other classes as the bases for the **ifstream**. The **ifstream** class is used for the disk file input. The **ifstream** class is described in the **<fstream.h>** header file. To use the **ifstream** class objects, include that file

```
#include <fstream.h>
```

C++ Standard Library Draft places this class in the **<fstream>** header file. You can check which one of those headers will work on your system. All the member functions of that class are declared as **public**. We will go over most important class members.

• The standard specifies only two overloaded constructor versions. Some compilers use four overloaded constructors. Their prototypes are:

```
ifstream ( );
ifstream (const char* pr, int Mode = ios::in,
          int PBuf = filebuf::openprot);
ifstream (filedesc fd);
ifstream (filedesc fd, char* q, int num);
```

Here, **pr** is a pointer to an array containing the name of the file to be opened during the object construction. The **Mode** is an integer containing the mode bits. The mode bits define, what operations could be done on the opened file. They are the enumerators of the **openmode** type of **ios** class (**app**, **ate**, **binary**, **in**, **out**, **trunc**, **nocreate**, **text**) given in Table 18.1, that can be combined with bitwise-OR (|) operator.

PBuf parameter specifies the file protection. It is not specified by the C++ Standard Draft, but used by a number of compilers. Its default value is the default static integer **filebuf::openprot**, that is equivalent to **filebuf::sh_compat**. The possible **PBuf** values are given in Table 18.6.

Table 18.6. The possible values of the **Pbuf** parameter.

Argument value	File protection mode
`filebuf::sh_compat`	compatibility share mode.
`filebuf::sh_none`	exclusive mode-no sharing at all
`filebuf::sh_read`	read sharing
`filebuf::sh_write`	write sharing

The **fd** is a file descriptor. It is an integer returned by the opening function. The type of the descriptor is equivalent to **int**, although we used the **filedesc** type. The **q** is a pointer to the reserved memory area with the length **num** bytes. This area will be used as a buffer. If **q=NULL** or **num** is 0, the stream will be unbuffered.

First constructor version constructs the **ifstream** class type object without actually opening a file. Second version constructs an object and opens a file whose name is stored in the string pointed to by the **pr** pointer in the mode specified by the parameter **Mode**. The file protection mode of such a file is specified by the third parameter. The second constructor version is specified by the proposed C + + Standard Library Draft without the third parameter. You can use two parameters, because the third one gets its value by default. However, many compilers have a three parameter version of this function. When the second constructor creates an object and opens a file, that file becomes associated with the created object. The third constructor constructs an **ifstream** class object and attaches it to (or associates it with) an *open file* specified by the **fd**. The last constructor constructs an **ifstream** class object, associates it with an *open file* specified by the file descriptor **fd**. It also uses a buffer pointed to by the pointer **q** of length **num** for that file I/O operations. The **ifstream** type object, that is associated with a file, becomes also associated with a **filebuf** object. The first three constructors allocate the reserve area by themselves. The fourth function permits a user-allocated memory area. The third and the fourth constructor versions are not specified in C + + Standard Library Draft. They are used by a number of compilers.

• The **ifstream** class has a virtual destructor. The destructor destroys an object of **ifstream** class along with corresponding to it **filebuf** object. However, it closes the file, from which its object performed an input only if that file was opened by the **ifstream** constructor or **open()** member function. Do not forget to close a file before destroying a class object. The **filebuf** destructor releases the reserved memory buffer only if it was allocated by the computer automatically. The synopsis of the **ifstream** class virtual destructor is

```
~ifstream ();
```

• The **ifstream** class declares the **open()** member function. Its synopsis is

```
void open (const char* pr, int Mode = ios::in,
            int PBuf = filebuf::openprot);
```

The proposed standard specifies the **open()** function without the third parameter. Some compilers use the **open()** function with three parameters. Since it is a function with default parameters, you can specify only two parameters. The **open()** function opens a disk file whose name is stored in the string pointed to by the pointer **pr** in the mode **Mode** in the file protection mode **PBuf**. It attaches the file to an object of the **filebuf** class. The function also associates the opened file with an object that opens it. If you try to open an opened file, or an opening produces an error, the **ios::failbit** is set on. If the file is not found, the compiler tries to create a file with a specified by you name. If you used the **Mode** parameter **ios::nocreate**, the error occurs and sets on the **ios::failbit**. The **Pbuf** parameter is not specified by C++ Standard Library Draft.

- The next one is the **close()** function. Its synopsis is

```
void close ( );
```

The function closes the file and disconnects it from the associated object. The object by itself is not destroyed. If the function fails, it sets on the **filebuf::close**.

- The member function **rdbuf()** prototype is

```
filebuf* rdbuf ( ) const;
```

The function returns a pointer to the **filebuf** object associated with this stream.

- The **is_open()** function tests if the file associated with an object, that uses it, is open. It returns a nonzero integral value if our stream is open. Otherwise, it returns zero. The synopsis of the function is

```
int is_open ( ) const;
```

Some of the compilers also define additional member functions.

- The **setbuf()** function prototype is

```
virtual streambuf* setbuf (char* arr, int num);
```

The function attaches the buffer to the stream's object, that has **filebuf** data type. In other words, it establishes a connection between a file and a stream via a reserve area buffer of length **num** pointed to by **arr**. If **arr** is a **NULL** pointer or **num** is equal to zero, the stream will be unbuffered. If the file is opened prior to use of the function or a buffer has been allocated already, the function returns **NULL** pointer. Otherwise, the function returns a pointer to the **filebuf** class type object, which is cast to the **streambuf** type. The reserve area is not released by the **ifstream** destructor.

- The next is the **setmde()** function. Its synopsis is

```
int setmode (int Mode = filebuf::text);
```

The **Mode** parameter accepts the values: **filebuf::text**, **filebuf::binary**. The function sets the binary or text mode for reading the data from a stream. The function returns an error or -1 if you type in an invalid parameter value, or the file is not open, or the mode cannot be changed.

- We will now review the **attach()** function. Its prototype is

```
void attach (filedesc fd);
```

The function establishes a connection between a stream and an opened file specified by the file descriptor **fd**. The function fails when the stream has been already attached to the specified file. Loosely speaking, you can attach an object to opened file, if it is not associated with any other file. The failure sets the **ios::filebit** on to indicate an error. The **filedesc** is equivalent to the **int** data type.

A file descriptor can be obtained by the next function. Its prototype is

```
filedesc fd ( ) const;
```

The function returns a descriptor of the file associated with the stream object.

The **fd()**, **attach()**, **setmode()**, **setbuf()** member functions of the **ifstream** class are not specified there by C++ Standard Library Draft. However, they are used by a number of compilers. So, we give them here as well.

18.6.2.3. *istream_withassign* class.

The `istream_withassign` class is derived from the `istream` class. The class
`istream_withassign` is not specified by C++ Standard Library Draft. However,
many compilers introduce this class. So, we study it. It has very minor differences with
the `istream` class. The `istream_withassign` class allows an object assignment,
i.e., we can reassign the input object `cin` to another one. It allows more flexibility in the
input operation. For instance, a program expecting an input from the `stdin` can be
redirected to read the data from the disk file. The `cin` is an object of the
`istream_withassign` class. It is connected to `stdin`, which is a standard input. Its
file descriptor is 0. This class is described in the `<iostream.h>` header file. It should
be included when the objects of that class type are used as

```
#include <iostream.h>
```

The `istream_withassign` class has an overloaded constructor

```
istream_withassign (streambuf* pr);
istream_withassign ( );
```

Here, the `pr` is a pointer to an existing object of the `streambuf` class. The first constructor creates an object of the class. That object has a `streambuf` object attached to it,
and, therefore, can be used for an input. In other words, that constructor creates the
stream interface, that enables the input. The second constructor creates an object. But it
does not initialize it. You still have to subsequently use the overloaded assignment operator to initialize this object.

The class destructor has a prototype

```
~istream_withassign ( );
```

It destroys an object of `istream_withassign` class.

The class also specifies an overloaded assignment operator with following prototypes

```
istream& operator = (const istream& yours);
istream& operator = (streambuf* yours);
```

The first overloaded assignment operator assigns the object **yours** of `istream` class
to the specified by you object of `istream_withassign` class. In other words, you can
assign any object of the `istream` class to any object of `istream_withassign` class.
The second overloaded assignment operator attaches (or in other words assigns) an existing object of `streambuf` class to `istream_withassign` class object. The second
function also initializes that object of the `istream_withassign` class. It is used with
the void-argument constructor.

18.6.2.4. *istrstream* class.

The `istrstream` class is derived from the `istream` base class, which is typically
inherited as public. The class is described in the `<strstream.h>` header file, that must
be included when you deal with the `istrstream` members and objects as

```
#include <strstrea.h>
```

C++ Standard Library Draft places this class in the `<strstream>` header file. You can
check which header will work in your programs on your particular compiler.

The **istrstream** class is used mainly for the input of the character array streams. The class member functions are declared as public. An object of this class is associated with the **strstreambuf** class object. Review following class member functions:

- There are four overloaded constructors in the **istrstream** class.

```
istrstream (char* narr);
istrstream (const char* narr);
istrstream (char* arr, int num);
istrstream (const char* arr, int num);
```

Two first constructors uses the string pointed to by **narr** to create an **istrstream** type object. The last two constructors create an **istrstream** type object, that consists of **num** number of characters, from a string pointed to by the **arr**. All constructors automatically construct a **strstreambuf** object, that handles the interface between the string and the stream. The standard draft can specify some other constructors. But we described the most important ones from our point of view.

- The class destructor has a following prototype

```
~istrstream ( );
```

It destroys both an **istrstream** and associated with it **strstreambuf** type objects. The string containing the characters is not destroyed, because it was allocated by the user. The constructor deletes an interface between a stream and a string (which is provided by the **streambuf** object) and an **istrstream** class object.

- The class also contains the **rdbuf()** function. Its synopsis is

```
strstreambuf* rdbuf ( ) const;
```

It reads and returns a pointer to a **strstreambuf** object, associated with this stream.

- The last is the **str()** function. Its synopsis is

```
char* str ( );
```

It returns a pointer to a character array, used to construct a **istrstream** object.

18.6.3. Output stream classes.

There are four major output streams: **ostream**, **ofstream**, **ostream_withassign**, **ostrstream**. The **ostream** is a so-called general purpose output stream. It is used as a base class for the other output streams. The **ofstream** is used for the file output. The **ostream_withassign** is the output stream that contains the **cout**, **cerr**, and **clog** objects. It is also used for the object assignments. The **ostrstream** class serves for the string output. We will now consider each of the classes in details.

18.6.3.1. *ostream* class.

The **ostream** class provides the tools for the sequential and random-access output. It is derived from the **ios** class, which is inherited as public. The **ostream** class works together with the objects derived from the **streambuf** class. The **streambuf** class provides the "interface" for the **ostream** class. The **ostream** class performs the formatting of the output. All the member functions of the **ostream** class write unformatted data. Formatted output is performed by the insertion operators.

The **ostream** class is described in the **<iostream.h>** header. Therefore, one should include that header, when the class objects are used as

```
#include <iostream.h>
```

C++ Standard Library Draft places this class in the **<ostream>** header file. You can check which header will work in your programs on your particular compiler. All the class member functions are declared as public. We will now consider each of the class member functions in details.

- The class declares a constructor as

```
ostream ( streambuf* pr );
```

The **pr** is a pointer to an existing object. That object should have a **streambuf** or **streambuf**-derived type. Some compilers declare additional protected constructor

```
ostream ( );
```

even though the class, according to the standard draft, does not have that second constructor. The constructors construct an object of **ostream** class.

- The class has a virtual destructor. Its synopsis is

```
virtual ~ostream ( );
```

It destroys an object of the class. It might also flush the output buffer. The attached **streambuf** object is destroyed only if it was allocated internally by the constructor.

Next two functions are so-called prefix/suffix functions.

- The first one is the **opfx()** function. Its prototype is

```
int opfx ( );
```

It is called before every insertion. It flushes a stream, if there is another **ostream** object tied to it. The function returns zero in case of error and a nonzero, otherwise.

- The **osfx()** function has a prototype

```
void osfx ( );
```

It is called after each insertion. It flushes the **ostream** object, if something sets up the **ios::unitbuf**. It flushes both **stdout** and **stderr** if **ios::stdio** is set on.

Following functions provide the output.

- We will begin with the **put()** function. Its synopsis is

```
ostream& put (char x);
```

It inserts a single character contained in its parameter **x** into the output stream.

- The overloaded **write()** function has a number of prototypes

```
ostream& write (const char* arr, int num);
ostream& write (const unsigned char* arr, int num);
ostream& write (const signed char* arr, int num);
```

The function copies a number of bytes specified by the **num** from a buffer (or an array) pointed to by the **arr** into a stream. If you use this function to write the data to a file that was opened in a text mode, it can insert additional carriage characters. The **write()** function is most commonly used for a binary stream output.

The **ostream** class also declares a number of miscellaneous member functions.

- The first one is the **flush()** function. Its prototype is

```
ostream& flush ( );
```

It flushes the buffer associated with a stream and calls the **sync()** function for the **streambuf** object. You, probably, still remember that there is a **streambuf** object associated with **ostream** class object.

- The overloaded **seekp()** function has following prototypes

```
ostream& seekp (streampos pos);
ostream& seekp (streamoff dif, ios::seek_dir qq);
```

The specified by a standard draft **streampos** data type corresponds to **long** for a number of compilers. The **streamoff** is an equivalent of **long** data type. The enumerator of **seekdir** or **seek_dir** type of **ios** class can accept only three values: **ios::beg**, **ios::cur**, **ios::end**. They are given in Table 18.2.

The first overloaded **seekp()** function changes the position of the cursor to that specified by its parameter **pos**. The position is specified with respect to the beginning of the stream. The second function offsets the cursor position by the **dif** number of bytes from the starting point specified by **qq**. There can be only three starting points. The **qq** parameter can accept only the following flag values, specified in the **ios** class:**ios::beg**, **ios::cur**, **ios::end**. They are specified in Table 18.2 of this chapter. Both functions can be used for any streams, including file and string streams. Both functions are not specified by C++ Standard Draft, but used in many compilers.

- The prototype of the **tellp()** is

```
streampos tellp ( );
```

It reads and returns the current put pointer position within a stream specified from the beginning of the stream. The **streampos** data type corresponds to **long**. The function is not specified in C++ Standard Library Draft

The class also declares and defines the overloaded insertion operator **<<**. The overloaded insertion operator function has following prototypes.

```
ostream& operator << (char ch);
ostream& operator << (unsigned char uch);
ostream& operator << (signed char sch);
ostream& operator << (const char* psz );
ostream& operator << (const unsigned char *pusz);
ostream& operator << (const signed char *pssz);
ostream& operator << (short s);
ostream& operator << (unsigned short us);
ostream& operator << (int n);
ostream& operator << (unsigned int un);
ostream& operator << (long l);
ostream& operator << (unsigned long ul);
ostream& operator << (float f);
ostream& operator << (double d );
ostream& operator << (long double ld); (16-bit only)
ostream& operator << (const void* pv);
ostream& operator << (streambuf* psb);
ostream& operator << (ostream& (*fcn)(ostream&) );
ostream& operator << (ios& (*fcn)(ios&) );
```

The overloaded insertion operator inserts its argument into a stream. The overloaded versions of that operator have been developed to accommodate different data types and different output cases. The last two prototypes of the operator permit to use the manipulators, which are defined in both **ostream** and **ios**.

The **ostream** class also specifies a number of manipulators.
- We first consider **endl**. It is used as

        endl

It should be inserted into an output stream. It inserts a newline character and flashes the buffer.
- The **ends** manipulator should be also inserted into a stream. Its synopsis is

        ends

It inserts a null character '**\0**'. It is used for the string output.
- The **flush** manipulator flushes the output buffer. It calls the **streambuf::sync** member function. It is easy to use it. Just insert it into an output stream as

        flush

18.6.3.2. *ofstream* class.

The **ofstream** class is used for the disk file output. This is why all of its constructors automatically create and attach a **filebuf** buffer object. The class is derived from the **ostream** class, which is inherited as public. It is described in the **<fstream.h>** header file, that must be included when using the **ofstream** class

        #include <fstream.h>

C++ Standard Library Draft places this class in the **<fstream>** header file. You can check which header will work in your programs on your particular compiler. All the class member functions are declared as public. We will consider the most important members of the class from our point of view.
- The class constructor is heavily overloaded. We will give you four constructors used in a number of compilers. C++ Standard Library Draft supports only two of them.

        ofstream ( );
        ofstream (const char* pr, int Mode = ios::out,
                  int PBuf = filebuf::openprot);
        ofstream (filedesc fd);
        ofstream (filedesc fd, char* q, int num);

All the parameters of those four constructors have the same meaning and values as the parameters discussed for the **ifstream** class constructors. First constructor version constructs the **ofstream** class type object without actually opening a file. Second version constructs an object and opens a file whose name is stored in the string pointed to by the **pr** pointer in the mode specified by the parameter **Mode**. The file protection mode of such a file is specified by the third parameter **PBuf**. C++ Standard Library Draft does not specify the **PBuf** parameter. You can use two parameters, because the third one gets its value by default. However, many compilers have a three parameter version of this function. The possible **PBuf** values are given in Table 18.6.
When the second constructor creates an object and opens a file, that file becomes associated with the object. The third constructor constructs an **ofstream** class object, attaches it to (or associates it with) an open file specified by **fd**. The last constructor constructs an **ofstream** class object, associates it with an open file specified by the file descriptor **fd**. It also creates a buffer pointed to by the pointer **q** of length **num** for that file I/O opera-

tions. All **ofstream** constructors also attach a **filebuf** object to that file. First three constructors allocate the reserve or so called memory area by themselves. The fourth function permits a user-allocated memory area. The third and fourth constructors are not specified by C++ Standard Draft, but are widely used.

- The class destructor has the following prototype

```
~ofstream ( );
```

It first flushes the buffer. It, then, destroys an object of the **ofstream** class. The destructor closes the file associated with **ofstream** object only if it was opened by the constructor or **open()** member function. If the associated buffer was automatically allocated by the computer, it gets released by the **filebuf** destructor.

We will now consider the operation functions.

- The prototype of the **open()** function is

```
void open (const char* pr, int Mode = ios::out,
           int PBuf = filebuf::openprot);
```

The proposed standard specifies the **open()** function without the third parameter. Some compilers use the **open()** function with three parameters. Since it is a function with default parameters, you can specify only two parameters. The **open()** function opens a disk file whose name is stored in the string pointed to by the pointer **pr** in the mode **Mode** in the file protection mode **PBuf**. It attaches the file to an object of the **filebuf** class. The function also associates the opened file with an object that opens it. If you try to open an opened file, or an opening produces an error, the **ios::failbit** is set on. If the file is not found, the computer tries to create a file with a specified by you name. If you used the **Mode** parameter **ios::nocreate**, the error occurs and sets on the **ios::failbit**.

- The **close()** function has a following synopsis

```
void close ( );
```

The function flushes an output if needed, closes the file and disconnects it from the **filebuf** object. However, it does not destroy the **filebuf** object. The file is also disassociated from the **ofstream** class object.

- The next is the **setbuf()** function. Its synopsis is

```
streambuf* setbuf (char* pr, int num);
```

The **pr** is a pointer to a previously allocated memory space of **num** length (in bytes). If either **pr** is a **NULL** pointer or **num** is zero, the stream is assumed to be unbuffered. The function attaches the buffer to the file (**filebuf** object). The **NULL** is returned by the function, if the file is opened and the memory buffer has already been allocated. Otherwise, the function returns a pointer to the **filebuf** object cast to a class type **streambuf**. This function prevents the class destructor to free the buffer memory.

- The **setmode()** function sets the opened file to a binary or text output mode.

```
int setmode (int nMode = filebuf::text);
```

The **Mode** can take only two values: **filebuf::text** and **filebuf::binary** in this function. The function returns -1 in case of failure.

- The **attach()** function has a following prototype

```
void attach (filedesc fd);
```

The function attaches the output stream to the file specified by **fd**. In other words, it provides an interface for the file. The error is generated and the **ios::failbit** is set on, if the stream has been already attached to the file. That function is not specified by the standard draft. However, it is used by a number of compilers.

- The prototype of **rdbuf()** function is

```
filebuf* rdbuf ( ) const;
```

It returns a pointer to the **filebuf** buffer object associated with the used stream.

- The **fd()** function returns a file descriptor that is associated with a stream. The **filedesc** is an integer type equivalent to **int**. The function synopsis is

```
filedesc fd ( ) const;
```

- In some cases you want to know, if a particular file is open. It can be done using the **is_open()** status checking function. It returns a nonzero value if a stream is attached to an open disk file. Otherwise, zero is returned. The function prototype is

```
int is_open ( ) const;
```

The **setbuf()**, **setmode()**, **attach()**, **fd()** are not specified as the member functions of **ofstream** class by C++ Standard Draft, but are used in compilers.

18.6.3.3. ostream_withassign class.

It is derived from the **ostream** class. The **ostream_withassign** class allows to assign the objects to each other. The **cout**, **cerr**, and **clog** are the objects of that class type on a number of compilers. They can be reassigned to different objects at the run-time. C++ Standard Library Draft makes those objects the members of the **ostream** class. It does not specify the **ostream_withassign** class, that is used by a number of modern compilers. You will not "feel" any difference between the **ostream** and the **ostream_withassign** classes in many practical applications.

The **cout** object is connected to the standard output, which is the screen. The **cerr** is a buffered standard error file. The **clog** object is a fully buffered standard error file. The **cin**, **cerr**, and **clog** are tied to the **cout** object. Therefore, the use of any of those objects can flush **cout**. The class is described in the **<iostream.h>** file. It should be included whenever this class objects are used

```
#include <iostream.h>
```

The class important members are: constructors, destructor and the assignment operator.

The class constructor is overloaded. The constructor prototypes are

```
ostream_withassign (streambuf* pr);
ostream_withassign ( );
```

Here, the **pr** is a pointer to an existing object that has a **streambuf**-derived class type. The first constructor creates an object and attaches a **streambuf** object to it. It establishes an interface with a file for copying the data to it. The second constructor creates an object but does not initialize it. It requires a subsequent use of one of the class assignment operators to either attach a **streambuf** object, or to initialize it.

The class destructor destroys a class object. It synopsis is

```
ostream_withassign ( );
```

There are two assignment operators in this class. Their prototypes are

```
ostream& operator = (const ostream& ros);
ostream& operator = (streambuf* sbp);
```

The first operator assigns an **ostream_withassign** class object to an **ostream** object. The second one assigns a **streambuf** type object to an **ostream** object.

18.6.3.4. *ostrstream* class.

The **ostrstream** class is used for the output of the character arrays. The class is derived from the **ostream** class, which is inherited publicly. The **<strstrea.h>** header file should be included when the **ostrstream** class objects are used

```
#include <strstrea.h>
```
C++ Standard Library Draft places this class in the **<strstream>** header file. You can check which header will work in your programs on your particular compiler. All the class member functions are declared as public. Let's review them.
- The class constructor is overloaded. Its prototypes are
```
ostrstream ( );
ostrstream (char* pr, int num, int Mode = ios::out);
```
Here, **pr** is a pointer to a reserved area, that will be used for the output streams. The **num** is the size (in characters) of the array **pr**. If **num** is zero, the **pr** array is treated as a null-terminated array. Its length is determined by the system. The array is assumed to have an infinite length if **num** is less than zero. The **Mode** parameter defines the stream creation mode. It is an enumerator member of the **ios** class, that can assume only **ios::out**, **NULL**, **ios::ate**, **ios::app** values.

The first constructor creates an **ostrstream** object, that uses the internal memory as a buffer for the data output. The buffer size is determined dynamically as needed. The second constructor creates an **ostrstream** object, that has first **num** characters of the array pointed to by **pr**.
- The class virtual destructor has following synopsis
```
virtual ~ostrstream ( );
```
It destroys an **ostrstream** object. It destroys an associated with it **strstreambuf** object. The destructor releases the internally allocated memory for a buffer, if you used a constructor without the parameters. Otherwise, you have to release the memory by yourself. An internally allocated character buffer will not be released, if you previously frozen it using **str()** or **freeze()** calls.
- Sometimes, you need to know the number of bytes stored in the buffer you use. The **pcount()** function returns that number of bytes in the used buffer. Its prototype is
```
int pcount ( ) const;
```
- The **rdbuf()** function returns a pointer to the **strstreambuf** class buffer object associated with this stream. The function prototype is
```
strstreambuf* rdbuf ( ) const;
```
- The **str()** function synopsis is
```
char* str ( );
```
The function returns a pointer to the internal array of characters. If you created an object of the **ostrstream** class with the second constructor, the pointer returned by the **str()** points toward the same character array **pr**. If you used the first constructor, the **str()** freezes the array. You cannot send any characters to that array. This array will not be deleted by the class destructor, when an object that is associated with this array goes out

of the scope. You have to delete that array. You can unfreeze it by calling **rdbuf->freeze(0)**.

• The **freeze()** function freezes an array. You cannot perform an output with the frozen array. But you can later unfreeze that array. If you call the function as

```
    ob.freeze (1);
```
it will freeze an array associated with that object of **ostrstream** class. Call to

```
    ob.freeze (0);
```
unfreezes that array.

18.6.4. Input/output stream classes.

The input/ouput classes are used for the stream I/O, as you would, probably, expect. We will review following I/O stream classes: **iostream**, **fstream**, **strstream**, **stdiostream**. None of those classes is specified in C++ Standard Library Draft. However, since they are used by a number of compilers, we give them in this book. The **iostream** class is used as a general I/O stream class. It is also a base class for other I/O classes. The **fstream** class is used for the disk file I/O. The **strstream** is used for the I/O of string streams. The **stdiostream** is used for the standard file I/O. Let's now review each of them.

18.6.4.1. *iostream* class.

The **iostream** class provides the tools for stream random-access and sequential I/O. It is derived from both the **istream** and **ostream** classes. So, it inherited all the members of both classes. It also inherited all the members of the **ios** class. The object of that class typically comes with attached object of the **streambuf** class. To use **iostream** class for the disk file I/O a **filebuf** object must be created. The class is described in the **<iostream.h>** header file, that must be included when an object of the **iostream** class type is used.

```
    #include <iostream.h>
```
The most important members of that class are the constructor and virtual destructor. The constructor function is overloaded. Its prototypes are:

```
    iostream (streambuf* pr);
    iostream ( );
```
The first constructor is a public one and the second one is protected. The **pr** is a pointer to an existing object of the **streambuf**-derived class type.

18.6.4.2. *fstream* class.

The **fstream** class provides the disk file I/O. It inherited the **iostream** class. The constructors of that class automatically create and attach a **filebuf** buffer object. The class is described in **<fstream.h>** header file. That file should be included, when the **fstream** class is used

```
#include <fstream.h>
```
All class members are public. Let's discuss important member functions of that class.

- The class has four constructors:
```
fstream ( );
fstream (const char* pr, int Mode,
           int PBuf = filebuf::openprot);
fstream (filedesc fd );
fstream (filedesc fd, char* q, int num);
```
All the parameters of those four constructors have the same meaning and values as the parameters discussed for the **ifstream** class constructors. First constructor version constructs the **fstream** class type object without actually opening a file. Second version constructs an object and opens a file whose name is stored in the string pointed to by the **pr** pointer in the mode specified by the parameter **Mode**. The file protection mode of such a file is specified by the third parameter. You can use two parameters, because the third one gets its value by default. Many compilers have a three parameter version of this function. The **PBuf** values are given in Table 18.6.

When the second constructor creates an object and opens a file, that file becomes associated with the created object. The third constructor constructs an **fstream** class object and attaches it (or associates it) with an open file specified by the **fd**. The last constructor constructs an **fstream** class object, associates it with an open file specified by the file descriptor **fd**. It also creates a buffer pointed to by the pointer **q** of length **num** for that file I/O operations. Each **fstream** type object becomes associated with a **filebuf** object. First three constructors allocate the reserve or so called buffer memory area by themselves. The last constructor permits a user-allocated memory area.

- The class destructor has the following prototype
```
~fstream ( );
```
It first flushes the buffer. It, then, destroys an object of **fstream** class. The destructor closes the file associated with **fstream** object only if it was opened by the constructor or **open()** member function. If the associated buffer was automatically allocated by the computer, it gets released by the **filebuf** destructor.

We will now consider the operation functions.

- The prototype of the **open()** function is
```
void open (const char* pr, int Mode = ios::out,
             int PBuf = filebuf::openprot);
```
The **open()** function is, sometimes, specified without the third parameter. However, some compilers use three parameter **open()** function. Since it is a function with default parameters, you can specify only two parameters. The **open()** function opens a disk file, whose name is stored in the string pointed to by the pointer **pr** in the mode **Mode** in the file protection mode **PBuf**. The possible values of **PBuf** are given in Table 18.6. It attaches the file to an object of the **filebuf** class. The function also associates the opened file with an object that has opened it. If you try to open an open file, or in case of an error, the **ios::failbit** is set on. If the file is not found, the computer tries to create a file with a specified by you name. If you used the **Mode** parameter **ios::nocreate**, the error occurs and sets on the **ios::failbit**.

- The **close()** function has a following synopsis

```
void close ( );
```
The function flushes an output if needed, closes the file and disconnects it from the **filebuf** object. However, it does not destroy the **filebuf** object. The file is also disassociated from the **fstream** class object.
- The next is the **setbuf()** function. Its synopsis is
```
streambuf* setbuf (char* pr, int num);
```
The **pr** is a pointer to a previously allocated memory space of **num** length (in bytes). If either **pr** is a **NULL** pointer or **num** is zero, the stream is assumed to be unbuffered. The function attaches the buffer to the file (**filebuf** object). The **NULL** is returned by the function, if the file is opened and the memory buffer has already been allocated. Otherwise, the function returns a pointer to the **filebuf** object cast to **streambuf** class type. This function prevents the class destructor from freeing the buffer memory.
- The **setmode()** function sets the opened file to a binary or text output mode.
```
int setmode (int nMode = filebuf::text);
```
The **Mode** can take only two values: **filebuf::text** and **filebuf::binary** in this function. The function returns -1 in case of failure.
- The **attach()** function has a following prototype
```
void attach (filedesc fd);
```
The function attaches the output stream to the file specified by **fd**. In other words, it provides an interface for the file. The error is generated and the **ios::failbit** is set on, if the stream has already been attached to the file. That function is not specified by the standard draft. However, it is used by a number of compilers.
- The prototype of **rdbuf()** function is
```
filebuf* rdbuf ( ) const;
```
It returns a pointer to the **filebuf** buffer object associated with the stream.
- The **fd()** function returns a file descriptor that is associated with a stream. The **filedesc** is an integer type equivalent to **int**. The function synopsis is
```
filedesc fd ( ) const;
```
- In some cases you want to know if a particular file is open. This can be done by the **is_open()** status checking function. It returns a nonzero value if a stream, attached to an open disk file, is open. Otherwise, zero is returned. The function prototype is
```
int is_open ( ) const;
```

18.6.4.3. *strstream* class.

The **strstream** class provides the tools for both input and output for the streams, that write or read from the character strings. An array of characters can be allocated by the class constructor dynamically or by the programmer. The **strstream** is derived from the **iostream** class, that is inherited as public. The **strstream** class is declared in **<strstrea.h>** header file, that should be included for using this class.
```
#include <strstrea.h>
```
We have described the constructors, destructors and all those member functions when studying the **istrstream** and **ostrstream**. All the member functions of those classes and the **strstream** class have a lot in common. The function parameters are the same.

They have the same values and similar meaning. All the functions work similarly. The difference is that the **strstream** class member functions operate with the objects of that class. They are used for both the input and output. At the other hand, the **istrstream** or **ostrstream** are used with the objects of their classes. The **istrstream** and **ostrstream** perform respectively input or output.

- The class constructor is overloaded. Its prototypes are

```
strstream ( );
strstream (char* pr, int num, int Mode = ios::out);
```

Here, **pr** is a pointer to a reserved area, that will be used for the I/O streams. The **num** is the size (in characters) of the array **pr**. If **num** is zero, the **pr** array is treated as a null-terminated array. Its length is determined by the system. The array is assumed to be of an infinite length if **num** is less than zero. The **Mode** parameter defines the stream creation mode. It is an enumerator defined in **ios** class, which can assume only following values: **ios::in**, **ios::out**, **ios::ate**, **NULL** character, **ios::app**.

The first constructor creates a **strstream** type object, that uses the internal memory as a buffer for the data output. The size of that buffer is determined dynamically as needed. The second constructor creates a **strstream** type object, that is associated with the array of **num** elements pointed to by **pr**.

- The class virtual destructor has following synopsis

```
virtual ~strstream ( );
```

It destroys a **strstream** object. It destroys an associated with it **strstreambuf** object. The destructor releases the internally allocated memory for a buffer, if you used a constructor without the parameters. Otherwise, you have to release the memory by yourself. An internally allocated character buffer will not be released, if you previously frozen it using **str()** or **freeze()** calls.

- Sometimes, you need to know the number of bytes stored in the buffer you use. The **pcount()** function returns that number of bytes in the used buffer. Its prototype is

```
int pcount ( ) const;
```

- The **rdbuf()** function returns a pointer to the **strstreambuf** class buffer object associated with this stream. The function prototype is

```
strstreambuf* rdbuf ( ) const;
```

- The **str()** function synopsis is

```
char* str ( );
```

The function returns a pointer to the internal array of characters. If you created an object of the **strstream** class with the second constructor, the pointer returned by the **str()** points toward the same character array **pr**. If you used the first constructor, the **str()** freezes the array. You cannot send any characters to that array. This array will not be deleted by the class destructor, when an object that is associated with this array goes out of the scope. You have to delete that array. You can unfreeze it by calling **rdbuf->freeze(0)**.

- The **freeze()** function freezes an array. You cannot perform an output with the frozen array. But you can unfreeze that array later. If you call the function as

```
ob.freeze (1);
```

it will freeze an array associated with object **ob**. Call to **ob.freeze(0)** unfreezes that array.

18.6.4.4. *stdiostream* class.

This class provides I/O for the standard I/O streams (such as screen, keyboard and so on). The standard I/O streams perform their own buffering. The object of this class calls the functions declared in the **<stdio.h>** header file. You can avoid using this class. If you choose to use it, set the **ios::stdio** format flag on by the function **ios::flags()**. Since the use of **stdiobuf** class may reduce the I/O performance due to double buffering, try to avoid using it. Use it to mix the **iostream** library with the standard I/O for the same stream. The class is described in the **<stdiostr.h>** file. Therefore, it should be included when you use this class

```
#include <stdiostr.h>
```

The class is derived from the **iostream** class, which is inherited as public. The **stdiostream** class declares constructor, destructor and **rdbuf()** function.

We will begin presenting the class functions with the constructor. Its prototype is

```
stdiostream (FILE* fpr);
```

Here, the **fpr** is a pointer to a standard file. This pointer can be **stdin**, **stdout**, or **stderr**. The constructor constructs an object of the class and associates it with an open standard I/O file. Unfortunatelly, the constructor also attaches a **stdiobuf** class object to an object, that is created. But the standard I/O system also provides its own buffering. This is the double buffering, that can affect the I/O performance.

The destructor destroys the object of the **stdiobuf** class, that is associated with this stream. But it does not close the attached file. The destructor prototype is

```
~stdiostream ( );
```

Sometimes, we need to have a pointer to the **stdiobuf** buffer object associated with our stream. It is returned by the **rdbuf()** function, which can be written as

```
stdiobuf* rdbuf ( ) const;
```

18.6.5. Stream buffer classes.

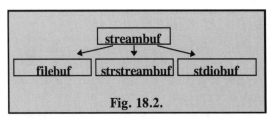

Fig. 18.2.

We will study classes, that provide the buffers for the I/O streams. The number of classes and their inheritance can vary for various compilers. One of the versions of this class hierarchy is given in Fig. 18.2. We will review the following classes: **strstreambuf**, **streambuf**, **filebuf**, **stdiobuf**. The base class **streambuf** is an abstract class, that is inherited by other classes. The **filebuf** is the stream buffer class, that handles the disk files. The **strstreambuf** is a buffer class for the string I/O. The **stdiobuf** is a buffer class for the standard I/O streams. Most of the member functions of those classes must be coded as protected according to C++ Standard draft. However, the style of using them illustrated by **Program 18.38** would work on many modern compilers.

18.6.5.1. *streambuf* class.

The **streambuf** class object, basically, controls the input and output streams. In many cases either input or output is performed. So, only input or output stream exists. If both input and output streams exist, the connection between them is not necessary. However, input and output streams are connected on a number of compilers. The **streambuf** class describes a very general way of I/O handling. Stream I/O classes create an attached **streambuf** or derived from that class object to perform the I/O operations. The **streambuf**-derived objects control the flow of information from and to a stream. This class serves as a base for a number of classes, which are also widely used with any I/O class objects.

All the objects of the **streambuf** class can provide a buffered I/O. In this case, the computer creates a fixed memory buffer, called reserve(d) area. That area is used for the input and output. It is dynamically divided on the parts that are used for the input or output. Those parts may or may not overlap. The part used for the input is called the *get* part. The part used for the output is called the *put* part. You can think about the reserve area as the memory allocated for storing an array consisting of a number of elements. Those elements are the characters, for instance. So, the whole area is a sequential set of memory cells. The computer divides this array on two parts. Before any of the strings will be written or read to or from the source, they will be placed into one of those array parts. One array part is used as a temporary storage of the input strings and called get area, as we said. Another array part called put area is used as a temporary storage of the strings, that will be written to some other location. So, before you write to a disk file, the computer will copy your string in the put area of the reserve buffer. After the string is written to that file, the put area might be flushed to empty it.

In general, the **ios** class performs all the formatting features, but the real I/O is done by the **streambuf** class. The class is described in the **<iostream.h>** header file, that should be included whenever the **streambuf** objects are used as

```
#include <iostream.h>
```

However, C++ Standard Draft describes this class in the **<streambuf>** header.

As we mentioned, the **streambuf** class objects control input and output sequences of characters. In other words, they control the input and output of the data structured as character arrays. The class declares six **private** member pointers:

char *gbeg, char *pbeg are the beginning pointers for an input or output sequence respectively. They point to the address of the first array element;

char *gnext, char *pnext are the next pointers for an input or output sequence respectively. It is an address of the next array element, that is now a candidate for input or output. The **gnext** and **pnext** pointers can be associated in our mind with the current cursor position. The **gnext** pointer contains the address of the element in the get area, that will be read next. This is why the **gnext** pointer is called the get pointer. Similarly, the **pnext** contains the address of the element in the put area, that will be written to some other destination (disk file and so on). This is why the **pnext** pointer is called the put pointer;

char *gend, char *pend are the end pointers for the input or output sequences respectively. They store the addresses of the next element after the last array element.

Those pointers can be called differently by different compilers. But their meaning remains the same. We give their names according to the C++ Standard Library Draft. We must review class member functions, starting with the constructor and destructor.

- The class constructor is a protected class member. Its prototype is:

```
streambuf ( );
```

It is a **protected** constructor. It does not have any parameters. It simply constructs a class object. Some compilers also declare another class constructor, although C++ Standard Library Draft does not contain it. Its prototype is:

```
streambuf (char* pr, int num);
```

Here, the **pr** is a pointer to the previously allocated reserve area. The length of that area is **num** characters or bytes. If **pr** is a **NULL** pointer or **num** is equal to zero, the stream will be unbuffered. This constructor not only initializes an object of the **streambuf** class. It also allocates the reserve area in the memory that will be used as a buffer. The **pr** and **num** determine the address and the length of that area.

- The **streambuf** class has a virtual public destructor. Its synopsis is

```
virtual ~streambuf ( );
```

It destroys a class object and flushes the buffer if the stream was used for an output.

We shell now describe different functions used for the character input.

- **in_avail()** function. Its synopsis is

```
int in_avail ( ) const;
```

It returns a number of characters in the reserved memory area, that are available for the input. As you will learn later, these characters are located between the **gnext** and **gend** pointers. Those characters can be fetched without any errors.

- The **sgetc()** is a public member function. Its prototype is

```
int sgetc ( )
```

The function returns a character that is currently located at the cursor position, i.e., it returns the value stored in **(unsigned char) * gnext**. So, it is a pointer to the current character to be read next. The function does not move the get pointer and returns an **EOF**, if a character cannot be returned.

- The **snextc()** is a public member function. Its prototype is

```
int snextc ( );
```

The function tests the current get area pointer position. The function returns an **EOF** if the end of the get area has been reached. Otherwise, the function moves the pointer one character forward. The function returns a character located at this new position, if the end of get area has not been detected at this position. Avoid calling this function.

- The **sbumpc()** is a public member function. Its synopsis is

```
int sbumpc ( );
```

The function reads and returns one character located at the current cursor position. It, then, advances the get area pointer **gnext** by one. The function returns an **EOF**, if the pointer points to the end of sequence.

- The **stossc()** function. Its prototype is

```
void stossc ( );
```

The function moves the get area pointer **gnext** one position forward. The function produces no action, if that pointer is at the end of the get area already. That function is not

specified by C++ Standard Library Draft.
- The **sputbackc()** is a public member function. Its prototype is

      int sputbackc (char x);

Here, the variable **x** contains the character that should be put back to the **streambuf**
object stream. The function moves the get area pointer one position back. It, then, compares **x** with the character that the get area pointer is pointing now to. If **x** does not match
that character, the function returns an **EOF**. Otherwise, it returns that character.
- The **sgetn()** is a public member function. Its synopsis is

      int sgetn (char* arr, int num);

The function reads up to **num** number of characters from the **streambuf** object's stream
into a buffer pointed to by **arr**. The function returns the number of characters, that it
actually read. It can read less characters than specified by **num**.
- The **out_waiting()** function. Its prototype is

      int out_waiting ( ) const;

The function is not specified in C++ Standard Library Draft, but is declared and used by
some compilers. It determines and returns the number of characters in the put area that
have not been sent to the final output destination. Thus, they are still contained in the
buffer. These characters are located between the **pnext** and **pend** pointers.
- The **sputc()** is a public member function. Its prototype is

      int sputc (int x);

The variable **x** stores a character to be written. The function stores a character in a put
area and increments a put area pointer. Thus, it writes a character to a buffer and advances
the pointer by one position. It returns the **EOF**, if it cannot write a character.
- The **sputn()** is a public member function. Its synopsis is

      int sputn (const char* arr, int num);

The **arr** parameter is a pointer to a buffer, that contains the data to be copied to the object
of the **streambuf** class. The **num** is the number of characters in the buffer. The function
copies **num** number of characters from the buffer pointed to by **arr** to the **streambuf**
buffer. Each copied character advances the put area pointer by one position. The function
returns the number of characters that are actually written. This number is usually equal to
num. It could be less in case of an error.
- The **sync()** is a protected member function. Its prototype is

      virtual int sync ( );

It flushes the put area and empties the get area. The characters that have not been sent
from that reserved area buffer to their destination are sent back to the source, if necessary.
If the get area is empty and there are no more characters to I/O, the function returns zero.
Otherwise, it returns an **EOF**. The **EOF** is returned in case of error. The **sync()** is a
protected member function. Its public member function version is called **pubsync()**.
The prototype of the last function is the same as for the **sync()**.
- The **setbuf()** is a protected member function. Its prototype is

      virtual streambuf* setbuf (char* pr, int num);

The **pr** is a pointer to a reserve area that should be allocated before using that function.
That reserve area has length of **num** characters or bytes. If **pr** is **NULL** or **num** is equal to
zero, the stream will be unbuffered. This means, there is no buffer in the input or output
stream. The data will be read or written directly. The function attaches specified by the **pr**

and **num** reserve area to a **streambuf** class object. The function returns a pointer to **streambuf** object, if the buffer is attached. Otherwise, **NULL** is returned. The **setbuf()** is a protected member function. Its public member function version is called **pubsetbuf()**. The **pubsetbuf()** prototype is equivalent to **setbuf()**.

• The **seekoff()** is a protected member function. Its prototype is

```
virtual streampos seekoff (streamoff dif, ios::seekdir
                  st, ios::openmode Mode =ios::in | ios::out);
```

Here, the **dif** is the offset in characters or bytes. The **streamoff** data type is equivalent to **long** for some compilers. The **st** is a variable of an enumerated type **seek_dir** or **seekdir** defined in the **ios** class given in Table 18.2. The **Mode** is an integer, that determines the stream mode. The **Mode** variable can accept only the values described in the **ios** class Table 18.1. The default value of that parameter is a bitwise-OR (|) combination of the **ios::in** and **ios::out**. The **seekoff()** function changes the stream cursor position by **dif** number of bytes from the point specified by **st**. Not all of the derived classes support the positioning. The **Mode** parameter defines whether the position changes for an input or output. The function returns a new position value in bytes from the start of a string (or file). It returns an output position, if both **ios::in** and **ios::out** are specified. If the derived class does not support the positioning, the **EOF** is returned. The **seekoff()** is a protected member function. Its public member function version is called **pubseekoff()**. The prototype of the last function is the same as for the **seekoff()**.

• The **seekpos()** is a protected member function. Its prototype is

```
virtual streampos seekpos (streampos dif,
                  ios::openmode Mode = ios::in | ios::out);
```

The function moves the cursor within a stream as specified by its first argument. The first argument is an object of the **streampos** class. The **dif.pos** member of that class has type **streamoff** (equivalent to **long**) and is used to specify the absolute cursor position. So, the first argument is assumed to be the value of that member. The **Mode** is an integer, that determines the stream mode. The **Mode** variable can accept only the values described in the **ios** class Table 18.1. The default value of that parameter is a bitwise-OR (|) combination of the **ios::in** and **ios::out**. The **seekpos()** function changes the stream cursor position by **dif.pos** number of bytes typically from the beginning of the stream. Not all of the derived classes support the positioning. If the derived class does not support the positioning, the **EOF** is returned. The **seekpos()** is a protected member function. Its public member function version is called **pubseekpos()**. The prototype of the last function is the same as for the **seekpos()**.

• The **overflow()** is a protected member function. Its synopsis is

```
virtual int overflow (int x = EOF);
```

The **x** parameter can contain any character or **EOF**. This function can be implemented differently by each of the derived classes. But the interface with the calling stream class remains the same. The function is usually called, when the put area is full. The function either writes a character stored in **x** to the put area or creates a position for adding that character. Thus, the function might expand a buffer, if needed. In order to expand an existing buffer, the computer might have to create a new buffer. In this case, the old buffer can be freed and the pointer to the old buffer can be readjusted to point to a new buffer. The derived classes, however, may perform a different operation. The function returns the **EOF** to specify an error.

- The **underflow()** is a protected member function. Its synopsis is
  ```
  virtual int underflow ( ) = 0;
  ```
It can be implemented differently by each of the derived classes. It is more often called, when the get area is sensed to be empty. The function gets a character from an input. If there is a character in the get area already, the function returns it. If there are no characters available, the **underflow()** function returns the **EOF** and does not place anything in the get area.

- The **uflow()** is a protected member function. Its prototype is
  ```
  virtual int uflow ( );
  ```
The function reads and consumes a character from a source of characters. It, then, moves the cursor one position forward. It can make a read position available, i.e., it can create a buffer with a character that can be read. It can read and consume a character from that buffer. The function returns the read character, or EOF on failure.

- The **base()** function. Its synopsis is
  ```
  char* base ( ) const;
  ```
The function returns a pointer to the first byte of the reserved memory area. This function is not defined by C++ Standard Library Draft, but is used in some compilers.

- The **ebuf()** function has a prototype
  ```
  char* ebuf ( ) const;
  ```
The function returns a pointer to the byte after the last byte of the reserved area. Imagine, the reserved area is a buffer for the I/O. Consider it as a memory allocated for an array of elements. The function returns a pointer to the element immediately following the last array element. For instance, if the memory is allocated for 4 elements, the **ebuf()** function returns a pointer to the fifth element. This function is not defined by C++ Standard Library Draft, but is used in some compilers.

- The **blen()** function. Its prototype is
  ```
  int blen () const;
  ```
The function returns the size of the reserve area in bytes. It is not defined in C++ Standard Library Draft.

- The **pbase()** is a protected member function. Its prototype is
  ```
  char* pbase( ) const;
  ```
The function returns a pointer (**pbeg**) to the first element of the put area.

- The **pptr()** is a protected member function. Its prototype is
  ```
  char* pptr ( ) const;
  ```
The function returns a pointer (**pnext**) to the next element in the put area that will be sent through a **streambuf** object. In other words, this function returns a pointer to the address of the element, that will be written next.

- The **epptr()** is a protected member function. Its prototype is
  ```
  char* epptr ( ) const;
  ```
The function returns a pointer (**pend**) to the byte after the last byte in the put area. If the put area is reserved for an array of four elements, the function returns an address of the fifth element.

- The **eback()** is a protected member function. Its prototype is

```
char* eback ( ) const;
```
The function returns the **gbeg** pointer.
- The **gptr()** is a protected member function. Its prototype is
  ```
  char* gptr ( ) const;
  ```
  The function returns the **gnext** pointer.
- The **egptr()** is a protected member function. Its synopsis is
  ```
  char* egptr ( ) const;
  ```
The function returns the **gend** pointer.
- The **setp()** is a protected member function. Its synopsis is
  ```
  void setp (char* pr, char* pe);
  ```
The function assigns **pr** pointer to both **pbeg** and **pnext**. It means, that both **pbeg** and **pnext** will be pointing to the same address as **pr** after calling the **setp()** function. The **pe** pointer gets assigned to **pend** pointer.
- The **setg()** is a protected member function. Its prototype is
  ```
  void setg (char* ps, char* pn, char* pe);
  ```
The function assigns the **ps** pointer to the pointer **gbeg**, pointer **pn** to **gnext**, and **pe** pointer to **gend**. So, the function assigns certain addresses to **streambuf** class type pointer members **gbeg**, **gnext**, **gend**.
- The **pbump()** is a protected member function. Its prototype is
  ```
  void pbump (int num);
  ```
The function increments the put pointer (**pnext**) by the number of positions specified by the **num**. The **num** parameter can be negative or positive. The function does not check if the pointer does not point over the limits of the put area.
- The **gbump()** is a protected member function. Its prototype is
  ```
  void gbump (int num);
  ```
The function increments the get (**gnext**) pointer by the number of positions specified by **num**. The parameter **num** can be positive or negative. The function does not perform the bounds checks, i.e., it does not check if a new pointer points beyond the get area.
- The **xsgetn()** is a protected member function. Its prototype is
  ```
  virtual int xsgetn (char* arr, int num);
  ```
The function reads the characters from an input. It does it in the same way as if you repeatedly call the **sbumpc()** member function. The read characters are stored in the first **num** successive elements of the array pointed to by the pointer **arr**. The reading stops when either first **num** characters have been read or a call to **sbumpc()** returns the **EOF**. The function returns the number of read characters.
- The **xsputn()** is a protected member function. Its prototype is
  ```
  virtual int xsputn (char* arr, int num);
  ```
The function writes the characters, stored in the first **num** successive elements of the array pointed to by the pointer **arr**, to an output sequence. It does it in the same way as if you repeatedly call the **sputc()** member function. The writing stops when either first **num** characters have been written or a call to **sputc()** returns the **EOF**. The function returns the number of characters written.
- The overloaded **unbuffered()** function. Its prototypes are
  ```
  void unbuffered (int stat);
  int unbuffered ( ) const;
  ```

The first overloaded function sets the way how the I/O will be performed. If the **stat** parameter is zero, the I/O will be performed through a buffer (buffered I/O). If the **stat** is nonzero, the I/O should be unbuffered. If the I/O is buffered, the reserve area will be allocated. Otherwise, no buffer will be allocated. The second function returns the current buffering state variable **stat**. You can determine, whether the I/O is buffered or not.

- The **allocate()** function. Its prototype is

```
int allocate ( );
```

The function attempts to allocate a reserve area. If that reserve area has already been allocated or an object of the **streambuf** class uses an unbuffered I/O, the function returns zero. If the space cannot be allocated, the function returns **EOF**. The function is used by many compilers.

- The **doallocate()** function. Its prototype is

```
virtual int doallocate ();
```

It is a protected and also a virtual function. It allocates a reserve area for the buffering. If such area cannot be allocated, the function returns the **EOF**.

The **unbuffered(), allocate(), doallocate()** functions are used by some compilers and are not specified for this class by C++ Standard Library Draft.

18.6.5.2. *filebuf* class.

The **filebuf** class is derived from the **streambuf**, which is inherited as public. The **filebuf** class performs buffered disk file I/O. The stream classes **ifstream**, **ofstream**, **fstream** use **filebuf** member functions. The **<fstream.h>** (or **<fstream>** according to C++ Standard) header file must be included, when the **filebuf** class is used

```
#include <fstream.h>
```

We will describe the most important functions of this class from our point of view. Some of these functions operate on a **FILE*** type data member **file** of the **filebuf** class. The **FILE** type is described earlier. This type is reserved to address the file pointers. Thus, the **filebuf** class contains a file pointer as its member. An object of this class can open and operate on a file.

The **filebuf** class typically has an overloaded public constructor. Its prototypes are

```
filebuf ( ); // this version is specified by C++ Standard
filebuf (filedesc fd);
filebuf (filedesc fd, char* pr, int num);
```

The **fd** is a file descriptor returned by a run-time opening function. The **filedesc** data type is equivalent to **int**. The **pr** is a pointer to the reserve area that should be allocated previously. It is a memory area for the I/O. The **num** parameter is the length of that reserve area in bytes. The first constructor constructs a **filebuf** object and does not attach it to any file. The second constructor constructs an object of the **filebuf** class and attaches it to the file specified by the file descriptor **fd** argument. The third constructor not only creates a **filebuf** object and attaches it to a file. It also specifies, that I/O to and from that file will be performed through a buffer. That buffer has an address specified by **pr** and the length **num** bytes.

The class destructor is virtual and public according to C++ Standard Library Draft.

```
~filebuf ( );
```
The destructor destroys an object of **filebuf** class and closes an attached file, if that file was opened by the **open()** member function of the **filebuf** class.

We can now consider operation functions. They are the following functions.

* The **open()** is a public member function. Its synopsis is

```
filebuf* open (const char* row, ios::openmode Mode,
               int PBuf = filebuf::openprot);
```

The C++ Standard Library Draft specifies this function, but without the third parameter **PBuf**. However, a number of compilers specify the third parameter. If you write this function with three arguments and it does not work, use only two of them. The third argument is a default one. So, you can use only two arguments anyway.

Here, the pointer **row** points to the string that contains the name of the file to be opened. The **Mode** parameter is an integer. Its values are defined in the **ios** class and are given in Table 18.1. The **PBuf** parameter is a file protection mode. It specifies the communication between the opened file, the system and other files. The **PBuf** values are specified in Table 18.6. The **filebuf::sh_read** and **filebuf::sh_write** can be combined using logical OR (|) operator.

The **open()** member function opens a file, whose name is stored in an array pointed to by **row**. The file is opened in the mode specified by **Mode** parameter. The file protection is specified by the **PBuf** parameter. The file is attached to the **filebuf** object that is used to call this function. The function returns a pointer to a **filebuf** object, or **NULL** in case of error or if the specified file has been opened already.

* The **close()** is a public member function. Its prototype is

```
filebuf* close ( );
```

The function flushes an output buffer, closes a file that belongs to an object by calling **fclose(file)** Standard C Library function described in **<stdio.h>** header. It disconnects the file from an object, that opened it. The function returns an address of the **filebuf** type object or **NULL** pointer in case of any error.

Following functions are not specified by C++ Standard Library Draft. However, they are used by a number of compilers, and we have to give them.

* The **setmode()** function. Its prototype is

```
int setmode (int Mode = filebuf::text);
```

We have discussed the **Mode** parameters when talking about **open()** function of file stream classes. The **Mode** parameter can accept only two values, when used in **setmode()** function. They are: **ios::text** and **ios::binary**. The first one sets the file to the text mode. The second one sets it to the binary mode.

This function sets the file associated with the **filebuf** object to the text or binary modes. It returns the previous mode, if there is no error. Otherwise, it returns zero.

* The **attach()** function. Its prototype is

```
filebuf* attach (filedesc fd);
```

The **fd** parameter is the file descriptor returned by the run-time file opening functions. The **filedesc** data type is equivalent to **int**. The function attaches a **filebuf** object that calls it to the opened file specified by the **fd**. It returns an address of the object of **filebuf** type. It returns **NULL**, if the file is already attached to the object.

* The **fd()** function. Its prototype is

```
filedesc fd ( ) const;
```
It returns a file descriptor associated with a **filebuf** object that called it. The data type **filedesc** is equivalent to **int**. The **EOF** is returned, if the object that calls it is not attached to a file. The function is not specified for this class in C++ Standard Library Draft. However, it is a member of this class in a number of compilers.
- The **is_open()** function. Its prototype is
```
int is_open ( ) const;
```
The function returns a nonzero value, if the **filebuf** object that calls it is attached to an open disk file. Otherwise, it returns zero.

The class also redefines a number of virtual protected functions. They are inherited from the base class. They all are specified in C++ Standard Library Draft.
- The **overflow()** is a virtual protected class member function. Its prototype is
```
virtual int overflow (int x = EOF);
```
The function appends a character stored in its argument **x** to the output sequence. It, then moves the cursor to the next position. Its action is equivalent to assigning that character to ***pnext++**. The function returns **(unsigned char) x**. The function can add another write position to a stream or a buffer, if it is not available. To do it the function evaluates the expression **fputc(x, file) == x**, that should be nonzero. The **fputc()** function is specified in the Standard C Library in **<stdio.h>** header file. The function returns the **EOF** if no file is associated with the **filebuf** object, or the **EOF** character is stored in **x**.
- The **underflow()** is a virtual protected class member function. Its prototype is
```
virtual int underflow ( );
```
The function reads a single character from an input sequence without moving the cursor one position forward. If it can be done, the function returns **(unsigned char)* gnext**. The function can also determine the character directly from an input and create a buffer for an extra character to read, if there is not enough space for reading a character. It acts, then, as if you call **(y=ungetc(fgetc(file), file)) !=EOF**. The **fgetc()**, **ungetc()** functions belong to Standard C Library and are described in **<stdio.h>** header. The **file** is the data member of **filebuf** class. The function returns **y** and assigns it to ***gnext** in the last case. If no file is associated with the **filebuf** object that calls **uflow()**. In case of faliure, it returns the **EOF**.
- The **uflow()** is a virtual protected class member function. Its prototype is
```
virtual uflow ( );
```
The function reads a single character from an input sequence. It, then, moves the cursor one position forward. If it can be done, the function returns **(unsigned char)* gnext++**. The function can also read the character directly from an input and create a buffer for an extra character to read, if there is not enough space for reading a character. In this case, it places it in object **y**, as if you call **(y=fgetc(file)) !=EOF**. The **fgetc()** function belongs to Standard C Library and is described in **<stdio.h>** header. The **file** is the data member of **filebuf** class. The function returns **y** and assigns it to ***gnext** in the last case. If no file is associated with the **filebuf** object that calls **uflow()**. In case of any faliure, it returns the **EOF**.

The **xsgetn()** and **xsputn()** are the virtual protected class member functions. Their prototypes and behavior are the same as specified for the member functions with the same names in the **streambuf** class.

• The **seekoff()** is a virtual protected class member function. Its prototype is

```
virtual streampos seekoff (streamoff dif,
                    ios::seekdir st, ios::openmode Mode);
```

The function alters the cursor position by the **dif** number of positions from the point specified by **st**. The **Mode** parameter specifies for what purpose this change is made (either to perform an input, or output and so on). The values of the argument passed to **Mode** are specified in Table 18.1. They can be combined by the logical OR (|) operator. The values of the argument passed to **st** are given in Table 18.2. The function constructs and returns a **streampos** object that stores the final cursor position. Basically, the function returns the cursor position, which is stored in the member of the object of **streampos** class type. So, for all practical purposes, the function returns a value, whose data type **seekoff** is similar to **long**. In case of failure, an incorrect position number is returned.

• The **seekpos()** is a virtual protected class member function. Its prototype is

```
virtual streampos seekpos (streampos dif, ios::openmode
                        Mode = ios::in | ios::out);
```

The function moves the cursor within a stream as specified by its first argument. The first argument is an object of the **streampos** class. The **dif.pos** member of that class has type **streamoff** (equivalent to **long**) and is used to specify the absolute cursor position. So, the first argument is assumed to be the value of that member. The second argument specifies the mode of the stream and is given in Table 18.1. If the file positioning fails or the file is not associated with the object that calls the **seekpos()** member function, the incorrect positioning value is returned. Otherwise, the function construct and returns a **streampos** object, that stores the absolute position in its member **pos**.

• The **setbuf()** is a virtual protected class member function. Its prototype is

```
virtual streambuf * setbuf (char* arr, int num);
```

The function specifies the buffer to be used for the buffered file I/O. The buffer will be an array of **num** elements pointed to by the pointer **arr**. The function returns the pointer ***this** to a **streambuf** object. It returns a null pointer in case of failure or if the file has not been associated with an object, that calls this member function.

• The **sync()** is a virtual protected class member function. Its prototype is

```
virtual int sync ( );
```

The function returns zero if the class member **file** is a null pointer. Otherwise, the function performs an action and returns the value equivalent to **fflush(file)**. The **fflush()** function is a C Standard function declared in **<stdio.h>** header file. In other words, when an object of **filebuf** class is associated with a file (or opens a file), the **file** class member points towards that file. This file is flushed by **sync()** member function. If no file is associated with the object, the function returns zero.

18.6.5.3. *strstreambuf* class.

This class is derived from the **streambuf** class, that is inherited as public. It is used for controlling I/O for the character sequences. Some of its member functions are virtual

and are defined in the base class. The **strstreambuf** class is described in the
<strstrea.h> (**<strstream>** acording to C++ Standard Draft) header file, that
should be included whenever the class is used as

```
#include <strstrea.h>
```

We offer you the most important functions of this class from our point of view.
The class constructor is public and heavily overloaded. Its prototypes are:

```
strstreambuf ( );
strstreambuf (int num);
strstreambuf (char* arr, int k, char* pr = 0);
strstreambuf (unsigned char* arr, int k,
                         unsigned char* pr = 0);
strstreambuf (signed char* arr, int k,
                         signed char* pr = 0);
strstreambuf (void* (*falloc)(long),
                         void (*ffree)(void*) );
```

Here, the **num** is the initial length of a dynamic stream buffer. The **arr** is a pointer to a
character buffer. That buffer will be attached to an object created by one of this constructors. The parameter **k** can be a positive number, zero, or a negative number. If **n** is a
positive integer, it specifies the length of **n** bytes of the **arr** buffer. If **n** is zero, **arr**
becomes a buffer, whose length is specified by a null-terminated string. If **n** is a negative
number, the **arr** buffer is supposed to have an infinite length. The **pr** is an initial value
of the put pointer. The **falloc()** is a memory allocation function, that has a prototype

```
void* falloc (long);
```

The first constructor constructs an object of the **strstreambuf** class. An object does
not contain any strings. The buffering for that object is assumed to be dynamic and is
allocated by the computer, as needed. The second overloaded constructor constructs an
object of the **strstreambuf** class. Its buffer is dynamic, but has **num** bytes initially.
That buffer is expanded by the computer, as needed. Following three versions construct a
strstreambuf object from the memory buffer. The address of that buffer is specified
by **arr**, the put pointer is **pr**, and the number of bytes is specified by **k**. The last
constructor constructs a **strstreambuf** class object, that uses dynamic buffering. It
allocates memory with its own run-time allocation functions.

- The destructor of the class has a familiar prototype

```
~strstreambuf ( );
```

It destroys an object of the **strstreambuf** class. The dynamically allocated area for an
object of that class is released, unless it is frozen. If a memory buffer has been allocated
by a user, it cannot be released by the destructor. It must be done by a user.

We will also discuss following functions.

- The **ffree()** is the function that frees previously allocated memory. Its prototype is

```
void ffree (void*);
```

- The **freeze()** is a public member function. Its prototype is

```
void freeze (int m = 1);
```

If **m** is zero, the current array or buffer can be deleted or expanded by the computer
automatically. If **m** is nonzero, the buffer cannot be deleted automatically. The
strstreambuf class objects use the dynamic buffers. Call to **freeze()** used with

nonzero parameter **m** freezes a buffer, that is attached to an object calling this function. No further input or output through this buffer is possible. You cannot delete or adjust a size of this buffer. You should not send any characters to a frozen array. A destructor does not destroy a frozen buffer. You are responsible for deleting the frozen array. Call to **freeze()** with **m=0** can unfreeze a frozen buffer, and allow I/O and adjustment of the buffer memory size.

- The **str()** is a public member function. Its prototype is

```
char* str ( );
```

The function returns a pointer to a buffer, that is associated with an object that called this function. If that buffer has been created by a user, the function returns a pointer to that buffer. If that object has been created automatically, the **str()** freezes that array. So, the array behaves as if it has been frozen by the **freeze()** function with a nonzero argument. If that array was empty, a **NULL** pointer is returned by the function.

- The **pcount()** is a public member function. Its prototype is

```
int pcount ( ) const;
```

If the **pnext** pointer to the output sequence is **NULL**, the function returns zero. Otherwise, it returns the part of the array, contained between **pnext** and **pbeg**. Thus, a difference **pnext - pbeg** is returned.

The class also redefines virtual protected member functions. They are inherited from the base class. They are: **overflow()**, **pbackfail()**, **underflow()**, **uflow()**, **xsgetn()**, **xsputn()**, **seekoff()**, **seekpos()**, **setbuf()**, **sync()**. Their prototypes are the same as in the base class. Their actions are identical or very close to those specified in the base class.

18.6.5.4. *stdiobuf* class.

The **stdiobuf** class provides the buffers for I/O through the standard C I/O system. The **stdiobuf** class is derived from the **streambuf**, which is inherited as public. The C standard I/O provides its own buffering. The double buffering by **stdiobuf** class and the standard C buffering can reduce the performance. Use the **stdiobuf** class only when you mix the **iostream** I/O with the standard I/O. The **stdiobuf** class is described in the **<stdiostr.h>** header file, that must be included as

```
#include <stdiostr.h>
```

We will consider constructor and destructor, although this class also declares a number of virtual and a few regular functions. Some of them are similar to the functions we have discussed before. The constructor has a following prototype

```
stdiobuf( FILE* fp );
```

Here, the **fp** is a pointer to a file, that allows us to operate with a file using standard C I/O system. The constructor constructs an object of the **stdiobuf** class. The object is associated with the standard I/O files (**stdin**, **stdout**, **stderr** and so on). The object is created as unbuffered by default.

The destructor destroys an object of the **stdiobuf** class and flushes the put area. However, it does not close the attached files. The prototype of the destructor is

```
~stdiobuf ( );
```

The class also redefines virtual protected member functions. They are inherited from the base class. They are: **overflow()**, **pbackfail()**, **underflow()**, **uflow()**, **xsgetn()**, **xsputn()**, **seekoff()**, **seekpos()**, **setbuf()**, **sync()**. Their prototypes are the same as in the base class. Their actions are identical or very close to those specified in the base class.

EXERCISES.

1. Run all the programs of this chapter, if you have an access to a computer.

2. Write a program that reads five integers from a standard input. It, then, displays the integers on the screen. Each integer is displayed on its field. The program must ask a user, what is the width of each field and what are the filling characters.

3. Write a program that reads the floating-point values from a keyboard and displays them on the screen. The program must ask how to display the values. A user should be able to set each of the flags that handle the floating-point values.

4. Write a program that reads and displays the integers in a user-defined base.

5. Write a program that reads a string from a keyboard and places it in a file. It, then, displays the content of the file on the screen. Use **iostream** library for doing it. Introduce checks for all known to you error flags.

6. Modify **Program 18.44**, so it reads the data from a keyboard and writes it to a file. A user must be able to extract the data from that file and to display it on the screen.

7. Write a program that uses a custom stream manipulator written by you.

8. Write a program that maintains the stock room records. It must read a part name, its price, stock number and the received quantity. The part name is entered like "Transistor 2N2222", or "Metal-film resistor 100 Ohm 1W" and so on. Some companies assign their stock number to the purchased parts. This part stock number is just an integer. The program must be able to read it for each entered part.

If you enter as new a part that already exists, the program must recognize it. Hence, the program must perform a search by both the part name and the stock number, when you enter a new part. If either the stock number or the part name already exists in your stock room, the program must display the corresponding part. A user must have a choice to change the record for the old or for the new parts. If a new part already exists in a computer, a user must also have a choice to add new quantity to the old one. Thus, the program updates the record on a quantity.

A user may request to display a record of any part stored in the stock room by the name, part number, quantity or price. Any record must be displayed on the screen in a form of a table. For example,

```
| Stock number |     Part name       | Quantity | Price |
     823          Transistor 2N3905      120       0.15
```

A program must also display all the records on request.

9. Write a program that reads data from a keyboard or from a file and places it in another file. The first file can also get its data from a keyboard.

10. Write a program that enters an array {100, -4, 29, -28, -293, 432, 28, 1, -48, -2, -4, 78, 95, -3} in a file from a keyboard. It, then, opens another file. The program, then, uses

these two files to sort that array using the sorting algorithms discussed earlier in this book. Any flips or placements of the values must be done to another file. The program performs a sorting and stores the final array in any file. That array is displayed on the screen.

11. Write a program that reads the data from a standard stream and stores it in an array. Other arrays and variables can read the data from the first array. Those other arrays display the data on the screen. Use **strstream** class objects.

12. Write a program that declares at least two strings. One of them reads the data from a standard input. Another one reads the data from the first one. Use the string class objects for performing manipulations with both strings. Try to write your own manipulators and operator functions for doing that. The content of the second array must be finally displayed in the screen to confirm, that the data has been copied to it from the first string.

CHAPTER 19

DATA STRUCTURES AND RUN-TIME ALLOCATION.

We have covered the run-time allocation functions in this book. But you do not know, how to use those tools to create, for instance, an array with the number of elements determined during the run-time. We still have not shown you how to create and handle the data structures, that will accept as much data as needed during the program run. This chapter covers some of these aspects. You should be able to create the programs that read different sizes of data and allocate the memory based on the size of that read data. You should also remember the computer memory has its limitations. Run-time allocation is performed in the heap memory region. When the whole region is occupied, a serious error can occur. Modern computers have pretty large memory available to a user. Hence, you should be able to allocate dynamically a sizable chunk of data.

A corner stone of run-time allocation in C is a self-referential structure. C++ uses a self-referential class for dynamic allocation. Both self-referential structures and classes are very powerful tools of C++ language. We will consider both, because we firmly believe, that C++ programmer should know all the C++ features along with all the tools inherited from the C language.

19.1. Self-referential structures and classes.

Self-referential structure is a structure, that contains a pointer to its data type among its members. We will review those structures on an example. Review following structure

```
struct race
{
int x;
char name[20];
race *next;
};
```

This structure contains three members: variable **x**, strung **name[]** and the pointer **next**. What makes it a self-referential structure? It is the presence of the **next** pointer. It is a pointer to a structure **race** data type. You can assign this pointer to point to any variable of **race** data type. It is just a regular pointer as a pointer to any other data type. The pointer is a member of a structure. As you will see, this permits a user to create those expandable arrays and other run-time expandable entities.

A self-referential class is a class containing a pointer to its class data type. Review following class

```
class Mine   {
public:
int mecal (float, float);
void setval (float, float, int);
void setpoint (Mine * );
Mine * retpoint ( );
private:
float x, y, ;
int z;
Mine * ptr;
} ;
```

The **Mine** is a self-referential class, because it contains a pointer to the **Mine** class data type **ptr** among its members.

19.2. Linked lists.

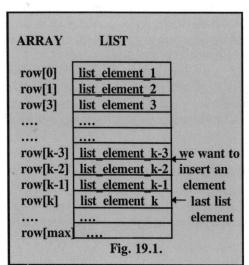

ARRAY   LIST

row[0]   list_element_1
row[1]   list_element_2
row[3]   list_element_3
....
....
row[k-3] list_element_k-3 we want to
row[k-2] list_element_k-2 insert an
row[k-1] list_element_k-1 element
row[k]   list_element_k   ← last list
....   element
row[max] ....

Fig. 19.1.

We will review linked lists, show how to implement them for the dynamic allocation with lists. Linked lists are used mainly for two purposes: creation of an array of variable size in memory, disk-file storage of databases. This way you can create a reasonable number of variables during the program run. The linked lists are good for databases. They allow you to insert and delete items without re-arranging the entire disk file.

List can be defined as a linear sequence of data like objects, that has a first element (called *head*) followed by successor (or next element), which can be followed by a successor and so on. Thus, each list element is followed by another element all the way up to the last element (called *tail*). The last element does not have any successors. One can perform certain actions on a list. For instance, you can create and delete a list and any element in it, search, insert, retrieve and update an element, sort and print a list. Each element of the list is called a *node*.

19.2.1. Array implementation of single lists.

A list can be implemented by a simple array. You declare an array. Each array element is a list element as shown in Fig. 19.1. You can declare an array with more elements than you need to accommodate all the list elements. The number of list elements cannot be greater than the number of array elements. You are familiar with how to handle the arrays. You can even use an array of arrays or an array of structures as a list. This is pretty useful, especially when each list element is a record. For instance, if a list represents students, so each element of the list can contain the first and last names of a particular student, his or her address, grade and so on. In this case, one has to deal with an array of structures.

You can use the memory allocation functions in a simple list implemented by an array. Its size is fixed, i.e., that list cannot grow in size, even if it is required during program execution. You should not have any problems to create a list or list element using an array. This means to declare an array and to enter a value of certain array element. You also know, how to search an array for a certain value or string characters.

To illustrate a list in an array implementation, we will give you an example of the most cumbersome insertion and deletion procedures. The insertion procedure is shown in the Fig 19.1. We have an array that has **max+1** elements, i.e., its last element is **row[max]**. Our list contains only **k+1** elements with **list_element_k** as the last element or the tail. We want to insert a new element between, let's say, **k-3** and **k-2**. How could you do that? Review following code

```
row[k+1]=row[k];
row[k]=row[k-1];
row[k-1]=row[k-2];
row[k-2]=new;
```

To insert an element between **row[k-3]** and **row[k-2]**, one has to move all the elements starting from **row[k-2]** one element up. The above code fragment illustrates it. This way the value of **row[k]** gets assigned to **row[k+1]**, then, **row[k-1]** value is assigned to **row[k]**, and **row[k-2]** is assigned to **row[k-1]**. Now we can assign a value of **new** to **k-2** element. The order of assignments is very important here. If we start with assigning the value of **k-2** element to **k-1** element, then, **row[k-1]** to **row[k]** and **row[k]** to **row[k+1]**, it will not work. Why? Look, you assign the value of **k-2** element to **k-1** element first. Now, **k-1** element holds the value of **row[k-2]**. When you assign the value of **row[k-1]** element to **row[k]**, you do nothing else but assigning the value of **row[k-2]** to **row[k]** and so on.

Remember following inserting an element in a list implemented as an array. When **row[k]** becomes **row[k+1]**, you have to check if **k+1** is not greater than **max**, that is, if the number of list elements does not exceed the number of array elements.

To delete an element you can simply move all the array elements above it one position down. **Program 19.1** illustrates both of those operations.

```
#include <stdio.h>
#include <stdlib.h>
#define MAX 10

int r;

void row_entry (char arr[MAX+1]);
void elem_ins (char line[MAX+1]);
void elem_erase (char str[MAX+1]);
```

```
void row_entry (char arr[MAX+1])
{
r=-1;
arr[r]='a';
while (r<=MAX && arr[r]!='\n')
{
r+=1;
scanf ("%c", &arr[r]);
}
r=r-1;
}

void elem_ins (char line[MAX+1])
{
int count, cal;
if (r >=MAX)
{
printf ("\nunable to insert\n");
return;
}
printf ("\nenter position to insert\n");
scanf ("%d", &count);
if (count>=MAX || count<0)
{
printf ("\ninsert number beyond the range\n");
return;
}
else if (count>r)
{
printf ("number outside the list\n");
return;
}
else
{
for (cal=0; cal<=(r-count+1); ++cal)
line[r+1-cal]=line[r-cal];
printf ("\nenter a character to insert\n");
scanf ("\n%c", &line[r-cal+1]);
r=r+1;
}}

void elem_erase (char str[MAX+1])
{
int k, m;
printf ("\nenter the element number to delete\n");
```

```
scanf ("%d", &m);
if (m>r || (m-1)<0)
{
printf ("\ncan't delete\n");
return;
}
for (k=0; k<(r-m+1); ++k)
str[m+k-1]=str[m+k];
r=r-1;
}

void main (void)
{
int p, choice;
char lis[MAX+1];
printf ("enter up to 11 characters\n");
printf ("push ENTER after you are done\n");
row_entry(lis);
for (p=0; p<=r; ++p)
printf ("%c", lis[p]);
printf ("\nwant to insert an element?\n");
printf ("enter 1 for 'yes' and 0 for 'no'\n");
scanf ("%d", &choice);
if (choice==1)
{
elem_ins (lis);
for (p=0; p<=r; ++p)
printf ("%c", lis[p]);
}
printf ("\nwant to delete an element?\n");
printf ("enter 1 for 'yes' and 0 for 'no'\n");
scanf ("%d", &choice);
if (choice==1)
{
elem_erase (lis);
for (p=0; p<=r; ++p)
printf ("%c", lis[p]);
}
printf ("\nend\n");
}
```

Program 19.1.

The output of the program is

```
enter up to 11 characters
push ENTER after you are done
```

```
compiler
compiler
want to insert an element?
enter 1 for 'yes' and 0 for 'no'
1
enter position to insert
4
enter a character to insert
x
comxpiler
want to delete an element?
enter 1 for 'yes' and 0 for 'no'
1
enter the element number to delete
4
compiler
end
```

The program consists of four functions: **main()**, **row_entry()**, **elem_ins()**, **elem_erase()**. The **row_entry()** function creates a list. If you go over this function, you will see a simple procedure of assigning the values to each array element. As we said earlier, each list element corresponds to one array element.

The **elem_ins()** function simply inserts one element at any position. It takes an array as an argument and prompts you, where to insert an element. After receiving an input from you, it checks whether the element can be inserted at this position. It, then, asks you, what element should it be. We have discussed an algorithm of insertion. The **elem_ins()** function just implements this algorithm.

The **elem_erase()** function erases the element whose number you specify by moving all the elements above it one position down. The **main()** function handles the control on the whole program. It calls each of those functions and passes the array to be changed to them.

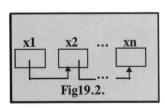

Fig19.2.

The memory allocation becomes useful when dealing with pointer implementation of linked lists. You can allocate as much space as you want, limited only by the available memory space. Lists implemented by the pointers are usually lists of self-referential structures or classes. There are following types of linked lists: single linked, double linked, circular lists using single link, circular lists using double links.

A singly linked list is the list, in which each element contains information about the next element or successor. In other words, the first element points to the second, second to the third, third to the fourth and so on up to the tail (last element). We illustrate it in the Fig 19.2. We will briefly consider how to create a single linked list, insert, remove list element using memory allocation functions.

19.2.2. Self-referential structures and single lists.

19.2.2.1. Introduction.

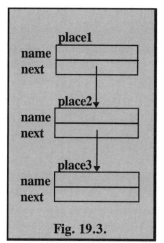

Fig. 19.3.

We will now concentrate on the self-referential structures first. As you know, they are the structures, that contain a pointer to themselves among the members. Consider a race. Suppose, we want to keep track of the runner names and their places in that race. One can do it by introducing a structure type

```
struct race
{
char name[20];
struct race *next;
};
```

This structure includes a pointer **next**, that is a pointer to a variable of structure **race** type. There is nothing wrong, if one of the structure members is a pointer to the same structure type. Again, it is just a pointer to the same structure **race** data type. This pointer can point to any of the variables of this data type. Let's now define three variables **place1**, **place2** and **place3** of the structure **race** type, that we might want to use for the first, second and the third runners crossing the finish line. Let's write those variables explicitly.

```
struct race {
char name[20];
struct race *next;
};
struct race place1, place2, place3;
```

One can now make a single linked list from those three variables. Simply arrange them in a way, so the first variable points towards the second one and the second variable points to the third one. In our case, second runner came to the finish after the first one and the third one came after the second one. If we print them in order, the first structure variable **place1** will give us the name of the first runner and will point us towards the second runner. The second variable will point us to the third runner, after giving the data about its runner. So, to implement a singly linked list, the pointer of the first variable must point to the second structure variable, and the pointer of that second variable should point to the third structure variable. It is shown in the Fig. 19.3, and coded below

```
place1.next= &place2;
place2.next= &place3;
```

Program 19.2 illustrates single linked list built from self-referential structures.

```
#include <stdio.h>                    /*line1*/
#include <string.h>                   /*line2*/
```

```
void main (void)                        /*line3*/
{                                       /*line4*/
struct race                             /*line5*/
{                                       /*line6*/
char name[20];                          /*line7*/
race *next;                             /*line8*/
};                                      /*line9*/
race place1, place2, place3;            /*line10*/
place1.next=&place2;                    /*line11*/
place2.next=&place3;                    /*line12*/
strcpy (place1.name, "Johnson");        /*line13*/
strcpy (place2.name, "Smith");          /*line14*/
strcpy (place3.name, "Robinson");       /*line15*/
printf ("%s  ", place1.name);           /*line16*/
printf ("%s  ", place1.next->name);     /*line17*/
printf ("%s\n", place2.next->name);     /*line18*/
}                                       /*line19*/
```

Program 19.2.

The output of this program is

```
Johnson   Smith   Robinson
```

The program begins with defining the structure and its variables at lines 5-10. We assign the pointers to make **place1** structure variable pointing towards **place2** and **place2** pointing towards **place3** at lines 11, 12. We copy runner names into corresponding variables using **strcpy** function at lines 13-15. Line 16 displays the **place1.name** structure member. The string "**Johnson**" is displayed. What member can be accessed by **place1.next->name** construction? It accesses the member **name** pointed to by **place1.next**. According to Fig. 19.3, **place1.next** points to the structure variable **place2**. Therefore, the **place1.next->name** accesses the member **name** of structure variable **place2**. That happens to be the string "**Smith**". It gets displayed by the **printf()** function at line 17. Then, **place2.next->name** accesses the member **name** of the structure variable **place3**. It is the string "**Robinson**" displayed by the third **printf()** function at line 18.

We have displayed a linked list by simply calling its elements. Since first structure variable points toward the second one and so on, it is seducing to try to use the loops. **Program 19.3** extends the operations with self-referential structures.

```
#include <stdio.h>
#include <string.h>

void main (void)
{
struct race
{
char name[20];
```

```
race *next;
};
race place1, place2, place3;
race *go=&place1;
place1.next=&place2;
place2.next=&place3;
place3.next=0;
strcpy(place1.name, "Johnson");
strcpy(place2.name, "Smith");
strcpy(place3.name, "Robinson");
while (go!=NULL)
{
printf ("%s ", go->name);
go=go->next;
}}
```

Program 19.3.

The output of this program is

```
Johnson   Smith   Robinson
```

This program is pretty much analogous to the previous one. It displays the runners in the order. We introduce the same structure **race**, containing pointer **next**, string **name**, same three structure variables **place1**, **place2** and **place3**. The pointer **next** of the first variable is assigned to point towards the second variable **place2**. Member pointer of **place2** is assigned to point to **place3**. We use the **strcopy()** function to fill in the content of each member **name**.

The difference between this program and the previous one is in following. We declare the pointer **go** and make it point to the first variable **place1** by ***go=&place1**. We make the member pointer of the last variable equal to **NULL** by **place3.next=0**. The pointer member of the last variable points to the null address. Null pointer is used in C to determine the end of the list. It is stored in the pointer of the last entry of the list. Thus, the last list node contains a null address. Assume, one accesses each structure in a list sequentially using loops. It is convenient to place a condition to stop the loop, when the null pointer is reached.

We display the list by the **while** loop in **Program 19.3**. Each loop cycle prints the string **go->name**. The **go** points to **place1** at the beginning of the first cycle. This prints string "**Johnson**", that belongs to **place1** variable. The first loop cycle also assigns the value of **place1.next** to pointer **go** by **go=go->next**. It is possible, because **go** points to **place1** before this assignment. Therefore, this assignment **go=go->next** is the same as **go=place1.next**. But **place1.next** points toward **place2**. So, **go** points towards **place2** after the first loop cycle, because this is where the first pointer **next** was pointing. Second cycle prints string **name** of **place2**, and refers the pointer to the third structure. This happens, because now **go=go->next** assigns the value of **place2.next** to the pointer **go**. This is the address of **place3**. The third cycle prints the third name and refers **go** pointer to the *null* address. When "**0**" address is encountered, the loop is terminated.

19.2.2.2. Run-time lists created from structures.

Program 19.4 creates a single linked list from the self-referential structures. This is an example of the run-time allocation. We create a list of runners by the name and the place. You can enter as many runners, as you need. You enter the runners at the program run-time. The computer allocates the memory space as the data comes. The number of nodes is limited only by the available memory.

```
#include <stdio.h>
#include <stdlib.h>

struct race
{
char name[20];
race *next;
};
race *first, *now;
void displ_place (void);
race *enter_name (void);

void main (void)
{

race *check;
int n;
check=enter_name( );
if (check==NULL)
printf ("can't create a list\n");
else
displ_place( );
}

race *enter_name (void)
{
int choice;
if ((now=(race *)malloc (sizeof (race)))==NULL)
return (now);
first=now;
do
{
printf ("enter runner's name\n");
scanf ("%s", now->name);
printf ("1-add another one, 0-no\n");
scanf ("%d", &choice);
```

```
if (choice)
if ((now->next=(race *)malloc (sizeof(race)))==NULL)
return(now->next);
else
now=now->next;
}
while (choice);
now->next=NULL;
return (first);
}

void displ_place (void)
{
int k=1;
now=first;
while (now!=NULL)
{
printf ("Runner #%d:%s\n",k, now->name);
now=now->next;
k=k+1;
}}
```

Program 19.4.

The program prompts the user to enter runner names in the order. One can enter as many names, as needed. When all the names are entered, the computer displays them in the order they were typed in.

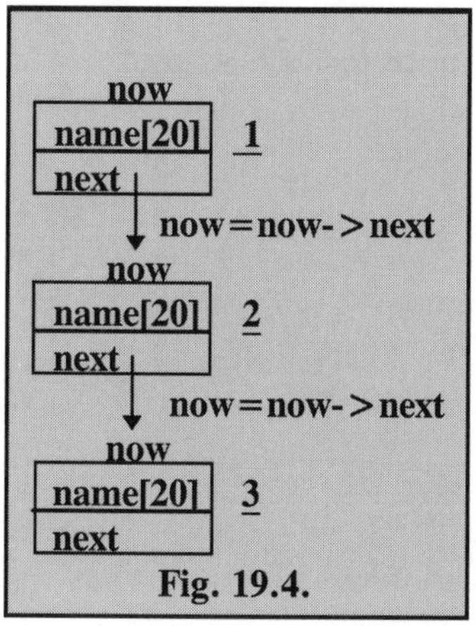

Fig. 19.4.

The code consists of three functions: **main()**, **displ_place()**, **enter_name()**. The structure **race** and two pointers to that structure are specified externally as global. The **main()** function just pulls the whole program together. It first calls the function **enter_name()** and checks the returned by that function pointer. If the list creation has succeeded, it calls the **displ_place()** function to display the whole list.

The run-time allocation is performed by the **enter_name()** function. It allocates the first node by

```
if ((now=(race *)malloc (sizeof
                           (race)))==NULL)
```

The **now** pointer is either returned if it is zero, or its value is assigned to the pointer **first**. This will be the beginning of the list. All additional nodes are added by the statements inside the **do-while** loop. Each loop cycle writes the runner's name to the corresponding **now->name** member. It prompts a user, if a new node must be added. If yes, a new node is created by

```
if ((now->next=(race *) malloc (sizeof(race)))==NULL)
return(now->next);
else
now=now->next;
```

This not only creates a new list element, but makes a member of the first structure variable **now->next** pointing towards a second structure with the address **now**. When we create a new structure next time, its address **now->next** will be assigned to the member **next** of that second structure pointer **now**. The process proceeds in the same way for as long as you enter new names.

New nodes creation in **Program 19.4** can be explained by the Fig. 19.4. We marked each structure with the numbers 1, 2 and 3 to make it easier to explain the drawing. Look at the most upper structure **now**. It is marked with the number 1 on the right of it. The first **do-while** loop creates the second from the top structure 2. But its address is held in the **now->next** pointer of structure 1. The first loop executes the first **now=now->next** statement. The pointer **now** is made equal to the address of the structure 2. The second loop creates the structure 3. Its address **now->next** is kept in the member **next** of the second (middle) structure **now**. The same loop executes **now=now->next** statement assigning the address of the third structure to the pointer **now**. This time **now** represents the third structure, so we can access its member **next** to create another structure and so on. To stop the loop, we must assign the **NULL** pointer to the last address.

```
now->next=NULL;
```

The loop is displayed by the **displ_place()** function, which is quite similar to the previous program.

19.2.2.3. Lists implemented with recursive functions.

We will review another example of linked lists, that uses recursive functions.

```
#include <stdio.h>
#include <stdlib.h>

typedef struct word
{
char let;
word *next;
} WORD;

WORD *first=NULL, *now=NULL;
int  m=0;
void displ_list (WORD *ord);
WORD *get_list(char *pr);


void main (void)
```

```c
{
WORD *check;
static char str[]="standartization";
first=get_list (str);
if (first==NULL)
printf ("unable to create a list\n");
else
{
printf ("list is:\n");
displ_list (first);
printf ("list has %d nodes\n", m);
}}

WORD *get_list (char *pr)
{
WORD *get_node (char one);
WORD *cur;
if ((cur=get_node (*pr))==NULL)
return(NULL);
if (*pr=='\0')
return(NULL);
else
{
pr=pr+1;
cur->next=get_list (pr);
return (cur);
} }

WORD *get_node (char one)
{
WORD *qq;
if ((qq=(WORD *)malloc (sizeof (WORD)))==NULL)
return (NULL);
qq->let=one;
qq->next=NULL;
return (qq);
}

void displ_list (WORD *ord)
{
if (ord==NULL)
printf ("\nend of list\n");
else
{
printf ("%c", ord->let);
```

```
ord=ord->next;
displ_list (ord);
m++;
}}
```

Program 19.5.

The program output is
```
The list is:
standartization
end of list
list has 15 nodes
```
The word is displayed using run-time techniques. The program consists of four functions: **main()**, **get_list()**, **get_node()**, **displ_list()**. The **main()** function calls the **get_list()** to create the list. It, then, calls the **displ_list()** function to display it. We initialize a string while declaring it in **main()** as
```
static char *str="calibration";
```
Since you initialize a string before the run, this would not be the best example of a run-time allocation. We introduce this program to illustrate a more sophisticated way of writing the lists. It teaches you how to use the recursive functions and modular programming for a run-time allocation. We recommend to use the technique similar to the previous program, when the nodes are created one by one, and the data is read one record at a time.

Fig. 19.5.

However, some tricks of this program can be very helpful for you.

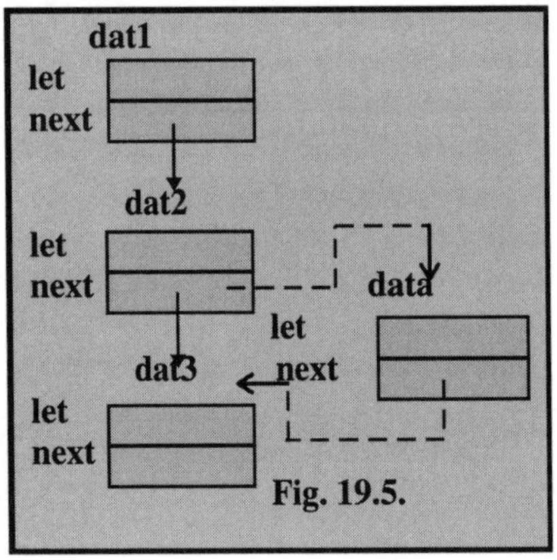

The **get_list()** function creates the list. It calls the **get_node()** function, that creates a particular node. Each letter is compared to '\0' by the **if-else** statement. The address of each node is obtained from the
```
if((cur=get_node (*pr))==NULL)
```
Then, the argument **pr** is incremented by one and the function calls itself
```
cur->next=get_list (pr);
return (cur);
```
It is a recursion. The function calls itself to create a list. Each call to **get_list()** returns a new pointer **cur**, that is an address of a newly created structure. Every time the previous **cur->next** will point to a new structure pointer **cur**, because
```
cur->next=cur;
```
The **get_node()** function creates a place in the memory for one structure **word**. It also assigns the values to each of its members. The **displ_list()** function displays the list elements. The reason we do not discuss those two functions in details is, that we have used similar solutions, and you should be able to follow those functions.

19.2.2.4. Insertion and deletion into a single linked list.

Another important step is to learn how to insert the elements in a list. Assume, we define the variables **dat1, dat2, dat3, data** of familiar to us structure **word** type.

Three of those variables are organized in a linked list of structure variables as shown in Fig. 19.5. Each list element points to its successor (i.e., next element). This is shown by the solid lines in Fig. 19.5. We want to insert a new variable in the list somewhere between two nodes. Let's insert a new variable **data** between **dat2** and **dat3**. Now think how could you do it. The pointer **next** of the variable **dat2** points towards **dat3**. Your new variable **data** must also point towards **dat3**. It can get this address from **dat2.next** pointer by

```
data.next=dat2.next;
```

It can also get that address directly from **dat3** by

```
data.next=&dat3
```

The address, contained in **dat2.next**, has been assigned to **data.next**. It points towards the structure variable **dat3**. Look at the dotted line in Fig. 19.5. The **dat2.next** also points towards the **dat3**. You can see, the solid line still exists in Fig. 19.5. However, nothing points to a new variable **data**. The link seems to be broken. In order to squeeze that new variable, one needs to break this solid line in Fig. 19.5. The **dat2.next** must point towards **data**. It is easily done by writing

```
dat2.next=&data;
```

This expression assigns the address of the variable **data** to the pointer **dat2.next**. Now **dat2.next** points towards **data**, and **data.next** points towards **dat3**. We insert a new variable or a new node between two other nodes. Node insertion should be performed in exactly the same sequence of statements. One cannot write them in opposite order, because when the address of **data** is assigned to **dat2.next**, the **data.next=dat2.next** directs **data.next** pointer to the same variable **data**. To improve the case, substitute by **data.next=&dat3** the **data.next=dat2.next**.

Now let's consider the program fragment, that will illustrate node insertion.

```
void ins_node (void)
{
WORD  *ptr1, *ptr2, *find_node (int n);
int num;
char cont;
printf ("press 1 to insert, 0-no\n");
scanf ("%d", &num);
if (num==0)
return;
printf ("enter the character to insert\n");
scanf ("\n%c", &cont);
printf ("enter after which node to insert\n");
scanf ("%d", &num);
if ((ptr1=(WORD *)malloc (sizeof (WORD)))==NULL)
```

```
{
printf ("can't allocate\n");
return;
}
ptr1->let=cont;
if (num<=0)
{
ptr1->next=first;
first=ptr1;
}
else if(num==1)
{
ptr1->next=first->next;
first->next=ptr1;
}
else
{
num=num-1;
ptr2=find_node (num);
ptr1->next=ptr2->next;
ptr2->next=ptr1;

}}

WORD *find_node (int n)
{
WORD *begin=first;
while (n>=1 && begin!=NULL)
{
n--;
begin=begin->next;
}
return (begin);
}
```

You can add this fragment as a separate program part to the end of **Program 19.5**. To incorporate it into that program, one has to write the function prototype somewhere before calling it from **main()**. The prototype of the above routine is

```
    void ins_node (void);
```

To call the function and observe its action add two lines to the end of **main()** routine.

```
    ins_node ( );
    displ_list(first);
```

Almost half of this fragment handles the data declaration and dialogs with the user. The computer asks, what character and after which node to insert. Then, it creates a new variable of structure **word** type, using **malloc()** function, and checks if the memory allocation is successful. If is done by comparing the returned by this function pointer to **NULL**. If the allocation is successful, it assigns a character to its member **let**. After that, the program compares the number stored by the node to zero.

If you enter zero or less, the computer assumes, that you want the inserted list element to be the first one in the list. Therefore, it reassigns pointer **first** to point to the newly created structure. If you want to insert a node after the first node, the procedure becomes relatively less complicated. We coded the insertion after the first node, according to our algorithm of insertion. If you want to insert after any other node, the function calls the **find_node()** function, that finds and returns the address of the corresponding node.

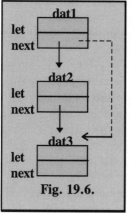

Fig. 19.6.

The **ins_node()** function does regular insertion after that list element.

We shell now review, how to delete the nodes. To delete a node **dat2** of already known to us structure **word** type follow Fig. 19.6. In order to delete the node **dat2**, one has to assign the address of **dat3** to the pointer inside of **dat1**, as shown below

        dat1->next = &dat3; or this is the same as
        dat1->next=dat2->next;

One can, then, assign a pointer to the old node

        ptr= &dat2;

and delete the old **dat2** cell using the command

        free(ptr); or free(&dat2);

Following fragment illustrates the node deletion.

```
void del_node(void)
{
WORD *fin=first, *aux, *tr;
int nod;
printf ("enter number of node after which to delete\n");
scanf ("%d", &nod);
if (nod<=0)
{
printf ("can't delete\n");
return;
}
while (nod>1 && fin !=NULL)
{
nod—;
fin=fin->next;
}
aux=fin;
fin=fin->next;
aux->next=fin->next;
free (fin);
}
```

The fragment deletes any list element after the node, whose number you enter. The fragment can be added to the end of **Program 19.5**. One should add the prototype of the **del_node()** function before calling it from **main()**.

```
void del_node(void);
```

To call the function and observe its action, add two lines to the end of the **main()**

```
del_node( );
displ_list(first);
```

You must understand more than half of this program without any questions. It declares and defines all the variables, pointers etc. Then, the program provides a dialog with the user, gets the number of the node after which to delete a list element. The **while** loop is used to find an address of the **nod** node, after which you intend to erase a structure. It decreases **nod** by one every loop cycle. When **nod** becomes 1, your pointer points to the right node. The node after that node will be erased. The statement

```
fin=fin->next;
```

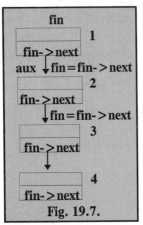

Fig. 19.7.

is also executed every loop cycle. Here, **fin** is the address of the current structure and **fin->next** is the address of the succeeding structure. Above statement assigns the address of the succeeding structure to **fin**. Therefore, each new loop directs **fin** to next list element. The loop stops, when **nod** becomes 1 or **fin** becomes **NULL**, i.e., you reach the last element and there is nothing to delete.

A few code lines of the above fragment can be very misleading. We will review them on the example of Fig. 19.7. We initially have 4 nodes pointing towards each other as 1->2->3->4. Let's start reviewing the code fragment from the last **while** loop cycle. It executes the statement **fin=fin->next**. Assume, it is the statement between the structures 1 and 2 in Fig. 19.7. The value of **fin.next** of node 1 is assigned to the pointer **fin**. This is also the address of the node 2. The value of that new **fin** is assigned to another pointer **aux** after the end of the loop. Now, the **aux** points towards the node 2 as well. The code goes one more structure forward

```
fin=fin->next;
```

Now, **fin** becomes the address of the structure 3. We, then, assign the value of the **fin->next** of the node 3 to the **aux->next**. The **aux->next** points now to the node 4. We effectively eliminated the node 3. It can be deleted now by the

```
free (fin);
```

We have shown you some of the operations on the singly linked lists. We hope, you got a feeling, how to create a list, insert and delete an element, display a list.

19.2.3. Doubly linked lists.

Everything stated for the single lists pretty much goes for the double linked lists. However, each element of the doubly linked list points to both previous (predecessor) and next (successor) elements. Usually, those lists consist of self-referential structures or classes.

Each structure includes data members and two pointers as shown in Fig 19.8. We called one of those pointers **next**. It points to the next list element. The second pointer, called by us **prev**, points to the previous list element. As you can see from the Fig. 19.8, the **prev** pointer of the first list element is equal to **NULL**. So is the **next** pointer of the last list element. They both are set to **NULL**, because they do not have where to point. When we go from the first to the last list element, we determine the end of the list by the **NULL** value of the pointer **next**. The **first** pointer points towards the first list element, and the pointer **last** points towards the last list element.

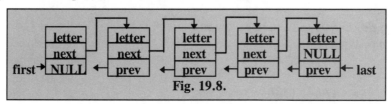
Fig. 19.8.

Same is true for another direction. If you go from the last to the first list element using **prev** pointer, you determine that first element by the **NULL** value of the pointer **prev**. Now we have to get an idea how to create, delete, insert elements into those lists. Let's review how to create a double linked list on an example.

```
#include <stdio.h>
#include <stdlib.h>

typedef struct word
{
char let;
word *next, *prev;
} WORD;
WORD *first, *last;

WORD *get_ent (char elm)
{
WORD *mynew;
if ((mynew=(WORD *)malloc (sizeof(WORD)))==NULL)
{
printf ("can't allocate\n");
return (NULL);
}
mynew->let=elm;
mynew->next=NULL;
mynew->prev=NULL;
return (mynew);
}
```

```
WORD *get_all (char line[ ], WORD *end)
{
WORD *cur;
if (*line=='\0')
return (NULL);
cur=get_ent(*line);
line++;
cur->prev=end;
last=cur;
cur->next=get_all(line, cur);
return (cur);
}

void displ_all (WORD *pq)
{
if (pq==NULL)
{
printf ("\nend of line\n");
return;
}
printf ("%c-", pq->let);
displ_all (pq->next);
}

void main (void)
{
static char arr[ ]="verification";
first=NULL;
last=NULL;
first=get_all (arr, last);
printf ("the doubly linked list is:\n");
displ_all (first);
}
```

Program 19.6.

The output of the program is

```
    the doubly linked list is:
    v-e-r-i-f-i-c-a-t-i-o-n-
```

The program creates and displays a double linked list, that gets its input from the string **arr[]**. The program consists of four functions: **main()**, **displ_all()**, **get_all()**, **get_ent()**. The **main()** defines and initializes the string **arr[]** to be represented as a double linked list. It assigns the **NULL** value to both **first** and **last** pointers. They are the addresses of the first and the last list elements. We want to clear them prior to their use. The **main()** routine also calls the **get_all()** function to create a list and the **displ_all()** to display the list.

The **get_all()** function creates the list. It reads the input string and compares each of its array elements ***line** to '**\0**' by **if** statement. If the current character is not a null character, a new list element is created by the

```
cur=get_entry(*line);
```

The **line** pointer is incremented by one to read the next string character, after reading the current one. The current structure pointers are assigned new values, so they point to the previous and next list elements. The **cur->prev** is assigned a value of pointer **end** by **cur->prev=end**. The **last** pointer gets the value of **cur**. The function calls itself by **cur->next=get_all(line, cur)** and returns the **cur** pointer.

The **get_ent()** function, basically, creates a node, assigns a value to the member **let**, and assigns **NULL** values to both of its pointer members. Let's review how does the creation of the list work. When the **get_all()** function is called for the first time, it creates a node by its call to the **get_ent()** function. The address of this node is **cur**. The **line** is incremented by one to get a new character from the input array. The **cur->prev** pointer gets the value of the **last** pointer, which is **NULL**.

The **get_all()** function is called with the **last** pointer as its argument for the first time. Therefore, the **cur->prev** pointer of the first list element is **NULL**. It is pretty much consistent with what we have indicated in Fig. 19.8. The **cur->next** pointer of that structure gets the returned pointer value from the subsequent structure, that will be created during the following **get_all()** execution. The **get_all()** function returns **cur** pointer and picks it up as an argument for the next call. Hence, the subsequent **get_all()** execution will create a new structure and assign the address of the previous structure to the **cur->prev** of that new structure. The address of that new structure will be stored in the **cur->next** of the previous structure variable. The execution of **get_all()** function, that will create that new structure, also contains a call to the **get_all()** function. It can create another node as well. The process lasts, until '**\0**' string character is encountered.

As you see, we take care of both **cur->prev** and **cur->next** member pointers, while creating the list. We use **displ_all()** function to display the list elements. It prints the current **pq->let** member and calls itself with the **pq->next** argument. It is quite analogous to **pq=pq->next** expression used in a loop, which is familiar to us. We can also use the **pq->prev** pointer to display the list in the reversed order.

Below, we give some additional functions to the **Program 19.6** for performing some other tasks. For instance, one can delete the above list by adding a routine

```
void del_all (WORD *ptr)
{
if (ptr==NULL)
return ;
ptr=ptr->next;
free (ptr->prev);
del_all (ptr);
}
```

To make this routine working, one would have to add one row to **main()**

```
delete_all (first);
```
The function **del_all()** must also be declared, if needed. This function uses familiar to us walk **ptr=ptr->next** to access the subsequent structures. It uses the **ptr->prev** member to free the preceding node.

One can insert and delete a node. It is similar to the singly linked lists. But you would have to redirect both **next** and **prev** pointers in the structure variables. One can search the list, going back and forth. In this case, it might be very convenient to have two pointers in the same structure. You can go either way using one of them.

19.2.4. Single and double linked circular lists.

As you have read, the last node member pointer of a regular single linked list usually has the **NULL** value. A single linked circular list is a regular single linked list, in which the last node member pointer points to the first node. This is the only difference. You already know, how to implement almost any operation on a single linked lists.

Let's now consider the double linked circular lists. You also know, that the **prev** pointer of the first node and the **next** pointer of the last node of the double linked list are equal to **NULL** according to Fig. 19.8. A doubly linked circular list is a regular double list in which: the **prev** pointer of the first node points to the last element of the list, the **next** pointer of the last node points to the first element of the list. In other words, the first and the last elements are connected to each other in those lists.

19.2.5. Self-referential classes and linked lists.

19.2.5.1. Introduction.

C++ uses self-referential classes to create the data structures. A class is very close to a structure. Lists of classes use the same algorithms as the lists implemented on structures. This is why we have begun building the linked lists using structures. Now, you can review, how to build a linked list from class objects. We demonstrate it below.

```
#include <iostream.h>                          //line1

template <class TYPENAME>                       //line2
class Newtest   {                               //line3
public:                                         //line4
Newtest ( ) { ptr=0;}                           //line5
Newtest (TYPENAME );                            //line6
void getval ( );                                //line7
Newtest <TYPENAME> * oneadd (TYPENAME);         //line8
void alldel (Newtest <TYPENAME> *);             //line9
private:                                        //line10
TYPENAME x;                                     //line11
```

```
Newtest <TYPENAME>* ptr;                    //line12
} ;                                         //line13

template <class TYPENAME>
Newtest <TYPENAME>::Newtest(TYPENAME q)     //line14
{                                           //line15
x=q;                                        //line16
ptr=0;                                      //line17
}                                           //line18

template <class TYPENAME>
Newtest <TYPENAME> *
Newtest <TYPENAME>::oneadd (TYPENAME var)    //line19
{                                           //line20
Newtest<TYPENAME> *cre = new Newtest<TYPENAME> (var);
                                            //line21
if (cre==NULL)                              //line22
return cre;                                 //line23
ptr=cre;                                    //line24
return cre;                                 //line25
}                                           //line26

template <class TYPENAME>
void Newtest <TYPENAME>::getval ( )          //line27
{                                           //line28
Newtest <TYPENAME> *readcur;                //line29
cout << "x=" << x << " ";                   //line30
readcur=ptr;                                //line31
do                                          //line32
{                                           //line33
cout << "x=" << readcur->x << " ";          //line34
readcur=readcur->ptr;                       //line35
}                                           //line36
while (readcur->ptr !=NULL);                //line37
cout << "x=" << readcur->x << " ";          //line38
}                                           //line39

template <class TYPENAME>
void Newtest
<TYPENAME>::alldel (Newtest <TYPENAME> * erpoint)//line40
{                                           //line41
Newtest <TYPENAME> *ercur;                  //line42
do {                                        //line43
ercur=erpoint;                              //line44
erpoint=erpoint->ptr;                       //line45
```

```
delete ercur;                                    //line46
}                                                //line47
while (erpoint !=NULL);                           //line48
}                                                //line49

void main ( )                                    //line50
{                                                //line51
Newtest<char > * startchpr;                      //line52
Newtest<char> * curchpr;                         //line53
Newtest <char> chobj ('A');                      //line54
Newtest <float> * startflpr;                     //line55
Newtest <float> * curflpr;                       //line56
Newtest <float> flobj (1.1);                     //line57
char y, m;                                       //line58
float a;                                         //line59

cout << " To enter characters hit 'C', for values"
     << " hit any letter." << endl;              //line60
cin >> y;                                        //line61

if (y=='C')                                      //line62
{                                                //line63
startchpr = & chobj;                             //line64
curchpr=startchpr;                               //line65

for (int k=0; k<3; k++)                          //line66
{                                                //line67
cout << "Enter a character." << endl;            //line68
cin >> m;                                        //line69
curchpr =  curchpr->oneadd (m);                  //line70
}                                                //line71
chobj.getval( );                                 //line72

chobj.alldel (startchpr);                        //line73
}                                                //line74
else                                             //line75
{                                                //line76
startflpr = & flobj;                             //line77
curflpr=startflpr;                               //line78
for (int r=0; r<3; r++)                          //line79
{                                                //line80
cout << "Enter a floating-point number." << endl;//line81
cin >> a;                                        //line82
curflpr =  curflpr->oneadd (a);                  //line83
}                                                //line84
```

```
flobj.getval( );                                    //line85
flobj.alldel (startflpr);                           //line86
}       }                                           //line87
```
Program 19.7.

The program prompts you

To enter characters hit 'C', for values hit any letter."
Assume, we pressed **C**. The program asks us to enter a character. We enter. It asks again. We enter another character. It happens, until we enter 3 characters. For instance, we entered **b c d**. The program displays them as

x=A x=b x=c x=d

The program consists of only one function **main()**. We declare the class template **Newtest** at lines 2-13. All the operations for creation of a linked list are done by the member functions of that class. They are handled from the **main()** routine. We must review the member functions of that class first, in order to understand the above program. The class declares following member functions: overloaded constructor, **getval()**, **oneadd()**, **alldel()**, destructor. The class has two data members: variable **x** of generic type and pointer **ptr** to an object of **Newtest** class data type.

The first class constructor does not have any parameters. It just sets the pointer **ptr** to zero. The second class constructor is defined at lines 14-18. It has one generic type parameter **q**. The constructor creates an object and assigns a value stored in its parameter **q** to class member **x**. It also assigns 0 to member pointer **ptr**.

The **oneadd()** member function is defined at lines 19-26. It has one generic parameter **var**. Its returned value type is **Newtest <TYPENAME> ***. It returns a pointer to a class object. The function creates a new class object using **new** operator at line 21. The **getval()** member function is defined at lines 27-39. It reads the **x** data member of all the objects in the list. The function defines **readcur** pointer to a class object. The first node is read by the **cout** object at line 30. The **readcur** is assigned the value stored in **ptr** pointer of the first node. Therefore, the **readcur** pointer must point to the second object in the list after that assignment. The function, then, proceeds executing the **do-while** statement at lines 32-37. The **cout** object at line 34 reads the **x** member of the current node.

```
cout << "x=" << readcur->x << " ";            //line34
```
The next node is selected by

```
readcur=readcur->ptr;                         //line35
```
The reading stops, after the computer encounters the **NULL** pointer in the last node. It is coded as the loop condition.

```
while (readcur->ptr !=NULL);                   //line37
```
The program also defines the **alldel()** function at lines 40-49. The function deletes the list nodes one by one. We offer this function just for the educational purposes. It illustrates how to walk along the nodes and erase them. You can modify this function to erase only the nodes, that you want to delete. In general, you can write a class destructor, that frees the allocated for an object memory. When the program goes out of scope, the objects will be deleted.

The list is created from **main()** function. The **main()** starts with defining and declaring all the objects and variables at lines 50-59. It, then, prompts, whether you enter the characters or the floating-point values. Since the class and its members have generic data types, you can use them to operate on any data type. This is why we define two objects. One of them must deal with the characters. The second one is used for the floating-point values. At this point, the **main()** function is divided on two almost identical parts. The part at lines 63-74 creates and displays the list of characters. Here, the generic class data type will be substituted by the **char** data type. The part at lines 76-87 deals with the floating-point values.

The list is created by the **for** loop in both parts in **Program 19.7**. For instance, a fragment of this program below creates a list of characters.

```
startchpr = & chobj;                         //line64
curchpr=startchpr;                           //line65
for (int k=0; k<3; k++)                      //line66
{                                            //line67
cout << "Enter a character." << endl;        //line68
cin >> m;                                    //line69
curchpr =  curchpr->oneadd (m);              //line70
}                                            //line71
```

We used the **for** loop to limit the number of entered nodes to three. You can use any loop with any condition. You can even code a loop with the dialog, that will prompt a user, whether to stop entering the data. This will make it truly run-time allocation decision. Our program displays the nodes by the **getval()** and deletes them by the **alldel()** function.

```
chobj.getval( );                             //line72
chobj.alldel (startchpr);                    //line73
```

Therefore, a linked list based on class objects not only permits to add the nodes at the run-time. It also allows to select the data type of the data to be written to that list at the run-time. It is an additional feature of C++ based linked lists.

19.2.5.2. Continuation on classes and linked lists.

We offer you another program illustrating the linked lists.

```
#include <iostream.h>

template <class TYPENAME>
class Newtest   {
public:
Newtest ( ) { ptr=0;}
Newtest (TYPENAME );
void getval ( );
Newtest <TYPENAME> * oneadd (TYPENAME);
void crelist ();
void alldel (Newtest <TYPENAME> *);
private:
```

```
TYPENAME x;
Newtest <TYPENAME>* ptr;
} ;

template <class TYPENAME>
Newtest <TYPENAME>::Newtest(TYPENAME q)
{
x=q;
ptr=0;
}

template <class TYPENAME>
Newtest <TYPENAME> *
Newtest <TYPENAME>::oneadd (TYPENAME var)
{
Newtest<TYPENAME> *cre = new Newtest<TYPENAME> (var);
return cre;
}

template <class TYPENAME>
void Newtest <TYPENAME>::getval ( )
{
Newtest <TYPENAME> *readcur;
cout << "x=" << x << " ";
readcur=ptr;
do
{
cout << "x=" << readcur->x << " ";
readcur=readcur->ptr;
}
while (readcur->ptr !=NULL );
cout << "x=" << readcur->x << endl;
}

template <class TYPENAME>
void Newtest <TYPENAME>
::alldel (Newtest <TYPENAME> *erpoint)
{
Newtest <TYPENAME> *ercur;
do {
ercur=erpoint;
erpoint=erpoint->ptr;
delete ercur;
}
while (erpoint !=NULL );
```

```
}

template <class TYPENAME>
void Newtest <TYPENAME>::crelist ()
{
TYPENAME m;
Newtest <TYPENAME> * dl;
cout << "Enter an element." << endl;
cin >> m;
dl =  oneadd(m);
ptr=dl;
for (int kk=0; kk<3; kk++)
{
cout << "Enter an element." << endl;
cin >> m;
dl->ptr =oneadd(m);
dl=dl->ptr;
}   }

void main ( )
{
Newtest<char > * startchpr, *curchpr;
Newtest <char> chobj ('A');
Newtest <float> * startflpr, *curflpr;
Newtest <float> flobj (1.1);
char y;
cout << " For characters press 'C', for values"
     << " hit other letter." << endl;
cin >> y;
if (y=='C')
{
startchpr = & chobj;
startchpr->crelist ( );
startchpr->getval( );
chobj.alldel (startchpr);
}
else
{
startflpr = & flobj;
startflpr->crelist ( );
startflpr->getval( );
flobj.alldel (startflpr);
}      }
```

Program 19.8.

The program prompts a user what type of data will be entered by displaying a message

```
For characters press 'C', for values hit other letter.
```

Let's assume, we have entered letter **C**. Now the computer expects to read the characters. The computer displays

```
Enter an element.
```

We enter **B** and press **ENTER**. The computer reads the letter, creates a list node and places the letter into the node. The procedure is repeated three more times. Suppose, we have entered letters **C**, **D** and **E** after the first letter. Each of the letters creates a new cell in the memory. The output of the program is

```
x=A x=B x=C x=D x=E
```

If we enter any other character but '**C**' after the first message, the program will expect to read the floating-point values. It will display four messages

```
Enter an element.
```

expecting us to enter a value after each message. We enter 2.2 after the first message and press **ENTER**. We type 3.3 next, followed by the **ENTER** button. We enter 4.4 and 5.5 after each of the last two messages. The program will display

```
x=1.1 x=2.2 x=3.3 x=4.4 x=5.5
```

The program declares the same class with almost the same members as **Program 19.7**. The class has one extra member function. It is the **crelist()** function. It prompts a user to enter a list element and creates the list using **for** loop. We also simplified the **oneadd()** member function and **main()**.

19.2.5.3. Node insertion in a list implemented with classes.

Program 19.9 demonstrates a node insertion into a list. It is based on **Program 19.8**. We intentionally made our next program long, so you would learn to read long programs. You will have to deal with them in the real life.

```
#include <iostream.h>                          //line1

template <class TYPENAME>                       //line2
class Newtest   {                               //line3
public:                                         //line4
Newtest ( ) { ptr=0;}                           //line5
Newtest (TYPENAME );                            //line6
void getval ( );                                //line7
Newtest <TYPENAME> * oneadd (TYPENAME);         //line8
void alldel (Newtest <TYPENAME> *);             //line9
void crelist ( );                               //line10
void oneinsert ( );                             //line11
Newtest <TYPENAME> *
retval (Newtest <TYPENAME> *);                  //line12
private:                                        //line13
TYPENAME x;                                     //line14
Newtest <TYPENAME>* ptr;                        //line15
```

```
} ;                                                 //line16

template <class TYPENAME>
Newtest <TYPENAME>::Newtest(TYPENAME q)             //line17
{                                                   //line18
x=q;                                                //line19
ptr=0;                                              //line20
}                                                   //line21

template <class TYPENAME>
Newtest <TYPENAME> *
Newtest <TYPENAME>::oneadd (TYPENAME var)           //line22
{                                                   //line23
Newtest<TYPENAME> *cre = new Newtest<TYPENAME> (var);
                                                    //line24
return cre;                                         //line25
}                                                   //line26

template <class TYPENAME>
void Newtest <TYPENAME>::getval ( )                 //line27
{                                                   //line28
Newtest <TYPENAME> *readcur;                        //line29
cout << "x=" << x << " ";                           //line30
readcur=ptr;                                        //line31
do                                                  //line32
{                                                   //line33
cout << "x=" << readcur->x << " ";                  //line34
readcur=readcur->ptr;                               //line35
}                                                   //line36
while (readcur->ptr !=NULL );                       //line37
cout << "x=" << readcur->x << endl;                 //line38
}                                                   //line39

template <class TYPENAME>                           //line40
Newtest <TYPENAME> * Newtest <TYPENAME>::           //line41
retval (Newtest <TYPENAME> *readcur)                //line42
{                                                   //line43
Newtest <TYPENAME> *retcur;                         //line44
int n=1, m=7;                                       //line45
char yy;                                            //line46
cout << "x=" << x << " ";                           //line47
cout << "To insert a character after that one press 'Y'."
     << "\nOtherwise, hit any other letter." << endl;
                                                    //line48
cin >> yy;                                          //line49
```

```
if (yy=='Y')                                    //line50
return readcur;                                 //line51
readcur=ptr;                                    //line52
for ( ; readcur!=NULL && n<m; readcur=readcur->ptr )
                                                //line53
{                                               //line54
retcur=readcur;                                 //line55
cout << "x=" << readcur->x << " ";              //line56
cout << "To insert a character after that one press 'Y'."
     << "\nOtherwise, hit any other letter." << endl;
                                                //line57
cin >> yy;                                      //line58
if (yy=='Y')                                    //line59
{                                               //line60
m=n;                                            //line61
n++;                                            //line62
}   }                                           //line63
return retcur;                                  //line64
}                                               //line65


template <class TYPENAME>
void Newtest <TYPENAME>
::alldel (Newtest <TYPENAME> *erpoint)          //line66
{                                               //line67
Newtest <TYPENAME> *ercur;                      //line68
do {                                            //line69
ercur=erpoint;                                  //line70
erpoint=erpoint->ptr;                           //line71
delete ercur;                                   //line72
}                                               //line73
while (erpoint !=NULL );                         //line74
}                                               //line75


template <class TYPENAME>
void Newtest <TYPENAME>::crelist ( )            //line76
{                                               //line77
TYPENAME m;                                     //line78
Newtest <TYPENAME> * dl;                        //line79
cout << "Enter an element." << endl;            //line80
cin >> m;                                       //line81
dl =  oneadd(m);                                //line82
ptr=dl;                                         //line83
for (int kk=0; kk<3; kk++)                      //line84
{                                               //line85
cout << "Enter an element." << endl;            //line86
```

```
cin >> m;                                       //line87
dl->ptr =oneadd(m);                             //line88
dl=dl->ptr;                                      //line89
}   }                                           //line90

template <class TYPENAME>
void Newtest <TYPENAME>::oneinsert ( )          //line91
{                                               //line92
Newtest <TYPENAME> *sinpr, *insp;               //line93
char w;                                         //line94
int z;                                          //line95
TYPENAME h;                                     //line96
cout << "Can't wait. Add a node now." << endl;//line97
cin >> h;                                       //line98
insp=ptr;                                       //line99
sinpr=oneadd (h);                               //line100
ptr=sinpr;                                      //line101
sinpr->ptr=insp;                                //line102
return;                                         //line103
}                                               //line104

void main ( )                                   //line105
{                                               //line106
Newtest<char > * startchpr, *curchpr;           //line107
Newtest <char> chobj ('A');                     //line108
Newtest <float> * startflpr, *curflpr;          //line109
Newtest <float> flobj (1.1);                    //line110
char y;                                         //line111
cout << " To enter characters press 'C', to enter values"
     << " hit any other letter." << endl;       //line112
cin >> y;                                       //line113
if (y=='C')                                     //line114
{                                               //line115
startchpr = & chobj;                            //line116
startchpr->crelist ( );                         //line117
startchpr->getval( );                           //line118
curchpr=chobj.retval (startchpr);               //line119
curchpr->oneinsert ( );                         //line120
chobj.getval( );                                //line121
chobj.alldel (startchpr);                       //line122
}                                               //line123
else                                            //line124
{                                               //line125
startflpr = & flobj;                            //line126
startflpr->crelist ( );                         //line127
```

```
startflpr->getval( );                        //line128
curflpr=flobj.retval (startflpr);            //line129
curflpr->oneinsert ( );                      //line130
flobj.getval( );                             //line131
flobj.alldel (startflpr);                    //line132
}        }                                    //line133
```

Program 19.9.

The output of the first part of **Program 19.9** is quite analogous to the previous program output. However, this program allows not only to create a list, but also to insert the nodes into it. Let's assume, you have selected **char** as the data type to be entered. Then, you entered **B**, **C**, **D** and **E** letters. The computer displays familiar to you

    x=A x=B x=C x=D x=E

It is followed by

    x=A To insert a character after that one press 'Y'.
    Otherwise, hit any other letter.

We hit any letter and message is repeated again.

    x=B To insert a character after that one press 'Y'.
    Otherwise, hit any other letter.

Now, we hit **Y** and press **ENTER**. The computer displays

    Can't wait. Add a node now.

We enter **q**, for example. The program displays

    x=A x=B x=q x=C x=D x=E

The program consists of function **main()** written at lines 105-133. The program declares class template **Newtest** at lines 2-16. All other lines define the member functions of this class. **Program 19.9** is similar to the previous one. Both programs have the same class with almost the same members. Common function members are defined very similar in both programs. Our class in **Program 19.9** has two data members: variable **x** of generic type and pointer **ptr** to an object of **Newtest** class data type. Class member functions are: overloaded constructor, **oneinsert()**, **oneadd()**, **alldel()**, **crelist()**, **retval()**, destructor.

One class constructor is declared and defined inside the class. The second constructor is defined at lines 17-21. The **oneadd()** function is defined at lines 22-26. The **getval()** function is defined at lines 27-39. The **alldel()** function is defined at lines 66-75. All those functions are similar to the previous program. We will not review them, because they must be clear to you. We will review the **oneinsert()** and **retval()** functions.

The **retval()** function is defined at lines 40-65. Its return type is written at line 41. It returns a pointer to an object of **Newtest** class type. It accepts a pointer to a class object as its parameter. The function reads the value stored in **x** for the current node. It prompts a user, whether to insert a character after that node. If you answer with '**Y**', it returns a pointer to the current node. The **oneinsert()** function actually inserts a node. It is written at lines 91-104. It utilizes the insertion algorithm, that we have discussed for structures.

We have discussed the single linked lists implemented with classes. We offered you a version of how to use the classes to create a list. It can be implemented in many other ways. It is more important, that you can understand the idea of the linked lists. We do not discuss the double linked lists in class implementation. We believe, you can write them. You would have to use the strategy offered in the last program and the algorithms discussed for the structures. Remember, a class is very similar to a structure. Therefore, you can transfer the algorithms learned for the structures to classes. But you can use class member and friend functions to operate with the lists.

19.3. Stacks.

19.3.1. Structure implementation of stacks.

We would like to acquaint you briefly with stacks and how to write them in C. It is an important subject. It is, usually, studied in more details in Data Structures course. A stack concept is an important tool for: parsing an expression by recursion by a compiler, windows and memory management by the operating system and so on.

A stack is a data structure that stores data objects or elements. The objects can be retrieved from the stack only in the *last-in-first-out* (LIFO) order. For instance, you have entered three numbers in the following order: the first number was 9, the second one was 5, and the third one was 2. Then, if you try to retrieve the data from the stack, the numbers will appear in the reverse order. The first one will be 2, then 5, then 9. So, the most recent data will be first to uncover from the stack.

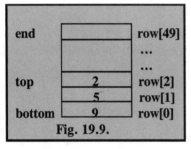

Fig. 19.9.

Review Fig. 19.9 for understanding a concept of a stack. A stack can store only finite number of data, because it occupies a finite memory space. Fig. 19.9 pictures a stack consisting of the cells. The "bottom" of the stack is used as a starting point for entering the data. A stack has one end, which is its last cell. The last cell containing the data is called "top". Let's consider how the data is entered and recovered from the stack on an example of our three numbers: 9, 5 and 2. It is shown in Fig. 19.9. The numbers are entered in the order: 9, then 5, then 2. When we enter number 9, it is placed into the bottom cell. The following number 5 is put in the cell, which is currently on top of the first cell. The third entered number 2 will be placed in the cell on top of the second cell. We can draw a conclusion. When you enter the data into a stack, each incoming value is put on top of the previous one. It is called the *push* operation. It is impossible to enter more values than there are cells. An attempt to do it will lead to the error state called *stack overflow*.

The data retrieval goes in an opposite direction. Look at Fig. 19.9. The data in the upper cell will be read first. It is number 2. When the number is read, it leaves the stack. Then, the second number will be on top of the stack and it will be read. It is number 5. Then, the last number 9 will become a top of the stack and will be read. The data retrieval is called the *pop* operation. An attempt to read more numbers, than there are in a stack will cause an error called *stack underflow*. The most important actions on stacks are: to create and clear a stack, to push and pop an element and to print the entire stack.

A stack can be implemented as an array or a list. An array implementation of stacks has a disadvantage of allocating a fixed amount of memory space for a given stack. One can avoid those problems by using linked lists. The first list element there becomes the first incoming stack element, the second list element is the second incoming stack element and so on. Each stack cell is implemented as a linked list node. When you push a new element, you add another node to the end of the linked list. You read a list in an opposite direction from the last to the first element. To perform popping procedure on the last element: read that last element, go to the second element from the end, destroy the last list element by **free()** function. Now, the second from the end element becomes the last element. If you want to read the new element, just perform a popping procedure on it again. To create a new node, you add a node to the last node in this list. In other words, you can add and read the stack elements only beginning from the top node. After you read a top node, it must be deleted.

List implementation of the stacks allows to use the memory space efficiently. The memory space can be increased or decreased depending on the size of the needed stack. The addresses of stack cells are random in the list implementation compare with an array sequential implementation. The disadvantage of that is the need in additional pointers to handle those linked lists. Review some of those operations on an example.

```c
#include <stdio.h>
#include <stdlib.h>

typedef struct word
{
char let;
word *next;
word *prev;
} WORD ;
WORD *first, *last;
int n=0;

WORD *get_entry(void)
{
WORD *mynew;
char one;
if ((mynew=(WORD *)malloc (sizeof(WORD)))==NULL)
{
printf ("can't allocate\n");
return (NULL);
}
scanf ("%c", &one);
mynew->let=one;
if (mynew->let=='\n')
return (NULL);
```

```
mynew->next=NULL;
mynew->prev=NULL;
return (mynew);
}

WORD *get_all ( WORD *end)
{
WORD *cur;
cur=get_entry();
if (cur==NULL)
return (NULL);
if (n==0)
first=cur;
n++;
cur->prev=end;
last=cur;
cur->next=get_all(cur);
return (cur);
}

void displ_all (WORD *pq)
{
if (pq==NULL)
{
printf ("\nend of line\n");
return;
}
printf ("%c-", pq->let);
displ_all (pq->next);
}

void retr_all (WORD *ptr)
{
if (ptr==NULL)
return ;
printf (" %c ", ptr->let);
ptr=ptr->prev;
free(ptr->next);
retr_all (ptr);
}

void main (void)
{
char one;
first=NULL;
```

```
last=NULL;
get_all (last);
printf ("the doubly linked list stack is:\n");
displ_all (first);
printf ("stack data retrieval order is:\n");
retr_all (last);
}
```

Program 19.10.

We can enter any word, for instance,

```
screen
```

The program output is

The doubly linked list stack is:

```
s-c-r-e-e-n-
   end of line
```

stack data retrieval order is

```
n  e  e  r  c  s
```

The program consists of five functions: **main()**, **retr_all()**, **displ_all()**, **get_all()**, **get_entry()**. The **main()** function makes **first** and **last** pointers equal to **NULL**, calls the **get_all()** function to create a stack. It, then, displays the whole stack in the order from the first to the last node by calling the **displ_all()** function. It is done only for your information. It is an incorrect retrieval order from a stack. We simulate the data retrieval from a stack by the **retr_all()** function.

The program functions are similar to those of **Program 19.6**, that illustrates a double linked list. The above **Program 19.10** also illustrates a double linked list. This list is used to implement a stack. The **get_entry()** function creates a node, that is a structure type variable. The function reads a character from a keyboard, places it into array member **let**. It also sets both structure pointers to **NULL** value and returns a pointer to created node. The recursive function **get_all()** creates a doubly linked list, using the **get_entry()** function for reading a character from the keyboard and node creation. The **displ_all()** function just displays the whole list on the screen, so we can see it. The **retr_all()** function reads the elements beginning from the last node. It also erases the nodes it has read.

19.3.2. Class implementation of stacks.

Following program demonstrates a simplified version of a stack written using self-referential class.

```
#include <iostream.h>                          //line1

template <class TYPENAME>                       //line2
class Newtest    {                              //line3
public:                                         //line4
```

```
Newtest ( ) { ptr=0;}                              //line5
Newtest (TYPENAME );                               //line6
Newtest <TYPENAME> *                               //line7
pushval (TYPENAME &, Newtest <TYPENAME> *);        //line8
void popallval (Newtest <TYPENAME> * poppr );//line9
private:                                           //line10
TYPENAME x;                                         //line11
Newtest <TYPENAME>* ptr;                            //line12
} ;                                                //line13

template <class TYPENAME>
Newtest <TYPENAME>::Newtest(TYPENAME q)            //line14
{                                                  //line15
x=q;                                               //line16
ptr=0;                                             //line17
}                                                  //line18

template <class TYPENAME>
Newtest <TYPENAME> *
Newtest <TYPENAME>
::pushval (TYPENAME &var, Newtest <TYPENAME> *pushpr)
                                                   //line19
{                                                  //line20
Newtest<TYPENAME> *cre = new Newtest<TYPENAME> (var);
                                                   //line21
if (cre==NULL)                                     //line22
return cre;                                        //line23
cre->ptr=pushpr;                                   //line24
return cre;                                        //line25
}                                                  //line26

template <class TYPENAME>
void Newtest <TYPENAME>::
popallval (Newtest <TYPENAME> * poppr)             //line27
{                                                  //line28
Newtest <TYPENAME> *readcur;                       //line29
cout << "x=" << x << " ";                          //line30
readcur=ptr;                                       //line31
delete poppr;                                      //line32
do                                                 //line33
{                                                  //line34
cout << "x=" << readcur->x << " ";                 //line35
poppr=readcur;                                     //line36
readcur=readcur->ptr;                              //line37
delete poppr;                                      //line38
```

```
    }                                              //line39
    while (readcur->ptr !=NULL);                   //line40
    cout << "x=" << readcur->x << " ";             //line41
    delete readcur;                                //line42
    }                                              //line43

void main ( )                                      //line44
{                                                  //line45
Newtest<char > * startpr;                          //line46
Newtest <char> chobj ('A');                        //line47
char y;                                            //line48
startpr = & chobj;                                 //line49
for (int k=0; k<4; k++)                            //line50
{                                                  //line51
cout << " Add a character as a node. " << endl;//line52
cin >> y;                                          //line53
startpr=startpr->pushval (y, startpr);             //line54
}                                                  //line55
startpr->popallval (startpr);                      //line56
}                                                  //line57
```

Program 19.11.

The program prompts
    Add a character as a node.
We enter **1**.
    Add a character as a node.
We enter **2**.
    Add a character as a node.
We enter **3**.
    Add a character as a node.
We enter **4**.
The program displays
    x=4 x=3 x=2 x=1 x=A

The program consists of **main()** function only. The program also declares the **Newtest** class template at lines 2-13. The class has two data members: generic variable **x** and a pointer to an object of **Newtest** class data type **ptr**. Therefore, it is a self-referential class. The class contains following member functions: overloaded constructor, **pushval()**, **popallval()**, destructor. There are two versions of the overloaded constructor, both used and described in the programs earlier in this chapter. The first version is defined and declared simultaneously. The second constructor version is defined at lines 14-18.

The **pushval()** member function is defined at lines 19-26. It adds new nodes on top of the stack. In other words, it just adds a new node to the last list element. It creates a new node using **new** operator. The function assigns the address passed to it as an argument to the member **ptr** of created node. The function returns the address of allocated node. This way, the allocated node becomes the last node of the list. Its member pointer points to the previous node. The **popallval()** member function is defined at lines 27-43. It reads all the data from the stack node by node. It destroys the nodes, that have been read. The **main()** program function defines and declares all the objects and variables. It uses **for** loop to create 4 nodes of the stack. The very first stack node is created by the object **chobj('A')**. We display the whole stack by

```
startpr->popallval (startpr);      //line56
```

19.4. Queues.

A queue is very similar to a stack. Consider a queue given in Fig. 19.10. One can introduce the *front* and the *rear* of the queue. When you enter the data, the first value occupies the front cell, second - the second cell from the bottom, the third value - the third cell from the bottom and so on. The last element to come will occupy the rear of the queue. Consider the same example with three numbers 9, 5, 2 entered in the same order as they appear here. This particular queue is shown in Fig. 19.10. When you enter 9, it will be stored in the first cell on the very bottom. The next number 5 will be placed in the second cell from the bottom. Number 2, which is the last to come, will be positioned on the top of the second one. Since there are only three numbers, the last number 2 will be the rear of the queue.

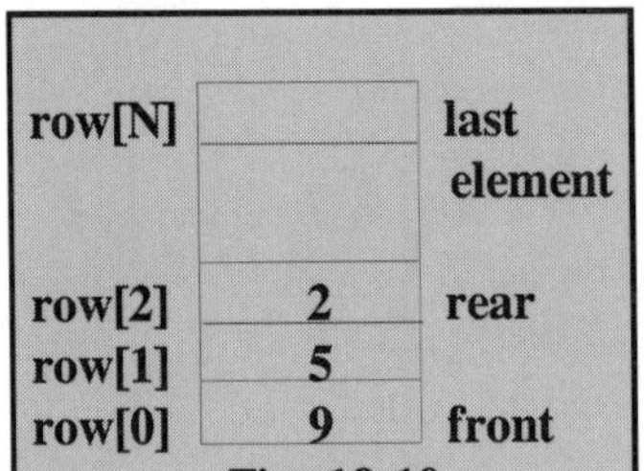

row[N]		last element
row[2]	2	rear
row[1]	5	
row[0]	9	front

Fig. 19.10.

The values are read from the queue in the order they come. It is called *first-in-first-out* or FIFO. The element, that came first, will be read first, followed by the second entered element and the third one. The elements are read, from the front of the queue. In our example, value 9 will be read first from the queue. Then, 5 should come one cell down to the front and be read, then 2.

Compare it with the stacks, where the values are placed in the memory cells in the same order from the bottom to the top, but read from the top to the bottom.

Queues are a particular type of data structures, and they have very wide application. You have probably called to phone company, airport, government agencies and were greeted with the message, that your call will be answered in the order received. This is a queue structuring. In computers, queue are particularly applicable in CPU, tape, disk and windows scheduling, printer spooling, in networks and so on.

Implementation of the queues is very similar to the stacks. You create a list from the first node up as we have done in **Program 19.10**. You add nodes to the rear of the queue. You read a queue from the first node up expunging the nodes, that you have read. Therefore, each subsequent element will appear the first queue node, after its predecessor has been read and deleted. You always read from the front of the queue. We do not give an example of the queue built from the self-referential structures, because it will be very similar to **Program 19.10**. We offer you a simplified version of a queue based on the self-referential classes. It is illustrated below.

```cpp
#include <iostream.h>

template <class TYPENAME>
class Newtest    {
public:
Newtest ( ) { ptr=0;}
Newtest (TYPENAME );
Newtest <TYPENAME> * addqueue (TYPENAME &,
                                Newtest <TYPENAME> *);
void readallval (Newtest <TYPENAME> * poppr );
private:
TYPENAME x;
Newtest <TYPENAME>* ptr;
} ;

template <class TYPENAME>
Newtest <TYPENAME>::Newtest(TYPENAME q)
{
x=q;
ptr=0;
}

template <class TYPENAME>
Newtest <TYPENAME> *
Newtest <TYPENAME>
::addqueue (TYPENAME &var, Newtest <TYPENAME> *adqpr)
{
Newtest<TYPENAME> *cre = new Newtest<TYPENAME> (var);
if (cre==NULL)
return cre;
adqpr->ptr=cre;
return cre;
}

template <class TYPENAME>
void Newtest <TYPENAME>
::readallval (Newtest <TYPENAME> * poppr )
{
Newtest <TYPENAME> *readcur;
cout << "x=" << x << " ";
readcur=ptr;
delete poppr;
do
{
cout << "x=" << readcur->x << " ";
```

```
poppr=readcur;
readcur=readcur->ptr;
delete poppr;
}
while (readcur->ptr !=NULL );
cout << "x=" << readcur->x << " ";
delete readcur;
}

void main ( )
{
Newtest<char > * startpr, *curpr;
Newtest <char> chobj ('A');
char y;
startpr = & chobj;
curpr=startpr;
for (int k=0; k<4; k++)
{
cout << " Add a character as a node. " << endl;
cin >> y;
curpr=chobj.addqueue (y, curpr);
}
chobj.readallval (startpr);
}
```

Program 19.12.

The output of the program is
    Add a character as a node.
We enter **1**.
    Add a character as a node.
We enter **2**.
    Add a character as a node.
We enter **3**.
    Add a character as a node.
We enter **4**.
The program displays
    x=A x=1 x=2 x=3 x=4

The program consists of only one program function - **main()**. The program declares class **Newtest**, that consists of following member functions: overloaded constructor, **addqueue()**, **readallval()**, destructor. The class consists of two data members: generic type variable **x** and the pointer to an object of **Newtest** class type **ptr**. Class declaration is followed by the definitions of all its member functions. We first define one of the constructor versions. It is followed by the definition of **addqueue()** member function, that creates a node and adds it to the end of the queue. The function returns a pointer to the created node. The function has two parameters. The first one is a reference.

It stores the content of the future node. The second parameter is a pointer to the node, that is currently the last node in the queue. The **readallval()** member function "walks" over all the nodes and displays the values stored in each of them.

The **main()** function defines the object of the class type and two pointers. It uses **for** loop to call the **addqueue()** function. This creates four nodes. We, then, display all the nodes of the queue by

```
chobj.readallval (startpr);
```

We used a loop with a fixed number of cycles to create a queue. We can use a loop, that will ask us when to stop creating the nodes. The loop could have been written as a separate class member function as we have shown before. We could have used the recursive functions to create a queue. Again, there are many solutions to this problem. We show you the simplified ways of doing it. It is enough for teaching you C++. It must be enough for making you write programs in C++ for solving practical problems. You will invent more complicated solutions, when you begin to program in C++.

19.5. Trees.

19.5.1. Introduction to trees.

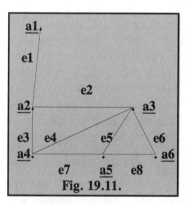

Fig. 19.11.

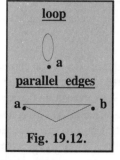

Fig. 19.12.

A tree is one of the most important concepts in computer science. They are widely used in the compiler design, databases, sparse matrixes, menus and menu-driven windows, hierarchical processes and file systems, decision trees, graphs and so on. A tree can be considered as a special type of **graph**. Before we discuss the trees, we will introduce you to the concept of a graph. We understand, reading about the graphs and trees can be boring and a bit too abstract for some readers. Some can wonder, why do they need it. Our advice, just read it and try to understand the concept. It will pay off in the future. A typical graph is given in Fig. 19.11. It consists of lines and dots and seems to be a pure mathematical abstraction. Do not hurry to conclusions. The dots on the graph are called *vertices* and the lines connecting the vertices are called *edges* or, sometimes, *arcs*. A graph, therefore, is a set of vertices and edges, where each pair of distinct vertices is associated with at list one edge. In other words, a graph is a set of dots and lines, in which every two points are connected by at least one line. Look at the Fig. 19.11. You can see a set of vertices {a1, a2, a3, a4, a5, a6 } and a set of edges {e1, e2, e3, e4, e5, e6, e7, e8}. Pick up any two points, for example, **a4** and **a5**. They are connected by the edge **e7**, edges **e4** and **e5** and so on. Loosely speaking, you must remember to call the dots the vertices and the lines the edges.

We should also introduce a few more definitions. The drawings explaining some of them are given in Fig. 19.12. A *loop* is an edge, that has an end and the beginning on the same vertex. *Parallel* edges are the edges beginning and ending on the same vertices. A *path*, in general, is a way or a trip that begins in some place and ends in another. For instance, review a path, that begins at **a5** going through **a3** and **a2** and ending on **a1** in Fig. 19.11.

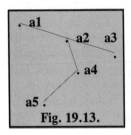

Fig. 19.13.

There are other paths connecting **a5** and **a1**. So, when one defines a path, it is defined by the order of the points or vertices through which it should go. A path length **n** is defined as a number of points through which it goes. In case of Fig. 19.11, our path can be written as {**a5**, **a3**, **a2**, **a1**}. And it has a length of 4, because it goes through 4 points. A *simple path* from one point to another one is a path, that has no repeated vertices. For instance, review two paths {**a5**, **a3**, **a4**} and {**a5**, **a3**, **a6**, **a5**, **a4**}. Trace them on the graph in Fig. 19.11. The first path begins at **a5** and goes through **a3** to **a4**. It is a simple path. The second one begins at **a5** and goes through **a3** to **a6**, then, back to **a5** and to **a4**. In the second case, the path goes twice through the same point **a5**. So, it is not a simple path.

Here we come to a definition of a tree. A tree is a graph, that has a unique simple path

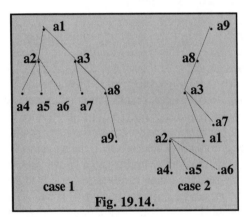

case 1   case 2
Fig. 19.14.

between any two points. The graph shown in Fig. 19.11 is not a tree, because for almost any of two given points on the graph, there can be many paths to go from one point to another one. A tree is presented in Fig. 19.13. Pick any two points. There is only unique simple path between them. Fig. 19.13 shows how to draw the lines to make a tree. A tree does not have any closed contours. If you have at least one closed contour or triangle and so on, there exists more than one path between two points.

There are three main categories of trees: *binary*, *binary search* and *general trees*. It is also important to define a few terms: *node*, *root*, *child*, *leaf*, *subtree*, *level*, *height*, *leftmost* and *rightmost leaf nodes*. A tree consists of data objects. Each of those objects is called a *node*. We simply marked them as points or vertices when considered graphs and trees. A node can be represented by an array element, structure, a class type object or a variable. A *node* can, for instance, contain data like name, salary, grades, address.

One of the vertices is called a *root*, and the tree is called a *rooted* tree. Any node can be chosen as a root. It is a matter of your preference. If you draw a tree, it is a convention to draw a root at the very top. We have shown the same tree in Fig. 19.14, where, in the first case, **a1** is a root drawn at the very top. In the second case, **a9** is selected as a root and placed at the very top of the graph. You will study, each tree can be divided into the subtrees. Those subtrees can be partitioned into the subtrees as well. Each subtree is a tree by itself. Therefore, it has a separate root. Each node can be a root of a subtree. In the case 1 in Fig. 19.14, the **a1, a2, a4, a5, a6** points form a subtree with the root **a1**. Other subtree of this subtree is formed by **a2, a4, a5, a6** with the root **a2**. Another subtree is **a1, a3, a7, a8, a9** with the root **a1**. Two more examples of the subtrees are: subtree **a7, a3, a8, a9** with the root **a3** and the subtree **a3, a8, a9** with the root **a3**.

The nodes in a tree are organized in a *parent-child (predecessor-successor)* relationship. Let's review Fig. 19.14 to study this concept on an example of **case 1**. The root node **a1** has no parents. The node **a1** is a parent for both points **a2** and **a3**, which are its children. Point **a2** is a parent to its children **a4, a5** and **a6**. Point **a3** is a parent to its children **a7** and **a8**. Hence, the nodes immediately following a root are its children. Therefore, the root is their parent. Those children are the parents for the nodes immediately following them and so on. A node that does not have any children is called a *leaf*. The points **a4, a5, a6, a7** and **a9** are the leaves in Fig. 19.14 **case 1**. The points **a7, a4, a5, a6** are the leaves in **case 2**.

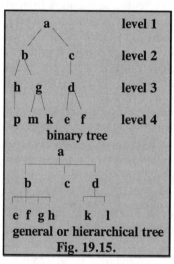

level 1
level 2
level 3
level 4

binary tree

general or hierarchical tree
Fig. 19.15.

The children with their children and so no are called the *descendants*. For example, all the nodes are the descendants of the node **a1** in Fig. 19.14 **case 1**. The parents, grandparents and so on are the *ancestors*. For example, the node **a3** is the ancestor of the node **a8** in Fig. 19.14 **case 1**.

A general tree, called also a hierarchical tree, is a tree, in which any parent can have any number of children, i.e., it has any number of disjoint general subtrees. A binary tree is a special kind of a rooted tree, in which every node can have none, one or two children. If there are two children, one is called *left* or *leftmost* and the second *right* or *rightmost* child. If a node has one child, it is designated to either right or left (not both). Thus, a binary tree has a root and can have only two disjoined subtrees at most. Fig. 19.15 shows the examples of regular and binary trees. One defines a *level* of a node in a binary tree as the total number of generations of ancestors plus one counted from the most upper root. Fig. 19.15 also illustrates how to count a node level. The binary search tree will be considered a bit later in this chapter.

So far, it has been an abstract notion to you and it will seem as such to you. We urge you to read the rest of this chapter. The material you are reading now is very important. You will definitely confront it in your future programs.

19.5.2. Implementation of trees.

19.5.2.1. Traversal algorithms.

We will review how to implement a binary tree using the linked lists, although it can be done by means of the arrays. The linked list approach allows you to create a list during run-time. Review Fig. 19.16, that explains the linked list approach for creating the binary trees. We have to introduce a pointer **ptr**, that will initially hold the address of the root node. Each node of the list is a structure variable or a class object. Each of those structures (classes) must have two pointers among other members. We called them **left** and **righ**. One of them will point to the left child, another one to the right child. Both pointers will be equal to **NULL** for the leaves. One can visit any node using those pointers. For instance, we assign the value of the **first** pointer to **ptr** by **ptr=first**. Then, **ptr** must point to the structure containing letter 'a'. Later, expression **ptr=ptr->left** can reassign **ptr** to the structure containing 'b'. Pointer **ptr** will point to the structure containing letter 'd' after another execution of **ptr=ptr->left**. Thus, we can move around the tree using the pointers and possibly loops. Therefore, you can create a tree node by node, keeping the address of the child node in one of the pointers **left** or **righ** of the parent node.

One of the important operations is to be able to put and get the information from the nodes of a tree after it is created. Sometimes, one has to visit all the tree nodes and get an information from each of them. Let's discuss some algorithms, that do it. Naturally, you would want to visit each node only once. It is called to *traverse* a tree or to go over the tree nodes visiting each of its nodes once. There are many ways of visiting all the tree nodes. To visit a node means to use its data members. We will review most commonly used traversal algorithms for the binary trees: *preorder*, *inorder*, *postorder*.

The *preorder* traversal algorithm consists of three steps:
1. Begin with the NODE (usually it is a root).
2. Traverse the left subtrees of a chosen node.
3. Traverse the right subtree of the node.

Let's apply the preorder algorithm to the binary tree in Fig. 19.15. We begin from the root **a**. We go over the left node first. This gives **a-b-h-p**. We, then, go to the closest node up, that has the right subtree. It happens to be the node **b**. We visit the right subtree, which has three points **g**, **k**, **m**. We first visit the right subtree point **g**. There, we are faced with two directions. We should go in the left direction first. Thus, we visit **m** node. After that, we return to the point **g**, and visit the right node **k**. Thus, the right subtree path is **a-b-h-p-g-m-k**. The left subtree is done in the order **c-d-e-f**. Traveling node by node using the preorder algorithm for the binary tree in Fig. 19.15 yields **a-b-h-p-g-m-k-c-d-e-f**.

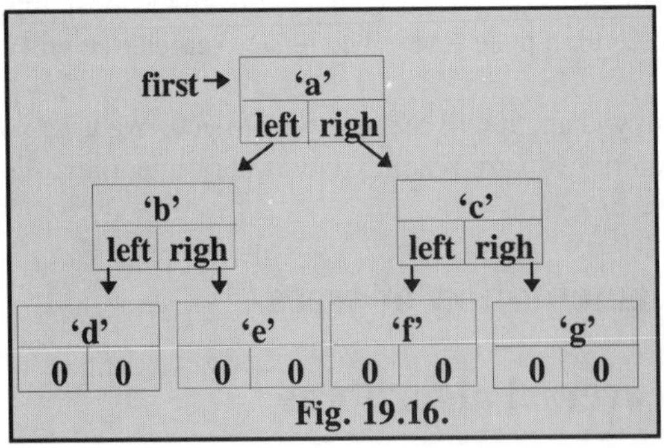

Fig. 19.16.

Consider another example of preorder algorithm used for the tree given on Fig. 19.17. We start from the node **1** and visit the left subtree. This produces a sequence **1-2**. We have a choice to go through the left subtree through node **4** or to go through the node **5**. We choose a left subtree according to preorder algorithm. So, the path proceeds through **4-6-7**. We, then, have to return to the closest node up, that has a right subtree (node **2**) and visit its subtree. This gives the path **5-8-9-10**. Let's now record the path through all the left subtrees **1-2-4-6-7-5-8-9-10**.

Now we have to visit the right subtree of the root node **1**. This subtree is a complex one. We first visit the left subtree of that subtree. It gives a path **3-11-13-14**. We, then, visit the right subtree of that subtree. This gives one point **12**. We, again, have two subtrees to visit. We must traverse through the left and, then, right subtrees. Going over the left part from the point **12** yields **15-17-18**. We return back to the node **12** and visit its right subtree. The path is **16-19-20**. The whole path through the right subtree of the root **1** is **3-11-13-14-12-15-17-18-16-19-20**. Let's add that pass to the left path and we get **1-2-4-6-7-5-8-9-10-3-11-13-14-12-15-17-18-16-19-20**. This is your path through the tree in Fig. 19.17 using the preorder algorithm.

The *inorder* traversal consists of following steps:
1. Traverse the left subtree of the node.
2. Visit that node.
3. Traverse the right subtree of that node.

We will apply this algorithm to the binary tree in Fig. 19.15. You begin with the leftmost subtree starting from the leaf. This gives **p-h-b**. You ran into the node, that has the right subtree. We traverse over it through **m-g-k**. We, then, visit the node **a**. So far, the path is **p-h-b-m-g-k-a**. We have to traverse over the right subtree. This yields the path **e-d-f-c**. The whole path is **p-h-b-m-g-k-a-e-d-f-c**. Consider more complicated example given in Fig. 19.17. We start with **6-4-7**. Next point is node **2**. The path, then, reads **9-8-10-5**. We, then, visit node **1**. So far, the path is: **6-4-7-2-9-8-10-5-1**. After that, we visit the right subtree of the root node **1**. We have to start from the left subtree of that subtree. We visit the path **13-11-14-3**. You can see the node **12** down from the node **3**. The node **12** has a subtree on its own. We cruise over that subtree as well, beginning from the left side. This gives **18-17-15-12**. We can now visit the right side. This yields **19-16-20**. Let's write the second part of the path **13-11-14-3-18-17-15-12-19-16-20**. Finally, the whole path is

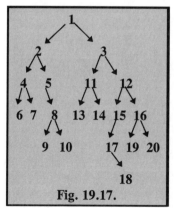

Fig. 19.17.

6-4-7-2-9-8-10-5-1-13-11-14-3-18-17-15-12-19-16-20.

The postorder algorithm can be formulated as
1. Visit the left subtree of the node.
2. Visit the right subtree of the node.
3. Visit that node.

Consider how to apply this algorithm for traversing over the tree given in Fig. 19.15. You begin with the left subtree of the node **b**. It is **p-h**. Its right subtree is **m-k-g**. Then, you visit the node **b** and **e-f-d-c-a**. The whole path is **p-h-m-k-g-b-e-f-d-c-a**.

More complicated tree for the postorder traversing is given in Fig. 19.17. We start with the leftmost subtree **6-7-4**. The point **2** has also the right subtree coming into it. We should traverse it before coming to that node. The path will be **9-10-8-5-2**. The path so far was **6-7-4-9-10-8-5-2**. We, then, visit the right subtree of the root node **1**. It is a complicated subtree, that has its own subtrees. The subtrees come to the point **3**. Therefore, we travel to the left of that node, and begin visiting the leaves on that side. We get **13-14-11**. We now have to pass across the right subtree of the point **3**. It has two subtrees coming to the point **12**. Remember, you have to begin with the last subtree, or even from the leaves, if they exist. According to the algorithm, we visit the left subtree coming to the point **12**. This yields the path **18-17-15**. We, then, visit the right subtree and the node **12**. The fragment of the path reads **19-20-16-12**. Now, we can visit the upper node **3**. This shell complete the subtree growing from the point **3**. Since we have visited both subtrees of the root node **1**, it can now be visited. The second part of the path is **13-14-11-18-17-15-19-20-16-12-3**. This completes the path **6-7-4-9-10-8-5-2-13-14-11-18-17-15-19-20-16-12-3-1**.

We will teach you how to create a binary tree on an example of a binary search tree. A

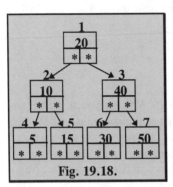

Fig. 19.18.

binary search tree (BST) is a binary tree, in which the nodes have a property: *the left subtree nodes store the values less than the root node, the right subtree nodes store greater values than the root node*. Thus, the binary search tree is a particular case of the binary trees. Why do we show you the binary search tree? Because this teaches you not only how to create a binary tree, but how to create a binary tree in which the nodes must be placed according to some rule.

An example of a binary search tree is given in Fig. 19.18. Here, the node 1 stores the value greater than node 2 and less than the node 3. None of the values in the left subtree starting from the node 2 is greater than the value stored in the node 1. None of the values in the right subtree initiated from the node 3 stores a value less than node 1. Same is true for the nodes 4, 2 and 5. Node 4 and any subtree that might be initiated from it will store the values less than the value stored in the node 2. Node 5 and any subtree starting from that node will store the values greater than the value stored in the node 2. It also holds for nodes 6, 3, 7.

19.5.2.2. An example of traversal algorithms.

Following program illustrates the creation of a simplified "pseudo" binary search tree and all three algorithms of traversing through it.

```
#include <stdio.h>                    /*line1*/
#include <stdlib.h>                   /*line2*/

typedef struct order                  /*line3*/
{                                     /*line4*/
int x;                                /*line5*/
struct order *left;                   /*line6*/
struct order *righ;                   /*line7*/
} ORD;                                /*line8*/
ORD *first=NULL;                      /*line9*/

ORD *make_n (int m)                   /*line10*/
{                                     /*line11*/
```

```
ORD *pr;                                   /*line12*/
if ((pr=(ORD *)malloc (sizeof (ORD)))==NULL) /*line13*/
{                                          /*line14*/
printf ("can't create a node\n");          /*line15*/
return (NULL);                             /*line16*/
}                                          /*line17*/
pr->x=m;                                   /*line18*/
pr->left=NULL;                             /*line19*/
pr->righ=NULL;                             /*line20*/
return (pr);                               /*line21*/
}                                          /*line22*/


ORD *find (ORD *start, int num)            /*line23*/
{                                          /*line24*/
ORD *q, *arp;                              /*line25*/

if (start==NULL)                           /*line26*/
{                                          /*line27*/
if ((q=make_n (num))==NULL)                /*line28*/
return (NULL);                             /*line29*/
first=q;                                   /*line30*/
start=q;                                   /*line31*/
return (start);                            /*line32*/
}                                          /*line33*/

if (num==(start->x))                       /*line34*/
{                                          /*line35*/
printf ("it already exists\n");            /*line36*/
return (start);                            /*line37*/
}                                          /*line38*/

if (num > start->x)                        /*line39*/
{                                          /*line40*/
if ((q=start->righ)==NULL || q->x > num )  /*line41*/
{                                          /*line42*/
if ((q=make_n (num))==NULL)                /*line43*/
return (NULL);                             /*line44*/
arp=start->righ;                           /*line45*/
start->righ=q;                             /*line46*/
start=start->righ;                         /*line47*/
start->righ=arp;                           /*line48*/
return (start);                            /*line49*/
}                                          /*line50*/
start=start->righ;                         /*line51*/
```

```
find (start, num);                        /*line52*/
}                                         /*line53*/

if (num < (start->x))                     /*line54*/
{                                         /*line55*/
if ((q=start->left)==NULL || q->x < num)  /*line56*/
{                                         /*line57*/
if ((q=make_n (num))==NULL)               /*line58*/
return (NULL);                            /*line59*/
arp=start->left;                          /*line60*/
start->left=q;                            /*line61*/
start=start->left;                        /*line62*/
start->left=arp;                          /*line63*/
return (start);                           /*line64*/
}                                         /*line65*/

start=start->left;                        /*line66*/
find (start, num);                        /*line67*/
}                                         /*line68*/
return (start);                           /*line69*/
}                                         /*line70*/


void cre_tree(void)                       /*line71*/
{                                         /*line72*/
int k, n, p;                              /*line73*/
printf ("How many numbers to enter?\n");  /*line74*/
scanf ("%d", &n);                         /*line75*/
for (p=1; p<=n; p++)                      /*line76*/
{                                         /*line77*/
printf ("enter integer number\n");        /*line78*/
scanf ("%d", &k);                         /*line79*/
if ((find (first, k))==NULL)              /*line80*/
return;                                   /*line81*/
}}                                        /*line82*/


void inor_tr (ORD *pin)                   /*line83*/
{                                         /*line84*/
if (pin==NULL)                            /*line85*/
return;                                   /*line86*/
inor_tr (pin->left);                      /*line87*/
printf (" %d ", pin->x);                  /*line88*/
inor_tr (pin->righ);                      /*line89*/
}                                         /*line90*/
```

```
void preor_tr (ORD *ppr)                    /*line91/
{                                           /*line92*/
if (ppr==NULL)                              /*line93*/
return;                                     /*line94*/
printf (" %d ", ppr->x);                    /*line95*/
preor_tr (ppr->left);                       /*line96*/
preor_tr (ppr->righ);                       /*line97*/
}                                           /*line98*/


void postor_tr (ORD *pos)                   /*line99*/
{                                           /*line100*/
if (pos==NULL)                              /*line101*/
return;                                     /*line102/
postor_tr (pos->left);                      /*line103*/
postor_tr (pos->righ);                      /*line104*/
printf (" %d ", pos->x);                    /*line105*/
}                                           /*line106*/

void main (void)                            /*line107*/
{                                           /*line108*/
cre_tree ( );                               /*line109*/
printf ("\ninorder traversing\n");          /*line110*/
inor_tr (first);                            /*line111*/
printf ("\npreorder traversing\n");         /*line112*/
preor_tr (first);                           /*line113*/
printf ("\npostorder traversing\n");        /*line114*/
postor_tr (first);                          /*line115*/
}                                           /*line116*/
```

Program 19.13.

The program first prompts you to enter, how many integral values you want to enter. We enter number 5. Therefore, only five values will be entered. The program, then, prompts you to enter a value. Thus, when you see a message

```
enter integer number
```

enter a value. You will see this message 5 times. Assume, we enter values

```
20   5   10   2   25
```

The program creates a binary search tree depicted in Fig. 19.19 and traverses it using three algorithms. The output is

```
inorder traversing
2   5   10   20   25
preorder traversing
20   10   5   2   25
```

```
postorder traversing
 2   5   10   25   20
```

You can ask, how do we know the tree is created and traversed correctly. Examine the program code and see, if Fig. 19.19 is consistent with the tree created by the program. Then, traverse the tree in Fig. 19.19 manually, using each of those algorithms.

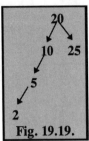

Program consists of functions: **main()**, **make_n()**, **find()**, **cre_tree()**, **inor_tr()**, **preor_tr()**, **postor_tr()**. Three of those functions read and display the data from the tree: the **inor_tr()** performs traversing using the inorder method, the **preor_tr()** utilizes the preorder algorithm, and the **postor_tr()** implements the postorder data reading. Each of those functions consists of a few lines. They are implemented as the recursive functions. Compare the code of every function with its algorithm described above and you shell understand them.

Fig. 19.19.

The **main()** function calls the **cre_tree()** function to create a tree. It, then, calls the traversing functions one by one to display the nodes of the tree. The **cre_tree()** function performs the interactions with the user. It reads the number of nodes to be created, which is used as as **for** loop condition. It displays a message prompting a user to enter an integer and reads it. Every time a value is entered, a new node is created. This is done by calling the **find()** function every loop cycle. The **find()** function belongs to the **for** loop body. One can enter as many nodes as needed. It is an example of a run-time allocation.

A node is created by calling the **make_n()** function from the **find()** routine. It allocates memory cell for the whole structure, assigns a numerical value to the structure member **x**, and assigns **NULL** value to both structure pointers.

The **find()** function has two parameters: **start** pointer and the read value **num**. As you see, it is called with the **first** pointer argument from the **cre_tree()** function. The **first** is the address of the foremost tree node. We have declared this pointer globally. Therefore, each function can change its value. The **find()** function begins with checking, if **start** is equal to **NULL**. If it is true, this means, that no node has been created yet. Thus, the first node must be created. It is done by calling the **make_n()** function. The address of that node is assigned to the **first** pointer by **first=q**. The same value is assigned to the **start** pointer by **start=q**. The function returns the **start** pointer, which is not used in this case.

Next couple lines of the **find()** function code check, if the entered value **num** has been entered previously. It is done by the **if(num==(start->x))** statement. If the value stored in any node is equal to the entered value, the corresponding message is returned and no new node is created. We describe the part of the code, that checks if the node value is equal to the entered value. You might not understand, how the computer moves from a node to a node to check their value. Read our explanations, and everything should be clear to you.

You always call the **find()** function and pass it the address of the first node from the **cre_tree()** routine. If the first node is created and the value stored in the first node is not equal to the entered value, the function executes the multiple **if** statements. The first **if** statement is

```
    if (num > start->x)                               /*line39*/
```
If the value of **num** is greater than the current node value, you check for following
```
    if ((q=start->righ)==NULL || q->x > num )         /*line41*/
```
Here, you check, if there exists the rightmost child of the current node. If **righ** pointer
of that node is **NULL ((q=start->righ)==NULL)**, there is no other node on the right.
Therefore, we can insert a new node after the current node pointed to by the current value
of **start**. If there exists a child node on the right (**q->x > num**), and its value is greater
than the value of **num**, the new node should be inserted between the parent and its right
child. In this case, a new node is created by the call to **make_n()** function at line 43. We,
then, rearrange the pointers to make the **righ** parent pointer pointing towards a new
node. The old address of that pointer is assigned to the **righ** pointer of the newly created
node. This is done at lines 45-48. The function returns the current value of **start**, which
is an address of the newly created node.

What happens, if none of the conditions in the **if** statement at line 41 is true? We know,
the current value of **num** in that case is greater than the value stored in the current node,
and the next right child is not the last one, and its value is less than the value of **num**.
Therefore, we should browse the tree to the right, until we find a first node, whose stored
value is greater than the value of the variable **num**. We will insert a new node containing
the value of the variable **num** right before that node. How do we do it? We call **find()**
function recursively with the current node address.
```
    start=start->righ;                                /*line51*/
    find (start, num);                                /*line52*/
```
Line 51 makes **start** pointer equal to the right child's address. It will be returned by the
present **find()** function invocation. Every time you call the **find()** function, the
current node value is compared to **num** variable. If it is equal to **num**, no new node is
created. This is one scenario of how a new node can be created.

The second case, when the node is created is a part of another **if** statement
```
    if (num < (start->x))                             /*line54*/
```
We check for the following condition
```
    if ((q=start->left)==NULL || q->x < num)          /*line56*/
```
If **(q=start->left)==NULL** condition is true, the current node does not have any
children. Therefore, the new node shell be inserted as its left child. If **q->x < num**
condition is true, the new node should
be inserted between the parent and its
left child. The insertion procedure in
this case is given at lines 60-63.

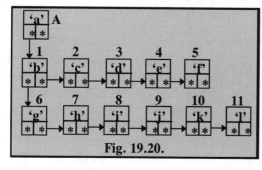

Fig. 19.20.

There might be a case, when none of
the conditions is true. Therefore, current node has a left child, and it stores
a value greater than the value of **num**.
So, we have to go over the left children, until one of the conditions at line
56 will be satisfied. It is done by the
recursive call
```
    start=start->left;                                /*line66*/
```

```
find (start, num);                              /*line67*/
```
The algorithm of the **Program 19.13** is somewhat simplified. It will create a very simple binary search tree, shown in Fig. 19.19. Here, each node can have only one child. We ask you to create such binary search tree, where each node can have two children as an exercise. This will also make the search algorithm more complicated.

A general tree can be implemented by means of a structure having two pointers as shown in Fig. 19.20. As we know, one node can have any number of children in the general tree. In Fig. 19.20, nodes 1-5 are siblings. Their parent is node A. Nodes 6-11 also are the siblings. They all are the children of the node 1. Therefore, one pointer should point towards the child. Another pointer is used to connect the siblings of the same parent.

EXERCISES.

1. Run all the programs of this chapter, if you have an access to a computer facility.
2. Write a program, that creates two linked lists. The program declares and uses two classes. Each class creates its own linked list. The first class reads vowels and is used to create a list of vowels. The second class is used to create a list of consonants. Each of the classes must be able to create a list, search for a character, display a list, count the number of elements in a list. Use friend functions, if necessary.
3. Write a program, that creates a double linked list of employees. Each node must contain both names of the same employee, his/her salary, position, employment starting date. Use a class for doing it. The program must permit to add, insert and delete the nodes. It must allow you to search for a certain employee by the name, salary, position, starting date. It must allow you to delete this node, or insert a node before or after that node. The program should permit to display the employees by their names in the alphabetic order, by the positions, by the salaries and by the starting dates.
4. Write a program, that uses two classes for creating two linked lists. Each list contains integers. You enter values from a keyboard. They are placed in a proper list. One list contains only odd integers. The second list consists of only even ones. After the data input is completed, the program merges those two lists in one. It is based on one of the existing lists. This list has all the (even and odd) integers placed in order. You should be able to display each of the lists and the final merged list as well.
5. Write a linked list, that represents a polynomial of the form

$$f(x) = a_n x^n + a_{n-1} x^{n-1} + a_{n-2} x^{n-2} + \ldots + a_2 x^2 + a_1 x + a_0$$

Use class for this list. Each node must consist of the coefficient a_i, **x** and its power. The program must prompt a user what is the highest power in the equation. It must, then, create all the nodes. It asks you to enter two variables for each node. The **x** is entered later for all nodes. The program must be able to go over each node and compute **f(x)**. The program should find an approximate value of **x**, when **f(x)=0**.
6. Read a number of characters. Put them in a stack and in a queue. Print them out. Find an algorithm of verifying if a word is a palindrome using a stack and a queue.
7. Write a program, that uses a stack to reverse the entered string.
8. Write a program, that puts a generic data type in a stack. It permits you to enter and to

read all the stack entries. It permits you to edit a stack entry, while it is in the stack.

9. Write a program, that puts a generic data type in a queue. It permits you to enter and to read all the queue entries. It permits to edit a queue entry, while it is in the queue.

10. Write a program, that creates a two child binary search tree using classes. You should be able to enter the values, to traverse the tree, to search for a value.

11. Write a regular binary tree. You should be able to place any kind of data in it. You should be able to traverse it in any of three orders, to search and to sort it. Write two versions of the same program. The first one uses the self-referential structures. The second one uses the self-referential classes. Write a recursive and a non-recursive version for each traversal algorithm.

12. Write a program utilizing a binary tree. You should be able to enter as many values of any type, as needed. You, then, display the tree on the screen, as we have shown in Fig. 19.17, for instance. The nodes of the same level should be printed in the same row. You do not have to draw the arrows on the screen, but one must understand which node is a parent or a child of which from your output. So, define the appropriate spacing between the nodes.

13. Write a program, that creates a binary tree. That tree is used to determine the number of occurrences of various characters in a line of text. Each node contains a character and a number of occurrences. Both variables are filled, when you type in a text. Each new character creates another node of that tree, when a text is read. If the program reads a character that has been read already, it increments a number of its occurrences. The program must display each of the characters appeared in the input in the alphabetic order and the number of its occurrences.

14. Write a general (non-binary) tree, that is used as a data base for a college library. Each node contains a name of the book, the author, subject and a publication year. The children of the same parent can be the books: of the same author, of the same subject, of the same word in the title. The program should prompt a user how to group the books. The nodes are created as you go. The program must allow you to search the library by an author, a subject, a word in the title. The found book must be displayed.

CHAPTER 20

THE STANDARD LIBRARY FUNCTIONS.

20.1. Introduction.

This chapter is dedicated to studying the Standard C Library header files, that C++ has inherited from C. We have discussed header files and **#include** preprocessor directive in this book. You should know by now, those header files describe the functions. You can use those functions. They expand the capabilities of C language. One cannot use them, unless the file describing a particular function is included in a program. You know how to include the files. Most of the modern compilers should have almost all the features described in this chapter. However, each compiler vendor is free to create additional features. They are compiler specific. We do not cover those features here. You should read the manuals to see, what are those additional header files. The information, that we give you in this book, will be sufficient for many problems, that you will have to solve working as a professional programmer. Let's first introduce the standard header files. They are:

`assert.h`	`ctype.h`	`errno.h`	`float.h`	`limits.h`
`locale.h`	`math.h`	`setjmp.h`	`signal.h`	`stdarg.h`
`stddef.h`	`stdio.h`	`stdlib.h`	`string.h`	`time.h`

We will discuss each of them in this chapter.

20.2. The <assert.h> header file.

The inclusion of **<assert.h>** header file

```
#include <assert.h>
```

enables us to use the macro **assert()**. The **assert()** synopsis is

```
void assert (int condition);
```

The macro **assert()** checks, if the *condition* inside the braces remains true during run-time. The *condition* can be any condition containing any operators. It should be of **int** type, i.e., it must contain integral numbers. If the condition is true, no action is performed. If it is false (or equal to zero), the text of the argument, the name of the source file and the line number, where the error occurred, are displayed. Then, the program execution is aborted. The macro calls the **abort()** function for that. It does not necessarily close any open file. It just stops the program execution and returns the control to the operating system. The **assert** macro returns no value.

```
#include <iostream.h>
#include <assert.h>

void main(void)
{
int x;
cout << "enter positive number\n";
cin >> x;
assert (x>0);
cout << "The number is: " << x;
}
```
Program 20.1.

If we enter a positive integer number, it will be displayed on the screen. If we enter a negative number, the program execution will be terminated with the message similar to

```
    Assertion failure x<0, file PLAY.CPP, line 8
```
  The use of this macro requires couple words about macro named **NDEBUG**. The presence of **NDEBUG** in the source file affects the **assert()** execution. If **NDEBUG** macro has been defined in the source file containing **<assert.h>** file and you still want to use the **assert()**, the **assert()** macro must be defined before using it as

```
    #define assert (ignore) ((void) 0)
```
Otherwise, it would not work in the program. The **NDEBUG** macro can turn on and off the **assert()**. Suppose, you want the **assert()** function to do nothing or, in other words, to be turned off as if it is not in the code. Then, simply write the **#define NDEBUG** preprocessor directive *before* the inclusion **#include <assert.h>** as

```
    #define NDEBUG
    #include <assert.h>
```
Try to add **#define NDEBUG** before the inclusion directive to **Program 20.1** and observe, that the **assert()** will be turned off.

  The abnormal program termination with **assert()** is highly undesirable, when it is used by a customer. Usually, the **assert()** is used while debugging the program. You can simply control if some variable inside a loop accepts correct values by imposing that condition as an argument of the **assert()** function. If **assert()** is not needed any more, when the program is ready to be made an application and go to the customer, you can turn it off by adding **#define NDEBUG**.

20.3. The <ctype.h> header file.

The **<ctype.h>** header file specifies following functions

isalnum	**isalpha**	**iscntrl**	**isdigit**	**isgraph**	**islower**
isprint	**ispunct**	**isspace**	**isupper**	**isxdigit**	**tolower**
toupper					

Before using any of those functions, the header file must be included in a program as

```
#include <ctype.h>
```
In some applications, one needs to test for certain characters, for instance, if entered character is a letter, or a number, or a special character. The **<ctype.h>** header file describes following functions, that allow to do this test.

The **isalnum()** function synopsis is
```
int isalnum (int x);
```
It returns 1, if its argument **x** is an "alphanumeric" character, i.e., if it is a letter from '**a**' through '**z**', or from '**A**' through '**z**' in the upper case, or a digit from '**0**' through '**9**'. Otherwise, the function returns zero.

The **isalpha()** function returns 1, if its argument is a letter from '**a**' through '**z**', or from '**A**' through '**z**' in the upper case. Otherwise, it returns zero. In some non-English environments it might test, if its argument is a letter in any other language. We will talk about it, when studying **<locale.h>** header file. The function synopsis is
```
int isalpha (int x);
```
The **iscntrl()** function returns 1, if its argument is any control (escape) character. Otherwise, it returns zero. As you know, there are following control characters: alert, backspace, carriage return, form feed, horizontal tab, newline, vertical tab and delete. In general, one can have more control characters. The function synopsis is
```
int iscntrl (int x);
```
The **isdigit()** function returns 1, if its argument is a decimal-digit character from '**0**' through '**9**'. Otherwise, it returns zero. The function synopsis is
```
int isdigit (int x);
```
The **isgraph()** function returns 1, if its argument is a printing character except space ' '. The function returns zero, otherwise. It, basically, checks if its argument is displayable on a paper or on a screen. The function synopsis is
```
int isgraph (int x);
```
The **islower()** function returns 1, if its argument is a lower case letter from '**a**' through '**z**'. Otherwise, zero is returned. The function synopsis is
```
int  islower (int x);
```
The **isprint()** function returns 1, if its argument is a printing character including the space ' '. Otherwise, zero is returned. The function, basically, checks if its argument is displayable. It is analogous to the **isgraph()** function. Its synopsis is
```
int isprint (int x);
```
The **ispunct()** function returns 1, if its argument is a punctuation character. If the argument does not belong to the group it is tested for, the function returns zero. The examples are ! " $ # & ( ) ` , . * + . ~/ ; : < = > ? [\] ^ {|}. The argument cannot be a space. The function synopsis is
```
int ispunct (int x);
```
The **isspace()** function returns 1, if its argument is a white space character. Otherwise, it returns zero. The standard white characters are the following: space (' '), form feed ('**\f**'), newline ('**\n**'), carriage return ('**\r**'), horizontal tab ('**\t**'), vertical tab ('**\v**'). Sometimes, it can be used to check for some implementation-defined white characters. The function synopsis is
```
int isspace (int x);
```
The **isupper()** function returns 1, if its argument is an upper case letter from '**A**'

through '**z**'. Otherwise, zero is returned. The function synopsis is

```
int isupper (int x);
```

The **isxdigit()** function returns 1, if its argument is a hexadecimal-digit character from '**0**' through '**F**'. Otherwise, zero is returned. The function synopsis is

```
int isxdigit (int x);
```

The argument of the above functions can be a variable, that is defined in the program as **int** or even **char** type or **EOF**. Each of those functions just tests the character, which is stored in the argument, if it belongs to a certain class of characters. The computer converts the argument character to its binary (ASCII or other) representation. This number is compared to the values, corresponding, for instance, to the binary (ASCII or any other) representation of letters from '**a**' through '**z**', or from '**A**' through '**Z**', or a digit from '**0**' through '**9**'. If the value corresponding to the function argument character lies in one of those ranges, the argument character is, indeed, a letter or a digit. Each function tests, if passed to it argument is a certain character or a digit. If it is so, each of the above functions returns 1. Otherwise, 0 is returned. So the returned value is of **int** type. It can be assigned to the different variables. Checking the returned value tells us, whether the argument, indeed, belongs to the tested group. Some of those functions are used in **Program 20.2**. The program is written in C style, so you do not forget it.

```
#include <ctype.h>
#include <stdio.h>

void main (void)
{
int x;
int y;
printf ("Enter any character \n");
x=getchar ( );
printf ("you character belongs to the classes:\n");
y=isalnum(x);
if ( y )          printf (" alphanumeric \n");
if (isalpha(x))   printf (" alpha \n");
if (iscntrl(x))   printf (" control character \n");
if (isdigit(x))   printf (" decimal digit \n");
if (islower(x))   printf (" lower case letter \n");
if (isprint(x))   printf (" printable \n");
if (ispunct(x))   printf (" punctuation character \n");
if (isspace(x))   printf (" white space \n");
if (isupper(x))   printf (" upper case letter \n");
}
```

Program 20.2.

The program prompts a user to enter a character. For instance, enter **a**. The program displays the message stating, that this character belongs to the groups: alphanumeric, alpha, lower case letter, printable. Therefore, one character can belong to a few groups.

We could also enter a character in the argument directly, as for example,

```
islower ('b');
```

Other two functions described in this header file are so-called character case mapping functions. The **tolower()** function converts an upper case letter, passed as its argument, to the lower case letter. It returns the same letter, if the argument is in the lower case. The **toupper()** function returns the upper case letter, passed as its argument, unchanged. If its argument is a lower case character, it returns its upper case letter equivalent. The prototypes of both functions are

```
int tolower (int x);
int toupper (int x);
```

Program 20.3 illustrates how to use those functions.

```
#include <ctype.h>
#include <stdio.h>

void main (void)
{
char x, y, z;
printf ("enter any character \n");
scanf("%c",&z);
x=tolower (z);
y=toupper (z);
printf ("The action of tolower( ) is: %c.\n", x);
printf ("The action of toupper( ) is: %c.\n", y);
}
```

Program 20.3.

For instance, you entered **A** and press **ENTER**. The output of that program will be

```
The action of tolower( ) is: a.
The action of toupper( ) is: A.
```

For instance, you enter **b** and press **ENTER**. The output of that program will be

```
The action of tolower( ) is: b.
The action of toupper( ) is: B.
```

20.4. The <errno.h> header file.

The **<errno.h>** header file specifies three macros: **errno**, **ERANGE** and **EDOM**. Whenever one uses any of them, the header file should be included promptly as

```
#include <errno.h>
```

One can make a mistake in a code. So, we want to have some kind of error reporting selection. We have studied functions returning some value in case of error. Some library functions may assign some integer values to a special symbol named **errno** in case of errors. A programmer can also use **errno** to test for an error. In order to use **errno**, one, sometimes, should assign it a zero value at the beginning of the program. Then, its value will be changed automatically by the library functions in case of error.

The ANSI standard specifies at least two possible values assigned to the **errno**: **EDOM** and **ERANGE**. The **EDOM** is used for indicating an invalid argument value or so-called *domain error*. It will occur, when you try to call functions using incorrect arguments. For instance, the square root function should have a positive argument. An attempt to use a negative argument will be interpreted as a domain error. The **ERANGE** is assigned to **errno**, when the result of some calculation can not be computed. For instance, the result is a large number. It is called a *range error*. Review **Program 20.4**.

```
#include <errno.h>
#include <math.h>
#include <iostream.h>

void main (void)
{
double x, z=-10.923;
errno = 0;
x = sqrt (z);
if (errno==EDOM)
cout << "argument error, negative value.\n";
cout << " The answer is: " << x;
}
```

Program 20.4.

This program cannot be executed, because we use negative argument for the square root function. Some compilers can display their own error message on top of ours. The output of the program is

```
argument error, negative value.
```

We used a standard library function **sqrt()** to take the square root. We will study this function later in this chapter. The **errno** has been set to 0 at the beginning of the code. After the library square function failed, it generated an error code passed to **errno**. We checked for that error message using **if** statement and displayed the error message. You should also notice, we included the **<errno>** header to enable the program to use **errno**. Some other headers were enclosed, because we had to use some other functions. You will understand them shortly.

20.5. The <float.h> header file.

Any floating-point number **x** can be defined by the formula

$$x = s \times b^e \times \sum_{k=1}^{p} f_k \times b^{-k} \quad , \text{ where}$$

s- is the sign of the number, that can be +1 or -1;

b- is a base of a number and it is an integer greater than 1. It is also called a *radix* of exponential representation. Some standard bases are: the binary (b=2), hexadecimal where b=16 and so on;

e- is the power that **b** should be raised to (it is an integer $e_{min} \le e \le e_{max}$);

p- is the precision, that gives the number of digits in the floating-point value mantissa. For example, each floating-point number can be presented as a mantissa, that is a value with one digit before the point and the fractional part, multiplied by a power of 10. For instance, 18.92 can be represented as 1.892*10. The 1.892 is called the mantissa;

f- is just a non-negative integer less than **b**;

For instance, according to the ANSI/IEEE standard 754-1985 one can represent single and double precision normalized numbers with the formula in the binary base

$$x = s \times 2^e \times \sum_{k=1}^{24} f_k \times 2^{-k} \text{ for floating-point value } \text{ where } -125 \le e \le 128$$

Basically, this formula is saying following. Suppose, we have any floating-point number and we define the base (let's say binary b=2) and precision **p** up to which we want to approximate this number. Then, the number can be decomposed on the sum according to the above formula. We can find **e** and each f_k in that formula to match any floating-point number.

You could read about this formula, but you might never have to use it, so we do not spend time on that. But the **<float.h>** header specifies the limits of each of these parameters for the concrete systems. This means, that you cannot have the floating or double type numbers greater or smaller than certain numbers. If the number is greater than the upper limit number, you have overflow. If the number is smaller than the lower limit, it is an error called uderflow. The third problem, occurring with floating-point numbers, is the significance loss. If one subtracts two numbers, which are very close, their difference can be smaller than the smallest possible number. Even though the numbers are different, but the difference between them can be equal to 0 due to precision limitations. The formulas can give the significance loss when coded.

The **<float.h>** header contains the following macros:

• **FLT_ROUNDS** indicates how the number will be rounded off. The standard floating-point number has 6 decimal digits after the dot, or 6 digits of precision. If you add or subtract numbers and get more than 6 digits after the point, they should be rounded off. If the **FLT_ROUNDS** is set to be equal to 0, the value gets rounded off to 0, i.e., the last digits get truncated. If the value of **FLT_ROUNDS** is equal to 1, the rounding goes to the closest value. If **FLT_ROUNDS** is -1, the rounding value is undetermined. If it is equal to 2, the rounding goes towards the positive infinity. If the value is 3, the computer rounds off a value towards negative infinity.

• **FLT_RADIX** defines the base **b** in which the number can be represented.

• **FLT_MANT_DIG**, **DBL_MANT_DIG** and **LDBL_MANT_DIG** determine the precision **p** for **float**, **double** and **long double** values respectively.

• **FLT_DIG**, **DBL_DIG** and **LDBL_DIG** are the numbers of decimal digits after the point for the **float**, **double** and **long double** values respectively, that can be converted to another base and back without change in any of the digits. The **FLT_DIG** is specified to be at least 6, while the other two constants are at least 10.

• **FLT_MIN_EXP**, **DBL_MIN_EXP** and **LDBL_MIN_EXP** are the minimum exponent **e** values for the **float, double** and **long double** values respectively in the above formula. At the other hand, **FLT_MAX_EXP, DBL_MAX_EXP** and **LDBL_MAX_EXP** are the maximum values of the exponent **e**.

• **FLT_MIN_10_EXP, DBL_MIN_10_EXP, LDBL_MIN_10_EXP** are the minimum values of exponent **e**, for the base of 10 for **float, double** and **long double** values respectively. Usually, it is a negative number. Therefore, a mantissa multiplied by ten to that negative power shell give you the smallest number of each data type, that the computer still recognizes as non-zero. Each of the minimum exponents is equal or less than -37. **FLT_MAX_10_EXP, DBL_MAX_10_EXP** and **LDBL_MAX_10_EXP** are the maximum values of exponent **e** for the base **b=10** for **float, double** and **long double** numbers respectively. A mantissa multiplied by 10 to that power gives the maximum possible value for each particular data type. Each of the maximum exponents is at least +37.

• **FLT_MAX, DBL_MAX** and **LDBL_MAX** are the maximum **float, double** and **long double** values respectively, which will not exceed the maximum presentable number for each of those types. The maximum presentable number of each of those types is at least 1E+37.

• **FLT_MIN, DBL_MIN** and **LDBL_MIN** are the minimum normalized positive **float, double** and **long double** values respectively, which will still be presented as the non-zero numbers of each type. The minimum presentable number of each of those types must be equal or less than 1E-37.

• **FLT_EPSILON, DBL_EPSILON** and **LDBL_EPSILON** represent the difference between 1 and the smallest value greater than 1 which is a **float, double** and **long double** value respectively. The **FLT_EPSILON** must be equal or less than 1E-5. The **DBL_EPSILON** and **LDBL_EPSILON** must be equal or less than 1E-9.

Those are the names or macros described in the **<float.h>** header file. They, basically, give the information about the floating-point, **double** and **long double** values, that one can operate with. You include the header file in the source file, when you want to use the values contained in those macros. Most of those values are implementation-dependent. You can, actually, recover the value of each of those macros by simply displaying them with the **printf()** function or **cout** object.

One of the very useful ideas those macros can be used for, is to check the floating-point value for the overflow or underflow, before actually using it in the formula. Let's say, you have to calculate an exponent **y=exp(x)** or $y = e^x$. You can check, if the result is not greater than the maximum possible **double** type value. The maximum double value is given in **DBL_MAX** macro. We know, that by taking a natural logarithm **x=ln y** or logarithm with the base **e**, we will get **x** back. Let's check, if $e^x \leq DBL\_MAX$. So, we should check if **x** is less or equal to the logarithm of **DBL_MAX**.

```
if (x<= ln(DBL_MAX))
y=exp(x);
else
printf( "value overflow\n");
```

Let's discuss another example. We want to find $y = 10^x$. The **float** type variable **y** must not exceed the maximum value presentable by a computer. We can go over the macros in the header and find **FLT_MAX_10_EXP**, which is nothing else but the maximum power that 10 could be raised to without getting an overflow. The check for an overflow in this case will be easy

```
if (x<= FLT_MAX_10_EXP)
y=pow (10, x);
else
printf( "value overflow\n");
```

The underflow, as we know, happens when the value is so small, so it is considered as a zero by a computer. It is wise to introduce an underflow testing in the programs, you feel might experience the underflow. The strategy is primarily the same, but one is testing for the minimum values in this case. Below we give two tests for underflow. You can code them, if you believe the exponent or the power of some value can be a very small value. The first test is

```
if (x>=ln ( DBL_MIN ) )
y=exp(x);
else
printf( "value underflow \n");
```

The second test is

```
if (x>= FLT_MIN_10_EXP)
y=pow (10, x);
else
printf( "value underflow\n");
```

The third mentioned problem is the significance loss. It happens when you subtract two very close values. The result can be such a small value, that it would be understood as zero by the computer. For instance, we offer a check below, if a result of a subtraction is at least a few orders greater than the minimum allowed for **float** type

```
z = x - y ;
if ( z > FLT_EPSILON * 100)
y=exp(x);
else
printf( "value significance lost\n");
```

Here we find, if the difference between two numbers is greater than 100 times the lowest possible difference between the numbers contained in the **FLT_EPSILON**.

Again, you will not deal with this header too often. It might be helpful to get a printout of all the values for the macros from the **<float.h>** header file. You would know the limits of the values you are dealing with for your particular computer.

20.6. The <limits.h> header file.

In the same way **<float.h>** specifies the maximum and minimum values, powers and so on for the floating-point numbers, the **<limits.h>** header file specifies the ranges and sizes of other data types. The standard header file specifies the limit values that can be exceeded by your computers. So, your computer systems must meet or exceed the specifications given below for different C data types. The macros described in that header are:

- **CHAR_BIT** is the number of bits contained inside the smallest object. Typically, the smallest unit of information is a byte, that contains 8 bits. So, any data is processed by bytes, one does an operation on at least 8 bits at once. As you remember, one can specify bit fields inside a byte. The information is still processed by bytes.

- **SCHAR_MIN** is the minimum value that a variable of the **signed char** data type can accept. It is at least equal to -127. **SCHAR_MAX** is the maximum value of the **signed char** data type variable. It is not less than +127. **UCHAR_MAX** is the maximum value of the **unsigned char** data type. It is not less than 255.

- **CHAR_MIN** and **CHAR_MAX** stand for respectively the minimum and maximum possible values of **char** data type variable. **CHAR_MIN** and **CHAR_MAX** values are equal to those of the **SCHAR_MIN** and **SCHAR_MAX** respectively. **CHAR_MIN** can be also 0. **CHAR_MAX** can be equal to **UCHAR_MAX**.

- **MB_LEN_MAX** gives the maximum number of bytes in a multibyte character. It is equal to 1 in the standard. It can be more than one, in general.

- **SHRT_MIN** and **SHRT_MAX** are respectively the minimum and the maximum values of a variable of **short int** data type. They are -32767 and +32767 respectively. **USHRT_MAX** is the maximum value of the **unsigned short int** data type and it is equal to 65535.

- **INT_MIN** and **INT_MAX** are respectively possible minimum and the maximum values of **int** type variable. **INT_MIN** is -32767. **INT_MAX** is +32767. **UINT_MAX** is the maximum value of **unsigned int** data type. It must not be less than 65535.

- **LONG_MIN** and **LONG_MAX** are the minimum and the maximum values respectively for the **long** data type. **LONG_MIN** can be less or equal to -2147483647. **LONG_MAX** is at least +2147483647. **ULONG_MAX** is the maximum value of the **unsigned long** data type variable and it is equal to 4294967295.

ANSI gives those values for each of the macros contained in the **<limits.h>** header file. The standard also specifies, that all the given numbers are implementation based, i.e., can vary for different computer systems. Each of those specified values can exceed the given numbers. This means, that the minimum range value can be made even less, and the maximum value even greater by the compiler vendors.

One does not have to include the **<limits.h>** header file in the program, when **char** or **int** types of data are used, because this header file does not in any way affect any of those types. It just provides the information for you as a user about the limits for the numbers The **<limits.h>** header file describes only given above macros. Those macros only tell us, the minimum and maximum values for some data types are such and such. You cannot change the limits by yourself. Whenever, you intend to use any of the macros, the header file should be included in the source file.

Let's review possible ways of using the macros. First possible application for you, is to display those numbers, to see and to remember them.

```
#include <limits.h>
#include <stdio.h>

main ( )
```

```
{
printf("%d \n", CHAR_BIT);
printf("%d \n", SHRT_MAX);
...... }
```

One can use the macros to check if the values of the variables do not exceed the limits.

20.7. The <locale.h> header file.

Following macros are specified in this header file

struct lconv	**NULL**	**LC_ALL**	**LC_COLLATE**
LC_CTYPE	**LC_MONETARY**	**LC_NUMERIC**	**setlocale**
localeconv			

The **<locale.h>** header file must be included whenever any of those macros is used.

Initially, there was an opposition to make the **<locale.h>** header file a standard part of ANSI C language. When the ANSI standard, which is the national C standard, had been almost developed, many European countries were unhappy with it. They even agreed, that the international standard for C language should differ from ANSI on that matter. It was unacceptable. The authors of ANSI C had decided to make all the changes necessary to accommodate international demands.

The main difficulties in Europe were related to the presence of many countries with different languages and cultures, while US had only one official language - English. There also were some differences in cultures. For instance, the integer and fractional parts of a floating-point number are separated by period (dot) in US and a comma in some other countries. Also, when people in US write the date, as for example 3/5/92, they put the month first and the day of the month second. In Europe, the day is put first and the month second. There are also other differences that might have been significant. Many of those differences had been tailored back by the very existence of that **<locale.h>** header file.

One should first introduce a concept of *environmental variable*. Environmental variable is a name, which identifies a null-terminated string. This string represents the value of the variable. One can delete, alter or add such a variable. System calls to them to begin a new process. The new process can simply ignore the environmental variables or it can copy them and get their values. One can use an environmental variable to write the file name when the program is executed. For example, you can give a user a possibility to select the file name for the application.

The way C language is adjusted to a particular culture or language environment is handled by so-called *locale*. The locales are in a way the object-oriented environmental variables. They provide information on many parameters and give it in a form suitable for a particular culture. The computer can interpret the characters differently in particular locales. There can be some other characters added to the set of available characters. Time can be displayed differently. It can affect the way of formatting monetary and nonmonetary values. The currency can differ for different locales.

Structure **lconv** defines some language specific attributes. It should contain at least following members in any order:

- The **decimal_point** points to a stored decimal point character used to format non-monetary quantities. It is declared as

```
char *decimal_point;
```

Some countries use comma and some use a dot to separate fractional and integer parts of a decimal number.

- The **thousands_sep** points to a stored character, used to separate groups of digits in the integral part of the values in formatted nonmonetary quantities. It is declared as

```
char *thousands_sep;
```

Usually three digits (thousands) are separated. A comma is used to separate thousands in US. For instance, 1,987,234,231. In some countries it can be a dot or a blank.

- The **grouping** is a pointer to a string whose elements actually determine the size of each group of digits in formatted nonmonetary quantities. This string contains a number of digits to be separated by the **thousands_sep** character. It is declared as

```
char *grouping;
```

In most countries, three digits are separated by a comma or a point. Hence, the string contains number 3. In general, the elements of **grouping** are interpreted as follows:

CHAR_MAX	It indicates, that no further grouping is to be performed.
0	It indicates, that the previous element is to be repeatedly used for the remainder of the digits.
integer	It gives the number of digits to form a current group.

- The **int_cur_symbol** points to a stored international currency symbol applicable to the current locale. It is declared as

```
char *int_cur_symbol;
```

The string consists of five characters including the null character. The first three characters contain the alphabetic international currency symbol according to the international standard ISO 4217:1987. The fourth character is used to separate the international currency symbol from the monetary quantity.

- The **currency_symbol** points to the local currency symbol applicable to the current locale. It is declared as

```
char *currency_symbol;
```

- The **mon_decimal_point** points to the monetary decimal point character used to format monetary quantities. It can be a point or a comma, for example. It is declares as

```
char *mon_decimal_point;
```

- The **mon_thousands_sep** is similar to **thousands_sep**, but it points to a character used to separate groups of digits in the integral part of numbers in formatted monetary quantities. Usually every three digits (thousands) are separated.

```
char *mon_thousands_sep;
```

- The **mon_grouping** is similar to **grouping**, except that it is used for the monetary quantities. It is declared as

```
char *mon_grouping;
```

- The **positive_sign** is used to denote a positive value in formatted monetary quantities. It is declared as

```
char *positive_sign;
```

• The **negative_sign** is used to denote a negative value in formatted monetary quantities. Usually, the '-' sign is used for that in US. It is declared as

```
char *negative_sign;
```

• The **int_frac_digits** indicates the number of digits after a decimal point that should be displayed in the internationally formatted monetary quantity. It is declared as

```
char int_frac_digits;
```

• The **frac_digits** indicates the number of digits after a decimal point that should be displayed in the formatted monetary quantity. It is declared as

```
char frac_digits;
```

• The **p_cs_precedes** is set to 1 or 0 if the **currency_symbol** respectively precedes or succeeds nonnegative formatted monetary quantity. For example, for $10.00 or $ 10.00, **p_cs_precedes** is equal to 1. It is 0 for 10.00$ or 10.00 $. It is declared as

```
char p_cs_precedes;
```

• The **p_sep_by_space** is set to 1 or 0 if the **currency_symbol** respectively is or is not separated by the space from a value of a positive formatted monetary quantity. For example, **p_sep_by_space** is 1 for $ 10, and 0 for $10. It is declared as

```
char p_sep_by_space;
```

• The **n_cs_presedes** is set to 1 or 0 if the **currency_symbol** respectively precedes or succeeds the negative formatted monetary quantity. It is declared as

```
char n_cs_presedes;
```

• The **n_sep_by_space** is set to 1 or 0 if the **currency_symbol** respectively is or is not separated by a space from the value of a negative formatted monetary quantity. For example, for -10.00$ or -$10.00 the **n_sep_by_space** is equal to 0. It is 1 for -10.00 $ or -$ 10.00. It is declared as

```
char n_sep_by_space;
```

• The **p_sign_posn** is set to a value specifying the location of **positive_sign** for a positive formatted monetary quantity. It is declared as

```
char p_sign_posn;
```

• The **n_sign_posn** is set to a value specifying the location of **negative_sign** for a negative formatted monetary quantity. It is declared as

```
char n_sign_posn;
```

Both **p_sign_posn n_sign_posn** can be set to the following values:

0 Parentheses should surround the quantity (the value) and **currency_symbol**.

1 The sign should precede the quantity (the value) and **currency_symbol**.

2 The sign should succeed the quantity (the value) and **currency_symbol**.

3 The sign should immediately precede **currency_symbol**.

4 The sign should immediately succeed **currency_symbol**.

We can now review the functions described in the header file.

We begin with the **setlocale()** function. Its synopsis is

```
char *setlocale (int term, const char *locale);
```

It sets all or some members of the **lconv** structure, so they are compatible with the local environment pointed to by the **locale** parameter. All C++ compilers support **"C"** string for **locale**. This is the locale with the English alphabet. For instance,

```
setlocale (LC_ALL, "C");
```

C++ compiler might support other locales, but it becomes implementation specific. The standard also mentions the (blank space) " " locale. It stands for the native locale. It is implementation dependent as well. Therefore, you should check your compiler manuals. The local environment or a locale is essentially a language or a culture specific region. It is specified by the string pointed to by the pointer **locale**.

The **term** specifies which parts of the structure to set. It can accept following values:

LC_ALL adjusts all the locale-specific items;

LC_COLLATE adjusts the controlling of the collation sequences. It affects the behavior of the **strcoll()** and **strxfrm()** functions in **<string.h>** header file.

LC_TYPE adjusts the classification of characters. It affects the behavior of the character handling functions and multibyte functions. It can affect the functions declared in **<ctype.h>**, printing and reading functions in **<stdio.h>**, numeric conversion functions declared in **<stdlib.h>** header file. The characters can be tested and altered differently for certain locales. The multibyte strings can be parsed and translated depending on locale.

LC_MONETARY can change the monetary formatting according to the local custom and in accordance with the international standards (ISO 4217). It also changes the nonmonetary formatting information returned by the **localeconv()** function.

LC_NUMERIC adjusts the decimal point character for the formatted I/O and string conversion functions. It alters the nonmonetary formatting information returned by the **localeconv()** function.

LC_TIME can change how the **strftime()** function declared in the **<time.h>** header file displays time.

The **setlocale()** function returns:

• a pointer to the string associated with the specified **term** and **locale**, if **locale** is a pointer to a string and the selection is honored by the system;

• if a selection is not honored, a **NULL** pointer is returned, the locale is not changed;

• a pointer to a string associated with the **term** for a program in current locale is returned, if the **locale** argument is **NULL**. The program's locale is not changed.

The **localeconv()** function prototype is

```
struct lconv *localeconv (void);
```

It sets the members of the structure **lconv** to the values according to current locale. We described all standard members of that structure. The function returns a pointer to that modified structure. The structure cannot be modified by the program after that.

20.8. The <math.h> header file.

The **<math.h>** header file should be included in the source file, if you use **HUGE_VAL** macro or mathematical functions described in this section. *All the functions described in this header file must have the arguments and the returned values of the **double** data type.* In case, if the argument is outside of the domain over which the mathematical function is defined, you will get the *domain error* message **EDOM**. It will be stored in **errno**. In case of overflow, i.e., the value of the result is greater than the maximum value for the data type you use, the math function returns the value of the macro **HUGE_VAL**. It would have the same sign as you would get in your calculations, if there were no overflow. The **HUGE_VAL** is described in the **<math.h>** header file. Only the **tan()** function does not necessarily return the same sign. The value of **HUGE_VAL** is supposed to be very large and is of **double** type. There is no standard value for it. On some systems it is equal to the value of **DBL_MAX** defined in **<float.h>**. The **errno** stores the **ERANGE** value in case of overflow. In case of underflow, or when the result is too small, the functions return 0. In this case, **errno** can store the **ERANGE** value, although some systems might not do it. Do not forget to include the **<errno.h>** header file, if you use **errno**, **ERANGE, EDOM**.

The **<math.h>** header file describes following functions:

`acos()`	`asin()`	`atan()`	`atan2()`	`cos()`
`sin()`	`tan()`	`cosh`	`sinh()`	`tanh()`
`exp()`	`frexp()`	`ldexp()`	`log()`	`log10()`
`pow()`	`sqrt()`	`modf()`	`ceil()`	`fabs()`
`floor()`	`fmod()`			

We must now review each of the above functions.

1. *Trigonometric functions:*

- **acos(x)** computes and returns the principal value of arc cosine of **x** within the range $[0,\pi]$ radians. **x** must be within the range $[-1,+1]$. Its prototype is
```
double acos (double x);
```
- **asin(x)** computes and returns the principal value of arc sine of **x** within the range $[-\pi/2, \pi/2]$ radians. **x** should be within the range $[-1,+1]$. The function synopsis is
```
double asin (double x);
```
- **atan(x)** computes and returns the principal value of arc tangent of **x** within the range $[-\pi/2, \pi/2]$ radians. The function prototype is
```
double atan (double x);
```
- **atan2(y, x)** computes and returns the principal value of arc tangent of **y/x** within the range $[-\pi,+\pi]$ radians. A domain error can occur, when **x** or both **y** and **x** are equal to 0. The function uses the signs of **y** and **x** to determine the proper quadrant of the angle. Its synopsis is
```
double atan (double y, double x);
```
- **cos(x)** computes and returns the value of cosine of **x**. The parameter **x** is measured in radians. Function synopsis is
```
double cos (double x);
```
- **sin(x)** computes and returns the value of sine of **x**. The parameter **x** is measured in radians. The function prototype is
```
double sin (double x);
```
- **tan(x)** computes and returns the value of tangent of **x**. Parameter **x** is measured in radians. The **tan()** function prototype is

```
double tan (double x);
```

2. Hyperbolic functions:

- **cosh(x)** computes and returns the hyperbolic cosine of **x**. Too large values of **x** cause a range error. The function synopsis is
```
double cosh (double x);
```
- **sinh(x)** computes and returns the hyperbolic sine of **x**. Too large values of **x** cause a range error. The function synopsis is
```
double sinh (double x);
```
- **tanh(x)** computes and returns the hyperbolic tangent of **x**. Its synopsis is
```
double tanh (double x);
```

3. The power and logarithmic functions:

- **exp(x)** computes the value of e^x and returns it. If **x** is too large you might get a result overflow, which will lead to the range error. The function synopsis is
```
double exp (double x);
```
- **frexp(x, ptr)** function has following prototype
```
double frexp (double x, int *ptr);
```
The function breaks the floating point number **x** on two parts: the normalized fraction **y** and the integral power **N** of 2. This function effectively rewrites a number stored in its parameter **x** as $y \times 2^N$. The value of **y** is returned as a **double** type and is greater or equal to 0.5 and less than 1. Since a function can return only one value, we cannot return the value of variable **N** as well. So, it is stored in a cell with the address, that will be contained in the pointer **ptr**. The **N** has the **int** data type.
- **ldexp(x, n)** has following prototype
```
double ldexp (double x, int n);
```
The function computes and returns the value equal to $x \times 2^n$ of **double** type. In other words, the function multiplies the floating-point value **x** by the integral power of 2 and returns that value. If the result of calculation is out of the range, the function sets **errno** to **ERANGE** and returns the value of **HUGE_VAL**.
- **log(x)** computes and returns the value of the natural logarithm of **x**. Domain error can occur, when the argument is negative. A range error occurs, if its argument is equal to zero. The function synopsis is
```
double log (double x);
```
- **log10(x)** computes and returns the value of the base-ten logarithm of **x**. A domain error can occur, when the argument is negative. A range error occurs, if its argument is equal to zero. The function synopsis is
```
double log10 (double x);
```
- **pow(x, y)** computes and returns the value which is equal to x^y. Its synopsis is
```
double pow (double x, double y);
```
You can get a domain error in following cases: **y** is not an integer value while **x<0**, **x=0**

while **y≤0**. If both **x** and **y** are large numbers, the result may be out of the range.

• **sqrt(x)** computes and returns a positive square root of **x**. Its prototype is

```
double sqrt (double x);
```

If **x<0**, a domain error will occur. It is faster than take a square root using **pow(x, 0.5)** function.

• **modf(x, ptr)** function has following prototype

```
double modf (double x, double *ptr);
```

The **modf()** function breaks the value of **x** on integer and fraction parts. The function returns the fractional part of the value stored in **x**. The returned value has **double** type. The integer part of the value **x** is stored in the memory cell as **double** type. The address of that cell is assigned to the pointer **ptr**.

4. Nearest integer, absolute value and remainder functions:

• **ceil(x)** function has following prototype

```
double ceil (double x);
```

It computes and returns the smallest integer value of the argument **x**, which is greater or equal to **x**. So, this function rounds the value off to the next integer up, if **x** has a fractional part. For instance **ceil(x)** if **x=7.3928** or **x=7.8392** would be equal to 8.0. The **ceil(x)** with **x=7.0** is equal to 7.0. The **ceil(-2.45)** is equal to -2.

• **fabs(x)** function computes and returns the absolute value of the floating-point number stored in its parameter **x**. The function synopsis is

```
double fabs (double x);
```

• **floor(x)** function computes and returns the integer part of the floating-point argument **x**. Both the argument and the returned value are of type **double**. Basically, this function rounds the value off to the first integer down. For instance, **floor(x)** with **x=7.3928** or **x=7.8392** is equal to 7.0. The **floor(x)** with **x=7.0** would be equal to 7.0. The function synopsis is

```
double floor (double x);
```

• **fmod(x, y)** function computes and returns the floating-point remainder of **x/y**. Returned value has the same sign as **x**. For instance, if **x=8.329** and **y=4.0**. The result of the division will be **8.329/4.0=2.0+0.329**. If **x=9.0** and **y=4**, then **x/y=2.0+1.0**. In the first case, the function returns the remainder 0.329, in the second - 1.0. Since **x** was greater than 0, both remainders are positive. If **x** were **-8.329**, the value of **fmod(x,y)** would be -0.329. The function synopsis is

```
double fmod (double x, double y);
```

Those are the functions given in **<math.h>** header file. **Program 20.5** illustrates, how to handle some of those functions.

```
#include <iostream.h>
#include <math.h>

void main (void)
{
```

```
double var=0.52, s=3.0, r=5.3, res;
res=cos (var);
cout << res << "   " << pow (s, r);
res=asin (0.5);
cout << "   " << res;
}
```

Program 20.5.

The program just computes the values of some functions. The output of the program is
```
0.867819   337.864568   0.523599
```

20.9. The <setjmp.h> header file.

A data type **jmp_buf**, two functions **longjmp()** and **setjmp()** are described in the **<setjmp.h>** header file. This header must be included in the source file for using any of these macros.

One cannot define nested functions in C and C++, i.e., the following is impossible
```
float func1(float x,float y)
{....
float func2( float z)
{...
}...}
```
Here, the **func2()** is the inner function of the **func1()**. A function can be defined (written) only outside of any other function, as we remember. Thus, both **func1()** and **func2()** must be written outside of each other. If we need to use **func2()** inside **func1()**, we just call it. This works very good for a vast majority of programs. Besides, this strategy makes functions visible from any point of a program. But, sometimes, while one of the functions is running, we might want to jump somehow to another function. It is like by-passing a normal function return. C and C++ have the **goto** statement for local jumps (called, sometimes, transfers) within the same function.

Both languages also use non-local transfers as part of the standard library functions. C and C++ programs can execute an *interfunction jump*, when in the middle of one function execution one can jump to another function.. Those jumps are the subject of our present discussion. We will first introduce to you the functions used for the jumps. Then, we will discuss their work.

We should first introduce the **setjump()** function. Its synopsis is
```
int setjmp ( jmp_buf x );
```
It is a function with one parameter. We called it **x**. As you see, the **x** variable has a special type. The argument **x** is declared as having the **jmp_buf** type, which is an array or structure type. This type specifies a structure. Each member of that structure stores one of the values from the CPU registers and the stack pointer. Therefore, the **jmp_buf** type of argument defines a buffer type, capable to store the current state of the stack and the CPU registers. The **setjmp()** function saves the current state of the CPU registers and stack for that particular program code line, at which it appears. The value of **x** is that state of the

computer environment for a particular line, at which the function appears. The function returns zero, when it is used before the jump. After the jump to the line containing that **setjmp()** function, it returns a value equal to the second argument of the **longjmp()** function. Do not put the book aside yet. At this point, not everything is clear for you. Just read to the end and you will understand.

The **long jmp()** function synopsis is

```
void longjmp ( jmp_buf x, int val );
```

Its parameter **x** specifies the state of CPU registers and the stack for a particular line of code. It should be the same argument as in the **setjmp()** function. When the **longjmp()** function is executed, the computer jumps to a line of code inside any function within the source file, where **setjmp()** with the same argument name is written. The program execution continues from that line down statement by statement. Hence, one can use the **setjmp()** in one function and **longjmp()** in another one. There are some limitations that we will discuss.

The second parameter of **longjmp()** function is an integer, which we called **val**. When the **longjmp()** function causes a jump to the **setjmp()** function, the value of the parameter **val** of **longjmp()** function is passed to and returned by that **setjmp()**. If we print the returned value of **setjmp()** function before and after the jump, we would get two different values. **Program 20.6** illustrates the jumps.

```
#include <iostream.h>
#include <setjmp.h>
#include <stdlib.h>

void hello (jmp_buf a)
{
longjmp (a, 5);
}

void main (void)
{
int x, m=0;
jmp_buf one;
x=setjmp (one);

if (x!=0)
{
cout << "jump completed\n" << "after jump: x=" << x
     << ", m=" << m << endl;
exit (0);
}

m=m+2;
cout << "before jump: x=" << x << ", m=" << m
     << "\nready for jump\n";
```

```
hello (one);
}
```

Program 20.6.

The output of this program is

```
before jump: x=0, m=2
ready to jump
jump completed
after jump: x=5, m=0
```

The program execution begins in **main()** routine. The **setjmp()** function is called. The value returned by **setjmp()** is assigned to **x**. It is zero before the jump. We display it by the **cout** object. The computer executes **m=m+2**. It, then, executes the **cout** object and warns you, that it is about to call the **hello()** function, containing the **longjmp()** function. It is done by displaying the message "**ready to jump**". Thus, the program execution is performed in a regular way, until the **longjmp()** function is encountered. The computer jumps to the line containing **setjmp()**. The returned by the **setjmp()** function value is equal to 5 after the jump. The **if** and following it statements are executed. The **exit(0)** terminates the program.

This explains, why do we have the second argument in the **longjmp()** function. We should be able to change the value returned by the **setjmp()** function. This value can be a condition in some decision statement (**if**, **switch** and so on). If a certain jump has been performed, that decision statement stops the program execution, or redirects it to another path. Think what would happen in **Program 20.6**, if we have not used the returned value as a condition in the **if** statement. The **if** statement stops the program execution, when the jump is performed. If we have not used it, the program would have performed an infinite loop.

It is interesting, but you cannot set the returned by **setjmp()** value back to zero after a jump. Even if we write the jump as

```
longjmp (one, 0);
```

the value returned by **setjmp()** will be 1.

Another interesting aspect is what happens with the values of the variables after the jump. We have introduced a local variable **m** in **Program 20.6**. Its value is made equal to 0 before the line, containing the **setjmp()** function. When the program is executed normally, it changes the value of **m** to 2. This is done by the **m=m+2** statement. We see the new value displayed before the jump. After the jump is performed, the new value is lost, and we are left with **m=0**. *The values, that the local variables will have after a jump, are implementation-dependent. You should expect to lose your data at all. Therefore, you should use global variables, if you want the variables not to change their values after the jump.*

The problem can happen, even if you declare some objects not only as local, but also as **register**. This problem occurs, because the code generator elects some of those objects to be stored in the registers. Those registers can also hold some intermediate values of an expression evaluation. The **setjmp()** saves the state of those registers. When the jump returns the program back to an earlier stage, the new values of the variables can be partially lost and substituted by the old ones. You can lose the data. So, if the object changes its value, declare it as having the **volatile** type.

The **volatile** data type warns the compiler that a variable of that type may be modified by some external event, as, for instance, some kind of interrupt. This type is not described in any header files. It is a part of the C language. The variable of that type is stored in the memory. A declaration of a **volatile** variable consists of word **volatile** followed by a data type and the variable name. Let's declare the variable **m**

```
volatile int m;
```

If we have used variable **m** of that type in the above program, it would have been equal to 2 after the jump. Thus, its value would have been saved in spite of the jump.

It is also a good idea to write each call to **longjmp()** in a separate (small) function, i.e., to put **longjmp()** in a separate routine. It is wise to use the **switch** rather than **if** statement to control the program before and after the jump.

We caution you against using the jumps just described in this section. They interrupt not only the normal program flow, but normal function return procedure and can lead to some unpredictable results. One should use them in case of some fatal error to terminate the program execution, or in outstanding circumstances. A good programmer usually avoids using them at all.

20.10. The < signal.h > header file.

The **<signal.h>** header file describes **sig_atomic_t** data type, **signal()** and **raise()** functions and macros: **SIG_DFL**, **SIG_ERR**, **SIG_IGN**, **SIGABRT**, **SIGFPE**, **SIGILL**, **SIGINT**, **SIGSEGV** and **SIGTERM**. The **<signal.h>** header file has to be included, whenever you use any of these macros, functions or data type.

When C or C++ program attempts to do something illegal like dividing by zero and so on, the hardware or software, in some cases, will detect the problem. A signal is a some kind of an extraordinary event, that occurs in a computer. All those signals are recognizable. Each corresponds to a certain kind of error or interrupt. There are two types of signals: *synchronous* and *asynchronous*. *Synchronous* signals occur as a result of program execution. Let's say, you mistakenly code a division by zero. Another example might be an improper access to a storage or to a file. *Asynchronous* signals are the results of the actions outside of your program. For example, somebody strikes an interrupt key, or other program, independent of yours, can signal to your program.

If you do not specify how to handle different signals, your program might terminate its execution. It is sufficient to use computer operating system for handling the signals for most programs. But, you might want to take much control over the incoming signals. Then, you use the tools given in **<signal.h>** header file. You can program a signal to be handled in three different ways: *default handling* or execution will be terminated upon the signal arrival, *ignoring* the signal as nothing has happened, *passing* the control to another function called *signal handler*. This *signal handler* function suspends the program execution, if the signal arrives. It can also display an error message, or try to do a change in the program. If the problem is not disastrous, the *signal handler* function can allow the program execution from the point it was paused.

Signals are a very delicate subject for a number of reasons. First, the very presence of a signal introduces a problem of control inside a program, synchronization and reliable operation. Second, the programs with signal handlers are not always portable. Third, asynchronous signal can occur, while a library function is running. It does not communicate properly with the signal handler and can cause a peculiar program behavior.

If you intend to use a signal handler, the **volatile** data type should be used where possible. This data type has some protection against synchronous signals. Another protection is offered by the very **<signal.h>** header file that introduces a new data type called **sig_atomic_t**. One can use this type in C and C++. For instance,

```
sig_atomic_t  x;
```

declares the variable **x** of **sig_atomic_t** type. We will show you later, how to use this type in the handler. You can also use this type for regular variables, for more protection of data. The **sig_atomic_t** data type defines an integral type object, i.e., you can only use it for the integral numbers. It handles the data differently. If you define a variable to be of **sig_atomic_t** type, the value assigned to this variable must be physically done in one machine instruction. Usually more than one machine instruction is needed to assign a value to an object. There is always a chance of interrupt occurrence while the data is transferred, and the value can be incorrect. If it takes only one instruction to assign a value, you cannot have an interrupt coming in the middle of assignment. Thus, you have better chances for the assigned value to be correct, if **sig_atomic_t** data type is used.

So, the scheme for creating your signal handler is simple. The **raise()** function sends a proper signal to the program, if any particular catastrophic event occurs. This signal can be received, or in other words, seen by the **signal()** function, that specifies what should be done about it. Now, let's review both functions.

We introduce the **raise()** function first. Its synopsis is

```
int raise (int sig);
```

It has a parameter of **int** type, which we called **sig**. The function sends the signal specified by its argument to the executing program. The values, that argument **sig** can take, are standardized and correspond to specific events occurring in the system. ANSI C Standard specifies following standard arguments and the events they correspond to:

SIGABRT is used to report unsuccessfully or abnormally terminated program as, for instance, program termination by **abort()** function declared in **<stdlib.h>** file.

SIGFPE is used to report so-called "floating-point exception". This signal occurs in case of any erroneous arithmetic operation, such as overflow, underflow or division by zero. The incorrect operations, which it reports, vary from compiler to compiler.

SIGILL is used to report an illegal instruction or function.

SIGINT is used to report the user interrupt occurrence. For instance, the user can press **Ctrl-BREAK** key to interrupt a program. It will generate this signal.

SIGSEGV is used to report an invalid storage access. It is used, for instance, if your pointer points outside the available memory, or you try to store a value of the variable in the same cell, where the *constant* was initially stored.

SIGTERM is used to report, that a termination request is sent to our program. This signal can be sent from the operating system or from another program, which is executed at the same time as your program. It is an asynchronous program, so it might occur at any time.

Those are the standard arguments, although your particular environment can have some additional argument options. Even those standard options can differ for different computers. Each argument is an integral constant. For example, we write

```
raise(SIGTERM);
```

We can assign a value, let's say, **SIGINT** to the variable **x** and write

```
x=SIGINT;
raise (x);
```

The **raise()** function returns zero, if it is successful and non-zero, if unsuccessful.

The synopsis for **signal()** function is

```
void (*signal (int sig, void (*func)(int x)))(int y);
```

Even though this form looks horrible, it looks nicer in the real life. First, let's discuss, what are the parameters of the **signal()** function. The first parameter is the variable **sig** of **int** type. It specifies a particular signal, on which the **signal()** function should react, i.e., if the **signal()** function "sees" this signal, it will do something. This argument can accept the same six standard values as we have described for the **raise()** function argument.

The second parameter is a pointer to a function **(*func)(int x)**. This function should have **void** type. It has standard values:

SIG_DFL is a pointer to a function, that causes the default handling of the signal. This is an implementation defined action.

SIG_IGN is a pointer to a function, that already exists in your compiler. It is used, when the incoming signal should be ignored by your program.

In these two cases, the **signal()** function can be written

```
signal (sig, SIG_DFL); or signal (sig, SIG_IGN);
```

One can use a pointer to any other written by you function as the second argument. In this case, the written by you function will be the *signal handler*. The *signal handler* function, written by you, can be terminated or ended only by **return**, **abort**, **exit**, **longjump**. Do not write a *signal handler* function, that ends with **return** statement and the **sig** argument **SIGFPE** or any other value, that your system uses to indicate a computational error. Let's say, you get **SIGFPE** and execute the signal handler. When it is terminated by the **return**, you will return to the same point of your initial program you started from, where an erroneous arithmetic operation has been done. So you can have **SIGFPE** again and go to the handler and so on, or get wrong result.

The **raise()** function sends the signal corresponding to its argument. If the **signal()** function recognizes a signal corresponding to its argument **sig**, it gives the control to a function (*signal handler*), to which its second argument points to. If the *signal handler* is a standard function, such as **SIG_DFL** or **SIG_IGN**, then, it is executed. If the signal handler is a written by you function, a program is interrupted and **signal(SIG,SIG_DFL)** is executed first. Only after that, your signal handler function is executed. Sometimes, if the argument **sig** is **SIGILL**, the **SIG_DFL** might not be executed before your signal handler. After your function execution is completed, **signal()** returns the control back to the program or stops the execution of that program at all. The **signal()** function, if it is honored, returns the value of the *signal handler* function. Otherwise, a special value contained in **SIG_ERR** macro is returned. That indicates an error. **Program 20.7** demonstrates the signal functions.

```
#include <stdio.h>
```

```
#include <stdlib.h>
#include <signal.h>

void main (void)
{
float x=1.0, y;
int arg=SIGFPE;
scanf ("%f", &y);
if (y==0)
raise (arg);
signal (arg, SIG_DFL);
y=x/y;
printf ("result:%f\n", y);
}
```

Program 20.7.

This program will perform **x/y** division, if **y** is not equal to zero. Otherwise, the signal will be generated, and the default action will be performed. Since the **<signal.h>** header varies significantly from compiler to compiler, we advise to read about it in your particular compiler manual before experimenting with it.

20.11. The <stdarg.h> header file.

C and C++ let you write the functions, that have variable argument lists. The header **<stdarg.h>** specifies macros used for that. It should be included, when **va_list**, **va_start**, **va_arg** and **va_end** are used.

One can create the functions, whose number of arguments and the type of each of them can be specified only when the functions are called. These functions are called the *functions with the variable argument lists* or the *functions with the variable number of parameters* (arguments). A function with a variable argument list must be declared prior to its use. For instance,

```
somefunc (double wy1, int x1,...);
```

will be a function with a variable number of arguments. The variable argument list functions should have at least one argument of any type. Their prototypes use comma and three periods (**,...**) after the last argument, to indicate that it is a variable-length argument list. Our function has two parameters: **wy1**, **x1** and comma with three periods. A function with the variable argument list must also be defined as a regular function. One must use the macros and functions specified in **<stdarg.h>** header file in the definition of such a function. After that, you can call this function. You can give such a function any name and write it to perform any operation, as a regular function.

After the above short introduction to the subject, we can discuss how to create the functions using **va_list**, **va_start**, **va_arg** and **va_end**. We will first introduce you to each of those macros. We will show how to use them after that.

The **va_start()** macro initiates the procedure for writing the variable list function.

Its synopsis is

```
void va_start (va_list obj, name);
```

It looks simpler, when written in the program

```
va_start (obj, name);
```

The return type of **va_start()** function is **void**, so it does not return any values. It has two parameters. The first one, is a special pointer **obj** of type **va_list**. The **obj** is just an identifier. The parameter **obj** points to the variable argument list, that will be passed to created function. The **va_list** is a special data type used for those lists. It is used by the functions of this header. The value of **obj** is undetermined for a user and cannot be changed. The first argument should be declared as

```
va_list obj;   or  va_list *obj;
```

Both declarations would work on some compilers. In general, one of them must work.

We called the second parameter **name** trying to emphasize, that it is, indeed, a name. Whose name is it? It is the name of the rightmost argument in the function prototype. The "rightmost argument" means, the argument right before the "**, ...**" characters. For example, the function prototype with the variable number of arguments contains

```
int somefunc (int n, ...);
```

Its rightmost argument is **n**. Therefore, the **va_start()** function used to create the **somefunc()** must have **n** as an argument

```
va_start (obj, n);
```

Suppose, we had more arguments in the prototype of some other function

```
float tryfun (double x, char *m, int k, ...);
```

The rightmost argument would be **k** in that case.

One cannot use **va_start()**, if the rightmost argument of the function: is a **register** variable, has an array type, is a function by itself, has a type that will not be compatible with the results. The behavior of the function in this case is undefined.

Next is the **va_arg()** macro, that has a synopsis

```
type va_arg(va_list obj, type);
```

Its first argument **obj** has **va_list** type. It is the same argument as in **va_start()** function. The second argument is **type**. It is just a data type, for example, **int**, **char**, **char ***, etc. It can also be a structure, union, class type. For instance,

```
va_arg(obj, int); second argument is of int type;
va_arg(obj, char); second argument is of char type;
va_arg(obj, float*); second argument is a pointer to float type;
```

Every time **va_arg()** is called, a new parameter is added to the function with the variable number of arguments. The second parameter **type** of **va_arg()** indicates the type of that argument to be added (**int**, **double** and so on). The **va_arg()** returns a value passed to an added parameter.

The **va_end()** must conclude the procedure of writing a function with variable number of arguments, that is initialized by the **va_start()**. The **va_end()** macro has **void** type and does not return any value. Its synopsis is

```
void va_end (va_list obj);
```

For example, we can write it as

```
va_end (obj);
```

The function has one argument of type **va_list**. It should be the same argument as in

va_start(), that begins the procedure of creating a function.

Program 20.8 illustrates how to write a function with variable number of arguments.

```
#include <iostream.h>          //line1
#include <stdarg.h>            //line2

int func (int n, ...);         //line3

void main (void)               //line4
{                              //line5
int m;                         //line6
m=func (5, 1, 2, 3, 4, 5);     //line7
cout << m;                     //line8
}                              //line9

int func (int n, ...)          //line10
{                              //line11
int k=0, r;                    //line12
va_list ptr;                   //line13
va_start (ptr, n);             //line14
for (r=1; r<=n; r++)           //line15
k=k + va_arg (ptr, int);       //line16
va_end (ptr);                  //line17
k=k/n;                         //line18
return (k);                    //line19
}                              //line20
```

Program 20.8.

The output of the program is 3. The program computes the average value of five numbers from 1 to 5. It consists of two functions: **main()** and **func()**. The **main()** calls **func()** function, that is a function with the variable argument list. After the **func()** function returns the calculated value, it is displayed by the **cout** object.

This program shows us, how to create a function with the alterable number of arguments. *You must declare the function explicitly with at least one argument and ending with comma and three periods (, ...). You can, then, write that function definition. The* **va_start()**, **va_arg()** *and* **va_end()** *must be used in the definition of a function with variable number of arguments.* The same identifier must be used as the first argument of **va_start()**, **va_arg()** and the argument of **va_end()** in the definition of the same function with variable number of arguments.

We wrote our function at lines 10-20. The function **func()** starts with declaring the variables. Variable **ptr** of type **va_list** is declared among them at line 13. The actual argument adding procedure starts from the

```
va_start (ptr, n);    //line14
```

The **ptr** argument of this function will be used later. The second argument **n** of **va_start()** is the rightmost parameter in the **func()** function prototype. The **func()**

function has variable number of arguments. We, then, call the **va_arg()** function as many times as needed. It is put inside the **for** loop body at lines 15-16.

The parameters of a regular function can be used in its body, because they have a function visibility scope. It is true for the functions with the variable argument lists. We can use any parameter of a function with a variable number of parameters. We can even use the parameters, that are added to such a function by **va_arg()** macro. We use the rightmost argument **n** of the **func()** function in the loop condition **r<=n**. The number of arguments in **func()** function in **Program 20.8** is given by its parameter **n**. You might get an impression, that only the rightmost parameter should be used for the loop condition. Again, a function with variable number of arguments can use any of its parameters. The rightmost argument of **func()** is specified by the **va_start()** function, because the computer must know its last existing parameter. *The rightmost argument gives a computer a point, after which it will insert the other parameters.*

Program 20.8 uses the existing argument of **func()** to regulate the total number of arguments. It illustrates, how to specify a total number of arguments by one of the arguments. We will show another way of doing it later in **Program 20.9**.

Let's go back to **Program 20.8**. Every time the **va_arg()** is called, a new argument is added. You specify the type of each argument to be added in **va_arg()** second argument. We specified the **int** data type of each added argument. The arguments are added in the same order, as they appear in the function call. We called the **func()** function in **main()** routine by

```
m=func (5, 1, 2, 3, 4, 5); //line7
```

Now we have to create five additional arguments, read their values and perform some actions with them. If we do not create five argument places, the call to **func()** will be rejected. *The argument creation is the procedure done by va_start(), va_arg() and va_end() functions.* The first call to **va_arg()** creates the first parameter after the rightmost argument of the function **func()**. Value 1 is passed to this parameter. This value is read and returned by the **va_arg()** function in the expression

```
k=k + va_arg (ptr, int);          //line16
```

The second call to **va_arg()** creates the second argument of **func()** and returns the value 2 to the expression at line 16. The program creates the arguments and reads consecutive values 1, 2, 3, 4, 5 from the **func()** call as many times as the **va_arg()** is called. The **va_end()** at line 17 concludes the procedure of creating the arguments.

Next program writes word "**hello**" to **onemy.dat** file. The function, that actually writes this word, has variable number of arguments. That function is created similarly to the previous one. Its rightmost argument is the pointer to the file, to which the word will be written. Pay attention to the way we call the **va_arg()** function, that creates the arguments. Its returned values are compared to '\n' character. When this character is read, we stop creating the arguments. As you see, this character is the last one in the call **func(pt, 'h', 'e', 'l', 'l', 'o', '\n')**. The program also reads the word from the file and displays it on the screen.

```
#include <stdio.h>
#include <stdarg.h>
```

```
void func (FILE *wa, ...);

void main (void)
{
FILE *pt;
char x;
pt=fopen ("onemy.dat", "w+");
func (pt, 'h', 'e', 'l', 'l', 'o', '\n');
rewind (pt);
while ((x=fgetc (pt))!=EOF)
printf ("-%c-", x);
fclose (pt);
printf ("\nend\n");
}

void func (FILE *wa, ...)
{
char b;
va_list q;
va_start (q, wa);
while ((b=va_arg (q, char))!= '\n')
fputc (b, wa);
va_end (q);
}
```

Program 20.9.

Word "**hello**" is written to the file **onemy.dat**. The output on the screen is
```
-h-e-l-l-o-
end
```

20.12. The < stddef.h > header file.

The **<stddef.h>** header file defines following types and macros: **ptrdiff_t**, **size_t**, **wchar_t**, **NULL**, **offsetof**. It should be included, when any of those macros is used. Some of those macros are described in other headers. In those cases, you have a choice, which header file to include.

C language can work in two environments: *freestanding* and *hosted*. The *freestanding* environment is the one, that cannot support the full Standard C library. The C Standard requires from a freestanding environment to support the C language features and four standard headers - **<float.h>**, **<limits.h>**, **<stdarg.h>** and **< stddef.h>**. The *hosted* environment must provide not only all the language features, but also the entire Standard C library. The subject of this book is primarily a hosted environment.

We know, some of the macros described in **<stddef.h>** header are defined in some other header files as well. For instance, **NULL**, **size_t** and **wchar_t** are described in other headers. Those replications are done, because some standard headers might not be available in freestanding environment. And each of the macros defined in **<stddef.h>** once has been a candidate for inclusion in the language proper. They are commonly used as the parts of the language. Let's now review each of those macros.

When two pointers are subtracted in C or C++ expression, the result has the **ptrdiff_t** type. It is a signed integer type, mostly **int** or **long**. The pointers can be subtracted only if: they have compatible data-object type, both pointers must point to elements within the same array data object. You would almost never have to use this macro. Besides, it has its limitations. The difference between two addresses can be greater than the maximum number allowed by **ptrdiff_t**, and cause an overflow.

The **size_t** is an unsigned integral type. The result of the **sizeof** operator has this data type. So, the **size_t** is an unsigned integral data type, that can be used for any object you want - variables, arrays and so on. It is the safest type for the integer data, which, sometimes, even makes the data more portable. It is helpful to use it for the array element referencing, or address arithmetic.

The **wchar_t** is an integral type, that can represent the largest character set. The **wchar_t** can be used with any character. The **wchar_t** type range can cover any character in the largest character set. The '**\0**' character has zero value, for instance.

The **NULL** is a null pointer and we have discussed it. We only want to add, that macro can be also written as **0, 0L, (void*)0**.

The **offsetof** macro returns an integral number of type **size_t**. This number is equal to the offset in bytes from the beginning of the structure to a specified structure member. It is written in a form

```
offsetof (type, member)
```

To understand it better, let's review a simple program.

```
#include <iostream.h>
#include <stddef.h>

void main (void)
{
struct check
{
int x;
float y;
} var ;
cout << offsetof (check, x) << ", "
     << offsetof (check, y);
}
```

Program 20.10.

The output of the program is: **0, 2**. So, the **offsetof()** returns the number of bytes from the beginning of the structure specified by its first parameter to the beginning of the cell, allocated for the structure member specified by its second parameter. The **offsetof(check, y)** shows, that the cell for **y** is allocated starting from the 2 byte from the beginning of the structure **check**.

20.13. The < stdio.h > header file.

This header file handles primarily input/output and describes following macros

BUFSIZ	**clearerr**	**EOF**	**fclose**
fflush	**feof**	**ferror**	**fgetc**
fgetpos	**fgets**	**FILE**	**FILENAME_MAX**
fopen	**FOPEN_MAX**	**fpos_t**	**fprintf**
fputc	**fputs**	**fread**	**freopen**
fscanf	**fseek**	**fsetpos**	**ftell**
fwrite	**getc**	**getchar**	**gets**
_IOLBF	**_IOFBF**	**_IONBF**	**L_tmpnam**
NULL	**perror**	**printf**	**putc**
putchar	**puts**	**remove**	**rename**
rewind	**scanf**	**SEEK_CUR**	**SEEK_END**
SEEK_SET	**setbuf**	**setvbuf**	**size_t**
sprintf	**sscanf**	**stderr**	**stdin**
stdout	**tmpfile**	**TMP_MAX**	**tmpnam**
ungetc	**vfprintf**	**vprintf**	**vsprintf**

They have been thoroughly described in Chapter 17 of this book. To use any of the above macros and functions, one should include the **<stdio.h>** header file in the source file. One can find some of those macros and functions described in other header files. For instance, the **size_t** macro is also defined in **<stddef.h>** header file. In this case, include any of the header files, where a macro is described.

20.14. The < stdlib.h > header file.

This header file essentially declares functions and defines macros that have no other sensible home. The macros and functions described in this header are:

size_t	**wchar_t**	**div_t**	**ldiv_t**
NULL	**EXIT_FAILURE**	**EXIT_SUCCESS**	**RAND_MAX**
MB_CUR_MAX	**atof**	**atoi**	**atol**
strtod	**strtol**	**strtoul**	**rand**
srand	**calloc**	**free**	**malloc**
realloc	**abort**	**atexit**	**exit**
getenv	**system**	**bsearch**	**qsort**
abs	**div**	**labs**	**ldiv**
mblen	**mbtowc**	**wctomb**	**mbstowcs**
wcstombs			

To use those macros, one should include **<stdlib.h>** header file in the source file. The functions described in this header can be subdivided into following groups:

- String conversion functions(`atof()`, `atoi()`, `atol()`, `strtod()`, `strtol()`, `strtoul()`) convert a numeric value contained in the string.
- Memory management functions (`calloc()`, `malloc()`, `realloc()`, `free()`) allocate memory space during run-time. We have already discussed these functions in the chapter on run-time allocation in this book. Hence, they will not be reviewed here.
- Pseudo-random number generation functions (`rand()`, `srand()`) create pseudo-random numbers.
- Math functions (`abs()`, `div()`, `labs()`, `ldiv()`) perform arithmetic actions.
- Sorting and searching functions (`bsearch()`, `qsearch()`, `qsort()`, `compar()`) sort and search the data.
- Functions for communications with the environment (`abort()`, `exit()`, `atexit()`, `getenv()`, `system()`) enable interactions with the host environment.
- Multi-byte conversion functions (`mbstowcs()`, `wcstombs()`, `mblen()`, `mbtowc()`, `wctomb()`, provide a match between multi-byte and wide characters.

20.14.1. String conversion functions.

We will give you the prototypes of the three string conversion functions at once.

```
double atof (const char *row);
int atoi (const char *row);
long int atol (const char *row);
```

The parameter, we called **row**, is a pointer to a character array (or string). One can also write a string right into argument instead of pointing to it, as for instance,

```
x=atof( "1234.38cm length" ); or z=atol( "192939cycles" );
```

Each of these three functions reads the leading number in the string **row**, converts it to the returned value type according to the prototype of each function, and returns it. For instance, **atof()** must return a **double** type value. The **atoi()** converts a numeric value to an **int** type. The functions read the leading numerical value as follows.

All three functions determine, if the first characters after possible white spaces and signs (**+, -**) in the string **row** is a number. The numbers in the strings to be read should precede letters or any other characters, except white spaces or signs. The leading white spaces are ignored, the signs (**+, -**) might be included in the converted value. The value is read from the string **row**, until white space or any other non-number character is encountered. Then, it is converted to proper data type and returned by the function.

For instance, **atof("1234.38cm length")** will read only the number 1234.38 and stop, when it gets to the letter **c**. This number will be returned as 1234.38000. The **atoi("123 Beacom Street apt.999")** will read and return the number 123 and stop, when the white space is reached. If we write **atoi("123.4567 Beacom Street")**, the number returned by **atoi()** is 123. **Program 20.11** illustrates it.

```
#include <stdio.h>
#include <stdlib.h>
```

```
void main (void)
{
double x;
int y;
long int z;
x=atof ("1234.38cm length");
y=atoi ("123 Beacom Street apt. 999");
z=atol ("192939cycles");
printf ("x=%.4f, y=%d, z=%ld\n", x, y, z);
}
```

Program 20.11.

As you would expect, the output of the program is:

```
x=1234.3800 y=123 z=192939
```

We will now review the prototypes of some other functions described in the header.

```
double strtod (const char *spr, char **epr);
long int strtol (const char *spr, char **epr, int base);
insigned long int strtoul (const char *spr, char **epr,
                           int base);
```

The first parameter **spr** in those functions is a pointer to a string to be read. When the string is read, any of those three functions split it on two parts. The first part is the numerical value that is returned. The second part consists of the remaining characters in the string. The second part of that initial string is placed in another string array pointed to by **epr**. The parameter **epr** points to that remainder of the initial string. It is a pointer to a pointer to **char** data type. If you do not intend to recover the remainder, use **NULL** as the second argument.

The third parameter **base** in **strtol()** and **strtoul()** indicates, what base do we expect the read number to have. In other words, you have to indicate the base of the number in the string. The number will be interpreted as having the base specified by the **base** parameter. The value of **base** argument can lie between 2 and 36. Even though binary, octal, decimal, hexadecimal bases are most known to us, but you can select any base within the range. The letters are ascribed to complement the numbers to the base value for the bases above decimal. For instance, hexadecimal numbers use letters from **a** (**A**) to **f** (**F**). For greater bases the whole alphabet from **a** (**A**) to **z** (**Z**) can be used. If **base** is equal to 0, the value will be interpreted as a constant and handled by the rules that handle the constants.

All three functions perform the same action. The difference between the functions is in the returned data type. You can read the returned data types from the prototype of each function. The **strol()** and **stroul()** functions also have the third argument, that should be set to the base of the expected number. If no value can be returned, all three functions return zero. In case, if the read value is beyond the range:

strtod() returns **+** or **− HUGE_VAL**; macro **ERANGE** is stored in **errno**;

strtol() returns **LONG_MAX** or **LONG_MIN**; macro **ERANGE** is stored in **errno**;

strtoul() returns **ULONG_MAX**; macro **ERANGE** is stored in **errno**.

Let's review how those functions read a string. For instance, value 923.58 in the string

"923.58 volts, 293.483milliamps." comes before all other characters. It will be read and converted. Second value 293.483 will not be read. The functions will not read a number from the string **"volts 923.58, 293.483milliamps."**, because the letters in this string go before the numbers. The **strtod()**, **strol()** and **stroul()** return only a leading value. That value can be preceded by the white spaces or signs (**+, -**). The white spaces are ignored and stripped by all three functions and the signs might be included in the converted numbers. The last three functions can substitute the previous three as follows: **atof()** function can be written as **strtod(spr, &NULL)**, **atoi()** - as **(int)strtol(spr, &NULL, 10)** and **atol()** as **strtol(spr, &NULL, 10)**.

Review an example of how to use these functions given in **Program 20.12**.

```
#include <iostream.h>
#include <stdlib.h>

void main (void)
{
double x;
long int n;
unsigned long int m;
char test[ ]="42.672 meters long";
char *line1, *line2;
x=strtod (test, &line1);
cout << "value:" << x << ", remainder: "
        << line1 << endl;

n=strtol ("110 killograms", &line2, 2);
cout << "second value as base 2: " << n
        << ", remainder: " << line2 << endl;

n=strtol ("110 killograms", &line2, 10);
cout << "second value as base 10: " << n
        <<", remainder: " << line2 << endl;
m=strtoul ("111110volts", NULL, 10);
cout << "third value read as base 10: " << m << endl;
}
```

Program 20.12.

The output of this program is

```
value:42.6720000,  remainder: meters long
second value as base 2: 6,  remainder: killograms
second value as base 10: 110,  remainder: killograms
third value as base 10: 111110
```

Every function is written fairly straightforward. We read the second value as a binary, and, then, as a decimal. We also use **NULL** to dump the remainder of the third string.

20.14.2. Pseudo-random number generation functions.

We want to review two pseudo-random sequence generation functions: **rand()** and **srand()**. The **rand()** function generates a pseudo-random integer between 0 and **RAND_MAX** and returns it. The macro **RAND_MAX** stands for a maximum integral number, that could be generated. Standard requires it to be at least 32767. You can display its value on the screen

```
printf ("%d \n", RAND_MAX);
```
The prototypes of both functions are

```
int rand (void);
void srand (unsigned int start);
```
The **srand()** function has one parameter, we called **start**. The **start** is used as a seed for getting a new sequence of pseudo-random numbers. This argument is a starting point for the **rand()** function generating the pseudo-random numbers. The **srand()** function does not produce a random sequence. It is used along with the subsequent calls to **rand()** function, that actually produces a random number. If **srand()** is called with the same value of the parameter **start**, the same sequence of pseudo-random numbers is generated by the **rand()** function. If **rand()** is called by itself before any call to **srand()**, it generates a special pseudo-random number sequence. The same sequence will be generated, if you call **srand(1)** and, then, **rand()**. The starting point can be coupled to some integer, or even the system time. We illustrate how to use the **rand()** function below.

```
#include <iostream.h>
#include <stdlib.h>

void main (void)
{
int n;
for (n=0; n<5; n++)
cout << rand ( ) << "   ";
}
```

Program 20.13.

The output of the program will be five random numbers displayed on the screen.

20.14.3. Integer math functions.

We will start from the **abs()** function. It computes and returns an absolute value of its argument. Its synopsis is

```
int abs (int x);
```
An absolute value of a positive integer is the very number. For instance, the absolute values of the numbers 4, 819, 66 are the same numbers 4, 819, 66. The absolute value of any negative integer is the same, but positive number. The absolute values of the numbers

-4, -819, -66 are the positive numbers 4, 819, 66.

The **labs()** function is similar to the **abs()** function, except that its argument as well as the returned value have **long** data type. The function synopsis is

```
long int labs (long int x);
```

An example of how to use both functions is given below.

```
#include <iostream.h>
#include <stdlib.h>

void main (void)
{
int n, m=-200;
long int k;
n=abs (m);
k=labs (-200000);
cout << "absolute values: " << n << ", " << k;
}
```

Program 20.14.

The output of the program is:

```
absolute values: 200, 200000
```

The **div()** function synopsis is

```
div_t div (int num, int den);
```

The **div()** function computes and returns the quotient and the remainder for division of the first argument (**num**) by the second one (**den**). Therefore, the **div()** function computes and returns a variable of a structure type **div_t**. The **div_t** is just a data type used for a structure returned by the **div()** function. To assign the returned value to any variable **x**, declare that **x** as having **div_t** data type. Both members of the structure, returned by the **div()** function, have the **int** data type

```
int quot;        /* quotient */
int rem;         /* remainder */
```

If the result cannot be presented, the behavior is unknown. Review the example below.

```
#include <iostream.h>
#include <stdlib.h>

void main (void)
{
int n=17, m=3;
div_t  fin, res;
fin=div (n, m);
res= div (7, 2);
cout << "17/3: quotient " << fin.quot << ", remainder "
     << fin.rem << "\n7/2: quotient " << res.quot
     << ", remainder " << res.rem;
```

```
}
```

Program 20.15.

The program output is:

```
17/3: quotient 5, remainder 2
7/2: quotient 3, remainder 1
```

This program is pretty clear. We access the quotient and remainder by accessing the returned structure members **fin.quot**, **fin.rem**, **res.quot**, **res.rem**.

The last function we introduce is the **ldiv()** function. It is similar to the **div()** function. It also computes and returns the quotient and remainder of division of the first argument by the second one. The difference is that both first and the second arguments have type **long int**. The function prototype is

```
ldiv_t  ldiv (long int num, long int den);
```

The returned value is a structure that has type **ldiv_t**. This is a data type similar to **div_t**, except the returned structure members have type **long int**.

```
long int quot;        /* quotient */
long int rem;         /* remainder */
```

20.14.4. Sorting and searching functions.

We will review the **bsearch()** function first. Its prototype is

```
void *bsearch (const void *key, const void *one,
               size_t num, size_t size,
     int (*compar) (const void *arg1, const void *arg2));
```

The first parameter **key** is a pointer to some data object. Three other parameters **one**, **num** and **size** are associated with an array or a collection of other objects. The **bsearch()** function searches that array of data objects associated with its second, third and the fourth parameters for an element, that matches the data object pointed to by the first argument.

For example, let the first argument of **bsearch()** function point to a variable having the value 25. Let the second, third and fourth arguments identify an array of values {**10, 20, 25, 30**}. The **bsearch()** function will search this array for the value 25. If that array contains that value, a pointer to a cell, storing that particular value, will be returned. One might ask, what happens if there are more than one value 25 in the same array? In this case, a pointer to any one of those values can be returned.

So, the function returns a pointer to a cell containing the value, that matches the object pointed to by the first argument. If no match is found, **NULL** pointer is returned. The first argument can point to the data object of any data type, for instance, **int**, **float**, **double** and so on. The standard specifies pointers to type **void** in the function prototype to be able to cast them to any data type. Our data object can be a variable, structure, string, an array, a class object and so on. So, the array defined by three other arguments can be a collection of any objects of any data type.

We postulated, the second, third and the fourth arguments of the function determine an array to be searched. The second parameter, called by us **one**, is a pointer to the first element of that array. Third parameter **num** is a number of elements inside that array. Our array {10, 20, 25, 30} had just 4 elements. Therefore, **num** was equal to 4 for our array. The number of bytes occupied by each array element is determined by the fourth parameter, we called **size**.

The last argument **compar()** is a pointer to a function. It is declared as

```
int (*compar) (const void *arg1, const void *arg2);
```

The **compar()** function has two arguments. The first one points to the **key** element and second one to an array element. Its arguments shell have the same data type as the data object pointed to by **key** pointer. Both arguments are the pointers to **void** type. One can cast them to any type. User writes the **compar()** function. Its returned value will be used to determine, if the search is successful. Typically, an array is presorted before using the **bsearch()** function. Pay attention, we use only presorted arrays for that function. Otherwise, it will not work. Consider example below, illustrating the use of the **bsearch()** function. We realize, you might have a feeling, that something is incomplete in the way the function is set up. For instance, you do not specify the **compar()** function arguments, when it is used in the **bsearch()** function. We can only reply, that a programming language is a formal language. You just have to write the **bsearch()** function according to the rules of the language. **Program 20.16** demonstrates how to use the **bsearch()** search function.

```
#include <iostream.h>                        /*line1*/
#include <stdlib.h>                          /*line2*/

int compar (const void *pr1, const void *pr2);/*line3*/

void main (void)                             /*line4*/
{                                            /*line5*/
int m, ob=3, *qa, x[5]={1, 2, 3, 4, 5};      /*line6*/
qa=(int *)bsearch (&ob, x, 5, sizeof (int), compar);
                                             /*line7*/
if (qa!=NULL)                                /*line8*/
cout << "number matches\n";                  /*line9*/
else                                         /*line10*/
cout << "not found\n";                       /*line11*/
}                                            /*line12*/

int compar (const void *pr1, const void *pr2) /*line13*/
{                                            /*line14*/
if (*(int *)pr1 == *(int *)pr2)              /*line15*/
return (0);                                  /*line16*/
else if (*(int *)pr1<*(int *)pr2)            /*line17*/
return (-1);                                 /*line18*/
else                                         /*line19*/
return (1);                                  /*line20*/
}                                            /*line21*/
```

Program 20.16.

The output of the program is the message displayed on the screen

```
number matches
```

The program searches the array **x** in order to find the value 3. This value is stored in the **ob** variable. We use the **bsearch()** function to do it.

```
qa=(int *)bsearch (&ob, x, 5, sizeof (int), compar);
```

As you can see, the function arguments are written according to its prototype. The **compar()** function does not have any arguments, when used in the **bsearch()** function. Since we compare the **int** type values, the returned pointer should be of that type. We use the type casting **(int *)** in the call to **bsearch()**. Now, look how do we write the **compar()** function. It is declared as having two pointer arguments to type **void**. When you write the definition of this function, both pointers are type cast to the **int** type at lines 15, 17. The **compar()** function returns -1, 0, or 1, depending on the outcome of **else-if** statement, that compares the values both pointers point to.

The **qsort()** function sorts the array specified by its arguments in ascending order (from smaller to greater values). It is written in the format

```
void qsort (void *one, size_t num, size_t size,
        int (*compar) (const void *arg1, const void *arg2));
```

Parameters **one**, **num**, **size** and **compar** are similar to **bsearch()** function. They just specify an array to be sorted. The **one** is a pointer to the first array element. The **num** stands for the number of elements in the array. The **size** still determines the size of each array element in bytes. Everything written about **compar()** function is true for its application in the **qsort()** function, except it now compares different elements inside the same array. The data type of **compar()** arguments is now determined by the type of **one**. The **qsort()** function returns no value. If two elements have the same values, their order in the sorted array is unknown. Review **Program 20.17** that illustrates the use of **qsort()** function.

```
#include <iostream.h>
#include <stdlib.h>

int compar (const void *pr1, const void *pr2);

void main (void)
{
int m, x[8]={100, 80, 1, 48, 35, 10, 39, 20};
qsort (x, 8, sizeof (int), compar);
for (m=0; m<8; m++)
cout << x[m] << ", ";
}

int compar (const void *pr1, const void *pr2)
{
if (*(int *)pr1 == *(int *)pr2)
return (0);
else if (*(int *)pr1<*(int *)pr2)
```

```
return (-1);
else
return (1);
}
```

Program 20.17.

The output of the program is
  1   10   20   35   39   48   80   100

20.14.5. Environment communication functions.

We will review the **abort()** function first. Its prototype is
```
void abort(void);
```
It causes an abnormal program termination and, therefore, is to be used only in the very bad situations. It does not return to its caller. The program execution is just terminated. The **abort()** function is not required to close any open files, although it flushes or closes the opened files in some implementations. Temporary files can be removed. The function prints abnormal termination message, usually, to **stderr**.

The **atexit()** function prototype is
```
int atexit (void (*fun)(void));
```
Its parameter is a pointer to a function of **void** return type, that has no arguments. The parameter of the **atexit()**, we called **fun**, points to a function, that should be called at the end of a program run. The **atexit()** function performs the registration of the function pointed to by **fun**. It means, that the function, pointed to by **fun**, will run at the normal program end. The specified function is, indeed, called at normal program termination. One can call up to 32 functions this way. The functions are called in the reverse order of their registration, i.e., the first registered function will be called last. The **atexit()** function has return type **int**. It returns zero, if the registration is successful, and nonzero, otherwise. The following program is a demonstration of the **atexit()** function application.

```
#include <iostream.h>
#include <stdlib.h>

void phrase1(void)
{
cout << "the program is over.\n";
}

void phrase2(void)
{
cout << "have a nice day.\n";
}
```

```
void main (void)
{
atexit (phrase1);
atexit (phrase2);
cout << "you'll see it at program termination.\n";
}
```

Program 20.18.

The program output is
```
you'll see it at program termination.
have a nice day.
the program is over.
```

We will review the **exit()** function next. It terminates a program normally, i.e., the program execution is stopped and control is returned to the operating system. But, first, all the functions registered with **atexit()** function are called for execution in reversed order of their registration. All open streams with unwritten buffers will be flushed. Open files are closed and temporary files, particularly created by the **tmpfile()** function, are removed. Typical application of this function is to terminate the program execution normally, if an error occurred. The function does not return to the caller. Therefore, it does not return any value in many compilers. Its prototype is

```
void exit (int stat);
```

If **stat** is equal to zero or **EXIT_SUCCESS**, the termination is successful. Other **stat** values, including **EXIT_FAILURE**, tell the system, that the program has been terminated abnormally. You choose the value of the function argument. If you expect an abnormal program termination, you can code a check for that condition leading to the **exit()** function with the proper argument. This function has been used in our book, and we do not give an example of its use here.

Let's review the **getenv()** function next. Its prototype is

```
char *getenv (const char *line);
```

Its parameter is a pointer to a string. The function searches the host environment (DOS, Windows, UNIX and so on) for a string that matches the string pointed to by the argument **line**. The **getenv()** function returns a pointer to a string, that matches the argument. If such a string cannot be located, a **NULL** pointer is returned. That string cannot be modified, in general. Most often the function is used to obtain a pointer to a string associated with an environmental variable.

The notion of an environmental variable is tied with writing the adaptive codes. Call to such a variable added to the system can start a new process. The environmental variables are sets of names with the open ends. Each of them identifies a string representing its value. Environmental variables can be created, altered and deleted. One of their common use is to locate the directories and support the temporary files.

The **getenv()** finds an environmental variable, that matches its argument. Function **system()** uses the environmental variables for the program execution. Its synopsis is

```
int system (const char *row);
```

The parameter is a pointer to a string. The **system()** function passes the string pointed to by the parameter **row** to the operating system of the host environment to be executed.

It is executed by a command processor. The way the command is executed is implementation dependent. For instance, in DOS the string will be typically executed, as if you entered it at the command prompt. One can use a **NULL** pointer as an argument to inquire, if the command processor is available. If the argument is a **NULL** pointer, a nonzero value is returned only if a command processor is available. If the argument is not a **NULL** pointer, the returned value is implementation dependent. **Program 20.19** demonstrates **getenv()** and **system()** functions in DOS. The **val** gets the current path, which is displayed. The action of the **system()** function in this program is, as you would have typed **TIME** command from the DOS prompt.

```
#include <stdio.h>
#include <stdlib.h>

main ( )
{
char *val;
val = getenv ("PATH");
printf (" %s \n", val);
if ( system (NULL)==0)
printf ("command processor is not available. \n");
else
system ("TIME");
}
```

Program 20.19.

20.14.6. Multibyte conversion functions.

We now must review the multibyte conversion functions. You might not use those functions in the real life. They are implementation dependent. Therefore, you must read your compiler user's manual for details on those functions.

Before we can talk about the functions handling the multibyte and wide characters, you must understand those characters first. You, probably, know, many languages use more characters than English. Some languages, as, for example, Chinese and Japanese use separate characters for different words. We live in the world, where people speak and write in many languages. The creators of the software have to anticipate, that their products can be used in a different language environment. The problem is how to represent the characters of different cultures. As you know, the set of the legal characters, that might appear in the source files, is usually an ASCII character set. But how to be with the characters belonging to other languages? Should the whole world just forget their languages and go only with English?

Since, at least for now, it is impossible, people invented the ways to get by. ANSI C uses two different approaches for handling those locale-specific characters: extended character sets and multibyte characters.

The *extended character set* approach uses the very **char** data type to represent the characters in addition to the minimum set of characters. The **char** type occupies at least one byte cell. Those eight bits can accept 256 values. It is quite enough to represent all the required characters in most locales. With the *extended character set* approach we can introduce up to 256 characters in each locale. The same value can specify different characters in different locales.

The *multibyte character* approach suggests to use different number of bytes to represent different characters in the same locale. Thus, one character may, for instance, still occupy one byte, while three or four bytes can be needed for another character. A multibyte character approach uses so-called *shift states*. We should refer to an analogy with the "shift lock" on a typewriter. When the "shift lock" is pressed, the upper case letters are typed. Pressing the "shift lock" again, results in typing the lower case letters. A multibyte character method may use a number of special *"shift characters"*. Each shift character causes all subsequent characters to be interpreted in a different way. The same number may correspond to a different wide character after entering another shift character. Therefore, the interpretation of the multibyte characters depends on the most recent shift character or shift state.

The multibyte character strings are assumed to start in some initial shift state. The null character cannot be used, except in the first byte of a multibyte sequence. Byte that contains all zeros is interpreted as null character and is independent of a shift state. Multibyte characters can be used only in the comments, strings, character constants and header names that shell begin and end in the initial shift state.

The *wide character* data type **wchar_t** is defined, usually, when one needs to accommodate extra characters not specified by ASCII. There is a unique wide character integer of type **wchar_t** associated with any multibyte character in any locale. This **wchar_t** data type is, usually, 16 bits long. The maximum length of a single wide character is defined by **MB_CUR_MAX** macro in the current locale. By having 16 bits for a character, one can accommodate many characters. It is always more convenient to work with a single integer rather than with the multibyte character. Therefore, there is one to one mapping between the mutibyte number and the wide character integer. The functions we will review in this paragraph provide this mapping.

We provide you with some functions to work with wide and multibyte characters. You shell consult your compiler user's guide to get more information about the particular characters supported in different locales. Some compilers work only in one locale at all. Thus, you might not even be able to use some of the functions given below.

The **mblen()** function prototype is

```
int mblen (const char *ptr, size_t n);
```

The **ptr** is either a null pointer or a pointer to a character string to be examined and **n** is a number of bytes to be examined. The **mblen()** function examines **n** first bytes of a string pointed to by the pointer **ptr** for presence of a valid multibyte character. If **ptr** is not a **NULL** pointer, **mblen()** returns a number of bytes a multibyte character occupies. If a valid multibyte character is not found, it returns -1. When **ptr** is a **NULL** pointer, **mblen()** returns zero, if a multibyte character does not change with the shift. It returns nonzero, otherwise.

The **mbtowc()** function synopsis is

```
int mbtowc (wchar_t *wid, const char *ptr, size_t n);
```

The **wid** is a pointer to a memory region, where the wide character will be stored. Other two arguments have the same meaning as in the **mblen()** function. The **ptr** is either a null pointer or a pointer to a character string to be examined. And **n** is a number of bytes to be examined.

The **mbtowc()** function examines first **n** bytes of a string pointed to by **ptr**. The function converts the first multibyte character, found in that string, into a wide character, which it stores in the location pointed to by **wid**. There can be a few cases with respect to what values can be accepted by the function arguments. First case is when the **wid** and **ptr** are not **NULL** pointers. Then, if a multibyte character is found, the function returns the number of bytes it occupies. All the bytes of that multibyte character must be in the first **n** bytes of the **ptr** string. Otherwise, the character is not considered to be found. The **mbtowc()** returns -1, if no character has been found.

If **wid** is a **NULL** the **mbtowc()** behaves as the **mblen()** function. It returns the length of the first multibyte character in the first **n** bytes of **ptr** string. It returns -1, if such a character has not been found. For **ptr** equal to **NULL**, the function returns 0 if the multibyte characters are shift dependent and nonzero, otherwise. In this case, the value of **wid** remains unchanged.

The **wctomb()** function prototype is

```
int wctomb (char *ptr, wchar_t wc);
```

The **ptr** is a pointer to a location in memory, where a multibyte character will be stored. It should be at least **MB_CUR_MAX** bytes long to be able to accommodate the largest character in the current locale. The **wc** is a wide character. The **wctomb()** function converts the wide character stored in **wc** into a multibyte character and stores it in the location pointed to by **ptr**. The function returns the number of bytes the multibyte character occupies or -1, if the conversion is impossible for the current locale. The returned value can be zero, if **wc** is zero. For **ptr** being a null pointer, 0 is returned if multibyte character is shift independent, and a nonzero value otherwise.

How the wide character is converted to the multibyte one by the **wctomb()** function can depend on a particular locale. A locale can determine how does a computer interpret a character. The **wctomb()** function keeps truck of the current shift state, if current locale is shift dependent. The function is called with its initial shift state by making the **ptr** a **NULL** pointer. Otherwise, the function assumes the last shift state.

The **wcstombs()** function prototype is

```
size_t wcstombs (char *ptr, const wchar_t *wid,
                 size_t n);
```

The **ptr** points to the memory area, where the resulting multibyte character string will be stored. The **wid** points to a wide character string, that will be converted to a multibyte character string. And **n** stands for the maximum number of bytes, that the multibyte string can hold.

The **wcstombs()** function converts the string of wide characters pointed to by **wid** to the multibyte character string pointed to by **ptr**. The function will stop: if all the wide characters were converted, or the first null wide character has been encountered, or a new character cannot be added because more than **n** bytes are needed. The function returns the number of bytes stored in **ptr** string. If a wide character value having no multibyte character representation is encountered, then, -1 cast to **size_t** is returned.

The **mbstowcs()** function is written in the format
```
size_t mbstowcs (wchar_t *wid, const char *ptr,
                 size_t n);
```
The **wid** is a pointer to the memory spaces, where the wide character string will be stored. The **ptr** is a pointer to a multibyte character string, and **n** is the maximum number of multibyte characters to be converted.

The **mbstowcs()** function converts a multibyte character string pointed to by **ptr** into a string of wide characters stored in the memory buffer pointed to by **win**. The conversion is stopped, when all the multibyte characters have been converted. It will be also stopped after converting **n** characters, if there are more than **n** characters in the string. The conversion will be stopped regardless of the number of read characters, if a null character is encountered.

20.15. The <time.h> header file.

The **<time.h>** header file defines following macros:

NULL	**size_t**	**clock_t**	**time_t**
struct tm	**clock**	**difftime**	**mktime**
time	**asctime**	**ctime**	**gmtime**
localtime	**strftime**	**CLOCKS_PER_SEC**	

One should include **<time.h>** header file, whenever any of them are used.

20.15.1. Basic components and definitions.

Before introducing the functions of that header, we want to introduce a few definitions. The *calendar time* presents the current date and time according to the Gregorian calendar. The *local time* is a calendar time given for some specific time zone. The *Daylight Saving Time* (DST) is a period in the calendar year (usually half a year) during which the local time is changed. The *Coordinated Universal Time* (UTC), which is now used more often than the *Greenwich Mean Time* (GMT), is the local time at Greenwich longitude.

The header defines the **NULL** pointer and **size_t** data type, that we described earlier. The **clock_t** is an arithmetic data type. A value of this type is returned by the **clock()** function and represents elapsed processor time. It can be used for integer or floating-point type values.

The **time_t** is an arithmetic data type. Several functions operate with values of this type. It presents calendar times that span years, sometimes, to the nearest second. One cannot perform arithmetic operations on a value of this type.

The data and time functions require from an operating system to maintain the date and time. The calendar time in C can be stored in its internal format by the **size_t** data type. It can be also stored as the *broken-down* time by the structure of type **struct tm**. Each member of this structure gives a particular component of date or time. This structure contains at least nine following members, written in any order:

int tm_sec; /* contains the number of seconds passed after the last minute, ranges from 0 to 61 */

int tm_min; /* contains the number of minutes passed after the last hour, ranges from 0 to 59 */

int tm_hour; /* contains the number of hours passed since midnight, ranges from 0 to 23 */

int tm_mday; /* contains a number of day of the month, can range from 1 to 31 */

int tm_mon; /* contains a number of months passed since January, ranges from 0 to 11 */

int tm_year; /* contains a number of years passed since 1900 */

int tm_wday; /* contains the number of days passed since last Sunday, ranges from 0 to 6 */

int tm_yday; /* contains the number of days passed since last January 1, ranges from 0 to 365 */

int tm_isdst; /* is called the Daylight Saving Time flag. It is positive if Daylight Saving Time is in effect, zero if it is not in effect and negative if no information is available. */

20.15.2. Functions for time manipulation.

We will begin our review with the **clock()** function. Its prototype is

```
clock_t clock (void);
```

The **clock()** function returns the best approximation of the processor time needed for a program execution. This time is typically measured from some beginning point down to executing a line, at which this function has been typed. In other words, this time is counted since some moment of that program execution. The point or the moment, from which the count starts, is implementation defined. For many compilers it is a start of a program execution. The value is returned in the special units **CLOCKS_PER_SECOND**.

The **CLOCKS_PER_SECOND** macro is just a number of counts per second that can be either integer or floating-point value. Each computer second corresponds to this particular number of counts. For instance, two seconds is two times **CLOCKS_PER_SECOND**. In order to determine the time returned by the **clock()** function in seconds, the number returned by it should be divided by **CLOCKS_PER_SECOND**. We advise to cast the **CLOCKS_PER_SECOND** to **double** data type to be sure to present the largest number.

Program 20.20 demonstrates the use of **clock()** for finding the time, that it takes to execute a double loop.

```
#include <iostream.h>
#include <time.h>

void main (void)
{
long int n, m, k;
clock_t begin, finish;
double begin_s, finish_s, sub_s;
for (k=0; k<400000; k++)
```

```
;
begin = clock( );
for (n=0; n<2000; n++)
for (m=0; m<500; m++)
;
finish = clock( );
begin_s = begin/CLOCKS_PER_SEC;
finish_s = finish/CLOCKS_PER_SEC;
sub_s = finish_s - begin_s;
cout << "started: " << begin_s << " seconds, "
     << "ended: " << finish_s << " seconds\n"
     << "loop duration " << sub_s << " seconds \n";
}
```

Program 20.20.

The program output for our system is

```
started: 0.010989 seconds, ended: 0.439560 seconds
loop duration 0.329670 seconds
```

We used **clock()** function twice in **Program 20.20** to show, you can use it any number of times in a program. It will measure the time from some starting point of program execution. We also subtracted two time values **begin_s** and **finish_s** to find the time spent on the second loop execution.

The **mktime()** function prototype is

```
time_t mktime (struct tm *timeptr);
```

The function converts the broken-down time of the familiar time structure **struct tm**, expressed as local time, into a calendar time value. Loosely speaking, you enter some members of the time structure **struct tm**. By doing this, you select a certain moment in time. The **mktime()** function sets the other structure members, such as **tm_wday** and **tm_yday**, for example. The members **tm_wday** and **tm_yday** ignore the input values. They are set by the function itself. The function returns the value of specified calendar time or -1, if the time can not be returned. The range restrictions for some compilers are not important, when you enter the data into the structure **struct tm**. For instance, one might want to know, what day of a week will be December 31, 1996. You do not have to be very careful with the number of days. For instance, if you enter December 33, it will be understood as January 2 and so on. Thus, the excessive number in a date will be credited to the next month. After the function **mktime()** is executed, you would get a right time corresponding to that date. Review the program below.

```
#include <stdio.h>
#include <time.h>
#include <stdlib.h>

void main (void)
{
struct tm *num;
```

```
static   char *const week_day[ ]= {"Sunday", "Monday",
         "Tuesday"," Wednesday", "Thursday", "Friday",
         "Saturday"};
time_t res;
num->tm_sec=0;
num->tm_min=0;
num->tm_hour=0;
num->tm_mday=31;
num->tm_mon=11;
num->tm_year=1996-1900;
num->tm_isdst=-1;
res=mktime (num);
if ( res ==-1 )
{
printf ("unable to set time \n");
exit (0);
}
else
printf ("%s \n", week_day[num->tm_wday]);
}
```

Program 20.21.

The output of the program is:

```
Tuesday
```

The **difftime()** function is written in the format

```
double difftime (time_t t2, time_t t1);
```

It computes and returns the difference in time in seconds between two calendar times **t2-t1**. The returned value can be positive or negative, depending on which argument is *later*. Each parameter **t2** and **t1** is a calendar time value of type **time_t**.

The **time()** function synopsis is

```
time_t time (time_t *ptr);
```

It determines and returns the best approximation of the current calendar time or -1, if the calendar time cannot be obtained. The argument can be a **NULL** pointer. If **ptr** is not **NULL**, the returned current calendar time is also stored in the memory space pointed to by **ptr**. Following program demonstrates the use of **difftime()** and **time()** functions. It measures the time before and after a double loop execution. The **difftime()** function computes the difference in that time. We intentionally called **time()** function with **NULL** pointer first time and a nonzero pointer argument the second time to illustrate, how to call it.

```
#include <iostream.h>
#include <time.h>
#include <stdlib.h>

void main (void)
```

```
{
time_t a1, a2;
double dif;
long int n, m;
a1=time (NULL);
for (n=0; n<500000; n++)
for (m=0; m<100; m++);
time (&a2);
dif=difftime (a2, a1);
cout << " a1=" << a1 << ", a2=" << a2 << ", dif=" << dif;
}
```

Program 20.22.

The output of the program is

a1=819306269, a2=819306284, dif=15

Both **a1** and **a2** values might look to you rather peculiar. But nothing is wrong. Function **time()** returns the values of the GMT or UTC in seconds starting from some date. Some systems take January 1, 1900, as the starting point for measuring time. This means, that the time in seconds at the beginning of that day is presumed to be equal to zero. UNIX, however, assumes January 1, 1970, as a starting point for measuring time. There are systems using other conventions of a starting point.

20.15.3. Time formatting functions.

Function **localtime()** would be the first one to review. Its synopsis is

struct tm *localtime (const time_t *ptr);

The argument has type **time_t** and is a pointer to a location, containing a value of the calendar time. The **localtime()** function converts the calendar time, expressed as local time, stored in the memory area pointed to by its argument **ptr** into a broken-down time. Loosely speaking, it just takes a value of a calendar time, converts it to the local time, which is set in your computer, and fills in all the values of the **struct tm**. The function returns an address of that broken-down structure. This is why the **localtime()** function return type is declared as a pointer to a structure **struct tm**.

For instance, you can take a calendar time measurement at any moment by the **time()** function. To fill in that structure **struct tm** for a local time corresponding to that particular calendar time, use a pointer to the time returned by the **time()** function as an argument of the **localtime()** function. Review an example below.

```
#include <iostream.h>
#include <time.h>

void main (void)
{
struct tm *num;
```

```
time_t  tv;
tv = time (NULL);
num = localtime(&tv);
cout << "Date is " << num->tm_mon << "/"
     << num->tm_mday << "/" << num->tm_year << "\n"
     << "Time is " << num->tm_hour << ":" << num->tm_min;
}
```

Program 20.23.

The output of this program is the current local date and time at the moment of execution. We use **time()** function to get current calendar time. A pointer **tv** to a location storing that time is used as an argument of the **localtime()** function.

  Let's say, there is a particular time point stored in the time structure, and you want to display this time in a normal fashion as a string. For example,

```
Mon Jan  10:20:44 1997
```

Is it possible to display the time in that format? The answer is: Yes. The function that can do it is the **asctime()** function. Its prototype is

```
char *asctime (const struct tm *ptr);
```

The parameter **ptr** of the function is a pointer to the broken-down time structure to be converted. Therefore, it is a pointer of **struct tm** type. The **asctime()** function converts broken-down time stored in the structure pointed to by **ptr** to a string like

```
Wed Aug 14 10:23:48 1997
```

The function returns a pointer to the converted string. Thus, the function returns a pointer to a type **char**. Its application is given in the **Program 20.24** below.

```
#include <stdio.h>
#include <time.h>

void main (void)
{
struct tm *num, val;
time_t *qp, tv;
tv = time(qp);
num = localtime(&tv);
printf ("%s\n", asctime (num));
}
```

Program 20.24.

The output of the program is the current time, like

```
Wed Aug 14 10:23:48 1996
```

  We use the function **time()** to get a calendar time in **Program 20.24**. That calendar time is converted to a broken-down local time by the **localtime()** function. The value returned by that function is used as an argument of the **asctime()** function to obtain the string output of the current time stored as broken-down time.

  One can convert a calendar time to a string by the **ctime()** function. Its synopsis is

```
char *ctime (const time_t *ptr);
```
The **ptr** is a pointer to a memory location, where the calendar time is stored. Hence, it is a pointer to a **time_t** data type. The **ctime()** function converts that calendar time pointed to by **ptr** to the local time displayed as a string. The function returns a pointer to that string. This is why the returned value is a pointed to a type **char**. The **ctime()** function is equivalent to
```
asctime (localtime (ptr));
```
Program 20.25 displays the calendar time in the same manner as **Program 20.24**.

```
#include <stdio.h>
#include <time.h>

void main (void)
{
time_t qp;
qp=time(NULL);
printf ("%s \n", ctime (&qp) );
}
```
Program 20.25.

We want to present the **gmtime()** function next. Its prototype is
```
struct tm *gmtime (const time_t *ptr);
```
The parameter **ptr** is a pointer to a memory cell, containing the calendar time value to be converted. The **gmtime()** function converts the calendar time pointed to by **ptr** into a broken-down time, that is the Coordinated Universal Time (UTC). The function returns a pointer to a **struct tm** type.

```
#include <stdio.h>
#include <time.h>

void main (void)
{
struct tm *univ;
time_t qp;
qp=time(NULL);
univ = gmtime(&qp);
printf ("%d\n", univ->tm_hour);
printf ("universal time:\n %s \n", asctime (univ) );
}
```
Program 20.26.

The output of the program is the UTC time. We display **univ->tm_hour** to show, that the function produces a time structure. We also use **univ** variable as an argument of **asctime()** function

The **strftime()** function allows to format date and time in the most flexible manner.

Its synopsis is

```
size_t strftime (char *row, size_t n, const char *ms,
                 const struct tm * num);
```

The first parameter **row** is a pointer to an array of **char** type, in which a set of characters
will be placed and stored. The second parameter **n** of type **size_t** is the maximum
number of bytes occupied by all those characters. The third parameter **ms** is a message
string, containing regular characters and one or more conversion specifiers. A conversion
specifier consists of **%** character followed by the letter. The conversion specifiers, along
with the possible action they cause, are given below. This string is somewhat like **printf()**
format string. It specifies the format of a message placed in the array pointed to by **row**.
The **ms** is a pointer to a string of type **char**. One can also type a string into the **strftime()**
function directly as shown in **Program 20.27**. The fourth parameter **num** is a pointer to a
time structure, that contains some particular time point to be displayed. Therefore, it has
struct tm type.

The **strftime()** function fills in the array, pointed to by the pointer **row**, with the
characters. The way the characters are formatted in that array is controlled by the string
ms. Only **n** bytes will be stored in the string **row**. The time data point is taken from a time
structure pointed to by the **num**. The **strftime()** function returns the number of characters (without a null character) placed into the string pointed to by **row**, if this number
plus a null character is not greater than **n**. Otherwise, the function returns zero.

Both strings **row** and **ms** can contain multibyte characters, supported in the current
locale. If the locale has any shift-dependencies, the strings shell begin and end in the
initial shift state. Each of the conversion specifiers represents the format of the data, that
should replace it. The specifiers are replaced by the following data:

%a   replaced by locale-specific abbreviated weekday name (**Sat**, **Tue**, etc. in En-
       glish);

%A   replaced by locale-specific full weekday name (**Saturday**, etc. in English);

%b   replaced by locale-specific abbreviated month name (**Jan**, etc. in English);

%B   replaced by locale-specific full month name (**January**, etc. in English);

%c   replaced by locale-specific appropriate date and time representation;

%d   replaced by a decimal number representing day of the month (01-31);

%H   replaced by a decimal number (24 hour clock: 00-23) representing an hour;

%I   replaced by a decimal number (12 hour clock: 01-12) representing an hour;

%j   replaced by a decimal number representing a day of the year (001-366);

%m   replaced by a decimal number representing a month (01-12);

%M   replaced by a decimal number representing a minute (00-59);

%p   replaced by locale-specific equivalent of the AM/FM for 12-hour clock;

%S   replaced by a decimal number representing a second (00-61);

%U   replaced by a decimal number representing a week number of the year, where the
       first week begins with the first Sunday (00-53);

%w   replaced by a decimal number representing a weekday (0-6), Sunday is 0;

%W   replaced by a decimal number representing a week number of the year, where the
       first week begins with the first Monday (00-53);

%x   replaced by locale-specific appropriate date representation;

%X   replaced by locale-specific appropriate time representation;

%y replaced by a decimal number representing a year without the century (00-99);

%Y replaced by a decimal number representing a year with the century, as in 1996;

%Z replaced by a name or an abbreviation of a time zone, or no characters at all, if a time zone cannot be determined;

%% replaced by **%**;

Many of those specifiers are locale-specific. C language should have potential capabilities for use in any part of the world. This is why multibyte characters can be used in the strings. This is the reason why many of those specifiers define locale-specific date/time representation. **Program 20.27** demonstrates the use of the **strftime()** function.

```
#include <iostream.h>
#include <time.h>

void main (void)
{
struct tm *num;
time_t  tv;
char tline[60];
tv = time(NULL);
num = localtime( &tv);
strftime (tline, sizeof (tline),
        "The time is %H:%M:%S on %A the %d,%Y.\n", num);
cout << tline;
}
```

Program 20.27.

The output of this program is the current calendar time. For example

```
The time is 10:15:31 on Monday  the  1, 1996.
```

20.16. The < string.h > header file.

The header file contains following pointer, data type and functions:

size_t	**NULL**	**memcpy**	**memmove**	**strcpy**
strncpy	**strcat**	**strncat**	**memcmp**	**strcmp**
strcoll	**strncmp**	**strxfrm**	**memchr**	**strchr**
strcspn	**strpbrk**	**strrchr**	**strspn**	**strstr**
strtok	**memset**	**strerror**	**strlen**	

The **<string.h>** header file should be included, if any of those macros is used.

All the functions defined in this header can be divided as follows:

• for copying strings (**memcpy()**, **memmove()**, **strcpy()**, **strncpy()**).

• for string concatenation (**strcat()**, **strncat()**).

• for string comparison (**memcmp()**, **strcmp()**, **strcoll()**, **strncmp()**, **strxfrm()**).

• for search (**memchr()**, **strchr()**, **strcspn()**, **strpbrk()**, **strrchr()**, **strspn()**, **strstr()**, **strtok()**).

• miscellaneous functions (**memset()**, **strerror()**, **strlen()**).

The header file also defines **NULL** pointer and **size_t** type learned in other headers.

20.16.1. Functions for copying strings.

We will review four string copying functions. The synopsis of first two functions is

```
void *memcpy (void *row1, const void *row2, size_t n);
void *memmove (void *row1, const void *row2, size_t n);
```

Both functions copy first **n** characters of an object from the location pointed to by **row2** into the location pointed to by the pointer **row1**. The copying does not affect the content of **row2**. We refer to the "object" to be copied. It can be a data of any kind, i.e., it can be a variable, an array, a structure variable and so on. Parameters **row1** and **row2** are the pointers to type **void**, so you can cast them to any needed type. Both arguments should have the same data type.

Both functions so far look very similar and you, probably, wonder why are they both used. They both are slightly different. The **memcpy()** function copies the data directly from **row2** to **row1**. So, if those memory areas overlap, the behavior is undefined. At the other hand, **memmove()** function copies **n** characters of data from **row2** into a temporary memory area first. It, then, copies the data from that temporary area into **row1**. This is why **memmove()** allows an overlap between **row2** and **row1**.

Both functions return a pointer to **row1**. If you want to assign the returned value to another pointer, make sure it is a pointer to the same data type as **row1**.

The prototypes of the next two functions are

```
char *strcpy (char *line1, const char *line2);
char *strncpy (char *line1, const char *line2, size_t n);
```

Both functions copy a sting (including the null character at the end) pointed to by **line2** to the array pointed to by **line1**. The difference between both functions is that **strcpy()** function copies the whole string, while **strncpy()** copies only up to **n** first characters. If **line2** copied by **strncpy()** function is shorter than **n** characters, a proper number of null characters is appended to the end of the string pointed to by **line1**. This makes the total number of characters equal to **n**. For instance, we specify

```
char stodata[10], havdata[4];
strncpy (stodat, havdat, 10);
```

Four characters from the **havdata** will be copied to **stodata** and six null characters will be added to the end of the string stored at **stodata** to bring it to 10 characters according to the third argument. If strings pointed to by the first and the second arguments of both **strcpy()** and **strncpy()** overlap, the behavior is undefined. One must make sure, the **line1** has a sufficient space to accommodate all the copied characters. The copying does not change the content of **line2**. Both **strcpy()** and **strncpy()** return a pointer to **line1**. Review an example given in **Program 20.28**.

```
#include <stdio.h>
```

```
#include <string.h>

void main (void)
{
char ini[30] = " It is a test. ";
char fin[40], fin2[40];
float num1[ ] = {10.5, 8.2, 39.0, 4.1, 3.33, 5.4};
float num2[ ] = {1.0, 1.0, 1.0, 1.0, 1.0, 1.0}, num3[6];
int n;
strcpy (fin, ini);
strncpy ( fin2, ini, 3);
printf ("initial string: %s \n", ini);
printf ("copied string: %s \n", fin);
printf ("partially copied string: %s \n", fin2);
memcpy (num2, num1, 3*sizeof (float));
memmove (num3, num1, sizeof num1);
for (n=0; n<6; n++)
printf (" %.2f, %.2f  ", num2[n], num3[n] );
}
```

Program 20.28.

The output of the program consists of four lines. It first displays the initial string, then, the copied one. They are identical. It, then, displays three copied characters (" **It**") of **fin2** string. The last line displays six corresponding pairs of numbers from the **num2** and **num3** arrays.

20.16.2. Functions for string concatenation.

Let's begin with the prototypes of two of those functions
```
    char *strcat (char *line1, const char *line2);
    char *strncat (char *line1, const char *line2, size_t n);
```
Both functions append the string pointed to by **line2** to the very end of the srting pointed to by **line1**. The difference between **strcat()** and **strncat()** is, that the first function appends the whole string **line2** to the end of **line1**, while the second function adds only first **n** characters (including null character) of **line2**. What happens with the null character at the end of the string **line1**? For both functions, the first character of **line2** substitutes the null character at the end of **line1**.

Both functions return a pointer to a string **line1**. If the first and the second string arguments overlap in any **strcat()** or **strncat()** functions, their behavior is unknown. The word "unknown" means, the behavior is not specified by the standard and is implementation dependent. In general, it might be treated as an error. Also, do not forget to provide a sufficient space in the destination string to hold the added characters. Review following example.

```
#include <iostream.h>
#include <string.h>

void main (void)
{
char part_begin[30] =" It is";
char part_end[30] =" only a test. ";
char part_more[30] =" Concatenation complete. ";
size_t n;
cout << part_begin << endl;
strcat (part_begin, part_end);
cout << part_begin << endl;
cout << "number of characters to add to this phrase\n";
cin >> n;
strncat (part_begin, part_more, n);
cout << part_begin;
}
```

Program 20.29.

The output of the program is

```
It is
It is only a test.
number of characters to add to this phrase
```

The program prompts to enter any number of characters, that you want to add from the string **part_more**. It will be read by the **cout** object. We enter 10 and get

```
It is only a test. Concatena
```

The program first concatenates the strings **part_begin** and **part_end**. It, then, appends the number of characters (including the null character), indicated by a user, from the string **part_more** to the end of already altered **part_begin**.

20.16.3. Functions for comparing the strings.

We will start with the **strcmp()** function. Its prototype is

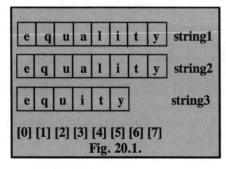

[0] [1] [2] [3] [4] [5] [6] [7]
Fig. 20.1.

```
int strcmp (const char *pr1,
            const char *pr2);
```

The function compares two strings pointed to by **pr1** and **pr2**. It stops, when an end of either string has been reached, or the first difference in characters has been found. The string is considered greater, if its character at the first position at which the difference occurs, has greater binary value. The **strcmp()** function returns positive, zero or negative integer, if the string **pr1** is respectively greater, equal or less than the string **pr2**. Both **pr1** and **pr2** are the pointers to the strings of type **char**.

The **strncmp()** function must be reviewed next. Its prototype is

```
int strncmp (const char *pr1, const char *pr2, size_t n);
```

It compares the first **n** characters of two strings pointed to by **pr1** and **pr2**. It stops, when first **n** elements have been compared, or an end of either string has been reached, or the first difference in characters has been found. The string is considered greater, if its character at the first position, at which the difference occurs, corresponds to a greater value (in ASCII or other standard representation). The **strncmp()** function returns positive, zero or negative integer number, if the string **pr1** is respectively greater, equal or less than the string **pr2**. Both **pr1** and **pr2** are the pointers to the strings of type **char**. The third argument **n** of **size_t** type stands for the number of characters to be compared.

We explain the string comparison on an example of the **strncmp()** function in Fig. 20.1. Let's compare two strings

```
strncmp (string1, string2, 5);
```

When you call comparison function to compare two strings, it compares first element **[0]** of **string1** to **[0]** element of **string2**. If they are equal, it, then, compares the second element **[1]** of both **string1** and **string2**. If the elements are also equal, the **strncmp()** function continues the comparison of corresponding elements of both strings. It stops, when the difference in characters is encountered, or **n** first elements of both strings have been compared, or an end of either string is reached.

In case of Fig. 20.1, first 5 elements of the **string1** are identical to the first 5 elements of **string2**. The **strncmp()** returns zero. Let's compare **string2** and **string3** in Fig. 20.1.

```
strncmp (string2, string3, 6);
```

The **strncmp()** function will compare strings element by element beginning with the first one. As you see, now element **[3]** is the first different element in those strings. The 4th elements of **string2**, **string3** store "**a**" and "**i**" characters respectively. The comparison will stop there. Each character is stored as a binary value. Those values of "**a**" and "**i**" will be compared. If the binary value of **string2** character is greater than the binary value of the character of **string3**, the **strncmp()** function will return a positive integer number. Otherwise, negative integer will be returned.

The function

```
int memcmp (const void *pr1, const void *pr2, size_t n);
```

compares first **n** characters of two memory regions (two objects) pointed to by **pr1** and **pr2**. It will stop, when first **n** elements have been compared, or an end of either region has been reached, or the first difference in characters is found. The object is considered greater, if its character at the first position, at which the difference occurs, corresponds to a greater binary value. The **memcmp()** function returns positive, zero or negative integer number, if the object pointed to by **pr1** is respectively greater, equal or less than the object **pr2**. Both parameters **pr1** and **pr2** are the pointers to any data type (**char**, **int**, **float**, etc.). They have been presented as having the **void** type, which, as you know, can be cast to any data type. Those two memory regions can contain any kind of data: variables, strings, arrays and so on. The third parameter **n** stands for the number of characters to be compared and has type **size_t**.

The function

```
int strcoll (const char *pr1, const char *pr2);
```

compares two strings pointed to by **pr1** and **pr2**. It will stop, when an end of either string has been reached, or the first difference in characters is found. The string is considered greater, if its character at the first position, at which the difference occurs, corresponds to a greater binary value. The **strcoll()** function returns positive, zero or negative integer number, if the string **pr1** is respectively greater, equal or less than the string **pr2**. Both parameters **pr1** and **pr2** are the pointers to the strings of type **char**. This function is similar to **strcmp()**, except that the results of **strcoll()** are locale-dependent. For instance, in a particular locale the uppercase and lowercase letters might have the same binary values.

Program 20.30 demonstrates the use of some of those functions.

```
#include <iostream.h>
#include <string.h>

void main   (void)
{
static char right[30] = "circumstances";
static char wrong[30] = "circumttances";
static float num1[6]= {6.3, 82.5, 9.5, 71.2, 6.3, 9.9};
static float num2[6] = {6.3, 82.5, 9.5, 71.2, 0.0, 9.9};
int n;
n = strcmp (right, wrong);
if (n<0)            cout << "right<wrong \n";
else if (n==0)     cout << "right=wrong \n";
else               cout << "right>wrong \n";
n = strncmp (right, wrong, 6);
if (n<0)      cout << "part of right< part of wrong\n";
else if(n==0) cout << "part of right= part of wrong\n";
else          cout << "part of right> part of wrong \n";
n = memcmp (num1, num2, sizeof num1);
if (n<0)            cout << "num1<num2 \n";
else if (n==0)     cout << "num1=num2 \n";
else               cout << "num1>num2 \n";
}
```

Program 20.30.

The output of the program is

```
right<wrong
part of right=part of wrong
num1>num2
```

We compare strings **right** and **wrong** using **strcmp()** and **strncmp()** functions. In the first case, the first string is greater than the second one. In the second case, we compare only 6 first elements of both strings. Since they are equal, two strings are equal. We also compare two arrays **num1** and **num2** using **memcmp()** function.

20.16.4. Search functions.

We will start with the **memchr()** function. Its prototype is

```
void *memchr (const void *pr, int x, size_t  n);
```

The function finds the first occurrence of a character equal to the one stored in **x**, converted to an **unsigned char**, in the first **n** character of the object pointed to by **pr**. It means, that only up to **n** first characters of the object, pointed to by **pr**, are searched. The **memchr()** returns a pointer to the object element, containing that character. It returns **NULL**, if a match is not found. The returned pointer has the same data type as **pr**. The parameter **pr** can be a pointer to a variety of data types (**char**, **int**, **float**, etc.). The object, pointed to by **pr**, can be a variable, array, etc.

Let's review the **strchr()** function. Its prototype is

```
char *strchr (const char *pr, int x);
```

The function finds the first occurrence of a character equal to the one stored in **x**, converted to **char**, in the string pointed to by **pr**. The **strchr()** function returns a pointer to the string element, containing that character. It returns **NULL**, if a match is not found. The null terminating character is considered as a part of the string.

We can now go to the **strrchr()** function. Its prototype is

```
char *strrchr (const char *pr, int x);
```

The function finds the *last* occurrence of a character equal to the one stored in **x**, converted to a **char**, in the string pointed to by **pr**. The **strrchr()** function returns a pointer to the string element, containing that character. It returns **NULL**, if a match is not found. The null terminating character is considered as a part of the string.

The **strpbrk()** function synopsis is

```
char * strpbrk (const char *pr1, const char *pr2);
```

It finds the first occurrence of any character from the string pointed to by **pr2** in the string pointed to by **pr1**. In other words, the function looks for presence of any character from **pr2** in **pr1**. The **strpbrk()** returns a pointer to a matching character found in **pr1**, or **NULL**, if the match is not found.

The **strstr()** function prototype is

```
char * strstr (const char *pr1, const char *pr2);
```

The function finds the first occurrence of the sequence of characters from the string pointed to by **pr2** in the string addressed by a pointer **pr1**. The **strstr()** function returns a pointer to the first element of that sequence found in **pr1**, or **NULL**, if match is not found. If **pr2** points to a string of zero length, the function returns pointer **pr1**. For instance, we have **pr1[20]="counterpart"** and **pr2[5]="part"**. The function looks for presence of sequence "**part**" from **pr2** in the string **pr1**.

We can review the **strcspn()** function. Its prototype is

```
size_t  strcspn (const char  *pr1, const char *pr2);
```

The function computes and returns the length of a segment from the beginning of the string pointed to by **pr1**, consisting of characters that do not match any character of the string pointed to by **pr2**. If no match is found, the length of the string **pr1** is returned.

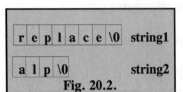

For instance, review an example given in Fig. 20.2. We write

```
strcspn (string1, string2);
```

The **strcspn()** function will search **string1**, until any of the characters "**apl**" of **string2** are found. One of those characters is found in **string1** at the third position. It is the letter "**p**". There are only two preceding letter "**p**" characters in **string1**: "**r**" and "**e**". The **strcspn()** will return the number of bytes (characters) from the beginning of **string1** preceding the first matched character. The returned number is 2.

We go to the next function. The **strspn()** function prototype is

```
size_t  strspn (const char  *pr1, const  char *pr2);
```

The function computes and returns the length of a segment from the beginning of the string pointed to by **pr1**, that consists entirely of the characters from the string pointed to by the pointer **pr2**. Suppose, we have string **pr1[20]="abcdowkal4jc0dk"** and **pr2[6]="dbac"**. We call **strspn(pr1, pr2)**. The **strspn()** function will look for presence of only "**dbac**" characters in any order at the beginning of the string pointed to by **pr1**. We have those characters in **pr1** in the order "**abcd...**". The order in which "**dbac**" characters follow in the string **pr1** is not important. But there should not be any other not matching character starting from the beginning of string **pr1**. So, if the string **pr1** is

pr1[20] = "abcdow...";   the function will return number 4;
pr1[20] = "accbcdow...";   the function will return number 6;
pr1[20] = "abjcdow...";   the function will return number 2;

Review **Program 20.31** illustrating the above functions.

```
#include <string.h>
#include <stdio.h>

void main (void)
{
static char  phrase[ ] = "You should understand it.";
int m;
char *qp;
qp = (char *) memchr (phrase, 'u', sizeof phrase);
if(qp !=NULL) printf ("memchr match 'u': %s \n", qp);
qp = strchr (phrase, 'o');
if (qp !=NULL) printf ("strchr match 'o': %s \n", qp);
qp = strrchr (phrase, 'd');
if (qp !=NULL) printf ("strrchr match 'd': %s \n", qp);
qp = strpbrk (phrase, "stog");
if (qp !=NULL)  printf ("strpbrk match: %s \n", qp);
qp = strstr (phrase, "You");
if (qp !=NULL)  printf ("strstr match: %s \n", qp);
```

```
m = strcspn (phrase, "hsl");
printf("strcspn match after %d: %s\n", m, &phrase[m]);
m = strspn (phrase,  "uoY");
printf ("strspn mismatch after %d: %s\n", m, &phrase[m]);
}
```
Program 20.31.

The program produces following output messages

```
memchr match 'u': u should understand it.
strchr match 'o': ou should understand it.
strrchr match 'd': d it.
strpbrk match: ou should understand it.
strstr match: You should understand it.
strcspn match after 4: should understand it.
strspn mismatch after 3: should understand it.
```

The program displays the **phrase** string from a point, where each function stops its search.

We can now review the **strtok()** function. It has the following prototype.

```
char  *strtok (const char *pr1, const char *pr2);
```
Both parameters **pr1** and **pr2** are the pointers to the strings of type **char**. Let's review this function on an example. For instance, we declare two strings and call the **strtok()** function.

```
line[ ] = " They are: Boston -first, New York -second,
           Chicago is the third.";
sign[ ] = ":,- ";
char *ptr;
ptr = strtok (line, sign);
printf ("%s \n", ptr);
```
When **strtok()** function is called, the string

```
They are: Boston -first, New York -second, Chicago is the
third.
```
is searched from the very beginning for the presence of " **: , -** " characters. It breaks the **line** string into parts called tokens. The beginning of the first token is the beginning of the string different from any of the characters specified in **sign**. The end is one of the characters contained in **sign**. Again, if " **: , -** " characters are found at the very beginning of **line**, the function looks for the first character different from them. This will be a starting point. All the characters from the starting point to any character from **sign** will be the first partition of **line**. The **strtok()** function returns a pointer to the beginning of the first token, if a string can be divided on tokens. It returns **NULL** pointer, otherwise. We get the first token in the above fragment, because our function returns a pointer to the first token. Our first partition is caused by the blank character contained in **sign**. Hence, the **printf()** must display

```
They
```
Pay attention, the first character before the word "**They**" was a blank, and it was ignored. Why? Remember, if the first string begins with any of the second string charac-

ters, they are ignored. The function will also save the next character after the first breaking character. If we intend to do the next search of the same string, it will begin from that
character. In our case, it is the next character after the blank space.

One can apply this function to the same string a number of times. You can call the
strtok() function again and print the second token.

```
ptr = strtok (NULL, sign);
printf ("%s \n", ptr);
```

The function will start from the position saved by the previous call to it. It will, again,
search for the first character different from " **:,-** ". This will be a new starting point.
The character saved in our case is the letter '**a**'. It will become the starting point of the
second token. The **strtok()** function will again search for any of " **:,-** " characters.
The last character before any of " **:,-** " characters will be the end point of the second
token. Our second token will be displayed as

```
are
```

Each following call will get you the next token. The third token is **Boston**. The
strtok() function is called with the first argument **line** pointing towards the string
only once. Each subsequent call to **strtok()** acting on **line** string has the **NULL**
pointer as its first argument. Consider following example.

```
#include <string.h>
#include <stdio.h>

void main (void)
{
static char line[ ] = " They are: Boston -first, \
       New York -second, Chicago is the third.";
static char sign[ ] = ":,- ";
char *ptr;
int  m, k=0;
printf ("how many tokens do you want ? \n");
scanf ("%d", &m);
ptr = strtok (line, sign);
while (ptr !=NULL && k<m)
{
printf ("%s \n", ptr);
ptr = strtok (NULL, sign);
k++;
} }
```

Program 20.32.

The program prompts the user to enter on how many tokens should the string **line** be
divided. It, then, parses the string on as many tokens as requested.

20.16.5. Miscellaneous functions.

We will begin with the **memset()** function. Its prototype is

```
void *memset (void *ptr, int x, size_t  n);
```

It copies the value stored in **x** converted to an **unsigned char** type into each of the first **n** characters (elements) of an object pointed to by **ptr**. The **memset()** function returns the value stored in **ptr**. The parameter **ptr** can be a pointer to a number of data types (**char**, **int**, **float**, etc.). The object **ptr** can be a variable, string, array and so on. The function is used to assign a known value to a region of memory.

The **strlen()** function has a prototype

```
size_t  strlen (const char *ptr);
```

It computes and returns the length of the string pointed to by **ptr**. That returned number does not include the null terminating character.

The **strerror()** function

```
char  *strerror (int errnum);
```

returns a pointer to the error message string corresponding to its argument **errnum**. Those messages are implementation dependent.

APPENDIX 1.

A1.1. ASCII Character set.

The ASCII characters and the numeric values corresponding to them are given in Table A1.1. We know, when a button is pushed on a keyboard, a character is sent to a computer. This character corresponds to a certain number. And this is how the computer "understands" each character. The computer evaluates its value, that is stored as binary. The ASCII is just one of the standard systems. There are other systems specifying the correlation between the characters and the numeric values. Next section shows how to convert a value to different bases. Here we just tell you which character corresponds to which value.

Table A1.1. ASCII characters

	0	1	2	3	4	5	6	7	8	9
0	nul	soh	stx	etx	eot	enq	ack	bell	bs	ht
1	nl	vt	ff	cr	so	si	dle	dc1	dc2	dc3
2	dc4	nak	syn	etb	can	em	sub	esc	fs	gs
3	rs	us	space	!	"	#	$	%	&	`
4	(	)	*	+	,	-	.	/	0	1
5	2	3	4	5	6	7	8	9	:	;
6	<	=	>	?	@	A	B	C	D	E
7	F	G	H	I	J	K	L	M	N	O
8	P	Q	R	S	T	U	V	W	X	Y
9	Z	[	\	]	^	_	`	a	b	c
10	d	e	f	g	h	I	j	k	l	m
11	n	o	p	q	r	s	t	u	v	w
12	x	y	z	{	|	}	~	del		

We used some abbreviations in the above table. Here they are:

CTRL-@ (null)
CTRL-A (soh) Start of Heading
CTRL-B (stx) Start of Text
CTRL-C (etx) End of Text
CTRL-D (eot) End of Transmission
CTRL-E (enq) Enquiry
CTRL-F (ack) Acknowledge
CTRL-G bell
CTRL-H (bs) Backspace '\b'

CTRL-P (dle) Data Link Escape
CTRL-Q (dc1) Device Control 1
CTRL-R (dc2) Device Control 2
CTRL-S (dc3) Device Control 3
CTRL-T (dc4) Device Control 4
CTRL-U (nak) Negative Acknowledge
CTRL-V (syn) Synchronous Idle
CTRL-W (etb) End Transmission Block
CTRL-X (can) Cancel

CTRL-I (ht) Horizontal Tab '\t'
CTRL-J (nl) Newline '\n'
CTRL-K (vt) Vertical Tab
CTRL-L (ff) Formfeed '\f'
CTRL-M (cr) Carriage return '\r'
CTRL-N (so) Shift Out
CTRL-O (si) Shift In

CTRL-Y (em) End of Medium
CTRL-Z (sub) Substitute
CTRL-[(esc) Escape
CTRL- (fs) File Separator
CTRL-] (gs) Group Separator
CTRL-^ (rs) Record Separator
CTRL-_ (us) Unit Separator

One can ask what are these abbreviations. They are different control commands, escape sequences, etc., used by the operating system and for some other purposes. Here we just specify what number they correspond to, or what number is sent to the computer, when you press these buttons.

Table A1.1 has an outer row and a column of numbers. They indicate the decimal number to which a particular keyboard button corresponds to. If you look, the column contains the numbers from 0 to 12. The row contains the numbers from 0 to 9. How do you determine the number? You write the number from the column first and the number from the row second. For instance, the character (or button) **$** corresponds to the decimal number 36. The character **a** corresponds to number 97. The button **del** corresponds to 127. The character **f** corresponds to 102. The greatest possible decimal number for the characters is 127. This is how C++ stores the **char** type data on a number of computer systems, that use ASCII convention.

A1.2 Number systems.

We were talking about decimal, octal and hexadecimal numbers. Here, we introduce each of those number systems. The decimal number system is a base 10 system. Each digit can be within the range from 0 to 9. The lowest digit is 0. The highest is 9. What does it mean a decimal number? We will begin with a few examples. Let's review the decimal number 7923. We show it in Table A1.2

Table A1.2. Decimal number.

7	9	2	3
$7*10^3$	$9*10^2$	$2*10^1$	$3*10^0$

The number 7923 consists of four digits. Each digit is nothing else by a power of 10. The whole number is a sum of the values produced by each digit. The first digit is 3. It means, that this digit contributes 3 times 10 to power 0, or 3. The second digit is 2. It is 2 times 10 to the power 1. The third digit is 9. It is 9 times 10 to the power 2 and so on. So, the whole number is a sum of $7000+900+20+3$. We are used to those numbers, when each position represents a power of 10.

An octal number consists of the digits ranging from 0 to 7. Each position represents a power of 8. So, the octal number 453 is $4*8^2+5*8^1+3*8^0$. Each hexadecimal number digit can be a number from 0 to 15. The numbers 0 through 9 are used for the first ten values. The rest is substituted by the digits: **A** substitutes 10, **B** - 11, **C** - 12, **D** - 13, **E** - 14, **F** - 15. Each digit is a power of 16. Thus, the number A9C is $10*16^2+9*16^1+12*16^0$. A binary number is a number each position of which is a power of 2. Each position can be either 1 or 0. For instance, 11101 is equal to $1*2^4 +1*2^3 +1*2^2 +0*2^1 +1*2^0$.

One can ask how to convert an octal and hexadecimal value to a decimal. Let's convert octal value 453 to a decimal. It is $4*8^2 +5*8^1 +3*8^0 =4*64+5*8+3=299$. Let's convert octal 1670 to a decimal value $1*8^3 +6*8^2 +7*8^1 +0*8^0 = 1*512+6*64+7*8+0=952$. Let's now convert the hexadecimal value 7BE3 to a decimal. It is $7*16^3 +11*16^2 +14*16^1 +3*16^0 = 7*4096+11*256+14*16+3 = 31715$. Thus, the hexadecimal value 7BE3 corresponds to the decimal 31715.

Let's now convert the octal value 437 to the binary one. It can be done, if we replace each octal digit by a three digit binary number and write them in the order they follow. Octal number 4 correspond to a binary number 100. Octal number 3 corresponds to a binary number 011. Octal digit 7 correspond to a binary number 111. So, the three digit octal number 437 gets converted to a 9 digit binary number 100011111. Let's convert octal number 642 to a binary number. The octal number 6 corresponds to a binary 110. Number 4 corresponds to 100. Number 2 corresponds to 010. The octal value 642 converts to the binary number 110100010.

Let's convert the hexadecimal value 9B4 to a binary number. You have to subsitute each hexadecimal digit by a four digit binary number, and, then, write them in the order they follow. The hexadecimal 9 corresponds to 1001. Hexadecimal B (11) corresponds to 1011. Hexadecimal 4 is converted as 0100. Thus, the hexadecimal number 9B4 is converted to a binary 100110110100.

Let's now convert a decimal value 792 to any other base, for instance hexadecimal. First step is to write the position values, stopping at the one that is greater than the number 792:

$16^3 = 4096 \quad 16^2 = 256 \quad 16 \quad 1$

792

As you see, the number 792 lies between 16 in the second and the third power. You first divide 792 by closest lower value obtained as a power of 16. It is 256. So, 792:256 produces an integer 3 and remainder 24. We, then, divide the remainder 24 by the next power of 16 down. So, 24:16 produces an integer 1 and the remainder 8. The last division happens to be 8:1. This produces number 8 without a remainder. So, the decimal value 792 is converted to the hexadecimal value 318. Conversion to the octal value is very similar. We place 792 between the greater and smaller power of 8.

$8^4 = 4096 \quad 8^3 = 512 \quad 8^2 = 64 \quad 8 \quad 1$

792

So, we divide 792: 512. It gives integer 1 and the remainder 280. We, then, divide the remainder 280:64. It gives the divisor 4 and the remainder 24. We, then, divide 24:8. It produces the result 3 and gives the remainder 0. We divide 0: 1=0. Our octal number 1430 corresponds to the decimal 792.

We can now obtain the binary equivalent using the same algorithm

$2^{10} = 1024 \ 2^9 = 512 \ 2^8 = 256 \ 2^7 = 128 \ 2^6 = 64 \ 32 \ 16 \ 8 \ 4 \ 2 \ 1$

792

You can perform the same algorithm and prove, that the binary equivalent of our number will be 110001100. Table A1.3 gives you some numbers in different bases.

Table A1.3. Number representations

Decimal	Hexadecimal	Octal	Binary
0	0	0	0
1	1	1	1
2	2	2	10
3	3	3	11
4	4	4	100
5	5	5	101
6	6	6	110
7	7	7	111
8	8	10	1000
9	9	11	1001
10	A (a)	12	1010
11	B (b)	13	1011
12	C (c)	14	1100
13	D (d)	15	1101
14	E (e)	16	1110
15	F (f)	17	1111

INDEX